D1598198

THE END OF
THE RUSSIAN IMPERIAL ARMY

The End of the Russian Imperial Army

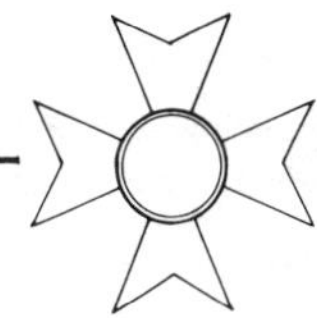

The Road to Soviet Power and Peace

VOLUME II

ALLAN K. WILDMAN

PRINCETON UNIVERSITY PRESS
PRINCETON, NEW JERSEY

CONTENTS

Published by Princeton University Press, 41 William Street,
Princeton, New Jersey 08540
In the United Kingdom: Princeton University Press, Guildford, Surrey

Library of Congress Cataloging in Publication Data will be
found on the last printed page of this book

ISBN 0-691-05504-1

Publication of this book has been aided by a grant from the
Whitney Darrow Fund of Princeton University Press

This book has been composed in Linotron Times Roman

Clothbound editions of Princeton University Press books
are printed on acid-free paper, and binding materials are
chosen for strength and durability. Paperbacks, although satisfactory
for personal collections, are not usually suitable for library rebinding

Printed in the United States of America by Princeton University Press
Princeton, New Jersey

Designed by Laury A. Egan

CONTENTS

LIST OF ILLUSTRATIONS

FIGURES

(following page 206)

MAPS

REMARKS AND ACKNOWLEDGMENTS

BECAUSE a preface setting out the rationale for this two-part study was included in the previous volume, *The End of the Russian Imperial Army: The Old Army and the Soldiers' Revolt* (Princeton: Princeton University Press, 1980), there is no need to repeat it here. For new readers, the "Transition" section will help establish the context of the beginning of this second volume. I again strongly recommend consulting W. H. Chamberlin's *Russian Revolution*, Volume 1, as the best general work available to prepare a reader for this or any specialized study of 1917.

The literature on 1917 has been greatly enriched by new works by Rex Wade, Donald Raleigh, Diane Koenker, David Mandel, Stephen Smith, and Tsuyoshi Hasegawa. A far more richly textured picture of 1917 is now possible, but the new contributions merely amplify my former prefatory remarks. The readers will judge whether I have properly interpreted my material. My object has been to convey as much of the original stuff of the Russian Revolution in the Army as possible without tainting it with preconceived views, but where appropriate I have introduced my more systematic interpretations so that readers can form their own judgments. Certainly a dialogue over the results of the most recent scholarship on 1917 would be welcome.

☆

As in the previous volume, I follow the Library of Congress system of transliteration and the Julian or Old Style calendar for dates (thirteen days behind the Gregorian or New Style calendar in 1917), except in those few instances where allusions are made to events on the Western Front or where non-Russian sources are employed (indicated by "N.S."). I continue to use my own system of designations for military units to maintain consistency—arabic numerals for regiments and divisions above the Tenth (105th Infantry Division, 462nd Stariiskii Regiment, but Second Siberian Rifle Division and Eighth Grenadier Regiment), Roman numerals for all corps (I Guards Infantry, IV Siberian, VII, XIV, XLI Army corps), and written designations for the fourteen armies (First, Twelfth, Caucasus, Special armies). I again use Army when it stands for the entire Imperial Army, but lower case when short for front army or one of the fourteen armies (e.g., "the army committee decided"), and Revolution for the Revolution as understood by contemporaries. I will also use "Right" and "Left" for the general political groupings to the right or left. I have tried to spare the reader a long list of special terms to remember for which a glossary would be necessary, but two important exceptions, since they are in general usage, are "Stavka" for the Supreme General Headquarters at Mogiliev, and VTsIK for the All-Russian Central Executive Committee of the Soviets after its establishment at the First All-Russian Congress of Soviets in June (a few reminders are provided). Until the Soviet Congress, the Executive Committee of the Petrograd Soviet of Workers' and Soldiers' Deputies functioned as a national leadership and is referred to in the text as "the Soviet Executive Committee." To facilitate electronic processing of the manuscript, the style used for footnotes is different from that in volume 1, for example *KA* 19 (1975): 24-25 is used for *Krasnyi Arkhiv*, XIX (1975), pp. 24-25.

As promised in the first volume, a bibliography covering both volumes, entitled "Source Abbreviations and Bibliography," is provided at the end of this volume. The abbreviations for sources cited in the footnotes are included there. Readers who are particularly concerned about my source base should first familiarize themselves with the list of keyed sources and perhaps also refer to the "Review of Sources" section at the end of the first volume.

☆

The research to complete this second volume was conducted mainly in the Soviet Union in the summer of 1977 supported by a grant from the International Researches and Exchanges Board. I wish to express special gratitude to L. M. Gavrilov of the History Section of the Academy of Sciences of the USSR for facilitating my speedy admission to the State Military-Historical Archives (TsGVIA)—a rare occurrence, but essential to the success of this study—and for making available to me other documentary materials at his disposal. I also owe a great debt to persons unknown who promptly handled my requests and added some unexpected treasures. It was also a pleasure to renew my acquaintance with my Soviet colleague V. I. Miller, whose scholarship has contributed significantly to this field. We resumed our fruitful exchanges where they left off on my visit of 1970.

It was a matter of regret that the help of L. F. Magerovsky was no longer available at the Russian and Eastern European Archive of Columbia University, but his generous help of times past continues to enrich this volume; the present staff also rendered me very efficient help in locating new sources. Several additional visits to the Hoover Institution at Stanford also uncovered new sources, facilitated by the much-improved organization and catalogue. I owe a special debt to the chief librarian of the Russian collection, Dr. Hilja Kukk, who among other things helped me locate some lost references, as well as to Anna Bourgina, former curator of the Nicolaevsky Collection and now deceased, who made available to me rich documentation on the Kornilov affair. It is regrettable that this assistance will not be adequately reflected in this volume, because a chapter on the Kornilov movement and the officer corps had to be sacrificed to keep the volume from becoming too unwieldy. Nevertheless, the Nicolaevsky materials were of great value to this study and will be utilized more fully in some future publication.

The writing of the manuscript was greatly facilitated by a fellowship from the Kennan Institute for Advanced Russian Studies in 1982, which is attached to that extraordinary institution the Wilson Center in the Smithsonian Building in Washington, D.C. The intellectual stimulus that comes from daily contact with the foremost scholars in a variety of different fields is an experience that no one who has been a part of it can forget. Thanks to the excellent facilities and staff, four chapters were written and a good half of the manuscript was retyped and put on word processor disks.

Generous grants from the research funds of the Humanities College of Ohio State University supported most of the costs of typing and photocopying; secretarial personnel from the History Department and the Humanities College were generously made available for word-processing the final version, and I would like to express my special admiration and thanks to those wizards of modern technology that make a vital task appear so routine, specifically to Chris Burton, Jo White, and Maria Mazon.

Finding colleagues these days who can spare the time from their own demanding projects to critique the work of another is a difficult task; therefore I wish to express my deepest appreciation to Donald Raleigh of the University of Hawaii, who carefully read, edited, and made useful comments on the manuscript, many of the latter incorporated into the final version.

Finally, on behalf of the entire scholarly community I want to pay tribute to the Soviet émigré scholar Professor M. S. Frenkin of Jerusalem, recently deceased, whose courage and extraordinary energy have rewarded us with two monumental works on the Russian Army during the Revolution, namely, his *Russkaia armiia i Revoliutsiia 1917-18* (Munich, 1978) and *Zakvat vlasti bol'shevikami v Rossii i rol' tylovykh garnizonov armii* (Jerusalem, 1982). It was my pleasure to have made Frenkin's acquaintance while he was still in the Soviet Union and to have renewed that friendship at a cordial reunion at the Second World Congress of Soviet Studies at Garmisch, Germany, in 1980. Frenkin stands behind the cryptic initials "M.S." (for Mikhail Samuilovich) in the dedication to the first volume; at that time, because of his recent emigration, I thought it discreet to withhold his identity, but it is now most appropriate that his remarkable accomplishment be recognized—not only did he for many years assemble an enormous amount of archival material, writing chiefly for "the bottom drawer,'' but he managed somehow to bring his entire storehouse of knowledge with him and to publish the results under the exceedingly difficult conditions of a new environment and culture. Our most heartfelt congratulations and gratitude for this achievement, Mikhail Samuilovich! Your work will long be remembered.

TRANSITION

DURING the first months of the Russian Revolution of 1917, which were covered in the previous volume, the various contenders for power were preoccupied more with internal politics and social perspectives than with the Gordian knot of the war. The sloganeering over "total victory" versus "no annexations and indemnities" served to mobilize the respective social sectors for political purposes, but failed to address the more serious diplomatic and military imperatives. Although the Soviet leadership persuaded its constituency that it maintained "control" over the Provisional Government by imposing on the latter a renunciation of conquests in a "Declaration" of March 27, Foreign Minister Paul Miliukov and socialist Minister of Justice Kerensky each interpreted the statement according to his own lights, which resulted in the "April Crisis" and the eventual resignations of Miliukov and War Minister Aleksandr Guchkov. A crisis was unavoidable, first because the game of deceptive rhetoric and calculated ambiguity could not forever postpone the resolution of basic issues, and second because the Soviet slogans, more than was realized, catered to a deep longing among the masses for a painless liquidation of the war and surety that the Revolution as they perceived it had triumphed.

The explosion of the April Days, which caught the Soviet leaders by surprise, was a moment of truth that they should have grasped but did not. The masses, reassured by the Soviet pronouncements of the preceding weeks, felt bitterly deceived when Miliukov's note to the Allies of April 18 was made public. Hitherto having limited influence over the masses, the Bolsheviks reaped the harvest of the Soviet leaders' ineptitude, making rapid gains in the metropolitan centers and, shortly thereafter, at the front, a development not heretofore brought out in the literature.

Much against the disposition of the Menshevik contingent, the Soviet representatives were obliged to enter the government to share the responsibilities of power, and with them the painful choices involved in securing the goal of a "democratic peace." As wielders of power, they were bound by constraints not obtaining in their capacity as watchdog: give-and-take with coalition partners, the pressures of allied governments, who dangled military supplies and other essentials, and finally the futility of their efforts in the absence of a revolution in Germany or leverage to persuade the Allies to modify "secret treaties." The latter consideration called forth the line of argument, first enunciated by Kerensky but soon adopted as dogma by the Soviet camp, that unless revolutionary Russia made a significant contribution to Germany's defeat, she would lack the authority to influence the peace settlement. Consequently, a termination of the de facto truce and a resumption of active operations proved necessary to prevent the German army from shifting a considerable number of its divisions to the Western Front. Only by inflicting a significant reverse on the Central Powers would the latter sense the futility of seeking to impose conquests by force and consent to negotiations. With rising revolutionary unrest and impatience over the war, a revived Socialist International could then generate sufficient pressure on all governments to agree to a settlement based on democratic principles.

The unforeseen consequence of this altered posture was a fundamental inversion of the former relationship between the democratic organizations and their constituency. The entire representational structure, above all the committees at the front, were now enlisted in the effort to restore discipline, to resume work and training routines, to speed replacements to the front, to halt fraternization, and to prepare for decisive military operations. The soldiers, aided and abetted by their committees, had hitherto regarded such notions as ''counter-revolutionary'' and the inspiration of the command and the bourgeoisie. Now their own revolutionary institutions were endorsing them.

If the trench soldiers were slow to absorb this lesson, it was not long before a flood of Bolshevik literature and agitators pressed it upon them. Disgruntled marching companies from the urban centers, harboring Bolshevik agitators, quickly brought to the front the virus of more advanced alienation and hardened political attitudes. With few exceptions, the committees followed the Soviet leadership in their defensist reconstruction and fostered a special personality cult of Kerensky. Consequently, they soon lost out in influence to nameless agitators broadcasting Bolshevik slogans and arguments. By June entire regiments and divisions were mutinying against the preparations for the offensive, and the morale of the balance was so drastically impaired that, despite considerable technical advantages, a massive failure was foreordained. The collapse of the offensive, coinciding roughly with the July Days, signified a crisis of the same magnitude, and like the latter deeply entrenched a feeling of disenchantment with the coalition arrangement and illicit admiration for the Bolsheviks' advocacy of land, peace, and Soviet power. If anything, the cleavage between the posture of revolutionary institutions and the temper of the masses was more profound and excruciating at the front than in the metropolitan centers; the soldiers were convinced that they had been sacrificed and maligned as cowards and traitors by the bourgeois press with the complicity of their revolutionary leaders.

The story in this volume is the enduring trauma of the summer offensive, which preordained the soldiers' response to the Kornilov affair, and subsequently the massive ''plebiscite'' against another winter in the trenches. This movement did not endorse per se the Bolsheviks' seizure of power in Petrograd, but it did regard the notion of Soviet power and immediate peace as axiomatic. The impetus was so overwhelming that the hitherto loyalist army committees yielded to it and thereby frustrated the frantic efforts of Kerensky and the old Soviet Executive Committee (VTsIK) to reverse the Bolsheviks' victory by drawing upon forces at the front. ''October'' may have been a ''coup'' in the capital, but at the front it was a revolution.

THE END OF
THE RUSSIAN IMPERIAL ARMY

CHAPTER I

THE COMING OF THE OFFENSIVE

THE RUSSIAN REVOLUTION had thrust itself unexpectedly into the ever-shifting balance between the contending alliances of Europe. The basic strategic problem of this third year of the Great War was still to break the stalemate of trench warfare, either by a decisive breakthrough (Verdun and the Somme had been costly failures) or by opening up fronts in other theaters where the enemy was presumably more vulnerable. The limited success of the Brusilov offensive and the entry of Rumania into the war in late 1916 exposing Austria-Hungary to a new front, was offset by the sudden collapse of the Rumanian army. The striking resiliency of the German war machine more than compensated for its weaker partner, so that at the close of 1916 the Central Powers had again restored approximate strategic parity. Nevertheless, the British blockade tightened and the Allied side still had significant mobile reserves, whereas the Central Powers were stretched to the limit and could only hope to defend along their vast perimeter. Their desperate plight led them to invest their hopes in unrestricted submarine warfare—and in the Russian Revolution.[1]

The military staffs of England, France, and Italy met at Chantilly in November 1916 and resolved to coordinate offensives on all fronts early in 1917. Russia was expected to reinforce the Rumanian army, to liberate

[1] For the German perspective, see *Ludendorff's Own Story, August, 1914–November, 1918*, 2 vols. (New York and London, 1919), 1:361-88; K. Novak, ed., *Die Aufzeichnugen des Generalmajors Max Hoffmann*, 2 vols. (Berlin, 1930), 2:164 and 167ff.; Paul von Hindenburg, *Out of My Life* (London, 1933), chap. 13; and *RWK* 11:1-10 and 32-41. The best account on the Allied side is *The War Memoirs of David Lloyd George, 1916-1917* (Boston, 1934). General Gurko's account (Gen. Basil Gourko, *Memories and Impressions of War and Revolution in Russia, 1914-1917* [London, 1918], chaps. 17-22) is quite disappointing, and General Alekseev has left no account. The two volumes of A. M. Zaionchkovskii in the series *Strategicheskii ocherk voiny 1917-1918 gg.*, 7 vols. (Moscow, 1923), vol. 6, *Period ot proryva iugozapadnogo fronta v maie 1916 g. do kontsa goda*, and vol. 7, *Kampaniia 1917*, chap. 1, offer a comprehensive, well-documented treatment.

Serbia, to knock Bulgaria out of the war, and to isolate the Turkish Empire. Despite Rumania's collapse and the enormous new strains on the Russian armies, Tsar Nicholas II and his temporary Chief of Staff, General Vasilii Gurko, affirmed the Chantilly decisions over the objections of the front chiefs on December 17, 1916.[2] The regular Chief of Staff, General M. V. Alekseev, recuperating from a serious illness, subjected the Chantilly strategy to a scathing critique in a detailed memorandum of January 4, 1917, arguing that the main blow should be struck where the enemy was weakest and that it was easiest to concentrate a large mass on the Galician sector; secondary operations would serve primarily to tie down the enemies' reserves. His plan, reluctantly adopted by Nicholas and Gurko, was communicated to the front chiefs and remained in force as the guideline for 1917 operations.[3]

General Gurko, however, ruled out a Russian offensive until May in order to implement his pet project of creating sixty new divisions by reducing the number of battalions per regiment from four to three.[4] A Conference of Allied Powers in Petrograd in January 1917, attended by the highest military and government representatives of all the powers, was another exercise in futility. Coming on the heels of the Rasputin murder and Nicholas' mental paralysis, the painful details of which were thrust on the embarrassed envoys, the conference reached meaningless compromises on operational matters: all Allied armies were pledged to begin major operations aimed at "decisive results" by May 1 (weather permitting), and only if the Central Powers attacked first were all Allied armies to respond with maximum force within three weeks. French General Castelnau's half-hearted efforts to secure a commitment from Gurko in accord with the wishes of General Nivelle, the Allied Supreme Command on the Western Front, was sarcastically noted in Ambassador Maurice Paléologue's diary.[5]

[2] Besides the version cited above, see the letter of French President Poincaré to Nicholas II of December 19, Nicholas' reply of reassurance of December 21, and the defense of the Allied strategy by the French military attaché to Stavka General Janin of December 21, in *KA* 29 (1928): 47-51.

[3] Text in A. G. Shliapnikov, *Semnadtsatyi god*, 4 vols. (Moscow, 1923-31), 4:217-21. The memorandum confirms that Alekseev was a strategist of the first magnitude, which Gurko and his Allied counterparts were not.

[4] The decision could easily have been postponed and was of doubtful military value, an opinion Gurko knew to be strongly held by Alekseev. See Gourko, 216-20, and telegram of Alekseev to Gurko of March 12, 1917, in Shliapnikov, 4:237.

[5] Maurice Paléologue, *An Ambassador's Memoirs*, 3 vols. (New York, 1923-25), 3:187. The formal request of the French representative General Castelnau at a conference session, and Gurko's evasion, are recorded in the protocol of the conference, published in *KA* 20 (1927): 45.

Undeterred by the outbreak of the Russian Revolution and by the certain knowledge that his plans had fallen into the hands of the enemy, Nivelle plunged recklessly forward on the Aisne sector in mid-April with his three scrupulously trained armies of twenty-seven divisions. Two weeks later his proud armies lay shattered, having but straightened out the line along the blood-soaked Chemin des Dames, and the remnants began to mutiny. In his memoirs, the German general Erich Ludendorff conceded his anxiety "what for our hard-pressed German armies the position inevitably must have been had the Russians attacked in April and May and met with even minor successes. . . . It was the Russian Revolution alone that saved us from serious trouble."[6]

In the month of March, Nivelle repeatedly reminded the Russians of the holy obligations of the Chantilly and Petrograd conferences and pleaded that the fate of his own operations depended on the fulfillment of those obligations. Revolution or not, he expected the Russian armies to undertake operations of "significant duration" aimed at "decisive results" no later than April 15 (April 2, O.S.).[7] Occupied with trying to calm the revolutionary storms, Alekseev at first argued that heavy snows precluded the resumption of operations before May, but on March 13 he candidly informed the French that the Russian army had been so severely disoriented by events that it would scarcely recover by June or July. He counseled Nivelle against major operations at the present time, citing arguments that to Nivelle must have sounded irritatingly similar to the carping of civilian politicians, the English ally, and even his own generals.[8]

At about the same time that Alekseev had decided to calm the waters at the front by authorizing committees (March 11), he also reconsidered his posture on the question of an offensive. He informed Guchkov that, despite the sorry condition of supply and turmoil in the troops, an offensive should be planned no later than early May, in view of the obligations to the Allies. He feared, first, that the Allies would cut off much-needed military supplies and loans and, second, that the enemy would probably not wait for Russia to recover to strike. At the same time, he laid the question with accompanying documents before his chiefs at the fronts, asking them when their armies would be ready to resume operations.[9]

General Ruzskii of the Northern Front replied that, though the worst excesses were over, discipline and supply were too shaken for Nivelle's

[6] *Ludendorff's Story*, 2:29.

[7] *KA* 22:28-29. Nivelle's appeal to the solemn obligations of the two conferences was disingenuous, as Russia was bound by Chantilly only with respect to Bulgarian operations and had never agreed to a date earlier than May 1.

[8] See Shliapnikov, 3:235-36, and *KA* 22:30.

[9] Both in Shliapnikov, 3:240-42.

request to be honored. On hand were food for only twelve days, fodder for ten, artillery reserves only for current needs, and he was understrength by 150,000 soldiers and 45,000 horses. Moreover, he opposed the current operational plan and pleaded that at least three full corps be transferred to his front to avert the danger of a German landing along the Finnish gulf.

Generals Smirnov and Brusilov accepted Alekseev's reasoning that the Germans would attack with the first dry weather, and since the Allies were already committed to an offensive it would be a betrayal not to tie down as many German divisions as possible. Although Smirnov was putting an optimistic construction on the reports he was getting from the field, his arguments were based on sound military considerations. But Brusilov claimed grandiloquently that his troops had been fired up by the Revolution, thirsted for victory, and had faith in their commanders and in the Provisional Government. Honor before Russia, the Allies, and the entire world demanded that the solemn commitments of Chantilly and Petrograd be observed. His indifference to the limitations of human and physical resources had already been demonstrated in the offensive of the previous year, and now he clearly believed in his star.[10] Quartermaster Lukomskii wryly scribbled in the margin of Brusilov's report, "Wouldn't it be a joy if these fancies corresponded to reality."[11]

General Gurko, who had just taken over command of the Western Front, now reversed his field, citing weighty reasons of state:

> Only if we render active support to our Allies are we in a position to demand from them the fulfillment of their obligations toward us. If they perceive our inability to conduct active operations, if they conclude that political difficulties have rendered the army inoperative, they will regard themselves as having a free hand.[12]

On March 30 Alekseev worked these replies into a memorandum to Guchkov and simultaneously instructed his chiefs at the fronts to choose a suitable point of attack where they would not require significant reinforcements. The main attack, however, was to be on the Southwestern Front in accord with the operative plan adopted in January. This was the quiet

[10] *Ibid.*, pp. 280-87, which includes Alekseev's preemptory rejection of Ruzskii's concern over the safety of Petrograd. Shortly thereafter, Ruzskii was dismissed and replaced by Gen. A. M. Dragomirov. For lower command reports on which General Smirnov's estimate is based, see *RazA*, pp. 25-27, and Shliapnikov, 2:121-33.

[11] *RazA*, p. 30. For a report of a conference of senior officers under Lukomskii's chairmanship for matters of supply, replacements, health, and railroads of March 18, which yielded alarming data in all these departments and concluded that active operations were now "unthinkable," see *ibid.*, pp. 10-11.

[12] Shliapnikov, 3:294.

but irrevocable step of which the Provisional Government as a whole was scarcely aware and which Kerensky inherited in the aftermath of the government crisis in May.[13]

☆

If Guchkov brought the matter before his ministerial colleagues, it finds no reflection in documentary sources or personal accounts. The political climate was such that it was almost impossible to broach the question of a new offensive and give it dispassionate consideration. By forcing on the government a renunciation of conquests (in the Declaration of March 27), the Soviet drowned the question of active operations in ambiguities that gave lip service to honoring obligations toward the Allies but permitted the Soviet to claim to its own supporters that it had thwarted the imperialist designs of the bourgeoisie. The Petrograd working class, galvanized by their encounter with the capitalist press of recent weeks, was alert for any sign that the Provisional Government might try to slip out from under the control of the Soviet, especially on the question of war aims. The garrison soldiers had learned to savor their role as guardians of the conquests of the Revolution, which meant that replacements need not be sent to the front and consequently that discipline and regular training exercises were superfluous. Guchkov, already steeped in pessimism, was not inclined to stir matters up again by advertising Alekseev's decision, or even to confide in his closest colleagues.[14]

Behind the facade of democratic harmony, the cabinet's inner masonic trio—Tereshchenko, Nekrasov, and Kerensky—hoped to utilize Kerensky's personal popularity to wean the masses from Soviet tutelage. Kerensky was not above insinuating to English ambassador George Buchanan and French socialist envoy Albert Thomas that Miliukov was a liability in the cabinet and that if the Allies made token concessions to the "no conquests" formula, the "democratic" elements in the government would be able to influence the Soviet and revive the fighting spirit of the Army.[15]

[13] *Ibid.*, pp. 295 and 291-93.

[14] "Iz vospominanii A. I. Guchkova," *Poslednye Novosti* (Paris), September 23, 1936. Guchkov claims that he was considering a military dictatorship enlisting the support of the cossack *voiska*. For evidence that this claim was not simply a fantasy of his declining years, see P. A. Polovtsev, *Dni zatmeniia* (Paris, n.d.), p. 32; and Gen. K. N. Khagondokov, "Vospominaniia" (Ms.), RA, pp. 780ff.

[15] In later years Miliukov was to claim that behind his back a treacherous bargain had been struck between his fellow cabinet members and the Allied ambassadors, whereby the latter would approve the idea of a coalition with the socialists, and Kerensky in particular as Defense Minister. Supposedly Paléologue, the French ambassador, brusquely rejected the plan, but his replacement, the socialist Thomas, approved it. See P. N. Miliukov, *Vospominaniia (1859-1917)*, 2 vols. (New York, 1955), 2:354-57; Sir George Buchanan, *My*

Miliukov's obsessive concern in these weeks was to uphold the integrity of the secret treaties with the Allies, specifically with reference to Constantinople, and to thwart the implications of the Soviet position on annexations. He had successfully carried through a wording of the Declaration of March 27 which in his mind nullified the revisionist import of the document: that the renunciation of conquests and acknowledgment of self-determination would on no account "allow the Motherland to come out of the war humiliated or undermined in her vital resources" or in any way affect "obligations undertaken toward the Allies."[16] When Kerensky announced to the press that the Declaration was to be officially communicated to the Allies, Miliukov publicly denied it and in a cabinet session threatened to resign if a formal refutation were not forthcoming.[17] Miliukov's intransigence may have been exceptional within the cabinet, but behind him stood the entire Kadet party, as well as most of the nonsocialist press and broad social circles of the center and right who had come to view Miliukov as their anchor of salvation. His presence in the cabinet was therefore regarded as almost axiomatic.

Renewed Soviet insistence forced the cabinet to consent to inform the Allies, but Miliukov insisted that there be appended an official interpretation which would make clear that existing treaties remained inviolable and took precedence over the vague terminology designed to appease the Soviet. The debate in the cabinet over the wording of this explanatory note was a continuation of the personal duel between Miliukov and Kerensky, the latter bickering over every phrase, but in the end Miliukov gained the substance of his own version, which twice included the code phrase "total victory." At his insistence the note was characterized as the unanimous view of the entire cabinet, and Kerensky, having exhausted himself in quibbles, declared himself satisfied.[18] This was the famous "Miliukov's Note" of April 18, which brought huge crowds into the streets, raised the specter of civil war, and unleashed a chain of events that led to the exodus of Miliukov and Guchkov from the cabinet and the formation of a coalition government with the socialists two weeks later.

Miliukov's action could not have been more calculated to arouse class

---

Mission to Russia and other Diplomatic Memoirs, 2 vols. (Boston, 1923), 2:117-18; and Paléologue, 3:311-12.

[16] *RPG* 2:1047-48. V. Nabokov, director of the Chancery of the Provisional Government, who helped Miliukov draw up these corrections, candidly admits that they were a calculated bit of "Machiavellianism to ensure that the document would not be interpreted by the Allies as a renunciation of the secret wartime agreements" ("Vremennoe Pravitel'stvo," *AR* 1 [1922]: 59).

[17] Miliukov, 2:354, and A. F. Kerensky, *The Catastrophe: Kerensky's Own Story of the Russian Revolution* (New York, 1927), pp. 134-35.

[18] Nabokov, *AR* 1:62-63, who alone provides convincing details of this session.

feeling, entrench dual authority, confirm the Bolshevik argument that the war remained imperialist, convince the garrison that its services were needed in Petrograd, and postpone to the Greek calends serious consideration of an offensive. All this did not transpire immediately, primarily because of the remarkable shift in the posture of the Soviet leadership in the course of the protracted crisis, and as a consequence the latter came to assume the power and responsibility for the conduct of the war. It is true that an incipient trend toward defensism had long been evident in Soviet circles and had already expressed itself in the resolution on war and peace at the All-Russian Conference of Soviets, which under the pressure of front delegates had been amended to support the idea of "preparedness" for active operations should the Central Powers ignore Soviet peace overtures. However, the Soviet leadership complacently neglected its garrison constituency and offered no wisdom on how the need of the front for replacements was to be reconciled with the agreement of March 2 not to remove "revolutionary troops" from the capital.

In the meantime, yielding to the euphoria of March patriotism and pressure from front deputations, a number of Petrograd regiments had consented to send modest numbers of replacements, though frequently hedged it with conditions that reflected considerable reluctance. The Semenovskii Regiment released two companies (500 men) on April 6 and three more on April 15, which amounted to roughly 22 percent of the total and perhaps one-third of those under training; the Petrogradskii Regiment released four companies (1,000 men), the Izmailovskiis released three, and five more guards regiments released one company or more.[19] Their departure was often accompanied by much fanfare and patriotic speechmaking, but Colonel Fomin, second in command of the Izmailovskii Regiment, notes that considerable *ugovarivanie* (persuasive agitation) was required and that spurious arguments were easily detected by the men; the banners, marching music, and rhetoric contrasted grotesquely with the dominant mood, which was that they should be exempt from front-line duty "as a reward for accomplishing the Revolution."[20]

In most of these cases, patriotically inclined battalion or unit committees responding to the appeals of front delegations foisted the decision on an unenthusiastic rank and file. In one characteristic instance, the Second Machine-gun Regiment consented to form a replacement company from

[19] See A. M. Andreev, *Soldatskie massy garnizonov russkoi armii v oktiabr'skoi revoliutsii* (Moscow, 1975), p. 110; G. L. Sobolev, "Petrogradskii garnizon v 1917 g.," *IZ*, No. 88 (1971): 69; *IzPS*, April 12; and *SS*, April 13 (scattered references in other organs of the contemporary press).

[20] B. V. Fomin, "Pervye mesiatsy posle fevral'skoi revoliutsii zap. bataliona Lb. Gv. Izmailovskogo polka," *Izmailovskaia Starina* 28 (1938): 155.

those entering the regiment after the Revolution, as presumably they did not share the privilege of not being sent to the front. Later, to refute the "vile slander" that their officers were about to leave for the front without them, the 19th company declared its readiness with "emblems and banners" to depart for the front. Two weeks later an angry deputation from the same company complained to the Soviet that the regimental committee had railroaded the decision through and were a "pack of counter-revolutionaries." The machine-gunners in particular believed themselves to be guardians of the Revolution.[21]

It is clear that instead of leading this movement the Soviet followed in its wake. No discussion of the question of replacements is recorded in the minutes of the Soviet Executive Committee for the first half of April, although it had been on the agenda since April 6. There was a chaotic debate on the issue in the Soldiers' Section of the Soviet on April 10, with Colonel Iakubovich of the Military Commission pleading that the matter urgently required regulation. On April 16 the hot potato was referred to the full Soviet, where defensist members of the Executive Committee and front representatives pleaded for the resumption of marching companies; several Bolshevik orators and soldier representatives were passionately opposed. N. D. Sokolov maneuvered a resolution through with some difficulty, accepting several hostile amendments, but four days later the April Crisis broke out.[22] In other words, the leadership finally took a position on the question precisely when the mood of the soldiers was moving sharply in the opposite direction.

In the same weeks, the Bolsheviks made their first serious inroads in the garrison by playing to the soldiers' mood. Although the majority of the soldier deputies and *komitetchiki* were ardent defensists, a handful of Bolsheviks who had participated in the uprising and helped in the framing of Order No. One, such as Paderin, Sadovskii, and Tarasov-Rodionov, constituted a militant, antiwar minority, as they were in their own party until Lenin's return. Although Bolshevik moderates such as Kamenev and Stalin dragged out consideration of Lenin's April theses for several weeks, the latter struck an immediate response among the activists of the Bolshevik Military Organization, which exploited the issue of marching companies to solidify soldier sentiment against the Soviet majority. The benefits were

[21] According to the *protokoly* of the regimental committee of the Second Machine-Gun Regiment, March 22-April 4, in A. K. Drezen, *Bol'shevizatsiia petrogradskogo garnizona 1917 goda. Sbornik materialov i dokumentov* (Leningrad, 1932), pp. 62-65.

[22] See record of the proceedings of the Soldiers' Section in F. I. Matveev, *Iz zapisnoi knigi deputata 176 pekh. polka. Petrogradskii Sovet, mart-mai 1917 g.* (Moscow-Leningrad, 1932), pp. 77-80. There is no record that it was ever discussed in the Executive Committee, though it was once on the agenda. See *PSPZ*, p. 86.

reaped on a significant scale only in May, and this hectic activity cannot be regarded as the prime mover of the April Days, which were a kind of weathercock of the changing mood to which the Bolshevik militants were attuned and the Soviet leadership was not.[23]

The soldiers' role in the April Days was secondary and more that of spectators, whereas the chief contenders for the streets were the thoroughly politicized workers of the Vyborg, Vasilevskii, and Petrograd districts and the ever-present middle- and upper-class public on the Nevskii Prospect, which fed on the patriotic drumbeating of *Rech, Russkaia Volia*, and other "bourgeois" organs. The forces of this public were augmented by students, officer trainees, staffs of military administrations, front officers on leave, and front soldiers in Petrograd on various missions to "straighten out the rear." Because of Lenin's recent return and lurid suggestions that he was bankrolled by the German General Staff, they were in a thoroughly alarmist frame of mind.

The exaggerated impression of soldier involvement is due primarily to the initial episode: the Finlandskii Guards Regiment, informed of Miliukov's note, gathered in full parade regalia in the mid-afternoon of April 20 before the Mariinskii Palace, where the government was said to be sitting, and demanded Miliukov's resignation. They were addressed in turn by General Kornilov, Chief of the Petrograd Military District, and several members of the Executive Committee. As time passed they were joined by elements of the 180th, the Moskovskii, and the Pavlovskii regiments, and the Marine Guards Equipage, a force of 20,000 to 25,000 in all.[24] This affair seems to have been the individual enterprise of an erratic, nonparty soldier-intellectual, F. F. Linde, who persuaded assembled battalion and company committees that they must come out in defense of the Soviet in response to Miliukov's brazen challenge.[25] Though doubtless hazy on the issues at stake, the soldiers were easily persuaded to defend the Soviet peace efforts against the intrigues of a "bourgeois" minister.[26] The slogan of the demonstrating soldiers was limited to "Down with Miliukov" and, as Linde later explained to the press, it was not meant to

[23] See the first few issues of *SP*, April 15-18, and documents in Drezen, pp. 75-82, for the most reliable information. Personal accounts, such as those of Podvoiskii and other Bolshevik activists, are self-advertising and less reliable. See the excellent treatment of Alexander Rabinowitch in *Prelude to Revolution: The Petrograd Bolsheviks and the July 1917 Uprising* (Bloomington, Ind., 1968), pp. 47-53.

[24] The best contemporary coverage is *NZh*, April 20ff.

[25] On the enigmatic figure of Linde, see I. G. Tsereteli, *Vospominaniia o fevral'skoi revoliutsii*, 2 vols. (Paris, 1963), 2:93, and Aleksei Tarasov-Rodionov, *February 1917* (New York, 1931), pp. 356ff., 368.

[26] See Kornilov's version, according to French journalist Claude Anet, *Through the Russian Revolution: Notes of an Eye-Witness from 12th March to 30th May* (London, 1917), p. 171.

be aimed at the Provisional Government as a whole.[27] After a few hours the soldiers were persuaded by Executive Committee members Skobelev and Gots to depart peacefully.

That evening and into the next day, column after column of worker-demonstrators, headed by armed militia and sometimes drawing in soldier participants, poured over the Neva bridges to Mars Field, the Palace Square, and Nevskii Prospect, clashing with patriotic groups and in several cases provoking gunfire and casualties. The placards of the worker-demonstrators reflected more militant attitudes and some Bolshevik inspiration: "Down with the War" "Down with the Provisional Government," "All Power to the Soviets."[28]

The Soviet Executive Committee mustered its full authority to restrain the demonstrators and sought to settle the matter as quickly as possible by negotiations with the Provisional Government. In spite of the awesome display of power on behalf of the Soviet, the Soviet negotiators allowed themselves to be hastily satisfied with a weakly worded explanation by the Provisional Government and did not even raise the issue of Miliukov's resignation. The basic contradiction remained unsolved: the self-deluded Executive Committee claimed to its constituency that the government statement of March 27 had been upheld, while Miliukov with just as little justification characterized the confrontation as a decisive victory for the government and his own point of view.[29]

The reason for the tractability of the Soviet Executive Committee was that the government weakness was all too obvious: during the crisis, Minister President G. E. L'vov had told Soviet spokesman Iraklil Tsereteli of his willingness to resign and to allow the Soviet to form a government, a prospect the Soviet leaders were by no means willing to contemplate. Not only was the Menshevik component shackled by its dogmatic Marxism (the inadmissibility of exercising or sharing power in a "bourgeois" rev-

[27] *NZh*, April 23.

[28] The best source on the workers' role is the collection of depositions of participants to a committee of investigation, published in "Aprel'skie dni v Petrograde," *KA* 33 (1929): 34-81. The slogan "All Power to the Soviets," which might have been due to Bolshevik participation, was not observed by the witnesses in the chief afternoon demonstrations on Nevskii Prospect, but it was seen at lesser demonstrations that evening. See *ibid.*, p. 78. Gerhardt Wettig has examined the evidence in considerable detail in "Die Rolle der russischen Armee im revolutionären Machtkampf 1917," *FO* 22 (1967): 291ff., and concluded that the Bolshevik leadership had taken no position on the demonstrations, and Tarasov-Rodionov (p. 368) portrays Lenin as outright against them. However, see Rabinowitch, pp. 44-45, on the militants of the Military Organization and the Petrograd Committee or local factory districts who on their own pushed the demonstrations toward overthrow of the Provisional Government.

[29] For the Executive Committee's claim, see *IzPS*, April 26. For Miliukov, see his *Vospominaniia*, 2:364; Paléologue, 3:370; and Buchanan, 2:124.

olution), but the leadership as a whole sensed that as bearers of power they would encourage expectations among the masses that they would be unable to satisfy. However, shying away from power did not free them from the underlying dilemma. On the one hand, they risked their credibility with their soldier constituency by instructing them not to come out for armed demonstrations except on a directive of the Soviet, which allowed the progovernment demonstrators to appear more imposing than they actually were. On the other hand, when Kornilov called out units of the Mikhailovskii Artillery School to uphold public order, the Soviet Executive Committee obliged him to countermand his order. Knowing that insistence would be futile, Kornilov consented to revoke the order if the Executive Committee would assume responsibility for clearing the streets. He understood, however, that the Soviet would act discreetly and covertly, so that an affront to command authority would not be evident,[30] but instead the Soviet advertised Kornilov's impotence to all the world in a proclamation: "Every directive to military units to come out on the streets (except ordinary patrols) must be issued on a form supplied by the Executive Committee, stamped with its seal, and signed by at least two of the following persons: Chkheidze, Skobelev, [and several others]. . . . Confirm every such order by telephone."[31] Kornilov's humiliation could not have been more profound, as even Order No. One recognized the legitimacy of orders of unit commanders "insofar as" they did not conflict with contrary orders of the Soviet. Kornilov resigned his command and was not inclined to forgive and forget.[32]

This incident revealed the absurdity of the situation in which the Soviet, the only reservoir of real power, enjoyed an almost limitless moral authority over the troops and workers of the capital without assuming direct responsibility for military and state administration. From the Left as well as the Right, voices began to multiply that Soviet figures should formally enter the government. First the voice of Left Internationalism, *Novaia Zhizn'*, then several "bourgeois" organs (but not *Rech'*), picked up the refrain as a "solution" to the unending crises of "dual power." Kerensky helped matters along by threatening to resign unless socialists joined him

[30] For Kornilov's version, see his letter of resignation to Guchkov of April 23 in "K istorii kornilovshchiny," *KL* 10 (1924): 206-7 (same details in *VVP*, April 26). Both claim that there was an understanding with the Soviet leaders. For Kornilov as otherwise flexible and forthcoming in the first few weeks with the Soviet, see *PSPZ*, pp. 34-35 (minutes of the Executive Committee for March 10, where Kornilov offers to maintain "contact" with the Soviet through their representatives on the Military Commission and even visits a session).

[31] *VOSR. Aprel'skii krizis*, p. 759, and *RPG* 3:1241 (from *IzPS*, April 22).

[32] For the unsuccessful effort of the Executive Committee to undo the damage, see V. B. Stankevich, *Vospominaniia 1914-1919 gg.* (Berlin, 1920), p. 127.

in the cabinet.[33] On April 26 the Provisional Government issued a statement, apparently backed by the entire cabinet except Miliukov and Guchkov, which raised the specter of civil war and anarchy if the government were not strengthened by "creative elements of the country which hitherto have not taken direct part in state administration."[34] Even the Kadet Central Committee on April 23 nearly endorsed the idea of coalition, falling short by a single vote (Miliukov was away at the time at Stavka).[35] But all this failed to overcome the ingrained reluctance of the Soviet Executive Committee, and it was pressure from their own constituency that ultimately tipped the balance.

Endorsement of the idea of coalition was first proposed from the Soviet side at a garrison conference on April 22, which the Executive Committee had called to elicit a congratulatory resolution for having peacefully liquidated the crisis. The Executive Committee discovered to its surprise that there was considerable skepticism in the barracks about whether the thorny issues had been resolved. The Armored Car Division proposed that the participation of socialists in the government should be affirmed as the only means of overcoming "deadly dual power." At first only the Semenovskiis supported them, but a number of the speakers expressed profound dissatisfaction with the existing arrangements. The eventual resolution instructed the Soviet "in the immediate future to put the matter of regulating relations between the Provisional Government and the democracy before the soldiers' and workers' assemblies."[36] In response, resolutions favoring coalition began to pour in from individual units and factories, as well as from the provinces and the front. The Mensheviks in the Executive Committee resisted as long as they could with their standard arsenal of arguments, but Guchkov's resignation finally broke down their resistance (May 1).[37]

The Mensheviks' behavior might be viewed as excessively timid in contrast to that of the Socialist Revolutionaries, who were more receptive to the idea of coalition. However, the Mensheviks' arguments were from their own point of view well grounded. Still traumatized by what they regarded as their fundamental tactical error of the revolutionary movement

[33] See *Catastrophe*, p. 137, and Tsereteli, 1:121. For the text of a letter of Kerensky requesting that the socialist leaders enter the cabinet, see *RPG* 3:1252.

[34] *RPG* 3:1251.

[35] See William Rosenberg, *Liberals in the Russian Revolution: The Constitutional Democratic Party, 1917-1921* (Princeton, 1974), p. 110. This is the best treatment so far on the politics of the crisis.

[36] Tsereteli, 1:108. Other details in *NZh*, April 29, and *IzPS*, April 25. Armored car resolution in Drezen, p. 77.

[37] Full account in Tsereteli, 1:107-37 (for Chkheidze's passionate opposition, see ibid., pp. 127-28); documents in *RPG* 3:1267-69.

in 1905-6 of trying to push beyond the framework of a bourgeois-constitutional order, they took as their Marxist text Engels' injunction that "the worst thing that can befall the leader of an extreme party is to be compelled to take over a government in an epoch when the movement is not yet ripe for the dominance of the class he represents, and for the realization of the measures which that domination implies."[38] Tsereteli's translation into the context of 1917 sounds almost prophetic:

> If by entering the government we arouse in the masses expectations we are unable to satisfy, we strengthen the left, maximalist tendencies. Then, together with the weakening of our influence on the masses, we lose our capacity to influence the government, regardless of the presence in it of our representatives. The disparity between the policies of the government and popular expectations will grow, and instead of strengthening the democratic power, the result would be the strengthening of the maximalist sentiments of the masses.[39]

Their haunting perspective was shortly to assume tragic dimensions, as their entry into the coalition amounted to propping up the faltering "bourgeois" component in the government, which Menshevik ideology dictated as essential. The combination could be maintained only by granting ever-new concessions, which served only to drive the masses over to the Bolsheviks.

An ardent proponent of coalition on the extreme Social Democratic Left, N. N. Sukhanov argued cogently that the real justification of coalition was to ensure consistent pursuit of the Soviet peace program and other Soviet policies, without unpleasant surprises like Miliukov's note.[40] But this policy could succeed only if the Soviet were willing to mobilize its constituency openly on behalf of the Soviet program, which besides a revision of the secret treaties should include a strong interim land law, a firm timetable for the Constituent Assembly, and effective economic controls to ensure full production and fixed prices on essential goods. These measures would have definitively alienated the Kadets and privileged social groups and provoked an earlier emergence of Kornilovism, still without satisfying the expectations of the masses, but it can be argued that such a confrontation was sooner or later inevitable. Since the actual intent of the Soviet leaders in entering the coalition was to avoid confrontation, its actions had to be directed toward conciliation. The April Days marked the beginning of the ever-growing frustration of the masses over the leader-

[38] Karl Marx and Friedrich Engels, *Werke*, 42 vols. (Berlin, 1964-83), 7:400.

[39] Tsereteli, 1:130.

[40] *NZh*, April 23ff. For Tsereteli's puzzlement and critique, see *op. cit.* (n. 25), 1:132; Sukhanov's version is in *Zapiski o revoliutsii*, 7 vols. (Berlin, 1922-23), 3:385-96.

ship's systematic policy of keeping their revolutionary energy under restraint, which exploded during the July Days in Petrograd and in virtually the entire country, and on the front in response to the Kornilov affair. Even then the Soviet leadership did not learn the lesson.

The prospect of power, paradoxically, sobered the Soviet leaders and transformed them, or rather completed their transformation, into partisans of order, structured authority, and a vigorous prosecution of the war, all clearly at variance with the predispositions of their constituency. Few Soviet figures were inclined to acknowledge this transformation in later writings, and their public statements of the time masked it behind clichés and ideological verbiage, but their critics on the Left, such as Sukhanov and the Bolsheviks, took note of it with gleeful sarcasm. Nevertheless, V. B. Stankevich, a Trudovik and defensist member of the Executive Committee, captures the psychological moment and the context with some persuasiveness. Shaken by the massive confrontations on the streets and faced with a faltering "bourgeois" government that extended the hand to them for help, the Soviet leaders were at this juncture approached by delegates of the Twelfth and Fifth Army committees (Kuchin, Vilenkin, Khodorov) who had just come from a conference of Northern Front committees. Laying out the appalling state of discipline and universal fraternization at the front, the delegates put the question squarely: "Are we to fight or not?" Rankled by the fact that neither the Allies nor German militarism regarded them seriously, the Soviet leaders answered to their own surprise, "We'll fight."[41]

In a memorable session of the Executive Committee, a surge of relief and enthusiasm accompanied by a new sense of purpose materialized in the form of unaccustomed applause for a militant call to arms composed by Wladimir Woytinsky:

> Comrade soldiers! Defend revolutionary Russia with all the strength at your command! Russian peasants and soldiers want peace with all their heart and soul, but this peace must be a universal peace for all peoples. What if the Russian Army should stick their bayonets into the ground and say it won't fight any more? What would become of our cause? Only this, that once defeating the Allies in the West, German imperialism would turn with all its strength against us. It would turn out that the German imperialists, German landowners, and capitalists would have their bootheel on our neck, seize our cities, villages, and lands, and lay a heavy tribute on the Russian people. Did we really overthrow Nicholas to bend our neck to Wilhelm?

[41] Stankevich, p. 122.

Even more startling was the open pronouncement of the forbidden words: "There are cases where the only way to ward off an offensive of the enemy is to take the offensive ourselves."[42] The inevitable chain of logic now led to the restoration of discipline and officer authority, the resumption of training and sending replacements, and the total mobilization of the country to secure the defeat of the enemy. Only then would both the Allies and the Central Powers be compelled to listen to Russian democracy's counsels of peace, only then would the democratic forces in Germany and Austria-Hungary take heart and struggle against militarism from within.

Such was the conscious rationale, but Stankevich also suggests that the subconscious logic worked in the reverse direction: all around them was social and political chaos, the militant workers were ever less amenable to Soviet appeals, and the armed and undisciplined soldiery was a threat both to themselves and to their fellow countrymen. The revival of an authoritative, undivided state power had become a social imperative. The necessity of waging war to make peace would give the soldiers a cause, a reason for discipline and order, and a new and more satisfying role for the Soviet leadership. Either way, the "circle of ideas was now complete," Stankevich concludes, and "everything was placed in the service of the new slogans."[43] The logical corollary of the "acceptance of the war" in Stankevich's scheme was the "acceptance of power," which within days brought Tsereteli, Skobelev, and Chernov into ministerial posts and gave Soviet benediction to Kerensky as the new democratic Minister of War. Kerensky by self-appointment epitomized democracy's determination to revive the "revolutionary army" from the ashes and to prove to all the world the superiority of "revolutionary discipline" and fighting spirit.

☆

The timetable for the offensive set by Stavka (as the Supreme Headquarters at Mogilev was called) had been seriously thrown off by April developments front and rear. Fraternization and chronic defiance of command authority showed no signs of abating, the few replacements that began to show up at the end of April were virtually untrained and more tumultuous than the front soldiers, and the delivery of munitions and supplies and was still far below requirements for active operations. To crown the Army's troubles, there was now renewed political unrest in Petrograd, which Alekseev himself witnessed. On April 20-21 he visited the capital to confer with Guchkov, and he was even present at the historic cabinet session that discussed the crisis. He also looked in on the Polivanov

[42] *RDRA*, p. 78.
[43] Stankevich, p. 124.

Commission, which to his consternation was then discussing the "Declaration of Soldiers' Rights" sponsored by the Soviet.[44]

A few days later Guchkov wired Alekseev that a government crisis was inevitable, as the Soviet had just laid claim to special jurisdiction over the troops of the capital. Thereupon Alekseev notified his front chiefs, that "Our fatherland may soon find itself in the hands of self-appointed government, whose leaders have already . . . brought about complete disarray in the Army." He proposed that the senior commanders collectively call on the government to exercise "firm power" (*tverdia vlast'*) vis-à-vis the Soviet, implying that it would be backed by the Army. An appeal was also directed to the general public to support the duly constituted government for the sake of victory. Alekseev's front chiefs all found objections to the project, and so he instead summoned them to Stavka for a conference.[45]

The Stavka Conference of May 1 was a remarkable but futile affair. Each of the front chiefs, General A. M. Dragomirov for the Northern Front, Gurko for the Western, Brusilov for the Southwestern, and Shcherbachev for the Rumanian Front, outlined the lamentable state of affairs on their sectors. Brusilov, abandoning his former optimism, etched a graphic picture of unrestrained, universal fraternization and collapse of discipline: soldiers recognized the moral authority only of the Soviet, dismissed their officers as *burzhuis*, and believed every Bolshevik orator who happened to come along. In one striking example, when a deputation of worker-Bolsheviks from Kiev actually exhorted the soldiers to obey an order to attack, the soldiers answered, "Let the workers and officers do it!" Brusilov asserted that the Soviet peace slogans brought out the soldiers' basest instinct of self-preservation, which reasoned: "Why should we fight and risk our necks when there will be peace without annexations and indemnities anyway?" "We now have freedom and we are going to get the land, so why should we go and get ourselves crippled?" He concluded that the prospects for an offensive at present were virtually nil because of lack of supplies and replacements. Brusilov, who alone of the generals at the conference had evinced an enthusiasm for the Revolution, was now the

[44] Press account in *Rech'*, April 21 (reprinted in *VOSR. Aprel'skii krizis*, p. 314). Kolchak's version of Alekseev's reaction is in his deposition of 1920, reprinted in *RPG* 2:880, and Alekseev's own version is in a private letter in "Iz dnevnika gen. M. V. Alekseeva, *Russkii istoricheskii arkhiv. Sbornik pervyi* (Prague, 1929), p. 17.

[45] For the text of Alekseev's invitation to front chiefs of April 26, see *VOSR. Aprel'skii krizis*, p. 324. The proclamation texts are not included, but Gen. A. I. Denikin, then Alekseev's Chief of Staff, confirms that they were distributed to all division commanders for their reaction; see A. I. Denikin, *Russian Turmoil: Memoirs, Military, Social, and Political* (London, 1922), p. 151.

most outspoken in his hostility to the Soviet. If the Soviet did not mend its ways, he declared, he would resign his command and take up the struggle against them in Petrograd as a private citizen.[46]

With Alekseev's encouragement, the other generals also unburdened themselves, fastening ever more specifically on the Soviet as the chief source of all disorganizing phenomena. At the appropriate moment Alekseev introduced the subject of the impending "Declaration of Soldiers' Rights," which evoked another rash of threats to resign if the government should yield. Shcherbachev declared himself against resigning, generally taking a more optimistic view, and assured his colleagues that the new coalition government would encourage a more responsible attitude on the part of the socialist leaders. Dragomirov unexpectedly proposed that they journey collectively to Petrograd to confront the Soviet—which apparently kindled an urge on all their parts for a heroic exploit to bring the country back from the abyss. Shcherbachev summed up the mood: "We have to go for broke." They departed for Petrograd the same night.

Exactly what they hoped to achieve or discuss with the Soviet was not clear, but the immediate objective seemed to be to forestall the approval of the Declaration of Soldiers' Rights. Why the Declaration should cause the most offense is puzzling, since most of its principles were already embodied in Orders No. One and 114, the shock of which had been absorbed. The controversial new points were the abolition of officers' orderlies (except at the front by mutual consent and for compensation) and of obligatory saluting. A fight for such marks of caste distinction would have been a poor line of defense in a confrontation with the Soviet, but probably the generals feared a new rash of conflicts over the Declaration's provisions. There could scarcely be any progress toward tightening up for the offensive if the soldiers possessed such a convenient weapon with which to harass officers. The period of turmoil had to be brought to an end once and for all, and the soldiers had to be persuaded that there would be no peace until the opposing army was defeated, which was impossible without a revival of discipline and strict obedience to command authority.

The generals arrived in Petrograd on May 5, just as the new coalition government came into being, so the generals unexpectedly conferred with the socialist leaders, not as representatives of the Soviet but as partners in the cabinet. This resolved an anxiety expressed by Gurko that by approaching the Soviet the generals would be acknowledging it rather than the government as the real power. Somehow the novelty of the situation caused the generals to temper their demands considerably. Although Bru-

[46] Zaionchkovskii, *Kampaniia 1917 g.*, pp. 134-35; the entire proceedings are published as an appendix in *ibid*. pp. 133-51.

silov again spoke with great passion about the harmful effects of Order No. One and the Soviet peace formula, his tone was conciliatory and pleading, and he failed to touch upon the delicate question of the Declaration of Soldiers' Rights. Dragomirov spoke in much the same tone, but with a stern admonition to "return authority to the commanding staff."[47] The only one to strike a belligerent pose was Gurko, who insisted that the Declaration of Soldiers' Rights would destroy the Army and that saluting had to be preserved as an indispensable mark of military discipline. He tactlessly suggested that "democracy" was playing into the hands of Wilhelm just as much as the old regime.

Alekseev's truculence also seems to have evaporated. He admitted, "We are all responsible for the current sad state of affairs," and he expressed his faith that the new War Minister would do all in his power to restore health to the Army. Incongruously, he pleaded with the Soviet representatives to "send their best people" to the front to repair the damage wrought by Order No. One, even calling for "new orders and explanations," while at the same time insisting on "firm, undivided rule" which precluded the circulation of any orders except those of the War Minister and the Commander in Chief. Still his basic plea was for help and cooperation.[48]

Thus, Tsereteli's claim that the generals, except for Brusilov and Shcherbachev, struck a preemptory tone seems exaggerated. However, the unanimous claim by the generals that Order No. One and the Soviet peace formula were largely responsible for the deplorable state of discipline struck a sensitive nerve. Tsereteli admonished the generals that only through the policies of the Soviet could health be restored to the Army, as they alone embodied the true aspirations of the people; soldiers had to be willing to fight, not because of the old discipline but because they were convinced they were defending the ideals of the Revolution.[49] Gurko correctly observed that the two parties were "arguing on two different planes" and that they had failed to make contact. Kerensky pleaded that both parties were pursuing the same goals according to their own lights and should not reproach each other, but this did little to bridge the gap. Minister President L'vov helplessly thanked the generals for "sharing your thoughts with us," and the latter departed, having achieved satisfaction on none of the issues that agitated them.

The scanty record of the coalition negotiations mentions no discussions

[47] N. N. Golovin, *Rossiiskaia kontrrevoliutsiia v 1917-1918 gg.*, 5 vols., 12 parts. (Tallin, Estonia, 1937), 1 (1):106 (from full text of proceedings).

[48] *Ibid.*, p. 111.

[49] Tsereteli also reproduces a good bit of the dialogue of this conference, including his own speech in *op. cit.*, 1:408-10.

of the Army, but certainly there were understandings, verbal or implied, as the new government program of May 5 formally stated the following:

> In the conviction that a defeat of Russia and her Allies would be a great misfortune for all peoples, and would delay or make impossible a universal peace, the Provisional Government firmly believes that the revolutionary army will never permit German troops to destroy our Allies in the West and then turn on us with their full military might. The strengthening of the principles of democratizing the Army, and the organization and strengthening of its military capacity for both defensive and offensive operations, shall be the first priority of the Provisional Government.[50]

Since the eight-point program was otherwise basically framed by the Soviet side, it is very likely that the Kadets did not withdraw their support as threatened because of their satisfaction with the above-formulated commitment. Despite the absence of direct testimony, it seems clear that a bargain had been struck, because the Soviet leadership registered no objection to Kerensky's prompt and vigorous efforts to prime the Army for an offensive. Kerensky was not only nominal co-chairman of the Petrograd Soviet and a prominent Socialist Revolutionary (S.R.), he was also formally accountable to the Soviet, along with the other socialist ministers, according to a determination of the Soviet Executive Committee of May 5.[51] Another indication is that around this time Allied representatives expressed a new optimism over Russia's contribution to the war effort and refer to the offensive as a matter decided, whereas a short time before they were advising their governments to the contrary.[52] Most press organs representing the Soviet majority immediately fell into line, the Soviet's own *Izvestiia Petrogradskago Soveta* (*IzPS*) setting the pace with a declaration on May 5 that "whether defending a fortified position or conducting an attack dictated by strategic or tactical considerations, the soldier may now believe that these operations serve one and the same goal—the defense of the Revolution and the earliest possible attainment of a universal peace."[53]

[50] *VOSR. Mai-iiun'*, pp. 229-30. For Tsereteli's detailed account of the negotiations, see *op. cit.*, 1:138-68. For it was basically a Soviet draft, amended only at the suggestion of L'vov to include rejection of "separate peace" and endorsement of "strong authority," see *ibid.*, pp. 138, 144, and 146; English text in *RPG* 3:1277-78.

[51] Text in *RPG* 3:1278-79 (from *IzPS*, May 6).

[52] See Buchanan, 2:128; Paléologue, 3:345, and *passim*; and Gen. Alfred Knox, *With the Russian Army, 1914-1917*, 2 vols. (New York, 1921), 2:618. The new Foreign Minister, M. I. Tereshchenko, expressed Russia's renewed commitment to the war to French Foreign Minister Ribot on May 7 (text in *VOSR. Mai-iiun'*, p. 235).

[53] Reprinted in *RPG* 3:1294. Lenin wrote in *Pravda* of May 9 with some discernment: "Prince L'vov has declared that the 'country must express its mighty will and send the Army

The defensist element in the Soldiers' Section could now surface and face Bolshevik agitators with the assurance of Executive Committee backing. At the front the beleaguered army committees greeted the new orientation with undisguised joy. They could now preach the brand of revolutionary militancy against German imperialism that corresponded to their own feelings. The former ambivalence of simultaneously "defending the Revolution" and upholding military order was overcome by the merging of the two sources of authority in the person of the new War Minister and revolutionary hero. Henceforward, the entire upper representational structure in the Army adopted as its own the revised Soviet program expressed in and through the Coalition Government. Cooperation with command authority could now replace conflict, because both were subject to the same authority and engaged in the common enterprise of preparing the Army for fighting. Kerensky's position as War Minister was, of course, pivotal to the new order of things. His initiative had brought the coalition into being, and he alone had the standing and moral authority to impose restraint on both parties within it. Unlike Guchkov, who was constantly badgered into concessions he found distasteful, Kerensky could pull the teeth from the many-faceted forms of Soviet "control" without risking being accused of counter-revolutionary intent. On the other hand, as "War Minister" he could oblige the generals to accept whatever innovations were necessary with the argument that the soldiers would fight enthusiastically only for goals sanctioned by an authoritative revolutionary government.

He carried through two immediate measures that without his personal authority would have entailed considerable difficulties, namely, the Declaration of Soldiers' Rights and the institution of "commissars" to the armies and fronts under the exclusive jurisdiction of the War Minister. Kerensky, apprised that the senior commanders contemplated collective resignation should the Declaration be approved, issued as his first order to the Army the forbidding of resignations as equivalent to desertion in wartime.[54] Although the Polivanov Commission approved the Soviet's version of the Declaration without significant alterations, Kerensky promulgated it on May 11 with changes designed to enhance command authority. He struck out the provision that granted committees the right to control officer appointments, and in article 18 he confirmed the command's exclusive authority over operations, training, "special duties," inspection, and supply. Unwelcome to commanders was that disciplinary powers re-

---

into battle.' That is the essence of the new government 'program'—offensive, offensive, offensive!" (*Sochineniia*, ed. L. B. Kamenev and N. I. Bukharin et al., 30 vols., 3rd ed. [Moscow-Leningrad, 1927-33], 20:354).

[54] See A. F. Kerensky, *Russia and History's Turning Point* (New York, 1965), p. 272; and *VVP*, May 6.

mained under the jurisdiction of elected committees and courts, as previously specified by Order No. 213 and other orders, but article 14 provided the important exception that, in combat, commanders retained the right to employ armed force against subordinates disobeying orders.[55] Guchkov would scarcely have been in a position to introduce these bold changes, but Kerensky basked in the praise of both the socialist and the nonsocialist press for ushering in a new era of the "citizen-soldier." *Pravda* and other Bolshevik organs, however, fastened mercilessly on articles 14 and 18 as transforming the Declaration into a "Declaration of Soldiers' Rightlessness."[56] General Gurko immediately resigned his command, but Kerensky informed him that his resignation was not accepted; instead, he was demoted to divisional commander.[57]

The Soviet Executive Committee had discussed the question of attaching commissars to military units since the first days of the Revolution and had even worked out a detailed instruction, which it never finalized.[58] The War Ministry was to provide the commissars with credentials to secure the cooperation of commanders, but in the exercise of their functions they were to be completely autonomous, responsible only to the Soviet.[59] The Provisional Government had even consented in principle, but Guchkov dragged the matter out in the Polivanov Commission until his resignation. In mid-April a conference of front delegates drew up new proposals: *three* commissars were attached to each army, one each from the government, the Soviet, and the army committee, and these commissars would jointly supervise *all* aspects of a commander's activities, countersign orders, and investigate commanding staffs with the right to recommend dismissals.[60] The Soviet Executive Committee even discussed whether commissars should have the right to make arrests, dissolve local zemstvos, and exercise other specified powers, but the objection was raised and sustained that if powers were defined too precisely they would in effect supplant the authority of commanders, and that therefore it was better to exercise control from without with undefined powers, interfering in a "revolutionary" manner when the situation called for it.[61]

Perhaps wishing to forestall the Soviet project, the Provisional Govern-

[55] Text in *RPG* 2:880-82.

[56] See *Pr* and *SP*, appropriate dates.

[57] See Gourko, *Memories*, pp. 310ff. See also the version of A. I. Denikin, *Ocherki russkoi smuty*, 5 vols. [Paris-Berlin, 1921-26], 1[2]:152), who replaced Gurko as commander of the Western Front and sympathized with his demonstration.

[58] For Soviet discussions of March 19 and April 11, see *PSPZ*, pp. 61-62 and 114.

[59] See *ibid.*, p. 77 (April 5).

[60] See *SS*, April 15, and Denikin, *Russian Turmoil*, p. 168.

[61] See *PSPZ*, p. 114 (April 17).

ment appointed its own commissars to the major fronts (but not to armies) at the end of April, but without providing them with specific instructions or defining their functions.[62] Finally, a compromise agreement that would have attached two commissars to each of the fourteen armies, one from the Soviet and another from the government, was about to be implemented at the end of April. Kerensky claims that shortly after taking office he persuaded Tsereteli and Skobelev to consent to a single commissar under the exclusive jurisdiction of the War Ministry. In practice, the appointments were negotiated jointly, the Soviet supplying most of the candidates and retaining the claim to accountability for their actions.[63] Thus Kerensky acquired primary jurisdiction over a network of commissars attached to army staffs, free to determine their functions as he saw fit and relatively free from Soviet interference (the claim of accountability to the Soviet was never effectively exercised). Later, in June, a more detailed regulation of their functions was introduced and supervised through a "Political Section" of the War Ministry.[64]

Finally, Kerensky quietly eliminated the major source of Soviet-inspired reforms and irritant with the command—the Polivanov Commission—a step Guchkov certainly would never have dared take.

☆

Kerensky's reforming activity was but a brief prelude to his chief concern—reshaping the psychological climate at the front for a new offensive. On May 12 he set out on a three-week, barnstorming tour of the front, determined to vindicate to friend and foe the fighting potential of an army animated by revolutionary ardor. The generals, he believed, were cynical about the Revolution because the latent power of "conscious revolutionary discipline" and willingness for self-sacrifice for the sake of freedom had not yet been clearly demonstrated. One can only marvel at Kerensky's confidence in his personal powers when one considers the magnitude of the task he faced. Though he had a ready audience among the higher committees, soldiers everywhere along the front were discussing orders at improvised meetings, ignoring their committees and the command, reveling in the confidence of an early peace, and above all passing resolutions or

[62] *Zhurnal zasedanii vremennogo pravitel'stva* (Petrograd, 1917), No. 61 (April 24). (Copy at HI.)

[63] *Catastrophe*, pp. 188-89. For the Soviet; involvement in the nominations, which almost without exception were of socialists, see Stankevich, p. 169, and Denikin, *Russian Turmoil*, p. 168.

[64] See Stankevich, pp. 140-50, and Fedor Stepun, *Byvshee i nesbyvsheesia*, 2 vols. (New York, 1956), 2:89-93. Stankevich served in the Political Section only briefly, but Stepun became a permanent fixture.

acting on the assumption that they would under no circumstances participate in a new offensive.

The arrival of marching companies, frequently loaded down with Bolshevik literature, were a new source of disruptive influence. Agitators, Bolshevik and otherwise, operated with impunity, deliberately undercutting the authority of the regular committees, thwarting efforts to restore discipline, and provoking animus and suspicion against officers. A state of paralysis and panic often prevailed among the latter, and entire regiments and divisions in effect opted out of the war. Even in the better units the committees and staffs were required to talk themselves hoarse, and any untoward incident could suddenly undo progress that had been made. In 1917 the leadership as well as the masses lived by the slogans and simple logic that flowed from the February Revolution—the defense of revolutionary conquests, vigilance against counter-revolution, peace without annexations and indemnities, the prospect of working-class revolutions in all belligerent countries which would bring the end of the war. The thrust of these slogans was to disorganize the army, to break down command authority, and to encourage friendly traffic across the trenches. If Kerensky were to turn this situation around, he was aware that he had to call into being a whole new mode of thought and discourse.

The opportunity for Kerensky's campaign came with the scheduling of a new round of army and front congresses to formalize the committee structure prescribed in Order No. 213, and the election of delegates to the forthcoming All-Russian Congress of Soviets. A Congress of the Southwestern Front already awaited Kerensky's appearance in Kamenets-Podolsk, and a joint congress of the Rumanian Front, the Black Sea Fleet, and the Soviets of the Black Sea region had also opened on May 10. The Southwestern Congress was the more critical, because in the contemplated offensive these were the armies that would have to carry the main burden. Fedor Stepun aptly expresses the expectation of the hard-working committeemen who sponsored the congress:

> The moment for the congress was propitious. The wave of mindless defeatism of the end of April began to recede gradually. The Army was disenchanted with the Germans, violating their fraternization with the Stokhod offensive, as well as with the Allies for not responding positively to the government declaration on peace. Displeasing to our democrats were also the Allied socialists who turned up in Petrograd—Thomas, Rambeau, and Henderson—revealing themselves to our S.R.'s and S.D.'s as "hearty chauvinists." In connection with all this, the thought took hold in the Army that the peace-loving word

> of free Russia would not gain the ear of either the enemy or the Allies unless behind it they saw the firm will of an army ready for battle.[65]

The characterization applies principally to the politically versed committeemen like Stepun himself, but it also expressed the less articulate but just as receptive mood of a great many of the rank-and-file committee activists. The majority of the delegates who turned up in Kamenets-Podolsk, however, were not yet settled in their attitudes, torn between their constituents' stubborn longing for peace and their own sense that "free Russia" should show itself strong and confident to the world. The instability of their mood was reflected in their responses to the high emotional moments of the congress. They wildly applauded General Brusilov's extravagantly "democratic" address, which nevertheless made a quite traditional patriotic appeal to defeat the enemies of "Mother Russia." But as the delegates reported one by one on the condition and mood of their units, the image of a "conscious revolutionary army" ready to shed its "last drop of blood for freedom" paled before the despairing reality: the soldiers seemed only to want immediate peace, with little regard for the consequences.

Climaxing this somber review was a passionate speech by the Bolshevik chairman of the Eleventh Army Committee, Lieutenant N. V. Krylenko, who was already a legend among the trench soldiers and a source of exasperation to the command. He offered a convincing rationale for the spontaneous feelings of the trench soldiers: the war had been started by the capitalists of all countries in the quest for colonies and profits, and so long as Russia remained allied to England and France without revision of the secret treaties, the war remained an imperialist war and Russian soldiers were shedding their blood to enrich the English and French bourgeoisie.[66] The formation of the coalition, Krylenko argued, did not fundamentally alter the situation; it merely broadened the base for the resumption of the war on old terms. Only when "all power" was in the hands of the people in their own soviets could the war take on a truly liberating character, for then it would become an international class war.

Krylenko, who had a long record of service in Bolshevik military organizations before the war and who had just returned from the All-Russian Bolshevik Conference, revealed himself as a literate exponent of Lenin's basic positions. Although the slogan "All Power to the Soviets" must have struck this audience of front delegates as startlingly new, the speech was greeted with thundering applause. Stankevich, who had been instructed

[65] Stepun, 2:73.

[66] As reported in *SP*, May 30. (For some obscure pretense Bolshevik organs in 1917 are dated in the New Style with Old Style [O.S.] in parentheses. We will use O.S.)

by the Soviet Executive Committee to put an end to qualified support for the Provisional Government and to secure a firm commitment to restoring the fighting capability of the Army, acknowledged his profound dismay: "Very loud applause and the obvious sympathy of many, but a majority or a minority? . . . Would the congress have to be disbanded?"[67]

First Stepun and then Stankevich spoke in behalf of the new Soviet policy, followed by several other members of the Executive Committee, including the "author" of Order No. One, N. D. Sokolov. Stepun eloquently evoked the emotional defensism of the front committeemen, while Stankevich carefully explicated the position of the Soviet leadership and buttressed it with all the characteristic arguments. Stormy applause greater than for Krylenko (so Stepun and Stankevich both claimed) rewarded their efforts; Brusilov warmly embraced the Soviet emissaries to cement the triumph.[68] The test came with the first vote on the question of coalition government. Some 570 voted for the resolution of the Soviet Executive Committee, and only 52 voted for the alternative introduced by Krylenko (64 abstained).[69]

The debate resumed on the more sensitive issue of war and peace, in the course of which Kerensky made his dramatic entrance. He spared nothing in his arsenal of gestures and rhetorical devices to arouse his audience to the highest pitch. "I have not come here to rejoice with you over the downfall of tsarism," he exclaimed. "No, it is my duty and right, thanks to my revolutionary past, . . . to say to you, 'Citizens! Stand to your arms!' " Kerensky's banal theatrics thrilled the present audience, which was thirsting for an uplift of spirits and responded to each invitation with ringing affirmations. Would they then at his call lay down their lives? "We swear it! Yes, we will die!" they replied. Turning to Brusilov, Kerensky solemnly affirmed: "And you, Mr. Commander, set your mind at ease. These men will go wherever you command."[70] As was his wont, having drained his oratorical resources to the utmost, Kerensky fell back in a faint in his chair.

It would seem that after such a spectacular performance no further swings in mood would be possible, but Krylenko again inveighed against restoring the Army to battle-readiness, fraternization, and endorsing the offensive. He discoursed on colonialism in Africa by the Great Powers, on broken

[67] Stankevich, p. 135.

[68] Stepun, 2:75.

[69] V. I. Miller, "Frontovoi s″ezd iugozapadnogo fronta (mai 1917 g.)," in *Istoricheskii opyt velikogo oktiabria* (Moscow, 1975), p. 214. Miller made use of the full proceedings published in the staff organ *Armeiskii Vestnik*, May 7-24.

[70] Anet, pp. 223-24, who also witnessed the proceedings; alternative version in *SS*, May 17.

resolutions of the Socialist International, on Lenin's and Rosa Luxemburg's views on the war, and a good bit more. Krylenko's compelling erudition and logic may have been lost on this unprepared audience, but at the climax Stankevich queried Krylenko point-blank: Would he as a Russian officer, if ordered by his superior, take his men into battle? Taken off guard, Krylenko replied that he personally would obey the order out of deference to the democratic majority. If he meant to qualify the statement, his reply was drowned in applause, and Stankevich extended his hand.[71] Thus the incident was reported in the press and carried by the delegates back to their units, where committeemen used it to persuade troublemakers to "submit to the majority," because *ideinyi* Bolsheviks like Krylenko opposed disorganizing actions and abided by the decisions of the Soviet.

Krylenko's eloquence had gained him respect, but he got no support beyond the dedicated Bolshevik minority. Some 554 voted for the main resolution, 38 voted for the Bolshevik resolution, and 69 abstained. The result was indicative of the sentiment of those who attended the congress and staffed the committee work in the regiments, but not of the mass of soldiers in the trenches. Figures of the mandate commission afford a striking profile of the makeup of the congress (the representational formula fixed the proportion of officers to soldiers at one to four). By occupation, roughly 28 percent were professional employees (including cadres officers), 24 percent belonged to the "free professions," and a mere 3 percent were landowners, businessmen, or owners of factories. Twenty-seven percent were classified as in agricultural occupations, 10 percent as workers, and 3 percent as artisans, but more than half of the agriculturists gained their primary livelihood through side occupations (certainly many of them were skilled artisans, since the figure for this category is inexplicably small). Thus half of the delegates consisted of educated, privileged elements, workers were represented at three times their usual numerical strength in the ranks (around 3 percent), and even peasants were represented by their more proficient, enterprising element, many of them doubtless with a considerable urban exposure.[72] A breakdown by party preference also indicates that party consciousness had penetrated well beyond the purely intelligentsia elements (see Table 1).

The handful of declared Kadets were of course officers, but two officers also confessed to being anarchists. Of the 312 Social Democrats, only 25 identified themselves as Bolsheviks, though their voting strength at the congress was twice as great. Most other counts of this kind show greater

[71] Stankevich, p. 137. Krylenko's speech is according to *SP*, June 3; the rest is in Miller. The text of the resolution under debate is available in *IzOA*, May 24.

[72] Data in Miller, pp. 210-11 and 216.

TABLE 1. Party Preference of Delegates to Congress of the Southwestern Front (1917)

	Members	Sympathizers	Total
Social Democrats	139 (22.0%)	173 (27.5%)	312 (49.5%)
Socialist Revolutionaries	85 (13.5%)	189 (30.0%)	274 (43.5%)
Nonparty Socialists			31 (5.0%)
Kadets	3 (0.5%)	1 (0.1%)	4 (0.6%)
Undeclared			9 (1.4%)
			630 (100.0%)

Source: Based on V. I. Miller, "Frontovoi s'ezd iugozapadnogo fronta (mai 1917 g.)," in *Istoricheskii opyt velikogo-oktiabria* (Moscow, 1975).

strength for the Socialist Revolutionaries (S.R.'s) in the committee structure, though the Social Democrats (Bolshevik or Menshevik) frequently held the key leadership positions. One can surmise that many officer delegates had been impressed by Tsereteli in the recent political crisis and realized that the credit of the Kadets was spent, while among the professional-intellectual element Social Democracy, mainly Menshevik, had always been strong. Workers naturally supported them also, and perhaps most of the declared artisans, while the true peasants and Populist intellectuals constituted the base of the S.R.'s. Until October this profile changed little, particularly in the top leadership of the army committees.

Kerensky repeated his performance at the Odessa congress, for which Stankevich's description will suffice:

> Again an auditorium heaving with the presence of thousands, indescribable enthusiasm, a sea of red banners, the singing of revolutionary songs. I remember the moment [of Kerensky's entry]: the overflowing audience goes delirious with ovations. . . . The work of the congress was no different from that of the preceding one and our resolutions were carried with nine-tenths of the votes.[73]

Kerensky, accompanied by Brusilov, then made the rounds of units at the front, making the same undeviating speech, using the same clever devices to discredit hecklers and hostile agitators, and usually (though not always) winning applause and vows to carry out orders to the death without question. One incident became a legend. A simple soldier at a mass gathering queried the War Minister: "What good are land and freedom to me if I'm

[73] Stankevich, p. 140.

dead?'' Kerensky turned gravely to Commander in Chief Brusilov and said, ''Send this fellow back to his home village and let them know that we do not need cowards in the Russian Army.'' In Kerensky's account the fellow fainted, pleaded not to be sent home, and turned into a model soldier.[74]

On May 16 Brusilov circulated to all units a glowing account of Kerensky's tour of the front. At each place he stopped, he introduced Kerensky as an ''old revolutionary and tested fighter for the ideals of freedom, equality, and brotherhood,'' using the standard device: ''Can I promise the War Minister that you will do your duty to the end, and if I order you to attack, will you attack?'' Brusilov capitalized on Kerensky's presence to remove a dangerous officer-agitator from the 23rd Finnish Rifle Regiment and to secure a pledge from the Eighth Trans-Amur Border Regiment to take up position at the front (they had staged a demonstration in Brusilov's presence with placards inscribed ''Away with the war!'').[75]

Other generals from army commanders on down also tried to make use of Kerensky's presence to put an end to fraternization, to apprehend agitators, to secure obedience to long-standing orders, and to gear up their units for the offensive. For example, on May 17 General P. N. Baluev, commander of the Special Army, appealed to recalcitrant units of the XXXI Army Corps: ''Remember the words of our own people's War Minister Comrade KERENSKY at the front congress, that if we do not restore discipline we will surely perish and the whole world will despise us, and even worse, will despise the ideals of Socialism and the Revolution.''[76]

There was a considerable contrast, however, between Kerensky's impact on the soldier committeemen and on the rank and file. Though to the former he had become overnight an inspiration to heroic exploits, his impression on the latter seldom outlasted the cheers and clouds of dust in the wake of his departing staff car. There is ample indirect evidence, which will be discussed below, but in one case direct documentation is available. Kerensky visited each regiment of the 159th Division (XXII Corps, Seventh Army) around May 20, and the division commander noted that the effect was ''excellent'' but regrettably ''was limited to the deputies who per-

[74] Kerensky proudly recounts the incident in *Russia and History's Turning Point*, p. 282. On its gaining currency in the press front and rear and becoming a legend, see *IzOA*, June 8, and *Go3A*, June 17. In both cases patriotic soldiers have written letters of protest to their army committee newspapers. (''Do we want to be slaves of Wilhelm and lose our Freedom?'' ''A coward not worthy of freedom!'')

[75] See *Iz8A*, May 23, for the first incident, and Orders of the Day of 329th Buzuliiskii Regiment (Special Army), TsGVIA, f. 2938, op. 1, d. 150, for May 30 for the second. The latter illustrates the propaganda use of such incidents by the staff machinery.

[76] *Ibid.*, May 22.

sonally heard the speech of the Minister.'' This judgment was based on reports from regimental commanders—one who denied any effect whatsoever, another who acknowledged marked effect on the direct hearers, which they were unable to pass to their comrades, and a third who said the same but noted important converts in the regimental committee who had formerly opposed an offensive. The last report made the significant observation that the better-inclined soldiers were now able to advocate the offensive openly, and officers and prowar committeemen now felt some ground beneath their feet.[77] This evidence confirms on the lower level the process that is much easier to document from the upper levels, namely, that whereas in April the chief concern of committee activists was to safeguard the Soviet peace program against the partisans of ''total victory,'' in May, owing in no small measure to Kerensky's whirlwind tour, it was to restore the fighting capacity of the Army and strict military discipline. In April the idea of an offensive was unthinkable to committeemen, but in May it was adopted as their device and symbol of loyalty to the Revolution.

☆

The committeemen-deputies, intoxicated by the front congresses, tried to replicate the results in a series of army congresses at the end of May. At these congresses an unapologetic cult of the person of the War Minister, abetted by the commander and officer contingent, stands out; in virtually every instance where Bolsheviks had previously had a foothold in the committee leadership, their influence was either curtailed (the Second and Special armies) or eliminated completely, whereas Mensheviks and prowar S.R.'s acquired uncontested ascendancy. Even Krylenko was obliged to yield his chairmanship of the Eleventh Army Committee when a Menshevik-S.R. bloc gained two-thirds of the delegate seats for the All-Russian Congress.[78] Nevertheless, it proved far more difficult than at front congresses to obtain satisfactory results; the Bolsheviks in most cases refused to be overwhelmed, and authentic voices from the trenches often belied claims of ''a new surge of the will to fight.'' The further the patriotic committeemen reached down to the lower levels, the more resistance they encountered to their dream of a revived army, and the more obvious and unpleasant became the gulf that separated them from the psychology of the soldier mass. The euphoria could be sustained only by fresh infusions of inspiration from above or by withdrawing into the world of committee

[77] See TsGVIA, f. 2222, op. 1, ed. khr. 1066, ll., 1-5.

[78] The turnover is recorded in the session of the army committee of May 26 in *RDRA*, pp. 114-15.

concerns (boots, forage, replacements) that were believed to be vital to preparing the Army for action but were in reality an escape.

The Special Army (Southwestern Front) held its own congress on May 17-21. The leadership was dominated by educated Menshevik intellectuals, but there was a cohesive Bolshevik minority, among them M. N. Kokovikhin, who headed the army committee's "Cultural-Educational Commission," and a Captain Babkin, talented writer for the organ of the Special Army Committee, *IzOA*. Although hitherto the army committee had functioned with little regard for fractional differences, the dominant group was determined to carry through a militant endorsement of the offensive at the congress. Special Army Commander General Baluev's opening address copied the style and arguments of Kerensky and leaned on his authority: "Do we want to surrender all our dearly won rights and freedoms to the yoke of the Teutons and their inspirer Wilhelm?" (Cries of "No! No! No!") "For Holy Russia, for the Army, for its chief, Citizen-Teacher Kerensky—Hurrah!"[79] Chairman Voitolovskii picked up on the refrain and expressed the hope that the congress would speak out firmly on the two most important issues before it—the offensive and the restoration of strict democratic discipline. There were no major political figures from Petrograd to lend authority to the program, but the newly appointed Commissar, V. N. Moiseenko, a veteran of the S.R. terrorist organization and now a staunch defensist, delivered an emotional appeal to end fraternization and keep faith with the Allies. He argued that active operations must be resumed because "here Kerensky and Chernov are at the helm and over there Liebknecht is in prison!"

Speech after speech paid tribute to "the rising spirit of the offensive." One officer held it a terrible crime not to trust Kerensky and the socialist ministers, while a soldier-orator exclaimed: "We must do battle not only for the Russian Revolution, but for the triumph of truth in the whole world, for a third International, for our Fatherland!" Another officer conceded that the reports gave little evidence of fighting spirit, but he perceived the winds of change in the rising mood of the congress itself: whereas on the first day one was afraid to utter the word "offensive," and on the second day one spoke of "active defense," now everyone was eager to go into the attack. Every invocation of "Comrade Kerensky" brought thunderous applause. Yet the draft resolution on the offensive was accompanied by a long list of conditions that seemed impossible to attain: a successful campaign against fraternization, "straightening out the rear," persuading the villages to deliver more grain. Finally, it would require a significant im-

[79] *IzOA*, May 19; this and following numbers have the complete proceedings.

provement in relations between officers and men (the chief theme of the reports) for which a purge of the higher command was necessary.

Debate on the resolution degenerated into a wrangling duel with the Bolshevik delegates, Kokovikhin revealing himself as a skillful interlocutor and deflater, if less eloquent than Krylenko. How could one afford "democrats" like Miliukov? Had his exit changed anything? How could the numerous intractable economic problems be resolved? Industrialists were sabotaging production, and grain would not last until the next harvest. Previous offensives had never gained more than small amounts of territory, yet they had cost millions of lives. Modern war has outlived itself. ("Away with him." "Enough." "Where, comrades, is freedom of speech? Can you refute my facts?") Did the socialists enter the cabinet, Kokovikhin continued, just so we could have an offensive? And what happened to the Socialist Conference in Stockholm? The self-confidence of the assembly had obviously been undercut.[80] Wearily Voitolovskii urged them to trust the coalition government and Kerensky, and not to cogitate unduly over the reasons. Babkin's final speech, however, was a *tour de force*, disarming his audience with a low-key parody of their enthusiasm. From Riga to Rumania not a shot was being fired, the economy was in disorder, the soldiers themselves were ruining the economy by jamming the railroads, and thousands of deserters crowded all the major cities and villages, yet from somewhere a "wave of enthusiasm" was supposed to come. Perhaps one ought to wait for the Soviet Congress or the Stockholm Conference to clear one's conscience, and in the meantime a revolution might break out in Germany. "Captain Babkin is about the only Bolshevik here, but if you send ten thousand agitators you might get the best of him." (Laughter, applause, and prolonged uproar.)

A resolution differing substantially from the previous one was passed unanimously: the question of "offense or defense" was a strategic question that should be left up to the Provisional Government, to whom one owed "unconditional obedience," since it had pledged that "not a drop of blood would be shed in vain." This was hardly the clarion call to arms the sponsors had hoped for, and it had been watered down to gain unanimity (if the Bolsheviks dissented, it is not recorded). Kokovikhin and Babkin no longer figured in the leadership of the Special Army Committee, and the Mensheviks and S.R.'s controlled the editorial line of the *IzOA*, but the militant offensive spirit proved stillborn, and the *IzOA* lapsed into humdrum organizational concerns. The leadership had undoubtedly learned a sobering lesson.

[80] *ONFV*, pp. 152-53; paraphrased from Kokovikhin's brief memoirs, in which he cites his own record of proceedings.

Other fronts reveal much the same forces at work. In the Fifth Army (Northern Front) the militantly defensist committee leadership sponsored an "assembly" of regimental committee chairmen on May 9, ostensibly to pay tribute to the new coalition government and to tackle practical problems to revive the fighting capacity of the Army. There were no grand addresses by authoritative figures; the meeting was advertised as "businesslike." After several orators held forth in particularly bellicose fashion, one of them claiming that his corps would go forward "driving ahead of us all the fraternizers with machine guns," others who refused to be steamrolled followed. Some were manifestly party Bolsheviks, voicing the standard critique of the coalition, but others were unblemished voices from the trenches. Only the rear called for the offensive, one claimed. In the trenches there was no enthusiasm, no common ground between officers and men, no agreement on the aims of the war. Socialists in the government could be trusted, but not the rest, who were a majority, said another. The land question should be resolved first. Most officers were hiding out. Capitalists should bear the full costs of the war. The soldiers themselves should decide whether an offensive was called for. And so forth.

The flood of objections had clearly gotten out of hand, and the leaders were obliged to intervene. Chairman Mazurenko chided that every "insofar as" had to be done away with, because the socialist Chernov was Minister of Agriculture, socialist Skobelev was Minister of Labor, and socialist Kerensky was Minister of War. Committeeman Khodorov opined that the Fifth Army Committee was respected in both Petrograd and Moscow for its efforts to "straighten out the rear," but the sentiments of the delegates undermined those efforts. The attention of the assembly was redirected toward practical organizational problems, but the mood of militancy could not be restored. The leadership arranged ritual tribute to Kerensky and to the Coalition, which was said to reinspire the delegates, but there was very little likelihood that this could be conveyed to the trenches.[81]

The Congress of the Third Army (Western Front) of May 21-27 was a more carefully orchestrated affair. General Kvetsynskii, a "democratic general," played his role to the hilt: "Comrade deputies! You are the salt of the earth, you are to choose the leaders who will sway the fate of Russia! Answer your leader Kerensky's call for an offensive!" The visiting French deputy Rambon brought warm regards from the Allies, Soviet Executive Committee members Erlikh and Borisov explained the Soviet positions on power, war, and peace, and several carefully selected workers and Black Sea sailors delivered passionate appeals for the renewal of active operations, which was required if the Russian Revolution and its peace program was to be revered by other nations. The self-induced hypnosis of the

[81] Proceedings in *Iz5A*, May 10-13.

assembly was exemplified by soldier-committeeman Tarasov: "Let only one regiment, one division, go into the attack, and all the guns, the whole Army as one man, will go against the enemy and bring on the tips of their bayonets human liberty and a lasting peace."[82] There were a few voices of subdued dissent: a corps resolution on immediate peace was read forth and ignored, another objected that the rear had to be straightened out first, while a third demanded that the Allies first renounce the secret treaties. But on the third day, on schedule, a resolution embodying the orthodox Soviet line of reasoning for the offensive was adopted with fourteen abstentions. The balance of the congress was spent passing standard resolutions on the Coalition, nationality and worker questions, supply, replacements, deserters, and so on. Most striking, however, was the overwhelming approval accorded a resolution on the land question that appeared to be identical with that passed at the All-Russian Peasant Congress.

Why this congress carried through the campaign for an offensive with relative ease, in contrast to the other army congresses and assemblies, is not clear, although the absence of articulate Bolshevik spokesmen was certainly a factor. The staunchly defensist Third Army Committee, located far from the urban centers beyond the Pripet marshes, had screened themselves off from the unwholesome Minsk Soviet and the semi-Bolshevik Front Committee. Careful preparation and screening of the delegates may have accomplished the rest, but it certainly did not mean that all lower committees, let alone the soldiers themselves, immediately fell into line. Three divisions in this army (the 55th, the 66th, and the 167th) were effectively out of control, owing to the activities of the skillful Bolshevik agitator known only as "Mikhailov."[83]

In general, the army congresses were less successful than the front congresses in generating enthusiasm for the offensive and inflating Kerensky and the Coalition into sacred cows. Even the most careful stage management could not avert the intrusion of the grim realities of trench life and the incorrigible pacifism of the soldiers. The committee press in the latter part of May was considerably more subdued and tentative, awaiting fresh moral reinforcement from the rear. Clearly only a titanic new effort backed by the highest revolutionary authorities and mobilizing legions of new persuaders would be capable of overcoming the inertia of the soldiers in the trenches, who until now had accepted as dogma that the Revolution meant imminent peace.

[82] Proceedings in *Go3A*, May 23ff.

[83] See A. K. Wildman, *The End of the Russian Imperial Army: The Old Army and the Soldiers' Revolt (March-April 1917)*. (Princeton, 1980), pp. 340-42. Cited hereafter as *The Old Army*.

CHAPTER II

BOLSHEVIKS AT THE FRONT AND "FRONT BOLSHEVISM"

THE DISORDERS occurring at the front up to mid-May were the spontaneous reactions of soldiers to events rather than clever inspirations of Bolshevik agitators, though sometimes the latter figure in reports of the time, because the capital press was then much exercised over Lenin's return in a "sealed car" and "German money" was rumored to be subsidizing Bolshevik agitation. The celebrated status acquired by Krylenko and a few others was exceptional, and it is difficult to find comparable examples before May. Although party Bolsheviks occupied key positions in a number of the higher committees (Eleventh and Special Armies, XLIII Army and III Siberian Corps) and dominated a dozen or so identifiable regiments scattered along the front, they were relatively subdued and scarcely distinguishable from other ardent partisans of the Revolution and the Soviet.[1] Until well into April there was little direction from the center. Communications were poor, and until Lenin's return the issues that were to become the hallmarks of Bolshevik agitation had not yet crystallized (immediate peace and land, power to the Soviets). Until the All-Russian Conference of Bolsheviks in late April, *Pravda* still reflected the qualified defensism of Stalin and Kamenev, and when Lenin's views became known they caused as much consternation among front Bolsheviks as among the upper leadership of the party. *Soldatskaia Pravda* and *Okopnaia Pravda*, the two organs that became the chief conduits of Lenin's militant positions at the front, only began publication on April 18 and 30 respectively, and their impact was not substantially felt until later.[2]

The April crisis galvanized the Bolsheviks behind Lenin's April theses

[1] The most complete survey of the entire front is V. I. Miller, *Soldatskie komitety russkoi armii v 1917 g.* (Moscow, 1974), pp. 172-46; see also collections of memoirs as *BOB* and *ONFV*.

[2] For the best treatment of the Bolshevik party in this period, see Rabinowitch, *Prelude to Revolution*, esp. opening chapters.

and stimulated the Bolshevik Military Organization to unfold a vigorous activity in the Petrograd and nearby garrisons. Meanwhile, a number of front Bolsheviks had journeyed to Petrograd, where they witnessed the April events firsthand, acquainted themselves with party positions, established contact with the Military Organization, loaded themselves up with agitational literature, and returned to their units primed for action on behalf of the party. Once fully apprised of the political situation, these Bolsheviks in most cases sympathized with the militant posture of the party toward the coalition government and the offensive.

The soldier masses at the front were in a quandary. Their disruptive actions—fraternization, arrests of officers, refusals of work details, and mass disobedience to orders—had been predicated on the vague notion that they were ''defending the Revolution'' and promoting the peace policy of the Soviet. Though not infrequently in conflict with their committees on the lower level, they still identified strongly with the representational structure as a whole and looked to the Soviet for realization of their aspirations. Regimental and divisional committees often took temporizing positions so as not to lose credit with their constituents and, sometimes themselves lacking a clear perception of Soviet policies, they drifted with the mass mood. The eventuality that neither the lower *komietetchiki* nor the soldier masses had anticipated was the entry of Soviet leaders into the ''bourgeois'' Provisional Government to promote a new offensive and the restoration of officer authority.

As the upper committee structure solidified in support of Kerensky's leadership, and the new ''revolutionary defensist'' position of the Soviet was defined in a proclamation of April 30, the soldier masses were progressively disillusioned and torn. Though most submitted grudgingly to the persuasions of their committees and maintained an unhappy silence, an ever-growing, turbulent minority grasped at the alternative revolutionary stance offered by the Bolsheviks. Very few of the unlettered soldier mass and lower *komitetchiki* absorbed the logic of the new Soviet position—that only by demonstrating the armed might of the Russian Revolution could the other powers be compelled to consent to a ''democratic,'' as opposed to ''imperialist,'' separate peace. Bolshevism was an attractive alternative in that it accepted the same premises as the Soviet position, and did not even repudiate loyalty to the Soviet, but provided a convenient rationale for their inner promptings and spontaneous actions. So compelling were the Bolsheviks' arguments that all other home-grown agitator types, and even enemy agents, caught them up as the most expeditious means of preventing the restoration of officer authority and the orderly implementation of plans for the offensive. The most articulate element promoting this line were the soldiers of replacement companies from the rear, many of them indoctrinated with the primitive Bolshevism of the garrisons and bitter about being compelled to go to the front against their will.

The consequence of this conjunction of forces was that in the course of May a vulgarized "Bolshevism" became the chief mobilizing force of the soldiers' mounting hostility to the new offensive, far outstripping the organized forces of the party and expressing itself in a new rash of major mutinies and disorders. Thus, one should distinguish carefully between Bolshevism subject to some kind of discipline and commitment and this new, more widely diffused "trench Bolshevism" or, as both detractors and moderate Bolsheviks called it, *shkurnyi bol'shevizm* (since they feared for their skin [*skura*], the equivalent of "yellow-bellied"). (Senior officers seldom troubled to distinguish between the two, regarding the one, at best, as the source of the other, whereas committee agitators, desperately trying to bring disaffected units into line, tended to plead a fundamental difference—that responsible Bolsheviks like Lenin and Krylenko opposed disorganized violations of military discipline—and argued their viewpoint loyally within the forum of revolutionary institutions.) While the massive revolt against the offensive was fueled in part by this new species of Bolshevism, its full dimensions will be developed in the next chapter. The present chapter has the more restricted aim of fleshing out the activities of party organizations at the front or immediate rear, defining their narrower constituency and presence, and determining how much responsibility for what transpired can be ascribed to them.

☆

Though Soviet sources allow one to identify a good number of front Bolsheviks in 1917, the list is incomplete and necessarily distorted. Recognizable members of oppositions and purge victims have been weeded out, whereas others lapsed into anonymity (many doubtless perished in the Civil War). A fair number of former Bolsheviks, passed over lightly in Soviet accounts, turned "revolutionary defensist," and an even greater number, especially experienced party intellectuals and workers, were partisans of "unity," that is, were against any immediate break with the Mensheviks and remained in "united" Social Democratic organizations even after direct orders from the center to split off.[3] Nevertheless, Soviet sources can be employed usefully with proper caution.

Only a handful of experienced party intellectuals were strategically located in scattered units across the front, most of them in staff and technical units of the rear or civilian Red Cross and Zemgor organizations. Only a

[3] The best-documented instance, the Minsk organization, is treated below, pp. 58ff. The most well known instance of a Bolshevik turned defensist is Wladimir Woytinsky (Voitinskii), who figures frequently in our narrative; others occasionally turn up in the sources, but even an approximate calculation would be futile.

few, like Krylenko, Dzevaltovskii (Grenadier Guards), and Sievers (436th Novoladozhskii Regiment), were officers in line regiments. More frequently in line regiments one encounters very young worker-Bolsheviks and petty intelligentsia recruited into the movement in the upsurge of 1910-12. These recruits were less reflective, more hardened in class attitudes, more deferential to party authority, more prone to violent actions and undiscriminating demagoguery.[4] The assertion of V. G. Knorin that every regiment had its troublesome worker-Bolshevik agitator is somewhat exaggerated, but not too far off the mark.[5] Considering the party schooling of these types and the excitable mood in the trenches, one need not be surprised that a single Bolshevik could easily spoil a regiment.[6] The ranks of front Bolsheviks were considerably augmented in April and May of 1917 by enlisting close comrades who shared their social origins and attitudes and by others who came in marching companies, either amnestied political prisoners or neophytes radicalized by the April events in the capital and processed by a quick course at the Kseshinskaia mansion (the Bolshevik headquarters in Petrograd).

The concentration was somewhat thicker in rear institutions and technical units, where the services of educated intellectuals, literate workers, and peasants with industrial skills were at a premium. This was often an advantage in that they were far less under surveillance, and the nature of their duties often gave them access to means of communication with units other than their own. N. G. Petrov, E. M. Sklianskii, and a certain Glezer (Second, Fifth, and Twelfth armies) were doctors, and M. V. Frunze, G. F. Ustinov, and I. E. Liubomirov were civilians in Zemgor units (Western Front), while A. M. Pireiko headed the printing shop of the Seventh Army staff. Many of the worker-Bolsheviks were motorcyclists, telephonists, and chauffeurs (collectively known as *sviazisti*), or sappers and artillerists.[7]

Because of the general shortage of politically informed activists at the front, it is not surprising that Bolsheviks were not infrequently propelled into higher committees, sometimes even playing key organizing roles, but they were greatly outnumbered by party Mensheviks and S.R.'s and newly

[4] For a characterization of this type of worker that became prominent in the so-called period of "revolutionary upsurge" (1912-14), see Leopold Haimson, "The Problem of Social Stability in Urban Russia, 1905-14," *Slavic Review* 23 (December, 1964): 633-37; and Victoria Bonnell, *Roots of Revolution: Workers' Politics and Organizations in St. Petersburg and Moscow, 1900-1914* (Berkeley and Los Angeles, 1983), pp. 431-34.

[5] V. G. Knorin, *1917 god v Belorussii i na zapadnom fronte* (Minsk, 1925), p. 2.

[6] A frequent remark in the sources. For examples, see *RDRA*, pp. 131 and 158 (17th and 80th Siberian Rifle regiments, Eleventh Special Regiment, all of Twelfth Army).

[7] Culled from sources mentioned in note 1 of this chapter and other cited works.

fabricated "March socialists." Moreover, in most instances they had not yet formed party organizations or even fractions within the committees. In the first phase of the Revolution, socialists of all persuasions put most of their energies into the practical tasks of the nonparty revolutionary organizations, where they were separated more by degrees of radicalism than by party identification. The specifying of party affiliation or preference at front congresses was understood to be for informational purposes only, and the rubric "Social Democrat" was usually not broken down into Bolshevik and Menshevik. In adjacent urban centers, such as Minsk, Kiev, and many minor towns, party organizations were primarily united Social Democratic organizations with minimal fractional loyalties. Menshevik Internationalists, Mezhraiontsy, Polish, and Latvian Social Democrats more frequently associated themselves with Bolsheviks than with Menshevik defensists and Bundists.[8]

In April a number of front Bolsheviks reestablished ties with the party, having occasion to come to the capital on various nonparty errands. Thus, Pireiko, a lone Bolshevik at the staff of the Seventh Army, came to Petrograd with a deputation from the Buchach garrison in time to witness Lenin's return and confer briefly with the secretary of the party, Elena Stasova. Pireiko stocked up with Bolshevik literature (also in Moscow and Kiev), which he distributed liberally at the Seventh Army Congress in session on his return. He claims that he was the sole professed Bolshevik at the congress and that many soldier delegates approached him afterward to find out more about the Bolsheviks. In his capacity as manager of the print shop that put out the army committee *Izvestiia*, he selected pro-Bolshevik printers and clandestinely reproduced *Pravda* and other Bolshevik literature.[9] At the end of April, F. V. Popov, a Bolshevik worker from the Don basin in the XXV Corps (also Seventh Army), came to Petrograd, where he was greatly impressed with the bustle of activity sponsored by the Military Organization ("uninterrupted conversations, meetings, lectures") and must have witnessed a good bit of the political turmoil following the April Crisis; he was one of the delegates from his corps to the congress of the Southwestern Front and recounts Krylenko's pyrotechnics in great detail. His claim that there were Bolshevik cells in every regiment of the 11th and 19th divisions, as well as in staff units, is probably considerably exaggerated (since it conflicts with Pireiko's as-

[8] Drawn from the author's general knowledge of 1917, which other researchers could easily augment but about which no suitable monographic work exists, particularly for the lesser groupings. Close attention to the distribution of votes in various soviets and representative bodies supplies the raw data. Examples will be encountered in Chapters X and XI, below.

[9] A. Pireiko, *Na fronte imperialisticheskoi voiny* (Moscow, 1935), pp. 71-78.

sessment), but could approximate reality in late May or June.[10] Lieutenant V. S. Denisenko and several others of the 143rd Dorogobuzhskii Regiment (Fifth Army) were also sent to the capital in early April to inspect the arms factories at Sestroretsk and Kronshtadt; they heard Lenin defend his April theses in the Soviet, registered with the Military Organization, and established permanent contacts with Kronshtadt sailors and Petrograd workers, whom they invited to visit the front.[11]

☆

The number of front Bolsheviks who actually "registered" with the Central Committee's Military Organization, however, could not have been very large, because the Military Organization was not yet primed for constructing a Bolshevik network at the front, as is sometimes claimed in Soviet accounts without evidence. There is no record, even in memoir accounts, of instructions or correspondence with front organizations, and it is doubtful that there was any. In practice, the Military Organization, which from April 10 on became "All-Russian" under the Central Committee, cultivated contacts primarily in the Petrograd and suburban garrisons, in the Baltic Fleet, and in garrisons and military formations surrounding the Finnish gulf (Helsinki, Vyborg, Peterhof, Narva, Reval). Later it sought to coordinate the activities of Bolshevik military organizations in other urban centers; there were major ones in Moscow, Tver, Ekaterinoslav, Kiev, Kharkov, Novgorod, Pskov, and several Siberian cities. In provincial and urban garrisons the mobilizing role of such military organizations with some prodding from the center cannot be doubted.[12] When an All-Russian Conference of Bolshevik Military Organizations finally met in mid-June, only a handful of delegates showed up from bona fide front units (perhaps 15 or 20), and none from the Rumanian or Caucasus fronts; most of the 150 or so who attended were from the rear garrisons and military installations, especially the large number designated from the "Northern Front."[13]

[10] F. V. Popov, *Rasskaz o nezabyvaemom (zapiski bol'shevika)* (Kiev, 1961), pp. 13, 21, 23-25, and *passim*.

[11] *ONFV*, pp. 83-94. When he was drafted and trained as an officer, Denisenko was a young petty intellectual, son of a village schoolteacher and a fresh graduate of the Kiev Commercial Institute. He had no previous association with the party, and like many others of his type he made his career in the OGPU-NKVD (*ibid.*, p. 87).

[12] V. V. Anikeev, who scoured the archives of the All-Russian Military Organization and constructed a systematic chart of contacts with front organizations (*Dokumenty velikogo Oktiabria. Istoricheskii ocherk* [Moscow, 1977], pp. 166-74), is able to identify only two before June 1917. For a systematic survey of party military organizations in April and May, see A. M. Andreev, *Soldatskie massy garnizonov russkoi armii v oktiabr'skoi revoliutsii* (Moscow, 1975), pp. 56-81.

[13] Most Soviet works cite the misleading figure of 167 delegates representing 44 front

The chief accomplishment of the Military Organization was in the realm of propaganda and agitation, and those were aimed at the soldiers at hand—the Petrograd garrison, commuters from the surrounding area—and front soldiers on various errands in the capital. Promising recruits were brought to the Kseshinskaia mansion, where they were treated to a "nonparty" soldiers' club appropriately called "Pravda" and a constant round of agitational speeches, comradely conversation, and quick courses for budding agitators. When possible the Military Organization would try to arrange meetings in the barracks, still difficult in early May because of the hostile climate created by officers and committeemen who portrayed Bolsheviks as "German spies." But mass meetings held outside the barracks were drawing an ever-growing clientele, while schooled agitators plied the streets engaging individuals and small groups in conversation; others were groomed for attending soldier meetings sponsored by patriotic groups, demanding to be heard in the name of "free speech" and exposing the "bourgeois lies" about Lenin and the Bolsheviks. Often the method was to introduce extraneous or deflating amendments to high-sounding resolutions, or to bring up items not on the agenda of the sponsors but known to appeal to the soldiers, such as the land question, marching companies, or pay for performing militia duty on the streets. The favorite topic, and one of the most effective in early May, was the "Declaration of Soldiers' Rightlessness," points 14 and 18 of which were characterized as restoring the officers' *palka* (stick).[14]

Before long the Bolsheviks gained entry to regiments where a short time before they had not been welcome (the Izmailovskii, Semenovskii, and Keksgolmskii Guards regiments) and were able without apology to introduce their own resolutions, which not infrequently carried. By the end of May and early June, because of the extreme anxiety over the forthcoming offensive, sending replacements, and rumors of the government's intent to transfer the garrison from Petrograd, the Bolsheviks were no longer swaying the masses, but were themselves carried with a powerful current toward the decisive encounter in July.[15]

---

organizations and 17 from the rear; however, details in S. E. Rabinovich, *Vserossiiskaia voennaia konferentsiia bol'shevikov 1917 goda* (Moscow, 1931), reveal that garrison representatives from Reval, Pskov, Venden (Latvia), and several in Finland were classified as front organizations (see pp. 18-20), whereas the primary materials on the conference, the so-called *Biulleten' vserossiiskoi Konferentsii Frontovykh i Tylovykh Voennykh Organizatsii RSDRP*, Nos. 1-5 (June 16-24), allow firm identification of only ten bona fide front delegates.

[14] The best sources for the early activities of the Military Organization are the early issues of *SP*, excerpts from which are included in *BPB*, pp. 151-62; see also memoir accounts of V. I. Nevskii, N. I. Podvoiskii, and A. F. Ilin-Zhenevskii, all utilized in A. Rabinowitch, *Prelude*. There is also good information based on primary documents in the above-cited work of S. E. Rabinovich (n. 13).

[15] For this development, see A. Rabinowitch, *Prelude*, chap. 4.

The Bolsheviks' most powerful instrument for mobilizing a soldier constituency was by far their spectacularly successful newspaper, *Soldatskaia Pravda*. Eventually printed in 50,000-60,000 copies, its significance for the front was twofold. First, by creating a devoted readership in the capital and surrounding area, it created a pool for recruiting and training agitators who later carried the message to other regions, including the front, and second, in soldiers' knapsacks large bundles could follow the route of marching companies or be dropped off at strategic points near the front for further redistribution (Dvinsk, Minsk, Kiev). The bread and butter of *Soldatskaia Pravda* was not high political reportage but simple, comprehensible expository items, such as "The Struggle for Land," "The Soldier and the Worker," "Fraternization," "What Is the Russian Social Democratic Workers' Party?" or "In Whose Interests Is the War?" By chronicling every meeting where Bolshevik views were presented, often reproducing the speeches in full and printing the text of every Bolshevik or militant-sounding resolution of units, however small (an auto repair unit, an electrotechnical battalion), they were able to repeat, elaborate, and refine their message and to create the sense of identity and community of a church under the cross.

Prominently featured in the early issues was the "slander" against comrade Lenin by officers and the bourgeois press, and the danger of openly invoking his name: such spokesmen were denounced as "spies" and "traitors," beaten, and dragged into militia headquarters to the screams of the street public. Extensive coverage was devoted to the April crisis and ensuing developments from a soldiers' perspective, including eyewitness accounts of street demonstrations and of meetings in the barracks, and texts of countless resolutions. All this implanted a firm image of aggressive intent by the bourgeois forces to snatch away the gains of the Revolution in order to further their own selfish interests and those of the English, French, and American bourgeoisie. Finally, a major feature was the abundance of contributions by "soldiers," some of them transparently written by members of the Military Organization, but others authentic and sometimes crude unburdenings of the soul of the average soldier. An ever-larger space was devoted to "voices from the trenches," which collectively are a monument to the bitter emotions now finding an outlet in the Bolshevik faith.[16]

This diet of reading soon became the daily fare for a devoted, semiliterate clientele in the region of the capital; initially not large, as pressure mounted to gear up for the offensive and to send marching companies, the

[16] Besides the relevant issue of *SP*, many such letters in the archive of *SP* but unutilized are published in A. F. Ilin-Zhenevskii, ed., *Pochemu soldaty i matrosy stali pod znamena Oktiabria* (Leningrad, 1933).

ranks swelled not only from week to week but also from day to day. Wladimir Woytinsky, who as an Executive Committee representative had the thankless task of persuading the reluctant reserve units to form marching companies, acknowledged the futility of his efforts:

> The Executive Committee had to "push" each company assigned to the front. . . . All marching companies departed according to schedule, with music and red flags, but we were paying a high price for each dispatch. . . . In retrospect, I think our effort to make the Petrograd garrison share in the defense of the country was the main cause of the soldiers' shift from us to the Bolsheviks, who demanded no sacrifice from men in reserve regiments and promised them the safe and serene life of the janissaries of the revolution.[17]

His more candid unpublished memoirs concede that in late May only *Pravda* (possibly meaning *Soldatskaia Pravda*) was read in the barracks, whereas the Menshevik organ *Rabochaia Gazeta* "enjoyed neither influence nor readers," and that at regimental meetings "the soldiers howled down their own deputies, listened to representatives of the Executive Committee with irritation, and greeted Bolshevik agitators with ovations."[18]

☆

Petrograd, of course, was only one center, and sent its replacements primarily to the two Guards Corps and the Finland Rifle Divisions of the Southwestern Front. But the six infantry and two machine-gun regiments from the suburban garrisons of Tsarskoe, Peterhof, Oranienbaum, and Strelna, which were even more subject to Bolshevik influence than the guards regiments, sent replacements to many other parts of the front. The same is true of the numerous technical units stationed in the capital and nearby (artillery, engineering, auto, and aviation units). One Soviet authority using General Staff data states that, up to the end of June, 103 marching companies and 34 technical contingents were sent from the capital to the front, or around 30,000 men.[19] Other Northern garrisons also supplied replacements, such as Novgorod with four reserve infantry regiments and Pskov with a garrison of some 40,000-50,000 consisting of recovering wounded, technical units, a school for *praporshchiki*, and large numbers being reassigned to the Northern Front. Thus a vast rear area easily accessible to the capital and subject to the same radicalizing forces funneled Bolshevik converts to all parts of the front in abundance.

Bolshevik party organizations in Moscow and Kiev were comparable

[17] W. S. Woytinsky. *Stormy Passage: A Personal History Through Two Russian Revolutions* (New York, 1961), p. 264.

[18] Vl. Voitinskii (Woytinsky), "Gody pobedy i porazhenii" (Ms.), 3 vols., HI, 3:145.

[19] Andreev, p. 122.

centers of the dissemination of propaganda. In Moscow a "Military Bureau" of the Moscow Committee was headed by the seasoned conspirator Olga Varentsova, a former member of the People's Will and an underground worker of the 1890s. She and her close collaborator Emelian Iaroslavskii were veterans of Bolshevik Military Organizations in 1905-7 and built up an operation as impressive as that in Petrograd. It claimed 200 registered members in April and 2,000 by July. In the same period they supplied 839 visitors from the front with literature, corresponded with others, and carried on extensive agitation in the Moscow garrison.[20] The *Sotsial-Demokrat* carried a report on June 27 that up to May 1 the Military Bureau had distributed to the front 7,972 copies of *Pravda*, 2,000 copies of *Soldatskaia Pravda*, 30,375 copies of *Sotsial-Demokrat*, 50,000 leaflets ("Soldiers and Workers," "Why Is There No Bread?"), and 12,350 books and brochures.[21] It also deputized members to other major garrisons of the Moscow Military District, which was a vast recruiting area, such as A. Ia. Arosev to Tver. In the course of the summer several provincial garrisons were wracked by disorders (Nizhnyi-Novgorod, Tula, Tver, and many others), upon which the Bolsheviks capitalized successfully.[22]

The Kiev Committee of the party also carried on extensive activity among soldiers headed for the Southwestern and Rumanian fronts, chiefly through its organ *Golos Sotsialdemokrata*, which regularly featured soldiers' letters and a column for soldiers. Though information on its activity is sparse, Pireiko claims that the committee regularly supplied the Seventh Army with literature and that a leading Bolshevik in the I Guards Corps, K. Pal'vadre, contacted it to plead for the special needs of the front. As a result, the Kiev Committee created its own Military Organization on May 20, and by July it claimed a membership of 1,000 in twenty different units of the garrison, mainly technical units.[23]

The work of the major military organizations was retailed in dozens of

[20] See memoirs of Varentsova, Iaroslavskii, and other Moscow activists in *Geroi Oktiabria* (Moscow, 1967), pp. 115-37. Such celebratory publications cannot always be regarded as reliable, but convincing corroboration of the vigorous activity of this group is to be found in S. Moravskii, "Deiatel'nost' moskovskogo soveta soldatskikh deputatov za vremia s marta po 25 oktiabria 1917 goda," in M. V. Miliutin (ed.), *Put' k Oktiabriu. Sbornik statei vospominanii i dokumentov*, 5 vols. (Moscow, 1923-26), 1:181-230.

[21] Andreev, p. 61 and *passim*.

[22] See T. F. Kuzmina, *Revoliutsionnoe dvizhenie soldatskikh mass tsentra Rossii nakanune Oktiabria* (Moscow, 1978), pp. 27-37. This is an exceptionally well researched monograph based on extensive archival and contemporary documentation, especially from the Moscow Military District, which comprised a vast area of the central provinces.

[23] See Pireiko, pp. 76 and 83; P. A. Golub, *Partiia armiia i revoliutsiia* (Moscow, 1967), p. 84; and Golub, *Soldatskie massy iugozapadnogo fronta v bor'be za vlast' sovetov* (Kiev, 1958), pp. 54-57.

rear garrisons and distribution points along the rail lines leading to the front by unsung local Bolsheviks, groups and individuals, most of them following their own lights without party direction. Where they held key positions in local soviets or were favored by such lax commandants as General Bonch-Bruevich in Pskov, they could carry on their activities with relative impunity, but just as often vigilant soldiers' soviets devoted to Kerensky and the new Soviet line obliged them to operate in semi-conspiratorial fashion. Some strategic locations near the front became centers of highly organized propaganda and the object of considerable complaints by garrison commandants. Venden, for example, in the rear of the Twelfth Army, was the conduit of Bolshevik influence in the reserve units of the Latvian brigades, having 426 party members; Gomel and Smolensk, redistribution points for the Western Front with garrisons of 10,000 and 70,000 respectively, had Bolshevik-dominated soviets based on a soldier constituency that circulated propaganda literature in huge quantities; and in Kharkov, a transfer point between the massive Moscow and Kazan military districts and the Southwestern Front, defensists dominated the soldiers' soviet, but ardently Bolshevik workers conducted extensive agitation among the soldiers passing through.[24]

☆

While one should be skeptical of the Soviet investigations that equate the sheer volume of publications or mere existence of party groups with influence on the soldier masses, military reports from all sectors of the front during the latter part of May and early June make it clear that an unprecedented flood of Bolshevik literature, "Bolshevized" replacements, and Bolshevik agitators arriving with the replacements were a major unsettling influence thwarting orderly preparations for the offensive. Many complaints were voiced in the First Army of the Northern Front, where the commander of the First Caucasus Rifle Division blamed troubles in two of his regiments on Bolshevik newspapers, particularly *Pravda*, and on "the corrosive influence of recently arrived replacements who are infected with the psychology of the rear, not excluding Leninism, and who are completely undisciplined, poorly trained and in the majority of cases totally ignorant."[25] In the same army the I Corps harbored a good many self-confessed "Leninists" (two regiments in the 22nd Division, one in the 24th Division), which the army commander ascribed to replacements from Petrograd; the three divisions of the XXXVII Corps (120th, 121st, 135th) were even more severely affected, the 538th Medynskii Regiment

[24] Andreev, pp. 56-57 and 64-66; for a personal account of Gomel, see memoirs of M. M. Khataevich in *BOB*, pp. 105-17.

[25] *RDRA*, p. 110 (report of May 20).

even advocating Lenin as War Minister. The report emphasized that the hostility to officers in these units was so great that "an offensive cannot even be considered" and that their mood was shaped by extensive reading of Bolshevik newspapers.[26]

Proximity to the capital was an obvious reason for the early and heavy registration of Bolshevik influence in the Twelfth and Fifth armies, but the same phenomena occurred almost simultaneously on other fronts, although not with the same degree of saturation. General Gurko informed Stavka on May 13 that arrests of senior officers were again on the increase because of the "harmful influence of replacements arriving from the reserve regiments of the interior military districts [i.e., Moscow District, not Petrograd], who apparently are under the influence of extremist parties, adherents of Lenin and others."[27] A report on the 188th Division on the remote Rumanian Front of May 20, while it does not specify replacements, notes the increasing frequency in soldiers' conversations of negative comments on the offensive and enthusiasm for peace, which it blames primarily on Leninist newspapers "which get through to our units in great quantities, whereas other papers arrive only after great delay."[28] At a later date, June 11, the commander of the 61st Siberian Rifle Division (Tenth Army, Western Front) pleaded: "I and my officers have no recourse but to save ourselves as best we can, as five companies of Leninists have just arrived from Petrograd. A meeting was called for 1600 hours, and it has been decided to hang myself, Morozhko, and Egorov."[29] This was but one of countless such incidents, great and small, prior to the offensive that were ascribed to the Bolshevik inundation and that will receive further discussion in the following chapter. The extent of saturation was vividly chronicled in a special investigation undertaken by the Quartermaster General at Stavka, based on commanders' reports from all sectors of the front for the month of June, of which the following excerpts are characteristic:

> [*From the Rumanian Front*:]
> N Corps has manifested a marked increase in Bolshevik influence due to the wide circulation of *Pravda*. . . . Normal life and service in several units, which were achieved with such great effort, have been destroyed in a few days by the arrival of agitators with replacement

[26] *Ibid.*, pp. 118 and 570 n. 21 (reports of May 21 and 28).

[27] *VOSR. Mai-Iiun'*, p. 335; there are also many documents on Bolshevik agitation in the Twelfth and Fifth armies in "Armiia v period podgotovki i provedeniia velikoi oktiabrskoi sotsialisticheskoi revoliutsii," *KA* 84 (1937): 139-50.

[28] *RDRA*, p. 110.

[29] *RazA*, p. 92.

units. . . . In Y Army reinforcements are a disintegrating influence spreading the teachings of the Bolsheviks.

[*From the Northern Front*:]
There is no possibility of insisting on the execution of orders, as a bitter agitational campaign is being waged against the offensive, emanating from the rear, chiefly Petrograd.

[*From the Southwestern Front*:]
X Division is temporarily incapable of active operations due to the arrival of replacement units from the Petrograd Military District. . . . In Z Corps the replacements arriving from Petrograd constantly cause unrest. The propaganda of ending the war immediately has found many adherents.[30]

While it is impossible in most instances to determine whether the "Bolshevik" turbulence was due primarily to specific agitators who had undergone a "short course" in one of the Bolshevik military organizations or to the more diffuse infection of Bolshevik newspapers, or simply to slogans clutched out of the air, clearly these forces were at work in tandem, which often comes out in the sources. For example, the guiding spirit of agitation in the Finlandskii Guards Regiment was a certain Vasilev, who claimed to be a Petrograd worker with credentials from the Soviet but appears to have been a party Bolshevik of the petty intelligentsia, possibly even a worker-intellectual, who had been groomed for his role by the Military Organization in Petrograd.[31] He cleverly undercut the authority of pro-offensive orators with seemingly reasonable objections: "How can we fight when new boots haven't arrived yet and we don't have enough machine guns and shells?" He deflated an effective committee orator, Dr. Nekrasov, by demanding, "Aren't you the brother of the bourgeois Minister of Communications?"[32] Also active in the regiment were two "bearded uncle" peasant types with "crushed caps and unbuttoned shirts" (the badge of home-grown agitators), who perpetually moved among the crowds shouting slogans like "Down with the war! Give us peace without 'nexes' and 'booshuns'!"

For the guards regiments at least, the situation does not seem untypical. In the Moskovskii Regiment the troublesome "Bolsheviks" are identified in several sources as former policemen and gendarmes, who made up an

[30] "Bolshevizatsiia fronta v prediiul'skie dni 1917 g.," *KA* 58 (1933): 87-94 (excerpts).

[31] See "Otchet kommissarov XI armii I. Kirienko i I. A. Chekotilo," *BA* 1 (1926): 26-27.

[32] B. V. Sergeev, "1917 god na fronte," *Finlandets*, No. 36 (May, 1958): 33, 36, 41, and *passim*.

entire company of replacements.[33] In other cases, such an identification is more doubtful, as it entered into the stereotyped formula along with "German spies," "counter-revolutionaries," "yellow-bellies," and "dark forces," all either "masquerading as Bolsheviks" or indistinguishably blended with them.[34] But there is overwhelming documentation showing that the stimulus of Bolshevik agitation originating in the rear and through the avenues of marching companies, newspapers, and otherwise had created a specific ethos of "Trench Bolshevism" affecting a large number of units with varying degrees of intensity.

☆

Although replacements from Petrograd and major urban centers were the worst sources of infection, a few important Bolshevik operations originated at the front itself or in areas immediately adjacent to it. Foremost among these was the newspaper *Okopnaia Pravda (OP)*, founded by an energetic Bolshevik group in the 436th Novoladozhskii Regiment of the Twelfth Army at the end of April, which soon acquired enormous influence in the Twelfth Army and far beyond.[35] The 436th Regiment had long been stationed in the environs of Riga and very early in 1917 had developed close ties with the Bolshevik-oriented Latvian Social Democrats, who soon dominated the Latvian representative institutions, particularly the Riga Workers' Soviet, the regional and district land councils, and the committees of the Latvian brigades.[36] This connection afforded the Novoladozhskii Bolsheviks a certain protection and freedom of action despite the presence in Riga of the army headquarters and the executive of the Twelfth Army "Soviet," Iskosol.

An episode of fraternization in March revealed the strong hold of the Bolsheviks on the regiment. A battery commander who had broken up a meeting between the trenches with artillery fire was shortly thereafter

[33] *BA* 1:26 and *RDRA*, p. 182 (report of B. P. Govechia, Commissar of the Southwestern Front, July 5).

[34] For a few examples, see *ibid.*, p. 128; *RazA*, p. 93; and *BA* 1:14.

[35] The chief source on this group is D. I. Grazkin, who wrote several accounts, each differing in details and emphasis, respectively: *Okopnaia Pravda* (Moscow, 1933); "Okopnaia Pravda," *IA*, No. 4 (1957): 168-83; "Revoliutsionnaia rabota v XII armii nakanune oktiabria," *Voprosy Istorii*, No. 9 (1957): 3-16; and *ONFV*, pp. 56-66. They are distinguished by the heroic Soviet style and such vagueness and inaccuracy that even one Soviet authority advises caution (V. I. Miller, "Fevral'skaia revoliutsiia i vozniknovenie soldatskikh komitetov na fronte," in *Sverzhenie samoderzhaviia. Sbornik statei* [Moscow, 1970], pp. 171-72).

[36] The thorough Bolshevik domination of Latvian elective organizations is recounted in detail in Andrew Ezergailis, *The Latvian Impact on the Bolshevik Revolution: The First Phase, September, 1917, to April, 1918* (Boulder, Colo., 1983). The best Soviet work of many is Ia. Kaimin', *Latyshskie strelki v bor'be za pobedu v oktiabr'skoi revoliutsii* (Riga, 1961). On the connection with *OP*, see pp. 116-19.

arrested by a soldier deputation headed by Lieutenant Khaustov, one of the founders of *OP* and chairman of the regimental committee. It was alleged at a "trial" that the "provocative action" of the commander had interrupted serious negotiations with the Germans. When a deputation from the battery demanded his release (implying the threat of bombardment), the court found that he had acted "unconsciously" under the spell of "old regime discipline," and he was dismissed with a reprimand.[37]

A short time later, the Novoladozhskii Regiment was removed from the front line for rest and reequipment, to be replaced by units of the Latvian brigades. According to N. I. Grazkin, a worker Bolshevik from Petrograd and an *OP* activist, officers and Mensheviks in the brigades spread the rumor that the Novoladozhskii Regiment had departed from the front without orders; he and co-activist Lieutenant Sivers agitated the ranks of the Latvian units, persuading them that the rumor was false. The result, he claimed, was a "committee revolution" in the brigades which left Latvian Bolsheviks firmly in control.[38] True or not, the close connection of the Novoladozhskii Bolsheviks to the Latvian organizations was certainly established around this time and, now stationed in a suburb of Riga, they acquired a solid reputation in the 109th Division, always challenging defensist committeemen at meetings, always proposing substitute resolutions or amendments designed to embarrass them ("We'll shed our last drop of blood for the Revolution *as soon as they supply us with new boots*"). They financed their enterprise partially by collections from soldiers (faithfully recorded in *OP*), but also by appropriating 5,000 rubles of regimental money earmarked for fallen and evacuated soldiers (as committeemen they supervised regimental accounts). They also received at least one remittance of 1,000 rubles from the Central Committee of the party through Latvian intermediaries.[39] By these means they acquired an unused printing establishment in Riga and brought out the first number of *OP* on April 30.

By the fourth issue the initials RSDRP (Russian Social Democratic Workers' Party) and the slogan "Workers of the World Unite" were proudly featured in the heading. The first few issues of *OP* recorded a struggle between Bolsheviks and Mensheviks for control over the Riga Soviet, in which the Bolsheviks gained a clear ascendancy. The Novoladozhskii Bolsheviks undercut the army Menshevik leadership by persuading the Riga Soviet to propose a merger with the Twelfth Army Soviet to form a joint Workers' and Soldiers' Soviet on the Petrograd model. As the Bolsheviks anticipated, the leaders of Iskosol (the army Soviet exec-

[37] Text of commanders' report in *VKDA*, pp. 67-68.

[38] *Voprosy Istorii*, No. 9 (1957): 5-6.

[39] Grazkin, *Okopnaia Pravda*, pp. 8-9, and Kaimin, p. 118.

utive committee) refused, as it would mean surrendering their official status recognized by the command structure, which was very sensitive to the danger of "dual power." But the army Mensheviks could not avoid becoming embroiled in local politics when the Thirteenth Conference of the Latvian Social Democratic Party (held in Moscow on April 19-22) adopted a Leninist agenda.[40] On May 7 at a meeting recorded in *OP*, the Latvian majority of the Riga party committee approved the decisions of the Thirteenth Conference over the vigorous objections of Russian Mensheviks G. D. Kuchin (a prominent leader in the Twelfth Army Soviet and its officer component Iskomof) and A. E. Diubua (Commissar of the Provisional Government to the Twelfth Army). *OP* noted gleefully that the Mensheviks had voluntarily separated themselves from the proletariat of Riga for the more interesting high-level work in the army in the company of officers.

With the Riga Committee now under firm Bolshevik control (functioning as a regional party organization with both Russian and Latvian membership), *OP* from May 10 onward printed a standing invitation to front-line soldiers to enroll in the Bolshevik party as members of the Russian Section of the Riga Committee; the address given was the headquarters of the city militia opposite the railroad station, which also housed the Riga Committee and the editorial offices of *Cina*, the organ of the Latvian Social Democrats. *OP* now carried the subheading "Organ of the Military Organization and the Russian Section of Social Democracy of the Latvian Territory."

A congress of the Latvian brigades took place on May 12-17, which after protracted and impassioned debate, despite the pleas of Iskosol representatives, Latvian officers, and civilian politicians of other persuasions, adopted a resolution denouncing the war policy of the Provisional Government and calling for all power to the Soviets.[41] On June 4 a conference of Latvian Bolsheviks in the brigades determined that there were 1,537 members of the party in their regiments and 200 in the reserve unit.[42] A delegate of *OP* to the All-Russian Conference of Bolshevik Military Organizations in June claimed that "the resolution of the Latvian Riflers enjoyed great sympathy in the Russian units, and it was passed at all meetings where it was put to a vote."[43] He claimed that the Bolsheviks had organizations of up to a hundred members in eight different regiments.[44] At the end of June there was a conference of Bolsheviks of the

[40] Text of the conference resolutions in *KPLOR*, pp. 66-77.

[41] Resolution text in *ibid.*, pp. 125-27.

[42] Kaimin', p. 160, and T. A. Draudin, *Boevyi put' latyshskoi strelkovoi divisii v dni oktiabria i v gody grazhdanskoi voiny* (Riga, 1960), p. 24.

[43] *SP*, June 20.

[44] Reports of A. G. Vasilev in *BVO*, Nos. 3 and 4 (June 18 and 20).

Twelfth Army attended by 400 delegates, according to Grazkin, but he does not specify how many were from the Latvian units, which easily could have made up the majority.[45] But Rimsha, the delegate from the Twelfth Army to the Sixth Congress of the Bolsheviks (July 26-August 3), reported 1,800 members in the Russian Section alone. Though the Bolsheviks constituted only a small fraction of an army of half a million—as organizational potential, given the enormous impact of their agitation—this figure, if accurate, is quite impressive.[46]

With its firm base in Riga, *OP* conducted an unremitting barrage of propaganda that kept the command of the Twelfth Army and Iskosol on tenterhooks and attracted attention far beyond the region. It could be purchased openly at kiosks in Riga and was distributed gratis to soldier deputations from the front. Other copies found their way to other fronts via soldier-travelers (railroad stations were a major distribution point). Though the number of copies apparently never exceeded 10,000, the newspaper's trenchant style and alluring slogans guaranteed a circulation far in excess of its mere numbers, taking on the characteristics of oral folklore (with such indelible slogans as "Burzhuis to the Trenches!").[47] Though the *OP* Bolsheviks' control over committees did not extend beyond the 109th, 110th, and 186th divisions and a few Siberian regiments, their upsetting agitation was pervasive and undercut discipline and order virtually everywhere, in effect making it impossible to consider an offensive on this front. For example, on May 19 the commander of the 18th Siberian Division thus despaired of his regiments:

> They no longer execute the orders of their commanders, but constantly enter into discussions and arguments. They don't believe their officers, nor even their committees. Anarchistic newspapers have persuaded them that the war is useless and was started by the capitalists and the *burzhuis* for their own benefit at the expense of the people. A particularly pernicious influence is exercised by *Okopnaia Pravda*, which can be bought at railroad stations for four kopecks.[48]

On June 24 General Radko-Dmitriev, commander of the Twelfth Army, without naming *OP*, complained of the "strengthened agitation of the Bolsheviks, who have woven themselves a firm nest in Riga" and named the Latvian brigades and the 439th and 17th Siberian Rifle regiments as particularly affected; a report of June 2 resumed the litany, now identifying

[45] *IA*, No. 4 (1957): 179-80.

[46] *Shestoi s"ezd RSDRP(bol'shevikov), avgust 1917 goda. Protokoly* (Moscow, 1950), p. 72.

[47] *OP*, May 16 (actually the title of a clever poem).

[48] *RDRA*, p. 107.

the three Pravdas (*Pr, SP*, and *OP*) as the source. Moreover, he noted that with the flood of new replacements, "a single agitator can set back on its heels an entire regiment with the propaganda of Bolshevik ideas."[49]

Various instances confirm the near literal truth of the latter assertion. In the 80th Siberian Regiment a Bolshevik military doctor named Glezer took advantage of a May Day celebration to deliver a blistering attack on the Provisional Government and the secret treaties; he defended the honor of the Bolsheviks against an attack by the division commander, who attended the affair sporting a huge red ribbon and claimed to be an S.R. (Lenin and his cohorts had been "bought off with Germany money.") The incident aroused continuing turmoil in the regiment, and Glezer became a hero and political consultant for the aroused soldiers. When he was arrested at the request of Iskosol, the soldiers took the regimental commander hostage until he was freed. On June 18, again in reserve, the regiment staged a huge armed demonstration in Riga, honoring the Congress of Soviets and openly proclaiming Bolshevik slogans.[50] In the 70th Siberian Rifle Regiment a similar situation developed as the result of a mass meeting organized by two soldier-agitators on June 29; a female student and a Latvian civilian urged their listeners to "end the war, fraternize with the Germans, overthrow the Provisional Government, and elect your own officers."[51] Other reports point to similar tendencies in the 10th and 17th Siberian regiments.[52]

The battle between Iskosol and *OP* for the soul of the Twelfth Army reached a climax in early June with the arrest on the streets of Riga of several Bolshevik soldier-agitators, among them a certain Stepanov, who had publicly humiliated Kerensky when the latter visited Riga. This was followed by a public accusation by Iskosol that Lieutenant Khaustov had received 10,000 rubles from the Germans and should be arrested on sight. *OP* carried daily protests, in one of which Lieutenant Sivers demanded that Iskosol produce evidence of their charges within one week or be declared "despicable slanderers" (since both Khaustov and Sivers were officers, this was meant as a mock challenge).[53] A few days later, Khaustov was lured into Riga on a bogus errand, arrested, and given over to the custody of the Provisional Government in Petrograd. The furor over the incident was not to subside until several weeks later, when the All-Russian

[49] *Ibid.*, pp. 158 and 166-67; see also Stavka survey for June 25 to July 1 in *VOSR. Mai-Iiun'*, p. 303.

[50] See his memoir fragment in "Na fronte v 1917 godu (iz vospominanii)," *KL* 7 (1923): 202-6.

[51] *VKDA*, pp. 217-18.

[52] See *ibid.*, p. 165, and *RDRA*, p. 158.

[53] *OP*, May 28 and 31.

Conference of Bolshevik Military Organizations managed to shame the Soviet leadership into securing his release.[54]

The first few issues of *OP* stamped out images of subservience to the Allies (''Tsar Buchanan the First''), of the imperialist nature of the ''secret treaties,'' of the gullibility of Soviet leaders who swallowed the government statement of March 27 on ''no annexations,'' and finally of the slaughter of millions of workers and peasants for the interests of the Russian and international bourgeoisie. N. S. Chkheidze, the Menshevik chairman of the Petrograd Soviet, was accused of getting a ''letter from Paris'' threatening the scorn of socialist opinion if Russia did not hold to its obligations under the Alliance. The new coalition government was cleverly compared to Krylov's fable of the cart drawn by a swan, a snake, and a cricket: the Soviet leaders were represented as harnessed to the same old war aims.[55] One might suppose that a good bit of the political satire would be lost on a peasant-soldier readership, but the purpose was to provide sustenance to agitators for whom the tone and cleverness of argument was as important as the content; for the less sophisticated there was plenty of additional fodder in resolutions, letters from soldiers, and simple lessons disguised as reportage. The overall impression conveyed was one of a great moral cause, but in a style and format that rivaled the prestigious capital press.

A second, oft-repeated theme was the land, pitched to the peasant readership. Typical vehicles were accounts of provincial peasant congresses, Bolshevik resolutions, Lenin's speech at the All-Russian Peasant Congress, and duplicitous actions of the government, but also insertions into extraneous articles, for example, pointing out that a ''People's Army,'' which would result from ''democratizing the command structure,'' would be able to settle the land question according to its own taste. The term *pomeshchiki* was always employed in couplets with *zavodshchiki, burzhuis*, capitalists, officers, and Kadet politicians. Workers were treated as honorary peasants, but worker issues were given far less billing than peasant issues.[56]

By far the most coverage was given to the twin themes of fraternization and the offensive. The opening issue vividly depicted the Easter fraternization and cleverly cited the speech of K. A. Gvozdev, a Menshevik member of the Soviet Executive Committee, at the Minsk Congress of the Western Front, which still innocently interpreted it as consonant with Soviet peace policy. ''Fraternization has tremendous significance as a means to spread revolution,'' argued *OP* in the first issue, ''as it facilitates socialist intercommunication, kills the war at its very roots, and prepares the ground

[54] See following issues *OP* and *BVO*, Nos. 3 (June 18) and 4 (June 21).

[55] See *OP*, May 7; ''Letter from Paris,'' May 10: ''Tsar Bukhanan I,'' June 6.

[56] For examples, see *ibid.*, April 30, May 3, and May 10.

for serious peace negotiations.'' The May 7 issue advocated a ''military general strike'' in behalf of the Stockholm Socialist Peace Conference and flooding the German trenches with revolutionary leaflets, to offset the efforts of the German Intelligence to exploit fraternization.

By mid-May the editors of *OP* were in a difficult position as Iskosol mounted a vigorous counter-campaign in favor of the offensive: they were now accused of ''treason'' and refusal to submit to the revolutionary authority of the ''majority,'' namely, the Soviet, which on all issues took an opposite position. A new line of defense was struck at a mass meeting, presumably of the XLIII Corps on May 6, at which the respective merits of fraternization and the offensive were vigorously debated. *OP* claimed that a resolution of its partisans was passed ''unanimously,'' but it did so through a carefully constructed argument: ''No sort of proclamation from whatever source will force us to take the initiative in an offensive until our Allies renounce their policy of conquests and *wholeheartedly* endorse our government's declaration of March 27.''[57] Thus an offensive was not rejected absolutely, but linked to a realization of the policy to which the Soviet leadership was committed. This was to become the standard defense against all future accusations of ''defiance of the will of the Democracy.''

The victory, however, was short-lived: two days later a second corps assembly was convoked by Iskosol, and Commissar Diubua demanded reconsideration of the previous decision, as ''now we have six socialist ministers in the government.'' According to *OP*, vehement protests broke up the assembly, but in all probability, sensing defeat, the partisans of *OP* resorted to obstruction. On May 16, *OP* argued that German soldiers would hardly be receptive to making their own revolution if their Russian brothers attacked them. Rather, the French proletariat should ''extend the brotherly hand'' across the trenches, and if Hindenburg were to answer this with machine guns, ''then you would see how we are willing to die for the French worker.''[58]

On May 17, *OP* was still calling openly for units to pass resolutions condemning the offensive ''until the Allies renounce conquests,'' but thereafter it was considerably more subdued.[59] It claimed that Bolsheviks never refused to relieve their comrades in the trenches and always favored obedience to ''legal orders'' having to do with defending the front and maintaining battle-readiness. Repressions against Bolsheviks only fomented anarchy, since the masses trusted the Bolsheviks and would listen to their counsels of restraint. *OP*'s defensiveness became even more evident once

[57] *Ibid.*, May 10, repeated in editorial on May 19.
[58] *Ibid.*, May 16.
[59] *Ibid.*, June 4 and 7.

the offensive was under way: on June 23 it declared, "We Bolsheviks never considered renouncing the offensive under all circumstances," but only after "getting rid of the ten capitalist ministers and turning power over to the Soviets, preliminarily declaring our conditions of peace and breaking with the imperialism of the Allies." Such qualifiers were cleverly calculated to shift blame on their adversaries in the minds of *OP*'s constituency.

If one took the editorial arguments at face value, the accusations of incitement to violence and of treason would seem to be greatly overdrawn. Nevertheless, behind the principled arguments was a subliminal appeal to the soldiers' deeper impulses, to release their inner restraints and doubts. If the war was unjust, if they were being deliberately used by domestic and Allied plutocrats, if their officers were inextricably tied to the interests of the *pomeshchiki*, if even their committees and the Soviet leadership were temporarily captive to these forces, then truly any sort of obstruction, systematic disobedience, or even violent rebellion seemed a justified course. *OP* provided them with the facile arguments and rationalizations for such disruptive actions as a means of preserving the goals of the Revolution with which they still profoundly identified.

Though the editors avoided overt incitement, soldiers' letters carried a more explicit message in every issue. One such letter cursed the *burzhuis* and *pomeshchiki* for causing the war, and thought it high time to go over the head of the diplomats; another complained that if letters from home mentioned anything about the land it was red-penciled by the "bourgeois censors," proving that "the *gospoda* capitalists don't want us to share our ideas on the land"; still another expressed profound disillusionment with the Soviet proclamation on fraternization, as he thought the time long past when simple people could be used for capitalist aims.[60] Even visceral issues became pretexts for outbursts of class rage:

> You tell us to take the offensive, but when are you going to approve the 25 ruble *paika* so our families won't starve? You don't hesitate to give pensions to the servants of Nicholas the Bloody. You live in luxury while we live in rags. How can we trust you? Send the propertied elements who are calling for "full victory" to the trenches.[61]

Thus, though the organizational influence of *OP* was extended to only a few units in the Twelfth Army, it helped define and give impetus to that unorganized "trench Bolshevism" which spread out across the entire front in the month of June.

[60] *Ibid.*, May 7, 10, and 16.
[61] *Ibid.*, June 14.

There is frequent and irrefutable documentation that the impact of the *OP* reached the most remote sectors. For example, early in June a circular to all lower committees of the Seventh Army (Southwestern Front) blamed opposition to the offensive in two regiments of the 159th Division on *OP*, which was eagerly read by the soldiers.[62] In the Eleventh Army (also Southwestern Front) General Kislii, commander of the V Siberian Corps, combed his units to find professional journalists and typesetters so that he could put out a popular staff organ to counteract the pernicious influence of *OP* and to inculcate the ideas of patriotism and discipline. It appeared as *Okopnye Dumy*, whose editor I. G. Savchenko has left an interesting personal account.[63]

Even more revealing, since complete materials are available, was a court case in late May against a group of agitators in the IV Siberian Corps on the Rumanian Front.[64] The defendants were simple, unlettered peasant soldiers who had served the entire war, among them a certain Bak, who was a veteran of the Russo-Japanese War; two were from Perm, two from Simbirsk, and one each from Tver, Kostroma, and Podolia. Nothing in the lengthy evidence suggests that they were other than what they appeared to be, though their professions of complete illiteracy and ignorance of politics is somewhat suspect. They were accused of having instigated serious breaches of discipline in the 40th Siberian Rifle Regiment. According to the testimony of witnesses (mainly noncoms), a certain Nesterov declared, "We don't have to work on repairing trenches. Let's go into Galats"; another, Gurianov, declared, "Since they won't give us peace, we should pitch our rifles and go home"; soldier Belkin was heard to say, "We don't have to take the offensive, and we don't have to do work details"; and still another defendant defied an officer's categorical order to resume assigned work. Only for Bak was the accusation more serious: he had made the rounds of units other than his own, persuading them that "they want to kill us off so the officers will have all the power." All the defendants under cross-examination claimed to be simple folk who followed the lead of others and did not understand politics (standard peasant defenses when confronted with authority).

One deposition, however, deviated significantly from the others. It pic-

[62] Copy of order in archives of XXII Corps, TsGVIA, f. 2222, op. 1, d. 1066, l. 6.

[63] Savchenko, "Okopnye Dumy. Iz vospominanii" (Ms.), RA. The author even staged debates on merits of the offensive between respective partisans of *OP* and *Okopnye Dumy* for which he claimed some success. General Kislii, however, strongly disapproved of Savchenko's use of revolutionary rather than patriotic rhetoric and his buildup of Kerensky as a popular hero, for which he repeatedly summoned the presence of his editor.

[64] Complete proceedings in TsGVIA, f. 2283, op. 1, ed. khr. 12, most of which is utilized above.

tured Gurianov as always citing *OP*, which he claimed ''explained everything.'' Moreover, the chief agitator, Bak, and another, Podzin, took frequent trips into Galats to fetch newspapers and ''telegrams'' and urged the soldiers to believe only *OP* and *SP*. One does not need to conclude that Bak or any of the others were party Bolsheviks or had direct associations with Bolsheviks. They were probably long-serving soldier-peasants who simply discovered in *OP* an effective means to vent their own feelings toward the war and to devise actions that might bring it to an end. In fact, *OP* did little to promote the sense of party identity or even to educate its readership in party political affairs; ''RSDRP'' was confined for the most part to the masthead, while the collective identity of workers, soldiers, and peasants over against the *pomeshchiki*, the *zavodshchiki*, and the imperialists was projected on every page.

☆

Organized Bolshevik activity on the Western Front was of a fundamentally different character. Through key positions in the Minsk Soviet and the front committee elected by the front congress in April, Bolsheviks enjoyed at an early stage of the revolutionary process a firm institutional base that had no counterpart elsewhere. Although the Bolsheviks were fortunate here in having an exceptionally large concentration of experienced party intellectuals, their strength was not in numbers but in their vigorous pursuit of revolutionary tasks in cooperation with other left factions that were equally well represented—the Mezhraiontsky, Polish and Latvian Social Democrats, and the Menshevik Internationalists. The Bolsheviks had no foothold among the less-numerous factory workers, who had been preempted by Bundists and Mensheviks; their chief following was in the garrison, where Bolsheviks I. G. Dmitriev, S. G. Mogilevskii, V. G. Knorin, and N. I. Krivoshein had organized the Soldiers' Soviet and served as deputies, and among Polish and Latvian refugees.[65] Their few modest positions on the Executive Committee of the Minsk Soviet (Knorin, B. P. Pozern, and I. E. Liubomirov) and 6-10 out of 74 of the Front Executive Committee can be ascribed to the personal standing and activism of individuals, not to Bolshevik support in the ranks, and their influence was often decisive in the practical affairs of these organizations.

There was even a small minority of Bolsheviks in the United Social Democratic Committee, where they revealed little inclination to form a separate Bolshevik organization or caucus, even after receiving explicit instructions from the Central Committee (a general determination of the

[65] See Miller, *Soldakskie komitety*, pp. 197-206, the memoir collection *BOB*, and documents in *VOSRB*, vol. 1.

April Conference).[66] United Social Democracy was a dogma to Bolsheviks in the White Russian area: with their disproportionate influence in the United Social Democratic fractions of the nonparty bodies, they were able to exercise a quite extraordinary leadership role in the mass organizations, promoting a "left internationalist" line even among the non-Bolshevik fractions.[67] It is noteworthy that there were few Great Russians among the Minsk Bolsheviks: Pozern, Lander, and Knorin were Latvian Social Democrats, Alibegov was a Chechen, Miasnikov was an Armenian, and Krivoshein, Pikel, and several others were Jewish. Moreover, the forces of the Bolsheviks were multiplied several times over through the control by reliable supporters of the United Polish Socialist Organization, which enjoyed undisputed authority among the Polish refugees and military units and embraced both the PPS (Pilsudski's Populist Socialists) and the SDKPL (Luxembourg's Social Democratic Internationalists).

The knowledgeable, pro-Bolshevik Polish socialist Waclaw Solskii supposes that Knorin and one or two others were informed "insiders" in touch with the Central Committee of the Bolsheviks, but he claims that Lenin's "April theses" were unknown to most Minsk Bolsheviks until the April Conference and that many were unhappy with those decisions of the conference that incorporated them. Resented most was the directive of the Central Committee to "split off" from the United Social Democratic Committee, and even the Polish and Latvian sympathizers were instructed to do the same, though it would have meant reducing Bolshevik influence to a fraction of its former strength. Knorin gave comforting assurances to the Central Committee while quietly sabotaging its implementation.[68]

Such heresies did not prevent the Minsk Bolsheviks from utilizing their positions of strength to pursue a course sharply opposed to the war and the offensive, and this soon brought them into conflict with those Mensheviks and S.R.'s who loyally supported the Coalition policies and Kerensky. In by-elections to the Minsk Soviet in mid-May, the Bolsheviks scored a surprising success, electing 184 out of 337 deputies (62 for the S.R.'s, 46 for the Mensheviks and Bundists) and securing absolute majorities on the Executive Committee and the Bureau. Their victory in the face of the almost universal opposite trend in elective organizations elsewhere at the front can be ascribed, first, to their control of the United

[66] The author was fortunate to have access to the very valuable manuscript memoirs of Solskii, a Polish socialist and activist in the Minsk organization, whose detailed knowledge of persons and events is often a corrective to the official Soviet materials, which are carefully edited and selective, above all on the sensitive "unity" tendencies of the Minsk Bolsheviks. See his "1917 god v zapadnoi oblasti i na zapadnom fronte" (Ms.), HI.

[67] See Miller, *Soldatskie komitety*, p. 206.

[68] Solskii Ms. (see n. 66, above), pp. 60-69.

Social Democratic organization, the so-called Obedinenka, based on the support of Polish and Latvian socialists (the Mensheviks and Bundists were bound by "party discipline" to vote the unified list of candidates in the nonparty bodies), and second, to a successful campaign for new recruits from the garrison based on opposition to the offensive (the Obedinenka was flooded with freshly baked soldier "Social Democrats").

For several weeks a "United" Social Democratic Military Organization headed by the militant Bolshevik Krivoshein carried on a vigorous activity on the model of its Petrograd Bolshevik counterpart. Soviet investigations reveal little about its activities, but Solskii, a reliable witness, declares that its agitators plied the rear garrisons (Solskii served as their agitator among the Polish units and frequently took trips to the front in this role).[69] They were all the more successful, he claims, because they deliberately low-keyed or denied their Bolshevik identity when proposing Bolshevik resolutions at mass meetings, but struck themes of inherent mass appeal, such as opposition to the offensive. The soldiers' attitude, according to Solskii, was: "What kind of revolution is it if you have to make conquests and you get just as little bread as you did before?"[70] Polish soldiers could be swayed, he asserts, by the promise of a speedier, less hazardous return to their homeland if the Bolshevik doctrine of self-determination of nationalities was adopted. In early June the Bolsheviks finally formed a "Party Bureau" and subsequently withdrew from the Obedinenka, but Knorin attempted to keep the coalition of Left Internationalists under Bolshevik hegemony together by using the recently converted moderate Bolsheviks as intermediaries, particularly with respect to the Polish component, which was one of the largest mass constituencies of the Bolsheviks at the time (a fact later reflected in elections to the Constituent Assembly). The Bolshevik Military Organization in Petrograd apparently deputized one of its members to the Minsk Military Organization, which, with the exodus of the non-Bolsheviks in early June, became a Bolshevik party organization.[71]

The activities of the Minsk Military Organization in front-line units is poorly documented, although the mushrooming of "trench Bolshevism" in connection with the approaching offensive was as pronounced here as elsewhere. Some influence was exerted by existing Bolshevik groups in certain units such as the 169th Infantry Regiment, the Seventh Siberian

[69] *Ibid.*, p. 84 and *passim*.

[70] *Ibid.*, pp. 69-70.

[71] See Knorin, *1917 god v Belorussii*, pp. 21-22, and Solskii Ms., pp. 83-84. The latter point tends to be confirmed by the memoirs of T. A. Liubovtsev (in *BOB*, p. 274), who names R. I. Berzin as his contact in Minsk "who had good connections to Petrograd" and supplied him with Bolshevik literature.

Division, and the Second Army Committee, some of which subsequently established connection with the Minsk Bolsheviks. The meteoric career of the agitator "Mikhailov" in the 55th Division in early May was clearly engineered from Petrograd. Nevertheless, an incident extensively chronicled in the organ of the Third Army Committee, *Go3A*, reveals that the Minsk Bolsheviks were indeed very active at the front under the covering mandate of the front committee and brings out the otherwise obscure interrelationships between the Minsk Soviet, the front committee, and the three army committees of the Western Front. Although the S.R.'s constituted a majority on the unwieldly front committee, many leading Minsk Bolsheviks were active in it, and with other antiwar Internationalists, including some S.R.'s, they imparted a particularly radical stamp to the work of the committee. In the honeymoon period, before the offensive became an issue, several Bolsheviks had obtained credentials as official "agitators" of the front committee and toured front units, presumably to explain Soviet positions on various issues. However, they continued to employ these credentials in May and June to agitate against the offensive and the war with considerable effect.

In the second week of June, *Go3A* initiated an editorial campaign against Bolshevik agitation, which was scoring heavily in their army on the eve of the offensive, and on June 14 they printed a statement of the Third Army Committee identifying the front committee as the chief source of the difficulty. The ensuing issues carried a verbatim record of conversations of the army committee with a representative of the front committee concerning antioffensive resolutions passed by the front committee on June 5 and by the Minsk Soviet on June 10.[72] The front committee "agitators" were representing these resolutions as the position of the "entire democracy" and not of the Bolsheviks and Internationalists alone. The front committee representative meekly claimed that the incriminating front resolution had been passed when the Mensheviks had absented themselves in an intramural argument with the Bolsheviks, leaving the S.R. defensists in a minority, and that since then the resolution had been retracted. But in stiff cross-examination it became apparent that the front "agitators" who opposed the offensive were still broadcasting the original resolution and concealing its retraction. Moreover, the chief agitator was identified as Krivoshein, the Bolshevik head of the "United" Military Organization in Minsk, and he was specifically blamed for provoking a mutiny in the Second Caucasus Grenadier Division during which N. D. Sokolov, the author of Order No. One, was severely beaten for agitating in favor of the offensive on behalf of the Soviet Executive Committee! This was one of

[72] See *VOSRB* 1:351-52 and 361-62 (texts of the two resolutions).

the major affairs in the general collapse of the offensive in the Tenth Army, and were it not for this fortuitous bit of evidence, there would have been no reason to link it to Bolshevik inspiration, let alone the front committee. Even if untrue, it demonstrates convincingly that the Minsk Bolsheviks must have played a considerable role in disseminating Bolshevik slogans on the Western Front.[73]

In early June, Bolshevik agitation on the Western Front was having a measurable impact, even on well-disciplined units. A report by the commander of the XXXVIII Corps (Tenth Army) of June 9 speaks for itself:

> Today a delegation came to me from the 43rd Siberian Regiment, hitherto one of the best in the corps, which declared that they can no longer cope with the propaganda of the Leninists and Bolsheviks. Noncoms and sergeants ask to be demoted to the ranks since they can no longer handle their men. In the region of the corps, some unknown soldiers under the cover of darkness penetrate into the bivouac and stir up the soldiers to refuse to go on the offensive and then they quickly disappear. To catch them is impossible, but their agitation is bearing fruit.[74]

Archival materials on the Fifth Grenadier Division (Second Army) offer an excellent case study of this penetration. The Grenadier Corps, under the enlightened command of General Parskii, had avoided the convulsions of the usual kind in the early weeks of the Revolution. A report on the Fifth Division of May 20, while still optimistic, introduced a note of anxiety:

> The mood and fighting spirit has not yet defined itself. One occasionally hears that an offensive is necessary, but there is no guarantee that these are not simply words. The over-forties and long-term servers are anxious to get home. Everyone complains of the lack of replacements. But no major breaches of discipline have occurred.[75]

However, the report ignored the warning of the commander of the 20th Regiment that ''discipline is declining, disintegration continues'' and that the ''majority of the soldiers want the speediest possible end to the war

[73] This is confirmed in the memoirs of D. I. Efremov of the 723rd Infantry Regiment, XV Corps, Third Army, in *BOB*, pp. 306-7. Efremov received literature from Minsk through N. V. Rogozinskii, another Bolshevik-oriented Polish socialist who was chairman of the Committee of the III Siberian Corps (Second Army).

[74] *RDRA*, pp. 128-30.

[75] TsGVIA, f. 2327, op. 4, d. 1, l. 309; see also l. 314 and *RDRA*, pp. 84-86 (a self-congratulatory order of May 30 on tranquillity in the corps and a report of May 7 noting problems but expressing optimism).

and the officers' mood is very depressed.'' Unexpectedly, on June 2 the division commander reported to the corps headquarters:

> Newspapers and proclamations of a harmful tendency, particularly of the Bolsheviks, are being circulated in considerable quantities and are having a disorganizing effect, as a result of which the soldier mass exhibits a negative attitude toward the performance of any work details or normal duties, and the commanders only have the force of persuasion.[76]

Shortly thereafter a very tense situation with overtones of lynching developed in the 20th Regiment over the news of the return of their former commander, who had taken a ''leave of absence'' in the early days of the Revolution over a ''red ribbon'' incident. Calm was restored with difficulty, but on June 11 replacements loaded up with copies of *Soldatskaia Pravda* arrived, after which the materials break off.[77]

Generalizations for an entire front are hazardous because the materials are incomplete, but it is safe to say that under the combined agitation emanating from Minsk and Petrograd, Bolshevik influence was more widely dispersed here than on any other front, including the Northern Front, and resulted in a more broadly based resistance to the offensive, involving a much larger number of total units. It was greatest in the Second Army, where for a time the army committee followed the lead of the front committee and Bolsheviks were firmly entrenched in the III Siberian Corps, and it was least in the Third Army, where the army committee carried on a vigorous counter-campaign. A number of units that drew replacements from less-affected places in the rear remained well disciplined and prepared for the offensive, almost as in prewar times. In a report of June 9, Front Commander General A. I. Denikin singled out as sound units the 20th Division of the Third Army and the First and 11th Siberian divisions of the Tenth Army, along with four others in the Second Army. But several of these were infected by Bolshevik agitation by the time the offensive began (the two Siberian divisions), whereas the 51st Division, estimated by Denikin to be ''incapable of military operations,'' performed the best of all.[78] Of the sixteen corps on the front, there was a badly affected division in all but two of them, and certainly there were many individual

[76] TsGVIA, f. 2327, op. 4, d. 1, ll. 311, 316, and 321.

[77] *Ibid.*, l. 331. See subsequent reports on Bolshevik activity in *RDRA*, pp. 207 and 527-29.

[78] See *RDRA*, p. 209, and Golovin, *Rossiiskaia kontrrevoliutsiia,* 1(1):159 (Denikin's speech at Stavka Conference, July 16, his own account of the action).

regiments or smaller units on which no information is available that had major or minor problems.[79]

☆

There was no base comparable to Riga or Minsk for Bolshevik operations on the Southwestern and Rumanian fronts. Here major urban centers were far in the rear, with Kiev and Odessa, the closest staging areas, performing a less vital role. A large share of the recruits (30-40 percent) came from the rural Ukraine and were more susceptible to the propaganda of the Ukrainian Rada than of the Bolsheviks, though the disorganizing impact of the campaign to form separate national units was often no less deadly than the latter.[80] Bolshevik activity here resembles a checkerboard more than a blanket, depending chiefly on the source of recruits. Though Soviet works identify a number of Bolshevik groups in these armies, they only occasionally coincide with those defined as troublesome in military reports.[81] Staff sources for the Seventh, Eighth, and Special armies seldom complained over Bolshevik agitation until the offensive actually began, though in some cases Bolshevik influence of some sort is evident. The Eleventh Army, however, which had been the arena of Krylenko's activities, was heavily carpeted with Bolshevik agitation, both of party origin and otherwise. Since the Eleventh Army was to be assigned a key role in the offensive, and because mutiny carried away a good share of the divisions at the most critical moment of the operations, Bolshevik activity is of particular relevance. The report of government commissars A. M. Chekotilo and I. I. Kirienko for June 8 to June 26 raised alarm over the deleterious effect of Bolshevik activity on plans for the offensive and described major disinfecting operations in the 20th Infantry and Sixth Grenadier divisions and the 13th and 21st Finnish Rifle regiments.[82] The 13th Finnish Rifle Regiment had been Krylenko's original unit, and clear

[79] Based on all sources available to the author, to be cited in Chapter III.

[80] See N. M. Iakupov, *Bor'ba za armiiu v 1917 godu* (Moscow, 1975), pp. 29-30; for disorganizing phenomena, see *RDRA*, pp. 128, 173, 188, 341, and 424. One suspects some "censorship" by Soviet editors on this issue, as the above are all incidental references, whereas major upheavals are documented in untainted primary sources (see examples below, pp. 274, 301). See also the major treatment by M. S. Frenkin in *Russkaia armiia i revoliutsiia 1917-1918* (Munich, 1978), pp. 211-24 and 525-40 (the turbulent 169th Division here appears to be plagued as much by Ukrainian separatism as by Bolshevism). Frenkin has informed the author that all his rich material on the Ukrainian movement within the Army was excised by censors in his earlier study, *Revoliutsionnoe dvizhenie na rumynskom fronte 1917 g.-mart 1918* (Moscow, 1965).

[81] Of V. I. Miller's survey of units with a Bolshevik presence, only the 165th Division of the Eighth Army (Southwestern Front, later Rumanian) is repeatedly complained about (see *RDRA*, pp. 43 and 155). See Miller, *Soldatskie komitety*, pp. 219-20.

[82] See "Otchet komissarov XI armii I. Kirienko i I. A. Chekotilo," *BA*, 1 (1926): 13-34.

evidence can be adduced for party-oriented agitation in the 20th Infantry Division; also, both archival and published sources indicate extensive agitation, some of it identified as Bolshevik, in the XXII Corps, which was made up of the First, Third, and Fifth Finnish Rifle and the 159th Infantry divisions, particularly in the 634th and 636th Infantry and the third and 20th Finnish regiments.[83] Beyond this, however, one can make few firm identifications.

The outstanding example of such turmoil was the Second Guards Infantry Division, made up of the Finlandskii, Grenadier, Egerskii, and Moskovskii regiments, where a talented Bolshevik agitator, Lieutenant I. L. Dzevaltovskii-Vintovt, who had spent some time in Petrograd in April in contact with the Bolshevik Military Organization, undertook a serious attempt to transform the entire division into a front version of Kronshtadt. The finale of this drama will be recounted in connection with the offensive, but a rich find of archival materials of which Soviet investigations seem totally unaware allows the reconstruction of an almost breathtaking enterprise that could have, had it succeeded, transformed the campaign against the offensive into a major revolutionary event; in fact, it did not fall far short of its goal.

Dzevaltovskii traveled to Petrograd on a routine assignment from his regiment to secure information on the political issues of interest to soldiers, particularly the platforms of political parties, but he returned an ardent evangel of Lenin's gospel. His subsequent actions reveal an ambitiously conceived and executed plan to transform the committees into a direct democracy of the masses. Dzevaltovskii was not the typical, gramophone Bolshevik agitator or party workhorse of 1917, but a highly talented, original demagogue akin to Krylenko, but with a greater flair for risky adventures and far less ideological sophistication. Indeed, one is tempted to see in him a Stavrogin, Dostoyevsky's prophetic vision of the future's charismatic Duces. Dzevaltovskii had no demonstrable Bolshevik past, but he seems to have been intrigued by Lenin's personality and political techniques. That Dzevaltovskii had a theoretical appreciation of the foundations of Bolshevism seems doubtful, but he must have observed the galvanizing effect of Bolshevik slogans on the masses and discovered within himself the capacity to exploit their possibilities on a grand scale. He was one of the few Bolshevik converts of aristocratic (Polish-Lithuanian) progeny, qualifying by social origin for admission to the Guards via the accelerated wartime program of the Pavlovskii Military School. He had participated

[83] Extensive materials in the archive of the XXII Corps, TsGVIA, f. 2222, op. 2, ed. khr. 1066, ll. 1-43; see also *RDRA*, p. 172 (report of July 3 on the XII Corps, which identifies two Bolshevik agitators in the Third Regiment).

in all the campaigns of the Guards since 1915 and was awarded several decorations for "valor in action." His defection to Bolshevism appears to have been a considerable puzzle to his peers, who heretofore had regarded him as "an excellent comrade and officer." One must conclude that it was something intensely personal in his mental makeup that drew him into his unheralded role.[84]

Dzevaltovskii first emerges in the archival records in early May as chairman of an "electoral commission" of the Second Guards Division to choose delegates for the forthcoming Congress of the Southwestern Front and the All-Russian Peasant Congress. That something unusual was afoot becomes evident in the electoral preparations: the delegates were to be elected directly by the entire division, making use of the complete paraphernalia of parliamentary elections: preelectoral assemblies, platforms, printed ballots, and so on. A local movie theater was turned into a bustling campaign headquarters, and the divisional staff was tapped for automobiles, typewriters, and communication facilities (a number of Dzevaltovskii's preemptory requests, which were apparently honored without protest, are in the archive). The preelectoral meetings were utilized, not only to give visibility to the candidates but also to publicize a *nakaz* (position paper), obviously inspired by Dzevaltovskii, which was ratified by an assembly of all regimental committees on May 7. On some issues it took ritual Soviet positions, but on the land, the relationship of the Soviet to the Provisional Government, and the war it followed a more radical line: all private lands were to belong to those who worked it, and buying and selling of land was to be prohibited (closer to the S.R. position than to that of the Bolsheviks); the Soviet was the sole authority of the democracy, whereas the government was a "purely administrative organ"; and on the war, though a separate peace was to be rejected,

> We must demand that the Allies come around to our position. Miliukov conducted a bourgeois and therefore duplicitous policy. Now we must declare sincerely and openly that we want an end to the war. The question of fraternization must be put up for discussion without predetermination.[85]

[84] Biographical information comes from text of indictment against Grenadiers for mutiny in July, in *RDRA*, pp. 234-62 (see pp. 234 and 251-52 for biographical data). Although he was identified as a Bolshevik and as later occupying important posts in the War Commissariat under Krylenko, Soviet works display great reluctance to claim him as their own; a footnote in *RDRA* (p. 583) notes only that he was the Bolshevik chairman of the Committee of the Grenadier Regiment.

[85] Archive of the Second Guards Infantry Division in TsGVIA, f. 2322, op. 7, ed. khr. 4, l. 161. Although ed. khr. 4 is the file for staff documents, reports, orders, etc., the affairs of the committee predominate, and it includes copies of many committee documents, pro-

Though not strictly Bolshevik, these formulations were designed to play on the latent radicalism of the masses without provoking the opposition of the committeemen of other persuasions. A few weeks later, when the battle lines between the Soviet leaders and the Bolsheviks were more clearly drawn, the strategy could not have succeeded, but in the still-tense atmosphere of the April crisis (a united front of socialists against Miliukov and the bourgeois factions) the statement was carried by the assembly unanimously.

Dzevaltovskii presented to the divisional assembly two other proposals designed to maintain the radical momentum of the electoral campaign. The first was to endorse and carry into action as a *fait accompli* the Soviet project for the Declaration of Soldiers' Rights, which at this juncture was thought to be tied up in the Polivanov commission. Coming before the announcement of Kerensky's implementation (May 11), the proposal was a direct challenge to the command on the sensitive issue of saluting. The divisional commander helplessly protested: "In general there is too much talk about rights and not enough about duties. The War Minister and the Provisional Government will concern themselves with your rights as citizens."[86] The force of this issue was removed a few days later by the announcement of Kerensky's Declaration, but the unbridled presumptuousness was revealed.

Of far greater consequence was the proposal to radically restructure the committees and call for new elections at all levels in the division.[87] Dzevaltovskii pointed out that many committeemen, particularly officers, obviously did not support the points in the *nakaz* unanimously approved by the delegate assembly. Moreover, the election of officer delegates in a separate curia, provided for in the existing regulations, was held to be "undemocratic." Dzevaltovskii was appointed the head of a new three-man electoral commission to carry through this reform.

Dzevaltovskii's draft statute for the new divisional committee clearly reflected his efforts to radicalize and politicize the division. Extensive discussions and preliminary resolutions on lower levels were required before the division committee could take a position on any issue, and on major questions an assembly of all regimental committees was to make the final determination. This had the effect of offsetting the demonstrable tendency of higher committees to take more moderate stands and impose them on lower committees. Other provisions, such as open committee

---

ceedings, draft resolutions, and communications, whereas the file for the division committee contains only a few documents from this period, duplicating information in the staff file (see ed. khr. 2).

[86] Various points in *ibid.*, ed. khr. 4, ll. 174, 186, and 188.

[87] *Ibid.*, l. 197, revisions in l. 199.

sessions, and the direct election of committee members, including the officer contingent, by the entire unit, were designed to neutralize the influence of officer representatives, as well as of Menshevik and S.R. intellectuals. Moreover, insisting on complete autonomy from command authority in the conduct of business, the proposed statute nevertheless imposed on the command the obligation to finance and facilitate through staff resources all undertakings of the committees. The most striking provision, however, was in electoral procedure: balloting was to be only for complete slates, which any organized group, including lower committees or political parties, could submit. The effect, of course, would be to bring about intense electoral campaigning between groups with specific political loyalties, and to afford the Bolsheviks the opportunity to ride the crest of constantly induced soldier radicalism to firm control over the division. The innovations would have rendered the division useless for normal military purposes, but could transform it into a suitable base from which to revolutionize the entire front.

The helplessness of the command is clear from an order of General Rylskii on May 3, shortly after he took over the division. "What is happening in the division," he complained, "does not allow me to regard myself as commander." "If you don't believe me, believe your leader Tsereteli" (that the Revolution will die if it does not show better discipline than the Old Regime), and "if you don't believe me, believe your Soviet" (on fraternization, citing the proclamation of April 30).[88] But Dzevaltovskii's high-handed methods also generated opposition among the soldiers. The committee of the Finlandskii Regiment formally protested the prescribed procedure and boycotted the divisional assembly of May 13 that was to ratify Dzevaltovskii's statute. On the other hand, a group of Bolshevik schismatics from the Pavlovskii Regiment belonging to the First Guards Division was illegally allowed to participate. Obviously Dzevaltovskii intended to create his Bolshevik base out of a rump parliament of the division, drawing in outside units on the basis of their Bolshevik commitment. That there were other absentees is clear from the list of delegates elected by the assembly to the Southwestern Front Congress, who were chosen proportionally to the number attending the assembly—10 from the Grenadier Regiment, 8 from the Finlandskii, 7 from the Moskovskii, 2 from the Guards Artillery, and none from the Egerskii.[89]

Despite the lopsided attendance, several amendments were proposed from the floor, the most important of which would eliminate the submission of slates by political parties (but not by other groups). The archival record

[88] *Ibid.*, ll. 20-21.

[89] *Ibid.*, ll. 122 and 180.

does not make clear whether the prescribed elections ever took place or whether a new divisional committee ever came into being. However, the Grenadier Regimental Committee met on May 16 under Dzevaltovskii's chairmanship with 46 members present. The "Organization of the Divisional Soviet" was on the agenda, but no discussion of it is recorded, whereas decisions were recorded on a rejection of the new courts instituted by the Provisional Government (order of April 17) and several "amendments" to a division order regulating the transfer of the Guards units to the Eleventh Army. Probably, faced with opposition or indifference in other units, the project was allowed quietly to lapse. Dzevaltovskii himself soon departed for the Congress of the Southwestern Front and rejoined his unit only two weeks later during their long march to the south. For that period there are no committee records, although Dzevaltovskii's almost hypnotic hold on the Grenadiers is well attested by other sources. The events that led up to the Grenadiers' mutiny during the offensive will be reserved for the following two chapters.[90]

☆

Although each of the above front organizations contributed significantly to the radicalization of the front, as organizations they comprised relatively few members and their direct control over units through the committee structure was very limited, extending beyond the original nucleus only in the case of *OP*. In the higher committees, with the few noted exceptions (Western Front and Second Army committees), their presence was little more than a nuisance if they pursued an antioffensive line, and in the course of May there was a considerable purge of the more articulate types (Krylenko, Kokovikhin, Fedotov). Since communications remained tenuous and nothing like a coordinated organizational strategy thus far existed, one can safely conclude that for all the appeal of "Bolshevism" to the trench-weary soldiers, the party forces were not yet in a position to reap organizational advantage from it.

The best proof of the above is the failure of the All-Russian Conference of Front and Rear Military Organizations (June 16-23) to make any significant impact on the front, either by establishing an organizational structure or by grooming a new breed of front activists. Of the handful of front delegates, only four clearly came from front units other than the well-known ones, among them a certain comrade Leges from an unidentified regiment on the Western Front (for whom he claimed a membership of

[90] *Ibid.*, l. 211. The official indictment contains no information confirming the above, and nothing at all on Dzevaltovskii's involvement with the divisional committee; it notes only that he was reelected chairman of the Grenadier Regimental Committee "on new principles" on May 13 (see *RDRA*, p. 234); for Dzevaltovskii's activities in connection with the mutiny on June 22, see below pp. 95-96.

150); another, Serov, from the "Dvinsk Front" (Fifth Army), who conceded that there were no organized Bolsheviks in his regiment; and one Filatov, from the 20th Finnish Rifle Regiment (Seventh Army, Southwestern Front). Only B. I. Burmatov, representing the strong Bolshevik fraction (8 out of 20) in the committee of the III Siberian Corps (Second Army), A. G. Vasilev of *OP*, E. Iurevich of the Latvian Riflers, and Krylenko rise above total obscurity.[91] The brief reports of the front delegates on their units are unremarkable and unenlightening, touching mainly on the favorable mood of the soldiers, the Easter fraternization, alarm over the offensive, and the unbelievable hounding of Bolsheviks at the front by the command and defensist committeemen.

The conference followed the standard formula of Bolshevik conferences of this period, with major reports by Lenin (agrarian question), Zinoviev (the April Conference resolutions), Stalin (nationalities), Krylenko (the Soviet Congress and the "Democratization of the Army"), Kaganovich, Volodarskii, Podvoiskii, and others. On June 18 the entire conference marched as a body with Bolshevik slogans in the gigantic demonstration sponsored by the Soviet Congress at which the Bolsheviks revealed their strength. It was indeed an exhilarating experience for the delegates, so much so that Vasilev created a sensation at a subsequent session by vigorously attacking the party leadership for excessive timidity.

> You want to know what is upsetting the front delegates at the present time? Without qualification the events of recent days, the unrest among the regiments and working masses. It seems to us that Comrade Lenin is not well informed on the conditions of the masses at the front, as he has given us no concrete recommendations for getting out of the current situation. One has to look the truth straight in the eyes. The Army at the front is being delivered over to the counter-revolutionary commanders. The offensive has now received the backing of the highest authority. . . . The Central Committee appears to us to be reacting too slowly . . . and is ill-informed about the mass mood. What are we to tell our comrades when we return? What is to be our line of conduct with respect to the offensive? For me, a worker, one thing is clear—I'd rather die here on the barricades than there for aims completely alien to the interests of the proletariat. . . . Right

[91] Leges, Serov, and Osipov figure in no other sources or secondary works of which the author is aware; Filatov is referred to in several sources as a Bolshevik in the 20th Regiment, for example, in *RDRA*, p. 310, and TsGVIA, f. 2222, op. 1, ed. khr. 1066, l. 168. On Burmatov, see Miller, *Soldatskie komitety*, pp. 201 and 214, and *BOB*, p. 269. On the Bolshevik influence remaining strong throughout 1917 in the III Siberian Corps, see below, pp. 273-74, 335, 339-40.

> now the bourgeoisie still carries the big stick to beat the masses into submission. We must tear that stick out of their hands and use it ourselves. Believe me, if we strike the front will support us.[92]

Vasilev, himself a Petrograd worker by background, had obviously picked up the electric mood in the capital and, like the workers and garrison soldiers, was frustrated by the counsels of patience of the leadership, which was still committed to the route of "peaceful propaganda" until there was a clear majority within the soviet structure. His attitude was echoed by an unidentified delegate named Shimaev, who asserted that "the time for just agitation has passed" because "there are whole divisions and corps virtually in the hands of Bolsheviks," while another remarked bitterly: "If we go on the offensive just because others do, it makes nonsense out of all our propaganda. Miliukov is telling us to make all the propaganda we want, but we 'must submit to the majority.' . . . I say even if the whole army goes over the top, I'll stay in the trenches myself."

Obviously the conference leadership was caught up short, and Kaganovich and Krylenko were obliged to defend the position of the Central Committee. Kaganovich pleaded that the comrades were in effect putting on the agenda the seizure of power for which the conditions were not yet ripe, whereas the correct line for the time being was "to put pressure on the Soviet leadership for by-elections." Krylenko even went so far as to assert that Bolshevik units had to take part in the offensive because it was obvious that most of their neighboring units favored it (apparently still under the spell of the Southwestern Front Congress) and one could not let one's comrades down. "Only when the ideas of Bolshevism are adopted by the broad masses of troops can we afford to pass over from words to deeds," he argued with finality. Krylenko proposed a resolution upholding the position of the Central Committee, but it passed only by a vote of 32 to 21. Though it is not clear that the front delegates voted as a block, the vote certainly revealed a deep split among the military Bolsheviks and must have had a demoralizing effect on the participants. Also, the fact that the vote revealed that less than one-third of the original delegates were still present points to a less-than-satisfactory outcome of the conference and a failure to achieve the hoped-for organizational unity between Bolsheviks of the front and the rear.

Whether for this or other reasons, the conference left no visible trace on the front forces of Bolshevism. Not only were the conference proceedings given no publicity—they were not covered in any of the leading Bolshevik organs, including *OP*—the near anonymous delegates carried no perceptible message back to the front (at least there is no documentary

[92] *BVO*, No. 5 (June 24).

trace of it). Any organizational advances that might have been made were cut short by the July Days and the collapse of the offensive, which not only demoralized front Bolsheviks (the July Days must have appeared to them as a failed opportunity) but also led to severe repressions and a wave of arrests that paralyzed their activities until after the Kornilov affair. The All-Russian Conference affords a brief glimpse of the ambitions of the leadership of the Military Organization, but it cannot in any sense be regarded as a turning point, as it is represented in Soviet works.[93] "Bolshevism" continued to spread apace, but spontaneously like a brush fire and primarily because of its appealing message, not because of any enhancement of its organizational framework.

[93] For the standard Soviet accounts, see Golub (n. 23 of this chapter), pp. 96-105, and Andreev, *Soldatskie massy*, pp. 78-81. Naturally, the above episode receives no treatment. Although extensive excerpts from *BVO* are reprinted in *BPB* (pp. 175-91), they are carefully edited, the speeches of Zinoviev and Kaganovich are omitted entirely, several objectionable passages in Krylenko's are excised (that soldiers should "obey orders" while peacefully propagating their views on the offensive), the reports of Vasiliev and the Latvian delegate are emasculated, and the entire debate in No. 5 is unrecorded.

CHAPTER III

THE REVOLT AGAINST THE OFFENSIVE

As a new offensive loomed on the horizon, the formless and sporadic disorders of April gave way to a more sustained and violent kind. Previously, the frequent resistance to orders and arrests of senior officers had been liquidated without major consequences through the intervention of committees, endless "persuasion," or revoking orders which were likely to precipitate unrest. Now that the Coalition Government and the command had resolved irrevocably on an offensive, major regrouping operations and morale-building exercises became an unavoidable necessity. The conjunction of dry weather, the resumption of sending replacements, Kerensky's whirlwind tours, and front and army congresses which debated the offensive gave rise to the first major front mutinies requiring drastic resolution. Though still exceptional, these affairs were deeply symptomatic of the unfolding general malaise which spawned numerous incidents of lesser magnitude, marked by increasing desperation and violence. Though these disorders exhibited many features of "trench Bolshevism," it is noteworthy that the most celebrated instances—517th Batumskii and 707th Neshavskii regiments, the 12th and 13th Siberian Rifle divisions (Southwestern Front, May 17 and 24 respectively), the Second and 17th Siberian Rifle divisions (Western Front, May 17), and the 163rd Infantry Division (Rumanian Front, May 22)—had no past history of Bolshevik influence.[1] Rather they were chiefly precipitated by major troop movements preparatory to new operations, and they occurred in units whose discipline had already been shaken by previous incidents, particularly the high-numbered divisions of recent formation. In these instances the persuasions of lower committees yielded meager results, and special measures by corps congresses, special teams from army committees, and government commissars were required.

[1] See Stavka's weekly survey of incidents for May 18-25 in *VOSR. Mai-iiun'*, pp. 348-39.

While punitive expeditions, forced disarming, and disbanding of whole units were often threatened, only in the cases of the 163rd Infantry and the 12th and 13th Siberian divisions were such measures actually carried out.

The double mutiny of the 517th Batumskii and 707th Neshavskii regiments on May 17, which ended in the arrest and severe beating of the 177th Division commander, General Ia. Ia. Liubitskii, can be taken as a major turning point.[2] En route as part of the XXXI Corps from the Western Front to the Special Army on the Southwestern Front, these regiments refused to obey an order to move from the railhead up to the front. The order was repeated three times, but only seven of the twelve companies of the 517th complied, while the other five companies and the entire 707th Regiment refused. Just what triggered the beating of Liubitskii is not clear, but agitation back and forth by obscure agitators had resulted in identically worded resolutions rejecting the offensive in both regiments. General Alekseev, shortly before his dismissal, concluded in a report to Kerensky:

> The internal rot has reached its ultimate limit and has nowhere to go from here. The troops are no longer a threat to the enemy, but to their own fatherland. Admonitions and appeals no longer have an effect on the masses. What is needed is authority, force, compulsion, the fear of punishment.[3]

Alekseev recommended disbanding the two divisions of which these regiments were a part and a comprehensive program for saving the Army, specifically restoration of the military code of justice in full force, prompt punishment of all offenders without exceptions or mitigations, and restoration of disciplinary powers to officers. He had in fact laid out the program that in July and August was to be promoted by General Kornilov.

Archival materials shed uneven light on the circumstances of this affair. The commander of the 517th Regiment cultivated a pseudo-revolutionary style and constantly berated his officers as compensation for his declining hold on the regiment. Several times in the preceding weeks he had consented to the removal of officers pending investigation at the request of the regimental committee.[4] The transfer from the Western to the South-

[2] The basic materials on this case are the daily orders of the 517th Batumskii Regiment (TsGVIA, f. 3054, op. 2, d. 23, part 1), which include the minutes of the regimental committee and various materials in the archive of the XXXI Corps (TsGVIA, f. 2440, op. 5, d. 1); they will be cited by folio and leaf number (f. and l. or ll.) only.

[3] *RDRA*, p. 111.

[4] On berating his officers, see f. 3054, ll. 142, 165, 185, and 215 (March 24, April 4, 17, and 28); on removing officers at the request of the regimental committee, *ibid.*, ll. 221 and 213 (April 30 and May 3).

western Front was a hazardous journey. Railroads in the vicinity were jammed with troops under transfer, replacements, discharged over-forties, and returning and departing deserters; railroad stations were the scene of intense agitation, "meetings," wine riots, and incidents of various sorts, such as the arrest at Vidibor of General Krasnov.[5] Two days before the regiment was to depart, on May 7, soldiers arrested a battalion commander Lieutenant Colonel Sliaskii, and two lieutenants, an incident the regimental committee quickly liquidated; nevertheless, they requested Colonel Sliaskii's removal for "sowing discord between officers and soldiers." The higher command, however, chose this unpropitious moment to appoint Sliaskii commander of the regiment, which either precipitated or greatly exacerbated the turmoil that ensued. This does not, however, explain the unrest in the 707th Regiment, and Alekseev must have had grounds for requesting the disbanding of both divisions; thus the incident is better seen as part of the general turmoil surrounding the massive transfers of troops then taking place at the front.

Sources document reactions to the crisis of the command and the committees more satisfactorily. On May 18 army commander General Baluev ordered "all personnel in the corps to comply immediately with operative Order No. 08532" or be declared "enemies of the Fatherland." He called all regimental and division committees of the corps into session as a "congress" to take appropriate measures to end the disorders. As of that time, seven of the twelve companies of the Batumskii Regiment had moved out, but the remaining five and the entire 707th Regiment had not. The congress accused the mutinous units of "the exclusive desire not to forsake a soft berth in the reserve," but curiously blamed the affair on certain unidentified "officer demagogues" who "curry the favor of the masses to buy themselves cheap popularity."[6] They requested the commander to issue the order one more time, after which the War Minister should be asked to disband the regiments. Kerensky did order the disbandment, but revoked it on General Baluev's request when the remaining units complied on May 22.

The committee of the Batumskii Regiment seems not to have held a formal session during this incident, but sometime before May 22 it passed a strange resolution, apparently intended to be exculpatory, denouncing certain "loudmouths, provocateurs, flatterers, and people on the take, hiding like spiders in every dark nook and cranny . . . , knowing full well that all filth and violence are repugnant to mankind."[7] In addition, a

[5] See P. N. Krasnov, "Na vnutrennom fronte," *AR* 1 (1922): 99, and Special Army order of May 7 (f. 3054, l. 254).

[6] See f. 3054, ll. 244, 278-82, 311, and 351-52.

[7] *Ibid.*, ll. 275-76.

congress of the 130th Division on May 30, attended by 130 delegates, proclaimed harmony between soldiers and officers and readiness to take the offensive, but at the same time sarcastically reminded the Staff "of the existence of our division" and called on it to "desist from strange methods hitherto causing unrest and disorders." The latter was possibly a reference to the untimely appointment of Colonel Sliaskii, as it also suggested that one way to avoid excesses in the future was "to devise a legal way to protest the harmful activity of one's nearest superiors and to promote truly revolutionary, deserving officers who have been intentionally shoved aside by hide-bound, bourgeois staffs."[8]

One should note that this was not merely a soldier-officer conflict. Two lieutenants, a staff captain, and several noncoms were among those who guided the proceedings of the congress. Regular commanders were not above using cheap demagogucry to circumvent the troublesome committees, the committees were divided between elements that played to the crowd and those that sought to cooperate with the more enlightened commanders to maintain order, and embedded in the soldier mass was an elusive "dark element" whose only aim was to create confusion and demoralization in any way possible. The materials suggest only the bare outlines of these groupings, but they suggest a situation very much in flux and threatening at any moment to slip into chaos and violence against the officer class.

In a second case the attempt of the Provisional Government to disband dissident units had a less-resolute outcome. On May 24 the 12th and 13th Siberian Rifle divisions of the Seventh Army refused orders to move to the fighting lines. When only half the regiments yielded to the persuasions of Commissar Boris Savinkov, Kerensky ordered the remaining regiments disbanded and published the fact in the newspapers.[9] Savinkov, however, was reluctant to employ force, and the rebel units, some 5,000 strong, dug in and prepared to resist; 3,000 others claimed "poor health" and demanded medical review, which was granted! Not until June 15 did Savinkov and the command agree on military measures to disarm the rebels. The villages where they were entrenched were surrounded by cavalry and artillery units, and after a few bursts of shrapnel they submitted. They were apparently not punished, but sent under convoy to rejoin their old divisions. The discharge of 800 of those under medical review caused further incidents on the eve of the offensive.[10]

Many other units not officially declared to be mutinous were in such a

[8] Record of the session in f. 2440, ll. 7-8.

[9] See *VVP*, May 27, and Stavka survey for May 18-25 in *VOSR. Mai-iiun'*, p. 349.

[10] Details in Knox, *With the Russian Army*, 2:637; telegram of Savinkov along with report of Seventh Army Commander Bel'kovich to Stavka of June 16 in *VOSRU* 1:426.

state of turmoil and indiscipline as to render any distinction superfluous. On the Western Front the 703rd Regiment of the Second Caucasus Grenadier Division, which had a history of violent disorders since March, indulged extensively in card-playing, plundering, rowdyism, and uninterrupted drunkenness; to support the latter they operated a network of eight to ten jealously guarded stills.[11] General Ia. K. Tsykhovich reported that on June 7 his 169th Division on the same front "ceased to exist as a fighting unit," being heavily penetrated with agitators whom he suspected of being "German agents who cover themselves with a veneer of Bolshevism" and who appealed to "the most sensitive feelings of exhaustion with the war."[12]

For most of May, major repressive measures had not been employed. Kerensky's personal prestige and the threat of disgrace were still forceful enough to persuade most reluctant units to take up positions at the front. Finally, at the end of May matters reached such a pass in the 650th Totemskii Regiment (Sixth Army, Rumanian Front) that Kerensky authorized the army command to break it up by armed force. In fact, because of their inadequate equipment and generally poor discipline, all the recently formed "third divisions" on the Rumanian Front were earmarked for dissolution, but the 163rd Division (of which the 650th Regiment was a part) resisted the order, and under the influence of an officer-agitator, Filippov, set up an independent "republic" in the Moldavian countryside. The soldiers encouraged local peasants to seize landlord property, while they themselves plundered the wine cellars of the estates. The regimental commander and a number of officers were severely beaten, one of their number left for dead by the roadside. According to the staff version, the slogans of the rebels were "No confidence in the officers!" "The speediest possible peace regardless of the consequences!" and "No confidence in either the Soviet or the Provisional Government!" The Sixth Army commander, after the failure of a peace mission, resorted to a punitive expedition, which was put under the command of the "liberal" General Biskupskii. (It consisted of two cavalry divisions, two infantry battalions, a battery of light artillery, and units of armored cars and airplanes.) Only the 650th Regiment, under Filippov's urging, held out, but when the expeditionary force began to move in they quickly laid down their arms and agreed to surrender their "agitators." Filippov and 220 soldiers were taken into custody. Thus the pattern for the repressive actions of the summer

[11] According to Denikin's speech at the Stavka conference of July 16, in Golovin, *Rossiiskaia kontr-revoliutsiia*, 1(1):155. See also *RDRA*, pp. 49-50 and 76 (arrest of commander in March, fraternization and threats to raise on bayonets anyone who fires at Germans).

[12] *RDRA*, p. 127.

months was established, and the Revolution no longer feared to use force where persuasion failed.[13]

☆

In the last week of May serious preparations for the summer offensive began. General Alekseev informed lower commands on May 21 that they should prepare for coordinated attacks on all three major fronts—the Northern, Western, and Southwestern—for around June 20. Alekseev's plan called for a major operation north of the Pripet marshes by the Tenth Army in the direction of Vilna, coordinated with a lesser operation by the adjacent Fifth Army of the Northern Front from the direction of Dvinsk; each would build up a reserve force of four to five divisions by drawing off units from other armies to exploit the breakthrough. But the chief arena of operations was to be the region of the Seventh and Eleventh armies in Galicia, where a strike force of twenty-seven to twenty-nine divisions was to be concentrated behind Tarnopol, ready to be deployed to any sector where a breakthrough was achieved in the initial attack. The entire front was to be provided with enormous superiority in artillery, including for the first time complete heavy artillery brigades, each with eight- and twelve-inch howitzers.[14]

It must have greatly pained Alekseev to be entering on major operations for the first time with the weaponry to assure a breakthrough, but with no assurance that his troops would fight. He was not, however, to bear this burden, as he was summarily dismissed by Kerensky the day after issuing this order. ("Like a house servant," he complained.)[15] Kerensky found in Brusilov a "democratic" general not offended by his extravagant style (indeed, Brusilov imitated him) and entrusted him with the command. Kerensky also removed General Gurko, commander of the Western Front, for challenging his new rule forbidding resignations. Both dismissals were meant to demonstrate Kerensky's authority to the military leadership and to deflate the Left's harping on the high command as the center of counterrevolution. There followed a series of swift changes in senior posts: Denikin was assigned to the Western Front, while Lukomskii replaced him as Chief of Staff at Stavka; General Gutor, commander of the Eleventh Army, took over the Southwestern Front from Brusilov, while General Erdeli replaced him; Kornilov was posted to the Eighth Army to replace Kaledin, who

[13] See *RazA*, pp. 38-41, and *RDRA*, p. 116.

[14] See Zaionchkovskii, *Kampaniia 1917 g.*, pp. 61-62. Stavka counted on an 84 to 53 superiority over the enemy in divisional strength on the Southwestern Front. According to Knox (2:641), in the region of the Eleventh and Seventh armies the Russians enjoyed an advantage in light artillery over the enemy of 683 guns to 284, and in heavy artillery and howitzers, 337 to 66.

[15] Denikin, *Ocherki*, 1(2):47.

likewise had earned the reputation of a counter-revolutionary. These appointments were designed to give the top leadership a more "democratic" image, as all except Denikin enjoyed the reputation of cooperating with committees and loyalty to the new order. Even Kornilov was not thought of at this time as being reactionary, because he had cultivated good relations with the Soviet until the crisis that brought his dismissal; moreover, the Eighth Army Committee and the new front commissars, Savinkov and Filonenko, found him quite cooperative, and they even encouraged his self-promoted personality cult.[16] Most other army commanders—Radko-Dmitriev at the Twelfth Army, Kvetsinskii at the Third, Baluev at the Special Army, and Danilov at the Fifth—likewise enjoyed "democratic" reputations.

A signpost of the new defensist attitude of the democratic forces was the institution of "revolutionary battalions of death" (also called "partisan detachments" and similar designations). A few entrepreneurs of the rear sold the idea to Kerensky and Brusilov in mid-May and sent deputations to every part of the country to raise volunteers and money. Brusilov's directive of May 22 defined their purpose to be "to arouse the revolutionary, offensive spirit in the Army . . . by giving [the soldiers] faith that the entire Russian people stand behind them" and to "carry along the wavering elements inspired by their [i.e., the revolutionary battalions'] example."[17] Alekseev pointed out the hazards of drawing in undisciplined, politicized elements, including civilians, from the urban centers, but allowed Brusilov to experiment with the idea on the Southwestern Front; when Brusilov became Commander in Chief he extended the practice to the entire army. The volunteers were to be given intensive training in "storming tactics" with grenades, quickly formed into battalions, and shipped off to the front with their own distinctive markings—a black and red chevron on their sleeves and a death's-head medallion on their caps. They pledged implicitly to obey their superior officers, to be at the forefront of all attacks, to fight with every sinew until wounded, never to reveal military secrets, and never to surrender alive to the enemy; moreover, they were to abstain from alcoholic beverages.[18] However, few of them were organized and trained by the time of the offensive.

[16] On the changes in command, see A. A. Kersnovskii, *Istoriia russkoi armii*, 4 vols. (Belgrade, 1933-38), 4:960-62. See also Denikin's acid comments on the "democratic" generals in *Ocherki*, 1(2), chap. 18, esp. his calculation that of the 40 top commanders and chiefs of staff in mid-May, 15 encouraged democratic practices, 11 were passive, and 14 struggled against democratic practices. Thus "opportunists" outnumbered the resolute almost two to one (*ibid.*, p. 7).

[17] *RazA*, p. 68.

[18] Text in *ibid.*, pp. 69-70; other relevant documents, pp. 65-70.

Far more important for their direct impact on the front were the "shock companies" or "shock battalions" (sometimes "storm companies") formed within existing regiments and divisions; even whole regiments were invited to designate themselves as shock regiments. In advance of any general directive, the 329th Buzuliiskii Regiment (Special Army, Southwestern Front) on May 11 received a divisional order to form a "shock company" by drawing thirty-five soldiers and noncoms from each battalion.[19] The committee of the Twelfth Regiment, Third Infantry Division (Eleventh Army, Southwestern Front) also discussed a statute for a "storm battalion" on May 16 but decided to postpone the decision (there is no further record). The unit was to be trained in the use of grenades and machine guns, including those of the enemy, and their insignia was to be a red patch in the form of an exploding grenade on the left sleeve.[20]

General Brusilov ordered the formation of shock units on the Southwestern Front at the same time as the "revolutionary battalions" (the front committee endorsed the idea in a circular telegram of June 1). Volunteers were to wear the distinctive black and red chevrons and seek to persuade their regiment to adopt the idea.[21] When the campaign to form units from volunteers flagged or met resistance, the emphasis shifted toward persuading existing units of any size to adopt the designation (e.g., "the third shock battalion of XYZ Regiment" or the "125th Shock Regiment of XYZ Division"); however, the unit was taking on itself the honor of spearheading the first attack against the enemy. The doubtful enthusiasm for the idea is recorded in the minutes of the committee of the Volynskii Guards Regiment of June 1, where it was decided not to form a shock unit "since the entire regiment considers itself as such," but nevertheless made the wearing of chevrons "voluntary."[22] On June 12 Kerensky proclaimed he would be happy "to see inscribed as true sons of Russia entire units of the Russian

[19] TsGVIA, f. 2938, op. 1, d. 150.

[20] *Ibid.*, f. 2333, op. 1, ed. khr. 1, l.267.

[21] Cited in *IzOA*, June 1; timing indicated in letter to Alekseev of May 20 while he was still Commander in Chief and Brusilov was commander of the Southwestern Front (*RazA*, p. 66); in a letter to Brusilov of May 18, Alekseev had expressed his skepticism over the idea (*ibid.*, p. 64). They were not introduced on the Northern Front until June 20, indicating that Brusilov did not immediately introduce them universally upon becoming Commander in Chief (secret order of the 186th Division of the Twelfth Army, TsGVIA, f. 2486, op. 1, ed. khr. 2, l. 76).

[22] TsGVIA, f. 2573, op. 1, ed. khr. 2, l. 16. Ia. Kal'nitskii, a soldier in the 35th Division (Eleventh Army, Southwestern Front), states that some units refused to adopt the designation on the theory that without shock units the offensive would have to be canceled, while others were pressured into it by overenthusiastic committees. The only enthusiasts for the idea he claims were committeemen, officers, student volunteers, and clerks. (Kal'nitskii, *Ot fevralia k oktiabriu. Vospominaniia frontovika* [Moscow, 1926], pp. 36-37.)

Revolutionary Army.''[23] The modest number of units assuming this designation is a testimony to the less than overwhelming enthusiasm of the lower ranks. More frequently they were composed of volunteers, mainly former officers, noncoms, and the subintelligentsia of noncombatant formations of the rear.[24] In the minds of most soldiers they were an alarming sign of the impending offensive and an affront to their own visceral rejection of the whole adventure.

☆

The coming of the offensive was advertised to the front soldiers, as well as to the enemy, by the hectic preparations of the remaining weeks. Roads were clogged with supplies and replacements, gun emplacements and dugouts were everywhere under construction, observation balloons and low-flying airplanes performed ubiquitous reconnaissance on both sides of the lines. Only the digging forward of salients and communications trenches proceeded at a painfully slow pace. A swarm of persuaders from the rear blanketed the front with their passionate appeals, among them a large deputation of Black Sea sailors under the colorful leadership of a student-volunteer Anisimov Batkin. The soldier soon felt no longer at home in his own element, as all and sundry were invoking the name of the Revolution and the Fatherland to dragoon him into acting contrary to his every instinct and feeling of what the Revolution was about.[25]

The command reports of early June, though registering numerous incidents and shaky units, manifest on the whole an unwarranted optimism on the prospects for a turnaround in the willingness to fight. On May 30 General Gutor's survey for the Southwestern Front characterized the Seventh and Eighth armies as not yet primed but steadily improving; the Eleventh and Special armies, on the other hand, were responding well to the intensive work of commanders and committees. Black Sea sailors had toured the worst units in the Seventh Army and found them quite receptive

[23] Cited in order to the Grenadier Corps marked ''for circulation to all units,'' in TsGVIA, f. 2327, op. 4, d. 1, l.290.

[24] A Stavka source cited in M. I. Kapustin, *Zagovor generalov (iz istorii kornilovshchiny i ee razgroma)* (Moscow, 1968), p. 81, indicates that by the end of July the designation ''shock unit'' had been adopted by 4 corps, 5 divisions, and 27 regiments but only 30 battalions and 33 companies. Obviously it was far easier for a larger unit to adopt the designation through committee action than on the levels closest to the soldiers. The number of composite shock units, usually of battalion size, is not available, but there are frequent references to them in the sources, usually performing some sort of police or guard role at headquarters, all the way to October. They became a much-hated symbol of the restoration of command authority and *kornilovshchina*.

[25] References to the persuaders are so frequent in the sources that specific references seem superfluous, but see Anet (who toured the front), *Through the Russian Revolution*, pp. 229-31.

to the resolutions of the Front Congress, and no Bolsheviks were in evidence. In the bad units the trouble was always due to a small, stubborn group of clever agitators who nevertheless could be faced down in confrontations.[26] Even General Denikin's report for the Western Front of June 11 notes the positive work of the committees in the Third and Tenth armies; the committee of the Second Army, however, was judged unsatisfactory, "following the Front Committee even in its most extreme manifestations." Fraternization and desertions had ceased.[27]

Reports from the Twelfth and Fifth armies were somewhat more alarming, due to the inordinate number of demoralized units and extensive penetration of Bolshevik agitation emanating from Riga, Petrograd, and the Baltic Fleet, but since the offensive there was to have a secondary character, it seems not to have dampened the spirits of Stavka.[28] Stavka's survey of the fronts for the week preceding the offensive, though cautious and unduly brief on the Northern and Western fronts, was decidedly buoyant with respect to the Southwestern Front: the Seventh Army had "noticeably improved," the Eighth Army was "generally satisfactory," and the Special Army was "sound in discipline, fired up in spirit, and ready to do battle."[29] Considering the chaos unfolding at that very moment, one marvels at the magnitude of distortion of information generated by the staff machinery as it filtered upward. In all probability, the official optimism ardently promoted by Kerensky and Brusilov fostered in lower commands an urge to see encouraging signs or desired results in the field reports and to minimize or screen out disquieting information. Characteristic were frequently claimed successes for treatments of "persuasion" which were practiced not only by commanders but also by higher and lower committees, commissars, Black Sea sailors, visiting firemen of all sorts, and even Allied officers and civilians (such as the French socialist minister Thomas). Senior commanders also tried, but seldom with success; Brusilov was the worst failure of all.[30] Often this resulted in cheaply bought resolutions to take

[26] See *RazA*, p. 86.

[27] *RDRA*, pp. 132-34.

[28] For pessimistic reports on the Twelfth and Fifth armies, see *RDRA*, pp. 130-32, and *KA* 84:145.

[29] *VOSR. Mai-iiun'*, pp. 366-67.

[30] On Brusilov's embarrassing failure as a persuader on the Western Front, see Denikin, *Ocherki*, 1(2):160, and Colonel V. Pronin, "Miting generala Brusilova" (Ms.), RA. Pronin characterizes Brusilov as "imitating Kerensky" and using elaborate circumlocution to avoid using the provocative term "offensive." He shook hands with soldiers, called them "comrades," and pretended not to hear hostile remarks and catcalls. (Pronin was an ardent monarchist, a co-founder of the Officers' Union and future lieutenant of Kornilov.) On the mixed success of French socialist minister Thomas in the Eighth Army, see Anet, pp. 30-37 and 248-52.

the offensive ("at the first call") or to obey orders ("without delay or discussion") or as recorded in this report of June 11: "The delegation visited N Rifle Regiment of the N Division which refused to move into position. After our presentation they decided unanimously to perform their duty as citizens."[31]

Such an Allied delegation, among them a French Colonel Rampon and Zinovii Peshkov (son of Maxim Gorky and presently a lieutenant in the French Army), visited the 28th Division (Tenth Army, Western Front). When their passionate appeals seemed to require some decisive gesture, Peshkov turned to the commanding officer and declared in a loud voice: "*Gospodin* Colonel! We request you to do us [the French delegation] the honor of enlisting us in the ranks as ordinary soldiers so that we may accompany these heroes to the front lines." The effect was magical, and the first battalion stepped off with their curious new companions in their midst. But from the rear ranks an anonymous voice cried out: "Hold on, comrades, do you really think those are Frenchies? Don't you know a *burzhui* trick when you see one? They just dressed up as Frenchies to put one over on us. No Frenchman ever spoke Russian like that!" A sergeant snapped, "They may or may not be Frenchies, but at least they are willing to march with us. But we know who you are getting paid by!" The soldiers marched on, subdued and uncommunicative, and that evening the "volunteers" quietly slipped out of the bivouac to try their hand elsewhere.[32]

The later famous author Victor Shklovsky and a veteran worker-revolutionary named Anardovich performed yeoman service as commissar-persuaders in Kornilov's Eighth Army. They worked themselves hoarse with marathon speech-making, as a result of which some of the most incorrigible units were moved to profess willingness to perform their revolutionary duty. In one instance they visited a particularly xenophobic "trench republic" tucked away in the Carpathians. The regiment was under the control of a junior officer-agitator, whereas the noncoms had all "fled to the shock battalions"; the thoroughly intimidated committee preferred to leave the men in peace. Nevertheless, the commissars managed to assemble a "meeting" during which agitators cried out: "Beat them! They're *burzhuis*! . . . How much do you get paid?" The crowd moved menacingly forward, but a soldier's impromptu outburst temporarily stayed the crowd; shedding his boots he exclaimed, "Look at our feet! They're rotting away in the trenches!" Throwing caution to the winds, Anardovich let loose a string of mother curses and *svoloches* surpassing the most

[31] "Bolshevizatsiia fronta v prediiul'skie dni 1917 g.," *KA* 58 (1933): 87.

[32] See Ia. M. Lisovoi, "Itogi odnogo iz ugovorov," *BA* 2-3 (1928): 18-19. Doubtless it was a standard ploy; Duma Deputy T. P. Demidov performed the identical feat in April to get a unit to occupy the trenches. See *VVP*, April 26.

grizzled noncom, and shamed his hearers into submission by reciting his services to the Revolution for which he had paid with years of prison and exile. The affair ended in hurrahs and the ceremonial tossing into the air of the revolutionary commissars. Anardovich stayed behind to shape up the unit, agitators were separated out, and a few days later it "went over the top, fighting no worse than the others."[33] But Shklovsky confesses that such successes were more than offset by the process of disintegration, bred of exhaustion, trench ailments, fear of new bloodletting, and the heady stuff of Bolshevism.

The most severe case of self-hypnosis was Commissar Boris Savinkov. His anonymous letters from the trenches published in Petrograd newspapers lyricize over the healthy *frontoviki*, who unlike the revolutionary heroes of the rear believed in deeds, not words. They cry as they depart for the front: "Wc will die for Russia, comrades! We will die for Land and Freedom! Long live Kerensky! Long live the Revolution! Hurrah!" But he also encountered other sentiments: "We'll fight once we've rested up, won't we comrades?" "We'll fight, if the priest's son and the sausage merchant's nephew fight too, won't we comrades?" "We'll fight if England and France publish their secret treaties, right comrades?" "But only if they back us up with plenty of artillery, right comrades?"[34] But these were ascribed to the Bolshevik citadel of Kseshinskaia's mansion and the German General Staff, brought to the front by returning deserters and replacements. With mystical determination he held aloft the image of God-fearing Russian peasants, reincarnated in tattered gray uniforms, cramped in the vermin-infested labyrinths, grimly ready to sacrifice their lives for LAND AND FREEDOM. Shortly, under testing, Savinkov's vision was to collapse.

As pressures mounted on the anguished muzhiks to give their moral consent to the offensive, and as the hour of reckoning drew near, angry defiance and mass disobedience grew to epidemic proportions. It was no longer a question of major troop movements along the railways or long marches of particular units, but reactions to the countless changes in position and tactical redeployment preparatory to battle which every soldier in every regiment keenly understood. The legitimacy of each order was challenged, open mass meetings thrashed them back and forth, orator after orator tried his hand at persuasion. Debate raged around whether the Soviets' views were being concealed, whether one's unit was adequately equipped or shod or up to strength, whether indeed an offensive was compatible with the goals of the Revolution and peace. A large number

[33] See V. Shklovskii, *Revoliutsiia i front* (Petrograd, 1921), pp. 39-40.

[34] N. Lugin (Fedor Stepun), *Iz pisem praporshchika-artillerista* (Moscow, 1918), pp. 198, 199, and *passim*, in which Savinkov's dispatches of 1917 are included as an appendix.

of regiments passed resolutions against the offensive at this time, a campaign obviously promoted by Bolshevik groups but spreading primarily by its own momentum. The 700th Elatomskii Regiment (Tenth Army, Western Front) was probably a typical case. On June 14 the regimental committee called a meeting to consider a pro-offensive resolution, but after passionate debate the assembly passed a resolution against the offensive instead. "Don't you trust the Provisional Government?" the chairman queried. "No, we don't!" "Whom do you trust then?" "The Soviet of Workers' and Soldiers' Deputies!" "And if the Soviet orders you to take the offensive?" "We'll think about it." The assembly finally agreed to send a deputation to Petrograd to determine the Soviet's position, but as the meeting broke up someone shouted: "If they force us to take the offensive and it fails, we'll run all the officers through with our bayonets."[35]

Refusals to take the offensive until the explicit sanction of the Soviet were obtained occurred frequently. For example, the Fourth and Sixth Finnish Rifle divisions, earmarked to spearhead the main attack in the Seventh Army, refused to move until the Soviet confirmed their orders.[36] A refusal of three regiments of the 83rd Infantry Division to move from the railhead toward the front was based on typical "misunderstandings," which Kerensky tried to clear up by telegram:

> A delegate of the 83rd Division returning from Petrograd claims that I said there would be no offensive in the near future to give Germany the opportunity to agree to our peace conditions. I request that the soldiers and officers of the 83rd be immediately informed that I never said anything of the kind. The delegate either misunderstood or deliberately led his comrades into error.[37]

A staff digest of lower command reports of this period is replete with further examples:

> [*From the Northern Front, June 6*:]
> Regrouping operations in several corps are being carried through with great difficulty, and it is necessary to convince whole regiments and

[35] *VOSR. Mai-iiun'*, pp. 364-65. Soviet scholar G. I. Zhuravlev identifies eight corps resolutions against the offensive and also for the 20th, 121st, 135th, 169th Infantry, and the 12th and 13th Siberian Rifle divisions. Since the first and the last two mentioned divisions later reversed themselves, while the corps units are suspect, the list loses its value as evidence. There can be no doubt that the issue was hotly debated up and down the front and that many resolutions (pro or con) went unrecorded. (See "Bor'ba soldatskikh massy protiv letnogo nastupleniia na fronte," *IZ* 61 [1957]: 12, 14, and *passim*.)

[36] See *IZ* 61 (1957): 15.

[37] Cited in orders of 329th Buzuliiskii Regiment of June 18, TsGVIA, f. 2938, op. 1, d. 319, l. 249. On the refusal of three of the regiments to move up to the front, see *ibid.*, l. 235 (June 14).

> divisions that these operations are vital to the offensive and require their transfer to new regions and positions.
>
> [*From the Western Front, June 6*:]
> In X Siberian Regiment it is impossible to carry out the order on forming storming units, as the soldiers refuse to allow the designation. The second battalion of Y Regiment passed a resolution endorsing the offensive yesterday, but today held a meeting and reversed the decision, declaring the orders of the government invalid. . . . In Z Regiment the soldiers declare that if the offensive takes place and it fails, they will settle accounts with the officers. . . . In another regiment the soldiers beat up the noncoms speaking in favor of the war.
>
> [*From the Western Front, June 15*:]
> In X Siberian Regiment, at uninterrupted meetings, the most extreme things are said of the officers and the commander, at one of which it was decided to hang the latter along with three officers and to deal with the rest according to their views on the offensive.[38]

Under these circumstances it was questionable whether the offensive would ever get off the ground and a deluge of last-minute requests for high-ranking "persuaders" ensued, preferably Kerensky or representatives of the Soviet Executive Committee. General Brusilov, fearing that the Germans and the Austrians would try to disrupt the offensive by an anticipatory attack, advanced the target date on the Southwestern Front to June 10, and to June 15 for the other two fronts. Five days later (June 2) he delayed it again until June 12, then again until June 16 to allow Kerensky to visit each of the attacking corps; Kerensky himself postponed it two more days to await an inspiring resolution of the All-Russian Soviet Congress; he might have spared himself the trouble, as the resolution merely repeated the formula of "readiness for offensive or defensive operations," while "strategic" considerations were left to Stavka. Even so, the vote was only 472 to 271 with 39 abstentions, revealing that many delegates besides the Bolsheviks had deep reservations. Nevertheless, Kerensky and the command chose to regard this as a solemn commitment binding on all loyal Soviet elements, though personally Kerensky was quite bitter.[39]

Details in accounts of Kerensky's visits by both friendly and hostile witnesses are always the same—incredible tension as soldiers assemble, uncertainty over the soldiers' mood, the awkward presence of senior commanders, unaccustomed stage management by the *komitetchiki*, the swift

[38] *KA* 57:87-90.

[39] For the Congress decision, see *IzPS*, June 21; for Kerensky's disappointment, see *Russia and History's Turning Point*, p. 284; and on changing the date for offensive, see Zaionchkovskii, *Kampaniia 1917 g.*, p. 66.

arrival of the staff car, Kerensky's comic-solemn visage and posturing, his yellow "French" jacket, high boots, and quasi-military yet "democratic" appearance; he bounds up to the tribune, immediately takes charge, and launches into his oration marked by dramatic gestures, rhetorical questions, and hysterical verbal assaults, playing for wild applause and solemn vows to die for the revolutionary Fatherland.[40] An urgent request for his presence came from the commander of the I Guards Corps, General Il-kevich, whose units were earmarked as a reserve in the Eleventh Army to exploit the breakthrough; the execution of its task was doubtful because of the incessant agitation of the Grenadier Guards Regiment and a huge last-minute influx of undisciplined Petrograd replacements.[41] On June 14 Dzevaltovskii called a mass meeting attended by 12,000 guardsmen from all units which passed a resolution of no confidence in the Provisional Government and condemned the offensive as "contrary to the interests of the Revolution."[42] A mass meeting of soldiers was arranged in a forest opening two days before the offensive was to begin.

The command made no effort to assemble the guardsmen in ranks for a review, and Kerensky's automobile pulled into the thick of an unorganized soldier mob of some 15,000 to 20,000, many lazily stretched out on the ground or sitting on an amphitheater-like hillside. The situation was tense, because Dzevaltovskii's Grenadiers and several hundred Bolshevik dissidents of the Pavlovskii and Finlandskii regiments gathered separately some distance away, making clear their intention to cause an incident. Removing his coat and rolling up his sleeves (which greatly offended or amused the senior officers present), Kerensky harangued the crowd at length in his high-pitched style, triumphantly extracting a pledge from all present to lay down their lives for the Revolution and Freedom. Although hostile officer witnesses blamed Kerensky's undignified behavior for spoiling the morale of the troops, others such as Preobrazhenskii diarist O. A. Mitrofanov and Lieutenant Sergeev of the Finlandskii Regiment, credit him for a sharp turn for the better in a situation otherwise laden with incipient violence.[43]

[40] For example, see B. V. Gerua, *Vospominaniia o moei zhizni*, 2 vols. (Paris, 1969), 2:187-90; Memoirs of General K. K. Akintievskii (MS.), HI, pp. 115-18; B. V. Sergeev, "1917 god na fronte," *Finlandets*, No. 36 (May, 1958): 37-40; V. Kamenskii, ed., *Leib-egeriia v voinu 1914-1917 gg. Sbornik materialov*, 2 vols. (Paris, 1935), pp. 204ff.; and G. Klimovich, "L. Gv. Moskovskii polk v voinu 1914-1917 gg.," *Biuleten' L. Gv. Moskovskogo Polka*, No. 131 (November, 1951): 8-14.

[41] See his report of June 15 in *VOSR. Mai-iiun'*, p. 363, which complains of the arrival of 13,000 Bolshevized replacements from Petrograd.

[42] *RDRA*, pp. 238-39 (trial record). Dzevaltovskii declared the meeting a legitimate division congress despite the lack of a quorum of regimental committees because "the Division Soviet is indifferent to its responsibilities." (TsGVIA, f. 2322, op. 7, ed. khr. 2, l. 245.)

[43] Mitrofanov, "Den' za den'. Kampanaia zapisnaia knizhka na 1917 goda" (Ms.), RA,

Nevertheless, the affair's outcome was far from pleasant for Kerensky, as the hecklers surrounded his staff car, renewing their challenge to meet the Grenadiers face-to-face. Kerensky yielded only when General Ilkevich pleaded that the whole point of the day's proceedings was to break the Grenadiers' hypnotic hold on the soldier masses. When Kerensky's car pulled up to the Grenadiers, Dzevaltovskii informed him that they were not interested in what he had to say, but wished to present him with the Grenadiers' resolution opposing the offensive. Kerensky rose to make a speech, but angry cries prevented him from giving flight to his talent. Stankevich, a witness, blamed the command for this gratuitous humiliation, suspecting them of deliberately orchestrating revenge on the symbol of the Revolution.[44]

Owing to Kerensky's last-minute efforts or those of hard-working committeemen and officers, there was a remarkable surge of enthusiasm, not only in the guards regiments but also in other units destined for major action. The transformation in the Finlandskii Regiment is vividly portrayed by Sergeev. Following Kerenskii's visit, the Bolshevik Vasilev called a meeting of his second battalion and argued cautiously at first that they were being sent into battle unprepared (not enough ammunition, too many sick, etc.). But Sergeev, who had been listening anxiously from his officers' bunker, noted that ever larger numbers were drifting in from other units. He bolted out, demanded to be heard, and delivered a passionate speech which found its mark; in response were cries "He's right, we already settled the matter at the corps assembly! Let's get some sleep!" The crisis had passed. Sergeev cites a letter he wrote on June 18:

> In just a few hours we will be moving up to the front and, however miraculous it may seem, into battle. Finally the "comrades" not only agreed to follow Kerensky's orders, but are doing so with great enthusiasm. What will happen when they are under fire is another matter.[45]

Mitrofanov's diary testifies to a similar enthusiasm among the Preobrazhenskiis. On June 18 his unit was on its way to the front, on June 19

---

entries for June 16-19, and Sergeev, *Finlandets*, No. 36, pp. 40-41. Before Kerensky's visit the soldiers in Mitrofanov's unit were ready to lynch their commander and the chairman of the regimental committee; afterward the mood was "very militant and pro-offensive"; Sergeev grudgingly acknowledges Kerensky's skill in working up the mood of crowds that were initially reserved or hostile.

[44] Stankevich, *Vospominaniia*, p. 44. Gerua and Akintievskii in particular seemed to delight in Kerensky's discomfiture, the latter citing General Il'kevich to the effect that he had "warned" his superiors that these troops would not fight and now the responsibility was in the hands of "the comrades" (Akintievskii [n. 40, above], p. 118). See also the version of the trial record of the Grenadiers of July 21 (*RDRA*, pp. 240-41).

[45] Sergeev, *Finlandets*, No. 37 (May, 1959): 41.

they responded encouragingly to a pro-offensive speech by a delegate to the Peasant Congress, and on June 20 they were already in the trenches awaiting the order to attack. "The mood is very militant and pro-offensive," he recorded on that day.[46] Growing resentment of the Grenadiers and other slackers was evident in a June 18 resolution by a company of Guards Sappers stating categorically that they would refuse to dig slit trenches for any unit that did not promise to take the offensive when ordered.[47] Kal'nitskii, a line infantryman, attributed the phenomenon to the same underlying thirst for peace, which the soldiers now hoped to achieve by a quick victory. He also attests to the marked cooling of Bolshevik agitation and the soldiers' indifference to the arrests and removal of agitators.[48]

☆

On June 16 commenced a two-day artillery bombardment along a 65 kilometer sector of the adjoining Seventh and Eleventh armies in Galicia, the equal of which had never before been seen on the Eastern Front. The men in the trenches were both exhilarated and terrified by the devastating cacophony of whizzes, whines, roars, crashes, and thuds of every conceivable kind of gun. Some units begged to go into action to escape the maddening ordeal; surely, they felt, the enemy trenches must have already been leveled, and the open battlefield could scarcely be more perilous than the trenches, where casualties mounted hourly. At the last moment Kerensky issued a clarion call to the troops:

> Soldiers! The Fatherland is in danger. Freedom is threatened, the Revolution stands before the abyss! The Army must at this solemn moment fulfil its duty. Your Generalissimo [Brusilov] . . . demands of you in the name of our free people and the Provisional Government to seize the offensive. . . . I order you, FORWARD![49]

Along the sectors of the main attack in the early morning darkness of June 18, soldiers of the attack units filtered into the forward trenches, and in the wake of saturation pounding of the enemy lines, then a moving curtain barrage, poured out of the trenches raising high their proud red banners inscribed with appropriate slogans. On the sector opposite Brzezany, the VII Siberian Corps (which included a composite division of the units that had mutinied) carried all three lines of trenches against both Austrian and German defenders and established themselves on high ground commanding

[46] Mitrofanov (Ms.), RA, entries for June 18-20.

[47] TsGVIA, f. 2322, op. 7, ed. khr. 2, l. 266. For the expulsion of the Bolshevik schismatics in the Pavlovskii Regiment, see resolution of the regimental committee (n.d.) in archives of Second Guards Infantry Division (*ibid.*, l. 275).

[48] See Kal'nitskii, *Ot fevralia k oktiabriu*, p. 47.

[49] *RPG* 2:942.

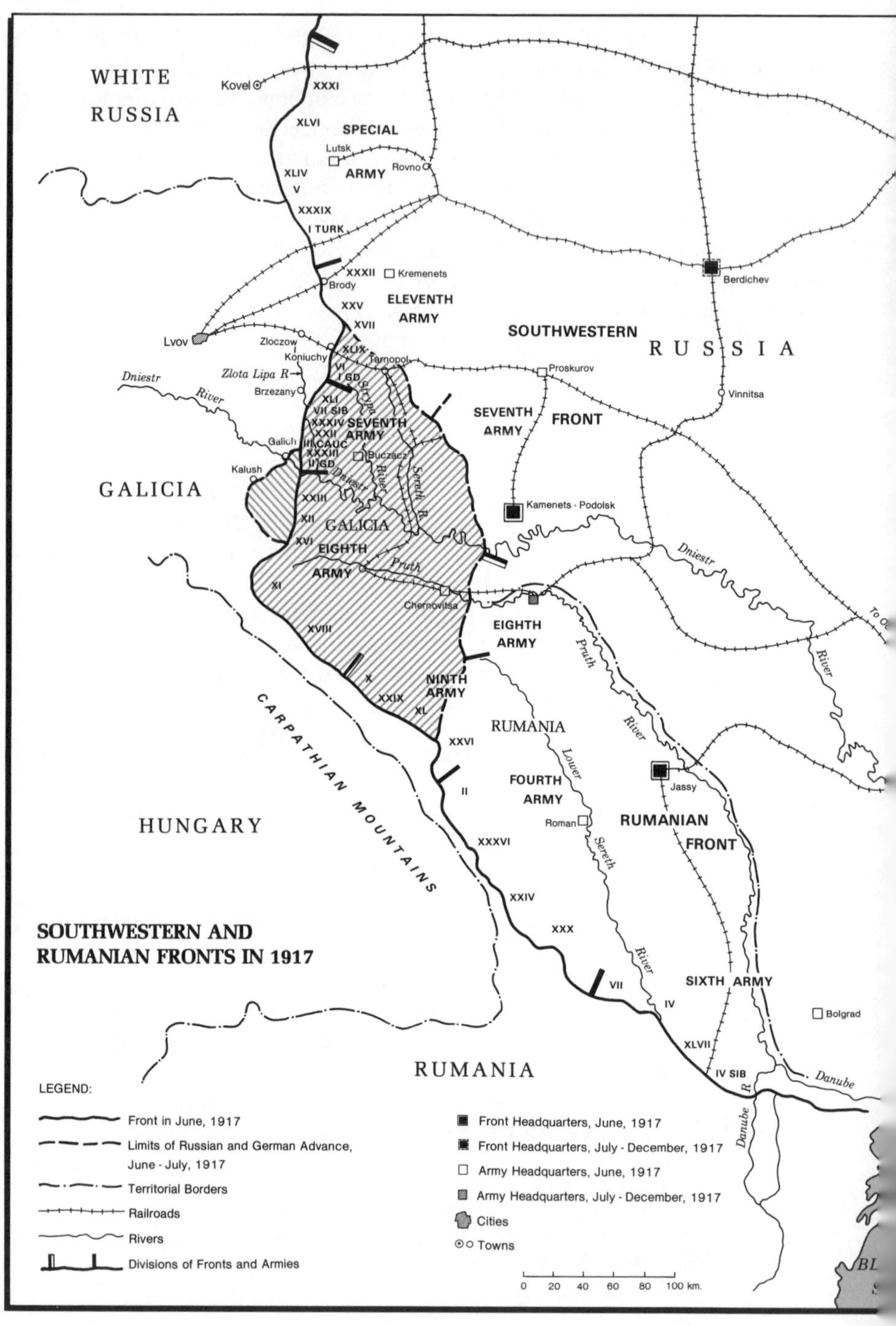

WHITE RUSSIA
Kovel
XXXI
XLVI
SPECIAL ARMY
Lutsk
Rovno
XLIV
V
XXXIX
I TURK
XXXII
Kremenets
Brody
ELEVENTH ARMY
XXV
XVII
Lvov
Zloczow
Koniuchy
XLIX
Tarnopol
VI
I GD
Zlota Lipa R.
Dniestr River
Brzezany
XLI
VII SIB
XXXIV
XXII
III CAUC
XXXIII
II GD
SEVENTH ARMY
Galich
Buczacz
Strypa River
Sereth R.
Kalush
GALICIA
XXIII
XII
XVI
Dniestr
GALICIA
EIGHTH ARMY
Pruth
XI
Chernovitsa
XVIII
X
XXIX
XL
NINTH ARMY
SOUTHWESTERN FRONT
RUSSIA
Berdichev
Proskurov
Vinnitsa
SEVENTH ARMY
Kamenets - Podolsk
Dniestr River
EIGHTH ARMY
Pruth River
RUMANIA
XXVI
II
FOURTH ARMY
Lower Sereth River
Roman
Jassy
RUMANIAN FRONT
CARPATHIAN MOUNTAINS
HUNGARY
XXXVI
XXIV
XXX
VII
IV
SIXTH ARMY
XLVII
IV SIB
Bolgrad
Danube
Danube R.
RUMANIA
SOUTHWESTERN AND RUMANIAN FRONTS IN 1917
LEGEND:
Front in June, 1917
Limits of Russian and German Advance, June - July, 1917
Territorial Borders
Railroads
Rivers
Divisions of Fronts and Armies
Front Headquarters, June, 1917
Front Headquarters, July - December, 1917
Army Headquarters, June, 1917
Army Headquarters, July - December, 1917
Cities
Towns
0 20 40 60 80 100 km.

the Zlota Lipa Valley. To the north the Third Transamur and 74th Infantry divisions accomplished the same feat on Mount Lysonia but were thrown back by a prompt German counter-attack. A bloody night battle ensued for control of the slopes, the Russians suffering particularly heavily because their artillery could not be brought into position. By evening of the second day they had lost all the ground previously won and the exalted spirits gave way to despair. Brusilov's repeated orders to renew the attack foundered on the stubborn unwillingness of the troops, who reverted to debating and voting on orders and demanded immediate replacement regardless of the consequences. In this brief surge the Seventh Army inflicted 12,500 casualties on the enemy (1,740 dead, 6,537 wounded, 4,250 captured), suffering approximately 15,000 casualties of their own.[50]

On the more important Zloczow-Koniuchny sector of the Eleventh Army, the Russian attack was more concentrated and achieved somewhat more significant results. The VI and XIX corps swarmed over both slopes of the key elevation, appropriately called the Mogila (graveyard), and rolled up a huge gap in the Austrian lines. On the northern slopes the Fourth Finnish Rifle Division was pushed back again, but in the center well-disciplined Czech brigades ultimately took and held the heights. Two Austrian divisions were virtually destroyed, one of them consisting primarily of Czechs who willingly surrendered when they heard familiar speech across the trenches. Again German units held in reserve averted catastrophe for the Central Powers, but the Russians had won and held five kilometers of cluttered, blood-soaked ground, including the coveted Mogila. The Austro-Hungarian IX Corps was reduced from 22,700 to 6,700 men, some 11,000 taken captive with little effort on the Russians' part. Kerensky exultantly congratulated his "revolutionary troops" and wired Prime Minister President L'vov that the "Regiments of the 18th of June" should be awarded special revolutionary banners.[51] But as happened all too often in this war, the unwitting public was led to believe that a significant victory had been won, whereas in reality an insignificant parcel of real estate had been purchased at an unacceptable cost. Of the units participating in the offensive, some refused to attack unless wider openings were made by the artillery in the barbed wire, others bolted at the last minute, leaving neighboring units exposed, and many more refused to press on with the attack even after all resistance had been broken, reluctant

[50] For the best and almost only reliable battle account, see *OHLK* 6:239-45.

[51] *Ibid.*, and Kersnovskii, *Istoriia*, 4:964-65, who relies on *OHLK*; Gerua's version (2:191-93) relies on Kersnovskii; Zaionchkovskii only names the units engaged and obviously has no concrete sources (*Kampaniia 1917 g.*, p. 70). Hence, there is no reliable military source from the Russian side; for an excellent and detailed personal account, see Kal'nitskii, pp. 48-57.

to get too far in advance of their field kitchens and familiar trenches; in the captured towns of Posuchow and Koniuchny the soldiers sought out liquor caches and gave themselves over to plundering and pleasant oblivion.

Kal'nitskii's 35th Division took heavy casualties, settled into the well-furnished Austrian trenches, and refused to budge despite the stinking water which threatened dysentery. Austrians filtered back, mingling with the Russians in adjacent shell holes, alternately fraternizing and tossing grenades. A battalion of the regiment which was ordered to replace Kal'nitskii's unit refused. A rump session of soldier-committeemen in blood-splotched, filthy clothing debated the situation. They felt the offensive had failed and that their sacrifices were in vain, but they were restrained from flight by the thought of opening up the front. A soldier named Miroshkin declared:

> Comrades! Whose land are we on anyhow? We're no annexationists and our government says "No annexations or contributions." Let's give the Austrians back their land and return to our own borders; then if they try to go further, over our dead bodies![52]

Others argued that this would expose other units and cause more casualties; someone suggested opening general negotiations with the Austrians, who after all were not that bad (the soldiers, not the generals, of course). A medic named Brezhnev pulled out of his jacket a copy of *Okopnaia Pravda*, which supplied the text for a Bolshevik sermon on the necessity of fighting one's class oppressors, the capitalists, and *pomeshchiki*, and not one's fellow workers across the trenches; his neophyte hearers found it enormously liberating. The assembly struck on a compromise formula: "Ours we won't yield, but others' [lands] we don't seek" (*Svoego ne dadim, chuzhogo ne khotim*). Though the command conceded they deserved relief, not only did their first battalion refuse, but so did two other regiments of the division that had remained unscathed. They languished thus for well over a week until the 623rd Regiment and several guards regiments relented.

Although most units attacked when ordered and only a few retreated under fire, there were a significant number in the rear or on neighboring, inactive sectors who refused to give support, even when the outcome hung in the balance. The command had quite logically employed the soundest units to launch the attack and kept dissident or shaky units on passive sectors or in the reserve. Thus, when it was necessary to replace the battered, exhausted units with fresh ones from the rear, a crisis inevitably arose. An inordinate number of the latter refused to move, endlessly de-

[52] Kal'nitskii, p. 61.

bated the matter, or attached dilatory conditions, such as "complete destruction of barriers" or "only if the Soviet directly orders us." The clamor of units like Kal'nitskii's for immediate replacement and prolonged rest in the rear is well attested. Stankevich, who was called upon to persuade a depleted division to hold the Austrian trenches until they could be replaced, was beseeched for respite in the rear "for a week, for a few days, even for one day!" No arguments or appeals to revolutionary conscience had the slightest effect.[53] Deputies of the 108th Division, which had been involved in the main attack on Brzezany, were less modest: they categorically demanded of the Seventh Army commander, General Selivachev, a stay of at least a month and a half in the rear for rest and reequipment.[54] Kerensky was subjected to the same humiliating experience in the unfriendly presence of General Gerua; receiving a deputation of the "heros of the 18th of June," the latter hotly argued: "We did our part . . . we're finished, let those in the rear who haven't fought yet take over."[55] On the second day of the offensive General Skoropadskii pointedly requested the Seventh Army headquarters to relieve his entire XXXIV Corps with the II Guards Corps and the request was granted! Shortly thereafter, the II Guards Corps itself was immobilized by unrest and could no longer be regarded as battleworthy. General Alfred Knox, the roving Englishman, reports that the XLI Corps also, after an unsuccessful attack on the first day, gave the commander to understand that the attack would not be renewed.[56] Whether any healthy units remained is open to question, but it is certain that after the second day the Seventh Army was never to renew the attack. As Selivachev reported on June 30:

> All corps of the army after the unsuccessful battles of June 18-20 are in the highest degree demoralized. The consistent flouting of battle orders, unauthorized departures from positions, and refusals to replace other units on the line have become an everyday occurrence. The work of committees of all denominations yields no results.[57]

Commissar Chekotilo of the Eleventh Army likewise characterized the dilemma: the Sixth Finnish Rifle Division suffered 50 percent casualties and demanded immediate replacement on the line; it was necessary to break off units of the 83rd Division from their designated tactical tasks, necessitating the cancellation of further operations on that sector. He notes that the 157th, 35th Infantry, and Second Finnish Rifle divisions demanded

[53] Stankevich, p. 157.

[54] "Iz dnevnika gen. V. I. Selivacheva," *KA* 10 (1925): 139 (diary entry for July 1).

[55] Gerua, 2:195-96.

[56] All according to Knox, 2:644-47.

[57] *RDRA*, p. 163.

replacement at the same time, virtually the entire shock group of the most successful area of attack.[58]

The most striking instance of a disastrous collapse of morale was the XXII Corps, consisting of the First, Third, and Fifth Finnish Rifle and 159th Infantry divisions. In spite of a blitz of Bolshevik agitation in early June, the corps had shaped up and played a key role in the attack on Brzezany. In a particularly bloody encounter, they took the enemy positions, but were thrown back with heavy losses the following day. Before the attack could be renewed, however, General Obruchev reported: ''The twelfth company, discarding all conscience and shame, not only willfully deserted the trenches in the night of June 19, but ridiculed those soldiers who remained in the trenches.''[59] The 20th Finnish Rifle Regiment, which had been heavily exposed to Bolshevik agitation, also fled under fire: 346 soldiers had disappeared with their rifles during the action, and 189 were driven by conscience and hunger to return but were spurned by their former comrades. The division committee determined that the entire division was no longer battleworthy and ''with a heavy heart'' requested the commander to report this fact to the higher command and the commissars.[60] Other sources confirm that in no less than eighteen divisions of the Seventh and Eleventh armies the mood was threatening, and that in nine of them major disorders had occurred.[61]

Several major incidents were triggered by transferring the XXV and XXXII corps from the Special Army into the Eleventh Army for follow-up operations. The Third Grenadier Division refused to move when it became clear that they were to replace the V Siberian Corps. At a mass meeting they voted not to take part in the offensive and nearly lynched the commissar when he called their agitators traitorous Bolsheviks, threatening punitive action by the VII Cavalry Corps. The 46th and 120th Infantry divisions apparently revolted in response. The Bolshevik Eremin, a telegraph specialist attached to the staff of the XXV Corps, describes the confusion and panic at headquarters when the commander, General Fogel, received a categorical order from Brusilov to put down the disorders by armed force without delay, even if it required the ''complete obliteration'' of the rebels; General Fogel helplessly screamed and flailed at all available staff personnel, especially demanding to know where there was an officer who knew how to operate the telegraph. He first called in the Fifth Don Cossack Division, but Eremin telegraphed his friend Kikvidze (a Left S.R.,

[58] See *BA* 1:28.

[59] Staff report of XXII Corps of June 24, TsGVIA, f. 2222, op. 1, d. 1066, l. 27.

[60] From divisional document of June 26, *ibid.*, d. 1185, l. 45.

[61] For example, *RDRA*, pp. 172-73, and *BA* 1:13-35 (Commissar Chekotilo's report on Eleventh Army for month of June).

to Eremin an honorary Bolshevik), chairman of the committee of the Sixth Cavalry Division, who sent out agitators to intercept the Don Cossacks.[62] Thus the XXV Corps, which was intended to restore operational flexibility to the Eleventh Army, was effectively immobilized.

☆

The other major unit held in reserve for follow-up operations was the I Guards Corps, which included the troublesome Grenadiers in the Second Division. After Kerensky's visit on June 16 the guards units received orders to move out to the area of the village of Danilovtsy in the immediate rear of the front to prepare to go into action. Dzevaltovskii tried to disrupt the order by again calling a mass meeting, but given the sharp swing in the mood of the corps it met with little response outside his Grenadiers and a few hundred Pavlovskiis and Finlandskiis.[63] Faced with increasing isolation, Dzevaltovskii ordered his Grenadiers to move with the rest of the guards to Danilovtsy. Knowing that a punitive action against him was being contemplated, he made it a point to assure the commissar (Stankevich) that the Grenadiers would obey all legitimate orders of the Provisional Government and would not betray their comrades during the attack. However, when they received a written order from divisional headquarters on June 20 directing them to take up positions for attack, they refused to move.[64] Although Dzevalstovskii and his supporters later claimed before a military court that they knew of no such orders, there is overwhelming evidence to the contrary. The helpless regimental commander had simply handed the order over to Dzevaltovskii, who responded by convoking a meeting of the regiment's "Soviet." Even had Dzevaltovskii intended to comply, he was now a captive of the mood he had created. In fact, he was actively promoting an ambitious plan to undermine the offensive, and perhaps even to escalate it into a major revolutionary event. On June 18, when it was clear that the Grenadiers had failed to win over the Second Division, he sent mounted messengers to units of the First Division, which had already taken up their positions, as well as to the infantry units they were to replace on the line (35th Infantry and Fourth Finnish Rifle divisions). Ostensibly to call on these units to endorse the Grenadiers' resolution against the offensive, the instructions to the messengers were to "make every effort to see to it that [the offensive] does not take place."[65] In response to this message, 365 Pavlovskiis and two companies of the 13th Finnish Rifle Regiment (Krylenko's home regiment) departed from

[62] K. G. Eremin, *Soldatskie versty. Voennye memuary* (Moscow, 1960), pp. 44-48 (uses archival material to augment a memory not above reproach).

[63] TsGVIA, f. 2322, op. 7, ed. khr. 2, l. 168.

[64] According to indictment, *RDRA*, p. 241. See also Stankevich, p. 158.

[65] TsGVIA, f. 2322, op. 7, ed. khr. 2, l. 246.

the front to join the Grenadiers in Danilovtsy.[66] The Grenadiers also tried to bring over units of their own division passing through Danilovtsy on the way to the front, but with little success.

The Grenadiers began to sense their isolation: by June 22 all supply and support units had moved on, and well-founded rumors began to circulate that a punitive force was gathering. That night a hasty meeting of the Grenadiers decided to return to their former berth in the village of Khorodishche, which they carried out in a highly secretive manner so as not to alert the command. On June 23 Dzevaltovskii reported to divisional headquarters that the officers had "deserted" and that the regiment was "awaiting further determination of our present situation."[67] The following day a force consisting of a cavalry division, two batteries of artillery, and two armored cars under the supervision of Commissar Chekotilo surrounded the rebels and gave them two hours to lay down their arms and hand over the leaders of the conspiracy. Defiant to the last, Dzevaltovskii surrendered with members of his Soviet ten minutes before the expiration of the deadline, marching out with the regimental band playing the Marseillaise. Around 100 were singled out as agitators and handed over to a military court, while 300 others were found innocent of criminal intent. The mutineers were dispersed in groups of fifty to seventy to other regiments, carrying their virus with them. Such was the outcome of the Bolsheviks' most serious attempt to transform the "imperialist war" into a "revolutionary civil war."

While the command and the loyalist committeemen had withstood the challenge of this "miniature Kronshtadt," they were rapidly losing the struggle for the souls of the guardsmen. On June 23, with the Finlandskii, Moskovskii, and Egerskii regiments in the trenches, and the Semenovskii, Preobrazhenskii, and Pavlovskii regiments in reserve, the guards divisions went into the attack. For some reason that was never cleared up, the promised artillery barrage failed to materialize, leaving the barbed wire undamaged, and the result was an unheard-of slaughter. The Moskovskiis were halted one hundred steps short of the wire by heavy enemy artillery fire; the officers who tried to get the troops to move forward were all killed or severely wounded. Two battalions sent in for a second wave, seeing the pounding taken by their comrades, took refuge in shell holes and refused to move.[68] The thought that had taken hold during fruitless battles of the previous year of treason in the high command was now revived with a

[66] *Ibid.*, l. 261, which is a semi-literate request from the 365th Pavlovskiis to Commander Rylskii to be transferred to the Grenadier Regiment, since they have the same "platform" and regard the offensive as a "lying slogan of the bourgeoisie."

[67] *Ibid.*, l. 270, all other details *passim* and in *RDRA*, pp. 240-48.

[68] See Klimovich (n. 40, above), pp. 8-14.

vengeance. Though in all probability the officers who moved ahead of their men were exterminated, the soldiers willingly believed that they had defected to the enemy.[69] Since none of the units succeeded in penetrating the enemy defenses, and demoralization was rapidly setting in, the attack was not renewed. The guards were again plagued by stubborn refusals of orders, chaotic meetings, and incidents with every rotation on the line. In Mitrofanov's regiment, one unit fled to the rear, another threw away their trench spades, and another voted not to replace comrades on the line.[70] General Mai-Maevskii, who had taken command of the corps, ordered each unit to "clean out" its Bolsheviks. Failing precise instructions, utter chaos and a reversal of the order under mass pressure resulted.[71] Sergeev was ordered to deliver up the well-known agitator Vasilev and his adherents, but Sergeev handled the matter with great circumspection: Vasilev agreed to submit to arrest if Sergeev would give him a written verification that he was not a coward and had followed orders during the offensive. Sergeev gratefully complied, grudgingly conceding that Vasilev was a worthy foe. A new order on July 1 stipulated that each unit was to lay down its arms and surrender their agitators. In the absence of a significant punitive force, the result was an utter fiasco. Sergeev inscribed in his diary: "Our regiment's song has been sung. . . . Of course they eagerly grasp at the opportunity to give up their rifles. Then along comes an orator who persuades them this is nonsense and they snatch up their rifles again and refuse to leave."[72] In disgust Sergeev requested permission to leave the regiment to get treatment for an old wound in the division hospital.

Accompanying this new wave of turbulence was Bolshevik agitation as never before, which could no longer be ascribed to the Grenadiers or other party Bolsheviks because they had been physically removed. *Pravda* circulated in massive quantities, brought in by recent replacements from Petrograd. A commissar's report of July 5 supposes that enemy agents were operating under the guise of Bolsheviks, since their agitation was aimed at sowing mistrust of all revolutionary authorities—committees, socialist parties, the Soviet, and the Peasant Congress. Of the latter it was said that they had been bribed with 3,000 rubles to pass a pro-offensive resolution.[73] The soldiers, having been buffeted back and forth by such titanic forces, easily lent themselves to such suggestions. The Grenadier's "Republic" had been defeated, but trench Bolshevism nevertheless prevailed.

69 See Kamenskii (n. 40, above), p. 115.

70 See Mitrofanov (Ms.), RA, July 4.

71 Kamenskii, p. 116.

72 *Finlandets*, No. 37, p. 30.

73 *RDRA*, pp. 181-82.

☆

Paradoxically, the Eighth Army, whose assigned role was to protect the flank of the main attacking armies, registered the only success of the summer offensive. Launching its own attack on June 23 after the other armies were mired in disorders, it unexpectedly broke through the enemy defenses on a broad front along a spur of the Carpathians and with bitter fighting pushed through to the valley of the Lomnitsa River, some 30 kilometers distant. The unexpected capture of the towns of Kalush and Galich on July 28-29 created a sensation in the patriotic press, which was starved for encouraging news since the stalling of the main operations; it also launched General Kornilov on his meteoric career. Although the same disruptive forces were present here as elsewhere, major mutinies were somehow averted. A command report of June 23 noted intense Bolshevik agitation in four regiments of the XI Corps and in two others of the XVIII Corps, as a result of which two mass refusals to move into position had occurred.[74] But the two main attacking corps, the XII and the XVI, ten divisions strong, seem to have been unaffected. Kornilov, his subsequent hatred of democratic novelties notwithstanding, authorized his army committee to form "battle committees," which were to function as troubleshooters and roving agitators during the attack.[75] Whether thanks to energetic command, democratic persuaders, or simply the sudden collapse of the Austro-Hungarian XXVI Corps (Croatian units were also seriously demoralized), the soldiers of the Eighth Army kept up the pursuit and heavily engaged the enemy for five straight days. Commissar Shklovsky, who until he was badly wounded was constantly on the move, cajoling reluctant units to move forward, comments that the Russian casualties were negligible and that the brunt of the attack was carried by officers, telephonists, sappers, and clerks ("even the doctors were cutting barbed wire").[76]

Brusilov repeatedly urged Kornilov to carry the attack to the north to relieve the two stalled armies of the Southwestern Front, but Kornilov kept his armies south of the Dniester, obviously having his eye on the prize of Lvov. As the gap opened up between himself and the Seventh Army, he desperately called for reinforcements. To his misfortune he was assigned the demoralized XXXIII Corps of the Seventh Army, among which were the thoroughly Bolshevized Transamur divisions. Of them a staff report of June 26 said:

[74] *Ibid.*, pp. 155-56. Recently arrived replacements were blamed.

[75] See *Iz8A*, June 13. They were established at an army conference of committeemen on June 10 and 14, and to their statute was affixed the resolution of Commander Kornilov: "I concur with the opinion of the conference."

[76] Shklovskii (n. 33, above), p. 53.

> In the Sixth Regiment, spirits which were raised by the army [committee] deputies and French officers are now flagging, due to the agitation of Tsaritsyn replacements and "yellow-bellies" claiming to be Bolsheviks. . . . In the 15th Regiment, delegates from Petrograd infected with Bolshevism . . . passed out banners bearing the slogan "Down with the war and the Provisional Government!"[77]

Three days later in the 23rd Division of the same corps there occurred the first mass flight under battle conditions.[78] General Kornilov ordered a punitive unit consisting of machine-gunners and artillery to fire on the fleeing soldiers to bring them to a halt (the order was confirmed by Commissar Savinkov).[79] In conquered Kalush the occupying troops went on a rampage, destroying property raping and brutalizing the civilian population, especially the Jewish, in the quest for booty and liquor.[80] With demoralization setting in and heavy rains swelling the Lomnitsa leaving Kalush and Galich exposed, Kornilov withdrew his troops to the east bank of the river. A few days later the breakthrough at Tarnopol sucked the Eighth Army into the vortex of the general retreat.[81]

☆

Offensive operations of the Northern and Western fronts were denied even a brief moment of success; the very effort of moving the troops into position and treating them to committee persuasion provoked massive reactions, and the order to attack on July 9 and 10 brought about the immediate disintegration of the better part of the Fifth and Tenth armies. It was, of course, no secret that an inordinate number of units in the Fifth Army had been affected by Bolshevik agitation and were in a state of thorough indiscipline; but the command cherished the hope that, inspired by successes on the Southwestern Front, they would yield to persuasion. Nowhere, except perhaps in the Eighth Army, was there an army committee more active and loyal in promoting the offensive. Agitational teams made the rounds of units constantly in the latter part of June and early July,

[77] *RDRA*, pp. 159-60.

[78] *Ibid.*, p. 162.

[79] *Ibid.*, p. 576 (footnote reference citing archival source).

[80] Lurid accounts were carried in the contemporary press, blaming cowardly soldiers perverted by Bolshevism; Savinkov, an eyewitness, claims he saw violence and plunder perpetrated only by tribesmen of the Wild Division, who purportedly had been sent into Kalush to restore order. Savinkov's fantasy about soldier-heroes probably affected his vision; he admits seeing a "few" Russian soldiers who were drunk. (See Lugin [n. 34, above], pp. 231-34.)

[81] See Zaionchkovskii, *Kampaniia 1917 g.*, pp. 72-73. This is the only campaign of 1917 to be described by Zaionchkovskii in detail, perhaps covertly intended to vindicate his hero, Kornilov.

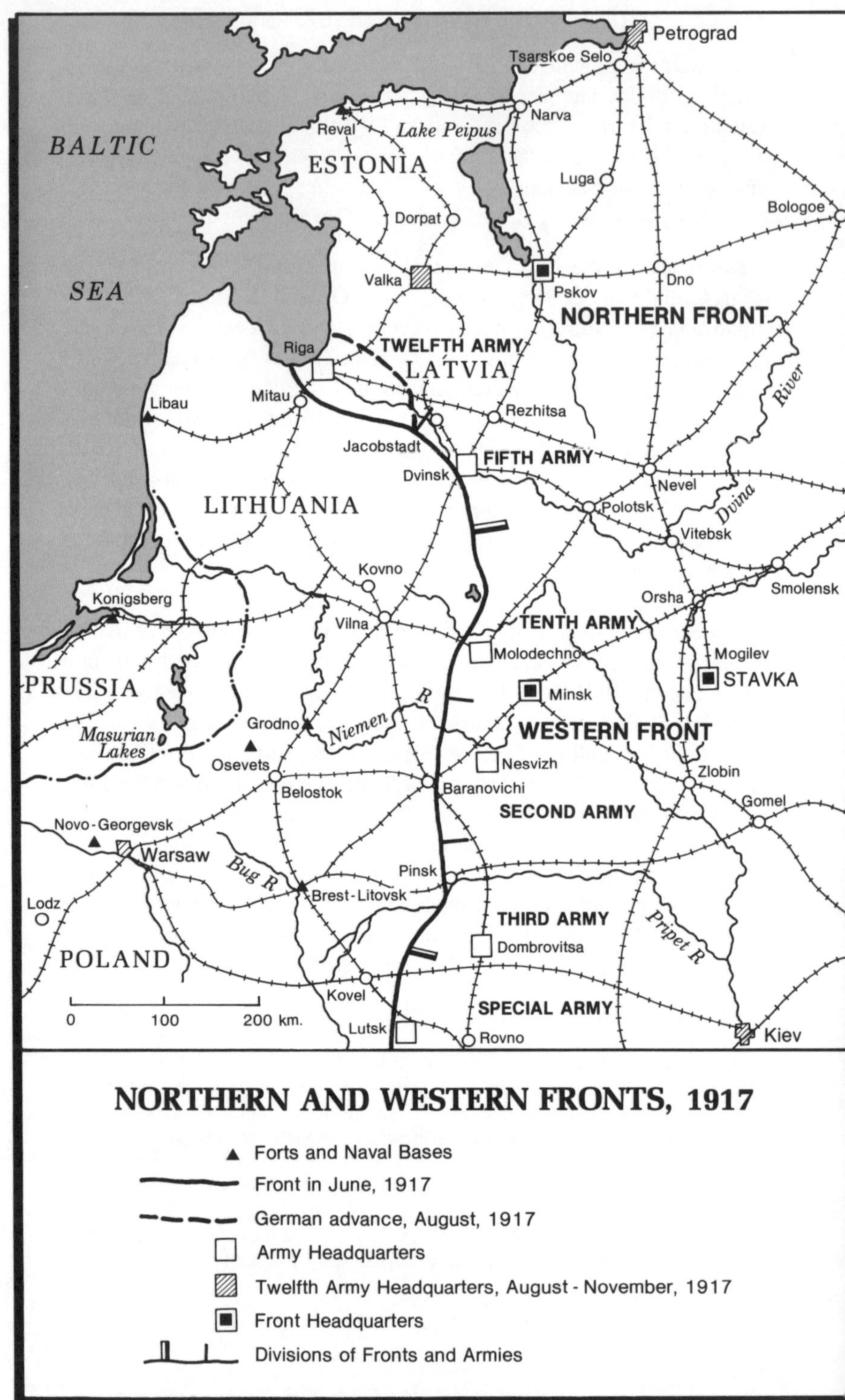

NORTHERN AND WESTERN FRONTS, 1917

sometimes succeeding in securing compliance with orders, but seldom in obtaining explicit endorsements of the offensive. By the end of June their official organ, *Iz5A*, recorded pro-offensive resolutions for a cavalry regiment, a death battalion, and a corps assembly, but for only one infantry regiment. In early July, three more regiments pledged in identical resolutions to "obey Comrade Kerensky" and their superior officers, and to answer the "first call" to attack without discussion.[82] On June 14 a committee team destroyed 1,000 bottles of wine from Count Platten's estate in Kreslavka and rounded up deserters.[83] On July 1, during persuasion, they were shot at and insulted, and their meeting was broken up by agitators (whom they characterized as German spies, gendarmes, and *okhranniki*).

A stark picture of the condition of the Fifth Army emerges from command reports of the weeks leading up to the offensive. The shakiest units were those from two corps of the former First Army transferred to the Fifth Army as a reserve for the attack. Particularly turbulent were the three divisions of the XXXVII Corps, the 120th, the 121st, and the 135th. The first two, stationed near Riga, had been exposed to the direct influence of the 436th Novoladozhskii Regiment, which put out *Okopnaia Pravda*. Transferred to a rural area, they joined Lativan and Estonian peasants in sacking the estates of German "barons." The 135th Division had been stationed at the Estonian town of Pernov, which was kept in a state of turmoil by agitators from Kronshtadt, during which a regimental commander was murdered (probably in mid-May). During their transfer to Dvinsk they rioted out of control. Officers slept with revolvers under their pillows, a mob threatened to lift General Benderev on bayonets, and Colonel Selivanov, commander of the 540th Regiment, was struck in the face with a rock. Because the commander believed the source of the trouble was a group of Bolsheviks in the 540th Regiment, he recommended its disbanding.[84] Around June 15 the commander of the 184th Division, General P. A. Noskov, fell victim to a sniper's bullet after a confrontation with soldiers over their transfer.[85]

The condition of the core divisions of the Fifth Army was little better.

[82] See *Iz5A*, June 28, July 4 and 9.

[83] *Ibid.*, June 24; other points *passim*.

[84] See report of Gen. M. A. Sul'kevich, commander of the XXXVII Corps to Fifth Army Commander Iu. N. Danilov, July 2, *RDRA*, pp. 168-71. See also *KA* 84:146-47 (reports of Regimental Commander Selianov to Danilov, June 28 and 29, respectively, which recommended disbanding).

[85] See *Iz5A*, June 25. A report of Division Commander S. Iu. Liatura of June 16 surmises that Noskov was murdered in revenge for his part in the bloody battle on the Stokhod of March 21, in which the soldiers claimed "ten thousand men gave up their lives for nothing" (*RDRA*, p. 138). On the XXVIII Corps, see the First Army commander's report on May 21 in *KA* 84:142-43.

Disturbances aroused by transfers into position were noted in every division of the I Corps (22nd, 60th, and 184th divisions), the XIX Corps (17th, 138th, and 183rd divisions), and the XIII Corps (180th, 38th, and 36th divisions). The only relatively well disciplined divisions in the entire army were the 70th and 18th in General Budberg's XIV Corps, though Bolsheviks were present in the 303rd Sennenskii Regiment, which later mutinied in July. A report by General A. A. Svechin, Chief of Staff of the Fifth Army, dated June 19, noted that in the 38th Division moderate Bolsheviks were the target; the Bolshevik chairman of the division committee, Dr. Sklianskii, claimed at a hearing of the Fifth Army Committee that the agitation was being conducted not by Bolsheviks but by former police and gendarmes.[86]

On June 22 there were renewed disturbances in the 17th and 22nd divisions: fifty of the latter marched in a demonstration carrying placards inscribed "Down with the offensive" and tried to bring over a neighboring regiment, even beating two orators who tried to dissuade them.[87] Finally, on June 29, after repeated defiance of orders to move into position, punitive action was taken against the 36th and 182nd divisions and one regiment of the 161st Division. They were surrounded by loyal troops and ordered to lay down their arms and to deliver up their agitators. In the 161st Division, 600 soldiers were arrested, of which 200 were identified as "instigators" and held for trial. In the other divisions 3,000 were disarmed, and the rest were disbanded and distributed to other units.[88] This action made it possible to move other divisions up to the line, but nevertheless the opening of the offensive had to be postponed from July 5 to July 9.

General P. A. Budberg, who commanded the corps with the loyal 18th and 70th divisions, has left a remarkable personal narrative of the operations on his front.[89] An old regime disciplinarian, he nevertheless acted with common sense in dealing with the revolutionary upheaval and maintained good relations with his committees, who backed up his authority and steered clear of politics. He worked very diligently to prepare his sector for the offensive, still able to get his men to work on salients and communications trenches.

[86] *RDRA*, pp. 141-42. On Sklianskii's role, see *Iz5A*, June 28.

[87] See *RDRA*, p. 159 (report of Northern Front Commander Vakhrushev of June 25).

[88] See *KA* 84:146-47 (reports of corps commander of June 27 and 28) and *V boiakh za vlast' sovetov. . . . Sbornik vospominanii i dokumentov* (Moscow, 1937), pp. 64-66 (report of Khodorov, Government Commissar of Fifth Army, July 8). For Brusilov's demand that the Provisional Government take decisive action against the Bolsheviks, who have ruined the Fifth Army, see *RDRA*, p. 157.

[89] See Budberg, "Vospominaniia o voine 1914-1917 gg." (Ms.), HI, pp. 1050-100. Excessively wordy and repetitious, but still one of very few gripping battle accounts by a competent commander.

The dispositions of his sector were particularly favorable for a breakthrough—his troops held the high ground on two sides of an inverted right angle, and thus the artillery could direct its fire along both sides of the angle directly into the enemy trenches. The army disposed of an unheard-of number of guns, over 500, many of them 6″ and 8″ caliber, and more than 200 were assigned to his corps, but he pleaded for more to take advantage of the favorable terrain. Budberg was graciously awarded the 120th and 121st divisions and categorically ordered to assign them battle tasks in spite of his plea that they would spoil his well-disciplined units. The 120th was placed between his two good divisions, and another high-numbered division—the 138th—was placed on his flank, necessitating remedial agitation in the adjacent battalions. He urgently requested to be assigned the well-disciplined rifle regiment of the 14th Cavalry Division, then in army reserve, but was ordered to hold it in reserve for the follow-up action. Budberg kept up a running complaint skirting insubordination over the unwanted divisions, but without effect.

On July 1 socialist ministers Skobelev and Lebedev arrived for the chore of persuading, and Commissar Khodorov credits them with getting the 17th and 22nd divisions to move into position. Budberg noted with caustic glee that they were nearly lynched by deserting soldiers whom they were attempting to "persuade" and had to be rescued by their chauffeur, who wisely kept the motor running.[90] Khodorov enthusiastically reported to Petrograd that "the Army will take the offensive as soon as it hears the sound of the artillery."[91] At this juncture came the startling news of the July demonstrations in Petrograd, and several well-disciplined units (cycle battalions, 14th Cavalry), whose services were very much needed at the front, had to be sent to the capital, causing a postponement of the offensive for several more days.[92] In the meantime, the 135th Division engaged in flagrant fraternization with the enemy, and the 479th Regiment of the 120th Division, under the guidance of its Bolshevik chairman Fedotov, passed a resolution declaring it would occupy and hold the trenches but would not attack.[93]

On July 9 the heavy guns opened up a two-day artillery barrage preparatory to the infantry attack, which destroyed the enemy trenches and barbed wire but failed to knock out a heavily fortified position at the apex of the right angle, endangering the success of the attack. Budberg called

[90] *Ibid.*, p. 1090.

[91] *V boiakh za vlast' sovetov*, p. 65.

[92] See order of the Quartermaster of the Northern Front, S. G. Lukirskii, July 4, in *RDRA*, p. 174.

[93] See his account in *V boiakh za vlast' sovetov*, p. 17. Text of resolution in *VOSR. Iiul'*, pp. 347-38.

for a postponement, but headquarters again overruled him.[94] His lead units attacked with enthusiasm and took two lines of trenches, but they were unable to reach the German batteries in the rear or to destroy the concealed machine-gun nests. Taking fire from all sides, the Russian troops lost all sense of orientation. Most of the officers, shock troops, and the better-disciplined units had all moved on ahead, leaving the mass of soldiers scattered in shell holes and caved-in trenchworks. On the Russian side of the wire the labyrinth of trenchworks was jammed with fainthearted backup units, intermingled with the lightly wounded and retreating first-wave troops. No amount of cursing and threatening could bring order out of the ensuing pandemonium. Budberg, unwilling to employ the demoralized 120th and 121st divisions, called on the cavalry riflers in defiance of headquarters. Budberg was deeply stirred as they filed past in perfect deployment: "the Old Russian Imperial Army in all its incomparable glory!"[95] But their path was blocked by the myriads of panicked, sobbing, leaderless soldiers clogging the forward trenches—Budberg noted that those who had refused orders to improve the trenchworks were now hysterically scratching out refuge for themselves with their bare hands. The day was lost as darkness fell, and the forlorn heroes from no-man's-land filtered back to their own lines. Budberg was determined to renew the attack, as the German front had been broken, his riflers were still intact, and he was sure he could still rally the remnants of his 70th Division. But he was soon informed that the operation had been canceled: his was the only sector that had broken through, whereas other units had deserted to the rear, arrested their officers, or otherwise precipitated havoc.[96]

Though no systematic picture is possible, it is clear that a new wave of disorders and mutinies ensued, so that the balance of July was spent in huge roundup and disarming operations. As summarized in a survey of July 18:

> In the 18th and 182nd divisions and the 303rd Regiment anarchist propaganda is growing: in the 65th Regiment of the 17th Division two battalions refused to take the offensive: in the 54th Regiment complete anarchy prevails, excesses and fraternization continue, and in view of the hopelessness of the situation 2,000 persons were arrested; the 480th Regiment of the 120th Division departed from the

[94] Budberg Ms., p. 1088.

[95] *Ibid.*, p. 1091.

[96] See report of Stankevich, Government Commissar for the Northern Front, to Brusilov, July 11, in *RDRA*, pp. 200-201. See also Stankevich's own account in *Vospominaniia*, pp. 167ff.

front under the influence of Bolsheviks, threatening to take active measures against the artillery.[97]

There was not much left of a "healthy core" in the Fifth Army.

The brief offensive of the Tenth Army was the most bloody, disorganized, and futile of all. This army was not thought by Western Front commander Denikin to be in irredeemably bad shape when he took charge in early July.[98] Only two of his twenty-three divisions were incorrigible—the Second Caucasus and the 169th—and he must have thought them capable of recovery because he assigned them battle positions in the forthcoming operations. Scattered regiments had undergone minor paroxysms of Bolshevik agitation, sometimes shaking the morale of their neighbors, but major incidents were less common than on other fronts. The First and Second Siberian Rifle, the First Caucasus Grenadier, and the 28th and 29th Infantry divisions were thought to be sound and willing to fight. The picture changed drastically, however, when orders for major regrouping operations came through around June 9. Alerted to what was in store, the 51st, 134th, and 16th Siberian Rifle divisions, hitherto relatively free of agitation, refused to pack up their gear and move out. For five days they held uninterrupted meetings, shouted down pro-offensive orators, threatened their officers with violence, and demanded to see Kerensky personally to confirm their orders. Two deputies of the Petrograd Soviet made the circuit of units, but were treated with as little ceremony as committeemen and commissars. The promise of Kerensky's personal appearance persuaded most units to move into position, but one regiment of the 16th Siberian Rifle Division voted to hang its commander, and the 675th Regiment (169th Division) approved a Bolshevik-inspired resolution, severely beating an officer who spoke against it.[99]

One June 20, soldiers of the 703rd Sumskii Regiment perpetrated a severe beating of N. D. Sokolov, author of Order No. One, and Verbo, another member of the Soviet Executive Committee. Sokolov and his entourage were trying to persuade the II Caucasus Corps to move into position, and before a crowd of some 4,000 from various units it seemed their credentials as Soviet representatives were about to yield success; then suddenly an agitator launched into a tirade, persuading the mob that the Soviet representatives might persuade other units to obey orders, which had to be prevented at all costs. Then a soldier exclaimed excitedly of

[97] *VOSR. Iiul'*, p. 149.

[98] See report of June 11, *RDRA*, pp. 132-34. Also reluctantly admitted in a vituperative speech at Stavka conference of July 19 in Golovin, *Rossiiskaia kontr-revoliutsiia*, 1(1):154.

[99] See compilative reports in *KA* 58:89-90 and editors' information in *RDRA*, p. 572, nn. 90 and 91 (presumably from archival sources).

Verbo: "He's an officer in disguise!" Another, indicating Sokolov, screamed, "I know him! He's a *pomeshchik* I used to work for!" The soldier-agitator struck Verbo a severe blow with his steel helmet, which signaled the crowd to take vengeance on the entire delegation. Sokolov himself was held prisoner bloody and half-conscious, while the crowd debated whether to shoot him, hang him, or throw him out on the barbed wire. He was freed when the 704th Regiment threatened shrapnel unless they did so.[100] The incident apparently sobered up other shaky units; for the time being regrouping operations proceeded without incident, though some declared they would occupy the trenches but not attack. Denikin resolved to disarm and disband the dangerous 703rd Regiment, but the mutiny soon spread to several divisions (First and Second Caucasus Grenadier and the 169th Infantry divisions). Unable to disarm such a large mass, Denikin ordered them to the deep rear, as he later explained, "depriving myself at one stroke without a shot being fired of 30,000 troops."[101]

Other divisions failed to settle down once they reached their new sectors. Colonel Ia. M. Lisovoi, a staff officer in the 28th Division, one of the best-disciplined in the Tenth Army, left a vivid account. He depicts a bright July day, a long gray ribbon of soldiers making their way along a dusty road through lushly wooded hills, on its way to hear the promised exercise in persuasion by "Comrade Kerensky." Soon the temptation to go into the woods to pick berries or pause for a nap was too great, and the unbroken ribbon became random clots of straggling soldiers. Someone cried "Halt!" and amid much bustle and shouting the clots reconstituted themselves as a "meeting." A sergeant declared: "Comrades! Kerensky isn't about to show up today—the command is going to send us an impostor who looks like Kerensky just to get us to take the offensive!" Someone replied: "He'd better show up, or there'll be hell to pay!"[102] The movement resumed and reached the rendezvous, but neither the division commander, the officers, nor the committees could get the soldiers to line up until Kerensky's staff car came into view.

With Denikin and other generals as set pieces, Kerensky went through his practiced routine, extracting the ritual of mass consent and carrying with him the moment of exaltation in a cloud of dust. Half an hour later, as he was about to board a train for another sector, a breathless, sobbing officer brought him the bad news: "Meetings are taking place in all the regiments . . . the soldiers are worked up to a frenzy . . . everywhere they

[100] See *KA* 84:145 (telegram of Tenth Army Committee to the Soviet Central Executive Committee, June 22, apparently based on Sokolov's own account) and *IzPS*, June 25.

[101] According to Denikin in Golovin, 1(1):155.

[102] "A. Kerenskii v armii gener. Denikina, XX k-s," *BA* 1 (1926): 36.

are passing resolutions against the offensive . . . many officers have been beaten.''[103]

The remaining days until the offensive were marked by a new round of disorders. A staff report for the week June 29 to July 6 notes that six more regiments passed resolutions against the offensive, accompanied by refusals to move into position. When the committee of the 115th Regiment conferred with a delegation of the army committee on how to secure compliance with an order, it was mobbed by soldiers throwing stones and bricks into the building. The soldiers seized supply trains, posted their own watches, and forced the officers to flee. Only the threat of disbanding quieted them down again. With great difficulty units were moved into the trenches prescribed by the battle plan, though many last-minute substitutions were necessary, which did not pass without incident.[104]

Convulsions had now wracked ten divisions and in nearly all the rest the mood was on the razor's edge. On the other hand, a few divisions, like the 51st, had surmounted past crises and now declared their willingness to fight; also there were shock units and composite units formed from volunteers from regiments that had been disarmed or quarantined. Denikin still enjoyed an overwhelming superiority over the enemy on the sector of the main attack, and he was aware that three German divisions opposite him had been detached to the Southwestern Front; thus he gambled on a change in mood once the artillery barrage began.[105]

The artillery barrage lasted three days (July 7-9), having been prolonged an extra day to give added confidence to the infantry and added time to get recalcitrant regiments to jump-off points. The attack on July 9 of the I Siberian Corps came off with textbook success, the advance troops and shock units overrunning the three lines of German trenches in the first half-hour and preempting serious counter-fire by the German artillery. As described by the corps commander, the sweet taste of success was all too brief:

[103] *Ibid.*, pp. 43-44 and 47. See also Denikin's speech in Golovin, 1(1):155.

[104] See *RDRA*, pp. 187-91 (summary of information on disturbances on the Western Front by Quartermaster's Section at Stavka for period June 29 to July 6).

[105] All according to Denikin's speech, Golovin, 1(1):162ff. Denikin claims he had 180 battalions facing 29 of the enemy and a threefold advantage in artillery on the 19 km. front of the main attack; Kersnovskii (*Istoriia* 4:986), citing a staff report, refers to an eightfold advantage in troop strength (85,000 to 10,300) for the three attacking corps. But on the sector of the nearby Third Army the Germans enjoyed a superiority which could easily be transferred without risk and German sources refer to a reserve force of 23 battalions, the equivalent of seven Russian divisions, so the numerical disparity was considerably less, perhaps two or three to one. (See *RWK* 14:157-58.)

> We crushed their artillery, took 1,400 captives, and seized many artillery pieces and machine guns. . . . But by nightfall I began to receive disquieting reports of massive movement to the rear of whole companies and disorganized mobs under no pressure from the enemy whatsoever. In several spots only regimental commanders with their staffs and a few soldiers occupied forward positions. The entire operation was hopelessly and definitively broken. . . . I sobbed bitterly for a long time.[106]

On the sector of the XXXVIII Corps, the bulk of the troops refused to attack, awaiting the outcome of meetings in the rear that endlessly debated the matter. A force of 44 officers and 200 volunteers tried to set the attack in motion but was wiped out to the last man.

Toward evening the women's battalion commanded by the indomitable Maria Bochkareva went over the top, broke through the German lines, and carried in their wake some of the reluctant regiments. By nightfall the Russians occupied the first two lines of German trenches, but there a new hazard awaited them—the soldiers discovered large stocks of liquor in the German trenches and fell victim to an orgy of drunkenness. Bochkareva was by now practically in command of what was left of the corps and succeeded in carrying the third line of trenches. But her lines were stretched out, her flanks exposed, half her women were dead or wounded, and the men began retreating to the rear. (In the midst of this hell she discovered one of her girls in a shell hole making love with a male soldier—she ran the girl through with her bayonet while the soldier bolted away.) Toward the end of the second day came the word that the corps that was to relieve her was still debating the matter and Bochkareva was authorized to extricate her remnant force. All the ground gained was surrendered.[107]

In the XX Corps, the 28th Division fell completely apart during the attack.[108] Having been cast back and forth between agitators and persuaders in recent days, one regiment, the 111th, occupied the trenches on their designated sector; the rest were somehow drawn into the routine of battle preparation. Debating ceased, restlessness gave over to resignation, supply trains, field kitchens, ammunitions boxes, and special details were moved up, other cogs and wheels meshed, and officers finally felt some ground

[106] Cited in Denikin's speech, Golovin, 1(1):161.

[107] See her autobiography *Yasha: My Life as a Peasant, Officer, and Exile* (New York, 1919), pp. 208-18.

[108] See Ia. M. Lisovoi, "Itogi odnogo iz ugovorov," *BA* 2-3:21-39. This is a staff document of the 28th Division, cited in full describing the exact course of events hour by hour, unit by unit, based on lower command reports and eyewitnesses. (Individual references are omitted because most of document is utilized.)

underneath their feet. At the last minute the 111th Regiment was to be pulled off the line and the other three regiments moved in. As the exchange was being consummated, there was a sudden reversal of orders: only one battalion from each regiment was to occupy the forward trenches, while the rest were to remain in slit trenches in the immediate rear. This change in orders broke the inertia of routine, rumors and angry questions popped up again, and as a result only a part of the 110th Regiment occupied the trenches. The 112th Regiment held an all-day meeting and sent a resolution to divisional headquarters demanding an explanation for the change in orders. When the hour approached that evening for all three regiments to move into the forward trenches, the 109th, except for 46 officers and 200 men, refused to budge. The 112th after a long delay complied, but once in the trenches prevented sappers from widening the salients and digging lateral trenches, even threatening to shoot them if they tried; also, the 110th appeared only in two-thirds strength. The 111th seemed ready to assume its assigned task (follow-up attack), but when it was ordered to replace the defecting 109th it refused. The attack was only a few hours away when the 111th was still occupying the slit trenches they had been ordered to evacuate to make way for a backup regiment.

At 4:30 in the morning came the disquieting report that in small groups the men of the 112th Regiment were slipping away toward the rear. The 110th Regiment was so badly shaken by the intensity of their own artillery barrage that they demanded its cessation, while the 112th declared they would not attack unless artillery fire were stepped up (later the artillery was blamed for their heavy losses). When the time came for the attack, only the storm unit and 200 or so of the 109th Regiment took part. The Germans soon noticed the confusion among the Russian troops and blanketed their rear positions with artillery fire, inflicting severe losses. Part of the 110th followed the lead units, but were soon forced to lie down and took heavy casualties. One battalion of the 112th reached the German wire but, unsupported by the rest of the regiment, retreated under withering fire. By evening, all units were melting away and collected in the rear in large numbers (1,000 men were rounded up near a railroad station). The Germans kept up an intense bombardment all day and far into the night, costing the Russians dearly. The attack had netted virtually nothing, yet the division had suffered 1,650 casualties, or 20 percent of its effectives; the storm battalion, one company of which had also fled under fire, suffered over 50 percent loss; 1,700 men were rounded up in the rear under the supervision of Commissar Bachinskii, but to the chagrin of the senior officers were immediately released to their units again.

Not only soldiers behaved less than heroically: the commander of the

111th Regiment failed to move up to his command post until categorically ordered, lied about the extent of his casualties, retreated with his men during the battle, and later claimed falsely to the commissar that he had been ordered to do so. A second commander tried to report in sick during the battle, but was ordered to stay at his post until killed or mortally wounded. The commander of the 110th Regiment demanded to be relieved even if it meant a court martial, as he refused to command men who would not obey orders; he had acted bravely in the initial phases of the battle, but apparently cracked under the strain of conflict with his soldiers. Five officer-demagogues who had been formally excluded from the officer fraternity for cowardice, but were ordered returned to their units by the commissar, fled with their men under fire.

The neighboring 51st Division succeeded brilliantly in its attack, two regiments reaching the enemy's rear in half an hour, but its backup regiment refused to move, blocking the path for yet another division, and the two advance regiments melted away in their tracks, suffering over 50 percent casualties, including nearly all their officers. Only half the 29th Division arrived before the conclusion of the battle, and then refused to leave the trenches. Unable to effect a foothold on any sector, Denikin canceled the operation on July 11, and Stavka confirmed it the following day.[109]

The 28th Division epitomized the fate of the offensive on the Western Front. Nowhere was the contrast between high expectations and miserable outcome so striking. Only here had such a large number of units seemed in relatively decent order until the offensive was at hand; only here had mass flights under fire assumed such grotesque proportions. There was not even the compensation of having given the enemy a good fight at the beginning. An assessment of the reasons is not quite so clear-cut as for other fronts. The Fifth Army had obviously been shot through with propagandized units, and the decision to proceed with the offensive must be reckoned particularly foolish. On the Southwestern Front, at least the Eleventh and Eighth armies put forth the maximum effort of which they were capable, given the specific circumstances created by the Revolution. There one should perhaps raise the question why so many units fought as well as they did. The Tenth Army did have its counterpart, however, in the Seventh Army, which seems to have had about the same degree of relative preparedness and discipline at the outset. Yet it too collapsed quickly in the contest of battle, although not as totally as the Tenth. In neither army could it be said that Bolshevik influence or outside agitation was the decisive factor; if anything, it was less a factor than elsewhere. It would seem that these armies reflected in most undiluted form the social

[109] According to Denikin's speech, Golovin, 1(1):159.

stresses of the Revolution and the spontaneous psychology of the soldier-peasant mass. Bolshevik arguments, where registered, simply articulated a deeply felt xenophobia toward the forces that were impelling them toward what they could only perceive as senseless slaughter, but with or without Bolshevism they were determined not to be consigned to oblivion.

CHAPTER IV

THE RESTORATION OF AUTHORITY

JULY was another month of deep crisis for revolutionary Russia. Hundreds of thousands of angry workers and soldiers took to the streets in Petrograd in a vain effort to force power on an unwilling Soviet Executive Committee (VTsIK), and contemptuously ignored the helpless government and the recently expressed positions of the All-Russian Soviet Congress.[1] The Soviet leadership escaped the frightening prospect of power chiefly because of Bolshevik ambivalence; the tidings of troops en route from the front and of Lenin's contacts with the German General Staff merely administered the *coup de grace*. But the skein did not cease to unwind there: the Kadets had withdrawn from the cabinet over the issue of Ukrainian autonomy, itself a signal of the fragmentation of loyalties; Minister President L'vov, the symbol of class cooperation, resigned shortly thereafter; the coalition partners haggled for weeks over the terms of a new government; and the Right gained a new lease on life, casting their eyes about for a suitable general.[2]

The magnitude of these developments left the political forces of various persuasions in a state of deep shock, which found scant compensation in anathemas hurled at the Bolsheviks. From the moderate Mensheviks to the far Right, the slogan of the moment was "the restoration of firm authority," which implied a willingness to forgo much of the libertarian freedom

[1] Besides the classic accounts of Trotsky, Chamberlin, and Radkey, see Rabinowitch, *Prelude to Revolution*. At the Soviet Congress the Executive Committee of the Petrograd Soviet was superseded by an "All-Russian" Central Executive Committee, known by its initials, VTsIK, which are employed hereafter. (See "Remarks and Acknowledgments," above.)

[2] Radkey is the most authoritative source on the cabinet crisis itself; the two best treatments of the political dynamics of this period are Rabinowitch, *The Bolsheviks Come to Power: The Revolution of 1917 in Petrograd* (New York, 1976), chaps. 3 and 4; and William Rosenberg, *Liberals in the Russian Revolution: The Constitutional Democratic Party, 1917-1921* (Princeton, 1974), chap. 6.

heretofore regarded as conquest of the Revolution. When it became apparent, however, that the revived right-wing forces were determined to shackle the Soviet-oriented organizations, the latter quickly changed fronts and girded themselves for defense. Rancorous name-calling and mutual recriminations permeated the metropolitan press and were carried over into speeches at an assembly of former Duma deputies on July 18 and at the Moscow State Conference in early August. When the Second Coalition was finally constructed at the end of July, it was essentially a personal cabinet of Kerensky, now the Minister President as well as Defense Minister, and without Tsereteli or authoritative Kadets it inspired little of the longed-for sense of "firm authority." Kerensky's efforts to ride the current to the right with firm measures against the Bolsheviks, and the appointment of Kornilov as Commander in Chief, simply whetted the appetite of the "bourgeois" groups for further concessions. The ground in the middle was fast eroding as Kornilov became the symbol for the mobilization of all "census Russia," including the Kadets, for the liquidation of the revolutionary adventure.

These currents evoked a strong reaction in the army committees and their following at the front, in the midst of unending crises in the aftermath of the offensive. Confidence in the prospects of recovery and the essential revolutionary virtue of the troops had not yet been utterly shattered. That at such a critical time irresponsible political groups in the rear should strike at the twin fountainheads of revolutionary authority, the All-Russian Executive Committee (VTsIK) and the Coalition Government with Comrade Kerensky at the helm of Defense, could only strike them as treasonous. Their indignation was first directed against the Kadets, a reflection of the fact that the earliest press reports erroneously connected their unilateral exodus with the actions of the First Machine-gun Regiment, but as the picture became more complete, the Bolsheviks were clearly identified as the "irresponsible element," abetted by counter-revolutionaries and German spies.

By July 5 and 6 the committee organs of the Twelfth, Fifth, and Third armies were already carrying reasonably full accounts of events. Those of the Tenth, Special, Eighth, and Ninth armies followed suit by July.[3] Reports in these organs confirm that nearly every army committee called an emergency plenary session, sometimes with lower-committee representatives present, to declare their loyalty to the Soviet Executive Committee (now officially VTsIK) and to condemn the Bolsheviks and Kadets. The reso-

[3] See the following committee newspapers for these dates: *RF, Iz5A, Go3A, GoXA, IzOA, Iz8A*, and *Iz9A*. Unfortunately *VGr* and *Iz7A* for this period were not available to the author, and in the others issues for the key dates were sometimes missing, so the account below is a composite.

lution of the Ninth Army Committee denounced "those irresponsible leaders who call for armed confrontation causing disorganization in the revolutionary ranks," affording the opportunity for "Black Hundreds, gendarmes, *okhranniki*, and adherents of the old regime to carry on a campaign against the Soviet and the government, covering themselves with revolutionary credentials," while the resolution of the Special Army Committee branded as treason assaults on the integrity of the Soviet or the government from both the right and the left (equating the Kadet walkout with the uprising) and, like other committees, offered armed support "at the first call" should it be needed.[4] The resolution of the Third Army Committee, conveyed in somewhat ungrammatical style its fear of "fratricidal war" which could "only lead to reaction and counter-revolution."[5] Such resolutions were carried by army committee members to units at the front for formal endorsements, which often were forthcoming.[6]

☆

Despite their passionate phrasing these resolutions still expressed fundamental optimism over revolutionary achievements, their current trials notwithstanding. Genuine despair at the front comparable to the Petrograd trauma was generated by the unexpected breakthrough of the German army above Tarnopol on July 6.[7] Three armies of the Southwestern Front, the Eleventh, Seventh, and Eighth, were thrust into pell-mell retreat until all of the hard-won ground of the Brusilov offensive of 1916 had been lost. The Eleventh, which absorbed the brunt of the initial attack, was at that moment being prepared for a renewal of a Russian offensive. The battered enemy troops facing it did not appear very formidable, and assurances had been given of a three-to-one superiority in divisional strength and of firepower several times over.[8] The Russian command was unaware that behind

[4] See *Iz8A*, July 7, and *IzOA*, July 8 (as is often the case these organs carry the resolutions of neighboring armies).

[5] *Go3A*, July 6.

[6] For example, the I Siberian Corps in *GoXA*, July 12 (congratulates the Provisional Government on "victory," which is characterized as a victory for "all the revolutionary democracy" and "firm revolutionary authority"). Resolution of the Special Army (supported by an artillery battery, in *IzOA*, July 9); that of the Ninth Army (by a radio-telegraph unit, *Iz9A*, July 15); that of the Twelfth Army (by two infantry and one Siberian Rifle regiment *RF*, July 9; by a cavalry regiment, *RF*, July 11); and that of the Third Army (*Go3A*, July 6, several units).

[7] This was immediately registered in panicky articles and resolutions: *GoXA*, July 12 ("The Country and the Revolution Are in Danger"); *IzOA*, July 12 ("The Country and the Revolution Are in Danger"); *RF*, July 11 (editorial blaming cowardly soldiers) and July 12 ("The Revolution Is on the Edge of the Abyss").

[8] For Brusilov's plan for a new offensive, see Zaionchkovskii, *Kampaniia 1917 g.*, p. 77, which was to be coordinated with the operations of the Fifth and Tenth armies and a renewed thrust of the Seventh and Eighth armies toward the key town of Rogatyn. On the Galician

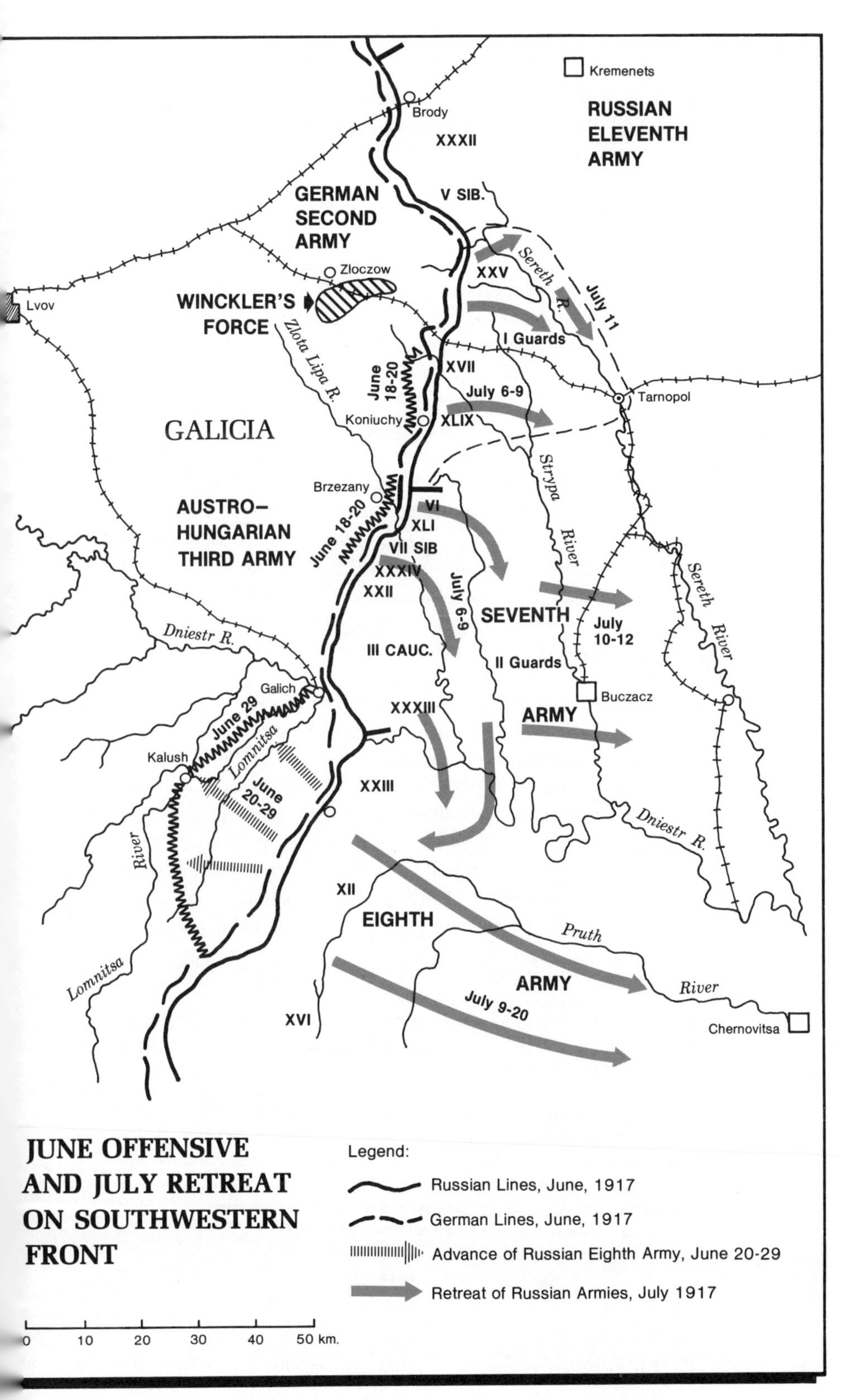

JUNE OFFENSIVE AND JULY RETREAT ON SOUTHWESTERN FRONT

the screen of used-up Austrian and Landwehr divisions was a crack force under General Winckler of nine newly equipped German divisions with enormous firepower, recently transferred from the Western Front. In fact, the German command had planned the operation the previous winter for the 1917 campaign, but had postponed it because of the Kerensky offensive.[9]

According to the Stavka version, endlessly repeated in the metropolitan press, the cowardly soldiers of the 607th Mlynovskii Regiment (Sixth Grenadier Division) abandoned their positions without resistance, allowing the enemy to pour through; units ordered in to take their place held meetings and debated the matter until it was too late. The debacle was laid squarely on the soldier masses crazed by Bolshevik propaganda, whereas the officers were lauded for their heroism and prodigal self-sacrifice.[10] In the coming days the public reeled with news of the magnitude of the disaster: all resistance in the Eleventh Army crumbled, as tens of thousands of disorganized soldiers streamed along both banks of the Sereth River in the direction of Tarnopol, crisscrossing or competing for the right-of-way with supply carts, caissons, staffs, and units still trying to hold their formations. The V and XVII corps on the left flank withdrew rapidly to prevent encirclement, leaving a huge gap with the right of the Seventh Army. Units of the XLIX Corps ordered to fill the breach resolved the matter in the negative by majority vote at a mass meeting.

By the evening of July 7 the Germans had driven a wedge 40 kilometers wide and 24 kilometers deep along the upper Sereth. At this juncture the German divisions wheeled southward, protected on both flanks by the Sereth and Strypa rivers, which were swollen with recent rains, and threatened the deep rear of the Seventh Army.[11] The commander of the latter, the doughty General V. I. Selivachev was ordered to bend and stretch out his lines to close the gap, but found himself equally incapable of controlling his units. In the meantime the Third Austro-Hungarian Army attacked all along the front south of Brzezany. The 159th Division on the Seventh

sector the prize was to be Lvov after the main Austro-Hungarian armies had been surrounded (orders to armies of July 8).

[9] For the plans of the German high command, see *RWK* 13:159ff. and *OHLK* 6:289-90.

[10] Text in *RPG* 2:66-67. Besides appearing in many newspapers, it was also carried in some front newspapers, for example, *GoXA*, July 9.

[11] Accounts in Zaionchkovskii, *Kampaniia 1917 g.*, pp. 78-84; Kersnovskii, *Istoriia*, 4:970-75; *OHLK* 6:294-310; *RWK* 13:163-72. Maps in Zaionchkovskii, No. 9, and *RWK* 14 and 15, but the best work for following the action is again *OHLK*. The Russian accounts reflect that commanders on the spot could not follow the course of the action and that Stavka was especially badly informed. Denikin, for example, was persuaded that no units stood and fought, whereas there is contrary testimony in *RWK, OHLK*, and some personal accounts, (e.g., Kal'nitskii's); see below, p. 122. (See Denikin, *Ocherki*, 1 (1):66-68.)

Army's left fled its positions, opening up a new gap in the line; neighboring divisions melted away and a mass retreat to the rear set in. A corps commander disconsolately reported to Selivachev that he no longer knew the disposition of his divisions.[12]

By July 9 the main units of the Seventh Army had retreated southward between the Strypa and Zlota Lipa rivers to a line 40 kilometers in a quarter turn from the former front. The German wedge along the Sereth now reached well south of Tarnopol, stretching 80 kilometers on one side and 64 kilometers on the other. Tarnopol, a major rail and supply center, was left undefended and surrendered without battle on July 11 despite Brusilov's categorical order to hold it at all costs. The chaos of the evacuation defies description: trains were piled over their rooftops with vital goods to be rescued from the enemy, but as they pulled out of the station, deserting soldiers threw off the goods to make room for themselves. At this juncture death battalions arrived in an armored train to restore order, summarily shot convenient culprits, and hastily withdrew. Before they departed, the Russian soldiers thoroughly raped and plundered the civilian population; all that could not be transported was put to the torch.[13] In the midst of this chaos a huge ammunition dump went up, sending off an otherworldly shockwave registered many kilometers away, which could hardly have been reassuring to the hard-pressed units trying to hold. (Sergeev, some distance away, recalls observing first the initial blinding flash, then countless secondary ones, and moments later a deafening thud; the gigantic plume, he thought years later, resembled an atomic bomb.)[14]

A Stavka communiqué blamed the surrender of Tarnopol on the Second Guards Infantry Division, which supposedly withdrew without pressure from the enemy. Sergeev, whose battalion was ordered to defend the town's perimeter, claims that he found the town undefended and that his men were taken under fire before they could take up their positions. They fought a brief skirmish in the streets against unequal odds and retreated under orders and in perfect discipline. A few days later he penned an angry refutation of the Stavka version and sent it through channels.[15] On July 10 the Germans tried to cross the Sereth south of Tarnopol, but for the first time

[12] *KA* 10:147 (other details in *ibid.*, pp. 144-50, entries for July 6-13).

[13] For graphic personal accounts, see Remter, "Epizody fevral'skoi revoliutsii na iugo-zapadnom fronte," *LR* 12 (1927): 60-65; Klimovich, *Biuletin L. Gv. Moskovskogo Polka*, No. 133 (April, 1952), n.p. (looting, armored train, shootings, burning of supplies, chaos on railroads, arrival of death battalion); K. S. Popov, *Vospominaniia kavkazskago grenadera 1914-20* (Belgrade, 1925), pp. 198-204 (grizzled cadre officer, several times wounded, heads death battalion, rounds up deserters, executes several on the spot).

[14] See *Finlandets*, No. 38 (December, 1939): 7 (other details *passim*).

[15] *Ibid.*, pp. 14-19.

they encountered stiff resistance. Nevertheless, after an intense engagement, the Russians were forced to yield.[16]

Having secured the line of the Sereth, the Austro-German armies turned their attention southward. As the Austro-Hungarian Third Army pursued the retreating Russian Seventh, pressing the latter from both the north and the west, the Russian divisions became hopelessly intermingled. Prompt flight, during which rifles, boots, knapsacks, and all other encumbrances were discarded, prevented an encirclement (an enormous booty in guns and ammunition was also left behind); still, the German high command was disappointed with the low number of captured.[17] It was now the turn of the Eighth Army to feel the threat of envelopment. In staged withdrawals involving heavy rear-guard fighting, the Eighth Army yielded successive positions south of the Dniester, until on July 20 Chernovitsa, for over a year the Eighth Army headquarters, was surrendered. Of the armies of the Southwestern Front, the Eighth Army retreated the longest distance, close to 160 kilometers and proportionately took the heaviest casualties (11,363, or 15 percent of the effectives).[18] Casualties of the other two armies are not recorded, but are not likely to be as high except in prisoners of war, which, according to German sources, were 42,000 (15 percent of those engaged).[19] Nevertheless, the German objective was unrealized—not a single Russian division had been encircled and destroyed. Though the number of deserters to the interior was extraordinarily large, for the most part deserters traversed only a short distance to the rear, where many were rounded up while others drifted back to their units. In the meantime, the Central Powers had expended enormous quantities of ammunition they could ill afford, their troops were exhausted, and their lines of communication were greatly overstretched.[20]

As the Russian troops drew near to their own borders, many of them underwent a sharp change of mood and firmly resolved not to yield any further. Along the Zbruch River they mounted a stout defense which took the Austro-Germans by surprise, and the latter called operations to a halt. The Central Powers did attempt to activate the Austro-Hungarian Seventh Army jointly with General Mackensen in Moldavia, but both the Russian

[16] See Gerua, *Vospominaniia*, 2:203.

[17] *RWK* 13:171ff.

[18] See M. S. Frenkin, *Revoluitsionnoe dvizhenie na rumynskom fronte g.-mart 1918* (Moscow, 1965), pp. 105-8. This monograph deals almost exclusively and in rich detail with the Eighth Army, which covered 250 km. of front, more than the Seventh and Eleventh armies combined with fewer divisions (13 as opposed to 14 and 20 respectively). (See also Zaionchkovskii, *Kampaniia 1917 g.*, p. 77.)

[19] *RWK* 13:178. No Russian source offers comparable figures.

[20] *Ibid.*, pp. 172 and 178-79.

and Rumanian troops counterattacked with great vigor, General Ragoza's Fourth Army scoring a textbook tactical success. These operations were also halted by mid-August, and except for the capture of Riga, also in August, the war on the Eastern Front was over.[21]

☆

The Stavka communiqué on the Tarnopol breakthrough, by firmly implanting the image of Bolshevized soldier hordes fleeing in panic to the rear, added considerable weight to the alarm and hankering for extreme measures which surged in the wake of the July Days. Quite naturally the press organs of the revitalized Right coupled it with the July Days, claiming a master plan of the German General Staff coordinated front and rear through paid Bolshevik agents. Kerensky lent his own authority to this version when he returned from the Western Front wielding a copy of the German propaganda sheet *Tovarishch* of July 3 which "predicted" the July Days, thereby "proving" Bolshevik connivance with the Germans.[22] The German organ claimed that the Russian offensive had aroused massive indignation and street demonstrations in Russian towns "protesting the murder of Russia's sons." An authentic touch was that cossacks were called out to beat the demonstrators while left-wing socialist leaders were arrested and exiled. This latter passage was to Kerensky the smoking gun, but probably it was simply an ingenious propaganda ploy designed to undermine the morale of Russian soldiers. Kerensky's version acquired wide circulation and credence in the Soviet-oriented public, not least of all among the front committeemen.[23]

A proclamation of the Southwestern Front Committee, endorsed by the Eleventh Army Committee and several army commissars and addressed to the War Ministry, the Soviet Central Executive Committee, the Peasants' Soviet, and the Commander in Chief with copies to all and sundry, laid on the colors even more thickly than Stavka's communiqués:

> Most units are presently in a state of all-embracing dissolution. There is no longer a trace of authority and obedience to command. Persuasion and appeals to conscience have lost their force, and are met with threats and even gunfire. Some units have abandoned their positions without even waiting for the enemy to show himself. For hundreds of miles the soldiers stream to the rear, with weapons and without.

[21] Further operations can be followed in the standard histories; on Riga's evacuation, see Chapter VI, below, pp. 185-90 and n. 9, p. 189.

[22] See Kerensky, *Russia and History's Turning Point*, pp. 290-91, and *Kerensky, Prelude to Bolshevism: The Kornilov Rebellion* (New York, 1919), pp. 26-27.

[23] *IzPS*, July 7, printed in *RPG* 2:962-66. For the front, see *Iz8A* and *Iz5A*, both for July 12.

> Knowing there is no risk of punishment, they flee without shame, sometimes by entire units.[24]

Moreover, it approved an order of the commanders of the Southwestern Front and the Eleventh Army to fire on fleeing soldiers and concluded: "Let the country . . . find in itself the resolution to act without mercy against those who by cowardice would destroy and betray the Revolution and Russia." This posture of ruthless revolutionary tutelage over the misguided masses became the characteristic refrain of commissars and upper-level committeemen during the period of the retreat, and it was sustained with little abatement until the end of July. Having invested the "heros of the 18th of June" with an aureole of unblemished valor, and having deluded themselves that only a handful of units had yielded to unscrupulous agitators, their psychic recoil was all the more hysterical when their illusions were destroyed. Their denunciations of "yellow-bellies," "traitors," "criminals," and "depraved hordes" yielded little in intemperance to the right-wing press. At best they bemoaned the "darkness" of the uncultured masses easily ensnared by appeals to the instinct of self-preservation. Thus the committee public was in a frame of mind not only to justify strong punitive measures against recalcitrant soldiers, but even to supervise them and carry them out.

The above sentiments represented a visceral reaction to the initial reports, before reliable facts were available either to the command or the committees. Both parties were feeding their respective ulcers: the command its past humiliations, and the committees their unrequited love. The notion of one cowardly regiment pulling the plug to allow the German hordes to pour through filled the need to identify a specific culprit, but it took no cognizance of the overwhelming German strength or of the ragged condition of the defending forces after three weeks of incessant fighting. An investigation carried out at Stavka's request by Generals Ilkevich and Goshtovt (both guardsmen) to justify the disbanding of the disgraced units turned in the opposite verdict: "The 607th Mlynovskii Regiment and the entire Sixth Grenadier Division cannot be accused of betrayal, treason, or arbitrary withdrawal from their positions. On July 6 the division fought and died." The materials of the investigation revealed that the Germans concentrated 200 guns at the point of attack, whereas the Russians had but 16, and that the division numbered only 3,400 effectives (normal strength, 14,000).[25]

Similarly, the I and II Guards corps, subjected to vilification by right-wing circles and higher staffs for retreating against orders, were subse-

[24] *RPG* 2:967-68; also in *Go3A* and *GoXA* of July 11.

[25] *RPG* 2:974 (from *IzPS*, August 18).

quently exonerated by the testimony of their own officers. The commander of the II Guards Corps, attached to the Seventh Army, asserted that during the retreat his units executed a difficult flanking maneuver through columns of retreating units and baggage trains, and left behind only 30 deserters and 230 physically enfeebled stragglers out of 20,000 men; thereafter, they gave battle to four enemy divisions, forcing them to suspend operations. Similar testimony vindicated the Egerskii and Finlandskii guards regiments (I Guards Corps, Eleventh Army), confirming Sergeev's account.[26] The archives of the guards units reflect considerable efforts at self-vindication by the committees. The Guards Sappers, for example, issued a detailed refutation of press reports on July 22; on August 17 the committee of the I Guards Corps called on all lower committees to submit information on the Tarnopol operations that would help rehabilitate the corps; on August 15 the committee of the Second Division was drafting a "protest," on August 21 they stated their case to the commissar, and on September 28 they were still disputing the assertion of a General Scheidemann that only the Preobrazhenskiis and Semenovskiis had forcefully engaged the enemy.[27]

The line between myth and reality is not easy to establish. The advertised preponderance of the Eleventh Army was in fact very misleading, since it was measured in much-depleted battalions. If the Mlynovskii Regiment was at a quarter of its regulation strength, other available divisions were in a similar state after heavy fighting. Also the Russian command seems to have never been aware of the magnitude of the German forces arrayed against them.[28] The claim of tens of thousands of troops streaming in disorderly fashion to the rear certainly had foundation in fact, as well as the unauthorized withdrawals of entire units, but one has to consider the unexpectedness of the breakthrough, catching many troops comfortably bivouacking in the rear by surprise. Often contact with headquarters or even with one's immediate superiors was broken off at once, and higher levels soon had no idea of the whereabouts of their units. Even the Eleventh Army headquarters, located close to the front lines and anticipating their own attack, had to withdraw under the cover of darkness on the first day.

[26] *Ibid.*, pp. 975-76.

[27] Committee *protokoly* of Volynskii Regiment, TsGVIA, f. 2573, op. 1, ed. khr. 2, l. 36, staff documents of Second Guards Division, f. 2322, op. 7, ed. khr. 2, l. 334, and *protokoly* of divisional committee, ibid., ed. khr. 4, ll. 23-25.

[28] Gerua, at the time Chief of Staff of the Eleventh Army, confesses he was made aware of Winckler's strike force from reading Kersnovskii, who in turn learned of it from *OHLK* (see Gerua, *Vospominaniia*, 2:200); Zaionchkovskii repeats the Stavka version and underestimates the enemy troop strength by several divisions and the number of guns several times over (see his *Kampaniia 1917 g.*, pp. 78-79 [400 light, 60 heavy], *RWK* 12:163 [600 light, 230 heavy] and *OHLK* 6:295 [500 light, 180 heavy].

Bewildered lower-level commanders on either side of the breakthrough withdrew in the absence of orders, quite logically fearing encirclement. Disorder and panic inevitably ensued when units took false directions, intermingled with neighbors on one flank, and broke contact on the other. Until communications with headquarters could be restored, the wisest course was to keep moving ahead of the enemy in the hope of reestablishing a line farther back.

Once defensible positions were reached, units often did reform and fight. Even Stavka credited the 155th Division with having done so. Kal'nitskii claims that his soldiers, getting their first rest after several grueling weeks of holding the line, nevertheless on hearing the thunder of gunfire automatically cleaned their weapons and doled out ammunition. They could observe the 623rd Regiment perched on the hilltop they had just vacated disappear in a curtain of fire; they also observed the spectacle of thousands of fleeing deserters, most of them barefoot and without packs or rifles, including Finnish Riflers who were supposed to be in Bukovina with the Seventh Army. Nevertheless, his division stood and fought, preventing an encirclement, though two of the regiments were overrun. Later remnants found their way back, then an entire battalion, then another until the division was able to reform.[29]

It seemed to the soldiers that their senior officers had lost their nerve or had strangely absented themselves. Kal'nitskii himself expressed the newly shaping mood: "One thing was clear to all conscious soldiers: the command showed less willingness to resist the Germans than the soldiers. Already in those days it was clear that the command preferred the Germans to the Bolsheviks."[30] Commanders even allowed their committees to discuss that "holy of holies," operative orders, he thought, hoping thereby to heap the blame for the defeat on the "democratic system." Commanders sometimes gave grounds for this opinion. General Selivachev, for example, berated commanders who "folded their hands" during the retreat and allowed committees to take charge, citing the example of the commander of the Fifth Transamur Division.[31] The commander of the Southwestern Front, General Gutor, normally quite cooperative with committees, also issued the following order: "Some commanding personnel have given up control over the units entrusted to them . . . to commissars and committees as if maintaining order were no longer their affair. . . . Such weak-willed commanders are to be removed by their superiors without reference to seniority."[32]

[29] Kal'nitskii, *Ot fevralia k oktiabriu*, pp. 97-99.

[30] *Ibid.*, p. 100.

[31] Entry for July 7, *KA* 10:145.

[32] Orders of 517th Batumskii Regiment of July 10, TsGVIA, f. 3054, op. 2, d. 23, part 1, l. 427.

Thus soldiers and many lower officers perceived events from their own, entirely different angle of vision, registered a different set of facts, and worked them into a distinct set of attitudes and conclusions that were quite the inverse of the official mythology. The conviction took shape during the retreat that they were being deliberately slandered, that they had bravely sought to withstand the Germans, that they had been ordered to retreat against their will, and that the high command had intentionally betrayed them to the enemy, because it was ridden with spies or had been bought off or sought to discredit the revolutionary army as a pretext to restore Old Regime discipline. In one instance, the careless lighting of a cigarette by an officer peering over the breastworks was interpreted as a signal to the Germans to attack and led to a major incident.[33] In the Eighth Army on August 5, two soldier deputies chosen by their comrades asked the division commander for permission to see the commissar to get the truth about Tarnopol, since "many soldiers are of the opinion that the retreat was the result of treason by the high command."[34] Nothing serves to stir up the human psyche or to burst the normal restraints of civilized behavior like a military catastrophe: the evil must be objectified, and involuntarily it is ascribed to those by whom one has been thwarted or humiliated in the past—it is they who have orchestrated the evil design, they who must be in league with the enemy, they who must be exposed, branded, and mercilessly punished. The vindictive impulse is masked as just retribution vital to the salvation of the fatherland. One feels no guilt for one's own behavior, because under the circumstances it seemed so logical and unavoidable. Thus, the psychology and behavior of soldiers, committeemen, commissars, officers, and the high command had much in common, even though the particular scapegoats and willingly believed myths varied from case to case.

☆

The myths and remedies that were being concocted over the soldiers heads, however, were molded by the Stavka communiqué of July 7 and the panicky appeal of the Southwestern Front Committee. For some time the sentiment had been taking shape that "the time for persuasions was past" and that measures tougher than those heretofore practiced were necessary to put an end to the collective acts of indiscipline; the collapse of the front acted like a catalyst, and new stern directives and laws poured forth like a fountain, culminating in the law of July 12 which reinstituted accelerated field courts and the death penalty at the front. The moment

[33] Stavka survey of condition of armies, August 10-19, in *RDRA*, p. 348 (incident in 12th Division, Eighth Army).

[34] Report of the corps commander, *RDRA*, p. 303.

coincided with Kornilov's appointment as commander of the Southwestern Front. His very first order of July 8 set the new tone:

> The willful withdrawal of units from their positions I regard as tantamount to treason, and therefore I categorically demand that all commanding personnel apply artillery and machine-gun fire against such traitors. I will take the entire responsibility for any casualties on myself. Any hesitation to carry out such measures I will regard as dereliction of duty and will remove such officers from command and hand them over to the courts.[35]

Simultaneously he demanded immediate reintroduction of the death penalty backed by front commissars Savinkov, Filonenko, and Gobechia on July 11, accompanied by the threat to resign were it not promptly done.[36] (Brusilov, not to be outdone, promptly wired Kerensky of his support, appending a grandiloquently argued memorandum that cited precedents from the revolutionary armies of France and America. He also threatened to resign if it were not executed.)[37] On July 9, without authorization, Kornilov proscribed all meetings in the region of the front and the breakup of any meetings that occurred with force of arms; moreover, he designated his order a battle order not subject to discussion, even by committees.[38] "Finally we are hearing a different kind of music," Selivachev gratefully noted in his diary, echoing a widespread sentiment in the higher command.[39] Kornilov's preemptory tone toward the government, which received immediate nationwide publicity, transformed him overnight into a symbolic figure for social and political groups to the Right. It could not be lost on them that these demands were served directly on the government, bypassing Commander in Chief Brusilov. General Denikin claims with good reason that even without exact knowledge of the circumstances many senior officers sensed that the moral leadership had shifted from Stavka

[35] From the orders of the 329th Buzuliiskii Regiment of July 11, relay of army order of July 8, TsGVIA, f. 2938, op. 1, d. 23, part 1, l. 369. Kornilov boasted in his deposition after his arrest that he had ordered the shooting of plunderers and deserters along the roads and the exposing of their corpses with the inscription of their crimes (see "Pokazanie gen. ot infantrii Lavra Georgovicha Kornilova" (Ms.), archive of R. R. Raupach, RA, in untitled folder; see also Denikin, *Ocherki*, 1 [1]:170).

[36] *VOSR. Iiul'*, p. 408, and Golovin, *Rossiiskaia kontr-revoliutsiia*, 1 (1):140. See orders of the 329th Regiment of July 13 for propaganda use of this telegram (TsGVIA, f. 2938, op. 1, d. 23, part 1, l. 385).

[37] See *RPG* 2:981. His claim in his memoirs that he signed the order on the death penalty only on Kerensky's insistence under the pressure of Savinkov is thus proven to be accurate. See Brusilov, *Moi vospominaniia* (Moscow-Leningrad 1963), p. 276.

[38] *RDRA*, p. 197.

[39] July 8, *KA* 10:146.

and Petrograd to the commander of the Southwestern Front.[40] It seemed that finally someone was prepared to challenge the sacred cows of the Revolution and to give backbone to the government without regard for the consequences.

Later, Soviet-oriented elements were glad to have Kornilov claim credit for the revival of draconic measures, but in fact a broad spectrum of the so-called "democratic forces," including the Soviet leadership, the commissars, and the soldiers' committees, had been moving in a similar direction and even helped frame the tough measures now being drafted. First of all, Kerensky himself, citing "grievous events in the Eleventh Army," on July 8 declared that "military discipline must be restored, implementing the full force of revolutionary power, including recourse to arms." The same day he circularized all front commanders, reminding them that they had at their disposal paragraph 14 of the Declaration of Soldiers' Rights, which recognized the right of officers under battle conditions to armed enforcement of obedience to their orders.[41] The following day a joint order with Brusilov directed commanders to halt individual or collective acts of disobedience of orders by armed force and to forbid any discussion of orders, either by improvised meetings or by committees.

In fact, Kerensky had been taking on a new orientation before the Tarnopol disaster: shaken by the failure of the offensive and the massive mutinies, he had already urged his government colleagues that "the time for persuasions and discussions is past."[42] During the July Days, Kerensky wired L'vov from the front:

> I categorically insist on the decisive cessation of these traitorous demonstrations, the disarming of rebellious units, and the trial of all instigators and mutineers. I demand the interdiction of all further demonstrations and military mutinies by armed force.[43]

On July 6, at Kerensky's urging, a new law was passed providing that all military personnel guilty of advocating disobedience to legal military orders be punished as traitors. The day before the news of the Tarnopol disaster,

[40] Denikin, *Ocherki*, 1 (1):171.

[41] Selivachev knew of it on July 9, which dates it (*KA* 10:146); published in the orders of the 329th Buzuliiskii Regiment on July 13, though the army order was undoubtedly earlier (TsGVIA, f. 2938).

[42] Secret report on the course of the operations of June 25, *VOSR. Mai-iiun'*, pp. 373-75. It was a detailed accounting of the failed operations and the mutinies, which indicates that, in private at least, Kerensky was cured of all illusions on the capacity of the troops to conduct active operations. See also Stankevich, *Vospominaniia*, p. 160, who accompanied Kerensky on his tours and pictures Kerensky as viewing the situation as "almost the failure of the Revolution."

[43] *VOSR. Iiul'*, p. 290.

he sent out an order to the Army to arrest and bring to immediate trial all agitators who advocated violence, violation of discipline, overthrow of the Provisional Government, or disobedience to superior officers; moreover, he specifically instructed the proscription of Bolshevik newspapers at the front, naming *Pravda*, *Okopnaia Pravda*, and *Soldatskaia Pravda*.[44]

The shock of the July Days created a receptive mood in the rump Provisional Government, now consisting primarily of Soviet figures in the absence of Kadets and Prince L'vov. (At this time Kerensky's candidacy for the premiership was being seriously considered.) In his memoirs Tsereteli concedes that the military catastrophe "compounded the internal crisis of the country" and "posed even more sharply the question of . . . the creation of a firm revolutionary power, capable of carrying through the most decisive measures both in the interior of the country and at the front." This sentiment was reflected in the alarmist tone of the program of the reconstituted Coalition Government of July 8. The introductory paragraph was sprinkled with references to the "threatening hour," "treason," "inner rot," "counter-revolution," "the German hordes," and so on. Overshadowing items on a "democratic" foreign policy, an interim land law, and an early convocation of the Constituent Assembly was a strongly worded point on the necessity to concentrate all efforts on fighting the "external enemy" and maintaining internal order for which "the most decisive measures are required."[45]

Whether the latter were already understood to include the death penalty is uncertain, but the frame of mind of the Soviet leaders was clearly evident when the socialist ministers' program was discussed at a session of VTsIK (the All-Russian Soviet Executive Committee) on July 9. Tsereteli and another leading Menshevik, Fedor Dan, presented the arguments for a "firm revolutionary power" and introduced a resolution that was to determine the authoritative Soviet position:

1. The fatherland and the revolution are in danger!
2. The Provisional Government is declared to be the Government for the Salvation of the Revolution.
3. It is hereby acknowledged to have *unlimited powers to restore order and discipline in the army*, and to struggle with all forms of anarchy and counterrevolution and to carry out a program of measures to this end.[46]

[44] See *RPG* 3:1358 and *RDRA*, pp. 197-98 (proves that circulation was to entire army); see also *IzGr*, July 14 (read by Corps Commander Parskii to assembled committee representatives).

[45] *RPG* 3:1386-87; for circumstances, see Tsereteli, *Vospominaniia*, 2:356-58.

[46] Tsereteli, 2:361-62 (italics added); speeches of Tsereteli and Dan supporting the reso-

The measure passed 252 to 47, all but a hardy band of Bolsheviks, Left Socialist Revolutionaries, and Menshevik Internationalists assenting. Receptivity to repressive measures was especially pronounced at the front. The committeemen and commissars of the Southwestern Front had endorsed Kornilov's measures without even knowing the position of the Soviet or the government. Skobelev, on a special mission to the Southwestern Front for VTsIK, reported on Kornilov's special execution detachments and noted with approval that the Eleventh Army Committee was cooperating in their organization.[47]

Though most Soviet-oriented elements were swept along this path by the force of events, some felt twinges of conscience and feared that the willingness to use force would be exploited by the Right for counterrevolutionary purposes. (Tsereteli used the instructive analogy of William Tell shooting the apple from his son's head.)

Nevertheless, the interim Soviet-dominated cabinet approved a statute reinstituting the death penalty and field courts (called "military-revolutionary courts") on July 12, which was implemented by telegraph.[48] The death penalty was prescribed at the front for treason, desertion, flight from the field of battle, refusal to execute battle orders, assaults on officers or fellow soldiers, interference in the execution of orders, rape, brigandage, and incitement to any of the above. In each division, military-revolutionary courts were to be instituted, consisting of three officers and three soldiers selected by lot from a list of sworn jurors (so many per unit). These courts were to be distinct from the existing regimental and corps courts in that they were to provide a swift, uncomplicated procedure for crimes of the highest order that impeded the conduct of military operations. Trials were to take place immediately upon ascertaining that a crime had been committed, and sentences were to be executed without delay. Guilt was to be determined by a simple majority of the court, which had no authority to mitigate the penalty prescribed by law, though it could recommend clemency to the front commander. Ten days later a provision was added that all sentences were to be confirmed jointly by the commander and commissar of the respective armies, which caused endless complications and virtually nullified the intended effect of the law.

☆

The front and army committees fell in with the general clamor for strong measures, publishing the text of most of the above-cited orders. Editorially

lution are in *RPG* 3:1390-92, 1394. The parallel of the circumstance of 1791, which led the French Convention to form the Committee of Public Safety, was not lost on this audience and led to considerable hair-splitting between Bolshevik and Menshevik orators.

[47] Tsereteli, 2:364.

[48] Text in *RPG* 2:982-84.

they argued for calm acceptance of the orders as a "sad necessity" for the sake of restoring the health and fighting capacity to the Army. Such articles were usually not very lucid, grasping at emotion-laden slogans and far-fetched historical precedents. "Let us not be slaves!" admonished *Iz9A* on July 15, blaming the "nightmare of recent days" not on the Germans "but on our own failure of will." "The Revolution is in danger!" was the device of *Iz5A* (July 12) as it flayed the "traitors" of the Eleventh Army and declared a "state of siege" and the suspension of civil liberties ("for power there must be!"). On July 11 the *IzOA* called on the Army to "save the Motherland" and "rally around revolutionary authority" (*vlast'*). It appealed to the civic heroism of the ancient Roman Republic and of Minin and Pozharskii of the Time of Troubles. The *Go3A* of July 18 even declared those who had fled the field of battle to be "outside the law" and asked the War Minister and the Soviet for authorization to deal with such traitors by summary justice, a sentiment echoed by *Golos Okopa*, the committee organ of the XXXII Corps (Eleventh Army), on the same date. Other committee newspapers conveyed the same message by their selection of the news, but in all cases the dominant mood was one of panic, desperation, and reconciliation to whatever means were necessary to restore order. The death penalty and the military-revolutionary courts, however, were seldom explicitly referred to, though the organs of the Ninth and Tenth armies published the text of the new statute without comment.[49] But the burden of the message of the committee leadership was that the days of conciliation and impunity were over and that revolutionary institutions must range themselves unequivocally on the side of stern military justice.[50]

The command, on its part, tended to cling to the new law as to the anchor of salvation and was quick to claim its "healthy effects." General Selivachev, for example, noted on July 19 that "all corps commanders without exception acknowledge that the death penalty has purified the atmosphere for the line commanders, who for the first time are breathing freely."[51] Lower command reports of Selivachev's Seventh Army (e.g., those of the First and Fifth Finnish Rifle Divisions [XXII Corps] of July 18) bear him out. The latter struck the formula that worked its way up the chain of command: "The officers declare that after they read out the order on the introduction of the death penalty in the theater of operations to the

[49] On July 14 and 18, respectively.

[50] A resolution of the committee of the XXXVIII Corps, for example, called for decisive measures up to and including the death penalty (*GoXA*, July 21); there were several divisional and regimental resolutions to the same effect in *Iz9A*, July 14 and 16, another in *GoXA*, July 18.

[51] *KA* 10:154.

companies and special units, they found it much easier to issue commands.''[52] General Baiov, commander of the 42nd Division of the Second Army (Western Front), took strong exception to a commissar's report that attributed the marked change in mood to the democratic institutions. On the contrary, he asserted:

> The introduction of the death penalty and other such orders . . . has made a very strong impression on the soldiers and left the so-called Bolsheviks thunderstruck. It is now possible for lower units to implement measures on the formation of disciplinary and regimental courts, the resumption of training exercises, the forbidding of card-playing, the improvement of the soldiers' appearance, and the normalization of relations between officers and men.[53]

These reports were accurate enough for the moment they describe, while soldiers as well as committeemen were still under the spell of events, but other reports of the same time or shortly thereafter register forebodings of possible negative consequences. The 20th Finnish Rifle Regiment was described on July 26 as reacting to the death penalty ''with suspicion.''[54] A Stavka survey for the end of July, while straining to observe the ''sobering effect'' of the new measures, also recorded negative reactions from several sectors of the Western Front:

> In the more tranquil units [the new measures] served to create a healthy climate, but in undependable units they only magnify the unrest, since the soldiers regard the orders on discipline and the death penalty as a return to the old regime and blame officers for their publication. The situation of the officers in many units is very bad, even critical.[55]

In fact, the report noted the sharp increase in recent days of major incidents traceable to attempts to apply the new measures. Clearly the units that were ''sobered up'' tended to be offset by those driven in the opposite direction.

The desired effect of the new law depended upon the credibility of the resolve of commanders to carry it through. A few instances of swift trial and execution of offenders might be expected to circulate rapidly and demonstrate the certainty of exemplary punishment for hitherto tolerated

[52] TsGVIA, f. 2222, op. 1, ed. khr. 1066, l 153; see also ll. 51 and 54.

[53] Report of July 2, *RDRA*, p. 264.

[54] TsGVIA, f. 2222, op. 1, ed. khr. 1066, l. 69. For indication that the new law was read and explained in every unit of the Third Grenadier Division (Eleventh Army), see corps order of July 19, which states that ''it must be explained to every soldier'' (TsGVIA, f. 2326, op. 4, d. 14, l. 1.

[55] *VOSR. Iiul'*, p. 437.

practices. Unfortunately command and commissar reports are spare in details on the application of the laws; nevertheless, there is sufficient documentary evidence to confirm that military-revolutionary courts were called into being and on occasion pronounced and carried out death sentences, though how many in proportion to milder sentences and acquittals cannot be determined. And it is just as certain that this was accompanied by a significant diminution in major and minor disturbances, discussions of orders, and impromptu mass meetings, particularly in those sectors affected by the military reversals. However, in purchasing short-term gains, the risk was run of a more fundamental and total breakdown if the momentum could not be sustained. Each new challenge had to be successfully met, and the command and the revolutionary institutions would have to maintain a common front. Events were to demonstrate that once Kornilov's star was on the horizon many commanders were unwilling to work in harness with the revolutionary authorities, and the effectiveness of the new arrangements barely lasted the month of July. By early August the committees and commissars were desperately defending themselves against the efforts of higher commanders to dispense with their role altogether, and as a result the committees were obliged to extricate themselves from the apparatus of repression and to resume their struggle against the threat of counter-revolution in the command hierarchy. Repressive actions, where they continued, more frequently turned into messy affairs, accompanied by a new string of lynchings and armed resistance that sometimes could not be overcome.[56]

In July and August, about a dozen death sentences by military-revolutionary courts can be confirmed. Most occurred in the last week of July or early August, that is, about the time interval one would expect for the new procedure to be implemented. Several, such as in the 174th Division of the Third Army and several in the Eleventh (46th and Third Grenadier divisions), were in connection with major mutinies and will be discussed below. Others were isolated acts of individuals or small groups, some of them quite trivial. In the Latvian brigades, for example, a stretcher-bearer was sentenced to death for "fraternization and conveying to the enemy information on his own troops," though he claimed only to have entered the German trenches to seek information about relatives in Courland and incidentally accepted cognac from German officers.[57] In the Fifth Army in one instance five soldiers of the 539th Regiment were condemned for fetching newspapers from the barbed wire, and in another case a soldier threatened an officer with a bayonet for arresting some comrades who had

[56] The turnabout of the committees on repressive actions and the attitude toward the command is the subject of the next chapter; all other points are documented below.

[57] See sentence of the court of August 1 is in *RDRA*, pp. 284-85.

forcibly prevented a gas attack from being carried out on the enemy. The commissar of the Fifth Army, Khodorov, was said to have witnessed one execution, and a member of the "Extraordinary Investigative Committee" of the Fifth Army witnessed another. In July none of the shootings provoked a major outburst or even formal protests, though one can be certain that knowledge of them was widespread. For example, the sentence of the court for the soldiers of the 539th Borovskii Regiment was announced in the daily orders of the 135th Division with the obvious intent that the ranks should take notice. Not many of the death sentences were actually carried out: the Latvian rifler was granted clemency by General Klembovskii, commander of the Northern Front, as were the five who were condemned in the Seventh Army. Filonenko, the merciless commissar, claimed never to have confirmed a death sentence, as did Stankevich, who doubts that any were carried out on the Northern Front. Other references, however, confirm that the sentences in the Fifth Army were carried out, as were several others.[58]

Nevertheless, neither the commanders nor the commissars were satisfied with the effectiveness of the new courts, once they were tested out. General Selivachev complained bitterly that Commissar Surguchev sought refuge in legal formalities to avoid confirming sentences for five accused in the 19th Infantry Division. The commissar insisted that the procedure follow the same rules of evidence as the existing regimental courts, which in Selivachev's view deprived the courts of their chief virtue—speedy execution of the sentence for the sake of example. Furthermore, he noted that even division commanders pleaded for leniency for the same reason as commissars—the fear of reprisals by the soldiers.[59] There is ample evidence of the commissars' touchiness over their responsibility to confirm death sentences and how it would affect their standing as representatives of "democracy." The commissar of the Third Army was furious over the announcement in the staff organ of the V Siberian Corps, *Okopnye Dumy*, of an execution and demanded that General Kislii dismiss the editor. General Kislii confidentially explained to the editor, Savchenko, that the commissar was worried about reprisals since the soldiers knew that he confirmed all death sentences.[60]

Other commissars, such as Grodskii of the Second Army, Khodorov of

[58] For the Fifth Army cases, see *ibid.*, p. 273; *VOSR. Iiul'*, p. 429; *KA* 84:153; and various documents in *V boiakh za vlast' sovetov*, pp. 73-76. All are command reports. See also Stankevich, *Vospominaniia*, p. 194, who in addition to his own claims cites that of Filonenko.

[59] See *KA* 10:170. Selivachev was especially vexed with the requirement for the signatures of both the commissar and the commander, who would seldom agree, and appeals would delay the proceedings. He rightly did not expect many death penalties to be thus confirmed (*ibid.*, p. 172).

[60] Savchenko, "Okopnye Dumy" (Ms.; see n. 63, Chapter II), p. 33.

the Fifth, and Anardovich of the Eighth, zealously made use of the powers laid on them. On the other hand, the commissar of the Western Front, V. Iamandt, claimed that the courts in practice "corresponded neither to the spirit nor to the sense of the new law" and "caused terrible conflict between commanders and their troops, discrediting the very idea of such courts."[61] Commanders seized at every insignificant offense, including impertinent remarks, "stealing apples from a local *pomeshchik*'s garden," or "instigation to do the same." The questionable nature of the accusations led to extensive investigations to collect evidence, delays, and equally questionable verdicts, thus depriving the courts of their chief justification—exemplary justice for the most serious crimes. Ordinary soldiers with some justice regarded them as a device of the command to bring back the old order of things. As this lesson sunk in, the committeemen were forced to choose between their divided loyalties—the voice of higher democracy in favor of "decisive measures" or the soldiers' universal rejection of them. In the fight for their own survival against Kornilovism, by August the committeemen almost without exception yielded to the soldiers' views.

The extent to which the military-revolutionary courts pronounced sentences milder than death cannot even be approximated, and it is possible that Iamandt's opinion that they were abused for petty offenses was exaggerated. But the following reconstruction from archival court records may have been the more typical case. A certain Arsenii Nikitin was accused of agitation against the lawful orders of the Provisional Government and was sentenced to twelve years imprisonment. He was apprehended in the act on July 30, the proceedings were initiated on August 3, and they were concluded on August 5. The dossier consists of three or four depositions by witnesses, the report of the investigator (the company commander of the unit where it occurred), and a brief protocol of the trial itself, in all eight pages of material. The circumstances were quite simple though puzzling: a few days before the incident, Nikitin tried to join a "partisan detachment" (one of the many varieties of volunteer formations formed during the offensive), but he was refused because he did not have identity papers. Thus rebuffed, that night he stole the sword of a platoon commander of the detachment and went directly to the bivouac of a "storm unit" of the 17th Regiment of the Fifth Infantry Division (Second Army, Western Front), where he called a "meeting." He claimed that the partisan detachment had been sent to subdue the Fifth Division and arrest its agitators according to the new laws, which he denounced as illegal and a return to the old regime. Apparently he did not carry along his audience: a sergeant handily apprehended him and took him to the partisan detachment for

[61] See *RazA*, pp. 112-13.

verification of his identity, where it was established he had used a false name and had stolen the sword (he apparently hoped to be taken as an officer of the partisan detachment to gain entry to the bivouac of the storm unit). He was identified as a literate Cossack peasant lad called up in 1915. The reason he had entered into this strange charade was not even raised in the proceedings. The charge was simply agitation against lawful orders of the Provisional Government, which was quite trivial and easy to prove, but the court did not note that he was obviously a deserter from another unit, that he had impersonated an officer, that he was obviously bent on causing a major disruption, and that he may have been groomed for this role by the enemy or by the Bolsheviks. If proven, any one of these facts could have been grounds for a death sentence and probably merited handling by a professional military prosecutor or the military counter-intelligence. That it was handled so perfunctorily probably reflected some unwillingness to make a big affair of it, but it is impossible to determine from available materials.[62] Clearly the procedure was designed not to get at the root of criminal behavior but to serve as a deterrent to others.

☆

The military-revolutionary courts were thus more of symbolic than practical significance. It was simply not feasible to round up, try, and shoot the masses of soldiers who had been and technically continued to be in violation of the law (starting with deserters), and the evidence shows that actual proceedings were relatively few. The thousands and thousands of deserters rounded up on the Southwestern Front by patrolling highways and railroad stations or combing the countryside were usually returned to their units with very little ceremony, except perhaps a lecture by the commissar; sometimes their units voted "not to accept them" or demanded that they "acquit themselves" by the performance of "exemplary service" on the front line or that they pay for the boots and rifles they pitched away.[63] Among the returnees were many who had assaulted officers and made trouble in the past and were likely to do so in the future.

It appears that in many such units command and peer pressure kept the restless elements subdued for a time, allowing discipline in the units to

[62] All according to "Proceedings and Materials of the Military Revolutionary Courts Concerning the Enlisted Man Calling Himself Nikita Arsenev Attached to the Gruzinskii Partisan Detachment of August 2-5," in TsGVIA, f. 2335, op. 1, d. 282. The division was attached to the IX Corps of the Second Army, in which some major incident occurred around the middle of July. See report of Army Commander Fedotov of July 13, *RDRA*, p. 207.

[63] The example of the Ninth Finnish Rifle Regiment is cited by Selivachev (*KA* 10:213). On the mood of the First Finnish Rifle and the 159th Infantry divisions of the same corps as strongly against deserters, see command reports of the XXII Corps of July 18 and 19 in TsGVIA, f. 2222, op. 1, ed. khr. 1066, ll. 50 and 54.

improve, but there were still many units, frequently specific companies in specific regiments, which harbored agitators and successfully defied command control. The precedent of rounding up and disarming incorrigibly mutinous regiments under the supervision of commissars had already been established during the offensive. Now, however, Kerensky and Brusilov had issued categorical orders to remove all agitators, Bolshevik or otherwise, and bring them to trial for treason. This led to new operations, large and small, stretching over the months of July and August, which did break up the previous pattern of entire regiments and divisions forming independent republics; many such units were now either totally disbanded or thoroughly cleansed of their known agitators. Not only were large numbers of the latter removed from their nests, but, as in Petrograd, the genuine Bolsheviks were obliged to go underground and assume protective coloration; in fact, many of them were suddenly converted to discipline and order to "disprove" the slander that all Bolsheviks were "yellow-bellies." The net effect of these developments was a sharp reduction in the number of unsubdued units and an almost complete, if short-lived, disappearance of the demagogic type of agitation that had flourished during the offensive.

Still, not all the operations ended successfully. By their very nature there was a limit to their effectiveness, as units were invariably stubborn and evasive in delivering over their agitators until threatened with bombardment, and disbanding only served to spread the infection all along the front to relatively healthy units; furthermore, new levies of agitators were constantly arriving in replacement units from the rear. By mid-August there was a considerable resurgence of all the old phenomena, and the Kornilov affair simply blew the lid off.

The greatest amplitude in the swing from one extreme to the other occurred in the Fifth Army. After offensive operations were called off, between July 12 and 16, massive repressive actions were undertaken against the 120th, 121st, and 135th divisions. On July 12 General Danilov inquired of front headquarters where he should send 2,000 or so soldiers of the 540th Regiment (135th Division) which consisted "exclusively of robbers and hooligans."[64] Apparently alarmed by the vast number of soldiers already accumulating from earlier roundups (36th, 112th, and 166th divisions), the higher command instructed Danilov to compel obedience at the first sign of a rebellion, but to arrest only the agitators.[65] In this instance the regiment was surrounded by Hussars and ordered to surrender its arms and its agitators. The second battalion offered resistance, but yielded when the Germans, observing the dust raised by the Hussars, opened artillery

[64] *KA* 84:152.

[65] Order of July 13, *ibid.*, and *V boiakh za vlast' sovetov*, p. 68.

fire. Some 785 men were taken into custody, of which 58 were given over for trial. The remaining 1,560 men of the regiment were redistributed as replacements to other units of the XXXVII Corps.[66]

Purging operations were also applied to the 120th and 121st divisions, which had a long history of disruptive activity. On July 14, some 150 soldiers of the 481st Regiment who had deserted from their units were apprehended. The following day the regiment was disarmed and unburdened of its worst agitators, after which it was restored to the command of its regular officers. Considerable telegraph traffic accumulated over drawing up lists of those against whom charges were to be preferred (49 from thc 5th and 10th companies, 63 from another, half of whom had already fled). The charges ranged from refusal to execute orders and insubordination to open agitation against the offensive. The commander of the 482nd Regiment was reluctant to go through the process of drawing up lists, claiming that, since the reintroduction of the death penalty, discipline was nearly normal and all orders were being carried out (probably a disingenuous claim, reflecting his desire not to stir up new trouble).[67]

A total of 178 accused from the division were turned over to a special commission of the Fifth Army and sent to Dvinsk for processing. All the well-known Bolsheviks, such as Fedotov in the 480th Regiment, Lieutenant Selivanov in the 484th, and Lieutenant Frolov in the 483rd, were arrested on separate occasions. On July 20, two companies of Cossacks with artillery and armored cars carried out a similar operation against the 303rd Sennenskii Regiment—138 agitators, including the entire Bolshevik-oriented regimental committee, were separated out. They too were sent to Dvinsk under convoy.[68] The 17th Division even planned an armed protest against the death penalty which was to feature a mass march into Dvinsk; however, the Bolshevik leaders were apprehended without resistance, and thereafter Commissar Khodorov reported that the division was performing exemplary service. He also reported on arrests in the 78th, 717th, and 732nd regiments and the First Caucasus Division, all of which had a history of Bolshevik agitation. His report concluded with satisfaction that the mood in the army had now considerably improved and that further repressive actions would be unnecessary.[69] Proceedings against the rebellious soldiers

[66] Order of Fifth Army Chief of Staff Svechin of July 18, *VOSR. Iiul'*, p. 420.

[67] Report of July 17 in TsGVIA, f. 2434, op. 2, d. 427, l. 12. Copious material on drawing up lists and formulating charges is in the same file.

[68] All according to Commissar Khodorov's report for the period July 16-23, in *V boiakh za vlast' sovetov*, pp. 71-72.

[69] *Ibid.*, and Stavka survey for July 23-31 (*VOSR. Iiul'*, pp. 436-37), which noted that, unlike the Twelfth Army where the Bolsheviks were not yet under control, the Fifth Army could now be regarded as "battleworthy," though it conceded that the cancellation of the

of the Fifth Army were all combined and handled by an "Extraordinary Investigative Commission" established by the Fifth Army Committee. No less than 12,725 soldiers and 37 officers were taken into custody, of which 10,390 were reassigned to new units, 1,399 were returned to their old units, and 968 (including 32 officers) were held over for trial. Fifty-four separate cases were filed (a special composite Corps Court was established for the purpose), of which considerably less than half had been completed by the end of August (23 cases, 221 accused). Of these, only 15 were given prison sentences of ten years or more, 71 were given lesser sentences, and 98 (44 percent of the total) were exonerated.[70]

Of the armies on the Western Front, the Tenth had been hit heaviest by mutinies because of its active involvement in the offensive. The notorious Second Caucasus Grenadier Division remained unsubdued after the unsuccessful disarming operation of June 25. An "Investigative Commission" temporized over the matter until July 20, when it was carried through by means of artillery bombardment. Also slated for disbanding were two regiments of the 169th Division, which had refused orders to move up to the front for the offensive on July 5; the operation was carried out on July 7, taking eight hours because of stubborn resistance. Some 250 agitators were separated out, and the remaining soldiers were sent to the headquarters of the Second and Third armies for redistribution. The same procedure was followed for the mutinous elements of the First Caucasus Grenadier Division (1,000 men), ten companies of the 134th Division, and most of the 203rd Sukhumskii Regiment (also around 1,000 men). A punitive action against the 18th Vologda Regiment on July 21 also required a bombardment, during which five were killed and eight wounded. Of the above, only the Second Caucasus Grenadier Division and two regiments of the 169th were actually disbanded.[71]

The Second Army registered few such actions, but it was notable for an ugly incident. On July 30, General Purgasov, commander of the 299th Dubenskii Regiment, was murdered by his soldiers in reprisal for his efforts to rid the 12th company of a dangerous agitator, Lieutenant Loginov, whom they had installed as their commander when the regular company commander went on leave. When the latter returned and the company refused to receive him back, Purgasov declared the company disbanded. In response, another officer-agitator, Captain Orlov, led a soldier mob from the

operation had something to do with the restoration of calm and that the mood could easily be reversed in the near future.

[70] Summary of the investigation of August 31 in *RDRA*, pp. 376-77.

[71] See respective reports in *RDRA*, pp. 193, 210, 270, and 311; see also *VOSR. Iiul'*, pp. 410-11 and 426-27. On the Second Caucasus Grenadier Division, see L. S. Gaponenko, *Soldatskie massy zapadnogo fronta v bor'be za vlast' sovetov* (Moscow, 1953), p. 56.

first battalion on headquarters; the guard, consisting of the second battalion and mounted scouts, melted away, leaving Purgasov undefended. After surrounding him and taunting him for some time, someone threw sand in his eyes, and others descended on him with bayonets. Thereafter the regiment resumed the routine life of their bivouac under its chosen leaders. A punitive detachment from the 75th Division did not arrive until August 7, subduing the rebels with the threat of gunfire. Taken into custody were 214 soldiers of the 12th company and 28 others, including Lieutenant Longinov and the alleged chief perpetrator of the crime, a Muslim named Hamidulla. Also arrested was a Captain Grebenshchikov, who was accused of organizing the whole affair because he was elected chairman of the regimental committee after the murder and exercised de facto command. Commissar Grodskii's report stated that the 299th Regiment was a hitherto well-disciplined regiment spoiled by replacements from disbanded units, whom he characterized as former police and gendarmes. Once these disreputable elements were removed, he claimed, the regiment resumed its former model discipline. Grodskii's version is somewhat suspect: two former rural policemen, one actually a simple forest guard, were indeed among the culprits, but unexplained were the excessive number of officer-agitators and an elected committee that had taken a conspicuous part in the affair.[72]

The Third Army commander, General Kvetsynskii, was particularly zealous in carrying out operations to purge agitators, for which he had the full cooperation of the Third Army Committee. He instructed all corps commanders to publish the War Minister's orders to this effect and to report back to him on measures taken; he summarized the results in a report of July 25 to front headquarters. In the XV Corps several arrests and court proceedings had already been undertaken and further investigations were in progress; in the XVI Corps the order had been read to all units, and seven arrests had been undertaken in the 221st Regiment; in the XX Corps agitators had been removed from three regiments that had mutinied on July 5, and two others, both officers, had been apprehended in the 532nd Regiment and proceedings initiated.[73] The only major punitive action was against the 174th Division on July 20; its outcome, described in a command report, merits citing at length:

[72] See report of Western Front Chief of Staff M. P. Alekseev of August 2, *RDRA*, pp. 287-88, and Commissar Grodskii's report of August 8 in *RazA*, pp. 98-99. For the sentence of the military-revolutionary court, see *VOA*, August 19. Fourteen soldiers, some of them "gendarmes," were found guilty; Hamidulla was sentenced to death, two "instigators" were given twelve years imprisonment. Also reported in *IzGr*, August 20.

[73] *RDRA*, pp. 271-72.

> Since the 293rd Regiment refused to surrender Shvaikin [the agitator] and several others subject to arrest, it was surrounded at 5:00 by a detachment under the command of Col. Krasnov . . . [who] gave them 15 minutes to consider. The regiment broke into small bands, part of them occupying trenches north of the village Bela, and others, breaking through the line of cossacks, seized the battery of the 28th Artillery Brigade, from which they fired seven rounds on Krasnov's detachment and the 174th Division headquarters. The rebels also occupied batteries of the 8th and 17th heavy artillery divisions, but could not compel them to take part in the rebellion. A training unit of the 29th Division deserted Col. Krasnov's detachment. At the present time the soldiers of the 693rd Regiment are still dug in north of Bela and are exchanging fire with Krasnov's Cossacks. . . . Part of the 694th regiment has joined the rebels.[74]

To put an end to the affair it was necessary to bring into action a storm battalion, another of grenadiers, a second brigade of cossacks with horse artillery, and loyal units of the 695th and 696th regiments. Shvaikin and two co-conspirators were tried on August 1 by a military-revolutionary court and shot, while twenty or so others received various prison terms. The 693rd Regiment and the training unit of the 29th Division were disbanded.[75] An investigation by the Third Army Committee revealed that Shvaikin was an extremely clever agitator who had trained a band of hecklers to disrupt meetings of the regimental committee and played heavily on antiofficer and even anti-Semitic sentiments. He also managed to divert regimental funds and grain alcohol from the infirmary to set up a still. Repentant soldiers of the regiment explained to investigators that delegates sent to Petrograd in April had somehow "fallen in with the Bolsheviks" and returned as hard-core agitators.[76]

In the Eleventh Army (Southwestern Front) there were a considerable number of unresolved mutinies and in nearly every division a stubborn, well-organized band of agitators. As of July 11, three out of four regiments of the 20th Infantry Division were still under the influence of certain officer-agitators headed by a Lieutenant Brechko. An attempt at disarming by Commissar Chekotilo using cavalry had failed, and thereafter, the commander complained, the soldiers turned into a band of hooligans, ambushing cavalry and artillerymen and intimidating them into passivity. It

[74] *Ibid.*, pp. 231-32.

[75] Report of the Quartermaster of the Western Front of August 2, *ibid.*, p. 289. In October, soldiers of these units dispersed through the Third Army were said to have disoriented the entire XX Corps. See staff survey for October 14-21, *ibid.*, p. 535.

[76] *Go3A*, July 26 and 27.

was difficult to go after them because two of the regiments occupied forward trenches which they agreed to defend, but they would not fire on the enemy. A congress of the XXXII Corps, in almost continuous session during the retreat to assist in maintaining order, tried to resolve the matter by inviting Lieutenant Brechko and Starozum, his loyal lieutenant in the 80th Kabardinskii Regiment, to present their case to the corps congress. The congress demanded that the recalcitrant units ''submit to the democratic majority,'' but the encounter ended in a shouting match. Assistant Commissar Dr. Israilantz claimed that only one regiment still held out and that he had to rescue Starozum, who was in danger for his life from his own regiment. Several days later Brechko and his chief supporters were taken into custody under unclear circumstances, and the corps congress thoroughly overhauled the committee system, bringing the lower committees under its control.[77]

A similar situation developed in the Turkestan Corps, but was peacefully resolved by committees in cooperation with the commissar and army committee representatives.[78] Two regiments of the 46th Division resisted pacification until pounded by artillery fire, and the 487th and 13th Finnish Rifle Regiments also yielded to force. All these units were ultimately disbanded. However, the Sixth Grenadier Division, which included the disgraced 607th Mlynovskii Regiment, was able to secure the reversal of an order on disbanding, probably because it was clear that a major military operation would be necessary to accomplish it.[79]

When Denikin took over command of the Southwestern Front in late July, he ordered a new purge of the I Guards Corps. Some 753 of the harmful element were successfully removed from the Moskovskii Regiment, but when the same measures were applied against the Pavlovskiis (a list of 147 harmful types had been drawn up) the company and regimental committees refused to cooperate. The commander of the Eleventh Army, General Rerberg, who already had a reputation as a tough pacifier, felt obliged to inform Denikin that this order was not only counter-productive, but unjust. He claimed that during the retreat the guards units, the majority of the Pavlovskiis included, had carried out orders and that if Denikin insisted on the execution of his order the entire I Guards Corps might slip out of control.[80]

The Staff survey for the Southwestern Front of July 23, otherwise reporting only comforting information, records that when Lieutenant So-

[77] *GO*, July 12 and 19.

[78] See report of commander of July 16, *VOSR. Iiul'*, pp. 417-18.

[79] From report of the Quartermaster of the Southwestern Front to Stavka of July 23, *RDRA*, pp. 268-69.

[80] Report of August 4, *ibid.*, p. 300. He noted that Commissar Chekotilo, the Pavlovskii officers, and all command personnel agreed.

kolovskii, the chief agitator in the 707th Neshavskii Regiment (the one guilty of beating General Liubitskii), was taken into custody, the first battalion surrounded staff headquarters and secured his release. Though committee persuasion restored calm, the regiment remained unsubdued, since the court case against Sokolovskii was dropped for "lack of evidence."[81] It seems likely that other such maverick regiments remain unidentified. In the Eighth Army, which was thoroughly exhausted by several weeks of rear-guard fighting that continued into August, Bolshevik agitators and other troublemakers were removed in half a dozen or so divisions, including the 117th, 79th, and Third Transamur. Major disbandings and punitive actions took place against the 47th, 79th, and 160th divisions.[82]

The outcome in the 160th Division illustrates the increasing difficulty of liquidating these affairs. Unrest affected three of the four regiments when an execution squad refused to carry out the sentence of a military-revolutionary court. A telephonist named Sidelev, said to be a Bolshevik, organized mass meetings of protest against the wishes of the regular committee. The persuasions of Commissar Arnadovich saved the officers from reprisals, but otherwise ended in stalemate: he could not dissuade them from passing a resolution against the death penalty or from sending a ten-man delegation to Petrograd to secure the revocation of the death penalty, while the insurgents posted machine guns outside the headquarters and dug in. Not until August 17 was a punitive operation with cavalry and artillery undertaken. The 638th Regiment defied the order to lay down their arms, using the officers as hostages. The cavalry, disgusted with the proceedings, allowed the revolting soldiers to slip through their ring and even threatened to arrest their own commander. The mutiny was never liquidated.[83]

Two further incidents in August illustrate the declining effectiveness of repression. On August 1 soldiers of the First Guards Rifle Regiment viciously murdered their acting commander, Colonel Bykov, and a company commander. The pretext was Bykov's attempt to liberate a Red Cross doctor whom the soldiers were convinced was a German spy. He later had organized the gathering of grain from the local peasants in pursuit of a command order to harvest all possible grain in anticipation of a new German attack (the remainder was to be put to the torch). The soldiers chose to interpret this as collusion between the officers and the local *pomeshchiki* to sell it to the Germans. The soldiers were simultaneously settling an old score for which they held Bykov and other officers responsible. (A few days previously a military-revolutionary court in the division had con-

[81] *Ibid.*, p. 269.

[82] Data in Frenkin, *Revoliutsionnoe dvizhenie na rumynskom fronte*, pp. 112ff.

[83] *Ibid.*, pp. 113-14, and report of XVI Corps commander of August 8, *RDRA*, pp. 302-303.

demned a soldier who had stolen a silver cigar from a local *pomeshchik* to life imprisonment.) For nearly a week the naked corpses of the two slain victims lay exposed on the bank of a river, subjected to profanations by the soldiers. Finally, on August 8, a punitive force of Orenburg Cossacks secured the surrender of the bodies and 814 rebels. Still, the rest of the division remained out of control until the Kornilov affair, and the order to disband the guilty regiment remained unexecuted.[84]

The second such case, the mutiny of the Third Infantry Division at the end of August, also ended in tragedy. Commissar Linde, the same who had brought out the Finlandskii Guards Regiment during the April Crisis, overreached himself in trying to carry through a disarming operation. Shouting curses in his thick German-sounding accent, hc ignored warnings of the threatening danger by General Krasnov, who led the punitive force. The cossacks witnessing the scene withdrew in disgust, leaving Linde exposed to the wrath of the soldiers. A short time later the commander of the division, General Girshfeld, who boldly tried to intervene, was seized and lynched.[85]

☆

What is most striking in this series of punitive actions is the relatively small number of units disbanded, compared with the great number guilty of disorders and chronic agitation. Even in the Tenth Army only the Second Caucasus Grenadiers and two regiments of the 169th were actually disbanded, whereas four others equally as bad were merely disarmed and obliged to disgorge their agitators. Disorders in this army had affected well over half the divisions (17 out of 23). Roughly the same situation obtained in the Fifth Army, where only a single division, two regiments, and a few lesser units had been broken up, though the numbers of arrested reached massive numbers. In most other armies only one or two major operations resulted in disbanding, and on the Rumanian and Caucasus fronts, none at all. Major disorders were very rare in July and only somewhat more frequent in August, while the evidence points to a much-improved climate of discipline and order.

Certainly the well-advertised tough measures and the knowledge of their application in a few instances had had their impact; nevertheless, they do not merit that exclusive potency ascribed to them by the command. The relative absence of major disorders was much more a function of the removal of their major cause, the ill-advised offensive; Kornilov ordered the cancellation of active operations on the Southwestern Front on July 9,

[84] See Vertsinskii's account (*God revoliutsii*, pp. 31-46), which includes his report on the affair. See also Selivachev's reaction, (*KA* 10:168-69 and 174) and report of Southwestern Front Quartermaster Orlov to Stavka of August 22 (*RDRA*, pp. 332-34).

[85] See account of General Krasnov, "Na vnutrennom fronte," *AR* 1 (1922): 105-12.

and Brusilov did the same for the Northern and Western fronts on July 12.[86] On the Southwestern Front, however, the decisive influence on the change in mood was the retreat itself, which more than anything else "sobered up" the troops.

Staff reports of the XXII Corps, which included three Finnish Rifle divisions, the 159th Infantry, and a Polish division, reflect this quite dramatically. The First Finnish Rifle Division registered a marked change for the better on July 18, which a report attributed to the fact that after a week of uninterrupted retreat the soldiers were "drawing near to the borders of the homeland." The sentiment was now heard that "we have to get down to business and stop the chatter." Not only was there an eagerness to do battle and a growing hostility to deserters, but even the death penalty was said to have been accepted with equanimity. Comments such as "The mood of the troops is improving," "Battle commands are being executed punctiliously," "Work details are being carried out without discussion" became commonplace. Agitators had either quieted down or deserted. On July 23 in the Fifth Finnish Rifle Division the 17th Regiment was rated "satisfactory," the 18th "excellent," and the 19th "improving"; in the 20th Regiment the agitators no longer operated in the open, but "secretly still do a good bit of harm."[87] Army Commander Selivachev expressed his satisfaction with a folklore image: "A remarkable thing—as soon as Mikula Selianovich touches the earth, he recovers his strength." He recorded the declared positions of the 159th and Third Finland divisions and the Volynskii Guards Regiment in favor of counter-attacks, the latter even taking the position of "no prisoners" (unless they were Austrians).[88] Willingness to fight, however, was apparently not incompatible with wild plundering and violence against the civilian population, as the same units sometimes engaged in both. A report on the Fifth Finnish Division of July 17, for example, observed that "plundering is not regarded by all soldiers as a crime" and suggested a few exemplary shootings.[89]

A report of August 3 on the XI Corps of the Eighth Army noted similar improvements, attributing them even-handedly to the latest measures of the government, the sobering effect of the disgrace of retreat, and successful counter-attacks which netted captives. Most units were described as welcoming the death penalty, though the 125th Regiment regarded it as a "return to the old regime."[90] The Stavka survey for the last week in July

[86] See Zaionchkovskii, *Kampaniia 1917 g.*, p. 83.

[87] See TsGVIA, f. 2222, op. 1, ed. khr. 1066, ll. 54, 55, and 74.

[88] Entry for July 17, *KA* 10:152.

[89] TsGVIA, f. 2222, op. 1, ed. khr. 1066, l. 53.

[90] *RDRA*, pp. 292-93.

notes fairly uniform trends on all fronts, the summary for the Rumanian Front holding for the average:

> The mood is improving under the influence of the most recent orders. Relations between officers and soldiers are improving. . . . The revolutionary courts have produced a sobering effect. The soldiers are beginning to recognize the need for a stubborn defense, and resistance to the attacks of the enemy has greatly increased. Desertions are diminishing. Cases of fraternization have not been observed. Resistance to military orders, work details, and training exercises has not been encountered, though there have been cases of instigation to the same. Relations with commanders have been worked out. The introduction of repressions is ascribed entirely to the desire of the officers to bring back the old regime. Awareness of the need for a renewal of the offensive and the bringing of the war to a victorious conclusion can now be observed.[91]

The glaring contradiction between the last two observations did not seem to draw the attention of the framers of the report, who manifestly strove for a buoyant tone. The command overlooked that the soldiers outwardly conformed for their own reasons: the Germans could not be allowed to sweep into the interior of Mother Russia. A primordial peasant patriotism did finally assert itself, but it did not transform underlying attitudes toward officers or the war in general.

The more typical attitude toward officers was expressed by a group of artillerists, normally the most disciplined soldiers, who were lined up to hear the reading of a Kornilov order that referred to the ''criminality'' of the troops during the retreat. On hearing this assertion they broke ranks and threatened the officers with violence. In their view, a report stated, the retreat had been ''prepared long ago by the officers themselves to have an excuse to reintroduce repressive measures.''[92] In early August, when General Vertsinkii took over the Guards Rifle Division, he was perplexed that the soldiers willingly lined up for parade, answered his greetings crisply as under the old regime, yet were determined not to continue the war and harbored a paranoid fear that the officers would deliberately ''open up the front.'' The latter sentiment sometimes took the most grotesque forms, as, for example, the rumor that when General Selivachev flew over the enemy lines to study their positions he was signaling the Germans the place for a breakthrough.[93] Sources attuned to the soldiers' views testify to an un-

[91] Stavka survey of armies for July 23-31, *VOSR. Iiul'*, p. 439.

[92] Report of the Commander of the Eighth Army, F. S. Rerberg, on the Third Artillery Brigade of the VI Corps, August 4, *RDRA*, p. 299.

[93] Vertsinskii, pp. 34-35.

diminished longing for peace. The commander of the First Finnish Rifle Division, for example, while giving his men high marks for improved morale and discipline during the retreat, commented on July 25 that "voices are now heard of a speedy peace as a matter already decided."[94]

The important battles that stabilized the line were fought on July 17-21 in Galicia and somewhat later in Rumania. Once the hot breath of the invading armies was no longer felt, life in the trenches and bivouacs resumed a routine character, and a typical August mood set in—the soldiers withdrew into themselves, lackadaisically observed military routine, avoided direct confrontations over orders, but dragged their feet in various ways to slow down military efficiency; least of all did they confide their true feelings to officers or even to their committees. The best description of the predominant mood which accords with other indicators was a commissar's report on the Western Front for August 12-19:

> No changes for the better have been observed. External order has not been violated, training exercises and work orders are being executed without murmur, but the mood is deeply apathetic. Service is rendered as a heavy burden. Interest in political questions has weakened. . . . Again the question of survival has taken the upper hand. In the trenches and in the reserve, conversations are only about peace, leaves, food, and finally the winter campaign.[95]

It also observed that while desertions and fraternization were down, card-playing, distilling spirits, fishing with grenades, and like behavior were up; committees were ignored and military tasks were no longer taken seriously. Incidents connected with the rotation of units on the line were again becoming more frequent, which seemed to be linked to the arrival of new replacements from the rear. This clearly shaping mood indicated that the gains from the "firm measures" and the "sobering effects" of military reverses were far from permanent and had not touched the soldiers' basic attitudes.

Kal'nitskii offers an intimate glimpse into the soldiers' life in this period. Relations with the command were very tense over a trivial incident: a soldier had been caught digging potatoes from a peasant's plot, and the commander had ordered a beating rather than turn him over to the non-functioning courts. Kal'nitskii, as chairman of the regimental committee, asked Commissar Chekotilo to remove the commander, but Chekotilo brusquely refused. The commander himself explained that he preferred "paternal exhortations" to shooting (the presumed verdict of a military-

[94] TsGVIA, f. 2222, op. 1, ed. khr. 1. 75.

[95] *RDRA*, p. 343.

revolutionary court) and read out to the committee Kornilov's order forbidding committees to interfere in matters of command responsibility. The makings for an ugly confrontation were present, but Kal'nitskii persuaded the committee to limit itself to a resolution: "All cases of beating are to be reported to us. . . . The commander is requested not to beat."[96] Each side contented itself with symbolic gestures, but tacitly agreed not to push matters to a crisis. Henceforward, Kal'nitskii states, routines were observed and confrontations were avoided.

Even a new incident failed to provoke a break. On August 20 Captain Belkin demoted several machine-gunners to the ranks, and his men demanded that he be removed. Kal'nitskii "mediated" the dispute, and both sides backed down. He characterized his policy as "by any truth or fiction to work out conflicts in a domestic fashion."[97] This suggests that the calm of August observed in many places up and down the front did not represent any fundamental reorientation by either officers or soldiers, but rather a respite from the unending conflicts of which both sides were tiring. Both were awaiting a new turn of events. The explosion of the Kornilov affair, which involved every layer of the army, is incomprehensible unless one correctly understands the situation in July and August.

One suspects that behind the bold rhetoric in reports of unit commanders lay many de facto compromises. The relative absence of major and minor incidents alone testifies to that. What seems untypical in Kal'nitskii's account is the claimed conscious calculation by his committee while maintaining the support of its constituency. More typical seems to have been estrangement between soldiers and committees, the latter yielding to pressure from commanders and commissars to draw in their horns. Their catharsis was to preoccupy themselves with routine housekeeping matters, forgoing direct contact with a deeply alienated soldier mass.

Thus, the general proposition which recent investigators have advanced for other mass constituencies in the rear (Rabinowitch, Raleigh, Koenker, Mandel) holds, namely, that the revolutionary ardor of the masses indeed cooled for a time, but was by no means extirpated, and the interlude is to be interpreted more as reflecting temporary confusion and reassessment (in Koenker's apt phrase, a period of "institutional malaise") than as disenchantment with the Revolution or visceral fear of reprisals. Soldiers at the front were more willing to hold the line against the Germans than soldiers and workers in the rear, but like the latter they viewed submission to "firm authority" (revolutionary or otherwise) as a truce or tactical retreat; more than the latter they were confident that counter-revolutionary

[96] Kal'nitskii, *Ot fevralia k oktiabriu*, pp. 107-13.
[97] *Ibid.*, p. 113.

forces could easily be dealt with in any new confrontation. Again the relatively handy victory over Kornilov is the best proof.

☆

The front Bolsheviks paid a very heavy penalty during the period of repressions, far more so than those in the rear. One reason was that except for Riga and Minsk they lacked an urban base which could protect their infrastructure and communications network. It was far less possible than in the rear to hide "underground" because usually the entire regiment, including the commanders and the committees, knew who the local Bolsheviks were. Along with countless homespun agitators and "instant Bolsheviks" from the rear, many party Bolsheviks were carried away in the roundups of July, including a number of the well-known personalities. Krylenko was apprehended handily on July 15 at a railroad station near Mogilev while returning to his home unit from his prolonged visit to the capital.[98] Lieutenant Sivers, one of the founders of *Okopnaia Pravda*, was lured to the headquarters of the XLIII Corps and arrested; in the same fashion other well-known Bolsheviks of the Twelfth Army were removed—Dr. Glezer, Captain Sobetskii, Lieutenant Zhuk, and a soldier-agitator, Ivan Vish.[99] In the Fifth Army the dangerous P. F. Fedotov and his close assistant Letunov in the 120th Division were arrested. Lieutenant V. S. Denisenko, the leading Bolshevik in the 143rd Dorogobuzhskii Regiment, names a long list of Bolsheviks, including himself, caught up in the net of mass arrests, chiefly from the 36th, 135th, and 22nd regiments, but how many of these can be regarded as bona fide party Bolsheviks cannot be determined. At the same time, he mentions several important Bolshevik leaders that remained at large and kept an underground network together (E. M. Sklianskii, A. I. Sediakin, I. M. Kriger, and N. D. Sobakin).[100] A study of the Eighth Army by M. S. Frenkin identifies a number of later prominent Bolsheviks who were arrested at this time—I. T. Dunaev, Ia. M. Muravnik, Lysenko, and I. F. Kuchmin—but he also names others who escaped arrest: Lieutenant Ovchinnikov, Shmelev, and Kniazev, all of the XXXIII Corps.[101] Muravnik and Lysenko later escaped arrest with the help of pro-Bolshevik soldiers and continued to work underground.

Soviet investigations provide few names of arrested Bolsheviks from other armies, but it seems to be primarily a problem of verification. Staff reports certainly identify a good number of arrested agitators as Bolsheviks,

[98] See *RDRA*, p. 224, citing *Kievskaia Mysl'* of July 16.

[99] See *ON*, July 23 and 26. Khaustov and Stepanovich had been arrested earlier (*ibid.*, June 21). For others, see *ONFV*, p. 63.

[100] *ONFV*, p. 104.

[101] Frenkin, *Revoliutsionnoe dvizhenie*, pp. 116-17. All of them later turned up as activists in MRCs of the Eighth Army in November. See below, pp. 368-70.

and of them it seems fairly certain that some were party Bolsheviks (e.g., Starozum of the 32nd Division and Vasilev of the Finlandskii Guards Regiment). Other identifiable Bolsheviks, however, were able to survive the repressions by remaining inconspicuous or by cultivating a devoted soldier clientele in disrupted units. In the XXV Corps, for example, prominent Bolsheviks M. N. Kokovikhin and G. V. Razzhivin, as well as less-prominent Bolshevik memoirists F. Popov and K. G. Eremin, were untouched. A good many front Bolsheviks weathered the storm, as evidenced by the number of them who resurfaced immediately after the Kornilov affair and the many experienced Bolshevik personnel who were available to take over army committees in November. The vagueness of many personal accounts in Soviet memoir collections concerning this period, which are quite vivid on the offensive and on later October events, suggests that most survived simply by keeping a low profile. For example, two Bolsheviks later to become key activists in the Seventh Army—V. A. Malakhovskii and I. V. Tuzhikov—were nested in the Sixth Regiment of the Second Finnish Rifle Division, which drew such glowing praise for its exemplary discipline during the retreat in the above-cited archival reports.[102] Though their political identity was undoubtedly well known to the soldiers of their units, they were in little danger of exposure. The Bolsheviks, like the soldier masses, were biding their time.

[102] See F. V. Popov, *Rasskaz o nezabyvaemom (zapiski bol'shevika)* (Kiev, 1961), pp. 45ff., and Eremin, *Soldatskie versty*, pp. 48-55; on Kokovykhin, Malakovskii, and Tuzhikov, see their respective brief (and rather schematized) memoirs in *ONFV*, pp. 154-56, 167-68, and 200ff. In all these accounts the months of July and August are dismissed with unrevealing clichés or ignored entirely.

CHAPTER V

REVOLUTIONARY ORGANS UNDER SIEGE

IN THE FIRST HALF of 1917, committees had become a seemingly indispensable part of the military landscape. Most commanders had accepted them and cultivated workable relations, though it was a humiliating admission of the diminution of their authority. Few had the hardihood to push matters to a confrontation, as that would have deprived them of the sole means for getting things done and risked their forcible removal. The commissars appeared as an even more direct rival authority, bearing implied though not yet codified powers to intervene, to call to account and even to remove commanders they thought unsuitable. Commissars and committees took their responsibilities in connection with the offensive very seriously, not infrequently overstepping the boundary into operative matters. However galling it may have been, most commanders, Denikin and Kornilov included, appealed to revolutionary organs for assistance no less frequently than in the early days of the Revolution, particularly when they were needed to secure the execution of orders. Some washed their hands completely and surrendered to their rivals the responsibility of carrying the troops into battle.

The failure of the offensive and the panic over the retreat brought a sharp change in attitude in many officers up and down the chain of command. The psychological recoil fostered the sentiment that commissars and committeemen were to blame for all the travails of the Army and that the moment had arrived to eliminate them altogether. Long-repressed resentments erupted through the surface, and, encouraged by the tough new measures of the government and the ultimative posturings of Kornilov, they took a stance of irreconcilable hostility to the committee system. Suddenly, committees faced a multitude of petty obstacles to their work, as well as tough reprisals for fancied infractions up to and including court proceedings. Commanders had to treat commissars more circumspectly, but acrimonious conflicts became more commonplace, and in certain instances (with Denikin, for example) reached an impasse. The outlook that was to distinguish the Kornilov camp was rapidly falling into shape: the officer-martyrs of the glorious Russian Army were now called upon to rescue the Army and the nation from the babel of partisan politics and to reestablish the integrity of command and state authority. Since the Provisional Government had proven itself incapable of imposing this discipline, a Leader from the ranks of the Army was to rise up and impose it for them. Kornilov lit up the path with his heroic stance on the death penalty, and around him quickly crystallized an agenda of counter-reform: the abolition or severe curtailment of commissars and committees, the restoration of disciplinary powers to officers, and the extension of the death penalty to the rear and to civilian as well as military corrupters of the body politic. The democratic camp was inclined to equate this movement with counter-revolution and the restoration of tsarism, though Denikin, Alekseev, and Kornilov in particular were stoutly to deny such designs. Rather, it was a Russian manifestation of the conservative military temperament which espouses the virtues of social order and discipline and finds little patience with the irregularities of democratic politics, particularly under the exigencies of war. The paradigm of the Army was instinctively transferred to the life of the state and the nation at large.

With Kornilov's appointment as Commander in Chief (July 20), a flood of positive signals coursed through the channels of command, and commanders no longer troubled to be subtle or devious. They flatly turned down committees' requests, transferred troublesome members, forbade officers to participate in committee activities, and trumped up charges against them. The committees, already in disarray in the latter part of July from other causes, were reluctant to counter in kind because they had just committed themselves to restoring the prestige of command authority for the sake of military order. Kornilov's audaciousness, coupled with disturbing signs of the revival of the political Right, persuaded them by the last week in July that a serious battle must be joined if they were to survive at all. Well before the Kornilov affair an intense struggle took place for ascendancy in the Army between the command and the organs of revolutionary democracy. This chapter will attempt to chronicle this struggle for power, which hitherto has attracted little attention, but must be taken into account as the prelude and backdrop to the Kornilov affair.

☆

Prior to the June offensive, the resentment of the commanders toward committees usually had to be suppressed. The penalties for overt hostility were revealed in an incident that occurred in the 741st Infantry Regiment of the Twelfth Army on June 10. A "conciliation commission" of the regimental committee tried to interview a company commander on the conflict but was rebuffed with the following comment: "I'm very busy right now with a session of the officers' committee and have no time to talk to you." Realizing the irreparable breach of decorum, he asked his superiors to be relieved of command.[1] The more characteristic method of dealing with obstreperous committees is documented for the 742nd Regiment: the committee had countermanded an order to send machine-gun ammunition up to the line, threatened the commander with removal for holding up mail, and otherwise committed flagrantly illegal acts, but the division commander referred the matter for adjudication to Iskosol (the Twelfth Army Committee).[2] Invoking command authority against committees was still regarded as too risky. Hostility expressed itself instead in mild symbolic gestures, as when General Gerua, vexed that committeemen during interviews draped themselves over his divan and available chairs, had the furniture removed and henceforward received them in front of his desk, riveting them to the entrance.[3]

Offensive operations immeasurably increased the occasions for friction, as committees were inclined to make their own dispositions and to make endless inquiries and suggestions, sowing confusion by their lack of expertise. Lieutenant General Baluev, commander of the turbulent 116th Division, protested to the indulgent General Radko-Dmitriev over the latter's instructions for cooperating with committees during the forthcoming operations in the Twelfth Army:

> Allow me, Mr. General, to point out a few serious conflicts with the principles of military organization. . . . During the conduct of operations no sort of joint work with elective organizations should take place. . . . Tacit dual authority is out of place and not permissible. By conversations and persuasions you are not going to prevent soldiers from fleeing their positions during battle. . . . Until the Army is delivered from regimental and higher committees, meetings, and *politikanstvo*, there will be no return of discipline to the Army.[4]

Such boldness, however, was possible only toward one's superiors, not toward committees. The frustration and resentment smoldered underneath the surface until the collapse of the offensive.

General Selivachev, appointed commander of the Seventh Army in early July, has left a remarkably intimate record of his relations with committees and commissars. On July 2 he had his first brush with the Seventh Army Committee, which had requested clarification of a rumor that the Seventh

[1] Archive of the 186th Division, TsGVIA, f. 2486, op. 1, ed. khr. 2, l. 65.

[2] *Ibid.*, l. 4.

[3] Gerua, *Vospominaniia*, 2:177.

[4] TsGVIA, Special Documents (f. 2031, op. 1, d. 1555, l. 94).

Army was to be disbanded. Selivachev accused the committee of fomenting panic and declared that even if such a preposterous order were given it was the duty of all concerned to obey it out without question. When a committeeman objected that this would disorganize the work of the army committee, Selivachev shot back: "I daresay operational imperatives take precedence over the convenience of committees; committees derive their existence from that of the Army and not vice versa." Observing the right of commissars to remove unsuitable higher commanders, the committee claimed for itself the right to remove staff officers. Selivachev rejoined that neither had such a right, as military law provided that officers were subject to removal only by their superior officers for cause. Moreover, Selivachev accused them of dereliction of duty in failing to nominate two members to the accelerated corps courts, a directive already ten days old. To his diary he confided: "The composition of the committee is outright anarchistic and it will scarcely be possible to work with it."[5] Selivachev had scarcely given the committee a fair hearing, but at the same time the committee's pretentiousness would have sorely tried the most tactful of commanders. The committee's demands clearly suggested that commanders were not to be trusted because they harbored counter-revolutionary designs. In fact, the thought was rapidly becoming the mother of the deed.

During the retreat, Selivachev's relations with the army committee rapidly deteriorated. On July 14 he noted with relief the War Minister's orders that committees confine themselves to the limits outlined in Order No. 213 of April 16. On July 16 he had a serious conflict with the army committee over his order forbidding appeals to higher committees or commissars over the heads of commanders, and he threatened to resign his command if it were not acknowledged. He demanded that henceforward they state all their requests in writing.[6] Selivachev began to collect a dossier on violations of legality by committees, which he intended to forward to General Kornilov (now his front chief) at the appropriate moment.

Selivachev ran into even more serious conflicts with the commissars. Savinkov had been the commissar for the Seventh Army, but had moved on to the front level before Selivachev took over command. His temporary replacement, Grigoriev, aroused Selivachev's ire over the use of cavalry in punitive actions without consulting him. The new commissar, Zagorskii, backed Selivachev in this dispute, dismissing Grigoriev, and brought in his own assistant, Surguchev. Relations with Surguchev went smoothly, the method of handling disorders being worked out amicably between them. Selivachev was impressed with Surguchev's toughness and loyalty, even

[5] *KA* 10:141-42.

[6] *Ibid.*, p. 150.

to the extent of ordering the arrest of an entire regimental committee that had balked at obeying a direct order. But Selivachev still had to deal with Grigoriev, now Savinkov's assistant, who demanded that Selivachev arrest an army prosecutor for insulting Savinkov to his face. In the midst of the German breakthrough, Savinkov showed up at the Seventh Army headquarters and demanded: "We insist that you hand over to the courts all culpable commanders. Thank God we now have the death penalty which doesn't apply only to soldiers." Selivachev replied: "You won't frighten with the death penalty those who have faced death many times in battle, but you might consider applying it against those who have ruined the Army."[7] The army committee even demanded the arrest and trial of the entire commanding staff of the Seventh Army. Zagorskii's good offices apparently cooled down tempers, which had been made edgy by the retreat, and no arrests were made. When Zagorskii was recalled by Savinkov a short time later, Selivachev was sure it was "for not arresting anybody, for not getting rid of generals and commanders, for not participating in shootings, and in general for not upholding the prestige of the commissar." Selivachev relished the telegram he fired off to Savinkov (with a copy to General Kornilov): "Why have you removed my commissar, my closest colleague on questions concerning internal politics?" Two days later the commissariat arrested Selivachev's own adjutant for having instructed a sentinel in the presence of an unfriendly orderly to "keep his rifle at the ready to drive off the commissar scum [*svoloch*]."[8]

Though Selivachev's bile was perhaps more developed than most, it is clear that the same issues were provoking similar clashes at other levels of command. On July 21 General Nazarbekov, commander of the Second Caucasus Rifle Division, outlined a proposal for the proscription of politics in the Army, the restoration of saluting, the forbidding of meetings, the abolition of higher committees, and tight restrictions on lower committees. In a similar minute of July 22, General Baiov, commander of the 42nd Division, argued that if a genuine, permanent restoration of authority in the Army were desired, then not only Bolshevik agitators should be removed, but "the entire system of deputies and committees, starting with the Petrograd Soviet."[9] It was symptomatic of the sharply altered climate that they felt bold enough to advance such proposals to their superiors.

Also raising its voice at this time was the Union of Officers.[10] Established

[7] *Ibid.*, p. 148.

[8] *Ibid.*, p. 153.

[9] See *RDRA*, pp. 263 and 264-66.

[10] For origins of the Officers' Union, see the excellent account in George Katkov, *The Kornilov Affair: Kerensky and the Breakup of the Russian Army* (London and New York, 1980), pp. 11-14.

in May by staff officers at Stavka, it then assumed the guise of a "professional organization" dedicated to the revival of the fighting capacity of the Army and the dissemination of technical military knowledge; at the same time, however, it vowed to defend the "honor" of the officers' corps besmirched by unspecified foes under the cover of the Revolution. How many officers adherred to the Union of Officers in May and June is open to question, but that it created an important communications network with the staffs of all parts of the Army cannot be doubted. The hidden agenda of the Union of Officers revealed itself in July in an open letter to War Minister Kerensky circulated through the staff communications network, endorsing Kornilov's call for the death penalty. A second point categorically demanded "the full restoration of the authority and disciplinary rights of commanders at all levels without restrictions by irresponsible collegial institutions."[11] Thus the army committees were alerted to the ultimate goals of the Union of Officers and began to suspect a conspiracy. A number of committee organs immediately raised the alarm, coupling this with provocative speeches by Duma deputies Purishkevich and Maslennikov at a private gathering of the Temporary Committee of the Duma, with like remarks of Miliukov cited in the press and with General Kaledin's address to a Cossack congress.[12]

☆

At this juncture Kerensky, not yet officially head of the government and still nursing his humiliation over Kornilov's public demand for the death penalty, was seeking to lay hold of the rising prestige of the military leadership in the patriotic camp without becoming swallowed by it. His expedient was to convoke a conference of prominent generals at Stavka for the purpose of "informing the government of the military strategic situation" and hearing their opinions on "measures necessary to restore the fighting capacity of the Army."[13] Commander in Chief Brusilov was instructed to invite any present and past senior commanders whose counsel he thought would be useful; aside from the present front commanders Klembovskii, Denikin, and Shcherbatov, Brusilov also invited the retired commanders Ruzskii, Alekseev, Gurko, and Dragomirov. Kerensky was deeply offended at the invitation of the latter two, whom he had removed in unpleasant confrontations which had been ventilated in the press; Kerensky curtly informed Brusilov that if their invitations were not revoked

[11] *VSO*, No. 4 (July 25, 1917).

[12] See examples in *Go3A*, July 23; *GoXA*, July 27; *IzOA*, July 26; and *Iz9A*, July 28.

[13] Ziaonchkovskii, *Kampaniia 1917 g.*, p. 152. The full text of the proceedings is given. Also in *RPG* 2:989-1010.

he would not honor them with his presence.[14] General Kornilov was not invited on the pretext of the critical situation on the Southwestern Front, though the personal motives of both Brusilov and Kerensky were suspected.

On the opening day of the conference, July 16, Brusilov failed to greet Kerensky at the train station with due pomp and ceremony, pleading urgent operational matters; moreover, the minister's train arrived an hour early, which left Brusilov no time to be adequately briefed for the conference. For Brusilov, who had hitherto catered to Kerensky's whims to a point of servility, this was a serious blunder. Kerensky stormed up and down his railroad carriage, fuming that "under the Tsar they would never have dared to behave so impertinently." Not bothering to rise when they appeared, he brusquely demanded a report on the situation at the front. Thus, the occasion was off to an inauspicious start.[15]

Ignoring the strategic and other items on the agenda, the generals, beginning with Denikin, descended on the democratic innovations in the Army as the chief cause of the recent reverses and the chief obstacle to prospects for recovery. Denikin's speech did not spare the government, the Soviet, the committees, the commissars, or Kerensky personally.[16] Commissars, he claimed, introduced an impermissible divided authority in the Army. However well intentioned, they could not make up for their lack of military experience. His own commissar on the Western Front was a very young man devoid not only of military experience but also of experience in general, who boasted he could remove from command anyone he chose. Another declared that paragraph 14 of the Declaration of Soldiers' Rights, reserving enforcement powers to commanders during battle, was not applicable on his front, and still another liberally used curses that were not allowed to officers under the old regime. The committees brought only harm and confusion. That of the Second Army claimed to be acting in behalf of the Soviet in Petrograd; half the members recognized the validity of paragraph 14, the other half did not. The front committee claimed for itself full state powers and the right to remove senior officers. No less than sixty commanders on his front had been removed by committees. On June 8 the front committee voted against the offensive and on June 18 in favor of it; the committee of the Second Army did the same on June 1 and June

[14] On this point, see Lukomskii, *Vospominaniia*, p. 165, and D. N. Tikhobrazov, "V stavke posle revoliutsii (1917 g.). Iz vospominanii Gen. Shtaba polkovnika Tikhobrazova" (Ms.), RA, p. 60. Tikhobrazov was a young general staff officer and communications officer at Stavka, in which capacity he was an eyewitness to many events.

[15] See Brusilov, *Moi vospominaniia*, pp. 278-79, whose recollections are often self-serving, uninformative, or even inaccurate; more reliable version in Lukomskii, pp. 166-67.

[16] Denikin, *Ocherki*, 1(2):173.

20 respectively.[17] When the Menshevik-S.R. majority of the front committee finally endorsed the offensive, the Bolsheviks on the committee continued to propagate the opposite view in the name of the committee. And such anarchistic institutions claimed to "control" the actions of the high command.

Denikin further systematically attacked the Declaration of Soldiers' Rights, pointing out that all the dire predictions made at the May Conference in Petrograd had come to pass. The Declaration, he pointed out, guaranteed that the soldiers could be disciplined only by court procedure, but the committees and the soldiers had successfully sabotaged the courts by not carrying out the prescribed elections of jurors. Finally, he turned directly to the War Minister and excoriated him for boasting that he could renovate the entire commanding staff in twenty-four hours and claiming that in tsarist times soldiers were "driven into battle with the knout and machine guns." Why had the War Minister expressed sympathy to Sokolov, the reputed author of Order No. One, when he was beaten by the infamous 703rd Regiment, but failed to do so when General Noskov was murdered?

Brusilov, fearing that the feisty general had gone a trifle too far, requested that he shorten his speech, but Denikin replied that if he could not speak his mind he preferred to pass the rest of the conference in silence. Kerensky nodded his assent, and Denikin proceeded to outline a program for restoring health to the Army: no politics in the Army, revocation of the Declaration of Soldiers' Rights, the abolition of commissars and committees, the restoration of the officer authority, military-revolutionary courts, and the death penalty for the rear, and finally a full acknowledgment of guilt by the Provisional Government for allowing officers to be slandered. The moment was saturated with melodrama as Denikin, shaking with emotion, asked to be excused; Brusilov was about to deny this incourtesy, but Kerensky solemnly rose, stretched out his hand, and thanked the general for his "forthright and courageous expression of opinion."[18]

Thus encouraged, the other generals—Klembovskii, Alekseev, Ruzskii—pursued Denikin's themes supporting his bold proposals, albeit moderating the content. Klembovskii, for example, noted that on the Northern Front his relations with committees were relatively cordial, though they always sought to "control" and command authority inevitably suffered.

[17] This and the following in Zaionchkovskii, *Kampaniia 1917 g.*, pp. 153-60, but also in *RPG*; Denikin, *Ocherki*; and Golovin, *Rossiiskaia kontr-revoliutsiia*, 1(1):154-68. For a list of arrested commanders on the Western Front, see *RDRA*, pp. 217-21.

[18] See opposing interpretations of this gesture in Lukomskii, p. 152, and Kerensky, *Prelude to Bolshevism*. p. 42. The latter consists of Kerensky's testimony to the Commission of Inquiry into the Kornilov affair in early October 1917, edited and heavily commented on in a self-serving way by Kerensky himself.

General Alekseev concurred, stating, "They simply have to be abolished!" In essentials the entire assembly embraced Denikin's outlined program. Denikin complained in his memoirs that Brusilov failed to support him, but the record indicates otherwise: after Denikin's exit, Brusilov strongly denounced the abuses of committees and called for restoring disciplinary rights to officers. It was not uncharacteristic of Brusilov to allow others to break the ice and then to make a bold display.

Kerensky's reply was a characteristic exercise in specious logic and self-serving apologia. He disclaimed responsibility for the Declaration of Soldiers' Rights, blaming the Polivanov Commission, and rejected outright that he had tolerated interference by committees in matters of command. He assailed General Ruzskii as an inveterate partisan of the old regime, whereas all present knew he had been instrumental in engineering the tsar's abdication (he had also initiated cooperation with the Soviet in March). Granting the justice of Denikin's complaints on the condition of his front, he cast the blame on the absent Gurko (Kerensky's grudge against the latter was known to everyone present). He suggested that committees and commissars were essential and that whoever could not reconcile themselves to their presence or dreamed of restoring the old regime should hand in their resignations. The generals quickly protested that none of those present were thinking of a return to the old regime or reversing the course of the Revolution. He declared his willingness to resign after carrying through all the proposed measures, but feared that the only result would be "complete anarchy and a slaughter of the officers." This proven technique swayed even Ruzskii to plead, "In vain you are taking the entire burden of this on yourself, Aleksandr Fedorovich." In the end, he made no concessions, yet he had blunted the resolve of his opponents.[19]

Kornilov submitted his views in a memorandum read into the minutes. It deviated significantly from the program of the other generals, much to everybody's surprise. To be sure, it recommended the restoration of the disciplinary rights of officers, the outlawing of meetings and assemblies at the front, and the extension of the death penalty to the rear, but it asked only for the "strict regulation" of committees and the limitation of their competence to "strictly household affairs." On two other points it differed in content and spirit from the others: it advocated, first, a thorough, merciless purge of the entire commanding staff (Alekseev had protested the rapid turnover in command), and second, the *strengthening* of the commissariat, introducing them even at the corps level and granting them the exclusive right to confirm death sentences!

Kerensky was so impressed with Kornilov's "political tact" that he was

[19] Zaionchkovskii, *Kampaniia 1917 g.*, p. 150.

persuaded that he had found his candidate to replace the faltering Brusilov, in whom he now saw a treacherous defector to the hard-line generals. It was not difficult to see behind this project the inspiration of Savinkov and Filonenko—in fact, Kerensky seems to have been the only one present not to notice it. Savinkov, doubtless anxious to have Kornilov's authority behind his proposals, in exchange extended his good offices in securing for Kornilov the Supreme Command.[20] Denikin himself suspected a cabal, but a few days later he was disarmed by a telegram from Kornilov, now Commin Chief:

> With sincere and profound satisfaction I have read your report at the Stavka Conference of July 16. I subscribe to such a report with both hands. . . . I firmly believe that with God's help we shall bring to a successful conclusion the rebirth of our beloved Army and restore its fighting capacity.[21]

The appointment on July 19 of Kornilov as Commander in Chief in place of Brusilov was the immediate sequel to the conference. Kerensky, of course, needed a scapegoat for the recent military failures; moreover, he needed a chief more readily identified with "strong authority" than the compliant Brusilov. He knew that Brusilov was despised by most of his confreres as a turncoat and that there would be little protest from them over his removal. Yet, with his eye on the premiership, he had to maintain his credit with the Soviet-oriented elements and could not appear to be buckling in to the hard-line generals. Kornilov was almost too obvious a choice to placate the Right, identified as he was with the restoration of the death penalty, and Kerensky still nursed an offense at Kornilov's public telegrams. Kerensky was still in an ambivalent frame of mind when he came to the conference, but the fact that Kornilov had submitted a program distinctly different from that of the hard-line generals, a program that offered Kerensky the important tool of a shakeup in the command and a stronger commissariat, now made him an acceptable choice.[22] Kerensky departed from Stavka with the matter still undecided, but before reaching Petrograd he abruptly informed Brusilov by telegram that he was dismissed from his post and should turn over his duties to Chief of Staff Lukomskii.[23]

[20] The above version is inferred from comparing personal accounts, which reveal attitudes but not always the desired facts, with the total known context of the relationships between the parties, including much that follows.

[21] Denikin, *Ocherki*, 1(2):188.

[22] Though again the above version is based on my own surmises, Denikin makes similar inferences in *ibid.*, pp. 189-93.

[23] See Lukomskii, p. 167.

☆

Kornilov's appointment was sensed by all ends of the political spectrum as a fillip to the program of strong state authority liberated from the embrace of the democratic organizations. It served to galvanize an already tentative alliance between the revived Right, the Kadets, and the military command. The euphoria was immediately reflected in the metropolitan press and resolutions of support from the Union of Russian Landowners, the Don Cossack Voisko, and not least of all, the Union of Russian Officers. These groups took considerable heart at the well-advertised "conditions" of Kornilov on accepting his appointment, which would have given him total control over the Army, including appointments to senior command posts, and committed the government to his "program." Again Kerensky was forced into a public contest with Kornilov for ascendancy at precisely the moment he was to be crowned Minister President of the reconstituted Coalition Government. The lines were drawn and the entire country, including the committees at the front, was aware of it.

Though the signs of thickening political reaction had been multiplying since the July Days (crowing in the right-wing press over the defeat of the Bolsheviks and suggestions that the Soviet should soon follow), the press organs of the army committees had held their peace until the third week in July. Then quite abruptly, within a few days of the Kornilov appointment, they without exception raised alarm over the "threat of counter-revolution" on the home front and proclaimed their readiness to do battle, specifically to strengthen the army committees as bastions of revolutionary democracy. *Rizhskii Front* (*RF*), the organ of Iskosol, the Twelfth Army Committee, took note on July 20 of the right-wing press campaign against the democratic organizations and warned that strengthening authority in the Army must not benefit the mounting "counter-revolution." The organ of the Third Army Committee (*Go3A*) made the same points on July 21. On July 23 the Tenth Army Committee organ (*GoXA*) reacted to utterances of Miliukov and the right-wing deputies Puriskevich and Maslennikov which blamed democratic organizations for the breakdown of authority in the country, and specifically held the Kadets responsible for prolonging the political crisis and forcing the resignation of Chernov.[24]

Several committee organs also launched an attack on the Union of

[24] Rodzianko had convened a session of the long-defunct Temporary Committee of the Duma on July 18, at which Purishkevich and Maslennikov publicly called for the execution of "several thousand traitors front and rear" and the destruction of "all the sinister forces that cling to the Provisional Government" (Rabinowitch, *Bolsheviks Come to Power*, pp. 45-46). Miliukov's press interview could not be located, but as described it accords with Miliukov's frequently expressed views of that time, particularly on the reconstruction of the government. See Rosenberg, *Liberals*, pp. 176-84.

Officers. In the Third Army it was a low-keyed exchange with a "section" of the Union which blamed the army committee for "partisanship"; the matter ended in a declared truce.[25] But the Ninth Army Committee directly associated the Union of Officers with the threat of counter-revolution for advocating the ostracism of politically undesirable officers, while the Special Army Committee attacked its circular telegram on the death penalty and the restoration of disciplinary rights to officers, characterizing it as "counter-revolution masquerading as salvation for the Fatherland." In *IzOA* of July 26, an editorial ("The Lord High Officers") denied that the Union of Officers could speak for "the officers who died on June 18 and had no opportunity to express their opinion."

Although committee organs on the southerly fronts were slower to take up an open campaign because of the retreat, they later published proceedings, indicating that army committees discussed the subject at length around the same date as the other armies. The Ninth Army Committee, for example, was in continuous session for three days, and on July 19 passed a resolution holding Bolsheviks and proponents of the old regime equally responsible for the current critical situation but placed the strongest emphasis on "decisive measures against counter-revolution." In the course of the debate, a proposal to endorse the Democratic Republic to rally the democratic forces was opposed by a VTsIK representative on the grounds that it would "arm the entire bourgeoisie against us." One comrade, Khavak, declared his impatience with the leaders of democracy: "The whole tragedy of our revolution consists in its fear of recognizing that in democracy is its strength. . . . By proclaiming the Republic we will force the enemies of the Revolution to shut their mouths."

When the VTsIK representative also requested that the death penalty and other strong punitive measures be approved, another warm exchange ensued; the army committee reluctantly approved them with the proviso that their execution be closely monitored. They even established a special commission whose function was "to prevent any attempts from any quarter whatsoever to limit the rights of soldier organizations or the exploiting of the recent orders of the Provisional Government and the higher command in the interests of counter-revolution." They also condemned the Union of Officers for publicly branding officer-Bolsheviks as outcasts, noting that it could become a convenient device to tar all adherents of revolutionary democracy with the same brush. The army commander was requested to deny further use of staff communications for circulars of the Union of Officers, which, unlike the army committees, had no "official standing."[26]

[25] *Go3A*, July 22.

[26] All recorded in *Iz9A*, July 26 and 28. Though the organ of the Eighth Army Committee

Thus, by the last week of July the army committees had become aware of the forces joined against them and had executed a sharp change of fronts: hitherto devoting their resources exclusively toward curbing military disintegration and Bolshevik agitation, they now perceived the major threat to be the forces of the Right and reactionary officers. They felt that it was no accident that this new coalition regarded the army committees as their chief target: the committees had proven during the July Days that they were the most powerful reserve force of the revolutionary establishment, having dispatched an expeditionary force from the Fifth Army under Lieutenant Mazurenko, a committeeman and now commissar. However, they deeply believed that it was the committees, not the command, that had held the Army together during the retreat and that now they, rather than the command, were carrying the burden of imposing ''firm revolutionary authority'' at the expense of their standing with the soldiers. The Soviet contingent in the government appeared to be on the defensive during the prolonged political crisis and was hard put to salvage its program of July 8 along with the symbolic personage of Chernov as Agricultural Minister. But the forces of reaction were aware that they could never be secure in any political victory in the capital unless they first finished off the soldiers' committees at the front—the Army had to be at the disposal of the bourgeois dictatorship, not of revolutionary democracy. Thus the committees had come to see themselves as engaged in a fight for survival against a formidable coalition of enemies, and this fight carried with it the fate of the country and the Revolution.

☆

The army committees' view that they were a source of strength to the revolutionary establishment could scarcely take comfort in the current state of lower committees or of the committee structure as a whole. Only at the peak of the committee hierarchy were the political stakes clearly perceived. Communications with lower levels had been disrupted by mass disorders and the retreat and had actually never been properly regularized. Strong, well-functioning corps organizations, such as that of the Grenadier (Second Army, Western Front), the Fourth Siberian (Fourth Army, Rumanian Front), and the XXXII Infantry (Eleventh Army, Southwestern Front) corps, were the exceptions, not the rule, and were plagued with the same difficulties of communication with lower levels; moreover, they had not been legitimized by Order No. 213 and existed on the sufferance of cooperative or passive commanders. Division committees had only in ex-

(*Iz8A*) resumed publication after the retreat only on August 2, the issue of August 3 records that on July 26 the army committee discussed ''slander'' against the committees in the Kadet organ *Rech'* and decided to draw up an official refutation to be sent to the capital press.

ceptional cases worked out a clear conception of their role and duties, and many during the period under discussion scarcely functioned.[27] Regimental committees carried on their routine duties for the most part, but the few available records indicate exclusive concern with replacements, leaves, rotten flour, boots, fodder, and occasional disciplinary cases. There was little change during the first two weeks of August, though the themes of reconstituting division committees, regimental libraries, and courses in political grammar (to prepare for the Constituent Assembly elections) occupied increasing attention. At all levels there were complaints of soldier apathy, chronic absenteeism at committee sessions (especially of officer deputies), isolation, poor communications, and lack of news from the capital.[28]

The efforts of the army committees to reestablish communications ran into considerable inertia from below. In the Twelfth Army a VTsIK representative who toured the units hoping to discover revived political consciousness since the July Days found quite the opposite: although Bolshevik agitation had substantially abated, the masses trusted nobody and preferred to send deputations directly to the capital for information rather than hear it from the command, the commissars, the committees, or even socialist newspapers. Officers who formerly cooperated with committees or participated as officer deputies no longer did so. Another inquiry ascertained that the masses were totally unaware what their committees were doing, whereas division committees functioned sporadically and ineffectively. Contact with Iskosol was nonexistent. Nowhere did they encounter awareness of events in the capital or serious preparations for the Constituent Assembly.[29]

Somewhat later, in mid-August, when the committee of the Special Army was making preparations for its first army conference since May, it found

[27] After all four regiments of the 46th Division had mutinied (see above, p. 94), the divisional committee was reconstituted on July 20 and held its first regular session on August 4; on August 7 it took up the matter of "counter-revolution" and did not meet again until August 24, possibly because of command reprisals (see TsGVIA, f. 2376, op. 1, d. 2); the committee of the Second Guards Infantry Division, disrupted due to the Grenadier revolt, was reconstituted on July 24 (TsGVIA, f. 2322, op. 7, ed. khr. 4, ll. 15ff.); that of the First Finnish Rifle Division met once in July and was reconstituted on August 5, and the same seems to be true of the Third and Fifth Finnish divisions (TsGVIA, f. 2222, op. 1, ed. khr. 1185, ll. 6, and *passim*); in the latter cases the agenda dealt exclusively with the distribution of medals and replacements.

[28] Details of the above are all set out in complete minutes (see appropriate dates) for committees of the 517th Batumskii and Volynskii Guards regiments and the scattered records of the Finnish Rifle regiments (TsGVIA, f. 3054, op. 2, d. 23, part 2; f. 2573, op. 1, ed. khr. 2; and f. 2222, op. 1, ed. khr. 1185 respectively).

[29] *RF*, July 25 and 27.

out much the same things. Almost none of the recommendations of the previous conference for committee work had been carried into effect, above all recommendations for coordination on the corps and divisional level. On none of the burning questions of the day had the lower committees taken positions or soundings of their constituencies, nor had they displayed the slightest initiative.[30] Likewise, a deputy of the Ninth Army Committee sent to investigate the state of affairs in a remotely situated corps on the Rumanian Front found "complete indifference to politics" since Tarnopol and "passivity in all ranks and total lack of initiative."[31]

The same reports ascertained a sharp increase in overt hostility toward committees on the part of officers. For example, in the Twelfth Army officers generally denigrated the government to the soldiers and threatened to use the new punitive measures for the most trivial purposes. An article of July 26 in *Rizhskii Front* noted that, whereas formerly most officers took the attitude "Let the committee do it," ever since "Purishkevich and company" declared war on the committees they became arrogantly defiant. As an example, it cited a colonel who screamed at soldiers who balked at cutting hay: "Enough of your taking liberties! Now we've got the death penalty for the slightest offense! You can forget about your freedom." An article in *Iz0A* of August 20 noted that a certain colonel, a "liberal" who had formerly served on the army committee, now snubbed the committee altogether; saluting and officer titles were "coming back in style." Many officers no longer felt constrained to speak civilly to their men. An inquiry into unrest in the 33rd Eletskii Regiment (Second Army, Western Front) revealed a number of examples: a sergeant questioning his commanding officer why the company was marching to field exercises with full pack was told, "Scum like you are always on the lookout for treasonous and agitational outbursts [*vykhodki*]"; another, who complained of short rations, was told, "We had enough bread for one-and-a-half years, but you surrendered it all at Tarnopol"; and still another who filed a complaint was told, "Committees don't exist anymore." When a battalion on the march broke order to get around a nasty slough, the captain shouted: "Get back into formation! No talking! Enough of your defending freedom! That's all in the past, and it's time to get down to business!" Even the Chief of Staff indulged in sarcasm with committee investigators: "They swore oaths to Kerensky and their little red rags with big-sounding slogans, but in the end they pitched them away and fled." These outbursts were associated with the tension of a major punitive action, but were not untypical of the officers' new demonstrativeness after months of tactful restraint.[32]

[30] *IzOA*, August 13.

[31] *Iz9A*, August 4, reporting committee session of July 31.

[32] *RDRA*, pp. 278-82. The purpose of the inquiry was to document violations by the

☆

The stage for major confrontations was being set by a host of new restrictive orders. Brusilov's instruction of July 12 forbade committees to engage in activities not expressly permitted in existing regulations (Orders No. 213 and 279) and specifically forbade discussion of operative orders. Meetings were now proscribed in all areas closer to the front than divisional headquarters; meetings in rear areas were to be approved by the divisional commander, and agenda items were to be submitted in advance.[33] On July 23 Kornilov extended the definition to include lectures sponsored by the cultural-educational commissions since the subject matter tended to be political and stirred up class hatred.[34] This order cast the command in the new role of political censor and threw a roadblock into the committee's extensive plans to institute courses in political education in preparation for the Constituent Assembly; moreover, it violated the letter of Order No. 213, which specifically authorized such activity, and in effect nullified the political and civil rights guaranteed by the Declaration of Soldiers' Rights or for that matter by Guchkov's Order No. 114.

Other restrictive orders followed in rapid succession, such as that of Chief of Staff Lukomskii of July 28 outlawing various "control commissions" that army committees had established to investigate the work of staffs during the offensive. A parallel directive forbade staff organs to supply information to "unauthorized private organizations" and specifically named the Defense Commission of the Petrograd Soviet.[35]

Major clashes between the command and higher committees were not long in coming. In the remote Fourth Army in Rumania, General N. L. Stremukhin, commander of the VII Corps, abolished his corps committee, which unleased a flurry of protest telegrams by the Fourth Army Committee.[36] Selivachev tried to strangle the organ of the Seventh Army Committee by denying it staff facilities and money, but was forced to relent after appeals to the commissar.[37] The most celebrated instance of harassment, however, was the confiscation without warning of the July 24 issue of *GoXA* and the denial to it of further use of the staff printing facilities.

---

command of the Declaration of Soldiers' Rights; it requested the commissar to have all soldiers detained on the above charges to be freed and their commanders investigated.

[33] Partial text in *VOSR. Iiul'*, pp. 302-3, full text in *GoXA*, July 18. A similar order gave senior commanders the right to forbid congresses and conferences in the region of the front (see *Iz8A*, August 2, and orders of Buzuliiskii Regiment, TsGVIA, f. 2938, op. 1, d. 2, l. 369 [July 11]).

[34] *RDRA*, pp. 267-68.

[35] *Ibid.*, pp. 275-76.

[36] See L. M. Gavrilov, "Soldatskie komitety deistvuiushchei armii v period podgotovleniia oktiabrskoi sotsialisticheskoi revoliustii" (Dissertation, Moscow, 1969), p. 34.

[37] Diary, July 22 and August 2, in *KA* 10:158.

For over a week the paper did not appear, and for several more days it was printed on other than staff facilities.

Just what had persuaded the army commander to undertake this precipitous action is not clear, because *GoXA* had hitherto been a very mild, loyal organ, though very strong against Bolsheviks and major breaches of discipline. The confiscated issue did carry a story that the commander of the XXXVIII Corps had dissolved the committee of the 175th Division and had ordered new elections, an almost unheard-of action. The army committee protested to the War Minister and the Soviet but urged the 175th division committee to comply pending resolution from above.

The closing immediately set off a flurry of activity. The army committee sent telegrams of protest to all relevant authorities, but in addition informed all other army committees. Resolutions of support came from the Twelfth, Third, Eighth, and Special armies. That of the Third Army urged the Tenth Army Committee to insist on its rights and ''categorically'' protested the ''unfounded and illegal action'' of the Tenth Army Commander, with copies to all and sundry, including the front commander, General Denikin.[38] A joint conference of the three army committees of the Western Front with the front committee to consider the implications of the incident was seriously proposed. Savinkov, now Kerensky's assistant minister, instructed the Tenth Army commander to remove all further obstacles to publication, but apparently did not secure immediate compliance, since Commissar Vengerov again wired Kerensky: ''In spite of your telegram, our newspaper has not resumed publication and the confiscated number has not been released. I request immediate disposition.''[39] Only after the direct intervention of General Kornilov did the army commander relent, and on August 10 it resumed publication.

A second landmark incident was the arrest of the entire Ninth Army Committee and the confiscation of all the documents on its premises, an affair which looked very much like a move to close it down permanently. The Ninth Army Committee had a long history of militancy, but at the same time was decisively pro-offensive and anti-Bolshevik. There had been a number of instances of flagrant interference in command authority in the matter of appointments. For example, on June 25 they recommended the removal from command of a Colonel Zakharov, who had received a vote of ''no confidence'' from his regimental committee and even from the officers of his regiment. They also determined that a garrison commander was unsuitable because he gave ''demoralizing lectures'' to re-

[38] See *Go3A*, August 3, which refers to resolutions of other armies. See also *Iz8A*, August 20.

[39] *GoXA*, August 11. On the chief commissar at Stavka, Filonenko, actually backing the commander in this conflict, see *Iz8A*, August 20.

placements on the agrarian question and requested the reinstatement of a captain who had been transferred to prevent "misunderstandings." Remarkably, the army commander complied with each request except the last, on which he asked for "more information." The record also reveals extensive interference in matters of supply and in the affairs of local Rumanian authorities, who complained bitterly to the army commander. All this could take place, a later front report alleged, "as a result of the dereliction of duty and connivance of the former army commander, General Stupin."[40]

The chief crimes for which punitive action was undertaken, however, were, first, that the army committee regularly cooperated with and was represented in Rumcherod, a regional soviet of the Odessa Military District, the Black Sea Fleet, and the Rumanian Front, and second, that they had created a "Control Commission" that interfered in all aspects of staff organization and demanded regular reports. Concerning the former, Rumcherod claimed full civil authority in the region and carried out de facto many governmental functions in open defiance of the Provisional Government.[41]

The issue of the "Control Commission" is worth some attention, since a number of army committees did not trust staffs and saddled them with supervisory bodies (e.g., in the Fifth, Twelfth, Seventh, and Eighth armies), but with perhaps less obnoxiously defined functions. The Ninth Army Committee, however, spelled out its functions in exact detail, for example, the supervision of the execution of army committee decisions by the army staff and lower units, and the verification of personnel lists of staffs. A command report verifies that this measure was the chief rock of offense, but one day previously they had passed an even more odious resolution: "To remove persons from command whose actions reveal a criminal attitude toward the execution of duties and to hand them over to military justice on democratic principles."[42] Though successfully defused by the commissar's intervention, it reveals the almost limitless pretensions of some army committees to function as a second government authority.

As the army committee was conducting its routine business on July 27, with no forewarning around 3:00 in the afternoon the duty member of the committee whispered the news to the chairman, who then solemnly an-

[40] From a Stavka survey for the week July 23-31, in *VOSR. Iiul'*, p. 440. The above material is taken from *Iz9A*, July 1, 3, and 7, which reproduce the corresponding committee records.

[41] For Brusilov's complaint against Rumcherod, see *RDRA*, pp. 221-22; see also *VOSR. Iiul'*, p. 439, and *Iz9A*, July 6.

[42] From *Iz5A*, July 16. Publishing material on other armies was a means of justifying such projects in one's own.

nounced: "Comrades! Be calm. The army committee is surrounded by troops. There is about to be a search." Indeed, a squadron of dragoons with armored cars cordoned off the building as if a major punitive action were in progress, and at each door guards were posted. The session continued for hours while investigative officers rummaged through the premises confiscating a mass of papers and records. Committee members were interrogated one by one, from which it emerged that the accusations ranged from "interference with operative orders" to "hiding machine guns" to "conducting anarcho-Bolshevik propaganda" to "surrendering an entire regiment to the Germans." In the meantime, the dragoons who surrounded the premises became restive and sent in an emissary to find out the situation. It turned out that they had been informed only that they were "to catch some anarchists and deserters." They assured the army committee of their loyalty while informing all surrounding units that the army committee's headquarters was being raided. Soon resolutions of support began pouring in from unit after unit and a huge crowd of soldiers and civilians assembled. Thus the arrest was lifted and a dangerous affair was in the making.

Late at night a telegram arrived from Commander in Chief Kornilov admitting that he had ordered the search on the basis of the army commander's complaint; however, on the basis of information supplied to him by Chief Commissar Filonenko he "found it possible to terminate the proceedings"; nevertheless, he admonished the army committee that "it must not exceed the limits of paragraph 43 of Order No. 51, which does not grant the right to control army staffs, and therefore the Control Commission must immediately desist from all activities in connection with the staff of the Army." The army committee, on its part, sent a long telegram to Kornilov explaining that the control commission did fall within the limits set by Order No. 51, that the army commander had already consented to earlier such resolutions (which was quite true), that they had scrupulously avoided touching operative questions, and that in any event the execution of the plan had been deferred pending clarification by VTsIK. It complained bitterly that among the confiscated records were not only those relevant to the alleged offense but also records of all the commissions set up by the committee, effectively paralyzing its work.[43]

These incidents revealed the lengths each side was prepared to go to meet the threat perceived from the other, but they halted short of a genuine test of strength. Kornilov was about to depart for Petrograd to confer with Kerensky on his "program," and perhaps he did not want to stake everything on the issue of committees. He needed Savinkov's support, and the

[43] Entire record in *Iz9A*, July 29, 30, August 2 and 4; detailed accounts also in *Go3A*, August 5, and *Iz8A*, August 20.

latter was committed to preserving committees under the strict supervision of commissars, to which Kornilov had already given his consent. In any event, Kornilov on August 1 circulated an instruction to the command which reaffirmed that he contemplated no drastic resolution of the matter of committees for the present. He also promised that he would shortly issue a comprehensive order governing the mutual relations between commanders, commissars, and committees which would clear up disputed areas. Savinkov announced the same intention in War Ministry Order No. 477, suggesting that some agreement had been reached to defuse the situation created by the Ninth and Tenth armies.[44]

The issue of conflict, however, had been seriously joined, and a new series of pronouncements and articles appeared in the committee newspapers, exhorting their constituency to conduct a firm defense of their organizations. An article in the organ of the Eighth Army Committee, *Iz8A*, of August 3 accused "certain reactionary groups" in the command structure of looking for a scapegoat for the military defeat and therefore gladly joined hands with "Shulgin and company" (i.e., the monarchists) to blame it on the committees. The command "folded its arms" during the retreat, whereas the committees had held the Army together after Tarnopol and had aroused in the soldiers the patriotic will to defend the borders of the homeland. The counter-revolutionary element front and rear were deliberately seizing on the recent orders of the government as a means of achieving a dictatorship. In twin articles of August 1 and 3, *Go3A* noted the "sudden resurgence of reaction in the higher staffs" and the "thickening atmosphere between the command and the committees, which can only result in the further deterioration of the Army." They looked with hope to Savinkov's pledge of an exhaustive new statute to protect the committees from the illegal acts of the command.

☆

This heightened perception of danger stimulated the army committees to intensified activity in two directions: first, toward reconstructing their organizational base and improving communications by means of visitations and conferences, and second, toward cultivating political awareness in their constituency through cultural-educational enterprises. There is enough information to characterize August as a month of sometimes feeble, sometimes fruitful efforts to revitalize the committees, though it took place against the background of massive indifference on the part of the soldier masses and continued harassment by the command. Thus, attempts were made to call new army congresses in the Sixth, Eighth, and Tenth armies and joint "conferences" of army committees on the Western and South-

[44] For both, see *GoXA*, August 20, which dates Order No. 477 to August 1.

western fronts.[45] Because of new rulings of commissars reflecting the negative attitude of Kerensky, none of these assemblies was authorized. A major concern was that the statutory mandate of three months for deputies to the army committees had expired or soon would fall due, and existing regulations provided that a committee's mandate could only be renewed by an army congress.

Army Commissar Liperovskii had endorsed the request of the Sixth Army Committee for a congress, but was overruled by Front Commissar Tizegausen on the grounds that still-active operations did not permit it; nevertheless, Liperovskii urgently renewed his request.[46] The Eighth Army Committee was also turned down, but insistently renewed their request on the eve of the Kornilov affair.[47] The Tenth Army Committee addressed itself directly to the War Ministry, but Fedor Stepun of the Political Administration replied that Kerensky "regarded as undesirable the calling of any further army congresses until the new statute on soldiers' committees is worked out."[48] The commanding staff henceforward utilized this declaration to forbid a congress or conference of any type, including those of nationalities, peasant organizations, political parties, and even cultural-educational conferences, a number of which were already scheduled.

Also on record are several instances of efforts to build up or restore corps organizations, and in all probability they were not exceptional. For example, the IV Siberian Corps (Sixth Army, Rumanian Front) laid plans for a congress on August 3 and had already secured the approval of Commissar Liperovskii. He warned them, however, that such assemblies "must not take on the character of political meetings" and must hold to the order prescribed in Order No. 213. Several days later he notified them that due to "battle conditions" it was canceled "until a new time can be set." The corps journal of this period does reflect vigorous activity and a good deal of tension with the command. It interfered extensively in supply matters and other areas of command responsibility, strongly recommending that a certain Colonel Martynov of a commissary unit be removed for crude behavior toward subordinates and threats to committees. On August 3 a committee rapporteur noted that "the campaign against the committees has reached into all armies of the front," and it praised Commissar Kharito's efforts in their behalf.[49] The committee of the XXII (Finnish) Corps of the

[45] See *VGr*, August 17; *Iz8A*, August 27; *GoXA*, August 15; and *Go3A*, August 13. On the Southwestern Front Conference, see *GO*, August 12, and *IzOA*, August 25.

[46] *VGr*, August 17.

[47] *Iz8A*, August 27 (citing committee *protokol* of August 8).

[48] *GoXA*, August 15.

[49] See TsGVIA, f. 2282, op. 6, d. 3, ll. 51 and 54; and op. 4, ed. khr. 11. On Kharito

Seventh Army, Southwestern Front, had not met in June, but became active again in late July, calling an extraordinary session with divisional committees over the dismissal of General Obruchev; it also planned for a major congress in September to renew its three-month mandate. Their session of August 3 took note of the low level of committee work and the need for revitalization, but also noted that they needed the cooperation of the command structure, which had recently become hostile.[50]

In the XXXI Corps, the efforts at revitalization enjoyed the encouragement of the command and more than usual success. In May there had been major disorders in both divisions, the 130th and the 177th, but in July they had been "tightened up" under fairly enlightened commanders. The regimental committee records reflect considerable command tolerance, particularly on household matters, and the commander of the 130th Division himself revived the flagging division committee by calling an assembly on August 3. The proceedings reveal a broadly based invigoration of committee activity: two delegates were sent to the army committee and the commissar to determine the exact rights and functions of division committees, which had always been a gray area in the statutes. A replacement deputy was sent to the corps committee and was attached to its permanent praesidium; the division assembly requested a visitation by the "Communications Commission" of the army committee to exchange information and "acquaint ourselves with the life of other units in the Special Army." The main business of the assembly was to establish courses of political education for the Constituent Assembly, for which a budget of 5,000 rubles was approved. The initiative can be credited to the 517th Batumskii Regiment, which already had an active program and was in touch with the Cultural-Educational Commission of the Special Army. The divisional assembly was followed by a conference on cultural-educational work, after which there was a corps assembly and a session of the corps Cultural-Educational Commission. The corps assembly seems to have been the work of several energetic officers, captains Stein and Savitskii, and a Lieutenant Sivokhin of the 517th Batumskii Regiment. It is also clear that they worked closely with the army committee's Cultural-Educational Commission.[51]

as probably replaced by Tizengausen as commissar because of his stout defense of committees' rights, see *Iz8A*, August 3.

[50] See Selivachev diary, *KA* 10:167, and TsGVIA, f. 2222, op. 1, ed. khr. 1185, l. 25, and d. 2, ll. 36-37 and 32-33. For an unnamed corps with a similar profile, see *IzOA*, September 2.

[51] See TsGVIA, f. 2440, op. 5, d. 1, ll. 35-36 and 45-47. The outlays covered books (670 rubles), paper, notebooks, blackboards (430 rubles), political pamphlets (1,880 rubles), and newspapers (1,000 rubles). Since sums of this order could only come from regimental

Thus, the XXXI Corps seems to have been an exception in the otherwise poor results of the revitalization campaign. The Ninth Army Committee, just prior to its arrest, deputized two of its number to each corps committee to reestablish communications.[52] The Special Army Committee claimed that as of August 20 the problem of communications was solved and summoned a conference of corps and division committees. Its Cultural-Educatonal Commission also instituted a course of instruction for "agitators," who were trained to organize political instruction in their units in preparation for the Constituent Assembly, though otherwise the activity of the army committee was very low.[53] The Eighth Army Committee, for all its newly discovered militancy, by mid-August was discouraged about the viability of its organization. Many members had dropped out and had not been replaced; the few active members performed multiple roles in the complex committee machinery, and new members were co-opted without elections. Thus a representative organization was being transformed into a self-perpetuating administrative apparatus (a parallel trend existed in all the army committees).[54]

Although the communications were still poor, some lower committees were also becoming concerned about "counter-revolution" independently of army committees. For example, on August 14 the 517th Batumskii Regiment called on all committees to "rally their forces in support of the Provisional Government and the Soviet of Soldiers', Workers', and Peasants' Deputies to form a bastion against the growing and threatening counter-revolutionary designs"; for this task they regarded the convocation of any army congress as essential. (Commander Anfinogerov declared himself "agreed" to the suggestion in the margin of the protocol.)[55] Similarly, on August 7 the reconstituted division committee of the mutinous 46th Division, far from showing penitence for past sins, passed the following resolution:

> The Division Committee notes the repeated and concerted attempts by certain members of the commanding staff to depreciate the dignity

---

funds, one must credit the beneficence of the commander, Colonel Anfingenov, who once before had granted 2,000 rubles (Minutes of committee of 517th Batumskii Regiment of June 27, TsGVIA, f. 3054, op. 2, d. 23, l. 405).

52 *Iz9A*, August 2.

53 *IzOA*, August 20 and *passim*. It appears as a colorless, two-page information sheet, giving the impression of total demoralization. On August 16 it complained of lack of money, personnel, and paper, implying that they were being deliberately squeezed by the command.

54 See esp. *Iz8A*, August 20.

55 TsGVIA, f. 3054, op. 2, d. 23, part 2, l. 547. The even more inert 518th Alashketskii Regiment passed a similar resolution on August 13, probably under prodding by higher committees; see TsGVIA, f. 2440, op. 5, d. 7, l. 28.

> and significance of revolutionary soldiers' organizations, at times even attempting to terminate their existence. Regarding this as the effort of certain dark, counter-revolutionary forces to restore the hated old order, the Division Committee declares it will struggle against them by all possible means, including closer and more permanent ties to all regimental, divisional, and even army committees and with all other revolutionary organizations.[56]

Such boldness carried certain risks. The committee organ of the XXXII Corps, *GO*, had hitherto scrupulously low-keyed politics, but on August 11 it blasted the critics of the government for "slander, insinuations, pogrom agitation, and other provocative undertakings." There was no suggestion of implicating command personnel; nevertheless, two days later it ceased publication, probably by order of the command, since it resumed publication the day after the Kornilov affair. On August 3 the Ninth Finnish Rifle Regiment of the XXII Corps (Seventh Army), ostensibly cured of Bolshevik politics during the retreat, passed a resolution, later endorsed by the divisional committee, denouncing the Temporary Committee of the Duma for blaming all the troubles of the country on "private organizations" like the Soviet and other democratic organizations, and accusing its supporters of "waiting for the moment to seize power from the hands of the people."[57] These instances reveal that lower committees sometimes reacted to the politics on their own and put pressure on higher committees to take action. Alarm over counter-revolution first rocked mainly the army committee leadership, but by mid-August had rippled through the committee structure as a whole; unlike some earlier instances it did not bear the earmarks of a well-orchestrated campaign.

☆

Although committees of the Twelfth and Fifth armies on the Northern Front reacted with vigor to the resurgence of the Right in Petrograd, it was not associated with the high command or senior officers. Considering that both armies in June were about to fall apart under the weight of mutiny and Bolshevik propaganda, the recovery of both armies to a respectable level in August is quite remarkable. These armies were distinguished by a unique accommodation between committees, commissars, and commanders. One of the reasons for this state of affairs was the different selection of the top leadership of all three institutions. There were few Denikins or Selivachevs in the senior command posts on the Northern Front. True, Front Commander Klembovskii complained about interference

[56] *TsGVIA*, f. 2376, op. 1, d. 2.

[57] *TsGVIA*, f. 2222, op. 1, ed. khr. 1185, l. 32.

by revolutionary institutions and had expressed them forcefully at the Stavka conference, but in practice he was yielding, even passive.

General Radko-Dmitriev, commander of the Twelfth Army, had been so pliant toward committees that Kornilov replaced him at the end of July with General D. P. Parskii, until then commander of the Grenadier Corps. However, Parskii was far from being Kornilov's creature. In March he not only accepted democratic organizations in the Army, but also promoted them with great vigor. He met with his committee almost daily, chaired their sessions, patiently listened to their desires, and employed the command apparatus to implement their decisions.[58]

General Iurii Danilov of the Fifth Army, formerly a professor at the General Staff Academy and Quartermaster General under Grand Duke Nicholas, had worked out business-like relations with the Fifth Army Committee. Fifth Army Commissar Khodorov was a former army committeeman and a strong partisan of the policy of "firm authority." There was a bond of mutual respect between commander, commissar, and committee that was quite unique. Danilov, in Stankevich's words, turned commissars and committees into "tools of military administration."[59]

Woytinsky and Stankevich have left vivid self-portraits of themselves as commissars. Neither was as imperious as Savinkov, whose qualities were often imitated by other commissars, but they took their role as spokesmen of the government and of "the democracy" quite seriously. They were prepared to rein in both committees and commanders, but above all they operated as effective mediators and problem-solvers. Stankevich, a long-standing member of the Soviet Executive Committee and a close associate of Kerensky, was thoroughly devoted to the cause of restoring the health of the Army. He rose above the knee-jerk reactions of most Soviet figures (including Tsereteli) toward "old regime" generals and easily disarmed the latter with his matter-of-fact composure in their presence. Although ideologically a Populist, he found it difficult to relate to the unpredictable soldier element or to indulge in the almost obligatory revolutionary speech-making and verbiage. Therefore, on one of his visits to Petrograd he persuaded Woytinsky, who excelled in precisely those qualities, to become his assistant. An ardent defensist and persuader, Woytinsky on more than one occasion becalmed an angry mob on behalf of the Soviet Executive Committee. By July he had become disenchanted with Petrograd politics, longed to get away, and at the front discovered

[58] See Stankevich, *Vospominaniia*, p. 179, and materials on the Grenadier Corps archive, TsGVIA, f. 2327, op. 4, d. 1 and 2, *passim*, esp. ll. 371, 373, and 376 (Parskii's initiative in forming soldiers' committees in March, which was in advance of army orders); see also Parskii's touching farewell speech to corps in *IzGr*, July 30.

[59] Stankevich, p. 179.

his true mission. A thorough master of the revolutionary jargon that so easily found resonance in the soldier masses, he combined it with commonsense logic, psychological devices, and, when necessary, the awesome authority of Revolutionary Democracy. Above all, he projected transparent sincerity and genuine sympathy for the concerns of ordinary soldiers. Commanders quickly came to value his services as a peripatetic troubleshooter in the Twelfth Army, even though he was not officially its commissar.

From the very first days of the Revolution, Iskosol had been run by a compact group of intellectuals close to the Mensheviks on the Soviet Executive Committee and frequently in touch with them. They became involved with the politics of the Soviet and functioned as local party representatives in Riga, apart from their role as army committeemen. Lieutenant E. D. Kuchin, a Menshevik, was the mentor of the group of Menshevik and S.R. intellectuals who operated the highly bureaucratized apparatus of Iskosol. His own dedication to extend and magnify the work of Iskosol infected the group as a whole and engendered a remarkable degree of camaraderie and unity of purpose. Vice-chairman Kharash was a young Jewish intellectual and soldier volunteer who like many others of his background remained uncommissioned. Not as self-confident or experienced as Kuchin, he was in effect the latter's protégé and soldier counterpart.

Though Kuchin's group firmly controlled the executive organs of the committee system, the Bolsheviks of *Okopnaia Pravda* (*OP*) and the Latvian brigades constituted a sizeable schism, claimed to consist of "seventeen regiments and comparable units." *OP* had made a distinct change in its editorial line after the debacle on the Southwestern Front, now claiming that it had never intended to encourage disorders but had merely tried to persuade Iskosol to consult its constituency before committing the army to the offensive.[60] They had always advocated a firm defense of the front and obedience to "lawful" orders duly discussed and ratified by the soldier masses.

Although Iskosol's organ, *RF*, did not soften its tone against *OP*, Iskosol did send an emissary to the "Left Bloc" in mid-July and apparently agreed to publish its grievances; a detailed account appeared without editorial sarcasm in *RF* of July 15.[61] For ten days thereafter *RF* desisted from further polemics, taking note of the Bolsheviks' more muted line; apparently they

[60] See *OP*, June 21, and *passim* (almost every issue).

[61] On July 13 in article "Much Ado About Nothing," editor Karash attacked the "Seventeen" and claimed that he welcomed an electoral contest; however, a "commission" was established to investigate the "causes" of anti-Iskosol agitation, and the compromise seems to have emerged out of this maneuvering.

felt the need for a "united front" against the mounting threat from the Right. After a two-week delay, *OP* was closed in pursuance of Kerensky's order. A joint meeting on July 25 with the commissars of Iskosol, Iskolastrel (the committee of the Latvian brigades), the Riga Workers' Soviet, and the Central Committee of the Latvian Social Democratic Party requested revocation of the closing of *OP*.[62] Stankevich and Woytinsky adamantly refused, claiming that *OP* had placed itself beyond the pale of democracy by openly advocating defiance of lawful orders of the Provisional Government and the command. The adamancy of the commissars apparently shook up the uncertain members of Iskosol, which had sponsored the meeting, and they decided to leave the matter up to the commissars.

The commissars on their part offered a striking proposal which was adopted without registered dissent: all obligatory measures for the region of the Twelfth Army were henceforward to be published jointly by the army commander, the commissar, and Iskosol. The significance of the resolution should not be underestimated, as it abruptly superseded the issues of conflict between the three pillars of authority. Iskosol had recently passed a resolution of "control" over the command, and even more recently had declared the commissar's actions invalid unless acted upon jointly with Iskosol.[63] But now the three organs were to be fused into a single authority with no explication of precedence. It was exactly the same dilemma the socialists faced when entering the Provisional Government. Iskosol was undoubtedly flattered by its new co-equal status, but suddenly it shared responsibility instead of "controlling" from the outside. The commissars, however, retained the initiative and effective control, since the reserve of ultimate state authority was there if needed.

Henceforward Iskosol loyally adhered to these arrangements, and ceased to harp on "counter-revolutionary generals," at least in their own army. Nevertheless, they blamed Stankevich for overruling their understanding with the Bolsheviks and tried to persuade Woytinsky to get him removed.[64] Woytinsky, however, stood four-square behind his colleague, and Iskosol was obliged to acquiesce. Why the Bolsheviks were not more vociferous over the rebuff at this session is not clear, but it appears that they were in genuine disarray after the closing of their organs and headquarters. Nevertheless, the clever Bolsheviks managed within three days to bring out a new organ, *Okopnyi Nabat* (*ON*), to the consternation of higher authorities, but in content it was far more subdued; *ON* even urged its followers to

[62] See Stankevich, pp. 186-87.

[63] Proceedings in *RF*, July 11, and the final resolution in July 25 (passed July 11).

[64] See Stankevich, p. 187.

observe military order and defend the revolutionary citadel of Riga against German attack (which everyone now expected). Bolshevism remained, but "trench Bolshevism" was no longer its stock-in-trade.

The commissars were able to deliver immediately on the new arrangements. On the very next day Parskii and his senior commanders met with Iskosol and worked out ground rules on political meetings. The conferees agreed that lectures and public meetings should take place only in the reserve with advance approval by Iskosol or corresponding lower-level committees. Committees controlled the agenda and were responsible for the course of the discussion; commanders were to be informed. Committeemen could not be removed for any offense, but could be put up for trial like any soldier or officer. Finally, the sessions of committees could not be restricted by the command in any way.[65] The new regulations, in other words, totally ignored the sharp curtailments of the Stavka directive of July 28. It was as if the Twelfth Army were totally immune to the disease that was then afflicting the rest of the Army.

On July 25 Woytinsky assembled the democratic organs and unrolled before them the imminent threat of a German attack on Riga; he then proposed a dictatorial collegium of commander, commissar, and Iskosol. Iskosol strongly supported the idea, while the representative of the Latvian brigades announced that they would henceforward observe "strict obedience to orders," and the Riga Workers' Soviet pledged loyalty to the majority of Revolutionary Democracy. A proclamation to the army and populace declared that the disgrace of Tarnopol must not be repeated and that all orders were to be promptly obeyed without discussion. It was signed by all the democratic organizations and political parties of the region including the Latvian Bolsheviks.[66] Missing was the imprint of the Russian military Bolsheviks, but on August 6 *ON* carried a close paraphrase of the appeal, failing only to note that it had originated with Iskosol. Woytinsky offers a very optimistic account of his labors in the Twelfth Army, describing touching encounters with Bolshevik units, including the Latvian brigades and the 436th Regiment, who were now anxious to restore their good name and present themselves as models of discipline.[67]

[65] See *RF*, July 26 and 30.

[66] Full text in Voitinskii, "Gody pobedy i porazhenii" (Ms.), 3:244-45. Soviet accounts are hard put to explain this sudden switch; Iskosol is invariably described as a lackey of the bourgeois-Entente combination. They concede only that the vote was a "tactical mistake" immediately reversed, the Latvian representative having been "deceived by Iskosol" and exceeded his mandate. See Kaimin', *Latyshskie strelki za pobedu oktiabr'skoi revoliutsii*, p. 223 and *passim*. M. I. Kapustin, *Soldaty severnogo fronta v bor'be za vlast' sovetov* (Moscow, 1957), mentions only a systematic struggle against Iskosol (pp. 112-15).

[67] See Woytinsky, *Stormy Passage*, pp. 227-29. See Parskii's own less optimistic assessment in report of August 4 in *RDRA*, pp. 295-97. His report stresses that particular units in

The Fifth Army Committee had been a staunch partisan of military discipline and command authority from its very founding and had promoted it with evangelical zeal in connection with the offensive. The committeemen did not nurture that visceral suspicion of the command or the passion for "control" so typical of other army committees. Vilenkin, Kuropatkin, and others were right-wing, undogmatic Populists and were not as obsessed with revolutionary politics as were Kuchin and his colleagues. They were ardent partisans of the Coalition and Kerensky, and the entire shift toward "firm authority" and "decisive measures" came to them quite naturally. Commissar Khodorov, Stankevich asserts, threw himself into the task of bringing rebellious regiments to heel with a "policeman's zeal."[68] He was always accompanied by an army committeeman to stress that they constituted a single democratic authority. Khodorov worked out a careful scenario to demonstrate solidarity between commanders and committees in support of the government's program to restore "strong authority" in the Army. On July 25 he and General Danilov issued parallel statements in the organ of the Fifth Army Committee, *Iz5A*, which were to be read out and explained in every unit of the army. Khodorov assured the soldiers that the new measures were designed exclusively to purge the Army of "cowards," which was the policy of the government and the entire democracy, not of the command alone. It called on committees and the command to work shoulder to shoulder to achieve the desired results. A hostile attitude toward committees by commanders was condemned, and harassment was a violation of military law and could be punished in the courts.

On his part, General Danilov declared his firm support of the present government and its policies and called for "iron revolutionary discipline." Tight curbs were to be placed on such disreputable practices as card playing, grenade fishing, robbing vegetable gardens, and trading in military uniforms, but commanders were to make it clear that they regard the soldiers as citizens, and committees as their colleagues in a common enterprise. Danilov, in other words, leaned over backward to divest the command of a counter-revolutionary image. The following day the army committee declared itself satisfied with these statements.[69]

For the next several weeks *Iz5A* was bland and uncontroversial, the forthcoming State Conference in Moscow notwithstanding. There were no

---

the Second and Sixth Siberian Rifle divisions persisted in disorganizing activities and the circulation of Bolshevik literature, though he recognizes an improvement in the 109th Division (where the notorious 436th Regiment put out *Okopnaia Pravda*) and others formerly noted for their turbulence (116th and 136th Infantry and 20th Siberian Rifle divisions).

[68] Stankevich, p. 175.

[69] *Iz5A*, July 26.

alarms over the gathering forces of the Right, the name of Kornilov was not mentioned once positively or negatively, and even the Union of Officers was left in peace, except for one mild reproach from Khodorov.[70] In general this army seemed immune to the tensions that were dividing the country and the Army as a whole. The Fifth Army Committee, though the best organized and most clearly identified with the command, was the least prepared for the crisis that was fast coming upon them.

The above examples demonstrate that not all commanders were implacable foes of revolutionary institutions and that despite legal and logical incongruities positive results could be achieved by collaboration. By contrast Denikin was the very incarnation of irreconcilability. Both his speech at Stavka and his memoirs bristle with graphic examples of the idiosyncrasies and unpredictable dabbling of committees that robbed commanders of their peace of mind. More questionable is the truth of his claim that "neither as commander on the Western or the Southwestern Front . . . did I cooperate in the slightest with committees, and where possible I put a stop to those of their activities I regarded as harmful."[71] In May and June, while still on the Western Front, he commented favorably on committee work. The committee organs of the Third and Tenth armies were very loyal to the command, particularly during the offensive, and very hostile to Bolshevik agitation.

Two incidents, however, reflect Denikin's sharp change in attitude toward committees under the stress of the offensive. Denikin became very upset over a proposal for "battle committees," which were to be used not only to "persuade" recalcitrant units but also to participate in drawing up the plan of attack in a clear violation of the stipulations of both Orders No. 51 and 213. Denikin exploded in every direction, threatening the precarious combination Kerensky had put together to get the offensive off the ground. Kerensky dispatched Stankevich to patch up the dispute. Stankevich practiced his skill as a mediator, shuttling back and forth between the two sides, who refused to speak to each other. Finally, he persuaded the committee not to assume responsibility in an area where they had no competence, and he swayed Denikin with the argument "Wouldn't you rather have the committees doing something useful for the offensive than busying themselves with politics and the counter-revolutionary danger?" Denikin yielded, but most likely resented being forced to agree against his

[70] *Ibid.*, August 9 and *passim*. Contrast the smugness of the committeemen with the sobering assessment in the Stavka survey for August 12-18, *VOSR. Avgust*, p. 272 ("Uninterrupted conflict between officers and soldiers continues. Activity of the Bolsheviks is becoming more open. Excesses within the army are becoming more frequent. Terroristic methods are being employed against officers." Examples of each are cited).

[71] Denikin, *Ocherki*, 1(2):34.

convictions. When the outcome was a humiliating defeat a few days later, it firmed up his resolve to fight to the finish.[72]

Denikin's army commanders, by his own admission, were all supporters of committee involvement, particularly the commander of the Second Army, but for three months he left them in peace.[73] However, in late July he removed General Kvetsinskii of the Third Army, quite obviously for his indulgent attitude toward committees.[74] The relationship between Kvetsinskii and the army committee was especially close. In June he held a conference of senior commanders and turned it into a seminar on the goals of the Revolution. Commanders who felt they could not live with revolutionary politics in the Army were urged to resign their commands! They were instructed specifically on the positive role of committees and encouraged to extend to them every cooperation. The army committee reciprocated with intense loyalty to the "revolutionary commander," and when he was dismissed they rendered him a glowing tribute in *Go3A* (August 1): "The army committee understood from its very first meeting with Kvetsinskii that it was dealing with a general devoted to the Revolution. . . . Bon voyage, Comrade General!" The same issue pinned the threat of counter-revolution specifically on higher staffs and commanders. It would seem that Denikin was meant.

When Denikin took over the Southwestern Front in early August his reputation preceded him, and both sides immediately assumed an adversary relationship. In the first week of his command Denikin banned proposed conferences of army committees in the most provocative fashion possible. He likewise vetoed the expenditure of 100,000 rubles by the front committee on "harmful literature" (undoubtedly political-educational literature expounding the views of socialist parties) and abolished the per diem expense account for committeemen on assignment (a long-standing "perk" of *komitetchiki*).[75] N. I. Iordanskii, commissar of the Southwestern Front, declares that in spite of his efforts to be supportive of command authority Denikin was irreconcilable, refusing the most trivial requests and consenting to a personal interview only twice during their joint tenure. Denikin, on his part, claims that Iordanskii's first act as commissar was to issue an "Order to the Troops" as if he were in command and that he curried the highly political Southwestern Front Committee. In the latter part of August, Iordanskii claims, Denikin assumed a threatening tone toward the Provisional Government and frankly expressed surprise to Iordanskii that he had

[72] See Stankevich, pp. 170-72, and Denikin, *Ocherki*, 1(2):155.

[73] See Denikin, *Ocherki*, 1(2):157.

[74] See *RazA*, p. 113.

[75] *Ocherki*, 1(2):202.

not been dismissed.[76] The front committee soon flooded the War Ministry with complaints against Denikin, requesting his removal. One such telegram of August 13 declared:

> From the very first moment of assuming command, General Denikin has expressed his hostile attitude . . . toward elective organizations, which has manifested itself in a whole series of limiting directives and interpretations of the rights of committees. . . . Also commanders violating the rights of committees are encouraged, and those who have worked out good relations with them are subjected to disgrace.[77]

Archival materials demonstrate that Denikin's campaign against the committees was extensive and systematic. First, he ordered commanders to report all decisions of committees which exceeded legal limits and statutes; later he even requested copies of all committee minutes. Second, he took a census of the membership of committees and subsidiary organizations all the way down to the company level, calculating the exact extent to which they were released from other duties or sent on assignment with support from regimental funds. He also instructed commanders to review election procedures and determine if present members of committees were elected according to the rules of Order No. 213. Finally, he inquired of all units whether there were worker, peasant, nationality, or political organizations, or any others not authorized, and, if authorized, by what specific directives.[78] The replies in most cases were less substantial than the queries. For example, on organizations: "The only organization in our regiment is the regimental committee, elected on democratic principles"; "Such organizations not noticed"; "None on hand"; "Don't exist."[79] These directives, on the surface quite routine, add up to a climate of calculated harassment and betray Denikin's intention to draw up a bill of indictment against committees to justify their abolition (waste of man-

[76] See his deposition to the Commission of Inquiry into the Kornilov affair, Raupakh Archive, "Berdichev," box 3, RA, and Denikin, *Ocherki*, 1(2):200.

[77] *RDRA*, pp. 318-19. Denikin (*Ocherki*, 1[2]:201-2) admits that there were repeated such instances. Selivachev's diary confirms that the army commanders were interpreting the new signals as the first steps toward abolishing the committees. See entries for August 5 and 6, *KA* 10:170-71.

[78] See TsGVIA, f. 2322, op. 7, ed. khr. 2, ll. 303-14 ("Are there electoral organs operating outside the directives of War Ministry Orders No. 213 and 277?"), 337 (request for full profile on committees to be reported by August 24), 365 (submission of minutes of all lower-level committee meetings to higher authority). All these directives emanating from Southwestern Front headquarters were addressed to all divisions, in this case to the Second Guards Infantry Division. See also TsGVIA, f. 2443, op. 1, d. 1, ll. 49 and 61 (similar instructions to 130th Division, XXXI Corps).

[79] TsGVIA, f. 2322, ll. 317 and 318, and f. 2443, ll, 62-68.

power, cost to the treasury, distraction with politics, chronic illegalities, interference in command affairs).

Other materials reveal Denikin's hostility toward the Soviet, but leniency toward the Union of Officers and groups to the Right, such as the Temporary Committee of the Duma. Commanders were forewarned of a traveling Soviet deputation and were asked to give a full report on their activities and utterances.[80] The only preserved replies must have been a disappointment: "In the Fifth Division they spoke only of the necessity to fight to the finish in cooperation with the Allies and to restore discipline, and of the 'crime' of the July Days."[81] Commanders were instructed to send over the wires no more resolutions critical of the Cossacks' Congress (which had just passed a resolution calling for an end to committees), and at the same time to circulate resolutions of the Union of Officers and the Cavaliers of St. George.[82] The most striking example of political bias was Denikin's rejection of a request of the Social Democratic fraction of the Southwestern Front Committee for a congress in Berdichev on September 1 in preparation for the Constituent Assembly elections, now set for mid-September. Denikin argued that committees were not permitted to function in behalf of political parties or to promote one at the expense of another. The Constituent Assembly elections were not presently the concern of committees, since a uniform procedure for the entire Army must first be worked out by Stavka in conjunction with the War Ministry; all congresses were now in any event forbidden, but the proposed representation formula of one deputy to twenty party members, if extended to all potential contenders, would denude the front and was therefore impractical; and finally, the state could not underwrite any partisan political activity (meaning no travel money, no per diems, no release from other duties).[83] It was a gauntlet thrown down before Soviet-oriented elements and even preempted decisions which rightfully belonged to the Provisional Government, but Denikin had already decided where the line should be drawn and prepared for a confrontation.

☆

Though committees were on the defensive and struggling from a position of weakness, they persisted in their efforts to reestablish their networks through August, just as the command persisted in its efforts to thwart them. Both sides hoped to reap some advantage from the War Ministry's promise of a comprehensive new statute that would define their respective rela-

[80] TsGVIA, f. 2222, op. 1, ed. khr. 1066, l. 126 (order of Seventh Army Commander Selivachev of August 10).

[81] *Ibid.*, l. 123.

[82] TsGVIA, f. 2322, ll. 362 and 363.

[83] All per TsGVIA, f. 2443, ll. 58 and 59.

tions.[84] The committees were hoping for a formal recognition of their status as ''democratic organs of self-administration'' and ''control'' function over the command in all except operative matters, whereas the command was hoping for the severe curtailment, if not the outright elimination, of committees. Savinkov seemed to champion the committees, but surreptitiously encouraged Kornilov to view him as an ally in bringing all democratic organizations, soviets included, under control through an all-powerful commissariat. Kornilov, calculating that to get his political program accepted he would have to temporarily string along with Savinkov, in his heart sympathized with Denikin and the hard-liners.

The committees, still viewing Savinkov as an ally because of his actions in behalf of the Ninth and Tenth army committees, were sanguine about the new statute. The Southwestern Front Committee, reeling from Denikin's assaults, devoted an illegal assembly of August 12-13 in Kiev to drafting a model statute on committees and hoped to get it approved in Petrograd over the heads of the command. Their intent was no less than to reverse the entire course of events since mid-July and to reduce the command to military technicians. Committees were to become the authoritative arm of democracy in the Army. The commissars, though titularly agents of state authority, would in fact become vehicles to force on the command the will of the committees. In the debates on the function of commissars, Chairman Dashevskii was at odds with the sentiments of the assembly for failing to recognize that corps and divisional committees, not the commissars, should be the ''watchdogs of the Revolution on the spot.'' The assembly also strongly favored the ''right of recommendation'' for candidates to command posts, but there was an argument whether the nominations should be routed through the commissars or higher committees. All agreed that an All-Army Committee should be located at Stavka, but the front committee wanted the exclusive right to select deputies, whereas the army committees argued that front committees were too far removed from the concerns of soldiers and that army committees should select them. Chairman Dashevskii was obviously quite uncomfortable with the proceedings because the most militant voices seemed to gain the most sympathy.[85]

The model statute confirms how far the sentiments of committeemen had shifted since mid-July. It claimed for committees unconditional, free discussion of all questions, including actions of representatives of authority, the right to review all military legislation before going into effect,

[84] For the text of Order 473, see *GoXA*, August 20.

[85] *GO*, August 12.

unlimited investigative powers, and much more.[86] Another section dealing with reciprocal relations between committees and commissars deviated considerably from the ideas of Savinkov. To be sure, they are defined as "accredited representatives of the Provisional Government," but every point that followed served to reduce them to co-equal or even subordinate status to committees. The commissar was to assist committees in carrying out their work (presumably through leverage on the command) and to undertake no action without consulting them; in the case of conflict he could not overrule them, but only appeal to a higher level.

Although the draft was distinguished by neither consistency nor political acuity, it is clear that the spell of "firm revolutionary authority" was broken and that the earlier militancy against counter-revolution had been fully recovered. In fact, a new model of self-governing democracy in the Army was taking shape: hitherto the Army had been treated as in certain respects exempt from the fragmentation and dispersal of authority in the country at large on the strength of its unique mission of defending the country. In this new version, the Army would come to resemble the mélange of local Soviets, Committees of Social Organizations, and autonomous bodies (trade unions, land committees, militias, cooperatives) that tended to usurp state authority and to foist policy decisions on passive administrative authorities, or even to create executive organs of their own. The militants of the Southwestern Front were slipping down this slippery slope.

In the meantime, the committees from all fronts took advantage of the Moscow State Conference to hold a first-ever conference. There is little record of the organizational steps which preceded it, but the Ninth Army Committee was aware of it in advance and gave instructions to their two representatives, so one may assume some type of advance preparation.[87] Only *Go3A* carried a record of the proceedings, which, while extensive, is obviously not complete. Indirectly one can infer that the conference either adopted a revised version of the model statute of the Southwestern Front or adopted a similar one of its own, as its version was subsequently submitted to the War Ministry. This version provided for extending commissars down to the corps level and, not in the Kiev model statute, for the right of committees to recommend removal (*otvod*) of commanders. Several proposals reflected a determination to have more influence over the centers of power. The most important was the creation of a central "All-Army Committee" at Stavka, pending the convocation of an All-

[86] *IzOA*, August 31 and September 2. Added later was a claim to "participate in the military preparations of the Army" as well as to evaluate operations at their conclusion (*ibid.*, September 1).

[87] *Iz9A*, August 12.

Army Congress which would maintain a regular, rotating membership in the Petrograd Soviet and post controls over the War Ministry. Moreover, it was charged with petitioning the Commander in Chief and the Supreme Commissar on the desires of the Army, with monitoring all actions of Stavka and its staff, and with coordinating the work of all army committees.[88]

These proposals were carried by a deputation to the War Ministry immediately after the Moscow Conference, where they were coldly received by Fedor Stepun of the Political Administration of the War Ministry (one can infer a snub by Kerensky and Savinkov). They were admonished to await the determination of the Provisional Government patiently.[89] It is not recorded whether they contacted any of the leaders of the Soviet, but since several of the proposals were carried out immediately following the Kornilov affair, specifically the All-Army Committee at Stavka and an Electoral Commission for the Constituent Assembly, one can assume they had gained the patronage of someone of influence on the Soviet Executive Committee.

[88] *Go3A*, August 23, 24, 25.
[89] *Ibid.*, August 19.

CHAPTER VI

THE KORNILOV AFFAIR AT THE FRONT

ALTHOUGH the Kornilov conspiracy involved but a handful of senior officers, and Krymov's expeditionary force dissolved readily under persuasive efforts, the entire "democratic" sector of the Army—committees, commissars, and soldiers—reacted convulsively, perceiving it as a monumental threat from the united forces of counter-revolution. Only Denikin and his narrow circle of confidants of the Southwestern Front were privy to Kornilov's plans, and once Kerensky announced Kornilov's treason and removal, no line of conduct was obvious to his general and officer sympathizers. On the other hand, weeks of anxiety had schooled committeemen and soldiers for this moment, from front headquarters down to the very last regiment. First, Stavka's communications had to be interdicted and Kerensky's passed through, which required immediate controls over radio, Hughes apparatus, telegraph, telephone, and all means of transport (cars, motorcycles, horses). Second, troop movements toward the capital and other vital centers had to be halted, which meant intervention in the operative apparatus of the command and the railroads. Third, all commanders and staff officers potentially sympathetic to Kornilov had to be arrested or quarantined. Finally, the entire representative structure from top to bottom had to be activated to declare loyalty to the Provisional Government and the Soviet (a split between the two was still regarded as inconceivable) and to coordinate the appropriate actions. The sources bear witness to mobilization on all these fronts, which if not total was far out of proportion to the pro-Kornilov forces, real or potential. The ease with which the Cossack and Caucasus units in Krymov's force were neutralized was a measure of the futility of the adventure; of units thought to be pro-Kornilov (cavalry, death battalions, officers' training units), few were activated, and those that were activated dissolved just as readily through persuasion. The significance of this episode, therefore, was the sudden revelation of the lack of real strength beneath the pro-Kornilov euphoria, and the enormous potential of the democratic organizations when leadership and following acted in concert.

This should have been a lesson for Kerensky and the partisans of coalition, but it was poorly learned, and even before the crisis was over, Kerensky (with the acquiescence of the Soviet leadership) was reconstructing the shattered edifice on the same foundations with other pro-Kornilov generals substituted for Kornilov. Well-broadcast directives of Kerensky promptly negated all the initiatives whereby the front was convinced it had saved the Provisional Government and the Revolution. The total effect was to undermine the last fund of prestige of the coalition government and its Leader, to paralyze the just released vitality of the committees, and to arouse in the soldier masses a renewed determination for Soviet-based power, coupled with a drastic resolution of all the dangling social and political issues, above all the war. The Bolsheviks were by no means the prime movers of these momentous developments, but under their protection they rapidly regained all the ground lost since June and easily disseminated their attractive programmatic appeals.

Consequently, the Kornilov epos, in a sense far more fundamental than conventionally understood then or since, was the decisive turning point, or watershed, of the Revolution. Thereafter events flowed ineluctably in the direction of a resolution based on Soviet power, land, and peace. The downward flow was not to be arrested by yet another coalition, appeals for restraint until the Constituent Assembly, or invocation of revolutionary authorities, not even of the current leadership of VTsIK. The destined outcome was not per se Bolshevik ascendancy, subject to other variables, but a credible realization of the masses' claims to their own Revolution. This fundamental postulate cannot be understood unless one fully appreciates the magnitude of the upheaval, not of Kornilov's partisans but of those who rose up against him. The present task therefore is to bring into appropriate perspective all the dynamic elements involved, from the peaks of authority to the deepest stirrings of the masses and comprising all the mediating structures in between—Soviets, commissars, committees at all levels, not to speak of new organizations that were now making their appearance at the front, namely, peasant, nationality, and party groups. Not all can be dealt with in equal depth, but a proper framework into which they can logically be joined will be attempted.

☆

Two events, the Moscow State Conference and the fall of Riga to the Germans, served to crystallize the hitherto inchoate preoccupation with counter-revolution into a firm conviction of a conspiracy centered at Stavka. The army committees were predisposed to regard the Moscow State Conference as the culmination of Kerensky's efforts to construct a strong revolutionary government as a bulwark any danger from the Left or the Right. Nor did Kornilov yet appear as irrevocably belonging to the hostile camp, as the distinctiveness of his views on committees from Denikin and other hard-liners was well known. Some committee leaders, particularly of the Fifth Army, placed great faith in a combination of Kerensky and Kornilov. At Moscow, however, the front deputies witnessed the thunderous demonstration of homage to the Savior-Supreme Commander and the orgy of vilification of soviets and committees. Undoubtedly they became politically more knowledgeable through the proceedings and informal contacts in the corridors with political figures. Any lingering admiration for Kornilov was dissipated by the fawning attention of Union of Officers types and his speech which though restrained on the subject of committees fed the appetite of the Right on the death penalty and the "cowardly soldier hordes."

The speeches of Alekseev and Kaledin were uncompromising indictments of the democratic organizations, civilian and military, and were pitched to crude responses from the right half of the auditorium. Alekseev contrasted the present situation—when agitators flooded the front, battle orders were settled at meetings, and committees and commissars tied commanders hand and foot—with idyllic prerevolutionary times when soldiers and officers trusted each other and the Army was able to fight. Lurid examples making little distinction between committee interference, mass disobedience, Bolshevik agitation, and German espionage elicited outcries of "Disgrace!" "Treason!" and "Bravo!" Kaledin's short speech was a sharp challenge to the democratic camp, leaving nothing to inference or innuendo:

> The army must be kept outside of politics (cries from the right: "Right!"). All Soviets and committees must be abolished (noise from the left, applause from the right). . . . Discipline in the army must be raised and strengthened by the most resolute measures (noise; cries from the right: "Bravo!" "Bravo!"; storm of applause, noise and whistles from the left); the leaders of the army must be given full powers ("Bravo!" "Bravo!").[1]

The honor of the committees required a forceful rejoinder, but only Kuchin of the Twelfth Army Committee, timidly rebutting Alekseev, claimed that the committees, not the command, had put a stop to fraternization and made the summer offensive possible, which brought forth a demonstrative reaction from the left. Kuropatkin of the Fifth Army read

[1] *RPG* 2:1479-80; Alekseev's speech in *Gosudarstvennoe soveshchanie. Stenograficheskii otchet* (Moscow, 1930), pp. 208-15 (not included in *RPG*).

a conciliatory statement on behalf of the front delegates, possibly reflecting the views of the Fifth Army delegation, which still looked to Kornilov to keep the Right in check.[2] Compared with their adversaries, the front delegates had failed to rise to the occasion, reflecting their relative lack of experience and acknowledged stature. Nevertheless, they came away from the conference wiser and more determined than ever to mobilize their own forces against the threat of counter-revolution.

The army committee press gave extensive coverage to the Moscow State conference, devoting whole issues to the verbatim record, but their commentary stressed the moments of harmony, such as Bublikov's celebrated handshake with Tsereteli. "Even Miliukov withdrew his 'insofar as' in support of the government," declared *Go3A* on August 19, a comment scarcely merited by the contentious and threatening tone of his speech.[3] Unlike their comrades at the conference, they had not witnessed the thickly drenched atmosphere of hostility, the thundering ovations and catcalls of Left and Right, and Kerensky's embarrassing impotence.

The committee delegates on their return conveyed their sense of alarm to their comrades. Aralov, the delegate from the Third Army, reported that "all the sessions were carried on under the banner of struggle against the committees and the Soviets."[4] He cited a few characteristic incidents, such as the slap delivered by a general staff colonel to Cossack Nagaev for denying that Kaledin spoke for the cossack rank and file. The Twelfth Army Committee, upon hearing their delegates report, protested to VTsIK and the Provisional Government that the speeches of Kaledin and Kornilov were "manifestly counter-revolutionary" and had provoked deep anxiety among the soldier masses.[5] Most of the committee public had now come to understand the significance of the demonstrations of the Right and mentally girded themselves for battle.

The Riga disaster called forth a repetition of the public outcry over the July retreat, but this time the committee public was not deceived. Kornilov's communiqué on the German crossing of the Dvina, provocatively mimicking the Tarnopol dispatch, referred to "the disorganized masses of soldiers streaming irresistibly along the road to Pskov," which conjured up images of German hordes pounding at the gates of Petrograd.[6] This version, however, was promptly refuted by Commissar Woytinsky, who

[2] *RPG* 3:1502 and *Iz5A*, August 24.

[3] Other examples in *GoXA*, August 19; *Iz5A*, August 24; and *IzOA*, August 20.

[4] *Go3A*, August 22.

[5] *RDRA*, pp. 326-27. Among other things, Kornilov had ordered the 56th Siberian Regiment "obliterated" for alleged desertion under fire, which they claimed never took place. For a similar reaction in the 426th Regiment, see *ibid.*, pp. 359-60.

[6] *RPG* 2:1037.

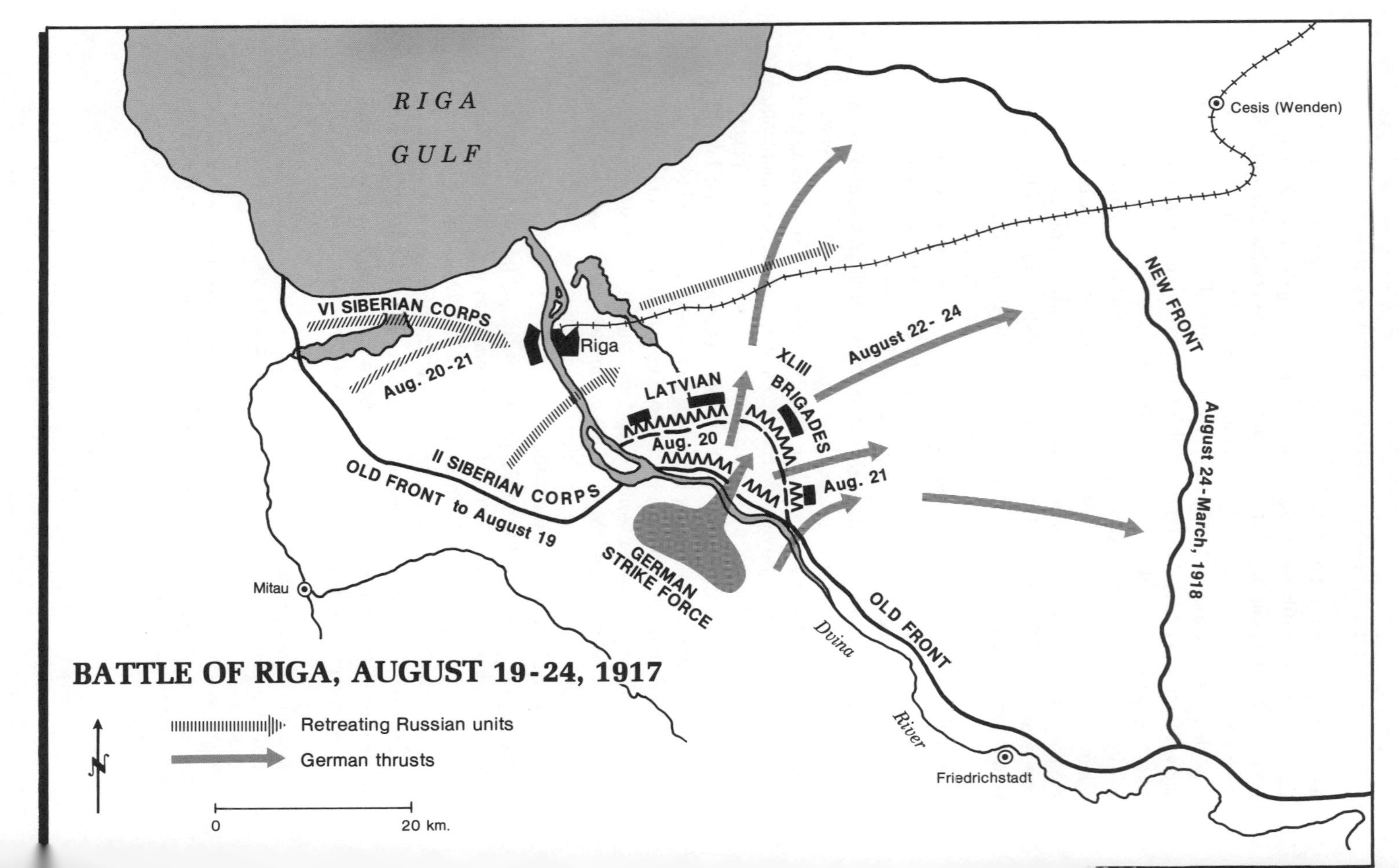
RIGA
GULF
Cesis (Wenden)
VI SIBERIAN CORPS
Riga
Aug. 20-21
LATVIAN
XLIII
BRIGADES
August 22- 24
NEW FRONT
August 24-March, 1918
Aug. 20
Aug. 21
II SIBERIAN CORPS
OLD FRONT to August 19
GERMAN STRIKE FORCE
Mitau
Dvina
River
OLD FRONT
Friedrichstadt
BATTLE OF RIGA, AUGUST 19-24, 1917
Retreating Russian units
German thrusts
0
20 km.

fired off a telegram to VTsIK: "I testify before all Russia that this misfortune was no disgrace to the army. The troops honestly carried out all the orders of commanders . . . [they] mounted bayonet charges and went out to certain death."[7] Woytinski's vivid account of the action appeared in *IzPS* and was reprinted in nearly all the army newspapers.

Shortly thereafter the II and VI Siberian corps were ordered to withdraw from the large pocket on the left bank of the lower Dvina without engaging the enemy, rendering a defense of Riga impossible. Riga was known as an impassable fortress, protected by elaborate concrete-reinforced entrenchments and gun emplacements, yet it was surrendered without a fight. The suspicious Left now read new meaning into Kornilov's cryptic words at the Moscow State Conference, to the effect that "the enemy is knocking at the gates of Riga, and if the shakiness of our troops does not allow us to hold the coastline of the Riga Gulf, the road to Petrograd will be open" and that "it may take the fall of Riga to bring about the restoration of order in the rear."[8] Thus, to the Right he became a prophet who forecast the inevitable fall of Riga, while to the Left, including Kerensky, the Bolsheviks, and the army committees, he had revealed his covert intention to deliberately surrender Riga to frighten the country into a dictatorship.[9]

[7] *Ibid.*, p. 1033.

[8] *Ibid.*, 3:1476 and 1478.

[9] A lengthy analysis of the Riga campaign that was meant to distinguish myth from reality has been eliminated here. What appeared to be "treasonous" command decisions were sometimes based on rational, even if mistaken, military calculations, and what appeared as "cowardice" was the normal confusion of battle conditions and loss of contact with the command. General Parskii, not Kornilov, decided on the evacuation of Riga; Kornilov offered no directives that can be determined, but he failed to provide reinforcements and could easily have dispatched the III Cavalry Corps had they not been earmarked for Petrograd. Parskii fully anticipated the German attack, pinpointed its exact location, and took prudent countermeasures, but the force of the attack spread out his units, and both lateral and vertical communications broke down. The Bolshevik-dominated Latvian brigades fought tenaciously for two days, taking heavy casualties, allowing the two Siberian corps to complete their withdrawal, which is acknowledged by both German and unfriendly Russian sources (*RWK* 12:194-98 and Stepan Posevin, *Gibel' imperii. Severnyi front* [Riga, 1922], pp. 15-27; Posevin was a mindless reactionary who blamed all adverse developments on a Bolshevik-masonic conspiracy, but lauded the heroism of the Latvians, who he said were the only troops to fight bravely). Commissar Woytinsky reaped the eternal gratitude of Parskii and XLIII Corps Commander Boldyrev for defending the honor of the troops with his dispatches and for providing the sole communications around the perimeter by racing from unit to unit by car, everywhere boosting morale, providing essential information on dispositions, and picking up stragglers and returning them to their units. (See Woytinsky's two accounts, "Gody pobedy" [Ms.], HI, 3: chap. 9, and *Stormy Passage*, pp. 338-43.) His superior, Front Commissar Stankevich, arrived on the scene late by the Pskov Road, saw only fleeing staffs and troops in total disarray, and was determined to undertake exemplary shootings until Kornilov's bloodcurdling telegrams and Woytinsky's information convinced him otherwise.

On the eve of the Kornilov affair an acrimonious debate raged in the metropolitan press between the ''democratic'' and Kornilovist versions. On August 22 *Russkoe Slovo* gravely stated: ''After six days the terrible warning has become a reality. . . . Unfortunately the voice of the Supreme Commander not only remains unheeded by our revolutionary democracy, but it is far from having the necessary effect on the Provisional Government.'' *Novoe Vremia* chimed in on August 25: ''The loss of Riga was prophesied—the Riga region was abundantly equipped with arms, artillery, military provisions, and a large garrison. . . . Everything was in vain because the northern army, devoid of military discipline, was no army at all, but simply an aggregate of armed men.'' *IzPS*, on the other hand, suggested on August 24 that ''the official communiqué regarding events near Riga have confirmed the suspicion . . . that Stavka is carrying on a calculated political game against the Provisional Government and the revolutionary democracy.''[10]

Despite the brevity of the controversy, it reached a broad sector of the front via newspapers, front and rear. The Twelfth Army became virtually obsessed with its own defense. Iskosol protested the ''brazen agitation of the Right,'' declaring it a ''stab in the back'' of a brave army that revealed ''amazing staunchness and dauntless courage'' and had endured unprecedented drumfire with enormous losses; it stoutly denied there had been a disorderly flight.[11] *Go3A* of August 24, citing Dashevskii, chairman of the Southwestern Front Committee, accused counter-revolutionary circles of ''criminal agitation'' and of ''taking advantage of sad events'' in the Army to ''terrorize Russian society and the revolutionary power into returning to the old regime.'' On August 26 *IzOA* noted the contradiction between Woytinsky's version and the capital press, which spoke of a ''new Tarnopol.'' The most forceful and politically significant, however, was an article in *Iz8A* of September 1, which accused Stavka of deliberate falsification in its accounts of both Tarnopol and Riga and publicly apologized to the soldiers of the 607th Mlynovskii Regiment for having swallowed the Stavka version. ''Fortunately, the soldiers didn't believe us and they were the first to see that treason was behind it.'' They also observed that the Officers' Union had woven itself a firm nest at Stavka, having full use

(See Stankevich, *Vospominaniia*, pp. 202-12.) Kornilov intended to bring Woytinsky and Parskii to trial for filing false reports, but the Affair intervened. The angle of vision determines everything.

[10] For the above, see *RPG* 2:1029-30 and 1034. Fifth Army Commander Danilov characterized as ''slander'' the assertion of the *Birzhevye Vedomosti* that the Fifth Army had refused to come to the aid of the Twelfth Army because they had disgracefully fled (*ibid.*, p. 1035).

[11] Telegram published in *IzPS*, August 26 (*RPG* 2:1036).

of official channels of communication which were now denied to the committees—the first suggestion of the complicity of Kerensky and Savinkov, which was to become a widespread conviction after the Kornilov affair.

After the Kornilov affair, soldiers frequently asserted that they had suspected treachery all along, often with more than a touch of self-congratulation, but in one case their presentiments can be confirmed: an army committeeman touring the front was buttonholed by angry soldiers who asked him: "When are you going to get rid of Kornilov and put a stop to the slander against the soldiers?" The author further states, "They complained specifically about the speeches of Kornilov and Kaledin at the Moscow Conference" and expressed willingness to support such a move with force of arms. He concluded, "The lying reports of Stavka about the flight of whole units from the front lines has definitely discredited all the staffs in the eyes of the soldiers."[12] These may represent the reactions of a few more articulate and well-informed soldiers, but the better informed often expressed the less articulate, sometimes fantastic, but just as firmly held convictions of the mass.

☆

Given the long period of psychological preparation, the Kornilov affair was liquidated with breathtaking swiftness, both in the environs of the capital and at the front. The crisis was precipitated on August 27 by the respective circular telegrams of Kerensky, VTsIK, and Kornilov, and by September 1 it was all over, even in remote areas of the front where communications were delayed. At its conclusion the grandiose plans for "strong authority" and the "restoration of discipline" by would-be strongmen—Kerensky, Savinkov, and Kornilov—lay in ruins: commanders and lower officers were once more at the mercy of the uncontrollable passion of their men, arrests and violent abuse of officers rebounded, and committees and commissars found themselves in charge of staffs, communications, and even operations. The heroic effort to reverse the course of the Revolution succeeded only in opening the floodgates of its downward course.

On August 27 the advance echelons of Krymov's force were fast approaching the capital along three different routes, reaching Iamburg, Luga, and Vyritsa by the following day.[13] Indeed, in another forty-eight hours

[12] *GF*, September 3.

[13] The hour-by-hour progress of the Krymov expedition on the basis of excellent documentation is given by E. I. Martynov, *Kornilov (popytka voennogo perevorota)* (Leningrad, 1927), chap. 6. See below, pp. 195-97. For the sake of brevity, an extensive discussion of the Kornilov conspiracy and the Krymov expedition is omitted here, though the author has researched the subject. The reader may consult the excellent account of George Katkov, *The*

the noose was to have closed around the revolutionary capital, as Krymov had been ordered to complete his concentration by the evening of the 28th; on the 26th Kornilov informed Savinkov, in keeping with their bargain, "The corps will be concentrated in the region of Petrograd by the evening of August 28. I request that Petrograd be declared under martial law on August 29."[14] There is no better proof that Kornilov was convinced that he had Kerensky in his pocket and was innocent of any thought that his plans could go awry. No sooner was the above telegram sent off than

---

Kornilov Affair: Kerensky and the Breakup of the Russian Army (London and New York, 1980), which portrays Kornilov and his supporters as the victims of Kerensky's failure of will and minimizes the clumsy conspiratorial activities of both Kornilov and well-wishers. For the best discussions, see Rosenberg, *Liberals*, pp. 205-12 and 220-28; and Rabinowitch, *Bolsheviks Come to Power*, pp. 146-49 and *passim*. Katkov's account is straightforwardly accurate on Kornilov's futile attempts to get Kerensky to implement his "program"; Kerensky did string Kornilov along, performing intricate gymnastics to avoid delivering on his promises and deceiving even his Deputy Minister of Defense, Savinkov, who was attempting to keep the combination together. Savinkov was pursuing a strong-man conspiracy of his own, which envisaged utilizing Kerensky and Kornilov as symbols in a revolutionary directorate which he and Filonenko, the chief commissar at Stavka, would manage behind the scenes through the commissarial network. He attempted to finalize this scheme in a long interview with Kornilov on August 25, during which he falsely pretended to be negotiating on Kerensky's behalf; Kornilov was thus led to believe that he had struck a bargain with Kerensky which allowed him "legally" to concentrate Krymov's cavalry corps toward Petrograd and reconstruct the government, but he also was guilty of deceptive conduct, since he had no intention of dealing with Kerensky as an equal partner once his forces occupied Petrograd. (For text of discussions based on Savinkov's notes, see *VOSR. Avgust*, pp. 421-23; see Lukomskii, *Vospominaniia*, pp. 234-35, for a reliable version of how Kornilov understood the agreement.) Kornilov's plans, however, had already been laid and did not depend on Kerensky's consent. Through the Union of Officers he was in touch with a number of officer and civilian patriotic groups which since April had been looking for a suitable dictator, loosely held together by a civilian-based organization called the Republican Center. Heavy financing was provided by a group of industrialists headed by A. I. Putilov called the Society for the Economic Regeneration of Russia. Krymov had been involved in plots against the Provisional Government since the early days of the Revolution and offered Kornilov the services of his Third Cavalry Corps under unclear circumstances sometime in early August. All essential ingredients of the plan were in place by the time of the Moscow Conference, since Kornilov confided the details to his Chief of Staff, Lukomskii, around August 6 or 7, when he was obliged to give orders on the transfer of the III Cavalry Corps to the Northern Front (see Lukomskii, pp. 220-22). Kerensky assembled a good bit of documentation on the different strands of conspiracy in *RPG* 3:1526-1613 which he subsequently utilized in his *Russia and History's Turning Point*, chap. 21. However, he arbitrarily construes them as a master plan concocted in April, whereas in reality a number of separate networks and scenarios were simply brought together in improvised fashion around the time of the Moscow State Conference, Kornilov attempting very inexpertly to keep them together. Soviet historiography parallels Kerensky's version. See N. Ia. Ivanov, *Kornilovshchina i ee razgrom* (Leningrad, 1965), and M. I. Kapustin, *Zagovor generalov* (Moscow, 1968).

[14] *VOSR. Avgust*, p. 439.

Kerensky called him to the Hughes apparatus to trap him into admitting that the message of V. N. L'vov to the effect that the government should surrender its powers to Stavka indeed proceeded from him. Kornilov was allowed to think that Kerensky and Savinkov agreed to the plan and would shortly come to Stavka for protection. So little was Kornilov aware of Kerensky's furious counter-measures that he sent off telegrams to a number of prominent political figures, including Miliukov and Rodzianko, to come to Stavka for consultations.[15]

Therefore Kornilov was stunned on the morning of August 27 to receive word of his abrupt dismissal and the order to Lukomskii to take over his duties, so stunned that he fell ill and played little direct part in the ensuing drama except by proxy.[16] Lukomskii took matters in hand and composed a long message to Kerensky recounting the bad faith of the government on Kornilov's program, the scourge of committees and commissars, the influence on the government of "irresponsible social organizations," and the solemn agreements entered into with Kerensky's emissaries, Savinkov and L'vov, which now were being repudiated. In conclusion he pleaded: "For the sake of the salvation of Russia you must go with General Kornilov and not replace him. His replacement would cause an explosion in the Army which would spell Russia's doom. I await further instructions."[17] Lukomskii immediately relayed all this information to the front chiefs, stating that "pending clarification of circumstances" Kornilov would not surrender command and that he, Lukomskii, had declined the appointment, as otherwise "civil war" and an upheaval in the Army would result.[18]

This open defiance of Kerensky's authority was nevertheless constructed to give him the opportunity to retreat gracefully. Though Kerensky himself

[15] See Lukomskii, pp. 240-41. V. N. L'vov was a Moscow politician and former Procurator of the Holy Synod in the first cabinet, not to be confused with Minister President L'vov. His was another of the circles who hoped to enlist Kornilov in plans of their own and secure Kerensky's cooperation. As a conspirator he was totally inept, fell into the clutches of Zavoiko (Kornilov's civilian adjutant and promoter, who was piqued at being left out of the main conspiracy), and manipulated L'vov into serving as a weapon to intimidate Kerensky into submission. The result was to alert Kerensky to the danger and the aborting of the plans of the conspirators. There are many accounts of L'vov's muddled interviews with Kerensky, for example, in W. H. Chamberlin's *Russian Revolution*, 2 vols. (New York, 1935), 1:209-12, but the bizarre story of Zavoiko's intrigues has yet to be told. See Martynov, *Kornilov*, pp. 39ff. and 85 and *passim*, and L'vov's deposition in *VOSR. Avgust*, pp. 425-28. L'vov's émigré account, which includes circumstantial details that seem incredible, is reproduced in *RPG* 3:1558-68.

[16] Text of telegram in Martynov, p. 101; on Kornilov's illness, see Tikhobrazov, "V stavke posle revoliutsii" (Ms.), RA, p. 96, who asserts that because of Kornilov's delirious condition he issued an offer to have himself and the entire staff at Stavka shot.

[17] *VOSR. Avgust*, pp. 447-48.

[18] Martynov, p. 102.

had crossed the Rubicon, he had considerable difficulty convincing his cabinet. After a stormy and confused discussion, Kerensky extracted from the weary ministers "full powers" to deal with the crisis (though they retained their portfolios), which he felt entitled him to send off the telegram of dismissal.[19] But throughout the day of August 27 he was under strong pressure both inside and outside the cabinet to reach a compromise. Savinkov insisted that he could straighten out the matter with Kornilov over the direct wire, which dragged out fruitlessly most of the day (each exchange was encoded and decoded).[20] Strengthened by Lukomskii's refusal, Kerensky was able toward evening to obtain ministerial approval of a final, irrevocable public pronouncement on Kornilov's removal. Reflecting the desire for compromise, the terms "rebel" and "treason" were scrupulously avoided; in fact, the affair was blamed on "certain circles of Russian society which desire to exploit the difficult position of the government to establish a state order contrary to the conquests of the Revolution." At the same time it announced the appointment of General Klembovskii, chief of the Northern Front, to replace Kornilov, and assigned him the task of halting Krymov's movement toward the capital.

Much to Kerensky's chagrin, not only did Klembovskii refuse the appointment, but he and all other front chiefs except Przhevalskii of the Caucasus Front strongly urged him not to remove Kornilov.[21] General Baluev of the Western Front, hitherto regarded as a loyal and "democratic" general, was particularly emphatic that Kornilov's removal would be interpreted as an unwillingness of the Provisional Government to carry through the necessary measures to restore authority in the Army. Of these responses, however, only Denikin's took a stance of open defiance of the Provisional Government. Stavka itself circulated these responses, Przhevalskii's excepted, as a package to all fronts through which they reached army and lower commands.

Thus, on August 28 the declared solidarity of senior commanders had some hope of persuading the government to back down. But two significant developments intervened to preclude this: first, Soviet circles were already alert to the movement of troops on the capital and were mobilizing their own forces for defense; second, Kornilov, through his surrogate Zavoiko, released an intemperate denunciation of the Provisional Government, accusing it of "outright lies" and a "great provocation." Declaring his refusal to step down, Kornilov appealed for support from the country:

> Russian people! Our great Motherland is dying! . . . Compelled to act openly, I, General Kornilov, declare that the Provisional Govern-

[19] See Kokoshkin's report in his Ms., Nicolaevsky Archive, HI.

[20] Complete text in *VOSR. Avgust*, pp. 448-52.

[21] Text of Kerensky's telegram in Martynov, p. 109; replies in *ibid.*, pp. 114-16.

> ment, under the pressure of the Bolshevik majority [*sic*], is acting in full accord with the plans of the German General Staff. . . .
>
> I, General Kornilov, son of a Cossack peasant, declare to each and all that I seek nothing for myself besides the preservation of Great Russia and swear to lead the people to victory over the enemy, and to the Constituent Assembly which will decide its own destiny and the form of the new state.[22]

This declaration cost Kornilov the support of generals Baluev and Shcherachev, as well as most of his civilian well-wishers, and scuttled all hopes for an accommodation.[23]

☆

The ensuing struggle took place primarily via telegraph, radio, and other media, since the forces of both sides were scattered up and down the front and along the railroads. A study of the copious published and unpublished communications reveals the utter hopelessness of Kornilov's cause once the contest was joined. Krymov could continue to concentrate his forces only to the extent that he could keep Kerensky's appeal and subsequent orders from his men and sell them on the cock-and-bull story of a Bolshevik rising. But there was no way of preventing railroad workers, telegraph operators, and local Soviets from getting these messages, and every pause in the journey became a great hazard.

The encounter in Luga of the lead echelons of the First Don Cossack Division, which Krymov joined on August 28, is typical. The chairman of the local soviet, N. Voronovich, relates how he was informed early that morning by the traffic manager that "the whole line back to Pskov is loaded with troop trains" and that cossack officers, who refused to reveal their mission, were demanding prompt expedition to Petrograd.[24] Only upon contacting the VTsIK by wire did Voronovich learn of Kornilov's dismissal. Through the General Staff apparatus he was informed that the Provisional Government expected the Luga garrison, consisting of merely 1,200 poorly armed cossack recruits, to hold up Krymov's full division, trainloads of which were stacking up outside Luga by the minute. Voronovich personally delivered to Krymov the order to reverse his march route and informed him that Klembovskii was now Commander in Chief. Krymov replied that he took his orders from his own Commander in Chief, Kornilov, and intended to carry out the mission entrusted to him. If the track were not cleared in a quarter of an hour, his Cossacks would push through by force. In the interim, railroad workers had let the steam out of

[22] *Ibid.*, pp. 116-17.

[23] *Ibid.*, p. 127.

[24] N. Voronovich, "Zapiski predsedatelia soveta sold. deputatov," *Arkhiv Grazhdanskoi Voiny* (Berlin, 1922), 2:75. Cf. Martynov, chap. 6.

the engines and blocked the tracks; cavalry sappers also mined the bridges over nearby rivers.

Voronovich moved most of the garrison across the river from Luga and ordered them to dig in. A small squadron was left behind with orders to fraternize with Krymov's Cossacks when they occupied the city and explain the true situation. The Don Cossacks had been told that the garrison was held by "Bolsheviks" who had disarmed the local cossack units, but an exchange of information revealed the deception. Krymov briefly occupied the telegraph office, but removed his troops before nightfall to prevent further infection. Meetings of cossacks took place throughout the night, at which the deceptive conduct of the commander was the chief subject of discussion. The next day agitators from the Petrograd Soviet arrived with bundles of newspapers. Krymov was obliged to persuade his troops by spurious arguments that they were being sent to rescue the Provisional Government from the Bolsheviks, but his Cossacks no longer believed him. They informed the Soviet representatives that if they had a direct order from Kerensky they would arrest their own commander.

On the morning of August 30, Krymov, realizing the game was lost, complied with Kerensky's order to proceed to Petrograd and report to his chief. After a violent encounter Krymov withdrew to the apartment of a friend and shot himself.[25] Just why Krymov decided to comply with Kerensky's order is still a puzzle, as it was to his fellow conspirators at the time, but surely the chief reason was sheer frustration at being unable to pursue his campaign by conventional military means and at the unexpected advantages of his opponents.[26]

☆

Senior commanders at most army and front headquarters were so completely overtaken by events that they could do little more than sit back and allow them to unfold. Denikin had shared his general knowledge of Kornilov's plan with a select group of senior commanders and staff at a conference he had called in mid-August. The meeting did not escape notice: a telegraph operator observed the unusual accumulation of staff cars,

[25] See Martynov, pp. 148-51, and Rabinowitch, *Bolsheviks Come to Power*, pp. 146-50.

[26] See informative article by Denikin in *Poslednye Novosti*, November 14, 1937. Krymov was persuaded by his friend and fellow general staff officer, Samarin, who was sent on this mission by Kerensky with the promise that he would not be arrested, a promise he nearly did not keep. Krymov was to give a deposition to an investigative commission that same day, but rather than comply he committed suicide. Denikin's facts still do not explain why Krymov complied if he had any hope of success. He does supply the circumstance that General Alekseev briefed Samarin before his departure and who possibly urged Samarin to comply. Krymov's suicide note was brought to Kornilov at Stavka, but Kornilov destroyed it without revealing its contents to anyone, thus sealing the mystery. (See Lukomskii, pp. 250-51.) It was apparently not complimentary to Kornilov.

learned from a chauffeur who was present, and immediately reported the fact to Assistant Commissar Kostytsin and the front committee.[27] Thus it was no longer a secret that something of considerable import was being prepared.

A few days before the break, an officer appeared to Denikin with a verbal message from Kornilov informing him of the details of the plot, including restructuring of the government, but the only action solicited was to send several dependable officers, officially to be instructed in the British mortars but actually to be sent to Petrograd to augment the forces of the officer conspirators. Thus, there was no plan of action, as Kornilov had not requested any, and the conspirators expected the matter to be resolved handily by Krymov in Petrograd. The complacent certitude of these generals is expressed by General K. K. Akintievskii, who was attached to Denikin's staff: "It seemed to us that Kornilov had a hand of four aces to liquidate Kerensky's government, and his entourage would disperse without any pressure in panic. . . . After chopping off the head, it would be easy to get rid of the commissars and the committees."[28] The first short telegram on Kornilov's dismissal, then Lukomskii's reply, "struck like lightning." Unlike the other front commanders, Denikin did not wait for further clarification to nail his colors to the mast. He fired off a telegram to Kerensky with copies to his army commanders:

> I am a soldier and am not accustomed to playing games. On July 16, at the assembly of senior commanders with the Provisional Government, I declared that a whole series of military measures have destroyed, rotted out the Army, and dragged our fighting banners in the mud. My retention at my post as front chief I understood as a recognition by the Provisional Government of its profound guilt before the Motherland and of its desire to rectify the evil. Today, General Kornilov . . . has been removed from his post as Commander in Chief. I regard it as the obligation of my conscience to inform the Provisional Government that I cannot follow it along this path.[29]

In a very short time Denikin received the endorsements of this telegram from all his army commanders—Selivachev, Erdeli, Rerberg—as well as

[27] Deposition to the Shablovskii Commission in the archive of R. R. Raupakh, "Materialy o sobytiiakh v gorode Berdicheve" (Ms.), RA (hereafter, Raupakh, "Berdichev"). Raupakh was a member of the Republican Center and a party to the Kornilov conspiracy whom Kerensky unwittingly appointed to the Shablovskii Commission; he was able to bring these invaluable materials into the emigration and deposit them at RA. That he was a conspirator is confirmed by Finisov in *RPG* 3:1537. See also Denikin, *Ocherki*, 1(2):202-3.

[28] "Memoirs of Gen. Konstantin Akintsievskii 1884-1962" (Ms.), HI, p. 153. Similar sentiments in Gerua, *Vospominaniia*, 2:211-12.

[29] *Ocherki*, 1(2):214, and elsewhere.

a number of chiefs of staff, quartermasters, and other senior officers. Kornilov sent Denikin a telegram of appreciation, but no additional instructions.

Denikin was thoroughly aware of his hopeless position—only a single regiment of Orenburg Cossacks guarded his headquarters, while nearby were the unruly garrisons of Berdichev and Zhitmor and a number of thoroughly propagandized staff units. Chauffeurs, orderlies, telegraph operators, messengers—none of them could be trusted. The *ordinartsy*, formerly field police but now performing security duty for staff buildings, had for some time been assembling dossiers on the "counter-revolutionary activities" of various staff personnel, which they submitted to the Southwestern Front Committee during the crisis.[30] The only available countermeasure was to interdict Kerensky's messages and let those of Kornilov and his supporters through, but even this had to be done cautiously. In the early morning hours Front Quartermaster Markov ordered all lower commands to "post immediate officer controls with guards over all telephones, telegraphs, and radio stations, both civilian and military" which were to "hold up all telegrams of hostile content to the Commander in Chief." General Erdeli of the Special Army ordered the telegrams of Lukomskii, Denikin, Markov, and his own endorsement of Denikin's telegram sent on to lower units, but held up that of Kerensky (received at 4:00 A.M.). He then ordered telecommunications closed until further notice, but when Kornilov's proclamation arrived at 8:00 A.M. he passed it through. All these orders were canceled at 3:00 P.M. the same day under pressure from committees.[31] As ineffectual as these gestures were, they sufficed to incur grave charges of counter-revolutionary intent.

Military moves were practically out of the question, but Denikin strengthened the guard of Orenburg Cossacks around the staff headquarters. The second company, one of the participants relates, was ordered out at 7:00 A.M. and informed of its mission to defend headquarters against 300 or so armed Bolsheviks. Kerensky's telegram was read to them, but so were those of all the other commanders. The company set off without incident, but their path was blocked by two armored cars and a squadron of cavalry. Someone shouted to the cossacks: "Your officers are backing the old regime!" A few shots were fired, but the cossacks proceeded to headquarters, where a colonel, speaking in the name of the Southwestern Front Committee, demanded to see their orders. The cossack commander, already losing control, sarcastically replied: "Ask the regimental com-

[30] *RDRA*, pp. 360-62.

[31] Telegrams in Raupakh, "Materialy otnosiashchie k delu gen. Erdeli," RA (hereafter "Erdeli").

mittee.'' His unit melted into a typical ''meeting,'' where he was reproved for misleading his men against freedom and the Revolution.[32] Denikin took no further measures in his own defense, and he and his staff turned to routine matters, awaiting their fate.

The events in Berdichev are not completely clear, since the self-advertising version of the front committee is manifestly overstated.[33] An account published in *Golos Fronta* of September 8 credits not the front committee but the 77th Mounted Militia Squadron (a second reserve, noncombatant formation) for initiating the action to take over headquarters. Hearing early on August 28 of cossack patrols, guards over telecommunications, and General Kornilov's rebellion, the militia men resolved that they were ''ready to die'' to defend the Revolution, mounted up, and informed the front committee of their intentions after the fact. Officers refused to take part in the operation, so a clerk, Popov, took command and in this account was the hero. If committees functioned in this affair, it is not recorded. Even *feldshery* (medics) and veterinarians armed with pistols and knives joined the force. They were able for starters to bring over the two armored cars and a company of *ordinartsy*. They picked up support as they made the rounds of units in Berdichev and disarmed cossack patrols along the way. Shortly a ''commissar'' (Kostytsin, Iordanskii's assistant) joined them and agreed to supervise the arrests of Denikin and his senior officers.[34]

From his headquarters Denikin could observe the soldier crowds gathering in Berdichev over a deep ravine; a dense column headed by armored cars with red flags eventually wound its way toward his headquarters. The arrest was carried out in polite form, Kostytsin courteously offering to have his effects fetched, but Denikin declined. There were two casualties—a Czech officer who tried to mediate was beaten by the soldier crowds, and an intelligence officer shot a soldier who tried to break into his section. Later the arrested generals were escorted through the streets in an open car as a trophy, exposed to the ''searching stares and jeers'' of the soldier mob and placed in the main guardhouse of the garrison.[35] That same night Kerensky wired his confirmation of the arrests of Denikin, Markov, and Elsner ''until further instructions'' and appointed the front committee's nominee, General Ogordnikov, as the new commander.[36]

Events in the Special Army closely paralleled those at the front head-

[32] Embodied in ''Resolution'' passed at a general meeting of the company; Raupakh, ''Berdichev.''

[33] In the form of two flyers entitled *Biuletten' Armeiskago Vestnika*, August 28 and 30 and a telegram to the VTsIK of August 28 in *VOSR. Avgust*, p. 552.

[34] All according to *GF*, September 8.

[35] Denikin, *Ocherki*, 1(2):217-18.

[36] *RDRA*, p. 360.

quarters. Kerensky's telegrams were picked up at a radio station before controls could be imposed and passed on by a clerk to a member of the army committee, Aleksei Karnovich. Karnovich carried it to the committee of the staff units of the Special Army (the army committee's executive was located elsewhere), which discussed measures. He tried to contact the army committee by telegraph, but his access was blocked by a communications officer (the hour was 3:00 A.M.). It soon became clear that incoming telegrams were being filtered, and during a temporary absence of the first officer Karnovich persuaded another to let a message to the army committee through. He then demanded of General Erdeli that communications be restored with Kiev and the front committee. Erdeli replied frankly that he supported Kornilov and that he would use force to block any counter-move of the committee. In the meantime the Dombrovitsa garrison reopened the radio station and learned that the Soviet had declared Kornilov a traitor and had called for active struggle against him. A general meeting decided that Erdeli should be arrested; a General Sarychev, was chosen to replace Erdeli, and he consummated the arrest in the name of the Provisional Government. General Valter, the Chief of Staff, declared he would submit to the Provisional Government, but he agreed with Kornilov in everything and was allowed to remain at his post.[37]

General Selivachev of the Seventh Army undertook the same actions as Erdeli, but soldiers attached to the staff prevented the closing down of the radio receiver. Selivachev had wired his support of Denikin's telegram, but when confronted by the army committee he asked to be relieved of his command on grounds of health, certainly not a display of courage for one of his convictions. Nevertheless, he was arrested on September 2 on the order of Commissar Surguchev, probably to satisfy the outcry against him.[38] In the Eleventh Army, General Rerberg must have acted with more circumspection, because in spite of endorsing Denikin's telegram he was left in command and no arrests took place. Later special charges were brought against General Gerua, the Chief of Staff, who had not bothered to hide his antipathy to the army committee. Commissar Chekotilo originally stated to the Commission of Inquiry that Gerua had "conducted himself the whole time absolutely loyally" and had cooperated with him and the committees during the crisis. The army committee, however, would not let the matter rest, testifying on September 8 that Gerua and General N. V. Sollogub (the Quartermaster) were zealous members of the Officers' Union, "circulating its views and resolutions on every occasion, even

[37] According to depositions of Karnovich and a Lieutenant Korotkov, chairman of the committee of the staff units of Special Army headquarters, in Raupakh, "Erdeli."

[38] Deposition of General Selivachev in Raupakh, File No. 1 (in 15 untitled files).

those which attacked the Provisional Government." Their reputation was such, it was alleged, that it cost the committee "great efforts to restrain the masses from excesses." It was countersigned by Chekotilo, who was probably intimidated into reversing his position by the ugly mood then shaping up.[39] Even though the only formal evidence against Gerua was his adherence to Denikin's telegram (which applied also to Rerberg, who was not arrested), the suspicions were not ill-founded. Gerua admits in his memoirs that General Markov had informed him of the details of the conspiracy and asked him to sound out reliable officers who would be ready to act when necessary, and that he confided this information to his close associate Sollogub. Denikin denies that he himself recruited adherents in lower commands, but since Markov was fully briefed and a zealot for the Officers' Union, this was undoubtedly the conduit which reached Gerua. Gerua probably failed to act because, like Denikin, he was "struck by lightning."[40]

Thus, by nightfall on August 28, two days before the liquidation of Krymov's force and four days before the arrest of Kornilov, the headquarters of the Southwestern Front and all its constituent armies were under the effective control of representatives of revolutionary democracy, who asserted their residual emergency powers and the right to appoint their own candidates to the high posts vacated by the conspirators.

On the other fronts, senior commanders were more cautious or drew back in time if they harbored sympathies for Kornilov. Most of them, however, did not. Parskii and Danilov (Twelfth and Fifth armies) were unwavering in their loyalty to the government, while Commissar Zhdanov of the Western Front reported on August 28 that "everywhere committees and commissars are working in full cooperation with the command."[41] On the Rumanian Front, Cheremisov, who commanded the Ninth Army, and Tsiurikov, who commanded the Sixth Army, had reputations as "democratic generals."[42] Northern Front Commander Klembovskii was under a cloud, however, because he had refused to assume command from Kornilov, and his Chief of Staff, Lukirskii, and a few staff officers were known to sympathize with Kornilov. Commissars Stankevich and Woytinski were stranded in Petrograd, and a Sergeant Savitskii, formerly chairman of the Pskov Soviet, was appointed acting commissar by telegraph. Klembovskii

[39] From unsorted documents in *ibid*.

[40] See Gerua, 2:212-13.

[41] *VVP*, August 28. This included a clean bill of health for Baluev, despite his telegram, and he was left in command; Commissar Zhdanov claimed that Kornilov's messages received no circulation on his front, which apparently convinced Kerensky of Baluev's loyalty.

[42] Cheremisov earned his reputation through his public statements opposing the "Kornilov program" (see Martynov, pp. 37-38); on Tsurikov, see Wildman, *The Old Army*, p. 286.

was completely passive during the crisis, appearing distracted and panicky, even complaining of being ill; according to General Bonch-Bruevich, the garrison commandant, he wore a soldier's overcoat over his uniform as if about to flee. An officer tried to forbid Savitskii to use the staff telegraph to contact Stankevich, but the telegraph operators and the soldier guard forced him to stand aside. Savitskii recommended to Kerensky that the popular Bonch-Bruevich be appointed to replace Klembovkii, which was promptly done (another "democrat," Cheremisov, was soon to replace him). Klembovskii departed unhindered, and except for a few spontaneous arrests of staff officers no major upheaval occurred.[43]

Active support for Kornilov, other than verbal, therefore did not go very far beyond the Southwestern Front, and this support was nullified on the first day of the crisis. On August 29 Kerensky sent an exultant telegram "to all! to all! to all!" proclaiming that "the rebellion of General Kornilov and the small circle of adventurers around him had been liquidated"; Denikin and Erdeli were already under arrest, and everywhere else the democratic forces resolutely supported the government. This was, of course, slightly exaggerated, as it ignored the other guilty army commanders, but its purpose was doubtless to influence the wavering and might well have had that effect on Krymov and his cohorts.[44]

☆

The direct threat to the Provisional Government may have been easily liquidated, but the perceived threat called forth a reaction from the entire democratic sector far out of proportion to the real danger. The effect of the telegrams and radio broadcasts was like a gigantic electric shock—within hours all the units within foot-carrying distance of headquarters were alerted, and on the next day meetings, explanations, and improvised actions were taking place all up and down the front. One should keep in mind two distinct lines of communication, because they were sometimes in phase, sometimes not. First, the committee-commissar network was mobilized from top to bottom via deputies back and forth, and resulted in statements of support and measures of defense on every level. This process took place in stair-step fashion over August 29 and 30, leaving the democratic institutions in total control of the command apparatus, or at least having demonstrated the capacity to do so. More overpowering was the surge through the informal networks of the soldiers, which frequently outpaced that of the committees and sometimes reached such a pitch of militancy and violence that the committees had to abruptly turn about and

[43] See Stankevich, *Vospominaniia*, pp. 238-40, and M. D. Bonch-Bruevich, *From Tsarist General to Red Army Commander* (Moscow, 1966), pp. 155-56.

[44] See *VVP*, August 29, Prilozhenie.

concern themselves with the safety and integrity of the command. Simply to keep the discussion organized, the activization of the committee structure will be dealt with first, although it did not necessarily precede the activization of the ranks in time, and sequences and patterns differed from sector to sector and unit to unit.

On the Southwestern Front, even before the front committee gained control of the staff network it found a means to inform the army committees of unfolding events. Dr. Gottlieb, committee chairman and deputy from the XXXII Corps to Eleventh Army headquarters, recounts that the army committee set up a bypass route of telecommunications during the day on August 28 through which lower units were kept informed. The army committee remained in permanent session, took measures to disarm staff officers, set controls over the telegraph and radio, and designated from its membership "commissars" to each corps with full powers to deal with the crisis on that level. By the following day these commissars were giving full reports on events to corps committees, some of whom already controlled communications, to divisions, and to regiments. It appears that some representatives, like Dr. Gottlieb, who had been sent to army headquarters for information, returned as commissars. In this capacity Gottlieb reported on events and outlined the measures expected of lower committees. He read out the proclamations of VTsIK and the Southwestern Front Committee, and the corps committee immediately approved a resolution of response, declaring that "at first call" it would be ready to fight in defense of the Soviet (no mention of the Provisional Government or Kerensky). Controls on the staff apparatus were automatically posted, and members dispersed to their respective units to ready their forces against possible counter-revolutionary actions on the part of commanders. All proceeded like clockwork; the next day resolutions of support were pouring in from lower units. Apparently most of them were unaware of pro-Kornilov telegrams, which had been successfully intercepted, but those of Kerensky and VTsIK were already broadly known. Gottlieb himself presided over the arrest of the corps commander, General Ivanovskii. (Asked whom he supported, General Ivanovskii replied, "The Commander in Chief"; asked what forces he would rely on, "A good many stand behind us." "Are you even sure of your own security guards?" "No.") Informed that he must declare his loyalty or be removed, Ivanovskii resigned his command. The committee summoned a General Safarov to assume command. Effective control over the command hierarchy in the corps now existed from top to bottom.[45]

Committee records of the 57th Division afford an excellent picture of

[45] All recounted in *GO*, August 29.

the comprehensive nature of controls in the Special Army. The decisive session took place on August 29, by which time a commissar, Dr. Razumov (whether of the army or corps committee is not clear), reported on the details of the plot, the role of the Union of Officers at Stavka, Kornilov's ultimatum, and Kerensky's response. He specified the measures recommended by the army committee together with corps and division representatives, which can be taken as fairly typical for the Southwestern Front:

1. To clarify the position taken by the commanding staff toward General Kornilov and the Provisional Government, and immediately to take appropriate measures
2. To have all instructions and orders counter-signed by commissars or their designees
3. To remove all counter-revolutionary officers and soldiers
4. To send delegates immediately to the army committee and nearby units for communications
5. To appoint replacements immediately for all commanding officers who have been removed
6. To report to the army commissar on the mood of the troops in the units
7. To determine the available troops which may be called out on a moment's notice by VTsIK

The "commissar" Razumov, who was asked to clarify the purpose and functioning of the commissars and regimental deputies (the latter a parallel authority called *upolnomochennye*), laid out a precise picture of how this improvised structure was intended to work. Division commissars were to be appointed by corps committees with the approval of commissars from the army committee, the regimental deputies to be appointed by the division committees with approval of the corps commissar; the obvious purpose was to exercise strict control from the top down, paralleling the command apparatus, but whether in the first instance of the government commissars or the committees remained ambiguous. However, the regimental representatives insisted that *upolnomochennye* be elected by the regiments themselves with the approval of the division commissar, revealing concern to maintain lower-level control. A resolution putting the entire division at the disposal of the Provisional Government and the Soviet was passed, following the precedent of the corps committee. Characteristically it also resolved that Kornilov and his co-conspirators were to be "handed over to a military-revolutionary court as traitors to the Motherland."[46]

[46] *RDRA*, pp. 367-70. On corps commissars appointed by committees functioning effectively elsewhere, see order of August 30 of the commander of the XXXI Corps, instructing his subordinate commanders to submit to their controls in TsGVIA, f. 2938, op. 1, d. 23, l. 635, and *protokoly* of the committee of the 46th Division, f. 2376, op. 1, d. 2 (the corps

This pattern, though typical, was by no means uniform for the entire Southwestern Front. The route the news traveled and the specific triggering item, whether Kerensky's telegram, the VTsIK resolution, or simply the garbled news of intercepted radio broadcasts, varied from unit to unit. In the records of the Third Grenadier Division (XXV Corps, Eleventh Army), for example, there are no references to the measures of the army committee or of the division committee itself, but nevertheless on August 28 the chairman, Captain Argunov, reported in detail to lower committee representatives on events in Petrograd—the formation of a "Temporary Revolutionary Committee" by the Soviet, the mobilization of support in the capital, the progress of the expeditionary force, even the farce of a bogus Bolshevik uprising and arrest of the officer-conspirators in the Hotel Astoria. They had apparently picked up a radio broadcast of the Soviet's Committee of Revolutionary Defense via the powerful transmitter at Tsarskoe Selo. On the 29th they picked up VTsIK's proclamation and the details of negotiations between the Soviet and Kerensky on the formation of a "revolutionary directory" (which did not materialize); in addition, they had by now received all the informational telegrams of the Eleventh Army Committee (arrests of Denikin, Erdeli, etc.) and the government commissar, Chekotilo (everything is under control, keep calm). The absence of references to concrete actions may be simply that the record has not been preserved.[47] However, the committees of the Second Guards Division and the Volynskii Regiment of the Third Guards Division, based on complete minutes, seem also to have been inactive, not even meeting during the crisis. Considering that the guards units had gone through extensive "deprogramming" in the aftermath of the Grenadier rebellion and the Tarnopol retreat, and that in August neither committee had been very active, this is perhaps not too surprising. Yet a reaction was bound to set in, and apparently did in the Second Guards Division on August 31, when an assembly of combined division and regimental committees passed the following resolution:

> Having discussed the current situation, [the assembly] declares that the treason and betrayal of the whole people has no support in the Second Guards Division. The entire division without distinction as to type of arms will rise to defend the Revolution at the first call of the Provisional Government with Kerensky at the head and the Central Executive Committee of the Soviets of Workers' and Soldiers' Dep-

commissar reads out telegrams of Kerensky and the VTsIK and issues instructions on posting controls).

[47] TsGVIA, f. 2326, op. 4, d. 14, ll. 16, 17, 21, and 22. On the same radio broadcast as picked up in the XXXII Corps, see *GO*, August 31.

uties. Against the criminal designs of the high-handed Pretender Kornilov and his adherents, who tried to abduct our freedom, won through incalculable sacrifice, we demand the application of the death penalty, introduced by Kornilov himself.[48]

The assembly further demanded the full restoration of the rights of committees and the abolition of the Officers' Union. This suggests that where committees had not been functioning regularly, the crisis served to revive and radicalize them. This resolution was the first in a rising chorus of demands for the death penalty for Kornilov.

The staff records on the Second Guards Infantry Division reveal that the government commissar, Chekotilo, collaborated with General Rerberg, rather than with the army committee. A "tough" commissar, like Savinkov, who had strongly supported the measures to restore discipline, Chekotilo feared that if the crisis were not confined to very narrow limits all these efforts would go down the drain. He therefore cooperated with Rerberg in imposing staff controls over communications and co-signed official communiqués. The first, at 4:15 P.M., urged all and sundry to remain calm and "not believe the various rumors connected with Kornilov's name"; the second urged that Kornilov's removal not be regarded as a "reversal of the measures to restore the health of the Army"; and a third, tending to exculpate Kornilov hinted at a compromise solution:

Regarding the present state of affairs in the country and the Army as fatal for Russia, General Kornilov on August 27 suggested to the Provisional Government that it hand over to him full military and civilian power. The Provisional Government, regarding this as contrary to its own intentions and plans, removed Kornilov from the supreme command and handed it over to General Klembovskii.[49]

Since Gerua and Sollogub were arrested against Chekotilo's wishes under pressure from the army committee, it becomes clear that Chekotilo was pursuing a policy of his own.

The XXII Corps of the Seventh Army, which was made up of Finnish Rifle divisions, represents yet another variant. The corps committee held its key session on August 29 to consider the army committee's instructions point by point. A "control commission" of eight members was to monitor the telegraph, radio, and Hughes apparatus and to transmit important political announcements. They took exception to the army committee's instruction to "obey no orders of Kornilov or other traitors." Operative

[48] TsGVIA, f. 2322, op. 4, ed. khr. 4, l. 43.

[49] *Ibid.*, op. 7, ed. khr. 2, l. 368; see also *ibid.*, ll. 369, 372 and 376-77, which confirm that higher staffs were still circulating telegrams to lower staffs.

1. Soldiers' demonstration in April Days (*Istoriia grazhdanskoi voiny v SSSR*, vol. 1. Moscow, 1935)

2. Street agitation outside Bolshevik headquarters at Kseshinskaia Mansion in May (Claude Anet, *Through the Russian Revolution: Notes of an Eye-Witness*. London, 1917)

3. Factory workers from Petrograd visiting Siberian and Latvian units in Twelfth Army, Riga Front (*Istoriia grazhdanskoi voiny v SSSR*, vol. 1. Moscow, 1935)

4. Conference of generals at Stavka in May. Denikin and Danilov on left. Seated center: Brusilov and Alekseev (Anton Denikin, *Ocherki russkoi smuty*, vol. 1[2]. Paris, 1921)

5. Two studies of Kerensky at the Front in May (*Belyi Arkhiv*, vol. 1 [1926])

6. A "meeting" at the Front, probably Bolshevik, in June (*New York Times Gravure*. N.d. [1917])

7. Pro-offensive meeting at the Front in June (*1917 Velikii Oktiabr': Kratkaia istoriia, dokumenty, fotografii*. Moscow, 1977)

8. French Socialist Albert Thomas addressing troops of Kornilov's Eighth Army before June Offensive (*Oktiabr' na fronte*. Moscow, 1967)

9. Bedraggled young soldiers after the July retreat (Laurence Stallings, *The First World War, a Photographic History*. New York, 1933)

10. Kerensky at the Moscow State Conference in mid-August (*1917 Velikii Oktaibr': Kratkaia istoriia, dokumenty, fotografii*. Moscow, 1977)

11. Kornilov's reception at the Moscow State Conference (Anton Denikin, *Ocherki russkoi smuty*, vol. 1[2]. Paris, 1921)

12. Revolutionary troops block advance of Kornilov's troops, August 26-27 (*1917 Velikii Oktiabr': Kratkaia istoriia, dokumenty, fotografii*. Moscow, 1977)

13. Soldiers en route to rear (Anton Denikin, *Ocherki russkoi smuty*, vol. 1[2]. Paris, 1921)

14. German and Russian soldiers celebrate the Armistice (A. F. Kerensky, *Russia and History's Turning Point*. New York, 1965)

15. Fraternization of Russian and Austrian soldiers. Uncertain date (*Istoriia grazhdanskoi voiny v SSSR*, vol. 1. Moscow, 1935)

orders signed by him relating to the defense of the front were to be obeyed without question, but those of "political content" were to be referred to the army commissar. They decided to circulate Kerensky's telegrams "as widely as possible" and ignored those of VTsIK and the Peasant Soviet, which had also been received. They rejected offering armed aid to the Provisional Government because they assumed the crisis would soon be resolved and that the conflict should not become overblown. (In fact, Krymov's force had not yet been liquidated.) Finally, the army committee's resounding appeal was "taken under advisement," that is, ignored. The committee was clearly alarmed over the possible collapse of authority and believed that the crisis should be contained rather than inflamed. One factor that shaped the mood of caution was the presence of many officer-deputies—two sub-lieutenants, three full lieutenants, and a staff captain, along with only seven soldiers. Among the divisional and regimental chairmen were two lieutenant colonels, three captains, a lieutenant, two sub-lieutenants, and a military doctor. The commission to monitor communications was also half officer in composition. This corps committee had been promoted by the command in the period when this was strongly discouraged elsewhere.[50]

The committees of the three Finnish Rifle divisions (First, Third, Fifth) by no means followed the lead of the corps committee. The Fifth Division Committee received its information directly from Commissar Surguchev on August 29, and by another avenue, the proclamation of VTsIK which was immediately passed on to committees. Its main resolution decisively condemned the "traitors to the Motherland who are guilty of a grave violation of discipline toward the Provisional Government" that could "only lead to civil war and open the gates to Wilhelm," but did not otherwise follow the model of the corps resolution. Minutes of a meeting of the First Division Committee refer to controls not only over the telephone and telegraph but also over packets and messages delivered by messenger, which were to be opened and inspected. The commander noted in the margin his approval of controls over messages, but declared the inspection of packages "illegal, as even the corps committee resolution does not provide for this sort of control."[51]

In the Third Division a combined session of divisional and regimental committees reacted only to the telegram of VTsIK and ignored the instructions of the corps committee:

[50] *Protokoly*, TsGVIA, f. 2222, op. 1, d. 2, l. 42; on the next day they voted to circularize Kerensky's telegrams (*ibid.*, l. 43).

[51] *RDRA*, pp. 372-73; on the Fifth Division, see TsGVIA, f. 2222, op. 1, ed. khr. 1185, l. 80.

> Having acquainted ourselves with the proclamation of the Central Executive Committee . . . concerning the treacherous politics of adherents of the old regime with Kornilov at their head . . . the combined session declares the entire armed might of the Third Finnish Rifle Division will be directed against those who oppose the Revolution. . . . We demand merciless struggle with counter-revolution, and call on all comrades to rally around their elective organizations.[52]

The same militancy and Soviet orientation was evident in a number of lower-level committees, for example, the Second Regiment, which reacted indifferently to Kerensky's telegram (''taken under advisement''), but when they later learned of the VTsIK resolution they declared Kornilov a ''traitor'' and clapped on controls. A like reaction took place in the Artillery Park of the Third Division. Even the most insignificant subunits put themselves on record.[53]

The evidence on committee reactions is more sparse for other fronts, but the Eighth Army Committee, now a part of the Rumanian Front, after hearing a report by Commissar Shklovsky on August 28 set up controls very much like those of the Southwestern Front.[54] Lower committees were authorized to arrest any officers suspected of counter-revolutionary activity, and many arrests did take place; operative orders were to be read, but did not require a counter-signature of the committee. In the IV Siberian Corps of the Sixth Army, the committee presidium received news on August 29 by a circuitous route and, without calling a full session, immediately monitored communications. Relations with the commander had been tense in past months over various jurisdictional disputes, but after discussing the affair among themselves, the committee called him in and persuaded him to sign a joint resolution, which was then circulated to the entire corps via the staff network. The intent was obviously to surmount the crisis without impairing command authority. The statement declared their joint support of the Provisional Government against counter-revolutionary attempts by soldiers or officers, and any such perpetrators were to be immediately handed over to a military-revolutionary court. A second part, not bearing the commander's signature, states that ''in connection with these events elective representatives and commissars are vested with special powers to

[52] TsGVIA, f. 2222, op. 1, ed. khr. 1185, l. 35; also in *RDRA*, p. 372.

[53] See TsGVIA, f. 2222, op. 1, ed. khr. 1185, ll. 98-99 (react only to the VTsIK resolution, impose complete controls on communications, including packages, read and report to division committee immediately upon arrival on all orders of the Provisional Government and commissars, and review all operative orders).

[54] See resolution of the army committee of August 29 in *RDRA*, pp. 366-67, and *Iz8A*, September 2; for controls in the XXXIII Corps, see record of session of September 1, *RDRA*, p. 382.

struggle with counter-revolution,'' and lower committees were urged to take all necessary steps to counteract such attempts. Clearly they wanted their own committee to be the locus of control.

The corps committee, while protecting the commander and the officers against humiliations, nevertheless insisted on the right to arrest and replace commanders, to control the communications and personal movements of suspected parties, and to countersign all orders and relayed telegrams. Moreover, a permanent ''Military Revolutionary Commission'' was established to supervise these arrangements and had the right to demand explanations from commanders for all orders. Committees were regarded as autonomous, not subject to regulation by the command, specifically in political and cultural-educational affairs.[55] In other words, the crisis was utilized to clear up all old scores in favor of the committees.

On the Northern and Western fronts the reactions seem mild on the surface by comparison with the two southerly fronts. The organ of the Third Army Committee, *Go3A*, was able to publish fairly complete information on August 29 based on telegraph traffic of the 28th and a radio telegram from the ''Military Bureau'' of VTsIK, calling on the front not to obey the orders of Kornilov or Lukomskii and to support the Provisional Government and the Soviet (this message was more loyal to the government than previously noted broadcasts). The army committee passed a *pro forma* resolution of loyalty calling for calm, but the impulse to prevent overreaction seemed to outweigh the impulse to action. It assured the troops that the measures undertaken by the Provisional Government would nip in the bud all the designs of counter-revolution. A pronouncement of Commissar Postnikov, formerly army committee chairman, stressed the same message, but added the urgency of upholding the prestige of the command. The following day an instruction of VTsIK was published, stating that committees should ''secure lines of communication to us, and establish control over all means of transmission of messages.'' If there were follow-up instructions to lower committees or requests for supporting resolutions, there is no trace of it in *Go3A* or any other available documentation on the Third Army. *Go3A* gave extensive coverage to other armies (Tenth, Twelfth, Special), mainly to reassure the readership that everything was under control, and on August 31 it published a declaration of loyalty to the Provisional Government by the Third Army Commander, General Tsykovich. On September 3 Commissar Postnikov declared, ''The Kornilov adventure has been definitively liquidated.''

The organ of the Tenth Army Committee, *GoXA*, gives the impression of almost total passivity in these critical days; nevertheless, on September

[55] See TsGVIA, f. 2282, op. 4, ed. khr. 11, l. 6.

5, long after the crisis was over, they recounted the actions of the army committee, which followed the pattern of the Southwestern Front precisely—an emergency session late on August 27, reception of all telegrams on the 28th, dispersal of the membership to each army corps circularizing the messages of Kerensky and VTsIK and holding up those of Kornilov, comprehensive controls on communications, and the formation of units to intercept troop movements northward along the railroads. One difference, however, was that commanders were on the whole cooperative. Thus, though information in the sources is sometimes sparse, this does not prove inactivity on the part of army and lower committees. The 129th Division of the Second Army (Western Front), for example, is noteworthy for the elaborate controls imposed by its committee, such as guard posts on all roads, requisition of horses for use by the committee, signature and committee stamp on the papers of all persons departing the corps, and so on; nevertheless, "all the above measures must be conducted with great tact, so as not to impair the authority of the commanding staff."[56]

☆

Within the above setting there began to occur a momentous groundswell of soldier determination to master their own fate which overflooded all institutional bounds, new and old, and recognized no counsels of restraint or accommodation. Through the trials of the summer the soldiers' rebellious impulses had flashed and played themselves out, leaving confusion, external submissiveness, and lethargy in their wake, but underneath the soldiers harbored deep resentments toward the forces that held them in check, particularly the "decisive measures" advocated by Kornilov and viewed by them as "counter-revolutionary." They had been certain where it would all end long before their ideological preceptors, and thus at the outbreak of the crisis they were more than ready to respond. If more and better concrete descriptions were available, one might safely conclude that the committees were activated by the soldiers and not vice versa, or at the very least that the committees acted with confidence because for a change they could be sure they were in accord with the elemental feelings of the soldier masses. However, the magnitude of the phenomenon can be measured by several indicators that are consistent with each other, broad in scope, and reliable in origin: first, resolutions and demands by lower units for a military revolutionary court and death penalty for Kornilov; second, an upsurge of antiofficer sentiments that expressed themselves in spontaneous arrests, violence, and humiliations of various kinds; and finally, the abrupt shift in concern of commissars and higher committees from the threat of Kornilov to the threat of a new wave of soldier anarchy. These

[56] *RDRA*, pp. 378 and 382.

phenomena occurred on every front and on a scale that evoked universal comment in reports and alarms of various kinds.

Several examples of resolutions crying for retribution against the conspirators have already been cited. A good share of those emanating from lower units specifically demanded the death penalty, though the model resolutions of higher committees seldom went beyond demanding a military-revolutionary court.[57] The greater militancy of the masses therefore expressed itself precisely in this demand, which could not but seem fitting for the one who was held responsible for introducing it. Two such instances emanate from Bolshevik-oriented units (a Latvian Rifle regiment and the 271st Regiment, Tenth Army, Western Front), but others seem quite average (one, for example, which combines it with a warning not otherwise to impair officer authority).[58] Since lower committees in this period usually met in expanded sessions, that is, together with the committees of their constituent units, they can be taken as reflecting the broad sentiments of their constituency. The uncompromising spirit that animated these resolutions is best reflected in that of the Seventh Battalion of the Fourth Supply Depot of the Ninth Army, which couples it with a warning to the leaders:

> It's time to forget the politics of forgiveness and loving-kindness. . . . The revolution of flowers and poets must be replaced by the revolution of fire and sword. Let those who lead it reflect what can happen when you hide a snake in your breast. For a long time we forgave you, but don't expect to be forgiven again. The Army must be cleared once and for all of those who dream about the old regime.[59]

The message ascending the committee hierarchy was that the soldiers expected the conspirators to receive the death penalty or the consequences would be quite serious. The Eleventh Army Commissar, who had just concluded a tour of the front and had conversed with many soldiers, states in a report of September 7 that the soldiers universally demanded the death penalty for Kornilov as a traitor, since there should be one punishment for treason for both soldiers and generals. Chekotilo, who can hardly be sus-

[57] For examples of those emanating "from above," see *GF*, September 2 and 3, and *IzOA*, September 2; for endorsement by the corps committee of the IV Siberian Corps of the resolution of the Sixth Army Committee on August 30, see TsGVIA, f. 2282, op. 4, ed. khr. 11, l. 10. See also several examples in the Finnish Rifle divisions in TsGVIA, f. 2222, op. 1, ed. khr. 1185, ll. 16 and 100-101, and *RDRA*, p. 383.

[58] *RDRA*, p. 389, and *VOSR. Avgust*, p. 573.

[59] *RDRA*, p. 373; in *Iz3A*, September 5, a divisional committee pronounced "curses on that traitor" and called for the death penalty, and in another case a session of regimental and company committees declared: "Away with the madness of counter-revolution; do not dare to touch with your filthy designs and hands our holy freedom. Death to all those who trespass!"

pected of currying soldier vengeance, declared that the work of rebuilding the Army could proceed only if this were done.[60] A telegram of Southwestern Front Committee Chairman Dashevskii to VTsIK on September 30 likewise states: "The slightest vacillation on this question threatens to provoke a great disturbance at the front and the most dangerous complications."[61] Commissar Iordanskii concurred, adding, "I regard this telegram as based on a correct understanding of the mood of the soldier masses." The very next day an even stronger plea was sent to VTsIK in reaction to the news that Kaledin had been released from arrest on the order of the government and was gathering a pro-Kornilov force on the Don.[62] The issue was particularly acute on the Southwestern Front because of the arrests of Denikin, Erdeli, and others, but one hears of the same sentiment elsewhere, for example, in the 59th Division (XXXIII Corps, Eighth Army, Rumanian Front) that "many soldiers want the death penalty for Kornilov."[63]

Equally striking was the wave of arrests of officers, forced removals from command, and votes of "no confidence," sometimes ending in violence or threats of lynching; in general there was a recrudescence of all the old forms of antiofficer hostility. Compared with March or April, more attention was paid to formalities, that is, specific charges, formal votes of committees, summoning of the commissar, depositions, and so forth, but they were no less resolute. Often the charges were simply expressions of sympathy for Kornilov, or alleged membership in the Officers' Union, or having been a party to military revolutionary courts against soldiers. The number of recorded arrests of commanders of regiments and divisions reached some dozens on each front, but a survey for the Northern Front declared that "to enumerate all the cases is impossible."[64] There was a greater incidence than in April among cavalry, artillery, and technical units, reflecting a deeper penetration of the malaise. Also, arrests of groups of officers or even of entire units accompanied by a vote of "no confidence" seems to have exceeded the April levels. In other cases, the committees under strong soldier pressure simply took over the management of units, leaving officers out in the cold. Sometimes this was orderly, sometimes not. An orderly case was the Kavalgard Regiment of the First Guards Cavalry Division, which became alarmed over the absence of senior officers during the crisis. On August 30 a general assembly of the regiment voted to arrest all the officers and to remove them from command, but no hand

[60] TsGVIA, f. 6978, op. 1, d. 357, ll. 68-69 (Special Documents, copy).

[61] *GoFr*, September 1, and *IzOA*, September 2.

[62] See *VOSR. Avgust*, pp. 594-95.

[63] See TsGVIA, f. 2134, op. 1, d. 28, l. 26.

[64] Stavka survey for September 2-10, in *KA* 84:163.

seems to have been laid on them; rather, the commissar of the Special Army was summoned and in the meantime the committee took charge of the regiment. When the commissar arrived, he could not persuade them to reverse their decision.[65] A more disorderly case is recounted in a soldier letter:

> I got back to the regiment just as they were meeting. It lasted until 3:00 A.M. We refused to submit to our officers and took all power into our hands. We won't let the officers go. They regard themselves as innocent in this thing, claiming they were only following Kornilov's orders. The whole lot were actually preparing a counter-revolution, but they didn't get away with it. . . . They stopped a company . . . that was intending to wipe out all the officers. At the meeting was a member of the army committee who did nothing but defend the officers. . . . "You send your officers into the trenches dressed like soldiers, they'll make speeches and carry the soldiers with them, because soldiers believe fellow soldiers." But we told him we have no intention of letting them go to other units, we've got plenty of work for them to do here—digging trenches. Many officers beg the soldiers' forgiveness, but we look on them as the worst sort of traitors to the Fatherland. Our company and all other companies passed a resolution that we won't submit to our officers and have no confidence in them, and are sending a deputy to Petrograd to the Soviet with it.[66]

Allowing for the tendency to exaggerate and self-advertise, the depth of animus against officers comes through, as well as the unwillingness to be dissuaded from such actions by committees or commissars.

A report by the corps commander on the Third Siberian Division (Twelfth Army, Northern Front) of September 6 offers a much fuller picture of the state of affairs than the usual dry weekly surveys. Here the situation was particularly tense over the retreat from Riga and mutual recriminations over who was responsible. The soldiers were particularly bitter about the fact that the officials had blown up the image of Kornilov and now he was revealed as a traitor, which they had suspected all along. It was now common, the report alleges, to hear that all officers were Kornilovites and should be done away with. Now orders were ignored with impunity, and all court proceedings against soldiers were halted. In one case a soldier who had been tried and found guilty for calling Kornilov a traitor before the affair was now freed and his accusers brought to trial. The committees were trying to maintain order, but the officer component was now absent

[65] *RDRA*, pp. 385-86.
[66] *Ibid.*, p. 379.

and demagogues from the ranks were acquiring more and more influence. The fate of the regimental commanders of the division is noteworthy: the commander of the Ninth Regiment was brought to trial for derogating remarks about the Provisional Government; the commander of the Tenth Regiment was removed for "unsuitability" and replaced by a soldiers' nominee; the commander of the Eleventh Regiment was accused by the committee of "humiliating inattention to our needs"; and the commander of the Twelfth Regiment was accused by his own officers of incompetence. The commander of the artillery battery, a supply officer, and a doctor were also arrested as Kornilovites.[67]

The crushing impact of the upsurge of antiofficer sentiment on the Northern Front is best conveyed in the weekly report to Stavka for the period September 2-10:

> The mood of the front armies has noticeably deteriorated in connection with the most recent events and exhaustion after the battle near Riga. . . . The situation of the officers is unbearable. They are accused of sympathy to General Kornilov and of adherence to the old regime. . . . In the 470th Regiment, for example, the regimental committee passed a resolution to interrogate each officer on his political convictions and to exclude any of them who think differently from the soldiers. In the 731st Regiment, when visited by the division commander, a huge crowd gathered and a soldier-orator declared that all commanders were counter-revolutionaries and traitors, and brought up the issues of special units of gendarmes and the execution of Sergeant Gordienko [by a military-revolutionary court for fraternization]. The 730th Regimental Committee passed a resolution of no confidence in the divisional and regimental commanders or in all officers in general. In the 19th Engineering Regiment they expelled eight officers. . . . The 19th Motorized Artillery Regiment did the same. . . . The Second Pskov Dragoons put all their officers under house arrest. . . . To name all the instances would be impossible.[68]

The wave of spontaneous arrests also became a matter of considerable concern on the Southwestern Front. On September 2, Commissar Iordanskii wired all army commissars and committees that the chief plotters had been apprehended and that therefore all further arrests should cease. Information

[67] "Vypiska iz donesenii komkora 6. Sibirskogo korpusa ot 6-go sentiabria" (Ms.), Bylevskii Papers, No. 8, HI.

[68] *KA* 84:163. Another report on the Fifth Army of September 3 notes that "there is extreme hostility to officers who are members of the Union of Officers" and that "leaflets are in circulation calling for a close watch on the officers and reporting everything to the committees" (*RDRA*, p. 394).

on suspected individuals should be forwarded to the commissars, by telegram if necessary.[69] On September 3 the chairman of the Eleventh Army Committee, Pipik, pleaded for the cessation of spontaneous arrests in his army.[70] Apparently matters also reached some urgency in the Special Army, as on September 5 a joint order of the acting commander, General Ogorodnikov, and Assistant Commissar Kudriavtsev declared that arrests of officers were continuing without the slightest pretext, even though all the conspirators had been apprehended and an investigating committee had been appointed. Those who did not comply with the order to cease arbitrary arrests would be "handed over to the courts."[71] The state of affairs must also have promptly reached Petrograd, as on September 2 VTsIK issued a proclamation urging soldiers to "desist from vengeance and assaults against officers."[72]

There were remarkably few cases of lynching, given the pitch of emotions; had it been widespread it would have attracted more attention in the military reports and more individual cases would have been cited. The murders of General Oranovskii and several officers in the XLII Corps stationed in Vyborg, Finland, were the most celebrated, though the Finnish gulf military stations had always been more violence-prone than the front itself. Several telegrams implicating the generals in the Kornilov affair (the First Don Cossack Division was to be moved in from Finland to join Krymov) had been discovered, and the generals were taken under arrest by the local Soviet and the corps committee. An enraged mob broke into the guard house, mercilessly beat the prisoners, taunted them, finally killed them, and threw their bodies into the gulf.[73] Several unrelated murders of officers took place in the same area. At the front there were more threats of lynchings than actual cases, but in one documented instance a captain was murdered by a soldier mob and his head was cut off and paraded around on a pole with a cigarette hanging out of his mouth.[74] If there were other such grisly dramas, there are no documentary traces, not even in the unit-by-unit surveys from which the above was taken.

[69] *GoFr*, September 2.

[70] *GO*, September 3.

[71] *IzOA*, September 5. The same issue cites a proclamation of the army committee of August 31 calling for "restraint and conscious discipline" and not to engage in "*samochinye vystupleniia*" (uncoordinated actions).

[72] Appears in *Go3A*, September 5.

[73] Details in front commander's report of September 3, in *RDRA*, p. 395.

[74] Report of XXXII Corps to First Army headquarters of September 14 (TsGVIA, Special Documents). Note that this is Dr. Gottlieb's corps, which put out *GO* and prided itself in its disciplined reaction to the Kornilov affair. The First Army on the Southwestern Front existed only briefly during the reshuffling of positions during the retreat, but the XXXII Corps was soon back in the Eleventh Army.

Few personal accounts or diaries cover this precise moment, but an exception is Kal'nitskii, the previously cited chairman of the committee of the 138th Bolkhovskii Regiment, whose account is based on a diary and full committee records for the critical days of August 29-31.[75] The crisis broke along the lines already familiar, Kal'nitskii being called to divisional committee headquarters to hear the key telegrams. When he got back to the bivouac a huge crowd had gathered and a mood and course of action had already taken shape ("The telegraph operators and *ordinartsy* are soldiers too," he observed), which was "Death to the traitors! Away with the officers!" The day before, the soldiers had been a herd of sheep, and now they were rushing headlong ahead of the committees, undertaking their own security measures without instructions. Goncharenko, an explosive Ukrainian, opened the discussion: "Kamrades, look how the awfisers sapport Karnilov in this shady bizniss. I say we arrist them awl, and send a tiligram sayin' we're cumin ta Pitrograd ta crush the contririvalushun!" (cheers all around; the rendition of quaint brogue is mine but based on Kal'nitskii).[76] Kal'nitskii drew up a toned-down version which was approved by the assembly and dragooned the reluctant commander into acceding "voluntarily" to committee demands. Nevertheless, the security company posted to headquarters was now at the disposal of the committee, and a committee representative was to be present at all officer meetings. The next day the committee discussed the current topics of grammar courses, a movie film, and an inspection of the regimental store. But to "avoid conflict" the security company was ordered to withdraw from headquarters, and it obeyed. The commander vigorously protested committee control of the security company and would not sign the committee resolution because it declared support to both the Soviet and the Provisional Government, whereas he recognized the Provisional Government alone. The officer delegates, present in full force at the committee session, unanimously supported the commander, whereas the soldiers were just as unanimously opposed. An officer demagogue named Bauman spoke passionately of the "long-suffering Motherland" and the Germans' envy of Russian land and wealth, cleverly sending over spies in sealed trains. "How about giving up your own land?" "Comrades, I have no land, I am just as much a peasant as yourself." "That's a lie! He has two thousand desiatins in Riazan." Goncharenko took the floor (the reader may now render his Ukrainian brogue): "Tavarishchi! He wants to get us into an argument with foreigners just so they can get the *palka* [stick] back in their hands and the tsar on our backs. If Kornilov wins out, that's what

[75] Kal'nitskii, *Ot fevralia k oktiabriu*, pp. 116-30.

[76] *Ibid.*, p. 126.

will happen. We have nothing more to talk about. We know what to do!" Another soldier, an artillerist, followed in the same vein: "Why fool around? Let's elect our own commanders . . . and make our own peace with the Germans! . . . It's time to go home and divide up the land." Turning to Kal'nitskii he continued: "Get rid of this gold shoulder-boarded scum and we'll all support you!" Kal'nitskii, realizing that to avoid violence some outlet for soldier anger was needed, proposed a brief resolution: "I move we categorically approve and carry out the resolution of August 29, irrespective of the wishes of the commander."[77] A roar of approval concluded the meeting, officers dissenting, and the soldiers immediately set about cleaning their rifles, doling out ammunition, and posting watches in perfect order. A collegium of three, including Kal'nitskii, now in fact commanded the regiment, and communications personnel reported directly to him rather than to the commander. The security company was again assigned to headquarters, but it took on the aspect of a collective arrest of the staff officers. The commander expressed his helpless rage and tried to issue orders, but found that only those of Kal'nitskii were obeyed. A further insult was that soldiers now marched with precision, saluted snappily, and kept their heads in and their chests out. However, Kal'nitskii did not allow the commander to be insulted or formally removed. The commander gradually accepted his new role as "military expert," appearing almost grateful to Kal'nitskii for securing the execution of his orders ("suggestions").

Kal'nitskii's account is perhaps somewhat dressed up, but it conveys an accurate sense of the dynamics involved. The committeemen were obliged to serve as the vehicle both of the democratic *verkushki* (higher leadership) and of the soldiers' feelings. He seems to have followed a judicious middle course with some tactical skill and personal authority, which was certainly not always the case, but he convincingly portrays the "objective" situation of committees during the Kornilov affair.

☆

Another casualty of the Kornilov affair was the personal reputation of Kerensky, and by extension that of the Coalition Government. The customary adulatory expressions attached to his name suddenly disappear from the sources, while sarcastic and critical notes crop up, reflecting that the nimbus surrounding his person had badly faded. This derived from Kerensky's misguided efforts to undo the damage of his change of fronts during the crisis, which in effect lent credence to the assertions of the generals, the right-wing press, and the Bolsheviks that Kerensky had been in league with Kornilov all along and simply panicked at the last minute.

Rumors concerning Kerensky's complicity were indeed in circulation at

[77] *Ibid.*, p. 128.

the front in these days. In the artillery brigade of the First Finnish Rifle Division a certain Dr. Kutuzov, arrested as a known Kornilov sympathizer, asserted in his defense that Kerensky "had an understanding" with Kornilov which he then broke. The divisional committee was disturbed enough to make inquiries of Commissar Surguchev.[78] This case was not exceptional, since yet another circular telegram of Iordanskii and Dashevkii was required to deny the rumors on the Southwestern Front.[79] Under normal circumstances such aspersions on the democratic idol would not merit consideration, but He Himself lent them credibility through a series of orders between August 28 and September 2. Kornilov, no longer Commander in Chief after Kerensky's first telegram, continued to process routine operational orders, which naturally were required despite the crisis, but inevitably their validity was subject to question. VTsIK's proclamation of August 28, broadcast up and down the front, flat out declared that Kornilov was a rebel whose orders were not to be obeyed. The soldiers' natural impulse was to view all Kornilov orders as "counter-revolutionary," regardless of time or intent, and eagerly subscribed to the VTsIK version.

Kerensky, advised of the danger of undercutting legitimate outstanding operational orders, sent out a clarifying telegram stating that only the orders of Kornilov after August 26, the moment of rebellion, were not subject to execution. Soldier logic resisted such a discrimination, and indeed it gave legitimacy to Krymov's outstanding orders. The waters were further muddied on the 30th, when at the insistence of Alekseev, whom Kerensky had just appointed Chief of Staff, he ordered the Army to obey all operative commands of Kornilov until Alekseev formally took up his duties. This immediately raised the possibility that Kornilov might legally send reinforcements to Krymov! Kornilov noted the irony himself in a secret message to Krymov, whom he still thought to be poised against Petrograd though in fact he was already dead: "What emerges is a situation unprecedented in human history—a Commander in Chief accused of treason and betraying the Motherland . . . receives an order to maintain command over the armies."[80] To repair the damage, Kerensky hastily sent a follow-

[78] *Protokoly* of respective units of September 8 and 9 in TsGVIA, f. 2222, op. 1, ed. khr. 1185, ll. 11 and 92. To counteract such anxieties, an army order reached the XXII Corps on September 1, which declared: "No sort of bargain has been struck between Kornilov and the Provisional Government, and the rumors circulating about this have caused a good number of protests" (*ibid.*, ed. khr. 1189, l. 369).

[79] *GO*, September 2.

[80] *VOSR. Avgust*, p. 469. Text of both orders registered as relays to lower commands by the Caucasus Front headquarters in *Revoliutsiia 1917 g. v istoricheskikh dokumentakh* (Tiflis, 1930), pp. 140 and 143. That the issue of Kornilov's operative orders immediately became a problem during the crisis came out at a session of the committee of the XXII Corps on

up instruction the same day, stating that he had meant to specify only operational orders at the front itself or concerning troop movements *to* the front, but any concerning troop movements *away* from the front were to be ignored.[81]

Every conceivable misinterpretation arising out of these confusing orders in fact materialized. The committee of the First Finnish Rifle Division on September 2 noted they were investigating Kerensky's recent orders and admonished lower committees "to take all measures possible to root out in their units all unfounded and manifestly false rumors through explanations and conversations with soldiers." ("Highly desirable," noted the commander in the margin.)[82] The 57th Division, which responded so magnificently to the crisis, debated at length whether to obey Kornilov's order before August 26, even though Kerensky's orders to that effect was at hand. They decided to consult the commissar in each case (the following day the army committee issued a clarifying bulletin).[83] The committee of the 13th Belozerskii Regiment (VI Corps, Eleventh Army), having the same information available, decided differently: "All orders and instructions of the former Commander in Chief, Kornilov, are to be regarded as illegal and not having force, since the aim is to abolish freedom, bought with so much blood."[84] The corps committee of the XXII Corps censured a supply unit on September 14 for refusing to obey an order of their commander based on an instruction of Kornilov issued in August.[85] *Golos Fronta* on September 3 carried the report that Commissar Surguchev and the Seventh Army Committee were doing their best to clear up all the misunderstandings surrounding Kerensky's order to leave Kornilov in charge of operations. That the wires were humming with messages of alarm is evident in yet another follow-up of Kerensky on September 2:

> To avoid all further misunderstandings, the temporary power of Kornilov to issue operative orders is due to absolute necessity. The Army must have direction, even if only for a few hours. In all other respects Kornilov's powers are restricted. All nonoperative orders of Kornilov

August 29, at which it was hotly discussed which orders were affected by the VTsIK's general revocation. They prudently decided to obey his operative orders, but referred all others to higher committees (see TsGVIA, f. 2222, op. 1, d. 2, l. 42). On the date causing problems, see *RDRA*, p. 369.

[81] In archive of the Second Guards Infantry Division, Staff Documents, with the accompanying signatures of the front and army commanders and Commissar Chekotilo, TsGVIA, f. 2322, op. 7, ed. khr. 2, l. 379.

[82] *Protokoly*, TsGVIA, f. 2222, op. 1, d. 2, l. 51.

[83] *RDRA*, p. 367.

[84] *Ibid.*, p. 384.

[85] *Protokoly*, TsGVIA, f. 2222, op. 1, ed. khr. 1185, l. 10.

are not subject to execution. I declare once and for all that the Provisional Government has already handed the rebellious generals over to the courts.[86]

It requires little imagination to infer from the above cases that Kerensky had incautiously appeared to be reinstating Kornilov's authority after having declared him a rebel, and to the unsophisticated soldiers and committeemen this raised the question of whether indeed the darker versions of his complicity had some substance.

Far more damaging to his reputation was his Order No. 907 of September 1, also issued under pressure from Alekseev with the ostensible intent not to impair command authority further. The force of this extraordinary decree can only be appreciated by examining the full text, each point of which was like a slap in the face to the proud committeemen and soldiers who felt they had just saved the Fatherland, and Kerensky in particular, from the clutches of Kornilov:

> In connection with the uprising of Kornilov, normal life in the Army has been disrupted completely. To restore order I command:
>
> 1. To cease all political struggle among the troops and to direct all efforts toward our fighting strength on which the salvation of the country depends.
> 2. All military organizations and commissars are to remain within the strict limits of their practical work, devoid of political intolerance and suspicion and without the slightest suggestion of interference in the official and operative work of commanding personnel.
> 3. To restore the uninterrupted movement of troop transports for tasks assigned by the commanding staff.
> 4. To cease forthwith all arrests of commanding officers, since the right to such action belongs exclusively to investigating authorities, the military procurators, and the Extraordinary Investigative Commission, which was appointed by me and has already begun its work.
> 5. To cease entirely the removal and replacement of commanding personnel, since this is the exclusive province of duly authorized organs of authority and in no way enters into the sphere of activity of democratic organizations.
> 6. To cease forthwith the formation of improvised forces under the pretext of fighting counter-revolution.

[86] From Second Guards Infantry Division, Staff Documents, relay of order of Eleventh Army Commissar Chekotilo, TsGVIA, f. 2322, op. 7, ed. khr. 2, l. 397.

7. To remove forthwith all controls over communications media established by military organizations.

The Army, having expressed in these difficult times confidence in the Provisional Government and in me as Minister President responsible for the fate of the country, must understand with its great wisdom that the salvation of the country resides only in legitimate organization and in the maintenance of complete order and discipline in all its parts. Therefore, I, vested with the confidence of the Army, summon all of you to duty. Let the conscience of each be aroused and prompt you to an awareness of his duty before the Motherland in this hour of danger when her fate is being decided.[87]

The rebuff must have been felt most acutely by the committees and commissars on the Southwestern Front, which had so promptly neutralized and apprehended Kornilov's most dangerous supporters; and by the democratic organizations of the Western Front, since under their eyes Kornilov was moving more reliable troops toward Stavka, and Kerensky had just appealed to them for help;[88] and on the Northern Front, as the concentration of Krymov's force had been followed with great alarm and it was not yet known if other forces were on the way. Finally, the chief culprit was still at Stavka, surrounded by his loyal Tekintsy, his operational orders still declared valid and replaced by General Alekseev, whose views were known to be identical. The entire catalogue of instructions must have seemed like a perverse piece of insanity on Kerensky's part to negate their revolutionary initiatives and to lapse back into the embrace of Kornilov.

The loyalties of the front and army committees were certainly being sorely tested. Those that had been the most nervous about the soldiers' overreaction greeted the new directives with relief (Tenth and Third armies), but the activist committees on the Southwestern front, including the corps organ of the XXXII Corps, published them as well.[89] Within a few days the coverage by army newspapers of anything in connection with the Kornilov affair disappeared, and they resumed the humdrum tone of previous times. The lily of heroism had bloomed luxuriantly for a precious moment as after a desert rain, then rapidly faded. One can infer that Kerensky's order was to a large extent responsible. The committee of the artillery brigade of the Third Finnish Rifle Division was actually discussing a resolution that no orders of Kornilov were to be obeyed, taking as a guideline the VTsIK telegram, when Order No. 907 arrived; without dis-

[87] *VOSR. Sentiabr'*, p. 470.

[88] For these facts, see V. A. Kolerov, *Kornilovskie dni* (Petrograd, 1917), p. 58, and Martynov, *Kornilovskoe delo*, pp. 159ff.

[89] See *GoXA*, September 3; *Go3A*, September 3; and *GO*, September 5.

cussion (it was an order, after all) they voted to "regard the controls established by our resolution of August 31 revoked."[90] A regiment of the Third Infantry Division (Eleventh Army) was so upset that it demanded that Commissar Chekotilo explain it.[91] However, an assembly of divisional and regimental committees of the IV Siberian Corps on September 14 passed an openly defiant resolution said to have passed unanimously:

> The normal life of the corps has not been impaired as stated in Kerensky's order, but political struggle has been thrust upon us by the criminal hand of General Kornilov. Regarding elective organizations as the bastion of democracy and the conquest of Freedom . . . the committees and commissars are controlling the operative and routine military actions of commanders to facilitate their execution based on mutual trust, and if arrests have been carried out, then this has been forced on us by the necessities of the situation which has arisen; . . . furthermore, the removal of unsuitable persons of the commanding staff by committees is fully in accord with the idea of democracy in the Army. The Provisional Government has always recognized the role of committees and the organs of Revolutionary Democracy in upholding discipline and establishing the fighting strength of the Army, and therein lies the strength of the Revolution; therefore the assembly of all committees of the corps recognizes the necessity of introducing broad democratization in the Army and the commanding staff, expanding for this purpose the rights of committees. In view of the lack of clarity of Order 907, which is regarded as contradictory to and a curtailment of the rights approved by the War Ministry in Orders No. 213 and 271 [which detailed the regulations on committees in March], the assembly requests that Order No. 907 be rescinded.[92]

The committees of the IV Siberian Corps obviously no longer stood in awe of Kerensky's authority and saw through the spurious and self-serving rationale of his order. Behind the heavy verbiage it seems they now understood Kerensky's problem—that under the pretense of "strong revolutionary authority" he coveted the claims of Kornilov to unlimited personal

[90] TsGVIA, f. 2222, op. 1, ed. khr. 1185, ll. 100-101.

[91] See TsGVIA, f. 2333, op. 1, ed. khr. 1, l. 485.

[92] TsGVIA, f. 2282, op. 4, ed. khr. 11, l. 17; and *RDRA*, pp. 413-14. The magnitude of this defiance can only be appreciated if it is realized that hitherto this committee had been quite moderate and loyal. The Special Army Committee also resolved to retain their own "commissars" despite the order, arguing that they were necessary "for the purpose of strengthening and democratizing the Army." (See "Protokoly ispol'nitel'nogo komiteta osoboi armii, sentribria 5-7," in TsGVIA, f. 2440, op. 5, d. 1, No. 14.)

power. For the front this was a new revelation. Woytinsky, now replacing Stankevich as commissar of the Northern Front, sums up the new attitude:

> Every soldier knew that the conflict between Kerensky and Kornilov had been preceded by negotiations between them, that the subject of these talks had been the death penalty, further restraints on soldiers' organizations, and the return of authority to the officers, in short, to put clamps on the soldier and return him to the control of the "old regime." . . . Thus, one heard that Kerensky had signed an agreement with Kornilov on August 23 [the Savinkov interview] and that Kerensky had *requested* a cavalry corps from Kornilov, and the latter complied, under the terms of which they would be used against the Provisional Government and the Petrograd Soviet.[93]

Order No. 907 could only confirm these suspicions. Examples such as these leave little doubt that Kerensky's orders were widely known in the ranks, provoked deep anxiety and alienation, and generated considerable pressure for responses from higher committees.

☆

One senses behind the scenes depicted above a tremendous movement, a new stage of the Revolution being born, and the finale of the stage in which Kerensky and the idea of "strong revolutionary authority" based on coalition between Soviet and bourgeois elements constituted the chief features. The psychological factors suggested by these examples entered into the dominant mood of September—a relapse of committees back into lethargy rebuffed by the Leader of Democracy Himself and a seething determination by the soldier masses not to allow it to happen, to find some alternative solution to cohabiting with the very forces that had betrayed them to Kornilov and would do so again. The next chapter will adduce an overwhelming body of evidence that while the committees maintained their composure through September, underneath were rumblings of the soldiers' mood, which literally exploded to the surface in October. In retrospect there can be no doubt that the experience of the Kornilov days, the culmination of a growing political struggle in July and August, set the attitudes that carried both the masses and the revolutionary institutions toward the October denouement.

93 "Gody pobedy" (Ms.), HI, 3:297.

CHAPTER VII

THE SOLDIERS' PLEBESCITE

AN UNRESOLVED PROBLEM in this study has been how to generalize safely about mass behavior while maintaining an accurate picture of diversity, of nuances of attitude and action within thc soldier milieu. The very nature of the sources and of the discussion—aggregate behavior which affects outcome—effaces the sense of particularity. Numerous subgroups have been neglected, each having their own determinants and justification for treatment, such as nationalities, distinctions by schooling or urban exposure, rank, skill, and endless other variants.[1] Moreover, mass soldier behavior often took abrupt turns under different stimuli and varied incredibly from unit to unit, for which there is not always a readily available explanation. For example, the cavalry and artillery, also made up of peasant recruits, long remained almost "old regime" in discipline and were far less politicized than the infantry. Few infantry formations maintained the same profile, whereas the more typical, politicized by the March events, remained long under their spell but might suddenly change orientation through Bolshevik replacements, an unfortunate incident, or battle experience. Some units, shaken by Bolshevik agitation or battle traumas in June, were successfully "tightened up" by disciplinary measures in July. Still others were awakened by the retreat to a "rebirth of patriotism," while still others were totally demoralized by misguided repressive actions. Yet one has to assume that all of these regiments and divisions were baked from the same peasant dough with roughly the same admixture of nationalities, hybrid peasant, urban, and educated types. Therefore, variations in behavior have to be attributed (not always demonstrably) to specific

[1] The nationalities in the army are given excellent treatment in M. S. Frenkin, *Russkaia armiia i revoliutsiia 1917-1918* (Munich, 1978), pp. 205-55, 529-46, and 683-720. Other groups present considerable difficulties because of the lack of sources. For example, one can identify peasant types who were obviously self-educated, intensely patriotic, strongly in favor of discipline, and true believers in the March ideology ("defense of our young freedom"), whose letters were sometimes featured in the committee press, but the lack of more substantial evidence makes a closer study impossible. Nevertheless, see below, pp. 253-55.

circumstances, such as the relative sanity of the commander, position and length of stay on the line, casualties, food supply, frequency of replacements, or exposure to German and Bolshevik propaganda. If the reader is distressed that the subject of discussion is frequently whole units with no reference to internal conflicts or diversity, the reason is that they appear that way in the sources, and the internal dynamics seldom find documentation. Undoubtedly also at work was an informal process of consensus-creation that eluded detection, a peer loyalty of peasant type, which subdued any inclination to dissent once consensus was arrived at, often at an unruly impromptu shouting match called a *miting* (the front counterpart of the village *shkodka*). Once a violent act had been perpetrated, the unit as a whole tended to defend the guilty parties or cover up the deed, even in the face of severe repression.

All this has been recapitulated at this point to underscore the magnitude of the phenomenon occurring in the wake of the Kornilov affair—a virtual tidal wave, first covert, then open and powerful, of self-assertion by the soldier mass in behalf of peace regardless of consequences or conditions, which now effaced all previous distinctions of behavior and affected all types of units whatever their previous history, including cavalry, cossacks, and artillery. The rumblings were clearly evident in the remaining weeks of September, although higher committees, commissars, and commanders tended to ignore them. Around the first of October, and thereafter with ever-increasing relentlessness and ferocity, the wave engulfed literally the entire front and immediate rear, sending shockwaves back to the capital with the very clear message: peace must be obtained before the winter sets in (by October 15, by November 1, by the first freeze) or not a soldier would remain in the trenches; if the government were unwilling to treat for peace, the Soviet should take over, and if the Soviet leadership were reluctant, the Bolsheviks should be put in. The higher committees, slow to come to terms with this phenomenon, became one of its victims—by the end of October and early November, coinciding with the Bolshevik assumption of power in Petrograd, a "committee revolution" at the front ensued from a powerful "soldiers' plebescite" and crushed any possibility of restoring the Provisional Government by raising a force at the front. Kerensky was to drink of the same bitter cup as Kornilov and Nicholas.

Even many contemporaries were in awe of the powerful unanimity with which the soldiers simply declared an end to the war and obliged all other parties to accede to it. Had the Bolsheviks not been there to legitimize it, it would have sought and found some other resolution, because the impulse was not to be denied. Many voted with their feet, though by far not as many as is usually supposed; but they voted in countless other ways—by refusing to build winter bunkers, by selling off warm clothing, by plundering railroad cars with winter supplies, by grilling commanders over each order, by renewing fraternization, by assailing committees with requests for leaves (for "family emergencies"), by holding meetings, passing resolutions, sending deputations to Petrograd, and every other device previously or recently invented; but this time they were pursued on a grand scale and with a determination heretofore unseen. To present this in an orderly, systematic way would leave a false impression of tidy compartmentalization—reality would be better served by dashing thick colors on a broad canvas at random—but the approach here will be to follow a certain logical progression flowing from the basic impulse with no pretense that it describes the sequence of events or rigid pattern.

☆

The climate at the front can be ascertained with some reliability from a number of available surveys that were now a weekly affair for both commanders and commissars, covering every army and front, sometimes unit by unit, but more often summarizing the substance of lower unit reports. This report of Commissar Surguchev of the Seventh Army (Southwestern Front) for September 7-14 can serve as typical:

> In most corps the troops perform their difficult service in the hope of an early peace, talk of which is universal. Questions of supply and warm uniforms have created a very anxious mood in the units, and military organizations [the committees] are urgently demanding an immediate resolution by efforts at the front and in the rear. The army has recently lived exclusively from local sources, which have now been utterly exhausted, and any interruption in transport would be deadly. Particularly acute in connection with the approach of winter is the question of warm boots and uniforms, which are in extremely short supply and are not coming in from the rear.
>
> A profound, often blind feeling of mistrust of officers, considerably reinforced at the time of the Kornilov affair, has not at all calmed down and will hardly be resolved in the near future. . . . Grudges over heavy losses find in "Kornilovism" a pretext to get rid of such officers [responsible for losses]. The spontaneous thirst for peace even generates in the soldiers hostility to lower officers over the performance of essential military duties, such as repairing the trenchworks and training exercises. On these grounds various excesses have taken place leading to the arrest of officers, threats, or beating by soldiers, the liquidation of which will require tremendous efforts and firm, decisive measures front and rear.[2]

[2] TsGVIA, f. 2003/c, op. 1, d. 36, ll. 52-55 (Special Documents, copy).

Although the connection with the Kornilov affair is clear, the impaired authority of the officers allowed feelings that had been held in check to surface, the source of which went far beyond Kornilov and now assumed a very precise outline. The first chilly nights in Russia occur at the end of August and to the soldier they heralded the approaching winter. This automatically led to thoughts of warm boots, underwear, and greatcoats, none of which had been resupplied since the previous winter. Committees and supply officers had busied themselves with the question all summer with paltry results. How this question could instantaneously unravel the skein of logic to all the others is very clear from the record of a joint session of committees of the V Corps (Eleventh Army) convoked on September 3-7. The formal agenda dealt with the roots of the Kornilov plot, but when they turned to polling the units on their "condition" they uncovered an obsessive concern with food supply (especially bread) and warm clothing. A spot check of supplies on hand or available through the usual sources revealed that "by December we'll be freezing and dying of hunger." A supply officer pleaded that his telegrams and urgent messengers to the rear bases remained unanswered, but such things took time and counseled patience. According to the correspondent the reaction was: "If you can't handle it, get out of the way and let us do it." A special commission was set up to "clean out the Augean stables" of the supply service. When it was observed that the press was blaming "marauding soldiers and deserters" for disorganizing supply, the recoil was broadened to the political and social arena. An inverse mythology was again counterposed to that of bourgeois society on a very sensitive issue.[3]

Naturally these versions were retailed to the soldiers (or the reverse) as they expressed their concerns to their committees. Scarcely a single state-of-morale report of September fails to make remarks such as the following: "The approach of cold and lack of provisions and warm clothing are leading to unrest and create fertile soil for Bolshevik agitation." "The shortage of warm uniforms, boots, and forage continues to excite the soldiers, adversely affecting their mood and evoking a positive horror over the winter campaign."[4] The connection or juxtaposition with the longing for peace is frequently registered: "The soldiers talk incessantly of the desirability of peace, warm clothing, and food." "The approach of the winter campaign has accelerated the process of disintegration of the armies of the Southwestern Front, strengthening the longing for peace."[5] Taking note that the

[3] *VVK*, September 17.

[4] Staff survey of the Rumanian Front for September 16-23, *RDRA*, p. 423.

[5] Stavka survey covering Seventh Army for September 16-23, *KA* 84:165; complete Stavka survey of fronts for September 20 to October 1 and October 1-15 are in Bylevskii Papers, Nos. 7 and 8, HI. Surveys of other armies and fronts are available in TsGVIA, Special

disorganization of supply in the rear was casting doubt on the feasibility of a winter campaign, the soldiers worked the logic in the reverse direction—why do anything to remedy the supply situation if it reduces the urgency of peace? For that matter, what was the point of building winter bunkers, stocking wood, contracting with local landlords and peasants for food supplies, or caring for weapons or training exercises? Thus, a good bit of the disorderly conduct of the soldiers in these weeks resembled a systematic campaign to sabotage all support activities for future operations or passing the winter in the trenches.

Many incidents resembled the April kind, but now took on a more purposeful, uncompromising vein and covered a far wider imaginative range. The most frequent complaints concerned refusals to carry out work details and training exercises, or to replace other units on the line. General Baluev reported that on the Western Front there had been twenty-one cases of refusals to perform training exercises, ten to repair trenches, eight to obey military orders, and four appeals for disobedience to orders; thirteen of these involved entire units.[6] The more detailed surveys and lower-unit reports make clear that these counts were only of major incidents and that the phenomena were virtually universal, marked not in every case by overt defiance, but invariably by ingenious forms of undercutting or averting the execution of orders. The 117th Division (Eighth Army, Rumanian Front) provides ample illustration. The commander of the 465th Regiment reported that the mood of his soldiers was good, that work was proceeding on winter quarters, that no refusals of orders, no insults to officers, no agitation, and only two desertions (and two returns) had occurred, but he conceded that there was persistent talk about poor food, lack of warm clothing and boots, and "ending the war no matter what." This commander doubtless suffered from selective vision, but reports on the three remaining regiments redress the picture. In the 466th Regiment, soldiers refused work on trenches or performed their work carelessly and fell far below the norms. Their excuse was poor food, "as if they were starving," and their confidence in early peace, making defensive emplacements unnecessary; they even refused to dig pits for warm winter bunkers, declaring, "We will never have to live in them." Persuasion by officers and committeemen only provoked surly reactions and threats. Every available plank in the passageway was scrawled with graffiti such as "Down with the war!" and

Documents, copies; for example, a commissar's report on the Special Army of September 9 states the condition of the troops to be "dangerous," requiring "heroic efforts," naming lack of food, winter clothing, and boots, and the thirst for peace, as the chief causes; another of a slightly later date for the front as a whole states that the soldiers talk only of peace, food, and warm clothing.

[6] TsGVIA, Special Documents, copies, Western Front of September 15.

"Beat the burzhuis!" The situation in the 467th Regiment was exactly the same, but included a distinctive reaction to news of the railroad strike: "That means peace, because there won't be anything to fight with"; in fact, they regarded the chief culprits for the war to be "the whole bourgeoisie, beginning with the commanding staff down to the lowest officer ranks." The last regiment was simply said to be very bad and getting worse, the hostility being specifically directed against the officers and rooted in "the striving to end the war as soon as possible," which rumors said would be over by October 15, "after which they can all go home." An engineering officer supervising work details noted that soldiers appeared for work solely to avoid being accused of refusing orders, but incessantly created "scandals." They seldom put in more than an hour, dug where they were not supposed to, and halted when they struck a rock or a root. A general phenomenon was the breakage of tools.[7] The real meaning of this behavior can be inferred from a committee declaration in the V Corps in early October in favor of a speedy peace, "as befits the honor and dignity of a free people," but not by the "false path of refusing to work on fortifications."[8]

Other actions great and small, which appear to express gratuitous violence and indiscipline, sometimes reveal traits of this hidden logic. For example, a huge riot of garrison soldiers in Gomel resulted in the plundering of 150,000 sets of warm clothing; commanders were often dismayed to see local peasants wearing soldiers' clothing and boots.[9] Soldiers who with local peasants plundered local estates, seemingly interested in wine and liquor caches, also burned down barns with inventory, destroyed food stocks, and slaughtered cattle badly needed by their own units. Soldiers refused to work on warm bunkers for officers, refused to allow them to send home for warm clothing, refused to allow them to be paid more than soldiers, forced them to close their separate mess, and in one recorded case moved into a winter bunker the officers had built for themselves. The argument here was that if the officers shared all the deprivations of their men they would also want peace.[10]

[7] Commander's report to headquarters of the XXXIII Corps of September 28, TsGVIA, f. 2143/c, op. 1, d. 28, l. 173 (Special Documents, copy). A staff survey for the Southwestern Front for September 1-7 records that in well over two-thirds of the divisions major instances of resistance to orders on transfers, work details, and training exercises occurred; in some they are overshadowed by open clashes between soldiers and officers or refusals to replace other units on the line (*ibid.* for Southwestern Front, but no folio reference).

[8] *VVK*, October 8.

[9] Stavka survey for September 20-October 1, Bylevskii Papers, No. 7, section on Western Front.

[10] See report on XXXIII Corps of October 6 with reference to Sixth Amur Regiment, TsGVIA f. 2134/c, op. 1, d. 28, l. 190 (Special Documents, copy). For other examples, see

A sign of the times reminiscent of April was the flood of requests for leaves and the release of "over-forties." The dockets of the committees and staffs were full of "letters from home" urgently pleading that Petr or Sidor was needed for a family emergency or field work.[11] Given the critical supply situation, there were grounds for leniency, and on September 5 the executive committee of the soviet of the Special Army decided to lift existing limits on leaves. In his survey for the Southwestern Front of September 7-14, Commissar Kostytsin noted the flood of requests as a general problem requiring swift regulation, as it was becoming a "terrible distraction" and was leading to a major increase in desertions.[12] Apparently as a result of the clamor of garrison units in the rear, the Provisional Government again allowed the temporary release of the age-group 42-43 in training; this unleashed a new wave of demands for release by the same age-group at the front, and the Stavka survey for September 20 to October 1 notes that it was being interpreted as the beginning of demobilization and that "no amount of argument can persuade soldiers of the absurdity of these rumors."[13]

☆

Desertions, said to be reaching massive proportions by this time, were not of great concern to front commanders, and the low figures reported defy credibility. For example, the weekly Stavka survey for September 20 to October 1 records only 15 desertions from the Fifth Army and 16 returnees. Official desertions from the entire Northern Front are recorded as 485 (50 returnees), and from the Caucasus Front as 283 (62 returnees).[14] Obviously the method of reporting was defective and varied considerably from unit to unit. Biweekly General Staff figures on desertions, available only through August 1, reached a peak of 23,432 for July 1-15, but fell back to 13,805 for July 16-30. Of the total of 84,086 for May through July, only 11,466 (13 percent) were from the front lines.[15] Though consistent with unit reports for that period, the lower staff cranked out numbers to satisfy higher staffs and had neither the machinery nor the incentive for accurate reporting. However, the author's opinion is that even in September and October desertions had not yet assumed massive proportions from the

TsGVIA, f. 2222, op. 1, ed. khr. 1066, l. 309 (removal of officers' messengers) and f. 3054, op. 2, d. 23, part 1, l. 33, *protokoly* for October 6 (officers warm clothing).

[11] For example, *ibid.*, TsGVIA, f. 3054, op. 2, d. 23, part 1, l. 23, September 25 (8-10 cases) and *protokoly* of committee of XXXI Corps of September 28, TsGVIA, f. 2440, op. 5, d. 1, ll. 72-73 (father requests leave for son for harvest, committee approves, commander affixes "agreed" in margin).

[12] TsGVIA, f. 366/c, d. 255, op. 1, ll. 73-78 (Special Documents, copies).

[13] Bylevskii Papers, No. 7.

[14] *Ibid.*

[15] *Rossiia v mirovoi voine 1914-1918 goda (v tsifrakh)* (Moscow, 1925), table 16, p. 26.

front lines, in part because of the expectation of an early peace (so why risk being branded a deserter?). On the other hand, there is every reason to believe that desertions from the garrisons, which had always been considerably larger than desertions from the front, were already massive. But no hard data can be gleaned from the sources, and the lack of commentary on desertions in military reports is noteworthy.[16]

By contrast, the military reports literally wail over the noxious influence of replacements, who were not only poorly trained, but also thoroughly Bolshevized and undisciplined—a major catalytic element in the rising sentiment for immediate peace. The front until the Kornilov affair having been somewhat screened from the day-to-day politics of the rear now came into contact with a vociferous element with ready-made slogans and identifiers for the culprits who were holding up peace—Kornilovites, *burzhuis*, Kadets, the Allies, compromising socialists, the whole system of coalition government, and not least of all Kerensky. Thus a marked politicization of various forms of unrest was a direct consequence of, or strongly reinforced by, the arrival of replacements. But first of all the magnitude must be assessed.

The offensive and the effort to build up depleted units thereafter had generated considerable demand to empty the pipeline of all training units. The recoil of the garrison soldiers to this pressure had resulted in the July Days in Petrograd, and massive unrest throughout the country. The rapid Bolshevization of the garrison soldiers in July and August was the consequence, and thus, particularly in the wake of the Kornilov affair, the arrival of any replacements from whatever region of the country could only intensify the radicalization of the front.[17] General Staff figures, available only to September 1, are as follows:[18]

May	181,000
June	293,000
July	437,000
August	260,000
Total	1,171,000

[16] See discussion in Wildman, *The Old Army*, pp. 362-71, where the difficulties in appraising desertions are treated in detail.

[17] See the excellent study of T. F. Kuzmina, *Revoliutsionnoe dvizhenie soldatskikh mass tsentra Rossii nakanune oktiabria* (Moscow, 1978), chap. 3. Also very useful is A. M. Andreev, *Soldatiskie massy garnizonov russkoi armii v oktiabrskoi revoliutsii* (Moscow, 1975), pp. 176 and *passim*.

[18] *Rossiia v mirovoi voine (v tsifrakh)*, table 4, p. 20. Frenkin, using the same or parallel data for the month of June, breaks it down into 697 marching companies of 138,000 men and 32 reserve regiments of 153,183 men (see Frenkin, *Russkaia armiia*, p. 313).

In August the rate slackened because of the policy of sending reserve regiments as complete units, rather than as dribbled-out marching companies, to speed up the process of "emptying the garrisons"; however, as the excellent data of the Soviet scholar T. F. Kuzmina shows, nearly all the reserve regiments ordered out in June and July were delayed by disorders or disorganization from three to eight weeks, over a third of the total arriving in August, and others (153rd and 159th Reserve regiments) not until mid-September.[19] Kuzmina's data does not include marching companies, which in the General Staff tables show an increase from 166,800 in July to 252,000 in August.[20] Citing other General Staff sources, M. S. Frenkin notes that in September 74 marching companies and 5 reserve regiments arrived on the Southwestern Front, and 40 companies and a reserve regiment on the Western Front, 88 companies and 2 reserve regiments on the Northern Front, and 68 companies and 5 reserve regiments on the Rumanian Front. If these units were up to strength, this would represent 106,500 men, but as Frenkin notes, reserve regiments seldom arrived with more than 2,000 out of a 3,000 complement and often with much less, and the same would be true of marching companies.[21] Thus there may have been a sizeable numerical dropoff in the course of September, but a bulge would have occurred early in the month.

However, the replacements of early and mid-September posed a problem far exceeding their mere numbers. The survey for the first week of September of the Southwestern Front blames the deterioration in the battleworthiness of the I Turkestan Corps, hitherto enjoying a good reputation, on poorly trained replacements, particularly in the 153rd Division. A similar survey of the Eleventh Army one week later specifies "harmful agitation in the Bolshevik style" in the 602nd and 604th regiments on replacements from the 159th Reserve Regiment; in the XXVI Corps (Rumanian Front) the poorly disciplined 311th Regiment suddenly turned worse with the arrival of replacements, resulting in refusals of work details and expressions of "lack of confidence in officers."[22] In the Sixth Army (Rumanian Front) several regiments refused to replace others on the line, even though they had recently distinguished themselves in battle: a detailed investigation blamed Bolshevik-dominated replacements who "inspire the soldiers with the hope that power will soon pass to the Soviet of Workers' and Soldiers' Deputies, which will bring immediate peace."[23] A survey of the Southwestern Front of late September observed: "Discipline is

[19] Kuzmina, Prilozhenie (Appendix) 6.

[20] *Rossiia v mirovoi voine (v tsifrakh)*, table 4, p. 20.

[21] Frenkin, *Russkaia armiia*, p. 509.

[22] TsGVIA, Special Documents, copies.

[23] Report on VII Corps of October 5, *ibid.*

declining with every passing day. . . . Units hitherto regarded as firm very quickly are transformed under the influence of dissolute and undisciplined replacements''; a survey of the Rumanian Front reported: ''Arriving replacements are not only depraved with Bolshevism, but are infected with outright hooligan instincts''; and a survey of the Caucasus Front stated: ''Arriving replacements are solidly Bolshevik, badly trained, and entirely undisciplined.''[24]

General Baluev regarded the whole issue so seriously that he twice requested Kerensky to disband entire reserve regiments. ''At the present time,'' he claimed, ''the majority of reserve regiments are in a state of total disorganization and instead of supplying the front with well-trained reinforcements are offering only uninstructed marching companies infected with Bolshevik ideas which only serve to work harm and cause disintegration among the regiments at the front.'' He also noted that in the garrison towns ''not a day goes by without major incidents,'' citing an instance in Kaluga, where the soldiers badly beat several doctors and their own committeemen because of their suspicion that one of their number had been medically poisoned; in Rzhev the garrison terrorized the local population and tried to break into a heavily guarded liquor warehouse.[25]

His chief example, however, was the Gomel redistribution point, where 8,000 to 10,000 soldiers went on a rampage on September 18-20. A street demonstration in behalf of immediate peace had just been broken up by ''armed intervention'' when two women, caught stealing bread and released, went to a nearby barracks crying, ''We are starving, but the burzhuis have all they want!'' A mob of 9,000 soldiers gathered before the headquarters of the local Soviet and shouted ''Beat the *burzhuis*!'' and ''Away with the war!'' threatening to trash the premises unless they received satisfaction. All movement of troops to the front halted, and the next day, when Assistant Commissar Kudriavtsev threatened the soldier crowds with cossacks and dragoons, they beat him and smashed his head with a rock. The disorders continued, the crowds now demanding ''immediate release to their homes and the conclusion of peace.'' The authorities did in fact release the 42- and 43-year-olds, after which the disorders subsided.[26] This is only one of many such disorders, though perhaps one of the more violent ones, that were occurring in the immediate rear of the Army as well as

[24] Stavka survey for September 20-October 1, Bylevskii Papers, No. 7.

[25] *RDRA*, p. 418.

[26] For the same incident, different details, see report of Western Front Chief of Staff Val'ter of September 23, TsGVIA, f. 2003/c, op. 1, d. 7, ll. 16-20 (Special Documents, copy), and Stavka survey of September 20-October 1, Bylevskii Papers, No. 7. These reports note that an organized group functioned throughout the disorders and sent emissaries to Kiev, Pskov, and elsewhere to raise similar demonstrations. Analogous events took place in Smolensk.

throughout the country, and that make up an important part of the general upsurge of anarchy and social disorganization which was a striking new phenomenon in September but universal in October and November.

☆

Accompanying the perturbations emanating from the rear was a marked rise in political concerns, connected not only with the urgency of peace but also with the Kornilov affair, the government crisis, the meeting of the Democratic Conference on September 12, the forthcoming elections to the Constituent Assembly (which sparked many conferences of party and other groups at the front), and a general climate of disenchantment with the coalition arrangement. Some of these influences were felt primarily by higher committeemen, others by lower committeemen, educated elements, or workers and peasants with a party exposure, and still others by the mass of soldiers. Some engaged the attention of all three levels, but from sharply differing perspectives. Bolshevism continued to be sharply differentiated between party-oriented and marching company-trench variety, though now a process of fusion rapidly set in along with a spectacular growth. Although Bolshevism was an increasingly important component in the broader political enlivening, clarity will be served by discussing the general phenomenon first and reserving the theme of Bolshevism for the following chapter.

Politicization at the front, of course, began in March of 1917 and never ceased to evolve among the masses as well as among committee elites even when it appeared to recede from surface consciousness. The masses had undergone a process of naive faith in the revolutionary authorities in Petrograd and then of deep disillusionment or quandary in the summer months in connection with the offensive and its aftermath. Bolshevism as an alternative faith suffered eclipse in the summer months (more so than in the rear) as its spokesmen were removed or went underground, and a climate of disapproval blanketed the peasant soldier from every side, including that of his committees. His withdrawal inward was accompanied by a lack of trust in or access to the normal sources of information—newspapers, agitators, committee spokesmen, government and Soviet pronouncements; the marching companies certainly brought with them their own feelings of class bitterness and confusion in connection with the punitive actions and forced embarkations, but political slogans, Bolshevik or otherwise, were subdued. Though the committees were strongly repoliticized with the rise of Kornilovism, the soldiers' August mood of brooding silence and passive resistance was related to that of other mass constituencies of the time—a disillusionment with politics, including revolutionary politics, a distrust of leaders, authorities, and institutions of all kinds, even blending in their consciousness the revolutionary and counter-revolutionary varieties, but at the same time a deepening of class feeling and resentment, seeking some kind of compensation, most clearly expressing itself in the popular mythology concerning Tarnopol and Riga. The Kornilov affair provided the sought-for outlet; it momentarily allowed the soldier to focus his feeling on the symbol of counter-revolution and to relegitimize, albeit momentarily, his faith in his committees, revolutionary institutions and—even more briefly—the Provisional Government. Kerensky's ill-advised post-Kornilov directives served to throw cold water on this rediscovered faith and raised searching questions and curiosity about what was going on in Petrograd.

Thus the repoliticization of September to a large extent came from within the soldier mass, a compulsion to find out whether the Provisional Government was worthy of rescue, whether in fact it served soldier-peasant interests, whether indeed it was going to conclude peace. The deeply disturbing rumors about the role of the Kadets and the "bourgeois parties" and that Kerensky had caved in to them made them wonder that a new coalition could mean anything else than a continuation of the war. Lower-level committees often had to respond to these promptings if they did not raise them themselves, and therefore one sees on both their parts a renewed interest in the politics of the center quite distinct in inspiration from the erstwhile loyalist politics of the higher committees. Thus, the purpose below is to examine in detail this rebirth of "politics from below."

The phenomenon was commented on extensively in the command reports along with disturbances and replacements. For example, on September 14 the commander of the XXXII Corps (Eleventh Army, Southwestern Front) declared: "All that is going on in the country, in the rear, in the capitals, in the government, is immediately reacted to among the troops, stirs them up and excites them. One reference to peace there brings a rash of resolutions and work refusals here." Another in the 59th Division (Eighth Army, Rumanian Front) of September 14 claimed that the soldiers "laid great hopes on the Democratic Conference in the assurance that it will bring peace."[27] But the chief evidence that committeemen and soldiers alike were following events with concern for how they might affect peace was the rash of collective statements by large gatherings. In September there were only a limited number, usually dominated by a tone of restrained reproach toward political authorities, but by October they became an angry flood.

The first such declarations of early September show few signs of so-

[27] TsGVIA, Special Documents, copy. A report on the 167th Division (also Eighth Army) around the same time records an appeal for "all power to the Soviets" and the execution of Kornilov without trial (f. 2134/c, op. 1, d. 28, l. 139, *ibid.*, copy).

phistication or sponsorship—otherwise they would not be so important—and each was uniquely eloquent in the expression of deep feelings. The first, an "instruction" (*nakaz*) of September 7 of an assembly of all company and special unit committees of the 15th Shlisselburg Regiment (VI Corps, Eleventh Army, Southwestern Front) to soldier and officer delegates to the soviets of Kiev, Moscow, and Petrograd, declares its definitive judgment on "the condition of the country at the present time in connection with and on the status of the question of war and peace." In rambling, florid style, paying due tribute to the "heroic efforts of the leading forces of Revolutionary Democracy in guarding the conquests of the Revolution," it stresses chiefly the imperative that the Soviet be informed of "the true state of affairs at the front," so that they "will not be led into fatal error in determining the cardinal question of war and peace." There followed an endless catalogue of hopeless conditions they faced in the forthcoming winter, starting with food supply and warm clothing and ending with the disorganization and anarchy in the rear. The "betrayal of the rebellious generals" and the deliberate surrender of Riga to frighten "the Democracy" get their due, but all of this is clearly a buildup to a vote of lack of confidence in the Provisional Government:

> The uninterrupted successes of the enemy on the one hand, and the compromising policy of the state power toward the bourgeoisie on the other, the insufficient influence of the Provisional Government on the Allied governments to get them to recognize Russia's peace conditions (evidenced by their successful blocking of the Stockholm Conference) . . . the imperialistic pressure from without and the counter-revolutionary attempts within . . . all this taken together is so unalterably horrible, so utterly depressing, that it kills any faith in the possibility of improvement and categorically demands that the question of peace be resolved now or never.[28]

A long series of rhetorical questions at the conclusion was meant to underscore for the benefit of Petrograd authorities the utterly helpless mood at the front: "Isn't fate laughing at us?" "Are we not falling into the abyss?" "Is the play worth the candle?" "Are we up to the role of selfless saviors?"

The combined committees of the 74th Infantry Division (Seventh Army, Southwestern Front) of the same date pronounced their own "decisive protest against the deadly policy conducted by the Provisional Govern-

[28] TsGVIA, Special Documents, copy (though from the Moscow Oblast State Archive). This and several others were reactions to the Bolshevik-sponsored resolution of the Petrograd Soviet of August 31, though there is no indication that the front resolutions were aware of the sponsorship. (See Rabinowitch, *Bolsheviks Come to Power*, pp. 160-62.)

ment'' and their sole faith in the Soviet, referring to the Bolshevik-proposed resolution of the Petrograd Soviet of August 31, which for the first time broached the idea of an all-socialist government (without specifying ''Soviet power''). That their own thinking was not in the Bolshevik orbit, however, is clear from its pledge: ''Regardless of hunger and disorganization the Army will continue to firmly guard our freedom against the external enemy, . . . but we nevertheless insistently and loudly demand—peace as soon as possible or everything will perish!''[29] Typically the resolution was to be hand-carried by a deputation to Petrograd to seek out the Soviet leaders.

A new militancy and political concern was manifest even in committees hitherto lacking in any definite political orientation, for example, that of the 46th Division (Eleventh Army), which had not passed a political resolution during the Kornilov affair, and in the first half of September met only once to discuss sanitary matters and forage. On September 15 it suddenly demanded the reinvigoration of the whole committee system, complaining that for two and a half months the Eleventh Army Committee had been silent:

> In the meantime many units have been undeservedly dishonored and their name dragged through the mud [remnants of the 607th Mlynovskii Regiment had recently been integrated into the division]. . . . The fate of the Republic [*sic*] is being decided, the suffering people is carrying an unbearable burden and making its last sacrifices. In such a decisive hour we must call an army congress so that by united forces we can work out our line of conduct and coordinate our actions with the democratic masses.[30]

Though its political views were unformed, the impulse was clear—the Army at the front must become organized so that it can influence political developments in the rear, implying a mistrust of the political center and the responsible democratic leadership.

The impulse to speak out was also keenly felt by individual soldiers and groups of soldiers outside the framework of their committees, reflecting

[29] *RDRA*, p. 401. Further points covered restoration of the rights of committees, protest against Kerensky's order on the removal of controls, the election of commissars, a purge of the commanding staff, and removal of repressive measures against Bolsheviks in recognition of their role in defeating Kornilov. *IzGr*, September 20, carries a resolution of a regiment addressed to the VTsIK insisting on ''no sort of collaboration with the Kadet Party'' and ''all power to the revolutionary democracy.'' Further points cover land to the land committees, publication of the secret treaties, a democratic republic, and freedom of agitation for the Bolsheviks; it is doubtless not Bolshevik-inspired, since it also expresses great alarm over the departure of Chernov, whom they regard as a ''great leader,'' from the government.

[30] TsGVIA, f. 2376, op. 1, d. 2, *protokoly*.

the same determination to get their message to higher authorities. The following pathetic letter received at Stavka in October addressed to Kerensky as Commander in Chief must have had numberless counterparts:

> Comrade Kerensky! We soldiers sitting in the trenches almost three years are awaiting that moment when we will hear that precious word "peace." In recent times rumors about peace are very widespread among us. From day to day we wait on pins and needles [*vot, vot*] for them to speak to us this precious word, but we still don't hear it [*net ego, net*]. We are all extremely tired both physically and morally, and therefore don't know if we will have the strength to spend another winter in the trenches. We are barefoot, unclothed, and starving, and therefore we turn to you as a comrade better informed—how long is all this going to last? We await your answer and hope you will take the trouble to write us a few lines here to the trenches, as they would be very dear to us. With deep regard, soldiers of the 270th Gatchinskii Regiment, Sixth Company, Third Platoon, N. Sergei Pishchuk [and two other illegible signatures].[31]

Though deferential in form like all peasant appeals to authority, there is an insistent tone, even an implied threat of violent reaction should a suitable response not be forthcoming, a reflection of proverbial peasant cunning. But that many soldiers were no longer troubling to appear deferential is expressed in another letter from a group of soldiers of the Rumanian Front to an unnamed newspaper of September 12:

> Did our new government really take power only to have its own way and continue the war for another three years? For what purpose did our brothers overthrow Nicholas II, and why did the soldiers put in Kerensky if not to get the war over with as soon as possible?
>
> . . . No, comrades, there is no use making fun of us and blinding our eyes with Kornilovite legends, or even the promises of Land and Freedom. What do we need your freedom in the future for? For what are you giving us land? Give us real freedom now and not in the future. . . . We are saying openly and directly that after October 1 we will no longer hold our positions, but will pick up our things and go home. Rather, let Wilhelm rule over us, at least we won't suffer any more; better that we have to pay indemnities, but at least our families won't die of hunger![32]

Perhaps these soldiers were consciously playing on the story of the soldier who confronted Kerensky in May with the question "What good is land

[31] Bylevskii Papers, No. 10, HI (handwritten copy of the orignal).

[32] TsGVIA, f. 2134/c, op. 2, d. 3, l. 69 (Special Documents, copy).

and freedom if I'm dead?'' but the notion by now was part of the authentic folklore of the trenches, reflecting the peasant's view of the war and those who made it. ''Land and Freedom'' and other high-sounding revolutionary verbiage were as much a subterfuge of the world of culture as ''Tsar and Fatherland.''

Corps and army newspapers are not good sources for the above development because they were too insulated and preoccupied with their own concerns; but, more important, such protests threatened to upset their own strategy of political survival, which was predicated on nursing along coalition politics until the Constituent Assembly. Importunities over winter supplies or peace at this juncture were treated as outright disloyal. Nevertheless, two committee organs, that of the Special Army (*IzOA*) and of the V Corps (*VVK*) gave some attention to the shaping mood, and their reaction to it is as revealing as the information on the mood itself. Around September 12 the *IzOA* began to print soldiers' letters, and inevitably the themes on the soldiers' minds began to take up quite a bit of space. One letter grumbled at the burden of training exercises, that every protest was treated with ''persecution'' and that ''the soldier is exposed to death every minute, but they laugh at us and slander us'' (again the extreme sensitivity to accusations in the ''bourgeois press''). He concluded pointedly: ''Where then is truth? From whom shall we seek protection? What government shall we trust? And when, pray tell, is this cursed war going to end?''[33]

On September 15, in connection with the ''peace question,'' *IzOA* fastened on a resolution of an unnamed corps congress, which argued that in view of the complete economic chaos in the rear and the universal longing of the soldier masses, the government absolutely had to undertake a ''decisive foreign policy aimed at peace, revising the secret treaties and making a serious offer of a democratic peace to all belligerent powers.'' The article ridiculed the shallowness of such thinking, as if Russia were in any position to dictate to the Allies, let alone Germany, unless she visibly demonstrated the will to fight. A second article excoriated the widespread rumors that ''if there is no peace by the first snow, nobody will be left in the trenches,'' ascribing such lies to ''traitors from the rear, German agents, Kornilovite adventurers, devilish minions of the former Emperor, but certainly not Russian soldiers.'' A third article also denied that ''real soldiers'' wanted ''peace at any price,'' but conceded that soldiers' distrust and cynicism had been bred by the myths of ''soldier cowardice'' at Tarnopol and Riga spread by the high command and bourgeois newspapers. In fact it acutely depicted popular psychology ''The *nachal'stvo* [general peasant term for authority] intentionally surrendered us to the Germans'' and the retreat

[33] *IzOA*, September 13.

was "ordered by the command" to deliver rebellious soldiers to the Germans. The command, *burzhuis*, and traitors all became synonyms. But the rumors of "peace by November 1" were still ascribed to marching companies.[34] Letters from soldiers again disappeared from the pages of *IzOA* and the complacent treatment resumed. A week later, like a bubble-burst, an editor who had just completed a tour evoked the true "mood" of the soldiers without illusions.

> Out of the soldiers' hearts pours forth a whole flood of hatred for the war and all it stands for. The chief culprits the soldiers see in the French, the English, and in general the whole bourgeoisie. They forget about the Germans. All our defeats and convulsions front and rear they blame on the generals and the bourgeoisie. The generals' uprising has definitely lowered the prestige of the command, which is no longer trusted. Nor do they believe the revolutionary leaders Kerensky or Tsereteli. They are deeply dissatisfied with our revolutionary institutions and deeply sympathize with the Bolsheviks. The Bolshevik mood is growing with each passing day. To them the Bolsheviks are their real friends and saviors of the Fatherland and the Revolution. They simply won't hear about continuing the war. . . . They reason that if we don't want to lose Petrograd, it is better to make peace now.[35]

Though the author bewailed the lack of elementary patriotism, he no longer minimized or explained away the phenomenon.

On September 20, *VVK* took cognizance of the soldiers' sentiment that "the war is being deliberately dragged out by the bourgeoisie to wipe out the *narod*," but they still ridiculed it as peculiar to marching companies. (When such types hear shots they dive for cover and shout, "Brothers, we've fallen into a nest of Kornilovites. It's the *burzhuis*, fellows, let's get them!") The moment of truth, however, came on October 6 in an article appropriately entitled "On the Volcano": it acknowledged that the striving for peace had taken on a massive character and could only be dealt with by a "decisive struggle for peace" that would restore the confidence of the men in the trenches. The committeemen-editors were now shaken in their confidence in the Petrograd leadership, which was expressed in a series of disconsolate editorials.

It was rapidly becoming impossible to ignore the mass mood. Between mid-September and mid-October at least a dozen large formations undertook some dramatic initiative to force the issue of peace. Invariably the

[34] *Ibid.*, September 17.

[35] *Ibid.*, September 24.

aim was to "get the message to Petrograd," either to expose the falsity of the information reaching them via the "commissars" and higher committees, or to demand an open shift in policy, or even to bring about a changing of the guard in political leadership. The pattern of these actions is so uniform, and so frequently do seasoned Bolsheviks turn up presiding over them, that one is tempted to infer a campaign orchestrated by the Petrograd Bolshevik leadership, but the verdict of the evidence is rather that the tide of events was so powerful in the direction of the Bolshevik program and so strongly against that of the loyalist Menshevik and S.R. committeemen that any Bolsheviks who happened to be on the premises were automatically drawn into them. If they weren't, then any available demagogue could be baptized a Bolshevik on the spot. Thus marching company Bolshevism and "politics from below" on behalf of peace were advancing hand in hand, the former fed by the reluctance of the existing committee leadership to yield to the latter.

If one were left with a random sampling of documents available in Soviet collections or printed in army newspapers, a good many perplexities might remain over how to interpret the evidence. However, two instances, coincidentally occurring in advance of the rest, are sufficiently documented to lend unmistakable concreteness to the nature of the process. It is fairly safe to conclude that these cases exemplify the chemistry at work nearly everywhere, even when the outcome was not so dramatic. In both cases specific units sought to mobilize as large a sector of their front as possible behind a demonstration for peace, the crown of which was to be a massive delegation to Petrograd.

In the first case, the XXXIII Corps in September consisted of the First, Second, and Fourth Transamur Border Guard and the 117th and 159th Infantry Divisions. All but the 159th had been in the corps since it was transferred from the Seventh to the Eighth Army just before the retreat. The core divisions suffered an episode of Bolshevik-inspired turbulence at the time of their transfer ("yellow-bellied Bolsheviks" from Tsarytsin in the Second Division, Bolshevik "delegates" from Petrograd loaded with literature opposing the war in the Fourth).[36] The Transamur divisions seem to have quieted down in August, but the 117th remained turbulent.[37]

A week-by-week profile of the corps augmented by other documents allows one to follow in detail the upheaval about to take place. The routine report for September 14 described most units as "satisfactory," except the

[36] Report to army headquarters of June 26, *RDRA*, pp. 159-60. Frenkin relates that Bolsheviks Muravnik and Lysenko headed a delegation to Petrograd in June, returned to the corps as ardent agitators against the offensive, and were subsequently brought to trial (*Frenkin, Revoliutsionnoe dvizhenie na rumynskom fronte*, pp. 115-16).

[37] Corps report to headquarters of the Eighth Army of August 25, *RDRA*, pp. 350-52.

Fourth Division, which remained "upset by events" (an allusion to the Kornilov affair) and anxious for a long rest in the rear. Three of the four regiments of the 117th Division were quiet, but the 468th was beset by an "undercurrent of unrest" ascribed to agitators recently transferred in from another division disbanded for mutinies in July.[38] On September 18 without warning a mass meeting of soldiers of the First and Second Transamur and the 117th divisions took place and passed the following resolution:

> Finding that a continuation of the war will lead to the final ruin of the country and loss of the conquests of freedom by the Revolution, we demand the most strenuous efforts to end the war. . . . Any delay in this regard under the present state of disorganization will lead to the collapse of the front. Realizing that the conclusion of peacc is only possible for a government clothed with the full confidence of the people, we greet the Democratic Conference, which will create a democratic power strong enough to obtain peace, land, and freedom.[39]

Who called the meeting, how large a gathering it was, or what had occasioned it is not clear, except that the regular committees had opposed it, standing instructions of the commissar forbade it, and the committee of the Second Division resigned as a result. The 467th Regiment came to the meeting with banners inscribed "Death to the Burzhuis!" In the 468th Regiment, arrested agitators were forcibly freed, and regimental headquarters were temporarily taken over by a soldier mob.[40]

The assembly decided to send a large deputation to Petrograd and that each division should elect delegates and provide them with an instruction (*nakaz*) which should cover the following points: (1) attitude on the coalition, (2) authorization of meetings and electoral assemblies at the front, (3) disbanding of all shock troops, (4) speeding up elections to the Constituent Assembly, (5) regular information on proceedings in the Soviet, (6) "renewal" of the commanding staff, and (7) clarification of why Kornilov's orders were still being passed on to the regiments. This was a typical political agenda of the time, logically derived from the soldiers' current concerns, and was to be repeated many times over in the coming weeks. Since the deputation was to arrive in Petrograd no later than September 25, a mass meeting of the entire corps was set for September 20. The unprecedented outcome of the affair was recounted by Commissar

[38] TsGVIA, f. 2134/c, op. 1, d. 28, l. 141 (Special Documents, copy).

[39] Text in *ibid.*, l. 51.

[40] Report of September 22, in *ibid.*, f. 2134/c. The First Amur and 159th divisions are recorded as still quiet.

K. M. Vendziagol'skii in a telegram to the War Ministry of September 21:

> In the reserve of the XXXIII Corps are five regiments in the village of Kliskovtsky, three kilometers from the position. Yesterday a meeting not authorized by my deputy or the regimental committees called an assembly for today to discuss the war, fraternization, and peace, having in mind to march in ranks with white flags and music to the trenches of the enemy. Since morning my deputy has been there. The mood is stormy: white flags, music, all is ready for a meeting of some 10,000 persons; the commanding staff is beside itself.[41]

The intervention of the commissars headed off the scandalous idea of a march to the enemy and secured a pledge to "hold the front," but only at the price of officially conceding the sending of a large delegation (36 persons) to Petrograd with a catalogue of political demands. Realizing the futility of enforcing the former rules, Vendzegal'skii asked permission to authorize meetings and assemblies, having learned anew the lesson of March that it was better to legitimize and guide into less harmful channels the spontaneous actions of the masses than to forbid them outright and expose one's inability to control the situation. Likewise, the prospect of legitimacy and the possibility of directly influencing the policies of the government tempered for a time the ungovernable spirit of the soldier masses.

The Fourth Transamur Division, stationed some distance away and not represented at the mass meeting, was an exception. It held a meeting of its own on September 19 and decided not to move up to the front when ordered, and in one regiment there was considerable agitation to desert by October 15 if there was no peace. During the night of September 19-20, two figures, one naked and the other minus his trousers, streaked through the bivouac shouting, "Let's go, everybody's retreating!" The streaking precedent did not catch on, but the incident became a legend and the culprits were not caught. A report of September 22 noted: "There is a party struggle going on in the regiment and passions are aroused by the newspapers." The committees had been spontaneously reelected several times recently because no one could satisfy the restless element.

Awaiting the outcome of the mission to Petrograd, the mood of the first two Transamur divisions seemed to have reached a plateau. Nevertheless, very little routine work was getting done, and the officers were powerless to do anything about it. The situation in the Fourth and 117th divisions, however, continued to deteriorate, the latter descending into a state of

[41] Text in *ibid.*, f. 366/c, op. 1, d. 304, l. 51.

absolute incorrigibility, and the former infected by frequent contacts between them. The 117th boycotted work details, abused their officers, and engaged in fraternization so assiduously that Austrian officers themselves broke it off. All officer deputies had been expelled from regimental committees, and a report of September 29 describes the latter as "having no influence whatsoever over the political thinking of the soldiers, who are only interested in something to the extent it promises peace."[42]

The minutes of a committee session of the 466th Malmyzhskii Regiment of October 1 reveal how seriously the routine military life of the division was impaired. It decided to abolish all training exercises and work details to give more time to prepare for Constituent Assembly elections (after all, they had come to the rear for a rest and were not adequately clothed and fed); it reviewed a number of court cases and petitioned the commander to release all the accused; it also petitioned the division commander to be assigned permanently to the army reserve because they had no intention of ever returning to the trenches; it abolished the separate mess of the officers and the shock battalion; it "recalled" the officers' orderlies to the ranks "to create a better climate between officers and soldiers"; and finally, it instructed the command henceforward to refer all court cases against either officers or soldiers to the regimental committee. All points are recorded as having passed "unanimously."[43]

One can see in the episode in the XXXIII Corps a pattern that was to be repeated many times on different sectors of the front in the coming weeks: inchoate dissatisfactions over strictly visceral issues suddenly expressed themselves in a bold initiative of a particular unit, which rapidly drew in as many of its neighbors as possible; the action then assumed an ever more organized and rationally expedient political form to which the authorities were obliged to yield to prevent a descent into anarchy; a temporary calm set in, but institutionalized controls and actions of committees and commissars in effect absorbed the soldier impulses. Military order in effect ceased to exist regardless of whether the unit remained "calm" or violent.

Events unfolded in the Finnish Rifle divisions (XXII Corps, Seventh Army, Southwestern Front) in very much the same way, except that one does not find a significantly demoralized element on whom to blame the affair. These units had recovered considerably after the retreat, and only the 20th Regiment of the Fifth Division remained troublesome, but it played no visible role in this affair. The Bolshevik memoirist Tuzhikov claims that his group controlled the committee of the Sixth Regiment, but if so

[42] Corps reports of September 29 and October 6 in *ibid.*, f. 2134/c.

[43] *RDRA*, pp. 445-46.

they must have been very subdued; no complaints against them in command reports are registered before mid-September. A corps report of September 20 was more concerned about replacements in the Fourth Regiment, which regarded training exercises as "*kornilovshchina*" and harbored agitators; in the Second Division work was proceeding normally, though without enthusiasm, and newspapers were blamed for too much talk about peace.[44] That same day the corps commander was obliged to report that a large group of soldiers of the Sixth Regiment had marched through the village of Andreevka carrying placards inscribed "Down with the war!" and held a meeting lasting until 7:30 P.M. They refused to listen to the entreaties of their own committeemen (the Bolsheviks?) to disperse quietly. Their intention was to gather on the next day and march with their placards and marching band to the village of Berezanka, where they hoped to bring over the Fifth Regiment to their slogans. The commander met with the regimental committee (again presumably Tuzhikov's Bolsheviks) early in the morning, and together they tried to bring the situation under control. A large crowd had already gathered for the march when the colonel himself urged them to formulate their demands, again yielding to the logic that it was better to be organized than unorganized. The resolution quite simply demanded that the Provisional Government immediately conclude peace, as a continuation of the war would ruin the country and destroy the Revolution. Other units of the division and the "Great Army" were invited to support it, and copies were sent to newspapers all over the country.[45] The nightmare of a huge demonstration was avoided when the commander persuaded them simply to send small deputations to other units instead of marching en masse. Within two days all regiments of the division had held meetings and endorsed the resolution. Again the legitimizing procedure probably widened the scope of the action and gave it a more purposeful political direction than it otherwise would have taken.

The repercussions of this affair were very far-reaching and fortunately well documented. Although the discipline of the Second Division remained intact, its action had a sensational effect on every unit of the XXII Corps, riveting their attention to the cause of peace and enhancing their sense of power to influence events. Proof that a sense of discipline prevailed in the Sixth Regiment after the affair is that two days later they were ordered to take up a position on the front lines, and they did so without incident or debate. The mood was described as "nervous, expectant, and impatient

[44] See *ONFV*, p. 203, and TsGVIA, f. 2222, op. 1, ed. khr. 1066, ll. 142, 158, 168 (complaints of Bolshevik agitator Filatov in 20th Regiment), 190, 214-25, and 232.

[45] Text in TsGVIA, f. 2222, op. 1, ed. khr. 1066, l. 273. Corps reports on incident, *ibid.*, ll. 238, 246, and 255, and reports of individual units, *passim*, esp. vivid account of commander of Sixth Regiment of September 20, l. 274.

to receive responses to their resolution on the speedy execution of peace''; in addition, a brief episode of fraternization occurred—a ''Down with the war!'' placard was raised over the trenches, which brought out a few hundred souls from both sides, but counter-measures were taken without protest, and the soldiers performed their duties normally.[46] Reports from all units reflect a general deterioration in the performance of training exercises and too much talk of peace, but no open defiance of orders or threats of violence toward officers. In fact, throughout the affair relations between soldiers and officers seemed relaxed, probably due to the accommodating stance of the commander. Relations of soldiers with committees are described as ''good'' even though most of the latter had opposed the demonstration.

One can clearly see the process of contagion, however, in the Third Division, which hitherto had been very disciplined. A report of September 24 claims that the 11th Regiment was considerably agitated over the resolution of the Sixth Regiment. ''Bolshevik replacements'' arrived precisely at this time, though the 12th Regiment seems to have been more affected by this than the 11th.[47] On October 3 one company voted not to engage in training exercises, and in response an assembly of company committees passed a peace resolution and requested the division committee to call a general meeting of the division for October 6. The division committee was apparently ready to comply, but instead the commander called a joint assembly of committees alone in hopes of quashing the affair. The soldiers from the offending company were allowed to present their case, which was that they had lost their faith that the war could be won because the rear refused to support them. They were particularly upset that the commissars were consistently misleading the Provisional Government and the ''organs of democracy'' with unduly optimistic reports on the condition of the army at the front. The commander requested the committee to explain to the soldiers the ''extreme danger of an open declaration of their desire for peace, which plays into the hands of the enemy'' and the ''criminality'' of refusing training exercises; however, he would allow them to express their wishes through their committees. He conceded that half their time could be devoted to self-education in preparation for the Constituent Assembly, but training exercises had to take place; furthermore, he strictly forbade any further meetings by soldiers or committees, particularly the one contemplated for October 6.[48]

On that date the combined committees of the division nevertheless met

[46] See division reports of September 23 and 24, *ibid.*, ll. 252 and 257.

[47] Division report of September 24, *ibid.*, l. 258, and corps reports of September 28, l. 255.

[48] Corps reports of October 4 and 5, *ibid.*, ll. 322-25 and 405-7.

(some 405 deputies), each reporting on its "mood," the result of which was another powerful statement:

> The never-ending slaughter has led the country to absolute ruin and exhaustion of all its resources. The anxious mood front and rear threatens to descend into anarchy, and this could lead to the end of the Revolution. . . . The united committees of the division, standing guard over the Revolution and state, find it absolutely necessary to undertake decisive steps to open peace negotiations. For the purpose of conveying the mood of our division, the assembly chooses a delegation of three soldiers and one officer to contact the Executive Committee of the Soviet of Workers', Soldiers', and Peasants' Deputies and the Provisional Government. Moreover, we call for an immediate Army Congress.[49]

On October 7 the 11th Regiment refused orders to occupy the trenches, which they regarded (not without reason) as an attempt to put an end to the agitation. The impasse lasted two days and ended only when the commander issued a third categorical order, threatening otherwise to disband the regiment.[50] This incident led directly to a rash of other incidents over disobedience of orders, punitive threats and counter-threats (to raise all officers to their bayonets), plundering, wine pogroms, and extensive soldier involvement in agrarian disturbances in the surrounding countryside, all of which did not cease until the October Revolution itself.

The missionary efforts of the Sixth Regiment, however, extended far beyond the Finnish divisions. In an order circulated to all units of the Seventh Army, Commissar Surguchev instructed that emissaries of the Second Finnish Rifle Division, who were broadcasting the demand that the Provisional Government make immediate peace, should be apprehended and turned over to the courts.[51]

The above affairs are only two more conspicuous and well-documented instances for the month of September, but they were not exceptional: in the Eighth Army, the 32nd and the 165th divisions (XI and XVI corps respectively) held large-scale assemblies, passed peace resolutions, and

[49] See *ibid.*, d. 2, l. 66 (text in corps committee archive). Incident is also covered in other corps committee documents in *ibid.*, ll. 61-64.

[50] Commissar Surguchev's instruction on the measures to be taken and the corps commander's response; see *ibid.*, ed. khr. 1066, ll. 376 and 377.

[51] See archive of the Second Guards Infantry Division, TsGVIA, f. 2322, op. 7, ed. khr. 2, l. 437 (the division order of September 30 is noted "to be strictly executed"). For telegraphed orders to all units of the XXII Corps to arrest the "delegates" of the Second Division on "orders from the commissar" of October 2, see f. 2222, op. 1, ed. khr. 1066, ll. 310-12. Tuzhikov claims to have been the emissary to the Eleventh Army (see *ONFV*, p. 206).

sent deputations to Petrograd, Moscow, Kharkov, and Odessa.[52] Another in the Eleventh Army published its resolution in the committee organ of the XXXII Corps:

> The time has finally come for the people itself to put squarely and firmly the question of its own life's blood, the question of ending the war. . . . We want the voice of our regiment and all regiments to resound throughout the land to tell those in power that the people cannot shed its blood without end or bear all the burdens—it cannot and it will not![53]

The 157th Imeretinskii Regiment (Sixth Army) stated unequivocally that "the mood of the regiment is peace regardless of the consequences, and if it does not come soon, we cannot be held responsible for the consequences."[54] Both sent delegations to the Soviet.

In the first eight days of October there were no less than ten verifiable instances of this order, among them the I Turkestan and VI Army corps (Special and Eleventh armies), and the First Rifle (Sixth Army, Rumanian Front), Second Grenadier (Second Army, Western Front), and Second Guards Infantry (Seventh Army, Southwestern Front) divisions.[55] There were also any number of regimental assemblies of the same type.[56] The significant new element in these cases was the more advanced level of politicization: frequently they took as their point of departure specific political events in the capital—the Democratic Conference, resolutions of the Petrograd Soviet and of VTsIK, the announcement of a date for the Constituent Assembly elections, pronouncements of the Kadets and other "census" elements, and so forth. Visible in the proceedings were now spokesmen of specific political persuasion, above all Bolsheviks, but also Left and Right S.R.'s, Peasant Soviet types, Menshevik Internationalists, and so on. The results were quite diverse, but only in exceptional cases can one say that Bolsheviks became entrenched in the leadership where they were not present before. Most noteworthy, however, was the enormous

[52] See Frenkin, *Revoliutsionnoe dvizhenie na rumynskom fronte*, pp. 156-57.

[53] *GO*, September 30.

[54] *RDRA*, p. 441. It was a plenary session of the committee with twenty-two deputies present, responding to a major incident in the 30th Division from which they feared repercussions.

[55] See *RDRA*, pp. 448, 461, 466, and 470-73; *IzGr*, October 18; and TsGVIA, f. 2179, op. 4, ed. khr. 2, l. 316; see also *VOSR. Oktiabr'*, p. 362, and *VKDA*, pp. 351, 354, and 358 for I Siberian Corps (Tenth Army), Fourth Rifle Division (Ninth Army), Sixth Infantry Division (Third Army), and IV Corps (Sixth Army).

[56] For example, see *RDRA*, pp. 447, 457, 458, 467, and 476, and *VKDA*, p. 347. Since the archives were scoured by the Soviet editors for the resolutions with close to Bolshevik formulations, the sample is far less complete and typical.

leftward pressure, not only on the war but on a whole range of issues, which definitely gave a tactical advantage to the Bolsheviks, obliging the loyalist committeemen to make concession after concession in programmatic matters to maintain a foothold for their basic political commitment, which at this point was to defend the legitimacy of the Kerensky coalition and the Pre-Parliament until the convocation of the Constituent Assembly.

The case of the Second Grenadier Division is interesting in that the committees had always been firmly in the hands of S.R.'s of the Left-Center (Chernov) type who were also ardently prowar and supportive of discipline. They had faithfully tried to indoctrinate their clientele with such attitudes through their corps organ, *IzGr*. Stubborn pockets of committed Bolsheviks survived the summer repressions, particularly in the Sixth Regiment, but of the ripple of Bolshevik agitation in June there was not a trace. Without warning on October 7 the combined committees of the Second Division passed a stirring resolution which connected unbearable exhaustion with the war with a long list of well-formulated political demands—a definite peace proposal based on the Soviet formula of March, a firm date for the Constituent Assembly, abolition of the death penalty, "democratization of the army" (the right of committees to nominate and remove officers), fixed prices on consumer goods, struggle against "sabotage" by the industrialists, immediate provisioning of the Army, and finally the transfer of all land (and "living and dead inventory") to the land committees. Although very sweeping, the program was not purely Bolshevik, since it vested "all power" not in the Soviets but in the Pre-Parliament and ascribed land not to "peasant committees" (the Bolshevik formulation) but to the nonclass land committees (the S.R. formula).[57] Delegations were to visit the Pre-Parliament, the Commander in Chief, and the War Ministry.

One can only guess at the combination of forces that produced the Grenadier document, but in the case of the Turkestan Corps one can observe the process firsthand because the complete record of an assembly of committees of October 2 is available.[58] Attended by 445 delegates, the assistant commissar of the Special Army, and a member of the Pre-Parliament, Dr. Zuker, it was earmarked as a political event of the first magnitude. The record of the corps in 1917 is obscure, but since the Kornilov affair it had been in a state of constant turmoil, mainly in connection with complaints over extreme exhaustion and inadequate supply. The occasion for this large gathering was the widespread demand for a prolonged rest in the rear, and the presence of authoritative political figures was doubtless arranged for

[57] See *IzGr*, October 18; text of resolution in *VKDA*, pp. 353-54.

[58] *RDRA*, pp. 440-52.

as an antidote. In any event, Zuker sought to put the Democratic Conference in the best light, arguing that prospects for peace were best served by securing the cooperation of the bourgeoisie rather than driving them into opposition. A popular Bolshevik committeeman, Razzhivin, argued that precisely the presence of the bourgeois groups undercut the prospects for peace, committed as they were to continuation of the war and the tsarist secret treaties.[59] Only a power based on the Soviets could save Russia. The S.R.'s stoutly defended Zuker's position, claiming that the Bolsheviks' strategy would lead straight to civil war.

Two resolutions were put to a vote, that of the committee leadership expressing confidence that only the Pre-Parliament could lead the country to the Constituent Assembly (''which will establish the kingdom of socialism on earth . . . and put an end to all grief, and stamp out the parasites that drink the blood of working people''), and that of the Bolsheviks denouncing the coalition and calling for an all-socialist government directly responsible to the masses (no reference to the Soviet), which alone could ''bring a speedy end to the fratricidal slaughter.'' The vote split the assembly right down the middle, giving a slight majority to the pro-coalition position (197 to 187). When a second resolution was introduced on ''war and peace,'' Razzhivin very cleverly insisted that each unit speak out for the opinion of its constituency. The result was a depressing series of statements on the utter weariness of the soldiers, who did not intend to spend the winter in the trenches. Principled discussion thereafter became impossible, and this time the Bolshevik position passed 235 votes to 155 (unilateral renunciation of the secret treaties, an immediate offer of a democratic peace to all countries, and if the Provisional Government refused, then ''All power to the Soviets''). When Razzhivin introduced a final resolution demanding that the corps be given at least a month's rest in the reserve, it passed without dissent. It should be noted that Razzhivin's skillful tactics could not gain the Bolsheviks control over the committees, since this was an expanded session of existing committees, not an official congress. But the reputation of the Bolsheviks must have soared.[60]

In the VI Corps an official congress was called and the Bolsheviks by

[59] According to K. G. Eremin, Razzhivin was chairman of the corps committee in June and became a hero when he defied the efforts of the Commissar Linde to engage units of the corps in repressions during convulsions in the Eleventh Army (see Eremin, *Soldatskie versty*, pp. 45-50). See also *VKDA*, pp. 256 and 556, where editor's note identifies him as a Bolshevik since 1911.

[60] On the continued escalation of the turmoil in the Turkestan Corps, resulting in a chain of refusals to obey orders, abuse of officers, fraternization, and total indifference to military order, see *RDRA*, pp. 508-9. There is no further information on the corps until after the October Revolution.

similar procedures were able to take control of the leadership. A reference by the Bolshevik Karakhan to the failure of the Democratic Conference brought "stormy applause," and another to the "treachery" of Kerensky brought him a reprimand from the chair and such a parliamentary snarl that the defensists walked out, allowing the Bolshevik-sponsored main resolution to pass with only one dissenting vote (199 to 1, with 67 abstentions). Without opposition, Bolshevik positions on a variety of issues were adopted, including the election of commissars, the universal arming of the workers, and an eight-hour day. The assembly ended in a state of euphoria over "the grandiose task before us . . . the now beginning socialist revolution."[61]

☆

Given the magnitude of the tidal wave rising beneath them, one can only marvel at the rigidity and complacency of the army and front committees. One can leaf through issue after issue of their official organs in late September and the first half of October and find nothing that forewarns one of the storm that was brewing. They even cease to be good sources of information on army and front committees, as they ceased publishing proceedings except in fragments after considerable delay. *Iz5A* and *Iz8A* were reduced to small broadsheets consisting almost entirely of military communiqués ("exchange of fire" on this or that front) or trivial news agency telegrams.[62] Editorials commented mainly on the Democratic Conference and preparations for the Constituent Assembly, both of which were treated in the most positive terms. More often, verbatim speeches or the text of electoral statutes were used as fillers. Since there are few other good sources (not a single higher *komitetchik* except Shklovsky ever wrote memoirs), one must reconstruct the picture from the total context.

Most active higher committeemen were party-oriented socialists of unquestioning loyalty to the Soviet leadership, and they deferred to the wisdom of the latter in political matters. All leadership cohorts in democratic institutions in 1917 tended to become estranged from their constituencies, and to hold rigidly to the dogmas of the coalition era. Even the Kornilov affair and the obvious duplicity of the Kadets failed to move the Soviet leadership to revise its political thinking. The Democratic Conference was only the most recent expedient to "control" the government in the name of the democratic program, only to founder on the danger of desertion by the bourgeois partner. Again Kerensky became the substitute solution.

[61] *RDRA*, pp. 470-73. On the hegemony of the Bolsheviks not lasting, see below, p. 355.

[62] It must be acknowledged that in both collections more than half the issues are missing, but it does not appear to have been a great loss. *GoFr* of September 17 bewails the dullness of the army press, but the best example is *GoFr* itself.

Measures on all other excruciating problems, therefore, were postponed until the Constituent Assembly, as it was obvious that Kerensky and the rump Pre-Parliament lacked the authority or will to carry them through. Thus the leaders tended to clap on blinkers and to rivet their attention to the mechanics of elections to the Constituent Assembly, which presumably would resolve everything. But neither at the front nor in the country at large were they to be given that respite. Thus, the democratic leaders were afflicted by a deep-seated political paralysis, and the army committeemen were simply a particular case of the general disease.

On a more practical level the committeemen were swamped with work. With the overall shortage of talent, the cultivated socialist activists tended to become drawn into a variety of different roles—editor, mediator, problem-solver, economic expert, parliamentarian, record-keeper, jurist, pedagogue, and party organizer.[63] At this juncture they were also burdened with the monumental challenge of organizing elections for the Constituent Assembly and working out the many associated practical problems—mastering the complicated instructions, working out voting procedures, printing up ballots, training local organizers and ballot watchers, and so forth. Moreover, enormous energies had to go into preparing the soldiers for their role as citizens—printing and distributing mountains of literature on political parties and issues, arranging for intensive courses for those who were to conduct lower-level courses of instruction. There are only fragmentary allusions to all this activity, but certainly it consumed an enormous amount of time and energy.

The Special Army will serve as an example, since it seems to have been the better organized than most and certainly is well documented. On September 26 the government published the statute for the elections which established front electoral districts and commissions, and set a firm timetable for procedures, which stirred the Special Army Committee to life.[64] All other political news disappeared from the pages of *IzOA* (nothing on the cabinet, nothing on the Pre-Parliament), but day after day in October extensive space was devoted to commentaries on the statute and explanations of the significance of the event. Various announcements confirm that the formation of electoral commissions, the drawing up of districts,

[63] Besides occasional complaints, one encounters the same names on commissions, party conferences, editorials, delegations, and committee sessions. The author has not attempted a systematic search, but Pipik of the Eleventh Army, Kuchin of the Twelfth, Titov of the Second, and Greiber of the Sixth would be examples. *Fr* of September 28 exclaims: "We must compile and verify lists of persons capable of supervising elections, we must master the electoral statutes, we must direct the agitational activity, and so on. All this responsibility lies on our army organizations."

[64] See *RPG* 1:463-64.

and the training of personnel for various roles was proceeding very well. For example, on September 30 a twelve-day course of instruction for lower-level instructors was announced, with sessions beginning on October 3, 15, and 27 respectively. On October 4 an invitation to turn to the Special Army Electoral Commission in Lutsk for information appeared. The October 8 issue announced the formation of a corps commission which had just held a conference of regimental representatives to work out procedures; subcommissions in most units were already functioning.[65]

Other evidence indicates that the lower-level committees were responding. On October 1 the committee of the 517th Batumskii Regiment called on each company to form task forces from their educated elements to conduct mini-courses, and on October 13 they allotted 700 rubles to supply literature. The work was to be supervised by a regimental cultural-educational commission that sponsored lectures and reading discussions.[66] On October 5, *IzOA* reported on another regiment that conducted extensive cultural-educational work: a number of soldiers and officers had attended the courses in Lutsk and a network of "schools" had been set up. Former teachers, officers, and educated persons were "ordered" to staff them by the commander. One cannot gauge how much genuine popularity these courses enjoyed, as there are complaints of apathy as well as enthusiasm. What is certain is the enormous expenditure of effort by lower and higher committeemen.

☆

The announcement of the elections also stirred to life the political parties, including the Bolsheviks, as well as peasant and nationality organizations, all of whom held army and front conferences in late September and early October about which there is extensive reportage in the committee press. The chief business of these conferences was to draw up electoral slates and to resolve tactical and programmatic matters.[67] The political intricacies are only of marginal interest here, but it is important to understand the role of these conferences in the dynamics of the current situation. On the

[65] In parallel actions the Western Front Committee announced in a two-week course for agitators on October 3 the schedule for candidates lists on October 11. *Iz8A* on October 8 carried a long article on the electoral procedures, as did *Iz5A* on October 3. On October 7 the latter announced the appointment of an eleven-man electoral commission. Missing issues make it impossible to trace the activities in more detail.

[66] See *protokoly* of the regimental committee, TsGVIA, f. 3054, op. 2, d. 23, part 1, ll. 32 and 39.

[67] The Tenth Army, on which there is the most complete record, is probably not untypical: a United Social Democratic Conference met on September 21-22 and was followed by a front conference on September 25; an S.R. Conference was held on September 22, a Peasant Congress on September 21-24, a White Russian Conference on October 3, and a Muslim Conference on September 25 (see *GoXA*, October 1, 6, and 8).

one hand, they reinforced the preoccupation of political activists with national politics and issues, rather than problems of the front, and for the first time partisan advantage became a primary consideration. On the other hand, by calling together delegates from lower units it might have again put the higher leadership in touch with the mood of the front. In fact, the only conference to mention lower-unit reports, the Social Democratic Conference of the Tenth Army, betrays a preoccupation with petty organizational matters, and they seemed as isolated from trench concerns as their colleagues higher up.[68]

On S.R. conferences there is little information relevant to the concerns here, but the peasant organizations are another matter. In several armies (Special, Tenth, Fifth) peasant organizations had existed since the time of the All-Russian Peasant Congress in June. They were mainly active in organizing "schools of literacy" which propagated the views of the All-Russian Peasant Executive Committee. In the army committees they usually formed their own "fraction," sometimes even a separate "soviet." Like the Peasant Executive Committee they were loyal to the Coalition, particularly to Chernov, and ardently defensist. This may seem paradoxical, but the organizers and promoters tended to be the more literate types with extensive contacts with the Populist intelligentsia, the dominant wing of which was staunchly defensist (Avksentiev, Gots). The Peasant Congress of the Tenth Army of September 21-24 affords the best profile.[69] There were forty-nine delegates, two in each division and one in each corps. The army "soviet" had been formed in August on the basis of a statute worked out with Savinkov, though strong peasant organizations already existed, notably in the II Caucasus Grenadier and XXXVIII Army corps. As in other armies they decided to bloc with the S.R.'s and drew up a list of ten names to be submitted to the combined list. On seven of them there are short characterizations. Five were authentic sons of peasants, one was a priest's son, and the last was the son of a political exile. All, however, were long-standing members of the S.R. party, one was a railway technician by occupation, two were primary-school teachers in zemstvo schools, another was self-educated and had resettled in the city, and the priest's son was a doctor. The chief organizer, Pasechnyi, is the most interesting, as he had left his village, acquired a gymnasium education, and returned to the *narod* as an agronomist and professional revolutionary. He was one of the initiators of the All-Russian Peasant Congress (whether of 1905 or 1917 is not clear) and was currently the commissar of the Tenth Army, a hard-headed partisan of discipline. Thus, the leadership, at least,

[68] See *GoXA*, October 1.

[69] See *ibid.*, October 8.

was clearly a "peasant intelligentsia" with considerable political experience, and it is not surprising that their attitudes did not coincide with those of ordinary peasant soldiers. Nevertheless, a surprising fact emerged from these peasant congresses: without exception they broke from the policy of the Peasant Executive Committee and demanded *immediate* transfer of all the land to the land committees without waiting for the Constituent Assembly, and sent urgent telegrams to the Provisional Government and the Peasant Executive Committee to that effect. For example, a resolution of the Tenth Army conference stated that "all the land should be given over to the land committees before the Constituent Assembly, as that is the only way to prevent agrarian disorders," while that of the Special Army stated: "The peasantry of the Special Army insists that the sole means of pacifying the *narod* and regulating the supply crisis is . . . the immediate transfer of agricultural lands to the land committees."[70] This was a marked change in tone for a conference that had just called for a national mobilization of industry to support the war effort, the drafting of all shirkers, and the severe punishment of deserters. While the conference was in session, delegates were receiving word from their units that soldiers everywhere were joining with peasants in plundering estates in the vicinity of the front.[71]

In the Fifth Army a strong Bolshevik faction made a bid to take over a peasant conference. The officially sponsored resolution was sharply critical of the Democratic Conference and called for an all-socialist coalition responsible to the Pre-Parliament in addition to the immediate transfer of all land to land committees. Nevertheless, the Bolsheviks voted against the resolution, because it did not support "All Power to the Soviets!"; the newspaper account interpreted this as "an attempt to disrupt the congress."[72] The peasant soviets were simply reflecting what had become the universal pattern in all democratic organizations at this time—the leadership was forced to yield to Bolshevik positions on item after item under mass pressure to keep the real Bolsheviks from taking over. It proved to be a game increasingly difficult to win.

☆

In October the blinkered stance of higher committeemen became increasingly difficult to maintain. Evidence kept pouring in that the mass of soldiery was truly restive, and not simply from marching companies and Bolsheviks, but over the same broad issues that were causing unrest and disorganization in the rest of the country. The rising incidence of major breaches of military order was rapidly blending in with a wave of agrarian

[70] *IzOA*, October 4.
[71] *Ibid.*, October 13.
[72] *Iz5A*, October 6.

disorders in the immediate rear, upsetting all the careful efforts of committees to regulate food supply through bilateral arrangements. The untimely announcement on October 8 of a new statute on committees (the delayed Savinkov statute of August, now modified) reminded the committee public of the long overdue need to renew their credentials (three months was the statutory rule) and aroused a clamor from lower committees for a new round of army and front congresses to resolve once and for all the rights of democratic organizations to control the command. And finally, upsetting entirely their own political agenda was the announcement by VTSIK on September 29 of a new Soviet Congress for October 20, the very time when the full resources of the committee structure would be required for elections to the Constituent Assembly.

The political dangers of the situation were immediately palpable. The "Bolshevik mood" of the masses was no longer a secret. Delegates to the Soviet Congress should be "accredited" by new army congresses composed of newly elected deputies. By-elections of existing committees, though long overdue, could only be bruising contests in which Bolsheviks would make significant inroads. It was also obvious that such electoral contests and congresses would fire up the expectations of the soldier masses beyond all measure, making moderate stands on issues such as the war and military discipline impossible to maintain. All this hustle and bustle would occur in direct competition with, even be seen as a substitute for, elections to the Constituent Assembly. In other words, the hard-working *komitetchiki* suddenly faced the possible collapse of the entire edifice of practical goals, strategies, and basic revolutionary values to which they had devoted six months of unremitting effort. Thus, in early October every higher committee and every official committee organ went through a sudden crisis of awareness, sometimes accompanied by signs of hysteria and imminent breakdown. The timing and triggering mechanism varied from case to case, but it was a direct function of all the factors discussed above and by mid-October had left none untouched.

Although the announcement of the Soviet Congress was made on September 29, there is scarcely a reference to it in the committee press until just before it convened, and then only to excoriate the Bolsheviks for using it as a screen to seize power. In these same weeks the elections to the Constituent Assembly were being promoted in large headlines on a daily basis. However, the minor notices of the back pages on army committee affairs indicate that the question had aroused considerable discussion inside the committees, and the boycott on the front pages was quite deliberate. First of all, the VTsIK announcement had been ambivalent, noting that it had been "compelled by the statutes" of the previous congress (which stipulated a three-month interval), hinting they were carrying out the commission with some reluctance. Then the Peasant Executive Committee announced that it would not take part, since all its energies were directed toward the Constituent Assembly. Finally, the Soldiers' Section (now "Military Section") of VTsIK announced similar misgivings and requested all army, front, and military district organizations to poll their constituencies on the matter and submit the responses.[73] Furthermore, Iskosol, the Twelfth Army organization, immediately fired off a circular telegram to fraternal army and front committees stating its own unequivocal position that "all creative forces of the country" had to concentrate on the timely convocation of the Constituent Assembly and that a Congress of Soviets could only "usurp the rights of the Constituent Assembly," presumably to the benefit of the Bolsheviks.[74] Thus all the higher committees had the issue on their agenda in the second week of October, and without exception they formally rejected sending deputies.[75] Though the record of these proceedings is scant, in the Seventh Army a complete archival record has survived: on October 10 an expanded session of army corps and division representatives was reviewing plans for Constituent Assembly elections, but in the course of unit-by-unit reports two divisions, the 19th and 64th, read out a joint *nakaz* adopted at a mass meeting on October 7 which was to accompany two deputies to the Congress of Soviets. The assembly was obviously taken by surprise, as few of those present were aware that the congress was to take place. The content of the *nakaz* was of the kind already familiar—exact aims of the war, a definite response from the Allies on a peace proposal, disclosure of all secret negotiations "of the capitalists," why the Stockholm Conference did not meet, extensive new rights for committees, enforcement of the Declaration of Soldiers' Rights, why the over-forties were released in the rear and not at the front, winter boots, and all the rest. Still it pledged to hold the front until answers were forthcoming. From this point on, the unit reports became ever more depressing—the First Guards Division was without meat and forage, relations with the command were passable, but the mood was "If you continue to feed and clothe us we'll continue to hold, but if not, look out!" The delegate from the Second Guards Division stated frankly that he thought the soldiers would all desert in the very near future—they were down to 60-70 per company and very poorly fed. The Third Guards Division was completely out of control, hostile to both committees and officers, the

[73] Both announcements appear in *Fr*, October 5.

[74] *Ibid.*, October 9.

[75] Scouring the back pages produced the following: *GoFr*, October 12 and 13 (Eighth, Special, and Seventh armies); *ibid.*, October 24 (Fourth Army); *VVK*, October 14 (Eleventh Army); others confirmed by later references.

courts were not functioning, and the soldiers had just perpetrated a massive wine pogrom involving many casualties. The XLI Corps was just as bad.

At this juncture the presidium announced the VTsIK telegram convoking the Soviet Congress (already ten days old), but explained that the Executive Committee of the Southwestern Front urged them not to send deputies. The spokesman argued that the time for congresses was past and that if the Democratic Conference with the flower of democratic leadership could not resolve the question of power, then a coalition was the only possible solution until the Constituent Assembly. Chudnovskii, the Bolshevik chairman of the First Guards Infantry Division, argued for the Congress because past experience had shown that without democratic control the bourgeois Provisional Government could not be trusted (if the record is accurate, it was hardly a principled Bolshevik argument). One comrade, Shumov, argued for the Congress from another standpoint: "We have to send representatives from the Army because otherwise only Bolsheviks will show up and we will lose out." After a hot debate Chudnovskii demanded a roll-call vote: forty voted against participation and only five voted with Chudnovskii, but there were ten abstentions, including the 19th and 64th divisions.[76] The result might seem to be a crushing defeat for the Bolsheviks, but this was a session of existing committees, not a freshly elected body. There would still be a reckoning to come, as the Bolsheviks had been handed a very effective issue for use in by-elections—the leadership had concealed the official announcement of the Soviet Congress.

The leadership in all committees could not be very happy about their situation as they could no longer be under any illusions concerning the dangers to which they were exposed. They could keep the lid on only by standing pat and allowing no by-elections to occur until the Constituent Assembly. Yet tremendous pressure was building up from below to reelect the committee leadership and to convoke army congresses as a forum for soldiers to vent their concerns. This issue came to a head at an expanded session of the Special Army Committee on October 12. A committee member acknowledged that the soldiers were demanding a new congress, but claimed that the Special Army Soviet lacked the resources for both a congress and the Constituent Assembly elections. "Which is dearer," he asked, "the Special Army or Russia?" Another referred to the idea as "another talking shop," and still another as a "crime." Finally one of them unburdened his torn conscience:

> We're all tired and would like to be dismissed or have a new mandate. Perhaps it is a crime not to give account of our activities. . . . Let them accuse us, let them drive us out with bayonets, but we have no

[76] All in TsGVIA, f. 2222, op. 1, ed. khr. 1185, ll. 159-77.

> right to throw down our weapons when the whole country should be concentrating on the Constituent Assembly.[77]

In other words, the uneasy committeemen were well aware of their outworn credentials and that any Bolshevik demagogue could effectively bring it to the attention of the masses.

In spite of their precarious position, most army committees remained loyal to the Soviet leadership and adamantly hostile to the Bolsheviks until the October coup, continuing their drudging preparations for the Constituent Assembly. But the process of slippage in support in both large formations and small continued relentlessly. In the Tenth Army, for example, some sort of assembly of "soldiers of the I Siberian Corps" passed a Bolshevik type of resolution on "All power to the Soviets," immediate peace, and land on October 3.[78] On October 8 the corps commander, Iskritskii, complained of an ugly mood in the 64th Siberian Regiment, fed by Bolshevik agitation emanating from a recently arrived reserve regiment, which openly declared its sympathy for the murder of a Colonel Makarevich in the neighboring 132nd Division. The infection spread to cossack and cavalry units sent in to subdue them. On October 8 the 63rd Regiment passed a resolution calling for immediate peace and the "obliteration" (*unichtozhenie*) of the entire officer component of the regiment. The regimental committee tried to calm the turbulent assembly, but were howled down and fled for their lives. Commissar Zhdanov reported on October 9 that in the Second Siberian Rifle Division no work orders were being obeyed and that he feared massive desertions from the front; moreover, the infection was spreading to units of the III Siberian Corps.[79] A conference of the combined committees of the 62nd Division, still holding out against the Bolshevik tide, informed the commissar that they had been able to avert mass desertion on their sector only by a solemn promise of immediate replacements and food supplies, and if this were not done the credibility of the committees would collapse. Moreover, they demanded the immediate convocation of an army congress so that the army could declare itself forcefully to the rear, that if the country was not prepared to back up the front they should immediately conclude peace.[80] The fact that such resolutions from October 17 on were regularly printed in the committee organ (*GoXA*) signified that now the higher committeemen felt it was time to get a message to Petrograd. Military reports covering the

[77] *IzOA*, October 8.

[78] See *VOSR. Oktiabr'*, pp. 362-63, from *Rabochii Put'*, October 14.

[79] Cited in full in report of army Quartermaster Samoilo of October 8 to front headquarters, *RDRA*, p. 482; Commissar Zhdanov's report in *VOSR. Oktiabr'*, pp. 378-79.

[80] See *RDRA*, pp. 499-501.

following weeks show that signs of disorganization and violence, fed by the demands for immediate peace, were escalating at an alarming rate and that now the targets were no longer merely the command, but the committees themselves.

The Tenth Army Committee began to show signs of cracking under the strain. At a plenary session of October 11, after considering the usual themes of the approach of winter, moral and physical exhaustion, and the lack of supplies, it reached the following conclusion:

> If the rear and the Provisional Government are not in a position to support the army, they ought to have the courage to admit it. In foreign policy it is high time to put an end to the abstract rationalizations on the question of peace and actively struggle for it, based on the formula which already has the endorsement of world democracy.

This position was telegraphed to VTsIK, the War Ministry, and all army and front committees. Such words of reproach had never before been uttered by higher committeemen to their acknowledged leaders. A week later, reacting to the news that the Bolsheviks were contemplating a coup, it sent to the Provisional Government a stiff new series of demands which included no delay in convoking the Constituent Assembly, a revolutionary court for Kornilov, firm prices on all items of primary consumption, immediate transfer of all the land to the land committees, and a "decisive struggle for peace." On October 20 a full conference of committee representatives from every division and corps, reviewing all the above issues and the condition of the army, came to a frank acknowledgment of the bind in which the committees were caught:

> The authority of the committees is declining with each passing day; in a few instances there have been efforts to overturn them, others are losing their former composition, but in the majority of cases they simply no longer enjoy confidence, and these are the only organizations capable of preventing a mass revolt. On the question of the war either the masses have broken with the committees or the committees have adopted the position of the masses.

This time their resolution condemned the government (by implication the Soviet leaders) for "seven months of collaborationism and lack of principle."[81] This was only the first army committee to confess openly its

[81] *Ibid.*, October 17, 19, and 21. In the issue of October 19 appeared another passionate resolution of an unnamed division informing the Tenth Army commissar of the "hopeless situation of the trench soldier, who has no winter boots or warm clothing, not enough bread and no moral support from the rear." "For six months we lived on the vague hope for

crisis of faith. In all armies in the latter part of October, such slippage of support unit by unit was occurring, undermining the integrity of existing committees and threatening the entire system with political collapse. On the eve of the October coup one observes a rash of such moments of enlightenment, a sudden willingness to depart from their former rigid stands, to concede the convocation of congresses and belatedly to send delegates to the Second Congress—anything to normalize their position or to relieve themselves of responsibility for presiding over the catastrophic trend of events. Because this development is inextricably bound up with the question of power, the details will be reserved for the following chapter, but here it is important to realize the enormous contradiction which had opened up between the strategies of the masses and those of their committees, which would have to find some resolution in the immediate future. The masses were declaring themselves in an ever-unfolding variety of ways and with ever more irresistible tenacity with every passing day, which finally, around the middle of October, bore into the consciousness of the democratic leaders at the front the impossibility of the political status quo and of their own position; unfortunately the Petrograd leaders were still oblivious to it.

---

peace,'' it complained, but now patience had given out. Doubtless many other such statements have gone unrecorded.

CHAPTER VIII

THE BOLSHEVIK REVIVAL AND THE CONTEST FOR POWER

THE SECOND, so-called "October Revolution" of 1917 was concurrently a *social upheaval* and a *contest for power*. The failing of so much writing on the subject is that it either confuses these two components or emphasizes one at the expense of the other, whereas the purpose here is to establish their vital interrelationship. The previous chapter laid out the ingredients of the incipient social upheaval, but also demonstrated that the peasant soldiers were very conscious of the problem of power—that unless they could somehow influence or reshape state authority, peace could not be obtained. Even when the soldiers' self-assertion took noninstitutional forms, a political rationale of sorts was discernible—to undercut or thwart the authority structure that carried on the war and prevented the Revolution as they saw it from being consummated. But beyond that their unmistakable determination to refurbish the committees, to get their message to Petrograd, to force the issue of the Second Congress, to vote in the elections to the Constituent Assembly, not to speak of their massive response to the new Soviet government's invitation to participate in the framing of an armistice—all demonstrate that the importance of institutionalized power was not unappreciated.

Still there was something primitive and irrepressibly utopian in the popular conceptions of power. The Soviet representational structure was an attractive symbol to the masses of the power that rightly belonged to them, as opposed to that of the educated, propertied, and prowar elements vested in the Provisional Government. From Soviet power they automatically expected the blessings of land, peace, and abundance. However vague their conception of politics in the capital, the fact that the new power based on the Soviets immediately "decreed" land and peace, as well as other measures that appealed to their view of things (abolition of the death penalty, the "democratization" of the army, workers' control, etc.), immeasurably inspired their confidence and their expectations. These mass sentiments were the fundaments on which the Bolsheviks erected their claim to power.

Conversely, the real power of the socialist leaders of the democratic institutions was rapidly slipping away because they failed to grasp that their power resided not in institutional means or mere claims to authority but in the capacity to generate popular assent, which if they could not offer the prospect of land and peace would no longer be forthcoming. In the course of 1917 they had so insulated themselves from their social base that they were no longer capable of mobilizing it. Their world of meaning now resembled those of their political and ideological opponents, the Kadets and other "bourgeois" groups, even tending to speak and think of the "dark masses" with the same vocabulary of mixed condescension and fear. Their notion of "revolutionary" state authority was based on the same conceptual fallacy as that of the Kadets and the Right, namely, that the elite of the nation was entitled to proxy for the whole, inasmuch as the masses were swayed by some unknown utopian impulses. The Democratic Conference, meant to legitimize a limp, all-class coalition until the Constituent Assembly, was as artificial a construct as the Moscow State Conference and equally lacking in authority. When this solution was likewise found wanting, only the solution of personal, charismatic authority remained: the Right and the Kadets had vested it in Kornilov, the Left was stuck with Kerensky.

Power gravitated toward the Bolsheviks after the Kornilov affair, not because of their superior organizational machinery or the genius of their Leader, but because they had already established credibility in the eyes of the masses in May and June. Daniels and Rabinowitch have effectively demolished the traditional historical myth that the seizure of power was engineered by slick technicians of revolution, and Rabinowitch in particular has demonstrated the significance of Bolshevik infrastructure organizations, above all the party's Military Organization. The importance of these subunits was that they were in daily contact with the masses, attuned to their visceral concerns, alert to the slogans that worked, which they then ground into the propaganda media. Rabinowitch has brought out that the slogan "Soviet power" was revived during the Kornilov affair, even though it had been officially discarded by the party and theoretically by Lenin, because the activists had quickly perceived in the turmoil its galvanizing potency. The "genius" of the Bolsheviks, and of Lenin in particular, lay in the ability to catch the motifs of popular folk-mythology and transform them into fighting slogans to generate mass action or belief in the validity of actions on their behalf. The potency of political myths in the twentieth century has been amply demonstrated; such myths tend to give the advantage to the party willing to exploit them over parties more rationally disposed and intellectually inhibited. Therefore the real basis of the Bolsheviks' power under the umbrella of "Soviet Power" was their ability to mobilize the mass constituencies by symbolic actions and claims. While not an exhaustive explanation of Bolshevik politics, a subject as vast as it is complex, this factor certainly accounts in large measure for their remarkable success at the front in October and November.

The magnitude of the Bolshevik achievement at the front in the weeks before and after the Petrograd coup was truly spectacular. In mid-October the Bolsheviks had no secure base on the order of Kronshtadt, the Vyborg Quarter, or the emerging majorities in local soviets and had only the most rudimentary beginnings of a party structure from conferences held in late September and early October. Nevertheless, they acquired at least formal control of the committee structure within a week to ten days of the uprising on the Northern and Western fronts, and on the Southwestern, Rumanian, and Caucasus fronts they gained secure bases of support at army congresses held in mid and late November. Everywhere they broke up or neutralized the cohesive Menshevik-S.R. majorities that had hitherto held sway in the higher committees. Army committees such as those in the Twelfth, Fifth, Third, and Tenth armies, which had built up organizations accustomed to carrying heavy responsibilities, to speaking with a confident voice for the "front" to the political institutions of the rear, to burning themselves out in practical endeavors believed to be vital to their constituency and the nation, were now unceremoniously dumped from the seats of authority as Bolsheviks and other leftists turned up at congresses and conferences in incomprehensible numbers. Once acquiring majorities or pluralities with Left S.R.'s, the Bolsheviks could proclaim Soviet power in the region and assume full civil and military authority on behalf of the Council of People's Commissars (Sovnarkom, or SNK, the government created by the Second Congress of Soviets). Military confrontations were few, as neither the command nor the former committeemen could raise military units willing to fight in the name of a discredited Provisional Government or its improvised "democratic" surrogate, the Committee to Save the Revolution and the Motherland (KSRR). On the more remote fronts, particularly on the Rumanian Front, the Bolsheviks lacked the numbers, talent, and moral authority to carry through a revolution of this order; but even here, where former committees managed to retain control, they veered far to the left, refusing to become entangled in efforts to rescue the fallen government, and on most program issues, sometimes including Soviet power, they took close to Bolshevik positions. In these areas the most frequently espoused formula was an "all-socialist government" (*odnorodnoe sotsialisticheskoe pravitel'stvo*), no civil war, and not a day's delay in the convocation of the Constituent Assembly. By the end of November, power was fragmented into dozens of components, army by army, corps by corps, with ascendancy exercised alternately by older committees, newly formed revolutionary committees with tenuous Bolshevik majorities, multiparty "Left Blocs," and Ukrainian "radas." The power balance remained stalemated and spilled over into local civil wars of unbelievable complexity. North of the Pripet, however, Bolshevik power exercised through revolutionary organs (Military Revolutionary Committees or MRCs) recognizing the authority of the Sovnarkom was ratified by decisive majorities in the elections to the Constituent Assembly, which proceeded like clockwork thanks to the careful organizational work of their political opponents.

☆

Until the Kornilov affair, Bolshevik groups at the front (where they survived) were obliged to exercise extreme caution or to forgo organizational work. The once-potent Bolshevik press was a shadow of its former self: a subdued *Okopnyi Nabat* (*ON*, replacing *OP*) continued until the fall of Riga but did not resume publication until October 12, and in Minsk a modest though militant Bolshevik paper, *Zvezda*, enjoyed but a limited circulation (3,000-6,000 copies) mainly in the rear and was closed down on August 23.[1] The respective organizational networks that supported them were in bad shape until their recovery in late September. The taking of Riga had deprived the Novoladozhskii Bolsheviks and the Latvian brigades of their secure haven, and the editorial group of *OP* showed no signs of life in September. Iskolastrel, the Bolshevik-dominated organization of the Latvian brigades, held up much better during the retreat, though its official historian, Ia. Kaimin', claims that their membership dropped from 3,000 to 1,450 because of heavy casualties in the Riga action.[2] Though lacking the protective umbrella of Riga, they were now in closer touch with their reserve regiment in Valmiera, where the Central Committee of the Latvian S.D. party also resettled. The Latvian organizations quickly rebuilt an infrastructure in the remaining unoccupied Latvian districts based on their striking electoral victories in local elections in August and on their ability

[1] Figures for *Zvezda* in *Russkaia periodicheskaia pechat' 1895-1917* (Moscow, 1957), p. 245, and other standard Soviet works. *Zvezda*, *Molot*, and *Burevestnik* were not available to the author, and dates of publication are culled from footnotes of Soviet publications. Soviet treatments of this period are sparse in facts, but the standard general work is P. Golub, *Partiia, armiia i revoliutsiia* (Moscow, 1967), and for documents, *Bor'ba partii bol'shevikov za armiiu v sotsialisticheskoi revoliutsii* (Moscow, 1977), cited as *BPB*.

[2] Kaimin', *Latyshskie strelki*, p. 268. For a general treatment of Latvian Bolshevism in English, see Andrew Ezergailis, *The Latvian Impact on the Bolshevik Revolution: The First Phase, September 1917 to April 1918* (Boulder, Colo., 1983), esp. chap. 5.

to provide many of the functions and services of a local government. The two organs *Brivais Strelnieks* and *Cina* resumed publication without interruption under slightly altered names (*Latvju Strelnieks* and *Musu Cina*).

In early September a new Bolshevik military organization became active in Cesis, a Latvian town adjacent to the new front, which put out a small sheet, *Otkliki Pravdy*, and several proclamations, mainly in reaction to the Kornilov affair. On September 20, in response to its request for recognition as the organ of the Twelfth Army Bolsheviks, this organization received a stern rebuff from Sverdlov, instructing them to take their directives from the Latvian Party and to avoid jurisdictional conflict at all costs; at the same time the Latvian Committee was instructed to renew the publication of *ON* as the organ of its "Russian Section."[3] A plenipotentiary of the Central Committee, S. M. Nakhimson, was deputized to the Latvian Party to direct the work of all military organizations in the region of the Twelfth Army, Latvian and Russian. His arrival marked the revival of Bolshevik activity in the Twelfth Army in October.[4]

The low fortunes of the Bolsheviks on the Western Front during the period of repressions was characterized in a report of A. F. Miasnikov of the Minsk organization to the Sixth Congress of the party on July 28:

> We have no direct tie with the Army because no literature can get through to them and we ourselves receive no literature. There are no party cells at the front. There must be close ties with the Central Committee. At the present time there is none on the Western Front.[5]

At an unofficial conference of front and regional party organizations in early September, the Minsk Bolsheviks were able to assess their strength. Some 52 delegates represented 6,061 party members, 3,651 of them from the front, but all organizations had suffered heavily, and there was no immediate prospect of reviving *Zvezda*. Rabinowitch has recounted how in Petrograd the Military Organization and its organ, *Soldat*, were put under the receivership of the Central Committee for exceeding their mandate during the July Days and were kept on a short leash during the Kornilov crisis. It was no longer the forward edge of party militancy, and its few records in early September suggest that it paid little attention to developments at the front.[6] The Central Committee's correspondence with the front seems entirely concerned with the drawing up of candidate lists for

[3] See *BPB*, pp. 290-91.

[4] See below, pp. 275-76.

[5] *BPB*, p. 273, from his report to the Sixth Party Congress (see *Shestoi s"ezd RSDRP [bol'shevikov], avgust 1917 goda. Protokoly* [Moscow, 1958], pp. 68-69).

[6] See Rabinowitch, *Bolsheviks Come to Power*, pp. 74-75, and *BPB*, pp. 316-24.

elections to the Constituent Assembly, and it is clear they are reacting to initiatives from the front rather than orchestrating a strategy of their own.[7]

In view of the organizational weakness, the conduit of Bolshevik influence at the front in September, as in May, was the stream of Bolshevized soldiers from the garrisons, but with the important difference that this influence now rested almost entirely on the ''mood'' of the soldiers rather than on schooled agitators buried in their midst or packets of literature stuffed into their tunics. Most local Bolshevik military organizations were not geared up to their former level, though they were beginning to recover, encouraged by rapidly growing representation in local soviets. *Soldat* was a far more modest sheet than *SP*, with considerably less content of interest to front soldiers and less than half the circulation (15,000-18,000 copies as opposed to 40,000-60,000).[8] References to *Soldat* or any other Bolshevik organ are almost wholly absent in the numerous military reports and staff surveys that otherwise complain of Bolshevik agitation.[9] Rather, Bolshevik propaganda motifs had already become a part of the soldiers' vocabulary and mode of thought, particularly in the garrisons, from whence they were again carried to the front. Bolshevism had become a tested device for soldiers of both front and rear to promote their longing for peace and no longer depended on prompting by party activists.

The revival of ''Bolshevism'' among the masses, however, was a strong stimulus to the party Bolsheviks at the front to regroup and organize their forces, particularly with Constituent Assembly elections, which now became the exclusive focus of their political activity, looming on the horizon. On every front and in nearly every army in late September or early October, conferences of Bolsheviks or of ''United Social Democrats'' took place, at which Constituent Assembly lists were the chief order of business.[10] These conferences apparently drew out of the woodwork a good many hitherto inactive Bolsheviks who preferred alliances with nonfractional Social Democrats (or at least Menshevik Internationalists) to a militantly

[7] *PSTsK* 1:41-42 and 57.

[8] *BPB*, p. 288 (session of Central Committee of August 31, report on Military Organization).

[9] *RDRA*, pp. 429-32. Its circulation was 8,000-10,000 copies, substantially more than *Zvezda*; see *VOSRB* 1:31. An exception is a long report of General Baluev of September 27 on the Minsk Bolshevik organ, *Molot*, which began publication on September 15 in lieu of *Zvezda*. It makes clear that it was scoring heavily on issues that appealed to soldiers, but there is no evidence it circulated at the front.

[10] A party directive of September 11 called for candidates' lists, and reports on preparations (see *PSTsK* 1:36), and more detailed instructions were sent September 27 (*ibid.*, p. 51), but there were no specific instructions on conferences; their rival parties were also preparing, and there was much discussion of the Constituent Assembly both by committees and by soldiers, so the front Bolsheviks were reacting chiefly to the situation.

partisan posture. The situation on the Rumanian Front was particularly unsatisfactory from the standpoint of the Bolshevik leadership in Petrograd. In the Ninth Army a joint conference of all shades of Social Democrats, consisting of delegates representing 3,000 members, was held on September 27-28. The Menshevik cohort had shifted sharply to the left under the pressure of events and was now dominated by Menshevik Internationalists; a resolution proposed by the latter condemning any further coalition with "census elements who supported Kornilov" passed 75-30, the Bolsheviks voting with them. Moreover, the resolution stipulated that if a new coalition government failed to carry out the Soviet program an "all-socialist government" should take its place. The conference agreed to draw up a joint list for Constituent Assembly elections consisting of three regular Mensheviks, two Menshevik Internationalists, and three Bolsheviks.[11] Out of touch with the center, it probably seemed to these front Bolsheviks that they were moving the more influential Mensheviks to the left and that a unified Social Democratic slate offered the best chance of stealing votes away from the formidable S.R.'s. In the Eighth Army, however, only the Bolsheviks and Menshevik Internationalists showed up at a conference on September 28 and took far more radical positions on every issue—an immediate armistice on all fronts, publication of the secret treaties, immediate convocation of the Socialist Peace Conference in Stockholm, and a new power based on the Soviets.[12]

The Rumanian Front Conference of Social Democrats turned out to be a disaster from the Bolshevik point of view. The purpose was to put up a unified list for the elections, and since half the delegates were Menshevik Defensists it could hardly produce a fighting document; the Bolsheviks and Menshevik Internationalists contributed five names each, whereas the Menshevik Defensists supplied ten. A profile of the delegates is instructive: 47 out of 58 delegates, or 80 percent, were between the ages of 25 and 35, 8 had a *stazh* (party affiliation) reaching back to the year 1900, and 29 (over half) to the Revolution of 1905; a like proportion (30) had had some higher education, 9 had completed middle school, and 14 had attended primary school only; half were soldiers, half were officers or military *chinovniki*; and finally, by social position, 25 were either workers or salaried employees, the rest were men of the professions, writers, or zemstvo employees. This reveals the kind of Social Democrats who became active at this time: they tended to be either the educated, experienced party veterans or workers with an above-average education. Thus they were not the typical 1917 recruit, or, with few exceptions, the worker recruits of

[11] Record in *BMRF*, pp. 63-65.

[12] *Ibid.*, pp. 66-70.

1912-14. There did not appear to be any great difference in this regard between the Bolshevik and Menshevik cohorts. In other words, the Constituent Assembly elections had reactivated primarily the intelligentsia layer of Bolsheviks who, by and large, had not played the role of militant antiwar agitators in 1917 and were far more susceptible to "unity" sentiments than the latter. Nevertheless, among them were a number who were to become the reliable, hard-line front Bolshevik leaders that were to staff the Bolshevik campaign to take over the committees in November.[13]

On the Southwestern Front the only documented army conference was that of United Social Democrats of the Special Army on September 22. Agenda items suggest that the conference took a decidedly left posture on most issues: a purge of the commanding staff, cessation of all political repression, abolition of the death penalty, immediate convocation of the Constituent Assembly, freeing all arrested Bolsheviks, and immediate peace negotiations. On the key point of power, the conference opposed coalition with census elements and favored a "firm revolutionary power enjoying the confidence of broad layers of the population." The latter formula was obviously designed to gloss over differences, but from the sketchy evidence "unity" sentiment seemed to prevail and was possible only on the basis of a marked shift to the left.[14]

Two front conferences of September 10-12 and 23-27 respectively cast further light on the complex process. The first was convoked by Mensheviks on the Southwestern Front Committee but made no stipulations as to factions, hence all types of Social Democrats turned up, including Bolsheviks. The account in *Soldat* on October 6 avers that the sponsors wanted to deprive of mandates all those who did not accept the positions of the United Social Democratic Conference of August 19-26, an affair dominated by defensists, which obliged the Bolshevik minority of 13 delegates to walk out and to call a second, purely Bolshevik conference. Not authorized as a legal gathering, the command and commissars put all possible obstacles in its way. Nevertheless, 107 delegates representing 7,000 members convened. The Bolsheviks claimed that Commissar Kostitsyn received orders from Petrograd to arrest the entire conference, but did not have the courage to do so.[15]

The Mensheviks enjoyed a secure position as fractions in higher com-

[13] *Ibid.*, pp. 71-74.

[14] Account in *IzOA*, September 5.

[15] Several documents of the Secretariat of late September and early October routed through the Kiev regional bureau appear in *BPB* (pp. 292 and 295-96), mainly concerned with supplying literature, but a telegram to the Secretariat of September 27 states that an army representative, G. I. Chudnovskii, requested instructions and a party representative for the conference (*ibid.*, pp. 359-60).

mittees mainly because of their talents and indispensable services, but they could be politically significant in elections only as adjuncts to the S.R.'s. Party Mensheviks who did not belong to the committee establishment revealed more concern for "Social Democracy" to make a good showing in the Constituent Assembly elections, and thus tended to be more accommodating toward the Bolsheviks and more willing to move to the left, if they were not there already. For the Bolsheviks it was sometimes advantageous to make common cause with such Mensheviks, even compromising on positions, because the anonymity of being just "Social Democrats" afforded them some protection from official harassment and a friend in court.

What this signified in practice will doubtless never be known, because the newspaper accounts are sketchy and the published Soviet sources have been carefully sanitized. One can surmise that these conferences allowed the Bolsheviks to become personally acquainted, to exchange information, to agree informally on tactics, and to lay the foundation for a revived organizational network, though only the rudimentary beginnings.

The greatest strides toward party organization were made on the Western Front. On September 15 the Minsk Bolsheviks convened a regional party conference officially billed as the "First Northwestern Regional Conference of the RSDRP(B)," whose task was to draw up Constituent Assembly lists. Since the previous unofficial conference, membership had increased to 7,132, of which 4,590 were said to be from the front (a 25 percent increase), probably representing a fuller representation of existing organizations as well as rising membership. The Second Army had by far the most registered members—2,388—whereas the Tenth and Third armies had 1,156 and 532 members respectively; in the Second Army the bulk were concentrated in the Grenadier and III Siberian corps.[16] Reports from individual units reflected the increasing influence of the party and the easy recruitment of new members, but also the dearth of experienced party organizers and suitable literature. The III Corps reported an easy preponderance of Bolsheviks over Mensheviks, but no literature and considerable harassment by the command. The Eleventh Siberian Division boasted 100 party members, the legacy of an energetic group of officer Bolsheviks who had since been arrested, while in the 55th Division, long a haven of Bolshevik agitation, many sympathizers remained, though they lacked sophistication in political matters and had few organizers. The hard-line Bolshevik A. F. Miasnikov, an army captain, chaired the proceedings and briefed the delegates on the Sixth Party Congress, sarcastically denouncing

[16] See proceedings of conference in *VOSRB* 1:686-96 (party membership figures on pp. 686-87).

unity enthusiasm, which was by no means dead among his Minsk colleagues. The question of party organization provoked heated debate, Miasnikov proposing a scheme of disciplined fractions in each soldiers' committee to be directed by a central Military Organization for the Western Front, in its turn attached to a new regional bureau for the Northwestern Region. The scheme was approved, and a new regional conference was scheduled for October 5 to choose party candidates for the Constituent Assembly elections.[17]

The First Regional Conference was followed immediately by a conference of Second Army Bolsheviks on September 29, which now claimed 5,124 members and 12,000 sympathizers, representing 104 organizations, nearly doubling the party's previously claimed total. The conference was buoyed by the arrival of thirty comrades just released from prison, where they had been held without charges since the July Days. This represented the influx of thoroughly primed veteran agitators who could immediately be put to work. Again the only item of business was the drawing up of lists for the Constituent Assembly.[18]

Although the September conferences of Bolsheviks and United Social Democrats considerably advanced the organizational and political self-consciousness of Bolsheviks at the front, it is important to keep them in perspective. They took place with no leadership or instructions from the center, but were fueled almost exclusively by the sense of opportunities in the forthcoming Constituent Assembly elections due to the sharp swing in the mood of the masses toward a Bolshevik orientation. Though the idea of Soviet power cropped up a time or two as a suggested alternative to coalition, it had not yet become a fighting slogan.[19] So far as can be determined, no front organization raised the question of a new congress of Soviets until VTsIK itself announced it on September 29.

☆

By the time the Second Northwestern Regional Conference convened on October 4, a decisive turn in tactics and scale of activity had taken place on the Western Front, doubtless spurred by the announcement of the new Soviet Congress and the striking success of the recruitment drive. A

[17] Announcement of September 28 in *ibid.*, p. 755.

[18] The only record of the conference is a short article in *Molot* of October 5, reprinted in *RDRA*, pp. 464-66. No references in *BOB*.

[19] The Minsk regional conference (discussed above) acknowledged the Soviets as "the sole recognized centers of the revolutionary camp," but skirted the notion of Soviet power (see *VOSRB* 1:705). The correspondence of the Secretariat with local organizations in September and October concerns almost exclusively tactics with regard to the Constituent Assembly and gives absolutely no directives on elections for the Congress of Soviets (survey of *PSTsK*, vol. 1).

considerable increase in membership and sympathizers at the front had occurred, the former from 4,590 to 21,138 (a four-and-a-half-fold increase) and the latter from 1,958 to 20,000.[20] Even allowing for distorting factors, the numbers must have reflected both intensive efforts and an enthusiastic response, which accords with other available evidence. Sensing their new opportunities, the organizers put by-elections to soviets and soldiers' committees at the head of their agenda. For the first time the Western Front Bolsheviks unequivocally declared their "immediate vital objective" to be "the fullness of power, both in the center and locally by means of coordinated revolutionary initiatives of soviets of workers, soldiers, and peasants deputies"; second, they laid the obligation on all party organizations to "apply every effort to guarantee through local action the convocation of the All-Russia Congress . . . through by-elections to army committees."[21] The new orientation was proclaimed in the October 5 issue of *Burevestnik* (successor to *Molot* and *Zvezda*):

> Comrade soldiers of the front and rear! The defensists have set themselves against the Congress of Soviets, hoping to wreck it. Half of the front committee voted against [participation]. In the army committees they agitate against the All-Russian Congress and army congresses. Comrades, all this stems from circles closely tied to the bourgeoisie, trying to bring the Army under its influence. Don't let them get away with it—force the calling of congresses of armies, corps, and divisions to elect representatives for every 20,000-25,000 soldiers to the All-Russian Congress! The Army must be represented at the Congress! Struggle against the divisiveness and conflict in our midst inspired by the defensists![22]

This was an ambitious program for the two remaining weeks before the scheduled opening, considering that existing committees could be counted on to put every possible roadblock in the way and that by-elections would have to be in sequence from the company level up through army congresses. The latter were in a double limbo: first, the formal suspension of congresses at the front had not yet been lifted, and second, most army and front committees promptly took the position that new congresses were incompatible with preparations for elections to the Constituent Assembly. The regional conference of Bolsheviks decided to turn these circumstances to their advantage by officially protesting against the just-announced decisions of the front and army committees (on the Soviet and army congresses),

[20] Report to Central Committee of October 18, *VOSRB* 1:830.

[21] *Ibid.*, p. 829.

[22] *RDRA*, pp. 494-95.

claiming that they "falsify the attitude and will of the revolutionary soldiers."[23]

Though the Bolshevik by-election campaign on the Western Front is poorly documented, the spectacular results by a later date are indisputable. However, for the Grenadier Corps and the Second Army there is a remarkable firsthand account by a young Bolshevik doctor, N. Petrov.[24] Arrested as a Bolshevik agitator in July for relatively mild infractions, Petrov was reassigned to the Sixth Grenadier Regiment with the help of a Bolshevik member of the Second Army Committee. He was in touch with other Bolsheviks in the Grenadier Corps and knew of the Northwestern Regional Conference in September, but he was definitively activated only by the directive of the regional bureau on by-elections. The opportune moment came with the convocation of an army "conference" of existing committees, a device utilized to ratify important decisions without the benefit of new elections. Petrov's regiment was represented by a superannuated volunteer jurist named Rovinskii, who claimed to be a Socialist Revolutionary. The small Bolshevik group decided to make an issue of the question of "confidence," that is, whether Rovinskii's views accurately reflected those of the regiment. Within twenty-four hours the Bolsheviks called assemblies of each company in the regiment, which "recalled" their former deputies, including Rovinskii, and chose new ones, mainly Bolsheviks, including Petrov.

The renewed regimental committee deputized Petrov in place of Rovinskii to represent the regiment at the army conference. The commander tried to have Petrov transferred, but he was bound by the rule that an elected deputy could not be prevented by the command from carrying out his duties. At the army conference a large number of Bolsheviks turned up, the same process obviously having taken place elsewhere. They met as a fraction before the conference began, some 50 out of 200, which grew to 80 by the time of the sessions. From the former Bolshevik fraction of the army committee, which had been substantial in the spring, were committeemen N. V. Rogozinskii and N. S. Tikhmenev, the former an officer of the Third Siberian Corps who apparently had attended the All-Russian Bolshevik Military Conference in June, the latter once a deputy chairman of the army committee. Others, such as F. Iu. Gzhel'shchak and P. I. Berzin, were veteran Polish Social Democrats who now supported the Bolsheviks. Thus, the group had both experienced leadership and many fresh recruits.

[23] *VOSRB* 1:831, and *Fr*, October 17; the Second Army also decided against on October 11 (see *IzGr*, October 11) and the Tenth Army around the same time (*GoXA*, October 22).

[24] In *BOB*, pp. 232ff. Petrov's account was originally written in 1919 and betrays little evidence of subsequent editing.

At the session they forced changes in the agenda, challenged the leadership on every point, and secured the adoption of positions considerably to the left of those of the S.R. leadership, for example, on the immediate redistribution of the land without waiting for the Constituent Assembly. The presidium claimed the credentials of the Grenadier delegation were falsified, but a verification succeeded only in revoking the mandate of a Menshevik delegate who claimed to speak for the corps committee. When Commissar Grodskii tried to make a grand speech, he was treated first to obstruction and then to a walkout. Thus, the Bolsheviks suddenly proved themselves a power in the Second Army and translated it into significant results. In the meantime, Petrov and several other Bolsheviks were coopted into the army committee in recognition of their undeniable strength.

Military reports of the time confirm that the Bolsheviks were making heavy gains throughout the Western Front, both in visibility and in inroads on the committees. A front staff report for October 14-21 notes their successes in the Grenadier Corps, not only among the soldier masses but also in the committees, which "now pass provocative resolutions, organize demonstrations, and discuss and dispute every order before they execute it, and sometimes don't execute it." A marked increase in demands for immediate peace and fraternizaion were laid to their account. The Second, Third, and Sixth regiments were said to be under their control as the result of by-elections. The only other active political group was a Ukranian rada, whose activity was just as disorganizing. In the three divisions of the IX Corps (Fifth, 42nd, and 15th Siberian) Bolshevism was also said to be engulfing whole units, though overt conflict was provoked more by Ukrainianization (i.e., separating out and consolidating Ukrainian soldiers into larger formations). In the III Siberian Corps, earlier a stronghold of Bolshevik influence, the Bolsheviks were said to be taking advantage of the electoral campaign for the Constituent Assembly to thoroughly demoralize the corps as a fighting unit. In the only remaining corps of the Second Army, the Fiftieth, the masses were said to be carried away by the Bolshevik promise of immediate peace.[25]

Though numerically the Bolsheviks were far fewer in the Tenth and Third armies, the same type of intensive campaign was obviously being conducted.[26] A front report notes intense Bolshevik agitation and a flood of Bolshevik literature in each of the three corps of the Third Army (XV, XX, and XXXV); committees trying to counteract it were being decimated in by-elections. It noted that agitators concentrated particularly on artillery

[25] *RDRA*, pp. 527-33.

[26] See account in *VOSRB* 1:782 (from *Burevestnik*, October 13).

and storm units, probably to forestall their use in punitive actions.[27] A commissar's report on the Tenth Army for the same period notes "total disintegration" in the Second, 11th, and 16th Siberian Rifle divisions, "not excluding the possibility of the opening up of the front," and held Bolshevik agitation responsible. Western Front Commissar Zhdanov added the comment that the campaign for elections to the Constituent Assembly was being effectively exploited by the Bolsheviks to bring about the collapse of the Army, hinting perhaps that the elections should be called off.[28]

On the Northern Front, where the Bolsheviks had been decimated by the repressions of July and disorganized by the retreat, they also made a spectacular recovery in early October. In the Fifth Army, where the summer arrests hit particularly hard and the Bolsheviks had always been organizationally weak, a conference met on October 8-9 and noted the "exceptional growth of party organizations . . . and of sympathy in the soldier midst for the RSDRP(B)." Though it went on record favoring a government of "soviets of workers, soldiers, peasants, batraks, and other deputies," it took no note of the Second Congress. Shortly thereafter a confidential message to the Petrograd Military Organization listed the Fifth Army Bolsheviks Sklianskii, Sediakin, and several others as their candidates for the Constituent Assembly and affirmed there was now a Bolshevik "bureau" of eleven persons for the Fifth Army.[29] Nevertheless, awareness and interest in the Soviet Congress was obviously on the rise in the Fifth Army independently of Bolshevik inspiration. Resolutions favoring participation and severely critical of the boycott pronounced by the Fifth Army Committee are registered for the 38th and 70th divisions, formerly renowned for their exemplary discipline and immunity to politics.[30] But the Bolsheviks' stock must have been rising rapidly in these weeks, because an army congress meeting on October 16 gave the Bolsheviks a slight majority, the only instance of a "committee revolution" before the October coup.

In the Twelfth Army, Nachimson's arrival led to a marked pickup in Bolshevik activity. On October 7 he addressed a mass meeting of 3,000 soldiers, denouncing the latest coalition as a "government of the all-powerful bourgeoisie and counter-revolution." On October 3, at a meeting of the "Little Soviet" of the Twelfth Army (an expanded session of the army committee with lower-unit representatives), Nakhimson introduced a resolution on behalf of the Left Bloc demanding peace, land, workers' control, purge of the commanding staff, and new elections to Iskosol. *ON*

[27] *RDRA*, pp. 533-36.

[28] *VOSR. Oktiabr'*, pp. 378-79.

[29] *Ibid.*, p. 379, and *BPB*, pp. 383-86.

[30] Session of respective committees of October 11 and 12 in *RDRA*, pp. 485-88. Both were joint sessions with lower committees.

resumed publication on October 12, calling on soldiers in every unit to discuss the resolution and to "force your representatives in the Little and Big Soviets to support it"; if they refuse "reelect those that do, elect Bolsheviks!"[31] *ON* reported that in one regiment a meeting of 2,000 soldiers approved the resolution with but one negative vote and 30 abstaining. Apparently the pressure was effective, as Iskosol called a general session of the "Big Soviet" for October 2. Literature, money, and subsidiary help flowed into the Bolshevik Military Organization from both Petrograd and the Latvian organizations, the latter supplying paper, type, premises, and some 3,000 rubles, while the Central Committee assigned another 1,000 rubles. Nakhimson was made co-editor of *ON*, and as a deputy of the Central Committee was given the right to veto content. On October 12 a conference of military organizations of the Twelfth Army selected a candidate list for the Northern Front for the Constituent Assembly: at the request of the Central Committee the names of Lenin, Nakhimson, Krylenko, and A. Gailis (chairman of Iskolastrel) headed the list; Vilks from the Latvian Brigades, Grazkin, Vasilev, and Sivers from *Okopnaia Pravda*, and two others from *Otkliki Pravdy*, completed the list. The Twelfth Army candidates would alternate on the list with those of the other two armies. *Okopnaia Pravda* was again recognized as the official organ of the "Military Organization" of the Twelfth Army, which was regarded as a "Russian Section" under the authority of the Latvian Party.[32]

On October 15 a conference of military organization of the entire "Northern Front" took place in Cesis, though the representation was rather lopsided. Grazkin claimed 3,600 members for the Twelfth Army, but the Latvian brigades must have made up the bulk of this number, as the Russian components were still weak. (The Iamburg Regiment, the only infantry unit mentioned by name, was denied voting privileges because its representative just "happened to be in town.") The Fifth Army was represented by a single delegate, who claimed a membership of 2,000, and the First Army (recently formed) was not represented at all. On the other hand, the XLII Corps stationed in Finland claimed a membership of 9,000, or almost two-thirds of the total. The record of the meeting clearly reflects the aim of tightening the structure of the military organizations: the Twelfth Army and Latvian organizations were well represented, and Nakhimson presided authoritatively over the proceedings, making clear that he had special credentials from the Central Committee. Although the discussions centered

[31] Cited in Kapustin, *Soldaty severnogo fronta*, pp. 179-80. The relevant issues of *ON* were not in the collection available to the author, but an account of the conference appeared on October 25.

[32] See *BPB*, pp. 386-87; D. I. Grazkin, "Revoliutionnaia rabota v XII armii," *Voprosy Istorii*, No. 9 (1957): 14-15, and Kaimin', pp. 288-89.

on how to gain control of Iskosol by forcing a new meeting of the "Big Soviet," in national politics the Constituent Assembly elections received far more attention than the Second Congress of Soviets. Ten days before the planned uprising in Petrograd, this important organization at the front with close ties to the Central Committee seemed scarcely aware of it.[33] Nevertheless, Bolshevik organization in the Twelfth Army had taken great strides toward recovery, though the Latvian component greatly overshadowed the Russian component. It was, moreover, the first front organization to enjoy supervision and support from the leadership in Petrograd.

The Bolshevik network in the entire southland from Kiev to the Black Sea was exceedingly tenuous and had few resources to devote to the front. Communications were irregular, dependable activists were few, and many nominal Bolsheviks preferred to work in unified organizations, even if it meant cohabiting with Menshevik defensists. In the spring a regional party bureau had been created with headquarters in Kiev headed by the indefatigable Evgeniia Bosh, but because of serious differences it did not cooperate with the Kiev Committee of the party, which had its own ties to the front. By the end of September, Bosh was in touch with key front Bolsheviks, such as Chudnovskii in the First Guards Division and B. I. Solers in the Eighth Army. She had failed to prevent the Rumanian Front Bolsheviks from entering a unified list with other Social Democrats for the Constituent Assembly and wrote to the Central Committee for further instructions. On October 10 the Central Committee sent word to the Rumanian Front Bolsheviks that blocking was against party policy and to take themselves off the list, which was complied with.[34]

The Bolsheviks of the Southwestern Front formed their own military organization following their conference and planned their own newspaper, for which they requested a subsidy from the Central Committee. Though this was approved on October 5 in the amount of 2,000-3,000 rubles, there is no evidence that the newspaper ever appeared.[35] In spite of these efforts, a party organization was never consolidated on the two southernmost fronts, though Chudnovskii, Kokovikhin, and Solers were capable of managing party work on a large scale if given the opportunity;[36] moreover, here as

[33] Complete proceedings in *KPLOR*, pp. 455-63.

[34] See Bosh, "Oblastnyi partiinyi komitet sotsial-demokratov (bol'shevikov) iugo-zapadnogo kraia (1917 g.)," *PR*, No. 28 (1924): 130ff., and her extensive report to the Central Committee of October 12 in *BPB*, pp. 387-89.

[35] Record of Central Committee session of October 5 in *VOSR. Oktiabr'*, p. 40, and Chudnovskii letter to Central Committee of October 7 in *BPB*, p. 295.

[36] Chudnovskii, when he heard of the planned coup in Petrograd, vigorously opposed it, went to Petrograd as a deputy to the Second Congress, and then led the Bolshevik forces in "storming" the Winter Palace nevertheless. See Rabinowitch, *Bolsheviks Come to Power*, pp. 223 and 281-84. Bosh claims that although she knew of the planned insurrection she

on the Rumanian Front the Bolsheviks had a serious competitor in the Ukrainian Rada, which was also rapidly expanding its constituency at the front, with a firm base in the political hinterland. In late October, the Bolsheviks on the Southwestern Front could claim strong points in the Second Finnish Rifle Division, the First and Second Guards Divisions, and several units of the XXV Corps; on the Rumanian Front, except for the 13th Transamur Border Regiment of the Eighth Army, there were virtually no strong points at all.

If the Bolshevik cause had depended on its organizational capacities, its prospects were very dim in October 1917. A rudimentary infrastructure was taking shape, but except on the Northern Front it was not yet in place or closely tied to the center. With the confusion still reigning in the counsels of the Central Committee even after the decision to put the armed uprising on the agenda on October 10, the front organizations could hardly be expected to do better. Events rather than directives were guiding the actions of Bolsheviks at the front: almost mechanically they prepared for the Constituent Assembly; the organizational steps were dictated by the schedule of submitting slates; their platform was scripted for them by the agitated masses and the legacy of past experience; the convoking of the Second Congress was an unforeseen godsend courtesy of a VTsIK that had run out of wisdom and inadvertently brought into focus the already gestating idea of Soviet power; and its early date determined the frenetic character of the campaign for by-elections. The "democratizaion of the army" was likewise an idea whose time had come, and nothing could have been more appealing to the peace-hungry soldiers than to install a new leadership at army and front congresses that would carry through the accumulated agenda and proclaim Soviet power at the front. Lenin had some grounds for asserting that the party was lagging behind the masses and that the Central Committee was bringing up the rear. His belaboring the Central Committee with the demand for an armed uprising was useless as tactical counsel but served to arouse the laggard leadership to the ripe opportunity of laying hold of Soviet-based power.

☆

But if fortune was thus smiling on the Bolsheviks, why did it continue to frown on the well-established and talent-rich leadership of existing democratic institutions? The shortcomings that straitjacketed the socialist leadership in Petrograd have perhaps been stressed enough and to dissect them further would be beyond the scope of this work, except to note that its key test was the Democratic Conference, which ended in fiasco. What

received no instructions from the Central Committee on tactics until after it took place (*op. cit.*, p. 132).

bears examination here is whether the leadership of the army and front committees, which throughout 1917 carried such an enormous burden of practical responsibility, were any more enlightened in rising to the challenge of the moment. Unfortunately, the verdict here is largely in the negative: though some belatedly recognized the failings of the national leadership, they were equally devoid of practical counsel. Eventually undeceived as to the temper of the masses, they were irrevocably committed to a strategy targeted on the Constituent Assembly and saw no means to extricate themselves from it. They unanimously rejected the Soviet Congress as an alternative, regarding it as a diversion of resources from the main task, and a snare and a delusion for the masses who would expect from it an immediate fulfillment of their aspirations. Though pressed every day by lower committees to call new army, front, and corps congresses, all army and front committees except the Twelfth and the Fifth had rejected the idea for the same reason. The Bolsheviks were able to exploit the twin issues of by-elections and the Soviet Congress to make the committee leaders aware of their isolation and lack of legitimacy. Though thoroughly unnerved by this situation, the committeemen saw no alternative but to hang on for a few more weeks, when they would gladly lay their mandates before the altar of a reconstituted democracy.

Again, political events in the capital served them an ill turn: on October 18 came the disturbing news of the Bolshevik plans to seize power in the capital. Not only were details of the plan leaked in *Novaia Zhizn'* (the indiscretions of Kamenev and Zinoviev relayed in the committee press in garbled and hysterical versions), but VTsIK sent all democratic organizations telegrams on the same date, mooting dark plans to seize power without naming the Bolsheviks; such an eventuality was likely to be accompanied by pogroms, which could only be regarded as a "stab in the back" to the Army with the Germans at the gates and hunger and economic ruin on the doorstep.[37] Here was material enough for panic and confusion, though reactions in army committees ranged from alarmist loyalty to total disillusionment with the Petrograd leadership and a sharp leftward shift in political stance. The Twelfth, Fifth, Ninth, and Special armies called for a solid patriotic front against the demoralized and anarchistic rear, as if all the Soviet leadership needed was to show a little more backbone and Bolshevism and Kornilovism would disappear. Iskosol appealed directly to the Petrograd garrison to defend the Revolution by joining their brothers in the trenches. An editorial in *Rizhskii Front*, the organ of Iskosol, began

[37] The text of the VTsIK proclamation appeared in full in *RF* on October 21 and to the author's knowledge is available nowhere else; references in *VGr* and *IzFR* both on October 20.

to betray disillusionment: Where was the voice of organized democracy? of the Pre-Parliament? Where was energy, where was wisdom?[38] The organ of the Special Army Committee, *IzOA*, of October 18 accused the Bolsheviks of intending to use the Second Congress of Soviets to stage a coup and repeated VTsIK's allusion to Black Hundred pogroms. If the Bolsheviks tried anything, it warned, they would have to reckon with the entire front democracy. The Ninth Army Committee boasted that it would "treat any such attempt just as decisively as it did the Kornilov rebellion."[39] Such statements, however, concealed a deep uneasiness and loss of faith in the conventional revolutionary verities, since when the crisis came few committees acted as boldly as their statements prescribed.

VTsIK contributed further to its own undoing by choosing this precise moment, October 18, to appeal to all army committees to send accredited delegations to the Second Congress of Soviets, as otherwise a rump Bolshevik congress would have an easy victory. The consternation and disorganization this caused among the committees was total. The army committees had predicated their strategy on denying the Soviet Congress legitimacy by their conspicuous absence, and now VTsIK had undercut that strategy with little prospect of affecting the outcome. Roughly half loyally fell in line as if obeying a military order (Twelfth, Fifth, Second, Third); the rest just as resolutely refused. The Southwestern Front Committee resolved to comply and urged all lower committees to follow suit:

> Taking into consideration the critical political situation in the country and particularly in Petrograd, where anarchist elements are preparing an uprising against the government and undoubtedly intend to utilize the Soviet Congress to seize power, the Executive Committee of the Southwestern Front regards it as absolutely necessary for the armies to send . . . sufficiently strong and authoritative delegations to offer organized and powerful resistance to attempts at violent overthrow by those who are sowing anarchy in the country on the eve of the Constituent Assembly, threatening the Army with new convulsions, trials, and deprivations.[40]

To its dismay not a single army committee supported its position, the Special Army Committee rejecting the idea as "insulting" to the integrity of democratic institutions, while the Eleventh Army Committee vowed to "fight [the Second Congress] with all possible means."[41] In other army

[38] *RF*, October 21 and 22; text of Iskosol appeal also in *Fr*, October 18.

[39] *IzFR*, October 20.

[40] *GoFr*, October 18.

[41] Response of the Special Army in *GoFr*, October 23; of the Eleventh Army in *VVK*, October 22.

committees, notably the Sixth and Tenth, wrangling over this issue led to a sharp split between Mensheviks and S.R.'s, the former favoring sending belated delegations, the latter adamantly opposed. In the case of the Sixth Army, it brought about a permanent realignment in the leadership, as the Menshevik group veered sharply leftward and within three days of the October coup formed a new left coalition with Bolshevik support and edged out the loyalist S.R.'s.[42]

The disorganizing effects of this sudden switch in signals is perhaps best seen in the Second Army. The telegram from VTsIK arrived during the session of the army conference at which the Bolsheviks turned up in such disconcerting numbers. Debate swirled around a Bolshevik resolution on Soviet power, and the army committee leadership had just secured a narrow majority for its own position to reject sending a delegation to the Soviet Congress and to await the convoking of the Constituent Assembly. But this result was achieved at the expense of resolutions for the abolition of the death penalty, for the transfer of all land to the land committees, and for a "decisive and open foreign policy." At this point the chairman was obliged to read out the VTsIK telegram. Forced to eat crow in front of the elated Bolshevik deputies, the conference sponsors now conceded new committee elections at all levels and the sending of a fully accredited delegation to the Soviet Congress (four Bolsheviks, six S.R.'s), while firm dates were set for corps and army congresses (November 9 for the latter).[43] The by-elections on lower levels that hitherto had taken place surreptitiously now acquired legitimacy.[44]

A similar upheaval took place in the Third Army, though not with as decisive results. Staff reports confirm the success of Bolshevik-inspired by-elections in the committees of the 31st Regiment of the XV Corps, and in the 55th and 67th divisions, while others are characterized as "going along with the masses, passing resolutions demanding bread, clothing, etc., and subscribing exclusively to Bolshevik newspapers."[45] The army committee must have been obliged to yield to this pressure because on October 20 it called an assembly of divisional and corps committees and, reversing its earlier decision, chose a delegation to the Second Congress consisting of two Bolsheviks, one Menshevik Internationalist, a Socialist Revolutionary, and a nonparty deputy. They must also have consented to

[42] *GoXA*, October 25, and *VGr*, October 25.

[43] Full account in *IzGr*, October 25; Petrov fails to record this drama.

[44] See Petrov's account in *BOB*, pp. 240-42; he even claims that the Bolshevik fraction immediately constituted itself as an underground MRC, using their status as army committeemen to gain access to military units.

[45] Survey of the Western Front for October 14-21 in *RDRA*, pp. 534-35 (the entire report, *ibid.*, pp. 527-40, is one of the most comprehensive available for any front for this period).

an army congress, as one was scheduled for November 2. Though barely withstanding the Bolshevik surge, the assembly approved the most ultimative statement yet to the Petrograd leadership:

> On the eve of a fourth winter campaign, when the army in the trenches is unclothed and starving, receiving no help whatsoever from the rear and seeing no prospects for improvement in its situation, . . . we the representatives of regiments, divisions, and corps of the Third Army . . . demand from the Provisional Government, the VTsIK, and the entire country in the name of saving the Motherland and the Revolution decisive steps for the conclusion of peace, the immediate provisioning of the Army, and unconditional cessation of anarchy in the rear. If these conditions are not fulfilled, the tortured Army will conclude the rear is not capable of satisfying its essential needs, and will itself take power into its hands until the Constituent Assembly.[46]

The Western Front Committee did not reverse its decision to boycott the Second Congress, but balanced between an orthodox Socialist Revolutionary and a Bolshevik orientation, it passed on October 17 a resolution that came down heavily on the left. It blamed the ''indecisive policy'' of the Provisional Government for the continuation of the ''imperialist war'' that was ruining the country and threatening all the gains of the Revolution. It outlined a detailed program for peace, including an immediate armistice proposal to all belligerents, the speedy convocation of the Stockholm Peace Conference, and an ultimatum to the Allies at the Paris conference then in progress. On land, the death penalty, and democratization of the Army it fell in with the leftward trend of other committees.[47]

In general, on the Southwestern and Rumanian fronts the leftward tide had not resulted in significant Bolshevik gains, and the committees were able to withstand the pressure to send accredited delegations to the Soviet Congress. On the Northern Front, however, the Bolsheviks were well on their way to de facto control before the October coup. The Fifth Army congress of October 16 sent a fully accredited delegation, half Bolshevik but purged of all the former defensists, to the Soviet Congress.[48] On the other hand, Iskosol was issuing broadsheets to the rest of the Army and the country as if the Twelfth Army was a bastion of revolutionary democracy and was prepared to conduct a national crusade to ''straighten out the rear,'' though there was almost no substance behind it. Its organ,

[46] Cited in full in *Fr*, October 24 (*Iz3A* for this period was unavailable to author).

[47] *Fr*, October 21.

[48] The Author's copy of *Iz5A* breaks off after initial session (see issue for October 22), but a recent Soviet monograph is based on the full record. See S. N. Bazanov, *V bor'be za oktiabr' na severnom fronte: 5-ia armiia* (Moscow, 1985), pp. 86-89.

Rizhskii Front, only resumed publication on October 20 after a two-month interlude, and immediately the disarray was apparent. Challenged by the Left Bloc to prove their support among the soldier masses, they consented to a new army congress for October 28 and authorized the reelection of all lower committees. The Bolsheviks claimed, probably justly, that Iskosol had agreed to an earlier date but delayed it when they heard of the postponement of the Soviet Congress to avert the possibility of the army congress choosing Bolshevik deputies.[49]

Iskosol defended itself against the accusation of high-handedness by turning the argument around: Nakhimson was represented as a creature of Lenin and as a Johnny-come-lately to the Twelfth Army who behaved like a "boss" within Left Bloc, which he succeeded in splitting; shrewdly calculating that the Iskosol leaders would be in Petrograd for the Second Congress, he was pushing for a session of the "Big Soviet" in their absence to take over Iskosol. Thus, the "Big Lenin" in Petrograd and the "Little Lenin" in the Twelfth Army were aiming at the "seizure of power" under that facade of democracy.[50] This was, of course, sour grapes. Iskosol was very aware that bona fide elections would bring in Bolsheviks and other extreme leftists, and all they could hope for was a delaying tactic. They succeeded in holding the Bolsheviks at bay until after the Second Congress, but it was scarcely worth the effort; in fact, it helped the Bolsheviks by giving them one more debating point in winning control of new units. If a congress had been held a week or so earlier with less fanfare, the former leadership might still have retained control.

With the army congress safely deferred, Iskosol could afford to respond positively to VTsIK's appeal for an accredited delegation. On October 22 it announced that the Twelfth Army was attending the Soviet Congress to pursue a "definite tactic," presumably a statement and a walkout, which it invited other army committees to join. How precarious the leadership's hold was evident from the fact that the delegation consisted of only three regular members of Iskosol, five Mensheviks and *six* from the Left Bloc (two or three of them Left S.R.'s). Clearly some infighting had taken place and resulted in compromise. Of the three bona fide Bolsheviks, only Peterson, a Latvian Rifleman, was a recognizable name.[51] Thus Iskosol had succeeded in minimizing Bolshevik representation and fielded a strong delegation of its own.

[49] See *ON*, October 18, and Kapustin, *Soldaty severnogo fronta*, pp. 180-81.

[50] *RF*, October 24.

[51] See *ibid.*, October 22, and *ON*, November 24. List of representatives in *Vtoroi vserossiiskii s"ezd sovetov R. i S. D. Protokoly*, ed. K. G. Kotel'nikov (Moscow-Leningrad, 1928), appendix.

⋆

In front and army committees the once-secure majorities loyal to the Petrograd leadership were fast slipping away, but at the time of the October coup control had not yet passed to the Bolsheviks. The amorphous Bolshevik mood based on the obsession with peace had not yet been translated into a firm hold on the committee structure and other levers of power, though it seemed only a matter of days or weeks. With such disarray the front representatives could not speak authoritatively at the Soviet Congress for or against Soviet Power, and in effect deprived it of an unambiguous mandate (peasant soviets were also conspicuously absent). Only the armies of the Western and Northern fronts sent sizeable official delegations, and these were fairly evenly divided between loyalists and Bolshevik-dominated leftists. In the cauldron of Smolnyi, with episodes of the uprising intruding every moment, the records of the Congress were kept very imperfectly, but a mandate commission reported figures that are at least approximate. It is best conveyed in tabular form (see Table 2).[52] The figures in Table 2 demonstrate that Bolshevik strength was concentrated almost exclusively in the Northern and Western fronts and that, as in the Congress at large, the Bolsheviks enjoyed a plurality only with the help of a substantial Left S.R. contingent. Still they represented less than 10 percent of the Bolshevik voting strength at the Congress (30 out of 390) and therefore did not weigh heavily in the result. Nevertheless, the front delegates made a major contribution to the drama of the historic session. Immediately following Martov's opening motion calling for a peaceful resolution of the crisis, which was passed unanimously (with Lunacharsky, not yet Trotsky, presiding), Twelfth Army Menshevik Delegate Kharash rose to be recognized and declared: "While we are sitting here passing resolutions . . . on the streets of Petrograd a battle is being fought. The Mensheviks and Socialist Revolutionaries disassociate themselves from these proceedings and leave to join the social forces resisting the seizure of power." His colleague Kuchin then pronounced the Congress "untimely and illegitimate" because the front was not adequately represented, and he invited "all true soldiers" to leave the hall; other voices responded: "For whom are you speaking?" "You represent the staffs, not the real Army!" "Kornilovites!" Latvian Rifleman Peterson then took the floor:

> What these two gentlemen have said would be fine if they really represented the Army. . . . As you well know, the Twelfth Army

[52] There was no official stenogram because the stenographers walked out with the Mensheviks and S.R.'s; the above figures are presumably based on registrations, but the fact that a long list of "supplementary delegates" were added to the official ones leads one to believe that the orderly process of registration broke down before completion.

> long ago demanded new elections for the [Twelfth Army] Soviet and Iskosol. They postponed a plenary meeting of the Big Soviet just so they wouldn't lose their right to attend the Second Congress of Soviets. The Latvian Riflers say with one voice: "It's time to act! It's time to take power into our hands." Let them go—the Army isn't with them![53]

Such was the prelude to the walkout by the Mensheviks and S.R.'s that handed the Bolsheviks their absolute majority. In short order the Congress approved the proclamation of Soviet power, the land and peace decrees, and the formation of the Council of People's Commissars (Sovet Narodnykh Komissarov, or Sovnarkom) with Lenin and Trotsky at the head. Trotsky's speech venomously assigned the old leadership of VTsIK to the dustbin of history.

☆

The events of October 25-30 gave the Bolsheviks a tenuous hold on power in Petrograd, but the issue of power could only be finally resolved in the rest of the country and at the front. Substantial urban and regional soviets already exercised considerable de facto power or could lay hold of it as handily as they did in Petrograd. All the military forces in Finland—soldiers and sailors—had long since exercised power through the Finnish Regional Soviet, where a firm Bolshevik majority ruled; in fact, throughout a wide swath of the northern and western regions (embracing Estonia, unoccupied Latvia and Lithuania, and White Russia) Soviets, rather than agencies loyal to the Provisional Government, controlled most aspects of civil power, and in most of them Bolsheviks already enjoyed an ascendancy. Thus, there were large areas of Russia where the writ of the Provisional Government had already been superseded by Soviet power, if one excepts the military command structure and front committee appendages (the rear garrisons were already a prop to Soviet power).[54] Elsewhere in the country the power equation was extraordinarily complex, with differing amalgams obtaining in each local area—radas entering the equation in the Ukraine, Cossack hosts in the Don and the Caucasus, peasant soviets and land committees in much of the interior. In October the authority of the

[53] *Ibid.*, pp. 5-6.

[54] Few Western works, with the exception of Ezergailis and Suny (on Baku), have as yet studied the accessions of Soviet power in the peripheral areas, and indeed the interrelationship between Bolshevik power and Soviet power has still received but minimal clarification. The above is pieced together from information in Soviet monographs or published documentation. Ezergailis (*Latvian Impact*, chap. 3) has exhaustively studied the electoral results of local city and land council elections in August in the Latvian Soviet, the Latvian Riflers, and the Constituent Assembly elections and has demonstrated the Bolshevik preponderance in all of them.

TABLE 2. Front Representation by Party and Army at the Second Congress of Soviets, 1917

	Bolsheviks	Left S.R.'s	Menshevik Interna-tionalists	Menshevik Defensists	Right S.R.'s	Center S.R.'s	Nonparty Delegates	Total
NORTHERN FRONT								
Twelfth Army	4	3	1	4	5	1	—	18
Fifth	11	1	2	—	1	3	—	18
First	—	4	1	—	—	2	1	8
	15	8	4	4	6	6	1	44
WESTERN FRONT								
Tenth Army	2	1	—	—	—	—	—	3
Second	5	—	—	—	3	2	1	11
Third	4	—	1	—	—	3	1	9
	11	1	1	—	3	5	2	23
SOUTHWESTERN FRONT								
Special	—	—	—	—	—	—	—	—
Eleventh	2	3	—	—	2	1	—	8
Seventh	1	1	—	—	—	—	—	2
	3	4	—	—	2	1	—	10

TABLE 2, cont.

	Bolsheviks	Left S.R.'s	Menshevik Interna-tionalists	Menshevik Defensists	Right S.R.'s	Center S.R.'s	Nonparty Delegates	Total
RUMANIAN FRONT								
Eighth Army	—	2	—	1	—	2	—	5
Ninth	—	—	—	—	—	—	—	—
Sixth	1	—	—	—	—	—	—	1
Fourth	—	—	—	—	—	—	—	—
	1	2	—	1	—	2	—	6
Caucasus Army	—	—	—	—	—	—	—	—
Total	30	15	5	5	11	14	3	83

Source: Data from Appendix of *Vtoroi vserossiiskii s'ezd sovetov rabochikh i soldatskikh deputatov. Protokoly*, ed. K. G. Kotel'nikov (Moscow-Leningrad, 1928).

Provisional Government was rapidly fading, while the large institutional constituencies of the Soviet sector, in defiance of their national leadership, were moving in the direction of a Soviet-based alternative. Many non-Bolshevik socialists were already half persuaded by the heady pace of economic and social deterioration that to wait for the Constituent Assembly to perform miracles was too risky and that something more urgent should be done—but as it became obvious that Soviet power would mean Bolshevik power, they were forced to draw back and seek other ground, the most frequent formula being an all-socialist government under the control of the Pre-Parliament. Ironically, the drawing back of moderates and leftists from the tangible prospect of Soviet power (Martov being a notable example) was precisely what gave the preponderance of power to the Bolsheviks. Following the Bolshevik victory at the Second Congress, various walkouts, boycotts, and questionable alliances with the military command were easily exploited by the Bolsheviks to finish off their reputation among the masses. Belated adoption of leftist positions on issues no longer helped.

Of concern in this picture is the position of the front in the constellation of power following the Second Congress. The various components and levels of power should be distinguished. First, there was the formal command and commissarial authority over the disposition of the troops. Had Kerensky been able to exert control over even a small part of this potential force, he could have handily retaken Petrograd. But the commander of the Northern Front, General Cheremissov, sensing the futility of a military solution, refused to help; almost conspiratorially Kerensky engaged the services of General Krasnov, commander of the Third Cavalry Corps, who was able to muster but eighteen companies of cossacks from his scattered divisions, and they deserted him after the Pulkovo confrontation on October 30. Dukhonin had ordered more troop movements from the Southwestern and Rumanian fronts on the eve of the coup (for what purpose is unclear), but these units were easily halted by local garrisons and soviets when the crisis occurred. At various railroad centers, headquarters, and other vital points the command was able to concentrate small units of cavalry, shock units, armored cars, and assorted units sufficient to protect communications and discourage for a time takeovers by pro-Bolshevik elements, but again these were minor delaying operations involving small numbers of uncertain steadfastness. The Bolsheviks had at their disposal the formidable Latvian Riflers, Baltic sailors from Helsinki and Kronshtadt, and indeterminate support in the Fifth Army, but again the insignificance of the numbers, compared with the magnitude of the upheaval swirling around them, indicates that the true fount of power lay elsewhere.

The second pivot of power lay in the soldiers' committees, from the army and front down to the regimental level, because they constituted the institutional framework of organized democracy at the front and on a practical level possessed an enormous capacity to get things done. As elements of real power their significance should not be underestimated, because control of the committee apparatus was precisely what enabled the Bolsheviks so swiftly to consolidate power over wide areas of the front and denied it to them in others. This may seem paradoxical in view of what has been said of the ineffectualness of committees in the period just described, but this was a reflection of their souring relations with their constituency, not of their institutional potential when acting legitimately in the eyes of the masses. The strength of the committees lay precisely in their credentials as the agencies of institutionalized democracy, which allowed them to act authoritatively in the name of the soldier masses on a whole range of matters from food supply to soldier-officer conflict. In tests of strength, command authority could not compete with them, as the Kornilov affair so vividly demonstrated. After the Kornilov affair the committees and commissars—not the command—effectively controlled communications, only grudgingly conceding the sphere of operations, and it was only after Kerensky cast his mantle of protection over commanders that the committees reluctantly held back. The command swam in a goldfish bowl, and further dabbling in politics was out of the question; their essential powerlessness had been amply demonstrated.

The ultimate determinant of power was the consensual power of the masses. If they chose to withhold it, no agency could be effective. Committees exerted authority only to the extent that their actions were in accord with the expectations of the masses. The committees' paralysis in October can be attributed mainly to their inability to respond any longer to concerns that mattered most to the soldier masses. The Bolsheviks' advantage was that they were prepared to avail themselves of mass consent through every artifice of propaganda and demagoguery. In the coalition era the committees had forfeited their status as popular spokesman to the Bolsheviks in the interests of the offensive and the restoration of state and command authority. Ironically, the Bolsheviks, as a result of the shock of the July Days, also temporarily abandoned the Soviet idea, but the masses clung to it tenaciously, convinced that it was their sole entitlement to power and that the leadership should be compelled to respond to their desires. The committee leadership failed to take advantage of the opportunity presented by the Kornilov affair to mend their relationship with their constituency, because it would have meant cutting themselves loose from "organized democracy" in Petrograd; the policies of VTsIK had come to mean, in the eyes of the masses, not "Soviet power" or even Soviet "control," but collaboration with bourgeois groups and suspected Kornilovites.

Thus the Soviet idea was forfeited and the Constituent Assembly was substituted for it as the fount of legitimate democratic authority. The committeemen at the front, unfortunately for themselves, invested their entire remaining political capital in this option. The soldiers, to be sure, endorsed the idea of the Constituent Assembly as well, but it never had the potency of the Soviet as a mythic symbol. Its power was more remote, shared by alien groups, and there was less perceived control over the final result. Who knew how the vote would turn out, how much it could still be swayed by *pomeshchiki* and *burzhuis*, or whether it would endorse the popular goals of land and peace? Nevertheless, the soldiers' remarkable degree of participation in the elections after the proclamation of Soviet power demonstrated that they attributed great significance to them. But the tricky evidence seems to indicate that it was chiefly because the Constituent Assembly would morally bind the propertied classes to the revolutionary settlement; the Soviet, on the other hand, alone represented the soldiers' own sense of power. Only with the Soviet did they sense an ability to control matters, to oblige deputies to respond to their wishes, and to reelect them if they did not; always they sent deputations directly to Petrograd, always to the Soviet, never to the government, and nearly always directly from a lower unit, seldom through "channels." The Soviet was in fact the hypostasis of their own power.

☆

The Bolsheviks in Petrograd staked their bid for power on a military insurrection, utilizing the Second Congress of Soviets and the Military Revolutionary Committee of the Petrograd Soviet as defensive cover. The Bolsheviks were by no means secure in a military sense in the days following the coup. Lenin, viewing insurrection as an "art," had been virtually obsessed with the military equation and, informed through his "experts" (Sverdlov, Podvoiskii, Antonov-Ovseenko), was well aware that the garrison soldiers and the Red Guards would count for little in a serious contest.[55] He assumed that such Bolshevik stalwarts as the Baltic Fleet sailors and the Latvian Riflers could be handily mobilized and dispatched to the capital to ward off the expected counter-measures of Kerensky's forces, above all the officer trainees and the expeditionary force Kerensky was expected to mount from the front.

To Lenin's surprise, he ran up against the newly discovered "defensism" of his own cohorts. Bolshevik propaganda in recent weeks had played heavily on Kerensky's treacherous intent to surrender the "revolutionary capital" to the Germans; Lenin himself had repeatedly expressed this idea in his writings of this period, and it was embodied in the resolution on

[55] See N. I. Podvoiskii, *God 1917* (Moscow, 1958), pp. 91-116, and V. A. Antonov-Ovseenko, *V semnadtsatom godu* (Moscow, 1933), pp. 267-69.

the armed uprising of October 10.[56] The Latvian and Baltic Fleet Bolsheviks needed no persuading on this score, as the former already had the instructive experience of the "surrender" of revolutionary Riga, and the latter of the battle of Moon Sound.[57] Antonov-Ovseenko, roving member of the Military Organization and Lenin's confidant in military matters, conveyed to Lenin that it would be dangerous for the Baltic ships to put out to sea after arresting their officers, and even if they came by rail, 3,000 was the maximum number of soldiers and sailors they could expect. "Not enough!" snapped Lenin. "And the Northern Front?" The mood there was excellent, Antonov replied, but to make an exact calculation he would have to go there. "Then get going!" Lenin shot back. When Antonov informed Dybenko, the leading Bolshevik in the Baltic Fleet, of Lenin's displeasure, the latter exploded: "Of course we'd come if we knew Piter [Petrograd] couldn't cope with the situation . . . but how can you not cope with 500,000 workers, 150,000 garrison troops and Kronshtadt into the bargain? . . . And who would go against you from the front after Kornilov?" Dybenko, worried over a possible German move in their absence, agreed to sink the battleships across the channel and to send four mine-sweepers and 5,000 sailors and soldiers. Thereafter Antonov made a hasty trip to Valka, the Northern Front headquarters, where a conference of Latvian Bolsheviks was in progress. Though greeting the news of a planned uprising with enthusiasm, their reply was another shock: "We feel we are defending Petrograd here. We reckon the Germans as allies of counter-revolution, its chief source of strength. . . . If the Latvians leave the front, there will be no stopping the Siberians!" They pledged only to occupy Cesis and Valka, to prevent the sending of troops from the Twelfth Army to the capital, but like the sailors would send two regiments only if Piter could not "cope."[58]

[56] Lenin's views of this period were embodied in a series of terse articles: "Russkaia revoliutsiia i grazhdanskaia voina," *Rabochii Put'*, September 16; "Krizis nazrel," *ibid.*, October 7; "Uderzhat-li bolsheviki gosudarstvenuiu vlast'," *Prosveshchenie*, Nos. 1 and 2 (September and October, 1917)—all in *Sochineniia*, 3rd ed., 21:200-210, 235-41, and 247-84, respectively, as well as in urgent letters to the Central Committee and other party bodies and individuals, for example, "The Bolsheviks Must Take Power" (to Central Committee, September 12-14), "Marxism and Insurrection" (September 23), and letters to Smilga (September 28), *ibid.*, pp. 193 and 229-31. For the Central Committee meeting of October 10, see *ibid.*, pp. 492-94, or *PVRK* 1:35-38.

[57] See Norman Saul, *Sailors in Revolt* (Lawrence, Kans., 1978), pp. 158-61. The Bolshevik sailors at the last moment threw themselves into battle, but the negative outcome was also blamed on "betrayal" by the command.

[58] Antonov-Ovseenko, p. 271. In the Central Committee session of October 10, Sverdlov reported that the Minsk Bolsheviks promised to send a full corps of troops, but this cannot be confirmed by any other source and is highly unlikely, since the Minsk Bolsheviks did not have any troops on which they could absolutely rely, like the Latvian brigades; moreover,

Lenin was well aware that Bolshevik prospects rested on the massive shift in popular sentiment after the Kornilov affair and that an isolated Provisional Government would have some difficulty finding units willing to fight should an uprising in the capital succeed. But he refused to underestimate the influence of the Menshevik-S.R. majorities in the democratic organizations at the front, who he was convinced would throw their last remaining authority into the effort to rescue the Provisional Government. The command, with the Kornilov bolt already shot, would cooperate fully. Marx's teaching applied to the present strategic situation dictated

> a coordinated, unexpected, swift-as-possible assault on Piter *both* from without *and* from within, from the workers' quarters, from Finland, from Reval, and from Kronshtadt involving the *entire* fleet, the accumulation of a *gigantic preponderance* over the 15,000 to 20,000 [and possibly even more] of the "bourgeois guard" [the junkers] and the "Vendee troops" [the cossacks] . . . to occupy the telephone, telegraph and railroad stations and bridges no matter what the casualties . . . would guarantee the success of the Russian and world revolutions.[59]

Though his battery of scenarios varied daily, the underlying concept was always the same—to concentrate a massive force so swiftly that "even if Kerensky manages to get one or two corps to the region of Petrograd" they would be unlikely to have the stomach to fight.[60] Once the main counter-assault was checked, Lenin was sure the magic of Soviet power, land, and peace would take care of the rest. Excessive caution is perhaps the earmark of a successful strategist, but Lenin would have been quite surprised that the sum total of Kerensky's "Vendee troops" was to be slightly over 1,000 and that the proletarian guards, though greatly outnumbering the enemy, responded with less than total strength and enthusiasm. After a few rounds of grapeshot, both sides, in defiance of their leadership, agreed to talk rather than fight. Pulkovo was a charade more than a battle; Valmy it was not.

The mustering of armed forces by both sides is more instructive about

---

the Minsk Bolsheviks, Miasnikov excepted, were staunchly opposed to the idea of an armed uprising. See *PVRK* 1:36 and below, pp. 330-31.

[59] A note "To the Petrograd Comrades" of October 8 was meant as an instruction for delegates to the Conference of Soviets of the Northern Region of October 10 (*Sochineniia* 21:319-20). Whether it reached its destination is uncertain, as another note of a more formal character, whose argumentation was less specific, was sent the same day (*ibid.*, pp. 321-35).

[60] Letter to the Central Committee and committees and membership of the Moscow and Petrograd organizations dated October 3-7 in *ibid.*, pp. 293-94, but October 1 in *PVRK* 1:30.

the temper of the army and the country than as an exercise in strategy. Both sides went through the motions of girding themselves for battle, but like Nicholas and Kornilov before them they found their human material wanting. In the final analysis the Soviet-Bolshevik cause prevailed, not because of the superior combative qualities of its few militant cohorts, but because its moral authority was ascendant in the "hearts and minds" of the millions.

Although the government and Stavka knew the Bolshevik intentions in advance, their counter-measures were half-hearted at best. With Woytinsky's help, Kerensky had managed a few days before the coup to transfer the heavily Bolshevized 128th Division stationed near Helsinki to the front and to replace it with the Fifth Caucasus Cavalry Division. Woytinsky simply printed up the resolution of the 128th Division defying Kerensky's order and circulated it to front units; a flood of protests over the slackers in the rear poured in, which Woytinsky forwarded to the 128th Division. He likewise extracted from General Cheremisov a formal request for the transfer of the entire Petrograd garrison to the front to stem the rumored German advance. The effort was in vain, as it gave the Bolsheviks precisely the issue they needed to galvanize the otherwise far from militant garrison behind the Petrograd Soviet's Military Revolutionary Committee (the organ the Bolsheviks used to carry out the uprising, hereafter MRC). Woytinsky cleverly arranged a conference of garrison and front representatives in Pskov to pit the Bolshevism of the front against the Bolshevism of the rear.[61] If Petrograd were truly in danger, Woytinsky argued from the Bolshevik lexicon, the revolutionary regiments of the rear should be more than happy to support their hard-pressed comrades at the front. General Cheremisov reluctantly seconded the opinion, unable to deny in the presence of his soldiers the urgency of replacements, yet it cost him his standing with the Pskov garrison, which backed the Petrograd soldiers. Woytinsky scored another rhetorical success, but the issue was left dangling until the uprising.

Though the intended coup was already an open secret, the commander of the Petrograd District, General Polkovnikov, displayed a remarkable complacency over the threat, calling in trainees of a few officers' schools and a female battalion from the suburbs, but he appeared to believe he could resolve the "crisis" by negotiations with the MRC (quibbling over the latter's "commissars"). Kerensky likewise seemed strangely calm and unconcerned. In a long conversation with General Dukhonin on October

[61] See Woytinsky, *Stormy Passage*, pp. 361-67; text of Kerensky's order in *VOSR. Vosstanie*, p. 356; for decision of Bolsheviks of XLII Corps to comply but insistence on right to review operative orders, see commissar's reports of October 5 and 6 in *RDRA*, pp. 463-64 and 468-69.

21, he ranged over the Italian campaign, the new statute on committees, the Shablovskii Commission proceedings, and other topics, but only in passing did he mention that "the Bolshevik MRC is presently attempting to detach the troops from the command . . . but I think we can easily handle it."[62]

If Dukhonin on his own initiative was taking precautionary measures there is no clear record of it. It is true that a number of units were under transfer from the southerly fronts (the XLIX Corps, for example), but their purpose was ostensibly to forestall a German push along the Estonian coast (if it served to cool the ardor of the Reval sailors and pro-Bolshevik Estonian workers, so much the better). The XVII and XXII corps were also under transfer, probably to afford more security to Stavka, which was surrounded by hostile garrisons (Gomel, Smolensk, Orsha).[63] When the crisis broke out they were the logical units to call upon, since they were already in transit northward.

Late on October 23 Kerensky instructed the Northern Front headquarters to be prepared to dispatch units to the capital. According to Woytinsky, General Cheremisov contemptuously handed the order over to him, declaring, "This is political and has nothing to do with me. . . . You can try to execute it if you think it can be done."[64] Woytinsky immediately set up his own "staff" headquarters with his own teletype (Hughes) apparatus, and over the next two days he furiously set about the task of drumming up units reliable enough to carry out this hazardous mission. The First and Fifth army committees refused to cooperate, and the commander of the Fifth Army, General Boldyrev, confirmed that he would be unable to secure obedience to such orders (the semi-Bolshevik committee had already put controls on his communications). Iskosol was sympathetic, but feared that any action might trigger the occupation of headquarters by the Latvian brigades (an accurate assumption). They cautiously readied the 17th Cavalry Division and units of the XLIX Corps west of Reval, as well as an armored car division from the army reserve, but advised Woy-

[62] *AR* 7 (Berlin, 1922): 284. On Polkovnikov, see Rabinowitch, *Bolsheviks Come to Power*, pp. 243-44, and on Kerensky's passivity, see Stankevich, *Vospominaniia*, p. 252.

[63] For a belabored Soviet version, which sees it as a preconceived "plan" to defeat the uprising, see V. D. Polikarpov, *Prolog grazhdanskoi voiny* (Moscow, 1976), chap. 2. My account benefits to some extent from archival materials on the XXII Corps in TsGVIA f. 2222, op. 1, ed. khr. 1185, ll. 250-54. These materials confirm that the original order was dated October 11 for transfer to Mogilev; hence they cannot be connected to the uprising.

[64] "Gody pobedy i porazhenii" (Ms.), HI, 3:329, and parallel account in Woytinsky, pp. 369-70. In the latter, Cheremisov almost comes across as a Bolshevik in disguise, deliberately plotting against the Provisional Government; this interpretation is disproven by his subsequent refusal to obey Sovnarkom directives or to recognize Krylenko as Commander in Chief, for which he was removed (see below, p. 391).

tinsky that not a single soldier would move toward Petrograd without a direct appeal by VTsIK. Repeatedly on October 24 Woytinsky pleaded with whoever was on the wire in Petrograd that success depended entirely on obtaining the imprimature of VTsIK.[65] Even as events were unfolding on the night of October 24-25, Woytinsky was vainly trying to get someone on the Petrograd end of the wire to speak authoritatively for VTsIK. He was reassured in the name of the Pre-Parliament but was not informed that it had broken with the government. Around midnight he received word from the "Presidium" of VTsIK authorizing him to send troops and pleading with him to "act with all speed."[66] Though a dubious mandate, Woytinsky acted on the premise that "democracy" had committed itself. He also passed on to lower units a distorted version of the day's events by the War Ministry spokesman ("a small band of Bolsheviks are trying to take over government institutions against the will of all organs of democracy").

Woytinsky soon discovered that the only unit available for dispatch was the III Cavalry Corps, the same unit utilized by Kornilov and now under the command of General Krasnov, who already had orders from Kerensky to move his First Don Cossack Division with artillery to Petrograd.[67] At the same time Kerensky summoned two cycle battalions from the front and the Fifth Don Cossack Division from Finland. Krasnov's headquarters were in Ostrov, 48 kilometers south of Pskov, but more than half of his companies had been dispersed to the rear to put down local disorders and were considerably understrength (70 per company instead of the normal 100). Only eighteen companies of his two divisions (First Don and Ussuriiskii Cossack) were on hand. General Krasnov, a guards cossack officer and a disappointed adherent of Kornilov, held no brief for Kerensky, the Petrograd politicians, or the Soviet, but he felt that the survival of the Russian state, above all by keeping the Army intact, took precedence over all else, and thus that the humiliation of serving under Kerensky had to be endured.[68]

Krasnov was thankful the order did not include his Ussuriiskii Division because he was by no means sure they would comply. At 11:00 P.M.,

[65] See teletype exchange with General Ia. G. Bagriatuni, Chief of Staff of the Petrograd Military District, erroneously dated October 22 (actually of the 24th), which refers to similar communications to Kerensky and General Levitskii, chief of the War Cabinet in *VOSR. Vosstanie*, p. 277. (Correction of date in Polikarpov, pp. 74-75.)

[66] *Stormy Passage*, p. 137. In his manuscript memoirs (3:333), Woytinsky cites an exchange with a Soviet Executive Committee member in which he asserted that "not one regiment or company will respond from the Northern Front to the call of the government."

[67] Text of order in *AR* 7:286-87.

[68] Krasnov's own detailed account in "Na vnutrennom fronte," *ibid.*, 1 (1922): 97-190; above details on pp. 135-45.

when the trains were ready to pull out of the station at Ostrov, Krasnov received an astounding order from the front commander to halt all troop movements to the capital. Krasnov sped by staff car to Pskov, roused Chief of Staff Lukirskii, and demanded an explanation. Lukirskii referred him to Cheremisov, who was at the time closeted with the Executive of the Pskov Soviet in a spirited discussion of current events and unwillingly came out to confer briefly with Krasnov: "The Provisional Government no longer exists," Cheremisov said wearily but insistently. "I order you to unload your echelons and stay in Ostrov. There is nothing you can do that will make any difference." A staff officer, who advised Krasnov that their front commander was a traitor, guided him to Front Commissar Woytinsky. Bolting the door, Woytinsky whispered to Krasnov, "You're here just in time. He's here!" "Who's here?" Krasnov queried. "Kerensky! Nobody knows. He just got here by staff car." Quickly Woytinsky filled Krasnov in on Petrograd events and told him that his force represented the only hope. Like conspirators they made their way through the dark to the quarters of Kerensky's brother-in-law General Baranovskii, Quartermaster General of the Northern Front. There Krasnov found an exhausted but strangely exhilarated Kerensky, who assured him that the entire front army would rise up as one man with him against the miserable band of scoundrels in Petrograd. On the spot Kerensky authorized Krasnov to raise an expeditionary force, offering him an extra cavalry and an infantry division, and the entire XVII Corps. Krasnov would command a considerable army, with the prospect of a triumphal march into Petrograd. Krasnov was naive enough to think his prospects excellent; he was convinced the "crowd" still worshiped Kerensky.[69]

Kerensky had been far from frank with Krasnov over the day's events. He had driven at breakneck speed from Petrograd, failing to encounter the hoped-for troops, and he yielded to despair after Cheremisov argued that sending troops would unleash civil war and the collapse of the front; he offered to resign as head of the government after appointing Cheremisov as Commander in Chief.[70] Later Woytinsky and Baranovskii persuaded Kerensky to reverse the decision.[71] Cheremisov was indeed playing an underhanded game, as when Dukhonin over direct wire demanded to confer with Kerensky on the decision to halt the troops, Cheremisov abruptly

[69] Details and quotations are all from *ibid.*, pp. 147-48.

[70] Kerensky's version is that the above was a crafty lie on Cheremisov's part to deceive Dukhonin and other front commanders. This is refuted by a direct wire exchange on October 26 between Northern Front Quartermaster Baranovskii (Kerensky's own brother-in-law) and Dukhonin, in which the former confirmed Cheremisov's assertion (see *VOSR. Vosstanie*, pp. 604-5).

[71] Voitinskii Ms., 3:343-44.

broke off the conversation, promising to call back in two hours, during which time he expected important matters to be resolved. In fact, he was conferring with the newly organized MRC of the Northern Front and hoped that in the meantime Kerensky would confirm him as Commander in Chief, which would enable him to present Dukhonin with a fait accompli. He had also claimed that the Provisional Government "no longer existed" several hours before the taking of the Winter Palace, concealed Kerensky's presence in Pskov from his subordinates, discouraged the latter from co-operating with Woytinsky's efforts, and made clear to the Pskov Soviet that he disapproved of the whole business of a rescue mission. Moreover, bypassing Stavka, he conveyed his special version of events to General Baluev, commander of the Western Front, and called on him to support his policy of not permitting any movement of troops to the capital for "political" purposes. General Baluev rebuffed the invitation and declared that only Stavka had the right to coordinate such policies.[72] Kerensky's initial submissiveness to Cheremisov may seem puzzling, though his propensity to manic-depressive fluctuations in mood is familiar enough. Undoubtedly, Kerensky felt isolated and defeated: the Pre-Parliament had refused him support, he fled Petrograd narrowly escaping arrest, he landed in Pskov simply because nowhere along the route were troops to be seen, he was out of touch with Stavka and could thus authorize no new troop movements, and from Baranovskii he learned that none of the armies of the Northern Front could assure him of more troops. Thus Cheremisov could easily play on his despondent mood.

Woytinsky, who might have encouraged him, was still tied up with the Pskov Soviet and the front committee, who were up in arms over the sending of troops. His assurances that VTsIK had called for the troops had persuaded these bodies to remain neutral, but when a telegram arrived stating that the Kadet Kishkin had been appointed Governor-General of Petrograd, and a suspected Kornilovite, Palchinskii, as his assistant, they reversed themselves; moreover, they formed on the Petrograd model an MRC whose sole task was to halt troop movements and prevent the outbreak of civil war. Flabbergasted, Woytinsky assented, resigned as government commissar, and graciously accepted the invitation to serve on the MRC![73] He then contacted the Political Section of the War Ministry, which informed him of the walkout of the Mensheviks and S.R.'s from the Second Congress and the formation of the Committee to Save the Revolution and the Motherland (KSRR) and assured him that VTsIK was determined to continue

[72] For the teletype exchanges, see *AR* 6:297-99 and 301-2.

[73] These details, not found in Woytinsky's two accounts, come from the deposition of an eyewitness to the Petrograd MRC of November 6 in *KA* 9 (1925): 190-92. For his telegram of resignation as commissar at this time, see *PVRK* 1:206-7.

the struggle against the Bolsheviks under this new democratic banner. Shortly thereafter he met with Baranovskii and learned of Kerensky's presence, and his attitude took a 180-degree turn: he joined Baranovskii in persuading Kerensky to reverse himself, took back his own resignation as commissar, and resumed his hectoring activity of raising troops. The following day, when he tried to explain his reversal to a mass assembly of the Pskov garrison, he was nearly lynched.[74] Woytinsky's turnabout was even more remarkable than Kerensky's.

General Krasnov's arrival rescued Kerensky from Cheremisov's clutches and allowed him to reactivate the expeditionary force that Cheremisov had canceled. There was no problem in moving out the units stationed at Ostrov (though some units required persuading by the Supreme Persuader): by midday on October 26 they had successfully passed through Pskov despite the attempts of railway personnel and the Pskov Soviet to stop them, and by midday on the 27th they had occupied Gatchina, easily dispersing and disarming the large pro-Bolshevik garrison, though only 850 or so cossacks and a few hundred soldiers of a shock unit from Luga now composed the force.[75] They easily moved on to Tsarskoe Selo, but the cossacks refused to move on to Petrograd without the promised backup troops, especially infantry. Kerensky, now attended by his Chief Commissar Stankevich, official representatives of the KSRR, and the eternal adventurer Savinkov (who claimed to represent the Union of Cossacks), kept up a flood of telegrams to Stavka and various headquarters along the Northern Front to speed up the sending of reinforcements. By the evening of the 29th, the day before the "decisive battle," only three more companies of the Ninth Don Cossack Regiment had arrived, increasing Krasnov's force to 1,200, but only 630 had mounts. By now he had also captured an armored car, an armored train, several airplanes that threw leaflets on Petrograd, and a mountain of weapons from the disarmed garrisons of Gatchina and Tsarskoe, but he had no means of confining those who had surrendered, and the 16,000 or so unarmed soldiers continued to hold "meetings." In the meantime it became clear that none of the promised reinforcements were on the way, not even the 17th Cavalry from the Twelfth Army reserve; moreover, Krasnov's Ussuriiskii Division was held up at Pskov on Cheremisov's orders.[76]

There were four days between the Petrograd coup and the "battle" of

[74] Text of teletype exchange in *VOSR. Vosstanie*, pp. 150-54, and for the near lynching, see Woytinsky, *Stormy Passage*, pp. 378-80.

[75] See Krasnov, *AR* 1:152ff.

[76] See Stankevich's account, pp. 266-83, for political developments, Krasnov, *AR* 1:155-69, for the military. Kerensky's telegrams are liberally reproduced in *VOSR. Vosstanie*, pp. 609, 610, 620-21, 626, 635, 637, 640, and 644.

Pulkovo Heights, more than enough time to assemble additional troops even from the more remote fronts. Already earmarked from the Northern Front were the remaining units of the First Don Cossack Division (two regiments near Reval, the rest scattered south and east of Pskov), the Ussuriiskii, Fifth Caucasus, and 17th Cavalry divisions, several armored car units attached to the headquarters of the Twelfth and Fifth armies respectively, the mysteriously missing cycle battalions, and the 44th Infantry Division also near Reval. En route from the south were the three divisions of the XVII Corps (35th, 156th, and Third) and at least one division of the XXII Corps (the Third Finnish Rifle). On October 26, General Dukhonin added the Second Kuban Cossack Division from his own reserve.[77] This was a formidable army, much larger than Kornilov's, but their "mood" was yet to be revealed, and those from the Northern Front were short of infantry, an essential ingredient to encourage the cavalry. In spite of Kerensky's flood of "categorical orders" and hysterical inquiries as to their whereabouts, as well as appeals by commissars and committees, very few of these units budged, and those that did advanced with incredible sluggishness.

First, nearly all the garrisons of the key nodal points (Reval, Pskov, Minsk), as well as many minor points (Viazma, Gomel), were already in a "Bolshevik" frame of mind or were becoming so (Orsha, Luga). Though easily curbed with relatively small security forces of cavalry, they could still enlist the help of railroad workers and work over the soldiers in transit with agitators. For example, the missing cycle battalions, hitherto very loyal to the government, were halted some 112 kilometers from the capital and after being persuaded by agitators sent a deputation to Petrograd; in three days of effort, the command never ascertained their whereabouts. A shock battalion was similarly halted near Novgorod, and an armored car division from the Fifth Army in Rezhitsa (the ranks turned the cars over to the Fifth Army Committee, the officers fled for their lives).[78] Bolshevized soldiers in Vyborg, Finland, dissuaded the Fifth Caucasus Cavalry Division, thought to be immune to disaffection.[79] The case of the Second Kuban Cossack Division en route from Mogilev was typical:

[77] Various orders and direct wire exchanges in *VOSR. Vosstanie*, for example, p. 599 (Second Kuban Cossacks), p. 614 (Fifth Caucasus Division), p. 621 (XVII Corps), p. 627 (17th Cavalry Division and armored cars from the Twelfth Army), p. 637 (Third Urals Cossack Regiment and armored cars from the Fifth Army), p. 646 (Third Finnish Rifle Division), and p. 640 (XLIX Corps). See other like examples in "Oktiabriskii perevorot i stavka," *KA* 8 (1925): 165 and 169, and 9:156-70, and "Oktiabr' na fronte," *KA* 23 (1927): 149-94 (see esp. Dukhonin-Lukirskii of October 27, p. 163, and of October 28, pp. 167-68).

[78] For cycle battalions, see *VOSR. Vosstanie*, pp. 607 and 624, and *KA* 23:152, 166, and 169; on shock battalions and armored cars, see *VOSR. Vosstanie*, p. 619, and *KA* 24:87-88.

[79] *VOSR. Vosstanie*, pp. 614-15 (Dukhonin-Lukirskii, October 27).

> At the Orsha station, an echelon of 800 [cossacks] armed with machine guns en route to Petrograd, having declared their unwillingness to proceed, have been meeting all morning, and under the influence of Bolshevik agitators, have seized the station and municipal institutions. The station is occupied by 100 cossacks, the city by 50. Request immediate instructions.[80]

In Vinnitsa on the Southwestern Front, a Bolshevized garrison of 30,000 blocked the path of the Third Finnish Rifle Division, which had just set out on its odyssey for the Northern Front. It resulted in a full-scale battle engaging armored cars and airplanes and causing a good many casualties, but the Bolshevik forces were routed and dispersed into the surrounding countryside.[81] The division obviously did not wish to be deprived of its berth in the rear, but its progress was significantly delayed.

The necessity to secure railway and other vital points along the way also caused delays. A vicious cycle set in: troop movements upset local garrisons and often solidified them behind Bolshevik MRCs; troops en route had to detrain, liberate local commanders, force the soldiers back into their barracks, and secure the railway point for echelons still to come, which in many cases were held up for similar reasons. The effect was to impose a time-consuming leapfrog procedure. In Pskov the lead echelons of the Ussuriiskii Division were halted to pacify the aroused garrison until the expected arrival of the Third Ural Cossack Regiment called in from the Fifth Army reserve.[82] The rest of the shaky Ussuriiskii Division themselves refused to move, and they sent a deputation to Pskov demanding cancellation of their orders. The departure of the Third Ural Cossack Regiment from Dvinsk provoked a major confrontation between the Fifth Army Committee and Commander Boldyrev, hitherto observing an uneasy truce: the army committee narrowly voted down a motion to send its own expeditionary force to defend Soviet power, whereupon the Bolshevik contingent withdrew, formed their own MRC, and readied such a force anyway (from the Fourth Special Infantry Division). General Boldyrev tried to prevent its departure with his last remaining loyal units, but he succeeded only in provoking the effective occupation of his headquarters by the MRC and the resubmission of the army committee to the Bolsheviks.[83]

[80] *Ibid.*, p. 628 (report of division commander to Stavka of October 29).

[81] *KA* 24:85 and 88 (two direct wire exchanges of Dukhonin and Baranovskii of October 31, the latter citing casualties of 1,500); detailed account in heroic style in I. I. Mints, *Istoriia velikogo oktiabria* (Moscow, 1967-73), 3:539ff.

[82] *KA* 9:166-67 (Lukirskii-Dukhonin, October 30).

[83] *VOSR. Vosstanie*, pp. 632-33 (Baranovskii-Popov, Chief of Staff of Fifth Army of October 29 and October 30).

Similarly, the XVII Corps was immobilized for two days south of Orsha. Railway personnel claimed insufficient cars and engines, and during the interval a regiment of the Third Infantry Division was worked over by agitators. Another more loyal regiment had to be used to disinfect the first and secure the point. The stretched-out corps was unable to proceed further because the 156th Division, which had a large Ukrainian component, received orders from the Ukrainian Rada to return to Kiev, where a desperate three-way struggle had broken out between the Bolsheviks (mainly Russian workers), the Russian command, and the Ukrainians. A regular battle ensued between the Russian and Ukrainian contingents of the 156th Division.[84]

One of the most critically needed units for the expeditionary force was the XVII Cavalry stationed near Twelfth Army headquarters at Valka. Iskosol had offered it in immediate response to Woytinsky's first call on October 24. Twelfth Army Commander Iuzefovich, fearing the threat from the Latvian brigades, pleaded with General Cheremisov to cancel it. Cheremisov was very willing to oblige, Kerensky's categorical order to the contrary notwithstanding.[85] Even more serious was the holdup of all troop movements through Reval, the sole artery from the right flank of the Twelfth Army to Petrograd. The commander of the special land and sea forces, General N. V. Khenrikson, went even further than Cheremisov in cultivating the radical mood of the port and region. When the local Soviet formed an MRC on the Petrograd model on October 26, he announced: "The commanding staffs [must] work in full accord with all committees. . . . All transfers of troops to Petrograd have been suspended. The commander is operating in full cooperation with the Reval MRC."[86] This clear act of insubordination held up the 13th and 15th Don Cossack regiments, the entire 44th Division, a brigade of the 29th Division, and two divisions of the XLIX Corps.[87]

Complicating the situation was the incredible tangle of communications and conflicting information. Unlike the February Revolution, when control remained with the command but information leaked like a sieve, or the Kornilov affair, when committees backed by the soldiers seized control of all the communications media, this time, both in Petrograd and at key

[84] *Ibid.*, p. 647 (Dukhonin-Baranovskii, October 31); *KA* 23:170 (Dukhonin-Lukirskii, October 28, on the XVII Corps' being ordered to secure Orsha and Dno); *ibid.*, p. 173 (Dietrichs, Quartermaster at Stavka-Malavin on the Western Front, on the Bolsheviks blocking of Orsha); *ibid.*, 24:84 (Dukhonin-Baranovskii, October 31); and *ibid.*, 9:162-65 (Dukhonin-Stogov, Chief of Staff of the Southwestern Front of October 30).

[85] *KA* 23:153 and 182.

[86] *VOSR. Vosstanie*, p. 601, co-signed with the MRC chairman.

[87] See *RDRA*, pp. 296-97, 208, 210, 244, 268-69.

points front and rear, control passed back and forth between progovernment and antigovernment forces, railway and telegraph personnel, local soviets, committees, MRCs, commissars, and even commanders. Most army committees supported by commanders and commissars filtered information coming from pro-Bolshevik sources in Petrograd, but there were usually roundabout channels: in Pskov the pro-Bolshevik Soviet and front committee enjoyed the patronage of General Cheremisov, whereas Woytinsky with the help of Baranovskii and Chief of Staff Lukirskii kept a seperate channel open to Stavka and the expeditionary force. In the First and Fifth armies, semi-Bolshevik committees monitored but could not completely control communications; nevertheless, they imposed neutrality on commanders in the political struggle, whereas in the Twelfth Army and all armies of the Southwestern and Rumanian fronts firmly anti-Bolshevik committees were in charge but wavered in their loyalty to Kerensky's government. Sometimes they held up pro-Bolshevik telegrams, at other times let them through with suitable comment.[88]

The Bolsheviks in Petrograd gained control of the General Staff building on October 25, but a separate apparatus allowed the Political Section of the War Ministry to keep Stavka and Woytinsky informed from its perspective for several more days. The Petrograd MRC sent out several radio messages from the powerful transmitter in Tsarskoe Selo on October 25 and 26 until Krasnov's forces occupied it.[89] Most telegraph personnel were anti-Bolshevik, and the Bolsheviks in Petrograd lost control of the telegraph exchange on October 27. In fact, the KSRR rapidly gained ground in Petrograd on the 27th and 28th in the capital, encouraged by Kerensky's occupation of Gatchina; they mobilized the support of a number of officers' training schools and persuaded many garrison units to declare their neutrality, while the commissar apparatus of the Petrograd MRC almost ceased to function (some were even arrested by their units).[90] There was even

[88] Based on the many sources already cited and others to be covered in the following chapters. It is often necessary to reconstruct mentally how messages were conveyed and to look for internal evidence to be sure that they actually reached their destination. Soviet *Sborniki* do not always indicate whether a message was a radiogram, a telegram, a leaflet, or simply a penciled draft.

[89] See lengthy exchange between the Political Section of the War Ministry and Baranovskii at Northern Front headquarters of November 5 in *KA* 24:105-7, in which they were still hoping to concentrate loyal troops in Luga; for MRC control of the radio at Tsarskoe, see *PVRK* 1:165, where Antonov, incensed over the loss of the radio to Kerensky on the 27th, orders an armored car and a battalion of Kronshtadters to win it back; on Kerensky "sending his radiograms everywhere" on October 29, see *ibid.*, p. 235.

[90] The materials on the Petrograd MRC frequently confirm the dangerous situation of the Bolsheviks in these days, for example, reports on October 28 on the loss of the telephone exchange, the still-real threat of the women's battalions, the easy disarming of soldiers from

great alarm over the security of Smolnyi, all of which resulted in wildly optimistic (and grossly inaccurate) bulletins broadcast by the KSRR. These bulletins were conveyed via the All-Army Committee (OAK) at Stavka all across the front, leading to considerable confusion as to who actually controlled Petrograd. Even more confusing was the fact that these bulletins were proclaimed by an obscure committee (the KSRR) which many front units, including the commanders of the First and Twelfth armies, took to be Bolsheviks.[91] With such vast quantities of uncertain information floating around, both pro-Bolshevik and anti-Bolshevik forces at the front were unwilling to commit themselves and assumed a stance of neutrality until it could be cleared up. The flow of information casting doubt on the Bolsheviks' hold on Petrograd was abruptly terminated on October 29 with the miserable collapse of the attempted uprising of the military schools. The Bolsheviks took courage, their wavering ranks regained strength, and again victory claims assaulted the communications networks.[92]

Out of this mélange emerged a very powerful current affecting both camps, as well as the noncommitted: civil war, having become a very real danger, had to be avoided at all costs. Thus, many units in transit halted by themselves or were easily persuaded to do so by others on the strength of this argument. Railroad workers in particular, even before the intervention of their union leadership (Vikzhel), deliberately sabotaged the expediting of troops, claiming absence of engines or fuel; they also blocked tracks with empty freight cars, locked switches, or tore up track. These forces played themselves out in countless local dramas which are impossible to follow, but the total effect was to halt the flow of reinforcements to Kerensky and to reinforce the general determination not to allow matters to come to a bloody result.

The Pulkovo confrontation itself was anticlimactic. The capture of Gatchina and Tsarskoe, the vigorous agitation of the KSRR in Petrograd, and the short-lived uprising of the junkers on October 29 had galvanized the Red Guards and Baltic Fleet sailors, the latter now arriving in significant numbers from Helsinki and Kronshtadt, but these events seem to have had the opposite effect on the garrison soldiers and many workers not integrated

the guards regiments sent to defend Gatchina, the open agitation on the streets on behalf of Kerensky, delegations from Kerensky's force agitating among soldiers in the barracks, unfriendly crowds on Nevskii Prospekt (*ibid.*, pp. 267-68, 277, 310, 317, 321, and *passim*).

[91] See the *BOAK*, No. 4 (October 31), in G. Lelevich (L. G. Kal'manson), *Oktiabr' v stavke* (Gomel, 1922), Prilozhenie (Appendix), which carried little but optimistic news. For an example of the commander's confusion, see *KA* 23:187 (Lukirskii-General Prievskii of First Army of October 29).

[92] The best account of the abrupt shift in mood in Petrograd is S. P. Melgunov, *The Bolshevik Seizure of Power* (Santa Barbara, Calif., 1972), chaps. 6 and 7.

into the Red Guards.[93] Though cited numbers fluctuate between 10,000 and 20,000, there were at least 5,000 sailors and large numbers of worker-volunteers (and their wives) who attached themselves to the mobilized Red Guard units, which Rex Wade puts between 8,000 and 10,000. Many of the latter were without arms and had no trained officers; one gets the impression of something more like a religious procession than an organized military force.[94] Podvoiskii, who was in charge of the undertaking, was so engrossed in securing supplies, especially spades and ammunition, that he neglected to give directives for the operations themselves. Lenin set up a "second staff" in Smolnyi, which created such confusion that Podvoiskii threatened to resign; Lenin ordered him to stay at his post or be turned over to a party tribunal and shot.[95]

The advantage of the defenders, besides their numbers, was that because they were dug in on the heights a cavalry assault would be subjected to withering fire even if the marksmanship were poor. Moreover, there had been heavy rains, turning a gully that Krasnov's forces would have to traverse into a bog. The sole eyewitness account from the command post on the Soviet side observed that the defenders' mood was determined but that there was an absence of officers or anyone in command; each detachment made its own decisions, and cyclists, telephones, and other means of lateral communication were lacking. The sole agreed-upon goal was to hold the occupied position.[96]

Although badgered by Kerensky to push on, Krasnov himself had no illusions about the day's prospects: his cossacks were grumbling about the lack of infantry, three companies of reinforcements immediately declared their neutrality, and his officers, like himself unrepentant Kornilovites, were far less inclined to pull Kerensky's chestnuts out of the fire. Savinkov generously offered to have Kerensky removed, but Krasnov claims he had

[93] Chudnovskii, Krylenko, Antonov-Ovseenko, and Podvoiskii all tried their hand at persuasion unsuccessfully in the barracks. See Podvoiskii, *God 1917*, pp. 161-62, and *PVRK* 1:310. On the poor mood of the Semenovskiis, the danger of their defection to the KSRR, the same for the Grenadiers, the neutrality of the Petrogradskiis, Keksgolmskiis, and Izmailovskiis, the latter's arrest of an MRC commissar, see the complete record of the sessions of the MRC in *PRVK* 1:277, 321, 334, 342, and 363 respectively.

[94] See Rex Wade, *Red Guards and Workers' Militias in the Russian Revolution* (Stanford, Calif., 1984), pp. 313-14; for the 20,000 figure, see Mints, 3:147n, which includes a questionable estimate of 5,000 soldiers. One published list specifies 3,200 Kronshtadt sailors (*VOSR. Vosstanie*, p. 706), but two supplementary lists mention 440 and 590 from Kronshtadt and Fort Ino respectively, and a further 4,000 from Vyborg (*ibid.*, pp. 719-20 and 733-34), which reaches a grand total of over 8,000, though whether all arrived on station is another question.

[95] Podvoiskii, p. 169.

[96] Report of two special deputies of the MRC to "Commander" Muraviev in *PVRK* 1:352-53.

no appetite to be a new Kornilov, and besides he had given Kerensky an officer's word. There was still the chance that the whiff of battle would light a fire in the Bolsheviks' rear and break their will to resist. But Krasnov knew their tactical position to be unassailable. From his vantage point he could survey the entire Soviet line, including the masses of reinforcements drawing up from the rear, and could even distinguish between the dark workmen's clothing and the bluejackets of the sailors, who were in more disciplined array on both flanks. They would be easy marks for concentrated light artillery and machine-gun fire, but alas, he disposed of only a few pieces of the former, and the latter could not be put in place without drawing counter-fire. Hearing that a column of soldiers was marching along the Moscow road on this flank, he easily neutralized them with the armored train. These were the Izmailovskiis, the only garrison unit to obey the summons of the MRC.

Krasnov somehow had to break their center or the day was lost. The Guards Cossack contingent volunteered to try—less than 100 against many thousands! As the cossack charge unleashed a vigorous exchange of fire, Krasnov noticed through his binoculars complete confusion and movement to the rear of the Red Guards in the center, even though they were not the main target of the attack. There was hope. But the more seasoned sailors held fast, and when the mounted attackers reached the gully the horses became hopelessly mired. Far more horses than cossacks became casualties, and the small unit was obliged to beat a hasty retreat, more than half of them on foot. The ''battle'' was continued for the rest of the day by the artillery at a safe distance, until by day's end they ''ran out of shell.'' The batteries drew back in disorder, and the sailors, sensing the cossacks' discomfiture, advanced on both flanks without resistance. Krasnov ordered a withdrawal to Gatchina, surrendering the prize of Tsarskoe (and its all-important radio transmitter), much to Kerensky's chagrin.[97]

Once this skirmish was over, the desire to end hostilities by accommodation became overwhelming on both sides. Krasnov's men declared they did not intend to fight again, and they refused to take up new positions outside Gatchina or even to fetch ammunition. They openly conferred with a sailors' deputation headed by the Bolshevik Dybenko, who proposed a truce and informed them of Vikzhel's appeal to halt the civil war. Krasnov tried to enlist the help of his committees, but they were also inclined to negotiate. ''Why not talk,'' they reasoned. ''They also want to stop fighting. Kerensky cooked up this mess, let him digest it.'' The outlines of a

[97] Krasnov, *AR* 1:162-69. There is no comparable account from the Soviet side, and almost immediately reality gave way to myth-making, beginning with a glowing account by Chudnovskii in *Pravda*, November 2 (in *VOSR. Vosstanie*, pp. 795-96).

settlement were quickly agreed upon—the surrender of Kerensky in exchange for amnesty and free passage to the Don. The temptation was irresistible, and Krasnov's last desperate appeals fell on deaf ears. The Baltic sailors' tactic of direct negotiations with the cossacks, ignoring commanders and politicians, was diabolically clever. The sailors assured the cossacks they would support the Vikzhel formula of a coalition of socialists with token Bolshevik participation, but not of Lenin or Trotsky. Krasnov even claims that Dybenko promised to deliver Lenin in exchange for Kerensky, but if so, this was doubtless a mere stratagem to suborn the naive cossacks into surrendering Kerensky; nevertheless, Dybenko had clearly exceeded his instructions (if he had any), as both Lenin and Podvoiskii argued against the agreement and for handing Dybenko over to a revolutionary court.[98] But when the advantages of an immediate liquidation of Kerensky's adventure and neutralizing the cossacks as a counter-revolutionary force became evident, they reconciled themselves to it. It became obvious that there was overwhelming sentiment for a compromise settlement based on the Vikzhel proposals from every part of the Bolshevik constituency—workers, sailors, garrison soldiers, and more than half of the Central Committee. There was no choice at the present moment but to go through the motions of negotiation.

☆

With Kerensky's flight and the intervention of Vikzhel (the two coincided on November 1) the political situation sharply changed. The anti-Bolshevik forces could no longer think in terms of restoring the fallen government or some surrogate by force of arms. Kerensky had fled and no longer enjoyed a shred of support; the KSRR, the improvization of the democratic camp, was divided between those willing to accept the Vikzhel proposals as the basis for negotiation and those who were not. The socialist parties were split along the same lines, as were nearly all elements of "organized democracy," such as the city Duma and the trade unions. However, there is no question but that the Vikzhel formula of "an all-socialist government from the Popular Socialists to the Bolsheviks" based on immediate peace and land proposals corresponded to the mass mood in the capital and a good part of the country in the wake of the Gatchina encounter, a mood that severely restricted the militant inclinations of the leaders of all socialist factions and obliged them for a time to go through the motions of serious negotiations. Melgunov, Lande, and other authorities cite overwhelming evidence on the worker and trade union element, while that of the garrison is attested to in the extensive published materials on the Petrograd MRC.[99]

[98] Krasnov, pp. 107-73, and Podvoiskii, p. 173.

[99] See Melgunov, pp. 160-61, and contribution of Leo Lande to *The Mensheviks from the*

Only four members of the Central Committee were willing to follow the hard line of Lenin and Trotsky, and nearly all the "people's commissars" temporarily resigned their positions to force continued negotiations. As will be seen below, the Vikzhel interlude corresponded also to a very widespread sentiment at the front, including both Bolshevik and anti-Bolshevik elements in the committees and the soldier constituency. The inertia of this mass sentiment determined that the Soviet Revolution was irreversible and could not be challenged by military means, but also that it was understood not as a veiled Bolshevik dictatorship but as the collective will of the popular masses to which all socialist-oriented groups should accede.

Revolution of 1917 to the Second World War, ed. Leopold Haimson (Chicago, 1974), pp. 67-68. In spite of the wide-reaching impact of the Vikzhel negotiations, especially at the front, the episode still needs complete investigation. The best account in English is that of Lande, pp. 58ff. On the soldiers' pressure on the negotiations, see session of the MRC of October 31 in *PVRK* 1:421-26.

CHAPTER IX

THE COMMITTEE REVOLUTION: NORTHERN AND WESTERN FRONTS

DESPITE the "victory" at Pulkovo, the situation of the Bolshevik government remained precarious. The ability of Vikzhel to compel Bolshevik participation in continuing negotiations on the structure of power with other democratic institutions and parties revealed the Bolsheviks' inherent weakness. They badly needed the legitimacy of democratic institutions to maintain credibility with the masses, and the Second Congress had failed to render a clear verdict. Not only had two major socialist parties, important organizations, and the old VTsIK withheld recognition, but only a fraction of the front had been represented, and peasant soviets not at all. Moreover, mass consent insofar as it had been genuinely mobilized extended to Soviet power, not to exclusive Bolshevik power, and until the Bolsheviks clearly controlled the elective institutions their claim to a mandate was under a cloud.

The formula of an "all-socialist government," that is, a coalition of all socialist parties according to their electoral strength as opposed to a coalition with bourgeois groups, had acquired some currency even before the Vikzhel proposals, not least of all at the front, and the narrow brush with fratricidal war gave it considerable impetus. The masses had little sympathy for the fractious hostility among socialist parties and were of a mind to force them to come to terms. Only certain Bolshevik stalwarts, such as the Baltic sailors, the Red Guards, and the Latvian Riflers, were prepared to settle matters through the raw exercise of power. In the capital the garrison soldiers, large factories, and trade unions demonstrated their preference for accommodation based on unity among the revolutionary parties. This was but a token of the Bolshevik problem in the country at large and more particularly at the front. Though still in the process of catching up to events, the front soldiers clearly expected Soviet power in the center to be legitimized through the network of democratic institutions of which their own committees were a part. The military insurrection, the delay and confusion in communications, and the tension over incipient civil war all served to becloud their awareness of the proclamation of power by the Soviet Congress and the land and peace decrees, which otherwise held such inherent appeal. Not infrequently, when told that the Bolsheviks or the garrison had "seized power" by force in advance of the Soviet Congress or in order to preempt the calling of the Constituent Assembly, they became quite upset. Though holding no brief for Kerensky's government, they could not understand why force was necessary, except against manifest "Kornilovites" when democratic solutions were available.

The masses expressed their orientation in a twofold manner, first, by participating enthusiastically at every opportunity in by-elections to lower and higher committees, and second, by sending deputations by divisions, regiments, and even smaller units directly to Petrograd to convey the message to pursue peace without partisan bickering and to undertake nothing of major consequence without consulting the front. The fact that by November 1 the Bolsheviks still lacked a secure hold on any of the army and front committees even where they held a slight majority (Fifth Army) or plurality (soon in the First, Third, and Twelfth armies), and that in most of them their inveterate foes were yet to be displaced (Tenth Army and all others to the south), deprived them of the authority they needed. When the Bolsheviks set up MRCs apart from the army committees, as in the Twelfth Army and numerous garrisons in the rear, they found it difficult to command mass support. Moreover, the old committees enjoyed very real advantages through their special relationship with the command, their control of communications, and their well-established reputation for getting things done. Soldiers, however unhappy with their committees, respected that kind of power and identified with it, because in the end they legitimized it (the lesson of the Kornilov times was not to be forgotten). Thus, their inclination was not to withdraw their assent from these organizations and transfer it to Bolshevik Military Revolutionary Committees (MRCs), but rather to avail themselves of the committees' authority with Bolshevik help.

The jockeying of armed contingents along the railroads was therefore far less vital to Bolshevik ascendancy than the battle for majorities in higher committees. Once the Bolsheviks gained control of the elective organs, they could spin off MRCs or grant recognition to their own, "legitimately" take over the command apparatus, remove uncompliant generals, claim power in the name of the Congress of Soviets, organize control of civilian administration in their region, and "execute" the decrees on land, peace, and democratization of the army. Thus, from the standpoint of understanding the consolidation of Bolshevik rule within the framework of Soviet legitimacy, the process of gaining control over the elective organs at the front was a key development. Though the "conquest" of the committee structure plays a ritualized role (the "triumphal march of Soviet power") in standard Soviet accounts, the subject remains virtually untouched by Western scholarship. If this monograph has any claim to adding a new dimension to the understanding of the Second Russian Revolution of 1917, it is precisely in this neglected area. The front, the regions, the cities, the countryside, and the border areas were all arenas of an incipient civil war that was to reach a final conclusion only three years hence. But these initial skirmishes were fought not on battlefields and streets with guns and armored cars but in countless electoral contests, improvised meetings, newspapers, and wrangling debates at army and front congresses stretching over the month of November and early December. It was here that Bolsheviks gained clear ascendancy over their rivals, resulting in a near monopoly of power on the Northern and Western fronts and sizeable chunks of power elsewhere; everywhere the rock-ribbed defensist committees went out of existence, replaced by leftist coalitions if not Bolsheviks, while new rivals for power arose in the peripheral areas (Finland, the Ukraine, the Don, Rumania, and the Caucasus). In all these outcomes the ingredient of popular assent by votes and debate was essential.

☆

The most striking feature of committee responses to Petrograd events is that they no longer followed the well-trod paths of previous crises, but instead a variety of uncharted modes that confounded the higher leadership and upset all political calculations. All through 1917 the army committees had been the most reliable and loyal extensions of VTsIK's authority and had successfully maintained the pretense that they spoke for the front with a single voice, which in political conflicts could be played off against adversaries to the right or left. If the upheavals of June and July took some of the shine off this assumption, the Kornilov affair had given it a new lease on life. It was Kerensky's grave miscalculation that he presumed he always had this card to play, however much he abused his position as the Savior of Democracy. But the Menshevik and S.R. leaders in the old VTsIK persisted in this illusion as well, and it lived on in the strategy of the KSRR and the OAK (the All-Army Committee at Stavka). National political figures not well acquainted with the front can be forgiven their error, but far less forgivable were the frenetic efforts of figures like Stankevich and Woytinsky, who could not plead ignorance yet persisted in conventional Soviet politics at the front even when they were in danger of being lynched or shot, and thus misled their colleagues in Petrograd. Just as remarkable was the misplaced braggadocio of the OAK committeemen at Stavka, of the Southwestern Front Committee, and of a few army committees like Iskosol, which against all evidence continued to pledge the "united support of the Army" against the Bolshevik adventure, including such stock phrases as "with our bayonets." It was particularly difficult for Iskosol to face up to the fact that its once-solid organization now rested on a vast pretense, no longer having a shred of foundation. Nevertheless, as demonstrated in Chapter VIII, many committeemen at the army level and below had somewhere along the line been shaken out of their complacency and were primed for radical new approaches; unfortunately for them, their message, even when forcefully stated, failed to make an impression on the higher leadership.

The assumption that the committees could mobilize the front behind the Provisional Government was counted on even more heavily by the commissar and command hierarchies. On the whole, the commissars were prowar socialists whose hypertrophied "state consciousness" tended to wall them off from reality (the legacy of the July repressions), and they continued to pontificate in splendid isolation in the name of revolutionary authority. Commanders, with copious disquieting reports from lower units at their disposal, were perhaps less sanguine, but they saw no alternative but to rely on existing modalities to avert the catastrophe of Bolshevism. Thus, all three pinnacles of authority in the Army acted in concert to raise the voice of "democracy" at the front against the criminal rebellion in Petrograd. When the lower committee structure failed to respond predictably, the strategy crashed to the ground.

At the outset of the crisis, General Dukhonin stressed that all troops headed for the capital should be met by accredited political representatives to explain events, that copies of all communications should be made available on demand to avert suspicion of Stavka's motives, and that committee representatives should accompany each unit.[1] In every communication he stressed that his actions were coordinated with the OAK and Chief Commissar Stankevich and enjoyed their support. Although Stankevich was at the time in Petrograd, deeply involved in the construction of the KSRR, he was in touch with Dukhonin by Hughes apparatus, and their full collaboration on both technical-military and political matters is well documented.[2] On its part, the OAK immediately announced its support of the

[1] "I regard it as imperative that all units be met by acknowledged leaders with copies of these telegrams to be explained to the troops; moreover, I have suggested to the Northern Front that units be accompanied by elected representatives of committees" (Dukhonin-Levitskii [military aide to Kerensky], October 25 in *AR* 7:289). See also Dukhonin-Baranovskii, October 26-27, *VOSR. Vosstanie*, pp. 607-8.

[2] *AR* 7:292. That the wires were humming with such communications between the Political Section of the War Ministry, Stavka, commissars, the OAK, and the various front networks, see *ibid.*, *passim*, and *KA* 8:155-57. For joint appeal of OAK Chairman Perekrestov, Assistant Chief Commissar Kovalevskii, and Dukhonin, see *Revoliutsiia 1917 g.* (Tiflis, 1930), p. 153.

government and requested the front committees to secure similar declarations from each of their respective armies as soon as possible. Stavka's communications reveal that it was counting heavily on these declarations to sanction the dispatching of expeditionary forces to the capital.

Although it would obviously take some time for the army committees to assemble and poll their units, the spokesman for the Rumanian Front Committee and the Executive Committee of the Southwestern Front responded that they expected such resolutions promptly, the former even volunteering to send troops. In addition, the commissar for the Southwestern Front, Iordanskii, assured Vyrubov, chief of the Political Section at Stavka, that troops would be forthcoming. The Western Front Committee spokesman declared the "likelihood" of support except for the Second Army, whereas for the Northern Front only Iskosol declared itself immediately and unequivocally. This was not yet the unanimity Stavka had hoped for, but nevertheless it informed lower commands that "the great majority of the army committees" had already condemned the Bolshevik uprising.[3]

The OAK firmly committed itself to the restoration of the Provisional Government as soon as it learned of Kerensky's expeditionary force, and it prodded the KSRR (which was wavering) to do likewise. The OAK chairman, Perekrestov, also in Petrograd on October 26, served as the chief conduit of communications between Woytinsky (who alone was in touch with Kerensky), the KSRR, and the Political Section of Stavka. He arranged the broadcasting through command and committee channels of Kerensky's "order to the troops," asking for support on October 26 and support of proclamations condemning the Bolshevik uprising by the old VTsIK, the Peasant Executive Committee, the KSRR, and the Union of Cossacks.[4] Henceforward, in political matters the OAK allied itself very closely with the KSRR, delegating three of its number to that body in Petrograd and after the collapse of the Kerensky expedition gave refuge to its survivors at Stavka.

The army and front committees had initially been hesitant to commit themselves because of the confusing information coming over the wires, but once they knew of Kerensky's expeditionary force and that the "official" organs of democracy, including their own OAK, were behind it, their loyalties were put to the test. Thus on 27 the mechanisms of front democracy were grinding out a good many resolutions at expanded assemblies of various kinds. Only a partial record of these responses is available,

[3] See *AR* 7:293-94, 296, 305, and 313; on Val'ter, see *KA* 8:159-60.

[4] On Perekrestov's role, see *AR* 7:312-13 (Political Section of War Ministry—Stavka, October 26); text of Kerensky's order in *VOSR. Vosstanie*, p. 595, and committee organs *Iz7A*, October 28, and *IzOA*, October 29.

particularly for lower levels, but General Val'ter, Chief of Staff of the Western Front, informed Stavka on October 27 that the front committee and all three of the army committees had condemned the Bolshevik uprising and supported the Provisional Government.[5]

Though based on information he had received, Val'ter's message was inaccurate and already outdated. The Tenth Army Committee agreed to support the Provisional Government only if it got rid of the bourgeois Minister of Foreign Affairs, Tereshchenko, who was "completely under the influence of the Allies," and if it "consistently pursued the Army's position on peace" (not defined).[6] In addition, the front committee organ, *Front*, failed to publish any such resolutions, and on October 28 took the position that "the Provisional Government is dead and will not be revived" as "the idea of coalition has outlived itself"; instead it called for the creation of a power "of the entire democracy," presumably including Bolsheviks. The same issue announced the formation of a Western Front KSR (Committee to Save the Revolution, parallel to the KSRR), but this body was based on an *accommodation* with the Minsk Bolsheviks, who received three places in it and it opposed any further movement of troops through its territory. Within four days congresses in all three of the armies gave results which divided the army committees roughly in half between those who recognized Soviet power and those who did not, but none supported the Provisional Government any longer. The Western Front Committee had always accommodated a substantial Bolshevik minority (10 members out of 25 to 30), and the army committees had all shifted sharply to the left before the coup, and thus were not disposed to give unequivocal support to the Provisional Government. After the army congresses it was out of the question.

There was a far broader base of support for the line of the OAK on the Southwestern Front. During the Kornilov crisis, Commissar Iordanskii and Committee Chairman Dashevskii had cooperated closely, thereby developing a strong sense of proprietorship over "revolutionary authority." Kerensky's "waverings" had caused them some problems, but they could easily identify with the line taken by the KSRR. Iordanskii was in constant touch with Stavka through political officer Vyrubov, and Dashevskii closely coordinated his actions with the OAK.[7] The front committee passed two resolutions on the current situation on October 27 and 28 respectively. The first condemned the Bolsheviks for disrupting elections to the Constituent Assembly and encouraging counter-revolution by dividing the

[5] *KA* 8:159-60.

[6] *GoXA*, October 27, but dated October 25, i.e., before receipt of the OAK appeal.

[7] See direct wire exchange of October 26-28 in *AR* 7:296-97, and *KA* 8:155-57 and 172-73.

forces of democracy, but failed to mention the Provisional Government or even VTsIK; in fact, it advocated energetic steps for peace and the immediate transfer of land to the land committees. The second, now aware of the formation of the KSRR and Kerensky's expedition, recognized the legitimacy of the Provisional Government but warned that it could avert further anarchy in the country and the army only if it gave real leadership to the longings of the masses for land and peace.[8]

Similar resolutions were passed by committees of the Eleventh, Seventh (both Southwestern Front), and Ninth (Rumanian Front) armies, though a full text is available only for the Eleventh, which urged the Provisional Government and the leading organs of democracy to "defend the Revolution against the small band of irresponsible Bolsheviks and other dark forces hiding behind their slogans."[9] This resolution was endorsed by expanded assemblies of the committees of the XXV and XXXII corps, and a number of regiments and divisions of the latter, prominently featured in their organ, *Golos Okopa*. However, the same issue that carried these resounding resolutions also carried an account of fraternization in the Volskii Regiment which the command broke up by shelling. The soldiers deserted the trenches en masse, demanded a cease-fire, and beat up a doctor and a noncom who tried to interfere. They afterward complained to the corps committee that their regimental committee "grievously errs in misrepresenting the mood of their comrades in corps and divisional sessions and thus deceives both themselves and higher authorities." This grotesque contrast between high-sounding resolutions and grim reality in parallel columns of a front newspaper underscores the fragile underpinnings for loyalist professions.[10]

Few divisions and corps on the Southwestern Front as yet supported the Bolsheviks, but many were doubtless like the 517th Batumskii Regiment of the Special Army, which on October 29 polled its companies and assembled representatives and found that with few exceptions the soldiers condemned the Bolshevik rising, but were also severely critical of the Provisional Government. Their conclusion was framed in the following resolution:

> The regimental committee after thorough discussion finds: (1) that the seizure of power by the Bolsheviks in Petrograd, leading to fratricidal war, was caused by the Provisional Government in deviating from the wishes of the majority of the democracy, and consequently it fell under the influence of the bourgeoisie; (2) that the forthcoming Con-

[8] See *IzOA* and *Iz7A* of October 29.
[9] *GO*, October 27.
[10] *Ibid.*, October 28.

> stituent Assembly is the sole authorized organ of the entire people, and it alone enjoys absolute power. Therefore, we demand of the Provisional Government that it without fail (1) convoke the Constituent Assembly at the scheduled time, (2) allows all parties in the country and the Army to campaign freely for their candidates in the elections, (3) undertake emergency measures to bring about a speedy peace, which alone can bring us out of economic chaos, (4) turn the land over to the land committees, (5) in the future listen only to the voice of the people and execute its will, and (6) any armed intervention from any quarter whatsoever is to be regarded as a death blow against the people.[11]

When committees took the trouble to sound out their constituencies, the response was not necessarily sympathetic to the Bolsheviks, but it was always disenchanted with the existing leadership and determined to be heard. Though the Constituent Assembly was accepted as the final arbiter, the critical issues of land and peace had to be resolved immediately, as the popular will was already manifest. This particular set of demands, recurring with remarkable frequency, reflected the efforts of much-harried lower committeemen to accommodate the assertive mood of the masses, and by this time had worked its way up a considerable swath of the democratic organizations.

Though the Eleventh and Seventh army committees seemed ready to follow the lead of the front committee and the OAK, the Special Army Committee, sobered by the mounting evidence of the mass mood, sharply shifted ground on the eve of the Petrograd uprising. A conference of divisional and corps committees on October 23-24, already aware of the planned Bolshevik uprising, condemned it as a "manifest attempt to disrupt the elections to the Constituent Assembly." It did not expect the floundering Provisional Government to measure up to the crisis and therefore resolved to "take upon ourselves active participation in the reconstitution of authority, not only at the front but also in the rear," and for this purpose it proposed the immediate convocation of an Army Congress. When the uprising did take place, the army committee set up an "Operative Commission" to assume complete control of military communications and manage all noncombat affairs in the Special Army; again harshly condemning the Bolsheviks and the cowardly garrison, it said not a word in defense of the Provisional Government.[12]

A number of army committees began to interpret events in the capital as a sign of the incapacity of the presently constituted government to cope

[11] TsGVIA, f. 3054, op. 2, d. 23, part 2 (*protokoly* of October 29).

[12] *IzOA*, October 27 and 28.

with "anarchy" in the form of plundering goods, wine riots, strikes in vital services, indiscipline in the garrisons, and general irresponsibility of the political leadership, all of which suggested that the "front" must take the initiative in restoring political authority in the country, in the first instance by taking control of their own units. The tendency to substitute committee power for fractured government power was most pronounced on the Rumanian Front. Here the Sixth Army Committee responded even more decisively than the Special Army. The following telegram, signed jointly with Commissar Liperovskii and the army commander, General Tsurikov, was addressed to all commands and lower committees:

> Part of the Petrograd garrison has revolted against the Provisional Government. The Northern Front is sending troops. Establish control over telegraph and radio. Undertake on your own authority all measures worked out at the conference of October 20 of the army committee and representatives of corps and divisional committees.[13]

Though there is no record of the October 20 conference, the three pivots of authority—command, commissars, and committees—had obviously collaborated in working out a contingency plan, ignoring their respective superiors, which anticipated the present situation and in essence ascribed "all power" in the army to the committees. The following day (October 27) the army committee passed a new resolution revealing how far removed its thinking was from the loyalist sentiments of the OAK:

> Discussing the events in Petrograd, the army committee declares (1) that the collapse of the coalition power was the result of its indecisive foreign policy, (2) that an authoritative revolutionary power must rest on all layers of the revolutionary democracy [i.e., including Bolsheviks], and (3) that all census elements must be excluded from power.

It also gave the highest political priority to convocation of the Constituent Assembly as scheduled and a "decisive struggle for peace."[14] The outlined program in essence anticipated what was to become the consensus of a good share of the committee public during the Vikzhel negotiations, and somewhat tardily of the OAK itself.

The IV Siberian Corps of the same army displayed the same spirit of localist independence and accommodation to the mood of the masses. Its official organ, *IzSK*, noted on October 22 that many units in the corps and on the Rumanian Front were demanding "immediate peace and the transfer of power to the Soviets," otherwise the troops threatened to desert the

[13] *VGr*, October 25.

[14] *Ibid.*, October 27.

trenches; this fact, combined with the obvious Bolshevik intention to seize power in the capital, made it imperative that "the Provisional Government and higher revolutionary organs reckon seriously with these threatening signs and take decisive steps to liquidate the war, regardless of how the Allies might react."[15] On October 28 an expanded session of the corps committee resolved that "the half measures and vacillating policy of collaboration with bourgeois groups . . . have reduced to nothing the accomplishments of the Revolution, and have failed to advance the cause of peace." Only those parties accepting a program of land and peace should participate in the reconstruction of the government. Until this was accomplished, all power locally was to be vested in a "Temporary Revolutionary Executive Committee for the Salvation of the Revolution" to consist of nine persons nominated by the committee who would enjoy the "broadest possible powers." The intent to force this policy on higher committees was evident in a request for support from neighboring corps and divisions.[16]

This survey of initial reactions demonstrates the rapid erosion of support for the Provisional Government in the committees at the front, even if recast according to the formulae of the KSRR and the OAK. On the Northern Front, Iskosol was totally isolated from the outset, the Western Front promptly shifted toward accommodation with the Bolsheviks, serious defections were materializing on the Southwestern and Rumanian fronts, and everywhere a new independent leftward course was making itself felt. Though Bolshevism was not everywhere instantaneously ascendant, it was certainly favored by the trend of events. The only possible political outcome had to be some sort of power based on the authority of the Soviets, discarding forever the idea of a coalition with bourgeois groups, and a commitment to a radically left program that included peace, land, and a "democratization" of the Army. For a critical period it seemed that the "Vikzhel solution" was a viable alternative to Bolshevik dictatorship. That it did not materialize must not be ascribed to Bolshevik (rather Lenin's) intransigence alone, but also to the serious political miscalculations of the moderate socialist groups and leaders.

☆

As long as there seemed to be some hope for the success of the Kerensky expedition, the OAK was cool to the Vikzhel's overtures, which were addressed to them directly by Vikzhel representatives at Stavka.[17] With

[15] On October 14 the corps committee itself had passed a resolution calling for an immediate armistice and an appeal to all belligerents to enter into peace negotiations (see *VKDA*, pp. 365-66).

[16] TsGVIA, f. 2282, op. 5, d. 11, l. 31 (Committee Journal, October 29). See also below, p. 370.

[17] The complete teletape of the exchange was published in *RF*, November 2. The con-

the collapse of the KSRR prospects in Petrograd and the decidedly ambiguous responses of the committees at the front, the Vikzhel alternative suddenly appeared more attractive. The OAK followed the Vikzhel negotiations in Petrograd very closely and on November 1 announced their full collaboration. It appears that the OAK representatives even applied pressure on the intransigent elements of the KSRR and the S.R. and Menshevik parties to bargain in good faith on Bolshevik participation in an all-socialist government.[18] Henceforward, the OAK was strongly allied with Vikzhel in pressing for the "all-socialist government from the Popular Socialists to the Bolsheviks," which was to be accountable to a long list of democratic organizations and committed to the threefold program of immediate convocation of the Constituent Assembly, immediate proposals on peace terms to all belligerents, and immediate transfer of all the land to the land committees. The progress and ultimate breakup of these negotiations were carefully chronicled in the daily "bulletins" of the OAK, and when the negotiations finally ceased on November 5, the Vikzhel team and leading figures of the socialist parties and the KSRR (Chernov, Avksentiev, Skobelev, Stankevich) transferred their operations to Stavka. The OAK then attempted to assume national leadership in constructing an all-socialist government built around the premiership of Chernov.[19]

☆

By the beginning of November the Bolsheviks had weathered the initial challenges to their power and were successfully pursuing a delaying tactic in the Vikzhel negotiations. The upheaval in the committees at the front had already denied moral as well as armed support to the old democracy, but whether the baton could be successfully passed on to the Bolsheviks remained to be seen. Generally speaking, committee revolutions took place on the Northern and Western fronts in a matter of days in a series of hastily called army congresses, in every case turning out the former leadership, but only in the Second Army yielding a firm Bolshevik majority. Elsewhere control was finely balanced with other leftist fractions, giving Bolsheviks a slight edge, while the party forces of the Bolsheviks were not as yet well organized. In the Fifth Army they held a formal majority, but some of their number wavered toward unity sentiments; in the First and Third armies

frontation was sharp: the OAK representative insisted that "neutrality only benefits the Bolsheviks," while the Vikzhel spokesman replied that without an agreement the railroad workers would strike; the OAK spokesman rejoined: "We know at least six lines that will not obey you." See also *BOAK*, October 31, in Lelevich, *Oktiabr' v Stavke*, Prilozhenie (Appendix).

[18] See *BOAK*, November 3.

[19] For the outcome of these efforts, see below, pp. 397-98, and colorful account in Oliver Radkey, *The Sickle Under the Hammer* (New York, 1963), pp. 73ff.

they shared control with other left fractions, and unity sentiments were pronounced, while the "congresses" of the Twelfth and Tenth armies, not yet based on fresh elections of lower committees, were so evenly divided between pro- and anti-Bolshevik elements that compromise arrangements were worked out pending new congresses on November 12 and 7 respectively. The latter finally yielded decisive Bolshevik majorities. On the Southwestern, Rumanian, and Caucasus fronts the process dragged out for weeks and resulted in the characteristic patchwork pattern of power that will be dealt with in the following chapter. Here of concern is the process of the consolidation of power on the two fronts where the Bolsheviks gained unquestioned ascendancy in the electoral process.

In the first half of 1917, the Northern Front was the haven of the strongest Bolshevik organizations, but also of the most ardently defensist army committees. The Riga disaster bred an instinctive defensism in the Bolshevik groups, while in October the soldiers' disenchantment with the politics as usual and the spontaneous longing for peace were forcing themselves on the committee structure. Of the three constituent armies, the Twelfth was most critical, as it had been the most highly politicized previously, the Latvian brigades and the Novoladozhskii Regiment forming the nucleus of a strong Bolshevik network, while Iskosol had been the best organized of the army committees. Iskosol, though disoriented since the retreat, was firmly ensconced at the army headquarters in Valka and enjoyed the advantages of command patronage and ready access to the staff communications network, whereas the Bolsheviks had nothing comparable. Prior to the uprising, both sides were girding themselves for the expected confrontation at the army congress scheduled for October 28 in Cesis, a Latvian town just behind the new front. When news of the uprising hit the front, the machinery for the congress was already in place, the deputies were selected, the instructions (such as they were) were already worked out. Iskosol carefully monitored the flow of information through the staff media, while desperately trying to locate loyal troops; meanwhile, the Bolshevik Military Organization situated in Cesis learned of events circuitously and imperfectly via the Estonian and Latvian Social Democratic networks.

On October 26, *ON* carried an announcement of the Twelfth Army Bolshevik Military Organization: "The ice is broken! The river has begun to flow!" Later the same day a proclamation announced the formation of a Military Revolutionary Committee (MRC) of the region of the Twelfth Army. It was composed of the various civilian and military Latvian organizations, the Bolshevik Military Organization, and the Left Bloc of the Twelfth Army Soviet, and its declared goal was to prevent troops from the Twelfth Army from being sent to put down the heroic struggle of Red

Petrograd, though specific information was lacking. In the next twenty-four hours the Bolshevik Military Organization caught up with essential communiqués, including the key radiogram of the Petrograd MRC announcing the overthrow of Kerensky's government: the latter called on all soldiers to report to revolutionary bodies suspicious activities of their officers and to arrest all who openly opposed the new government of Soviets.[20] Though a considerable role in directing the struggle in the Twelfth Army is ascribed to the Cesis-based MRC in Soviet works, only the actions of the Latvian brigades are well documented. Probably its chief activity for the moment was to agitate on behalf of Soviet power through *OP* (now reappearing under its old name) and the Riflers' *Latwju Strehlneeks*, in order to counteract the doctored version of events of Iskosol and the command network.

Sometime on October 25 the committees of the Latvian brigades were alerted to carry out their previously agreed upon mission of occupying the key towns and railroad junctions of the rear—Cesis, Valmiera, Iurev, and Valka. The operation in the First Brigade (First and Third regiments) went smoothly: the few unsympathetic officers were arrested and replaced by reliable nominees. The brigade commander, Colonel Penike, cooperated fully, issuing appropriate marching orders but claiming to his superiors that he acted under duress.[21] Things went less smoothly in the Second Brigade (Sixth and Seventh regiments), which were earmarked to occupy army headquarters at Valka, as one regimental commander and most of the officers refused to cooperate; moreover, in and around Valka were stationed the Fifth and 17th cavalry divisions and several units of shock troops (armored cars from Pernov were on their way), so that a real battle was in prospect. Nevertheless, General Iuzefovich was obliged to ignore Kerensky's orders to part with his last reserve troops to reinforce the Gatchina operation, so the net effect of the Latvian brigades' action was to sink the fortunes of the Provisional Government.[22] On October 29 the reserve unit occupied Iurev, giving the Latvian units effective control over both rail lines leading from the Twelfth Army region to the rear via Pskov

[20] Details in Kaimin', *Latyshskie strelki*, pp. 315ff. Documents including announcement in *ON* in *KPLOR*, pp. 493-98. Text of Petrograd MRC radiogram in *ORA*, pp. 14-15.

[21] *ORA*, pp. 21-22. Penike's official report explained: "Around 5:30 A.M. today a representative of the MRC appeared at staff headquarters accompanied by a company from the Vidzemskii Regiment, disarmed the officers of the staff, and declared that they received an order for the First and Third regiments to occupy Venden [Cesis]. Since power was now in the hands of the Petrograd Soviet of Workers' and Soldiers' Deputies, they claimed that all orders of the brigade staff must be under the control of their MRC. Guards have been posted on the telephones, and all conversations are monitored." Text of Penike's order of the day, which appears to cooperate with the MRC, is cited in Kaimin', p. 318.

[22] See Iuzefovich's report to Cheremisov of October 28 in *KA* 23:118.

(a line along the coast from Reval to Petrograd still lay open). The occupation of the army headquarters in Valka, however, was not to take place until November 5.[23]

On October 28 the army congress assembled in Cesis in surroundings controlled by the Bolsheviks. The luminaries of Iskosol, Kuchin and Kharash, were present, as was Victor Chernov, just then making a tour of the front, while Nakhimson was the chief spokesman for the Bolsheviks. The atmosphere surrounding the Lutheran church where the sessions were held was extraordinarily tense; large numbers of curious soldiers, armed and unarmed, milled about, while patrols of Latvian brigaders moved through the city streets and stood guard at the premises.[24] The opening skirmish over the chairmanship, accompanied by much shouting and confusion, revealed the even split in the congress: the first vote gave the Bolsheviks a majority of one vote and Nakhimson took the chair; the opposition set up such a din that a re-vote was taken, which gave them the chair.

Both factions presented resolutions on the "current moment" over which debate raged for two days. The resolution of the Left Bloc denounced the "hellish plan of the bourgeoisie and the commanding staff to open up the front to the German imperialist robbers . . . to drown socialist Petrograd in blood," and claimed that only Soviet power and "iron defense" by revolutionary troops could thwart this plan. It hailed the land and peace decrees of the Soviet Congress as great victories, and called for the abolition of the death penalty, the "complete democratization of the army, and the purging of the commanding staff of all counter-revolutionary elements." While it ruled out any further coalition with census elements, it was curiously vague on where power was to reside: ignoring the Second Congress, the Petrograd MRC, and Sovnarkom, it called for a government of "workers, soldiers, and peasants responsible to VTsIK"; power was not yet claimed for local Soviet bodies (under the formula "all power to the Soviets"), whereas the speedy convocation of the Constituent Assembly occupied a prominent place.[25] Perhaps the Twelfth Army Bolsheviks were still uncertain over the outcome of the contest in Petrograd, or they were already yielding to the shaping "no civil war" sentiment, but either way it reflected hesitancy and uncertainty on the part of the Twelfth Army Bolsheviks.

The opposing resolution of Iskosol condemned the Bolshevik seizure of power and called for support of the KSRR, but it ignored the plight of

[23] Further details in Kaimin', *loc. cit.*

[24] See account of T. Ia. Draudin in *ONFV*, p. 81, who apparently was a participant. Most complete Soviet account is Kapustin, *Soldaty Severnogo fronta*, pp. 272-75, which is based on *OP*, November 15, the only cited record of the proceedings.

[25] Text in *RDRA*, pp. 385-86.

Kerensky and the Provisional Government; in fact, it called for a new government of "united democracy" until the Constituent Assembly, which should work for a speedy peace and turn land over to the land committees. Thus, it was following the general movement of democratic organizations, like them too late and too little. The assembly voted 248 to 243 in favor of the Iskosol resolution. Though the antagonists seemed almost exactly balanced, it soon became obvious that the hard-line Bolsheviks were obliged to yield to a considerable Left S.R. and moderate Bolshevik contingent. Serious negotiations took place, brokered by the moderates from both sides, over the composition of a new Iskosol and the terms of a temporary accommodation.

A new temporary Iskosol was to be based on equal representation of both blocs at the congress, but only on the condition that no members of the old Iskosol serve on it. Once that issue was settled, a detailed compromise proposed by the Left S.R.'s was readily accepted: (1) "political neutrality" by the front army and "not one soldier" to either side of the opposing camps outside Petrograd, (2) the "old power is dead" and should be replaced by an "all-socialist government from the revolutionary democracy," (3) complete freedom of the press and agitation during the Constituent Assembly elections, (4) "unrestricted authority" for the new Iskosol in the region of the Twelfth Army, and (5) a new congress to convene on November 14 based on new elections: the final and most revealing point, however, was "the immediate disbanding of all other organizations claiming executive functions, that is, any sort of MRCs." In fact, it specifically forbade the MRCs to undertake arrests, confiscations, or any other arbitrary actions with the use of force. It seemed an almost incredible act of forbearance on the part of the Bolsheviks, considering their large measure of de facto power through the Latvian organizations, but the alternative would have been to sacrifice the legitimacy of an accomplished committee revolution. In return they had secured an official repudiation of the old government (no rescue operations for Kerensky) and the definitive demise of the old Iskosol; moreover, they could temporize with disbanding their MRC and await the outcome of events.[26]

When the new Iskosol formally instructed the Latvian regiments to return to the front, the Bolshevik MRC refused to cooperate, and its members never took their seats in Iskosol, while the brigades remained in place. Thus a rump Iskosol headed by the Left S.R. Medvedev took up residence at Valka, while *RF* continued for a time to support the KSRR and to publish resolutions condemning the Bolsheviks (and none in favor), including a

[26] Texts of both Iskosol and compromise resolutions in *RF*, November 2. Mentioned in Iuzefovich-Cheremisov, November 1, *KA* 24:73-74.

few of Kerensky's orders from Gatchina. Only with Kerensky's collapse on November 3 did it shift to "neutrality" and defend the decisions of the army congress.[27] The Bolsheviks moved very cautiously for the time being, undertaking no new military actions and avoiding armed clashes, as they doubtless respected the deep anxiety of the soldiers over the possibility of civil war. They were probably encouraged by the fact that General Iuzefovich's repeated requests for reinforcements from the XLIX Corps (near Reval) had gone unheeded, that a regiment of his cavalry defected to the Bolsheviks and others were shaky, and that his sole remaining shock battalion had been summoned to Pskov to secure the transfer point.[28]

The delay in the occupation of Valka was ascribed by the Soviet historian Kaimin' to the treachery of officers and the lack of experts who knew where to place the artillery, but in fact, finally, on November 5 the Second Brigade talked its way in, in marching order to the accompaniment of martial music.[29] On November 7 Chief of Staff General A. A. Posokhov reported to Northern Front headquarters that the army was now divided into "two equal halves" and that the 14th and 17th Siberian Rifle regiments were now under the control of MRCs; a similar dispatch of November 14 acknowledged that MRCs existed in all parts of the army and that the results of the upcoming congress would "undoubtedly strengthen the authority of the Army MRC and consequently the number of units no longer subject to command authority." Since Posokhov mentions no overt clashes, one can infer that both parties agreed to live and let live, awaiting the outcome of the new army congress.[30] As expected, the latter ratified the positions of the Left Bloc on every issue by a large majority (396 to 123, with 26 abstentions on a typical vote) and in effect, after a long delay, legitimized the authority of the Bolshevik MRC. Nakhimson now took over as chairman of Iskosol, augmenting his role as chief of the MRC, which now was recognized as wielding supreme executive power on behalf of Sovnarkom over the territory of the Twelfth Army, while the regional Latvian Soviet, controlled by the Latvian Social Democratic Party and represented in the MRC, functioned as the civil authority.[31]

On the recently reconstituted First Army, with its headquarters in the Latvian village of Vitsgolben (Altshvanenberg) to the immediate south,

[27] See *RF*, November 5, and Kapustin, p. 274.

[28] *KA* 24:74-75 (Iuzefovich-Chermisov, November 1 and 4).

[29] Kaimin', pp. 334-36. There is a curious discrepancy between the lengthy discussion of the tactical difficulties and the ease with which it was consummated, deepening the mystery of why there was a delay of nearly ten days.

[30] *VRKDA*, pp. 154 and 161 (confirms the picture of "march-in").

[31] Account in Kapustin, pp. 277-80, based on *RF*, November 22 and 23, and *OP*, November 19, neither of which were available to me. Text of main resolution in *KPLOR*, pp. 535-36.

there is little information prior to the Petrograd coup: a military report of October 22 recorded disorders in the 51st and 184th divisions, and another report of October 27 described the army as exhausted, bitter, and determined to end the war without delay. Committees were characterized as generally willing to support discipline but totally without influence, while "the great majority of replacements are . . . badly instructed and shot through with strong Bolshevik tendencies."[32] The army committee, apparently newly elected, responded with immediate enthusiasm to the news of the Petrograd uprising: "Having discussed the situation in the country, the First Army Committee . . . regards the new revolutionary power in the form of the Petrograd revolutionary committee as legitimate . . . and regards its orders and instructions as binding and subject to immediate execution." They had obviously received the radiogram of the Petrograd MRC of October 25, but did not yet know of the outcome of the Second Congress of Soviets. The army committee immediately reconstituted itself as an MRC, removed the commissar of the Provisional Government, assumed "full civil and political powers," including "control over the commanding staff," and instructed lower committees to do the same. At the same time, it called for "strict revolutionary order," resolute defense of the front, and an orderly continuation of work on elections to the Constituent Assembly. Nevertheless, the chairman, Ossovskii, was a Left S.R. and the committee was of mixed party composition, with Left S.R.'s and Menshevik Internationalists predominating.[33]

The committee promptly convoked an army congress on October 30, which proved to be exactly evenly split between Bolsheviks and non-Bolshevik leftists (old-line defensists were absent). The congress declared itself in favor of Soviet power both in the center and locally on the basis of a coalition of all socialist parties. Kerensky's government was declared devoid of authority, and the KSRR was denounced for not recognizing the Second Congress of Soviets.[34] Ritual endorsements on land, peace, and the Constituent Assembly followed. However, the congress was divided on whether to send armed aid to the Soviet government: the Bolsheviks and the Left S.R.'s presented opposing resolutions. They compromised by sending deputations to both sides to plea for a peaceful resolution of the conflict, but Kerensky was definitely to step down or be forced out. However, if "counter-revolutionaries" made a move on Petrograd, up to half the units of the First Army were to be sent to support the new power. When they learned of Kerensky's defeat the following day, they called for

[32] *RDRA*, p. 548.

[33] *TrSh* 1:433-34, and *VRKDA*, p. 134.

[34] See *IzlA*, November 23; main resolution in *VKDA*, p. 392.

an all-socialist coalition based on the new VTsIK elected at the Second Congress of Soviets, roughly the position of the Left S.R.'s and moderate Bolsheviks during the Vikzhel negotiations.[35]

Though Voitov, a Bolshevik, was elected chairman, the First Army MRC followed a temporizing, nonpartisan line; its official organ, *IzlA*, covered mainly the Constituent Assembly elections, the Ukrainian question, and other secondary mattters, and not once paid tribute to Sovnarkom as the official government; it even published without comment a resolution of the former army committee denouncing the Bolshevik government for entering into negotiations for a "despicable separate peace" and instituting political terror.[36] Resolutions of lower committees also chiefly called for nonpartisan support for Soviet power, for example, of the First and Third Caucasus Rifle regiments (October 26 and November 2), the 60th and 185th divisions (November 6 and 8), and staff units of the XX Army Corps (November 9).[37] Unqualified support of the orthodox Bolshevik position was not evident in the First Army until after the armistice.

Although the committee victory in the Fifth Army of mid-October allowed the Bolsheviks more freedom to maneuver, it did not give them much real power. The command and the commissars functioned independently, and there was more or less a standoff until the Soviet Congress.[38] The Bolsheviks on the army committee were in direct communication with Smolnyi on the night of October 25, and at 9:00 P.M., as events were still unfolding, they sent telegrams to all units of the army proclaiming the advent of Soviet power.[39] They declared committees to be the guardian of Soviet power, for which purpose commissars responsible to the army committee were to be chosen in each unit. At the same time they urged soldiers to defend the front, avoid violence against officers, and execute only orders countersigned by the authorized commissars. The message was signed "the Bolshevik fraction of the army committee and the Bolshevik Military Organization," but the following day a new proclamation identified an MRC as the executive organ of the Fifth Army Committee in pursuance

[35] All according to account in *Pr*, November 5, reprinted in *TrSh* 1:442-43. Text of resolution in *VOSR. Vosstanie*, p. 778.

[36] See *IzlA*, November 25.

[37] See *ORA*, pp. 20, 44, 67, 70, and 89.

[38] Sklianskii and several key Bolsheviks were in Petrograd for the Second Congress, leaving the less-experienced Captain Sediakin and a twenty-two-year-old soldier, Shapurin, in charge. See the latter's account in *ONFV*, pp. 106-7.

[39] See telegrams in *PVRK* 1:122 and *TrSh* 1:433; confirmed by General A. P. Budberg in "Dnevnik barona Alekseiia Budberga," *AR* 12 (1923): 229-30 (this represents a fragment of his voluminous manuscript memoirs on deposit at HI and frequently cited above). For decision of the army committee of October 25 to ready an expeditionary force, see *VKDA*, p. 321.

of instructions of the Soviet Congress.[40] Response to one or the other of these proclamations was very widespread. The first was read and discussed on October 26 by the committee of the XXXVII Corps, which chose its own commissar and instructed each division and regiment to do the same.[41] General Budberg, commander of the XIII Corps, records that a commissar and watches were posted to his headquarters, which he accepted with equanimity and supposed they existed elsewhere. His commissar behaved with circumspection, promising to uphold the authority of the commanding staff in purely military matters, whereas Budberg was expected "not to get involved in politics."[42]

Thus far in the Fifth Army, Bolsheviks followed the instructions of the Petrograd MRC with exactitude, but as news of the Kerensky expedition spread, the Bolsheviks behaved with considerably more hesitancy. First, non-Bolsheviks on the army committee hotly disputed the Bolshevik version of events in Petrograd and insisted on the distribution of *all* telegrams, including those of Kerensky. Second, as General Budberg noted in his diary on that day, while the soldier masses rejoiced at the overthrow of Kerensky, they were "against the Bolsheviks taking power for themselves, and in fact favored giving power solely to the Central Executive Committee of the Soviet."[43] The Bolsheviks were also shaken by the fact that railroad workers, hearing that the army committee intended to send their own troops to the capital, tore up 10 kilometers of track.[44] Furthermore, General Boldyrev began to chafe at controls, reporting to Cheremisov, "At first they tried to take charge and countersign my orders but, having received my categorical refusal, have given it up."[45] Cheremisov boldly asked Boldyrev to put an MRC representative on the wire and extracted a promise that no further interference would occur. When he asked point-blank whether the army committee was sending troops to oppose Kerensky, the MRC spokesman replied that "the army committee has taken a neutral position" and wished above all to "avoid slaughter."

The Fifth Army Bolsheviks, however, were only suffering from momentary confusion and soon reversed their stand. On the evening of October 28 they received a direct appeal from the Petrograd MRC to send troops to counter Kerensky, but when they raised the issue in the army committee

[40] *VRKDA*, p. 135, for the latter proclamation.

[41] *ORA*, pp. 18-19. On the 77th Regiment informing the Fifth Army MRC that it had elected a commissar in response to the order, see *ibid.*, p. 21.

[42] Budberg, *AR* 12:230-31 (diary entry of October 26).

[43] See *ibid.*, p. 234.

[44] See circular telegram of November 2 (*VRKDA*, p. 147), which acknowledges the fact and reassures units that a peaceful solution is being sought.

[45] *KA* 23:192 (undated, but October 27 or 28).

they were voted down by a bare majority, one or two of the Bolsheviks apparently defecting. The Bolsheviks withdrew from the army committee, but still in their capacity as the MRC they tried to raise a force from the pro-Bolshevik Fourth Special Division and the 488th Regiment.[46] When Boldyrev, responding to urgent new demands from Kerensky, tried to dispatch the Third Ural Cossacks and the First Armored Car Division stationed in Dvinsk, the fortunes of the Bolsheviks were restored, as the alarm over civil war again gave the Bolsheviks control within the army committee. By a majority of three votes it now approved the readying of twelve battalions of infantry, machine-gunners, and support units.[47]

When Boldyrev refused to approve the necessary operative orders, the army committee ordered his arrest along with that of Commissar Pirogov. Boldyrev countered by calling on loyal units to interdict the Bolshevik expeditionary force.[48] Though the encounter was a standoff, the news of Kerensky's flight rendered the issue moot—the Bolshevik MRC again gained control and Boldyrev again became a hostage.[49] The net effect of Boldyrev's actions was to shift the balance in lower committees of the Fifth Army decisively in favor of the Bolsheviks. The committee of the 70th Division voted on October 29 to "put its bayonets at the disposal of the military organization of the Bolsheviks of the Fifth Army." The 38th Division must have made a similar determination around the same time, as on November 3 the committee of the 151st Regiment discussed and approved it.[50] Budberg notes that his corps came back under the control of the Bolsheviks on November 4 and that the next day a new commissar from the MRC arrived.[51]

No sooner did the Bolsheviks take charge, however, than the limited nature of their authority became apparent. On November 1, the 277th Regiment carried out its long-standing threat to take up quarters in Dvinsk by force, ignoring a direct order of the Bolshevik Commissar Sobakin to replace the 18th Division on the line; when he tried "persuasion" the soldiers of the regiment threatened to drown him in the Dvina. A similar fate befell a Bolshevik commissar in the 480th Regiment. Budberg noted in his diary that the Bolshevik commissars were obliged to resort to "old

[46] Text of appeal in *VOSR. Vosstanie*, p. 689. Report on action of the army MRC by Chief of Staff Popov to Northern Front headquarters on October 29, *ibid.*, 631.

[47] See Dukhonin-Baranovskii of October 31, *ibid.*, p. 649.

[48] Popov-Baranovskii, October 30, *KA* 23:190.

[49] Details in Boldyrev-Cheremisov of November 1, *KA* 24:71-72, and Dukhonin-Baranovskii of October 31, *VOSR. Vosstanie*, pp. 650-51.

[50] See *RDRA*, pp. 28-29 and 56-57.

[51] *AR* 12:240 and 243. That on this day there was probably a general directive of the MRC proclaiming power in the Fifth Army on behalf of Sovnarkom, see Kapustin, p. 284, who cites an undated archival source.

regime'' methods to enforce their authority.[52] In fact, the Fifth Army Bolsheviks were floundering like their counterparts elsewhere for lack of clear direction from the center, where the Bolsheviks were still divided over the Vikzhel negotiations and Sovnarkom had not yet asserted itself as the organ of Soviet power.

Though each army on the Northern Front had followed a distinct pattern, the underlying forces were everywhere very much the same. The Bolshevik peace program was an irresistible allurement to the masses which could be countered only by imitation. Although the Bolsheviks' single-minded pursuit of this issue paid handsome dividends in by-elections and general popularity, they faced definite limits to their capacity to act in their own name and pursue the tactics prescribed from Petrograd. Menshevik Internationalists, Left S.R.'s, or anyone committed to immediate peace could get elected as readily as Bolsheviks. The masses, though bewildered by the conflicting versions of events in the capital, were very clear on certain matters. They definitively rejected government based on coalition with the bourgeoisie or the personal authority of Kerensky, and they welcomed the proclamation of Soviet power once the confusion had lifted, as it was irrevocably identified with peace. The Bolsheviks were broadly perceived as its champions, but no ill will was harbored toward other socialist parties, whose factional divisions were but hazily understood. Instinctively the masses felt that any squabbling among the socialists could only benefit counter-revolution, which they were persuaded was waiting in the wings. Thus, they were not too patient with Bolshevik partisanship toward the S.R.'s and Mensheviks or vice versa, and gave little credit to the accusations they hurled at each other.

Consequently, in a number of instances front Bolsheviks, despite the wishes of Lenin to the contrary, followed a conciliatory line on sharing power within the democratic organizations to obtain a tactical advantage for their program. For the most part they did not have a clear line of conduct laid down by instructions from authoritative party organs, but took their cue from the few radioed and telegraphed proclamations that got through, and otherwise improvised as events unfolded. Well-instructed party figures were a rarity, but the apparent exception, Nakhimson, had consented to the remarkably lenient compromise in the Twelfth Army. In the Fifth Army the enthusiasm of the Bolsheviks for armed intervention cooled rapidly when it threatened to erode their base of support in the committees, and they were rescued only by the corresponding military moves of their opponents. In the end the arms of either side counted for little; inertia, not militance, defeated Kerensky. The soldiers demonstrated

[52] *AR* 12:240-41 and 243-44.

by their inaction that they did not wish to see matters resolved by force of arms.

The mandate, if there was one, was not for Bolshevik power but for Soviet power and peace, or, alternatively, the Constituent Assembly and peace or any variety of a socialist (as opposed to coalition) government, so long as it stood for the same basic program. It was assumed that if all socialist parties agreed to a settlement, counter-revolution was impossible and peace was secure. The consciousness of Soviet power being vested in Sovnarkom as ratified by the Second Congress of Soviets had not yet taken firm root due to the confusion and delay of communications, but the general concept of Soviet power was well understood and approved. MRCs, whether still purely Bolshevik or authorized by the committee structure, were not yet widely perceived as legitimate extensions of democratic Soviet power. By the second week in November there was a certainty that the old authorities had passed into oblivion forever, but the shape of the new Soviet power was yet to be determined. Given the current mood of the soldier masses, the predilections of committeemen of all stripes, including many Bolsheviks, and the politics swirling around the Vikzhel negotiations, a settlement based on the idea of an all-socialist coalition and the ''Soviet'' program of land and peace seemed a far greater likelihood than a settlement based on a Bolshevik dictatorship with a Left S.R. adjunct. The solidification of Bolshevik power under the umbrella of Soviet power was the result of developments still to be discussed, namely, the collapse of the Vikzhel negotiatons, Lenin's dramatic telegram to General Dukhonin removing him as Commander in Chief for refusal to initiate armistice negotiations, and the invitation sanctioned by Sovnarkom to every regiment to initiate its own negotiations on peace.

☆

On the Western Front the ''Bolshevik mood'' of the masses was reaching a climax precisely at the time of the Petrograd uprising, and it led to prompt Bolshevik ascendancy within the committee structure in all three armies. A conciliationist front committee lingered on until a front congress renewed its membership on November 20, but the Bolshevik-dominated Minsk Soviet formed their own MRC on November 1 and established control over front headquarters by November 5. Its authority was immediately recognized by the Second Army Committee and shortly by the other two. The Constituent Assembly elections yielded a 66 percent majority for the Bolsheviks, a higher total than for any other front. Yet many of the same ambiguities were present as on the Northern Front, and reality was even further removed from official Soviet hagiography.

The ritual account faithfully followed in numerous fragmentary (and heavily edited) memoirs is that the Minsk Soviet, under resolute Bolshevik leadership, responded immediately to the radiogram of the Petrograd MRC, proclaimed Soviet power in the region, released imprisoned Bolsheviks and soldiers, formed them into a "revolutionary regiment," seized the primary institutions, assigned commissars, occupied the staff headquarters of the Western Front, placed General Baluev under firm "control," formed their own MRC, and invited all public organizations and military units that recognized Soviet power to join it—all on October 27.[53] In other words, events replicated the Petrograd pattern. But a week intervened before the new revolutionary authority actually functioned, because in the interim a rival Committee to Save the Revolution (KSR) claimed power for itself and was recognized by the command, the commissariat, most committees, and, curiously, by the Minsk Soviet itself. During this period no MRC functioned and the Minsk Soviet quietly relaxed its claims to power. The standard accounts claim that the command in collaboration with Front Commissar Zhdanov and the Menshevik-S.R. majority of the front committee moved into Minsk an overwhelming military force, comprised (according to some accounts) of as many as 20,000 troops, variously identified as the Second Caucasus Cavalry Division, shock battalions, the "Savage Division," "Tekhintsy," Cossacks, Ukrainian units, Polish legions, or Ossetians, all with armored cars, artillery, and machine guns.[54] These accounts concede that there was a formal agreement between the KSR and the Minsk Soviet, but represent it as a mere ruse to give the Minsk Soviet time to call in its own troops (in other words, purely military considerations). On November 1, with the arrival of an armored train commandeered by loyal Bolsheviks and units of the 60th Siberian Regiment from the Second Army, the tide was turned, the KSR disbanded, the MRC asserted its total power, and by November 5 even General Baluev yielded to superior force, calling on his commanders to recognize Soviet power.[55]

The version bears an external resemblance to the facts, but the substance was quite different. Solskii, a Polish socialist who was close to the Minsk Bolshevik leadership, insists that most Minsk Bolsheviks, like Kamenev

[53] See Mints, *Istoriia*, 3:611-15; Gaponenko, *Soldatskie massy zapadnogo fronta*, pp. 116, 135-38; and *Pobeda sovetskoi vlasti v Belorussii* (Moscow, 1957), pp. 262-76. Even the memoir accounts in *BOB* are carefully tailored to fit the official version, though incongruities and contradictions can be detected.

[54] Lander cites the figure of 20,000 (*BOB*, p. 66) and other memoirists contribute various identifications of units; Mints (3:376) scrupulously records them all, including Lander's preposterous figure. Knorin, who names cossacks, artillerists, machine-gunners, and armored cars, perhaps inadvertently reveals the truth—that the defection of the Second Caucasus Division was the chief force and subsequently came over to the Soviet side (*BOB*, pp. 35 and 37).

[55] On Baluev's surrender, see his circular telegram enjoining subordinate commanders not to resist the controls of the MRC in *VOSRB* 2:109.

and Zinoviev, opposed the Petrograd uprising and sought to obstruct its implementation. Their unity sentiments, he claims, were quite genuine, and they conceived of Soviet power as shared by all parties represented in the Soviet; their chief hopes were pinned on the elections to the Constituent Assembly, where they had invested considerable efforts and anticipated (correctly) an impressive Bolshevik majority on the Western Front. He is also convinced that they entered the agreement with the KSR quite sincerely. Even K. I. Lander, he claims, who was closer to the Petrograd leaders than the others and had just returned from Petrograd on October 28, fully approved of cooperation with the KSR, which he regarded as a working arrangement until the convoking of the Constituent Assembly. He expected the Bolsheviks to dominate the latter, but if not, he was prepared to see it disbanded.[56]

The Minsk Bolsheviks certainly did receive the radiotelegram of the Petrograd MRC on October 25, and in reaction to it they proclaimed Soviet power in Minsk, but there is no hard evidence that they formed an MRC.[57] Under the authority of the Minsk Soviet they did free many prisoners, put patrols out on the streets, and in other respects laid claim to civil authority in the city and region. Solskii claims, however, that Miasnikov had acted on his own without consulting his party colleagues and that the latter reversed the decision and reached an accommodation.[58] It is also incontestable that garrison soldiers loyal to the Minsk Soviet temporarily occupied front headquarters and that General Baluev made no effort to resist them. It is interesting, however, that publicly the Minsk Soviet laid claim to authority only in "political questions" in the army and urged that "all military orders of an operative character of Front Commander Baluev are to be executed without question."[59] Baluev conveyed his own version to Dukhonin by direct wire on the 26th:

> Last night a telegram arrived from a revolutionary committee in Petrograd which has seized power and calls upon all troops to acknowledge its authority. . . . In Minsk the Soviet of Workers and Soldiers has taken power, but the front committee opposes them. I doubt that the front committee can gain the upper hand over the Soviet, because I cannot rely on the local garrison. . . . The 37th [Reserve] Regiment has posted a watch over me and has declared me and my entire staff

[56] Solskii Ms., pp. 192-93 and *passim*. This remarkable manuscript by a Polish socialist who supported the Bolsheviks and himself played a key role in the events described is a rare alternative to the official Soviet version.

[57] Radiogram and proclamation published in *Burevestnik*, October 27 (*VOSRB* 2:29-31).

[58] Solskii Ms., p. 211.

[59] Also in *Burevestnik*, October 27 (*VOSRB* 2:33-34).

> under arrest, and demands that I conduct my work under the control of their revolutionary staff. The situation is rotten and I have no idea how I can get out of it, as the commissar also can do nothing.[60]

Baluev's captivity, however, proved to be only temporary, as the front committee initiated a vigorous counter-offensive the same day, buoyed by the resolutions condemning the Bolsheviks which came in from the three armies.

Sometime during the day, troops loyal to the front committee moved into Minsk and patrolled the streets, and the patrols and guards of the local garrison disappeared as if by magic.[61] Just what units were involved in this operation and how many is impossible to determine because the documentary evidence is both conflicting and suspect, but it is certain that on October 27 a KSR was formed consisting of representatives of all democratic organizations, civil and military, and that it was based on a formal bargain with the Minsk Soviet whereby the latter agreed to yield power to the KSR.[62] The KSR's chief political position was that the "Revolutionary Committee" in Petrograd (presumably the MRC) and VTsIK immediately convoke a congress of all democratic organizations for the construction of a new power. For the time being no government would be recognized, and all authorities in the region of the Western Front, civil and military, would be subordinate to the sole authority of the KSR; the Minsk Soviet, on its part, would recognize the supremacy of the KSR and delegate its own representatives to it; both parties agreed that the ultimate resolution of legitimate power would be resolved in Petrograd, not on the Western Front, but meanwhile no troops should move through the territory of the Western Front to support either side in the current conflict.[63]

Several factors doubtless swayed the Bolsheviks to enter into this curious agreement. First, they were caught by surprise by the resolute action of the front committee and the quick evaporation of their support in the garrison units, and second, conciliatory sentiment was strong in their own ranks. They now knew of the formation of the KSRR in Petrograd and of

[60] *AR* 7:315.

[61] See above, note 54. An account published in *Zvezda*, November 1, the only contemporary documentation, refers only to "cavalry companies" having been called in to which the garrison soldiers yielded "to avoid bloodshed" (see *VOSRB* 2:69).

[62] The official announcement with details of the agreement (but no text) was published in *Fr* on October 28, which is the only contemporary record.

[63] Knorin had at his disposal the text of the agreement, which he cites extensively, but either through genuine confusion or subsequent editing it is characterized as an agreement between the Front MRC and the Regional Soviet, which makes no sense because both were already Bolshevik-controlled (*BOB*, p. 36). Fortunately the references in *Fr* confirm the nature of the agreement.

Kerensky's expedition, yet had received no news of support from the respective armies, only of the loyalist resolutions of higher committees. Finally, the incredible concession of the Western Front KSR not to use armed force in behalf of the old government or to allow troop movements through its territory bought the Bolsheviks time to reap the advantages of the strong shift in sentiment in their favor at the front.

Why the Bolsheviks' opponents were so forthcoming when they had so easily faced the Bolsheviks down in the streets is equally puzzling. Here the strength of conciliatory sentiments bears equal weight. There had always been a precarious balance within the front committee between the Bolsheviks and the other left-oriented elements, on the one hand, and the firm defensists, on the other. The latter by themselves had never had a secure majority and depended on the support of several swing votes. The defensists, together with Commissar Zhdanov, had doubtless initiated the action against the Bolshevik takeover, but they could not command a majority without significant gestures toward accommodation. Thus, the moderates on both sides pressured the intransigents to yield; the strongest argument in favor of a compromise on both sides was their fear or, perhaps more correct, the aroused sentiment of their mutual constituency that an armed clash between the wings of the democracy could only benefit counter-revolution.[64]

The Bolsheviks held to the spirit of this agreement over the next few days much more than did Commissar Zhdanov and the defensist hardliners on the front committee, Zlobin and Kolotukhin (an S.R. and a Menshevik respectively), who saturated the communications media with a distorted version of events—that all democratic organizations had condemned the Petrograd coup, that the Bolsheviks were without mass support and collapsing of their own weight, that the Petrograd garrison was on a drunken rampage and despoiling the Winter Palace, and that Kerensky was marching triumphantly toward the capital and would arrive in a matter of hours. The news from Kiev, Moscow, Odessa, and the Rumanian Front was supposedly equally favorable to the anti-Bolshevik forces.[65] The Petrograd KSRR was reported to have the backing of all the junker schools and cossack units, who had occupied the Mikhailovskii Palace, seized the armored cars and motorized artillery, and retaken the telephone and telegraph stations, whereas the Bolsheviks were holed up in Smolnyi and the

[64] Knorin and Alibegov both concede the existence of conciliationist sentiment in the Bolshevik ranks but ascribe it to others, not themselves, and do not concede that it influenced the actions of the Minsk Soviet and the MRC (*BOB*, pp. 37 and 57).

[65] *Fr* initially maintained a neutral tone editorially, but soon was swayed by the OAK position and carried some of the misinformation published in its *BOAK* of October 31 and November 1.

Peter-Paul Fortress. All this, of course, was miserable self-deception banking on the success of Kerensky's venture, but as the Russians are fond of saying, this was "skinning an unkilled bear."

This propaganda bombardment, however, did not reflect the actual posture of the Western Front KSR. In the critical days October 28-30 it followed the policy laid down in the agreement fairly consistently, and secured the enthusiastic cooperation of local Soviets, KSRs, and MRCs, as well as railroad workers, telegraph operators, and garrison soldiers. Once Baluev was liberated from the embrace of the Minsk Soviet, he came under strong pressure from Stavka to allow the troops from the Southwestern Front through and to dispatch units from the Western Front to Moscow, where an armed struggle was shaping up. On October 28 the lead echelons of the 156th Infantry Division had entered the territory of the Western Front but were held up by local garrisons at Zlobin and Orsha. On the 29th Dukhonin pleaded with General Baluev to reroute the division through Minsk. General Baluev wearily objected that "if they come through Minsk and get stuck, they will tear the place apart" and tip the scales in favor of the Bolsheviks. Nevertheless, he agreed, on the condition that the trains pass through without stopping and their mission be kept secret.[66] The same day, Commissar Zhdanov persuaded a Turkestan Rifle Regiment from the Third Army to liberate Smolensk, which lay on the route from Orsha to Moscow.

On October 30, the Minsk KSR again issued a general order to stop all troop movements, and the plans of Stavka were brought to grief. As General Maliavin informed General Dietrichs at Stavka on November 3:

> The question of sending armored cars to Moscow has not been resolved, because the Minsk KSR has forbidden their departure, which means they cannot come to the relief of Viazma, which is in the hands of the Bolsheviks, or Gomel, where they occupy the telegraph. . . . In all operative matters and nonoperative matters we are tied hand and foot by the Front and army KSRs.[67]

The stance of neutrality of the Minsk KSR in the emerging civil conflict therefore weighed strongly in the Bolsheviks' favor without the latter having to lift a finger.

The decline of the Minsk KSR was dramatic after November 1: on that day the representatives of the Minsk Soviet announced their withdrawal, and the last recorded act of the KSR was an appeal on November 3 for an "agreement of all the democracy" in Petrograd, obviously alluding to

[66] *KA* 7:165.

[67] *Ibid.*, 23:174.

the Vikzhel negotiations.[68] The resurgence of the Minsk Bolsheviks is equally striking. Official accounts ascribe it to the arrival of the armored train, which had the additional bonus that the hard-line committeeman Kolotukhin was caught planting a demolition charge under a bridge to intercept the train, but the charge went off after the train had passed.[69] It is doubtful that this episode was the decisive one, as there is no record otherwise of military clashes or even arrests of the culprits. *Front*, the organ of the front committee, continued to appear for three more weeks and incessantly appealed for an understanding between the two wings of the democracy and condemned the intransigence of both sides. It ardently promoted the Vikzhel solution, but spent its remaining capital when it opposed the armistice negotiations; a Bolshevik-dominated front congress on November 20 finally consigned it to oblivion.[70]

Although Kerensky's defeat was a considerable psychological lift for the Minsk Bolsheviks, the news of the string of Bolshevik victories in the committees of the various armies raised their spirits even more. By November 1 they were informed of Bolshevik ascendancy in the I and III Siberian and the IX Army corps, as well as in the Sixth, 42nd, and 15th Siberian and Fifth Grenadier divisions and numerous smaller units, but above all, of the spectacular victory at the congress of the Grenadier Corps on October 30.[71] Thus, they could be certain that the existing front committee would soon lose its credentials and could raise no substantial military force. The KSR faded for the same basic reason.

In any event, over the next three days the Bolshevik organs and organizations displayed a vigorous activity, taking over the civilian sector through the apparatus of the Minsk Soviet and front headquarters through controls imposed by a newly surfaced MRC. An article in *Zvezda* on November 1 ("Away with the Mask!") denounced the KSR for breaking the agreement and collaborating with counter-revolutionary Stavka. It declared:

> What sort of Committee of Salvation is this that spreads false information on events, calls for disobedience to the new government of Soviets, and misrepresents the mood and opinion of the masses? that allows echelons to pass through from the south to Kerensky, that arms certain units against unspecified enemies for unspecified aims while

[68] *Fr*, November 3.

[69] See the colorful personal account of the hero of this episode, V. Prolygin, in *BOB*, pp. 254-59. That the episode is not fiction is confirmed by account in *Zvezda*, November 3 (*VOSRB* 2:92-94).

[70] See the corresponding issues, which cease to appear thereafter.

[71] All these units are specifically referred to in *Zvezda*, November 1 (*VOSRB* 2:67-68).

> disarming revolutionary troops consisting of liberated prisoners, the victims of Kerensky's vengeance?[72]

All civilian and military organizations that supported Soviet power were invited to send representatives to the MRC of the Western Front, now formed under the auspices of the Minsk Soviet. From November 3 on, the Western Front MRC issued a series of orders which reflected that it had become a serious wielder of power. An Order No. 2 called on the population not to believe rumors and leaflets spread by the enemies of Soviet power and to obey only the orders of the new government (Sovnarkom) and its organs, the MRCs; it ordered the garrison to resume drill and rifle practice and forbade the sale of alcoholic beverages.[73] Order No. 3 of November 4 declared that "since Minsk is now under the power of the MRC of the Western Front and the city is entirely peaceful, all units called in recent days are to return to the front." Pogroms and plundering were to be dealt with ruthlessly by armed force, and the streets were to be patrolled by garrison units according to a system then being worked out. Kudos were given to the First Revolutionary Regiment of freed prisoners and to Lieutenant Prolygin, the commandant of the armored train. All institutions and persons were to obey only the orders of the MRC, except those of the commanding staff of a purely operative character.[74] Proof that the power claimed by the MRC had become effective is a circular telegram of General Baluev of November 5:

> In Minsk the KSR has disbanded. Commissar Zhdanov has resigned. The Soviet of Workers' and Soldiers' Deputies, having formed a Military Revolutionary Committee, has gained the upper hand and is now maintaining order. The task of military commanders at the front at the present time consists of holding the front and not allowing intramural, fratricidal clashes among the troops. Since all power now devolves upon the MRC, I have declared that until a new power has become established in all of Russia and order is restored, I will conduct no political struggle and will undertake no adventures, and I suggest that you also hold to this policy and devote all your attention to keeping the troops at the front, and without the sanction of the revolutionary committee not to allow troop movements or transfers to the rear, utilizing in this respect the authority of the MRCs.[75]

[72] *Ibid.*, p. 69.

[73] *Ibid.*, pp. 91-92.

[74] *VRKDA*, p. 263. Order No. 4 announced the appointment of commissars for military, economic, communications, and international affairs, the removal of Commissar Zhdanov from his post, and preparations for a regional peasant congress. Order No. 5 announced a series of further appointments (*ibid.*, p. 264).

[75] *VOSRB* 2:109.

Baluev's order closed the book on the past and finalized the revolution in authority on the Western Front. Baluev had not yielded as readily as Cheremisov, but he was doubtless swayed by the same logic—to persist in attempting to mobilize resistance in the name of the old government or the Petrograd KSRR against the clear preference of the soldier masses would simply lead to open civil war and invite a slaughter of the officer class. In that case the front would collapse, the soldiers would head for home leaving chaos in their wake, and nothing would stand in the way of a German advance. Not having any illusions about his new masters or their permanency in power, Baluev was for the time being content that the apparatus of military authority remained intact, as the Bolsheviks also had an interest in it. The Bolsheviks, on their part, were happy to have his cooperation, as it obviated the need for an armed struggle, and the communications of the staff were now at their disposal to consolidate their power.

The absence of armed confrontation in all this is quite remarkable, confirming once again that, whatever poses each side might take, the overwhelming preference of those being called upon to fight was to resolve matters through talking and votes in the democratic organizations. The most popular slogans of the moment were "no civil war within the democracy" and "not a day's delay in the convocation of the Constituent Assembly." The leaders in this regard were the captives of their own instruments. The "dictatorship" of the MRC was exercised with a very light hand: the KSR dissolved without the use of force, the city Duma continued to function and was even scolded for failing to keep up city services, and the opposition organ *Front* continued to preach its independent line unimpeded. The Bolsheviks had no reason to rush the liquidation of their rivals, as they already enjoyed a preponderance in all committees of the respective armies and were confident that the front congress scheduled for November 20 and the elections to the Constituent Assembly already under way would settle the matter with finality.[76]

☆

The most remarkable committee victory of the Bolsheviks was in the Second Army. In three out of the four corps (the Grenadier, the IX and the L), the Bolsheviks gained control of nearly the entire committee structure from the regimental level on up in direct response to the Petrograd events. The process was more drawn out in the III Siberian Corps, once a Bolshevik stronghold, but before long that also was rectified.[77] The

[76] The above can be followed through the organ of the MRC, *BZF*, for November 9-14. On scolding of the city Duma, see issue for November 9.

[77] See Petrov's complaint in *BOB*, p. 243. There is no other direct documentation or information on the III Siberian Corps.

Grenadier Corps is the best documented. After their electoral success of mid-October, which gave them positions on the army committee, the Grenadier Bolshevik leaders established reliable contacts in each regiment of the corps.[78] Petrov recounts that he returned to Nesvizh on October 24 for a regular session of the army committee to find the S.R. presidium members in a state of great agitation.[79] On the morning of the 26th he discovered the reason: hitherto concealed telegrams from Petrograd, which were reluctantly handed over. When Petrov tried to contact comrade Berzin, chairman of the L Corps Committee, a guard posted on the direct wire informed him he was forbidden access "on the orders of the commissar." At the committee session the Bolsheviks tried to push through a resolution recognizing Soviet power and exited when it was voted down; in their absence a loyalist resolution was apparently passed. Suspicious moves of a cossack regiment toward Nesvizh led Petrov to believe that Commissar Grodskii was planning to arrest the Bolshevik faction, so they discreetly dispersed to their units by circuitous routes.

Petrov and a fellow Grenadier Bolshevik, utilizing their army committee credentials, assembled the staff units of corps headquarters, read them the appropriate telegrams, and extracted a resolution in favor of Soviet power, a prudent tactical move that secured control of communications in the corps. By the morning of October 28 they had secured resolutions of support for Soviet power and forced through by-elections in all four regiments of the Second Division, followed by a divisional assembly of 200 representatives, in which they secured all but 35 of the votes. That same evening, along pitch-black slimy roads, newly elected division deputies made their way to corps headquarters where other deputies of by-elected committees were assembling. The corps committee objected to the legality of a meeting, displaying a spate of telegrams from the Petrograd KSRR and Commissar Zhdanov to the effect that Kerensky was about to enter Petrograd and that now was no time to "divide the democracy." But the Bolshevik deputies, easily having a quorum, assembled in a dugout just behind the front lines that barely housed the ninety or so present. The Germans selected this moment to launch a furious artillery and infantry attack, and to the deafening roar the Bolsheviks rammed through a resolution on the current moment without a dissenting vote (the defensists boycotted). The new corps committee consisted of twenty-two Bolsheviks, six Left S.R.'s, and two Menshevik Internationalists. The deputies then seized their rifles and dispersed to the trenches. The action, the last on this front, cost the corps 1,300 casualties, among them, Petrov claims, "many good Bolsheviks."[80]

[78] See above, pp. 273-74.

[79] *BOB*, p. 239.

[80] *Ibid.*, pp. 245-47. The figure is credible, as the heavy action is confirmed in a report

The main resolution reflected a consistent, hard-line Bolshevik position, though no instructions from the center can be pinpointed. The entire military strength of the Grenadier Corps was declared to be at the disposal of the Petrograd MRC and Sovnarkom (an exceptionally specific reference), while warm personal greetings were sent to "the new leader of the Revolution, Comrade Lenin." A seven-point program covered peace, land, control over banks and factories, the regulation of the distribution of consumer goods, the democratization of the army, the Constituent Assembly, and "a just and equal social order." Army and front congresses should meet "by revolutionary means" if necessary, and the Western Front KSR should be disbanded by force if it did not recognize the Soviet power in Petrograd. The resolution was printed up and circulated in large quantities, with copies to Sovnarkom, the Petrograd MRC, the front committee, the Western Front KSR and the Minsk Soviet.[81] No other front resolution of the time was as precise and forceful in following the scenario of the Petrograd MRC.

A morale report by Commissar Zhdanov for the week ending November 1 confirms that committee revolutions of the same magnitude occurred in the IX and L Corps. In the IX Corps two of the three divisional committees (Fifth and 42nd) and two regiments of the third division (15th Siberian) voted "full confidence" in the Petrograd MRC on the day the news arrived (obviously a response to the radiogram of October 25); the Fifth Division, possibly in response to the appeal of the Western Front KSR, revised its position on October 28, withholding support for either side in the civil conflict and expressing its opposition to all troop movements. The resolutions of both divisional committees had called for the prompt reelection of corps and army committees. The mood of all the units was described as "definitely Bolshevik," and postal and telegraph communications were said to be already controlled by Bolsheviks. In the most tranquil division of the IX Corps, the 15th Siberian, four officers (including the Chief of Staff) were arrested for refusing to recognize Soviet power and the validity of the orders of the Petrograd MRC. In the III Siberian Corps, described as the least affected by events, the as-yet unreelected corps committee passed a resolution condemning the seizure of power by the Petrograd MRC, but also condemned the Provisional Government and called for a new one based on VTsIK (presumably the old one), the Peasant Executive Committee, and the Pre-Parliament purged of census elements.[82] In short, a committee turnover on the order of the Grenadier Corps was occurring

of the Second Army Commander, General Suvorov, of November 9, who generously praised their heroism and sacrifice (see *ORA*, p. 94).

[81] *Ibid.*, p. 32.

[82] *Ibid.*, pp. 47-49; see also Suvorov's report, above (n. 80).

in the entire Second Army, the III Siberian Corps simply lagging a bit behind.

Given the upheaval in the lower units, it was a foregone conclusion that the Bolsheviks would soon control the army committee. The Bolshevik activists decided not to wait until the scheduled army congress on November 9, but to press on with their luck. The soldiers of the 32nd Siberian Regiment at the Bolsheviks' behest arrested their officers and occupied Zamire, a town adjacent to army headquarters.[83] When Petrov entered the town on October 31 he found the walls plastered with copies of the land and peace decrees, which soldiers on the streets were avidly drinking up. The following day, November 1, the "illegal" army congress convoked by the Bolsheviks assembled. Nevertheless, the S.R. Chairman, Titov, opened the assembly and formally turned over his mandate and that of the former army committee. Though puzzled, the Bolsheviks were grateful, because now they could not be accused of usurpation. Since the Mensheviks and the S.R.'s had boycotted the congress, the Bolsheviks in short order formed a ten-man MRC, sent greetings of recognition to the Petrograd MRC and Sovnarkom, passed an orthodox Bolshevik resolution on the "current moment" (almost a copy of the Grenadier resolution), heard a detailed report on the Western Front KSR and the activities of Commissar Zhdanov, who were formally condemned, and passed a six-point declaration instituting the total power of the new army committee in the Second Army. The declaration was virtually a textbook execution of the injunctions of the original radiogram of the Petrograd MRC and subsequent directives. All commanders acting against the Soviet power or refusing to recognize it were subject to immediate removal and arrest. The commissars of the Provisional Government were formally removed, and their acts were declared null and void; they and their agents were subject to immediate detention. Committees were authorized to nominate their own commanding officers with the approval of the next highest committee; supply and operative functions of the command were retained, but with "strict control" and the counter-signature of commissars of the army committee.[84] A separate resolution accused the front committee of "betraying the Revolution" by sanctioning the Western Front KSR, and it formally recalled the rep-

[83] According to report of its commander of November 3, cited in L. M. Gavrilov, "Soldatskie komitety deistvuiushchei armii v period podgotovleniia oktiabr'skoi sotsialisticheskoi revoliutsii" (dissertation, Moscow, 1959), pp. 70ff.

[84] For Petrov's account, consult his full-length memoirs, *Bolsheviki na zapadnom fronte 1917 g. Vospominaniia* (Moscow, 1959), pp. 70ff., since this material is not included in *BOB* version. On the congress agenda and for a summary of the proceedings, see *VOSRB* 2:75-80; for the main resolution, see *OAR*, pp. 394-95; and for an account, see *IzGr*, November 8.

resentatives of the Second Army. The KSR could prove a change of heart by arresting Commissar Zhdanov, whose dispatches were regarded as particularly odious. They sent deputies to other armies to raise the issue of a front congress.

The organizational measures approved by the congress were implemented without delay. The MRC issued its first order on November 2, giving instructions on committee controls over the commanding staff and authorizing the arrest of all officers who did not submit. All committee decisions were to be issued as binding orders by the command, with copies to the corps commissars of the MRC.[85] A staff report of November 8 bears witness that the controls were effectively carried out in all four corps of the army down to the divisional level: in the L Corps the officers were said to be the captives of the soldier masses and subjected to various humiliations, abetted by the committees, which pronounced various reprimands and offenses; the principle of counter-signature was recorded for the 129th Division, as were a number of instances of removal and arrest.[86] A report of the MRC commissar to the Grenadier Corps to the new Bolshevik Stavka of November 29 proudly recited the measures taken to implement the new order:

> All telegrams and radiotelegrams coming into the corps staff are reviewed by the corps commissar and are distributed only after due consideration of their content. . . . The commanding staff undertakes nothing without the knowledge of the commissar and the committee, nor can anybody depart from the region of the corps. All orders and instructions proceed only through the committees to the units. The elective principle of command has been carried out according to Order No. 4 of the Western Front Commander [Kamenshchikov, a Bolshevik]. . . . Those found unfit are demoted to the ranks.[87]

A briefer telegram from the L Corps affirms the same vigorous execution of the above instructions, while the IX Corps had sent a similar report to the Petrograd MRC on November 8.[88] In the Second Army at least, the committee revolution held very closely to the prescriptions of the Petrograd MRC and all organs were tightly controlled by reliable Bolsheviks.

The Third Army was likewise convulsed by a committee revolution in direct response to Petrograd events, but it was far less a Bolshevik-monopolized affair. Commissar Zhdanov's survey for October 14-21 noted

[85] *ORA*, p. 91.

[86] *Ibid.*, pp. 91-95. All instructions of the army MRC, including those above, were published in *IzGr*, November 8.

[87] *Ibid.*, pp. 221-22.

[88] *Ibid.*, pp. 229-30, and *VRKDA*, p. 403.

the sharp decline in influence of unreconstructed committees and that by-elections had brought in Bolsheviks in others, but the process was far less advanced than in the Second Army. His report of a week later noted a sharp response to "current events" in the XV Corps, greatly exciting the mass mood; an expanded session of the corps committee with two divisional committees (Sixth and Eighth Infantry divisions) passed a resolution "greeting the accomplished revolution and expressing confidence that at long last it means an end to the plundering war, a guarantee of the meeting of the Constituent Assembly, and the transfer of land to the peasants." The XX Corps still appeared subdued though tense, but the committee and the command structure of the XXXV Corps had "lost all weight and influence" to a spontaneously created MRC, which took the part of the Bolsheviks and had "posted its controls everywhere." The MRC held up and read all telegrams, letting them through selectively to lower units.[89] For the most part, the Third Army appears to have reacted to Petrograd events spontaneously, forcing existing committees to declare for Soviet power and peace or to yield to new elections of those that would. Although army committeemen were sophisticated enough to know of the Bolshevik inspiration of the Petrograd uprising, at the lower levels the news came primarily in the form of the radiogram of the Petrograd MRC which General Baluev had unwisely transmitted to the lower units; since the MRC was represented in this communication as an organ of the Petrograd Soviet, whose name still worked magic, the coup was easily understood as a necessary step to protect the Second Congress and force the issue of peace. Since this logic swayed many soldiers who were not Bolshevik-oriented, the MRC order served to crystallize a broad, militant mood that the Bolsheviks could exploit but certainly did not create or control.

The spontaneous reactions can be separately documented for the Sixth and Eighth divisions of the XV Corps. Both heard the news on October 26 through the MRC order, and both immediately formed MRCs and took the prescribed actions, such as arresting hostile officers and establishing controls; however, confused by conflicting telegrams, above all over sending units to aid Kerensky, they suspended actions and sent delegations to Petrograd.[90] An "assembly of reserve companies" illustrates the temper of lower units: it protested the loyalist resolutions of the Second and Third armies and denounced the use of armed force by Kerensky and "other organizations," since "this is not the rebellion of mindless Bolsheviks, but an organized action of the conscious proletariat against the counter-

[89] Front report, *RDRA*, pp. 533-55; second report, *ORA*, pp. 49-51.

[90] See reports of delegates to the Petrograd MRC of November 3 and 6 in *PVRK* 2:43 and 173 respectively.

revolutionary Provisional Government.'' It declared its readiness to support Soviet power by force of arms, but was against sending troops from the front for the moment to either side, since ''these units are needed to defend the Motherland against German militarism.''[91] A lengthy list of specific demands and detailed controls over staffs completes the picture.

Though there is no record of divisional and corps congresses, a congress of the Third Army met on November 2-6 in Polotsk against the declared wishes of the army committee and Commissar Postnikov; it registered a party composition of 173 Bolsheviks, 119 S.R.'s, 26 S.R. Maximalists, 28 nonparty, and 14 Mensheviks.[92] Since Left S.R.'s were not listed separately, a good many of the S.R.'s were doubtless also left-oriented, since only a small handful of those present defended the position of the old army committee. The Bolsheviks with their left allies easily commanded a majority, yet the two most authoritative Bolsheviks present, Dr. Kogan from the Regional Party Bureau and Gromashevskii from the Bolshevik fraction of the front committee, were dedicated conciliationists and worked out a resolution on power which endorsed the idea of an ''all-socialist coalition''; it ratified the land and peace decrees and other acts of the Second Congress, but it did not specifically recognize Sovnarkom as the legitimate government.[93] Moreover, the new army committee and a separate MRC both mirrored the exact fracitonal makeup of the congress (the army committee consisted of 29 Bolsheviks, 19 S.R.'s, and 4 each of S.R. Maximalists, Mensheviks, and nonparty deputies). The MRC, however, was designated not as a permanent organ of power but as having the limited mission of interdicting troop movements toward the capital.[94]

The new army committee was paralyzed by its even split between those who wished to recognize Sovnarkom and those who favored the Vikzhel formula. During that time the MRC scarcely functioned, since the conciliators were very jealous of the residual powers of the army committee. The stalemate dragged out until mid-November, when the crisis over the armistice negotiations shifted sentiment strongly in favor of recognizing Sovnarkom, a subject reserved for the final chapter. Embarrassment in the Third Army was real, as practical decisions concerning the armistice had to be made on the lower levels, following guidelines laid down by the Western Front MRC and Sovnarkom, bypassing the army level entirely. By November 17 the Bolsheviks secured enough votes in both the MRC and the army committee to effectively consolidate their control and function

[91] *VOSR. Vosstanie*, pp. 687-88.

[92] *IzVK3*, November 27, and slightly different tabulation in *Pr*, November 9, cited in *VOSRB* 2:85.

[93] See memoirs of A. A. Vashnev and B. I. Efremov in *BOB*, pp. 309 and 321 respectively.

[94] *Ibid.*, p. 309, and *IzVK3*, November 23.

as legitimate organs of Sovnarkom in the army. As late as mid-November the conciliationists still held the upper hand at congresses of the XV and XX corps, but a new army congress of December 3-8 completed the committee revolution in favor of the orthodox Bolsheviks.[95]

One might legitimately ask why the conciliationists gained such a strong foothold in the Third Army and not in the Second. The question is not easy to answer on the basis of available materials. Of course, the party-oriented Bolsheviks were more numerous and better organized in the Second Army, but authoritative party Bolsheviks in the Third Army were conciliators, whereas in the Second Army they were not. Moreover, the Second Army had always been more open to the left, until July tolerated a Bolshevik minority in the army committee, always had a more tense relationship with the command, and always followed a more demagogic line on soldier-officer relations. In the Third Army the command from the generals on down patronized the committees, officer "socialists" provided the leadership, and moderate, defensist Populism had dominated its politics. Nevertheless, after the Kornilov affair and even earlier, committeemen in the Third Army sensed the growing gulf between the leadership and the mass mood, and many moderate types without strong party affiliations began to move left on many issues. Whether the striking presence of so many left-oriented S.R.'s and "S.R. Maximalists" at the army congress of early November represent moderate S.R.'s who moved left or a secret levy of some hitherto inactive radical element simply cannot be determined on the basis of available materials. One has to assume that the peasant-soldier element in both armies was the same and that the desire for peace and repatriation dominated everything. Perhaps the most significant lesson to be drawn is that the original stimulus—Baluev's transmission of the radiogram of the Petrograd MRC—could arouse sufficient mass reactions in the Third Army to force through a committee revolution without relying exclusively on Bolsheviks to carry it through. Here neither the Petrograd MRC nor the Second Congress nor Sovnarkom decrees were perceived as patented by Bolshevism—only as the first true revolutionary word in a long time. The Soviet Revolution in the Third Army, as in the First, did not depend on Bolshevik activists and organizing skills. The masses found their own leaders.

Materials of the kind employed above are for the most part lacking on the Tenth Army. Even the two commissars' reports before and after the

[95] *Protokoly* of corps congresses in *VKDA*, pp. 418-21 and 424 respectively; *protokoly* of army congress in *VOSRB* 2:405-66. A vote by fractions for candidates' lists to the army committee establishes that of 290 delegates, 217 voted for the Bolshevik list, 18 for the S.R.-Maximalists, 28 for the Left S.R.'s, and 27 for the bloc of Defensist S.R.'s and Mensheviks. On the crisis in leadership over the armistice, see below, p. 390.

October Revolution bear witness only to intensified spontaneous unrest, such as fraternization, plundering of local estates and supply depots, and more frequent and violent clashes with officers, but they essentially ignore political phenomena in general, including that of committees and the Bolsheviks. Soviet accounts identify no active Bolshevik groups since the disbanding of the notorious 169th Division in July, though a report of General Rylskii on October 15 complained of the extensive circulation of the Minsk Bolshevik organ *Burevestnik*, which "is eagerly read by the masses and exerts an extremely disintegrative influence."[96] There does appear to have been a delayed reaction to Petrograd events, possibly due to a more stringent control of information by the committee and commissar networks. In only one instance, that of an artillery unit, is the reception of the radiogram of the Petrograd MRC recorded.[97] In fact, the Committee organ *GoXA* is useful primarily as a source for the unsuccessful efforts of the old committees to hold back the waves by censoring the news. It is also virtually a complete record of the efforts of democratic authorities at all levels to mobilize sentiment against the "Bolshevik adventure"—resolutions of a galaxy of loyal committees and organizations, pontifications of front and army commissars, and editorializing on events ad nauseum. On October 26 appeared the texts of army committee resolutions condemning the uprising, including its own, a statement by Tenth Army Commissar Pasechnyi that it meant "death to the conquests of the Revolution," Commissar Zhdanov's announcement that Kerensky was amassing revolutionary troops in Pskov, a press agency dispatch on the destructive bombardment of the Winter Palace, details of the formation and composition of the Petrograd KSRR, and the telegraph appeals of Kerensky himself. Editorials lamented that here was one more illustration of the indifference of the rear to the needs of the front, that now the Constituent Assembly probably could not meet, and that the Bolsheviks and Black Hundreds together were drowning freedom in Russia. The issue of October 28 carried pronouncements of the Executive Committee of the Peasant Soviet, of Chief Commissar Stankevich (a boost for the KSRR, the "isolation" of the Bolsheviks), as well as of the committees of the Second, Ninth, and Special armies. On this date also they published the full text of the radiogrammed order of the Petrograd MRC, probably on the mistaken assumption that its "adventurous" content would be self-evident, as well

[96] *RDRA*, p. 495.

[97] The First Caucasus Artillery Brigade assembled on October 28, heard the texts of Radio One of the Petrograd MRC and communiqués of Kerensky and the KSRR, and decided "not to believe" the latter two but to support the MRC (*PVRK* 2:314). The information was conveyed by delegates sent to Petrograd directly to the MRC on November 9.

as the texts of the land and peace decrees.[98] Over the next few days *GoXA* continued to purvey the misleading version of events, above all Commissar Zhdanov's dispatches to the effect that the Bolsheviks were isolated and afraid of their own constituency, whereas Kerensky was on the threshold of his triumphal entry (Minsk events were given a like treatment).

Amid this flow of premasticated news, the issue of October 29 casually mentioned that an "army conference" was in progress, marked by heated debate over the "unending fatigue and thirst for immediate peace," often accompanied by calls for Soviet power and the immediate convocation of the Constituent Assembly. The issue of October 31 revealed that in fact an assembly of lower committees had already convened on October 27, probably to ratify the army committee resolution on the uprising, but a noisy minority of fifty or so Bolsheviks "tried to break up the congress [*sic*] into two irreconcilable camps." The officially sponsored resolution blamed the Bolsheviks for fomenting civil war and sabotaging the Constituent Assembly, but nevertheless called on democratic groups to break completely with the "census elements," whose policies were bankrupt, and to form a "unitary socialist government" which should be entrusted with convoking the Constituent Assembly, turning the land over to the land committees, and working out concrete proposals of peace. Further points covered the repeal of the death penalty, a revolutionary court for Kornilov, immediate resupply of the front, and a complete democratization of the army, including the rights of recommendation and removal for command positions. The programmatic part would seem to have left little for the Bolsheviks, but the Bolshevik resolution called for the immediate recognition of Soviet power, the complete reelection of committees from top to bottom, a new peasant congress, an immediate armistice on all fronts, universal labor service, and abolition of all taxes on goods of primary consumption. Clearly it was difficult to outdo the Bolsheviks in radical program items.[99] A "reconciliation commission" was formed to work out a compromise resolution, but at the last minute the Bolsheviks forced a vote on the two resolutions separately, revealing a division of 81 votes for the committee resolution to 38 for the Bolsheviks, with three absentions.

It would seem that the existing leadership had won a clear-cut victory by "moving left" and that it was foolhardy for them to yield on the issue of a new congress, but the pressure on the leadership was relentless. For

[98] The radiogram itself contained the threat that "any concealment by army organizations of this order is tantamount to the most serious crime against the Revolution and will be punished with all the strictness of revolutionary law" (*ORA*, p. 15 and in most Soviet *sborniki*).

[99] Text of the resolution in *VOSRB* 2:64-65 and *ORA*, pp. 33-34.

example, an expanded session of committees of an unnamed division resolved on October 28:

> Accepting the revolt of the Petrograd garrison and proletariat as an accomplished fact, enjoying the sympathy of the entire front, and having lost confidence in the ability of the coalition government to satisfy the essential needs of the people, the congress demands the cessation of civil war, the unity of all socialist parties, and the creation of a single revolutionary authority until the Constituent Assembly, which must meet at the appointed time.

It called for an MRC to control the commanding staff, but as in the Third Army for the restricted purpose of halting troop movements and averting fratricidal strife. Although clearly more Left S.R. than Bolshevik, the resolution nevertheless excoriated the army committee for "acting not only precipitately but in manifest disregard of the interests and will of the masses they represent."[100] Likewise the committee of the II Caucasus Corps at some unspecified date before November 4 endorsed the idea of no civil war, land, peace, and immediate Constituent Assembly. It could have simply been an endorsement of the leftish conference resolution, but it seems more likely to have been one of those that persuaded the army committee to move left.[101]

Whatever the circumstances, a new congress was called for November 9; in the meantime the army committee shifted first to the OAK-Vikzhel proposals and subsequently to the OAK proposal of a national government with Chernov as premier. Editorially *GoXA* continued to attack the Bolsheviks and selectively present the news. On November 2 the chairman of the army committee, Pecherskii, returned from Petrograd with optimistic expectations of the outcome of the Vikzhel negotiations and assurances that Lenin and Trotsky were finished even among the Bolsheviks.[102] But by that date the Minsk-based KSR had collapsed, and two days later the Vikzhel negotiations stalled. Clearly the ground was slipping from beneath every halfway position. The theme that preoccupied the paper in the few days before the new army congress was the total breakdown in supply, occasioned by the overloading of the railroads with moving troops, which left the front staring outright starvation in the face. Whether this was a genuine concern overriding political considerations or simply an oblique attack on the Bolsheviks (as the fathers of anarchy) is not quite clear, but at least the political faculties of the Tenth Army loyalists were at the end of their tether.

[100] *GoXA*, November 2.

[101] *Ibid.*, November 4.

[102] *Ibid.*, November 3 and 4 (editorials by Pecherskii).

When the congress met on November 9 with a clear Bolshevik majority, it immediately degenerated into total chaos. Before chairman Pecherskii could report for the old army committee, the agenda was revised from the floor to allow for "greetings from the Baltic Fleet," a report from the MRC of the Western Front (Alibegov), and the election of a new presidium (the Bolshevik list received 326 votes, the non-Bolshevik, 187). A representative of the front committee was howled from the podium, and only persistent banging of the gavel gained him a hearing. A motion of lack of confidence in the old army committee stirred up further angry debate. A broad-gauged, hours-long speech of Miasnikov on behalf of the Minsk Soviet and the Bolshevik Party recounted the entire history of the Revolution from the very beginning to the rapt attention of his audience and stormy applause at the end.[103] From this point on, with the partisans of Soviet power in clear control, the sessions became more orderly and even generous toward the defeated minority.

Four days of grueling debate were brought to a close with the approval of a ten-point resolution on the current moment and the election of a new army committee. The main point on Soviet power clearly defined power as vested in the new VTsIK, which it expected would be augmented by representatives from the forthcoming Congress of Peasants' Deputies. The decrees and authority of Sovnarkom were upheld on the assumption that it was responsible to VTsIK and would be expanded to include several ministers representing the peasant interest. Whether this was meant as a cautionary note to the all-Bolshevik Sovnarkom or was simply a defense against unfair accusations of dictatorship is not clear, but it was an unusually explicit qualifier. Likewise it attempted to avert the danger of "dual power" by carefully outlining the respective functions of committees and MRCs. Both were to exist at all levels, but committees were in charge of all routine work carried out by commissions of a technical or educative nature, while MRCs were responsible for all policy decisions and actions necessary to conduct the "political struggle." Otherwise the positions taken were typical of the army congresses of this period.[104]

A Tenth Army MRC was formed on November 10 and immediately assumed "full powers" and control over the command. All lower committees were instructed to institute MRCs or rename themselves such, whether they were Bolshevik-dominated or not, depriving them of any specific identity as extensions of the Petrograd MRC.[105] A known exception proves the rule: on November 17 the MRC of the III Corps reproached

[103] All in *protokoly* in *VOSRB* 2:148-51.

[104] *Ibid.*, pp. 154-56.

[105] *VRKDA*, p. 270.

the committee of the 73rd Division for not subjecting itself to reelection and instituting an MRC; failure to execute the congress order by November 20 would lead to a loss of credentials. The 132nd Division (I Siberian Corps) on the other hand carried out the transformation on the same date and immediately exercised its new powers by countermanding an order of the new Bolshevik chief of the Western Front, Kamenshchikov.[106] The committee revolution in the Tenth Army was complete, but Bolshevik control was marginal.

The Tenth Army differed in pattern from both the Second and Third armies. There was no visible "conciliationist" tendency among either the Bolsheviks or the old leadership, nor did the formula of an "all socialist government" gain currency except as a device to embarrass the Bolsheviks. The contest had been won as a straight fight at the army congress, and the Bolsheviks were the clear winners by virtue of their superior numbers but revealed a primitive grasp of the Bolshevik program. It seems that the outcome was almost purely the result of the surge of the soldier masses that overwhelmed the old leadership before it became organized. If there were organized, party-oriented Bolsheviks guiding the proceedings they were well concealed. Miasnikov was able to exert a considerable influence by virtue of his mastery of Bolshevik apologetics and his formidable credentials representing the Minsk Soviet and Bolshevik fraction of the front committee; but his very presence seems to have been a last-minute improvisation rather than a carefully planned move. If the victory of the Bolsheviks in the Second Army can be attributed to the organizing skill of the Bolshevik activists, in the Tenth Army it was the spontaneous appeal of their program.

[106] *Ibid.*, pp. 267 and 280.

CHAPTER X

REVOLUTION DELAYED: SOUTHWESTERN AND RUMANIAN FRONTS

THOUGH THE LONGING for peace and the restiveness of the soldier masses were as strong on the Southwestern Front as elsewhere, October events did not serve to focus them politically, and a massive turnover in the committees did not ensue. The army and front committees remained for the most part in the hands of the former leadership through the first half of November, and the same appears to be true on the corps level and divisional level. When congresses did take place in the latter part of the month, Bolsheviks were everywhere substantially represented, and with other left fractions, they usually acquired a plurality. Yet they shared the field with a rapidly rising Ukrainian movement, which held the balance of power. Although the slogans of Soviet power and peace were obviously a strong factor in favor of the Bolsheviks, other left parties and groups likewise capitalized on them, and the number of units dominated by conscious, party-oriented Bolsheviks remained few—in the Special Army only the Turkestan Corps and the 126th Division (XXXIX Corps), and in the Eleventh Army only the V Army Corps and the Sixth Siberian Division (V Siberian Corps); their strongest presence was to be found in the Seventh Army in the II Guards Corps (chiefly Egerskiis, Petrograskiis, Volynskiis, and Keksgolmskiis), the 74th Infantry Division, and the Sixth and Eighth Finnish Rifle regiments (XXII Corps). Some corps that had passed pro-Bolshevik resolutions, notably the VI and XXV corps, remained fluid and did not define themselves in relationship to Soviet power until the latter part of November.[1]

If the formation of MRCs is taken as an index of the shift from old loyalties to the new, here also the ''revolution'' was delayed. With few

[1] See below, pp. 356 and 359, and above, pp. 250 and 314.

exceptions, only Bolshevik-dominated units formed them in response to the appeal of the Petrograd MRC, the main reason being the effective control over communications by existing committees. Pressure mounted on the old committees by mid-November with the collapse of the OAK-Vikzhel strategy, the establishment of a vigorous Ukrainian government, and the forcing of the armistice issue by Sovnarkom. A number of MRCs came into being at the corps and army level, albeit with varying degrees of compromise, in connection with the convening of a front congress on November 18 (XXV, XXXII, XII, and V Siberian corps), but in the XXXI Corps a congress formed a KSR instead. An MRC of mixed party composition was formed in the Eleventh Army around November 9, but following a series of corps congresses the Bolsheviks gained the upper hand; still, the MRC and the army committee functioned separately until the army headquarters was occupied by Ukrainian units in early December. In the Seventh Army the army committee was disbanded by force around November 20 by the pro-Bolshevik Sixth Finnish Rifle Regiment, which took over the army headquarters at Proskurov much as the Latvians had taken over Valka; a Bolshevik MRC claimed power, but commanded little loyalty from non-Bolshevik units until the result was ratified by an army congress early in December.[2] By this measure the committee revolution was not only delayed, but incomplete.

The turning point was probably the front congress of November 18-24, whose delegates were split three ways: the Menshevik-S.R. bloc and the Bolsheviks had approximately the same number of deputies (260 and 267 respectively), though the S.R. fraction included an indeterminate number of Lefts, while the Ukrainians and nonparty socialists had around 115. The old leadership missed the opportunity to ally themselves with the non-Bolshevik groups and suffered shipwreck in a parliamentary tangle not unlike that which had destroyed the Democratic Conference and the Pre-Parliament. The Bolsheviks engineered the formation of an MRC on which they held eighteen of the thirty-five seats, the Mensheviks and S.R.'s held 11, and the Left S.R.'s and nonparty members held six.[3] The MRC lasted one week, able to accomplish nothing, as troops loyal to the Ukrainian Rada occupied front headquarters in Berdichev on November 30. The most significant effect of the congress was that it stimulated by-elections in many lower formations where they had not already taken place. The end result, however, was not unchallenged Bolshevik ascendancy, but frag-

[2] The formation of MRCs can be surveyed primarily in the documentary collection *VRKDA*. For the Seventh Army one must rely chiefly on Bolshevik memoirists, such as L. P. Malakovskii and E. P. Krasnov in *ONFV*, and F. V. Popov, *Rasskaz o nezabyvaemom*, though all are heavily edited and inflate the extent of Bolshevik influence in the first half of November.

[3] See detailed account in *IzVIu*, November 28 and 29.

mentation of power, unit by unit, which drifted without firm leadership, preoccupied with survival and spontaneous demobilization. In this competition the Bolsheviks controlled a certain cohort and constructed around it an apparatus of military authority, but so did their dangerous competitors, the Ukrainian Rada, and clusters of cossacks, shock units, and officers, whose eyes were now cast Don-ward. December was a month of truce with the Germans, but also of unfolding civil war.[4]

One cannot ascribe the above developments merely to the rising Bolshevik tide. As the Constituent Assembly elections demonstrate, the Bolsheviks' mass support still lagged far behind the S.R.'s on this front, except in the Eleventh Army, where they polled 38 percent and the S.R.'s polled 29 percent.[5] Rather, the old leaders, having unwisely put themselves on record in support of Kerensky, and then of the OAK at Stavka, found it increasingly difficult to maintain a foothold even by drastically revising their politics leftward. When Lenin and Krylenko boldly broadcast to the entire Army that Dukhonin refused to initiate armistice negotiations and authorized all units at the front to initiate local armistices of their own, the former leaders were forced to show their colors and lost out if they even equivocated. Therefore, when the OAK supported Dukhonin it could no longer provide the symbol of the Army's unity; in fact, it was rapidly disintegrating anyway due to the recall of representatives of the Northern and Western fronts. Finally, Krylenko's occupation of Stavka on November 20 and the final liquidation of the OAK left the anti-Bolshevik socialists without an anchor, symbolic or otherwise, to play off against the Soviet government. Furthermore, their twin props in the commissar and command hierarchies no longer sustained them. Calls for the removal of commissars of a nonexistent government were frequent in the early weeks of November,

[4] While the account below systematizes the information available, it should be noted that the documentation in Soviet *sborniki* becomes more fragmentary and one-sided, and army committee newspapers become less informative or cease publication (*Iz7A*, *IzOA*; an exception is *VGr*). This is compensated for by a number of new organs, of MRC's or renewed committees (*IzVK7*, *IzVK3*, *BOA*, *IzVIu*, *Iz2S8*), which continue into December. Archival sources available to the author are fewer, but those for the XXXI and XXII Corps (Special and Seventh armies) continue to yield invaluable insights.

[5] See *VVK*, December 3. In the same tabulation the Ukrainians received 21.5%, the United Social Democrats (mainly Mensheviks) 5.3%, and all others combined, including Kadets, 4%. Incomplete results for the Special Army record S.R.'s receiving 50%, the Bolsheviks 21%, the Ukrainians 16%, and United S.D.'s 7%, while in the Seventh Army the S.R.'s received 56%, the Bolsheviks 24%, and the Ukrainians and United S.D.'s 7% each (according to *IzVIu*, November 29). I. I. Mints (*Istoriia*, 3:394) cites the figures for the front as a whole, attributing to the S.R.'s 40%, the Bolsheviks 29.8%, and the Ukrainians and other nationality groups 28.8% (Kadets 1.4%). A total of slightly over one million soldiers are recorded as voting, 70% of those registered (a lower figure than for the Northern and Western fronts), which indicates that mass desertion had not yet taken place.

even in non-Bolshevik units, and where not forcibly removed by Bolshevik MRCs they simply quietly faded away. Senior officers were in a quandary as to what symbol of authority to lean on and often found it politic to distance themselves from the passionate appeals of commissars and committees on behalf of the Petrograd KSRR or the OAK. A new wave of arrests of officers and affronts to their authority at all levels again engulfed the Army, and again accommodation of some sort was the only mode of survival. Bolsheviks, where they gained uncontested control through MRCs, invariably introduced the "elective principle" of command and otherwise carried through measures of "democratization," which proved to be very popular among the soldiers. Non-Bolshevik lower units sometimes obeyed such directives without scrutinizing the source. Those officers who could not abide them looked for the first opportunity to escape, many of them in the direction of the Don.

☆

The two available organs of army committees *IzOA* and *Iz7A*, and the organ of the XXXII Corps, *GO*, vividly record the attempts of the old committees to guide events on the basis of outworn loyalties. They were for the most part faithful conduits of the information, misinformation, and disinformation coming through the staff and commissar networks. On October 28 they portrayed Kerensky as rallying forces at the front, and the KSRR in Petrograd as mobilizing the political forces of the capital; on October 29 they published various army and front resolutions, commissars' appeals, the position of the OAK, and selective news conveying the impression of the "unanimity of the democracy" in condemning the Bolshevik adventure. Over the next few days they featured resolutions of lower units which condemned the Bolsheviks for usurping the rights of the Constituent Assembly.[6] They also continued to publish considerable material on the Constituent Assembly elections to persuade the readers that they must proceed as scheduled despite the Bolshevik sabotage.

The Seventh Army Committee was obviously floundering, unable to strike a line of its own, but the Special Army Committee revealed a firmer grasp of political realities and in more timely fashion adjusted its policies. On November 2 it condemned the "one-sided portrayal of events" and called for the cessation of all troop movements to the rear and the formation of an all-socialist government committed to land and peace. With other local democratic organizations they created a "Committee for the Defense of the Motherland and the Salvation of the Revolution" (in effect, a local KSR) and set a conference of the sponsoring groups for November 10 in

[6] Around a dozen such resolutions of regimental and lesser units appeared in *IzOA* and *Iz7A* in the appropriate dates.

Rovno, but there is no record that it actually functioned. *IzOA* carefully chronicled the Vikzhel negotiations, utilizing extensively the OAK bulletins. Resolutions favoring the idea of an all-socialist government were now carried regularly with approval. On November 9 the *IzOA* recounted in excruciating detail the final deadlock of the Vikzhel negotiations, reflecting equally badly on both camps, including the S.R.'s intransigent opposition to an all-socialist government unless Bolsheviks were excluded and, even more painfully, its ultimatum to Chernov to withdraw his candidacy for the premiership.

The political bankruptcy of the democratic forces could not have been more self-evident, and this time the committee organ made no effort to conceal it. *IzOA* also objected to the candidacy of Chernov, though from its own position in favor of an all-socialist government based on the party distribution of the newly elected VTsIK and the legitimacy of Sovnarkom decrees; it also supported the claim of the Ukrainian Rada to the exercise of sovereignty over its territory until an all-socialist government came into being in Petrograd. The Special Army Committee even more clearly struck out on its own in denouncing Dukhonin and the OAK for their refusal to obey the Sovnarkom directive on armistice negotiations. They were given twenty-four hours to reverse their stand or the committee of the Special Army would open its own negotiations with the Germans.[7] On November 19 the Special Army Committee in fact signed a three-day cease-fire with the Germans pending the anticipated general armistice.

All this took place against the background of considerable turmoil that was not recorded in *IzOA* but that doubtless swayed the thinking of the army committee. On October 26 a "Revolutionary Committee" was formed in Rovno by garrison soldiers and peasant deputies in opposition to the local Workers' Soviet, which supported the local KSR; its chief object was to block the movement of troops toward the capital. When the army commissar threatened reprisals, the "Revolutionary Committee" invited the army committee to form an MRC and "take power." A similar revolutionary committee in Lutsk headed by a "Bolshevik" agitator named Dmitriev proclaimed a local "social revolution" and invited the Bolshevik-oriented 126th Division to occupy the town and army headquarters. Commissar Kudriavtsev, with several assistants, the editor of *IzOA*, and possibly the entire army committee, were arrested by this committee, while imprisoned Bolsheviks were freed. It appeared to be a successful coup, but the artillerists of the 126th Brigade were upset over the arrest of their popular commander and threatened to bombard the town unless he and

[7] *IzOA*, November 11. It also published two divisional resolutions supporting the *OAK* and criticizing the position of the army committee. See *ibid.*, November 12 and 22.

other arrested individuals were released. Lacking further support from front units, Dmitriev's enterprise collapsed, and other local Bolsheviks disavowed him.[8] The stock of the old army committee actually rose after Dmitriev's supression.

This episode persuaded the army committee to take charge of events and call an army congress to resolve the question of power. When the congress finally met on November 27, a Bolshevik resolution declaring "no confidence" in the old army committee was carried by a slim margin of 208 to 207 votes, an acknowledgment of its role in bringing about the armistice. A vote declaring that the Constituent Assembly must defer to Soviet power passed by 240 to 159 votes, with the help of Left S.R., nonparty, anarchist, and Polish socialist votes. The account of the congress notes a conciliatory spirit in the debates.[9] *Nakazy* from lower units published in the bulletin of the new army committee make clear why the Bolsheviks low-keyed their partisanship: virtually unanimously lower units supported the idea of an "all-socialist coalition" coupled with an immediate armistice; moreover, a good half specified that the Constituent Assembly rather than the Soviet should be the final arbiter on power. Clearly the more strident Bolshevik formulations did not enjoy great popularity in the Special Army, and a conciliatory line was necessary to gain them a broader base of support. The congress did, however, establish an MRC staffed by Bolsheviks which reported to Commander in Chief Krylenko on December 2 that it had assumed "full power."[10]

Paradoxically, the only corps in the Special Army to go on record in support of Soviet power was the I Turkestan Corps, which held a congress on November 11.[11] It called for a government based on the Second Congress of Soviets with a majority of Bolsheviks in the cabinet and endorsed the "decrees" on land and peace, but at the same time it called for "the immediate restoration of civil liberties," the "cessation of fratricidal war," and the participation of all socialist parties in a government to be formed by the Constituent Assembly, reflecting some unease over the most recent actions of the Bolshevik government. They did not form an MRC, a delegation to Petrograd explained, because they had not received the radiogrammed order of the Petrograd MRC and their own Operative Commission was an equivalent.[12]

[8] Details of both episodes in *BOA*, November 30 (report of MRC of the Special Army to the army congress).

[9] Account in *ibid.*, November 20 and December 3.

[10] *VRKDA*, p. 413.

[11] Text of main resolution in *ORA*, p. 108.

[12] Response to questionnaire of the Petrograd MRC in *VRKDA*, pp. 375-76 (also in *PVRK* 3:99-100).

By contrast the committee of the XXXI Corps voted 20 to 7 on November 9 to support "full powers" for the Special Army KSR. However, it approved the OAK position on the candidacy of Chernov and *withdrew* recognition from the army committee and the KSR when the latter broke with the OAK over Dukhonin's refusal. It now asserted its own claim to "all power" within the area of the corps.[13] The XLIV and XLVI corps seem to have resembled the XXXI Corps while the XXXIX Corps, which harbored the 126th and another tumultuous division, resembled the Turkestan Corps.

The peculiarities of the Special Army were probably a function of the relatively weak Bolshevik forces, the talent-rich old leadership, and the fact that it had not felt the full force of the summer offensive. In the Eleventh Army, by contrast, corresponding factors were weighted in favor of the Bolsheviks: Krylenko had established a firm Bolshevik tradition, the loyalist committee leadership which took over in June lacked vigor, and the bitter experience of the summer offensive inclined the soldier masses to radical solutions for their peace-longings. Except for its loyalist resolution of October 31, the old committee was scarcely heard from.[14] On November 10 Assistant Commissar Sheiner (Chekotilo mysteriously disappeared) convoked a conference of corps representatives which formed an MRC claiming "highest authority in the army" pending an army congress and the election of a new army committee. Sheiner brokered this compromise upon the arrival of a Lieutenant Mironstev, a deputy of the VI Corps to the Second Congress of Soviets, who now claimed credentials as a "commissar" of the new government to the army.[15]

The party composition of the MRC is unclear, though initially the Bolsheviks were probably in a minority, since no massive turnover in lower-level committees, except in the V Corps, is recorded; it remained inactive until November 16, when it issued a proclamation recognizing the authority of the Second Congress of Soviets and Sovnarkom, signed by a Lieutenant Ustriantsev, who can be identified as a Bolshevik. On November 18 it announced its assumption of power and control over the command "not excluding operations" and instructing all lower committees to do the same.[16] A congress of the Eleventh Army, however, was not held until December 3-5, by which time the Bolsheviks had acquired firm control.[17]

Documentation below the army level is very meager, but only the V Corps turned Bolshevik in direct response to events in Petrograd. The old

[13] TsGVIA, f. 2240, op. 5, d. 1, ll. 85-91 (*protokoly* of sessions).

[14] See *GO*, November 4 and 7.

[15] Record of session in *VRKDA*, p. 368.

[16] See *ibid.*, pp. 373-74 and 377-78.

[17] Excerpt from *protokoly* in *ibid.*, pp. 416-17.

committee, which had moved far to the left on the eve of October, called a congress based on new elections on November 2 to discuss the Petrograd uprising; this resulted in a Bolshevik majority and the formation of a Bolshevik MRC.[18] A certain lack of confidence on the part of the MRC leaders, however, is reflected in the fact that the MRC agreed to allow the old committee to continue routine commission work and publish its organ, *VVK*; in case of conflict between the two, joint sessions would be held. The MRC doubtless felt it could not dispense with the expertise of old committeemen in matters of supply, cultural-educational work, and above all preparations for the elections to the Constituent Assembly, which were about to take place. The old committeemen probably refused to take on these responsibilities unless guaranteed some freedom of action. This co-operative arrangement continued for the rest of November, as *VVK* maintained its former editorial line highly critical of the Bolsheviks and Lenin in particular.[19] New elections based on detailed instructions of the MRC were carried out around November 10 in preparation for the front congress, and the V Corps supplied the most solid bloc of Bolshevik deputies. The most notable innovation was the abolition of the separate officers' curia and the direct election of all deputies by the companies. Finally, a new corps congress on December 1-5 refurbished the membership of both the MRC and the army committee, and the old leadership finally passed from the scene.[20]

The V Corps is the only one on the entire front for which the detailed results of the Constituent Assembly elections unit by unit are available; they demonstrate not only clear Bolshevik preponderance but also how their support varied by category of unit. The Bolsheviks outpolled their nearest rivals, the S.R.'s, not only overall but in nearly every infantry regiment by three or four to one. They also dominated the engineering, railroad, and division staff units, while the S.R.'s did better on the corps staff, auto transport, and half of the supply units. The Bolsheviks polled 51.5 percent of the overall vote, and the S.R.'s polled 27.5 percent, the Ukrainian Socialists 10.25 percent, and the United Social Democrats (Mensheviks) 5 percent.[21] This was a considerably better showing for the Bol-

[18] Text of congress resolution in *ORA*, p. 61; text of Order No. One of MRC of November 3 in *VRKDA*, pp. 365-68; account of congress in *VVK*, November 16.

[19] All in *VVK*, November 16ff.

[20] For regulations on by-elections and announcement of MRC on results of congress, see *VRKDA*, pp. 365-68 and 430.

[21] *VVK*, December 3, appendix. The Muslims polled better than the Kadets (2.2% and 1.4% respectively). In no unit, not even in the corps or division staffs, did the Kadets poll more than 50 votes, and in infantry regiments they averaged between 15 and 20, less than the officer component of the units. In only one regiment out of eight did the S.R.'s outpoll the Bolsheviks, receiving 1,633 out of 3,447 votes (47%), whereas the Bolsheviks received

sheviks than in the Eleventh Army as a whole, where they polled only 38.5 percent (only slightly ahead of the S.R.'s) while the Ukrainians polled 21.5 percent.[22] Since the Ukrainian movement expressed many of the same psychological factors as the Bolsheviks for their constituency, specifically the longing for peace and a power on which soldiers could pin their expectations, the sum of the two figures reflect the depth of the mass mood (also at least a third of the S.R. vote must be allotted to Left S.R.'s and Maximalists).

Of the other corps in the same army, only the VI Corps had previously expressed Bolshevik sentiments. A brief resolution of October 29 welcomed the fall of Kerensky and characterized the Bolsheviks as "principled fighters for the ideas of the Revolution."[23] Status reports shed little additional light, noting unrest only in the 16th Division over the question of Ukrainianization. By contrast, the committee of the XXXII Corps, chaired by the eternal Dr. Gottlieb, promptly endorsed the position of the army committee and loyally polled its subunits: the Black Sea, Atkarskii, and Luganskii regiments condemned the Bolshevik rising, but "several units stood for all power to the Soviets and the impermissibility of civil war," whereas the Serdobskii Regiment sent a deputation to Petrograd to ascertain the true situation. All resolutions reflected concern for the Constituent Assembly on which "the masses pin their hopes for peace." This polling was not very scientific, but one militantly anti-Bolshevik and pro-Kerensky resolution was said to have passed unanimously at a division assembly of 700 persons. The result was a tribute to the well-organized and disciplined committee leadership, which had endured mutinies and Bolshevik agitation in June, but it is doubtful that it expressed the genuine attitudes of the mass of soldiers. Dr. Gottlieb himself conceded that the masses were "seized only with the thought of peace," whereas the committees had lost all authority and proposed that their position be "Away with civil war!" "Not one drop of blood of workers or peasants on the front!" and "United democratic government!" By November 3 the corps committee had shifted to a "united socialist government." At a congress that met on November 13 the Bolsheviks, coached by a special commissar of the Petrograd MRC, M. N. Kokovikhin, disposed of a bloc of 100 votes, but Gottlieb's unshakeable majority of 300 rammed through a strong endorsement of the line of the OAK, including the premiership of Chernov, even though this strategy had already collapsed. Complacently the leadership declared,

only 1,183 (34%). Clearly the V Corps was not typical of the front as a whole and helped considerably to boost the showing of the Bolsheviks in the Eleventh Army.

[22] See above, p. 352.

[23] *VOSRU* 2:486. Like many others of this time, it was a joint session of corps and divisional committees.

"There is no wave of Bolshevism in the Eleventh Army." As of November 21, Gottlieb's forces were still in control, but by November 22 the Bolsheviks must have gained control, because the committee organ, *GO*, ceased to appear, and an MRC that recognized Krylenko began to function.[24] Again the armistice issue was the most probable cause.

Bolshevik ascendancy in the XXV Corps was achieved at a congress on November 13 of 399 representatives elected directly by the companies. The tone of the debate was not rancorous, the former majority being hopelessly outnumbered by Bolsheviks, Ukrainians, and devotees of a congenial "nonparty" committeeman, Dr. Matusov, who apparently believed in swimming with the stream. On the key vote on power, the Bolshevik resolution passed 193 to 163 with 26 abstentions, and the old committee resigned. A new "reconciliation resolution," which endorsed Soviet power, the legitimacy of Sovnarkom, and the decisions of the Second Congress of Soviets, passed 261 to 25 with 51 abstentions. The reason for the lopsided vote was that Dr. Matusov and a representative of the Ukrainians urged the assembly to support it.[25] An MRC was broadly constructed, including representatives of each regiment and many non-Bolsheviks like Dr. Matusov. It began to function only after the front congress on November 22, by which time the leadership had been reduced to a presidium of eleven under firm Bolshevik control. On November 29, however, it became obvious that the MRC was not functioning well as an administrative apparatus; the Bolshevik chairman Chulkin resigned, pleading exhaustion and ill health, and no one could be found to replace him. Someone suggested coopting two officers from the Fanagoriiskii Regiment who were both competent and willing. Conducting a revolution was one thing, but operating a complex administrative apparatus to deal with supply, demobilization, pogroms, and acts of violence against officers without alienating one's constituency was another.[26]

The Seventh Army had also been thoroughly disoriented by the summer offensive, but it harbored a much larger contingent of party-oriented Bolsheviks with connections to the center. Units with strong Bolshevik influence reacted instantaneously to the news from Petrograd by forming MRCs, whereas few others did. On a good half of the units of the Seventh Army, which was by far the largest (seven corps and eighteen divisions) and the most isolated (from the rear and from each other), there is no information of a political nature whatsoever. The higher committeemen, though loy-

[24] See *GO*, for November 14ff. On Kokovikhin's being deputized by the Petrograd MRC, see his credentials dated November 15 to the Eleventh Army in *PVRK* 3:22. For his former activities in the Special Army, see above, pp. 32-33.

[25] See *VRKDA*, pp. 371-73.

[26] See *ibid.*, pp. 386-87 and 402-3.

alist, were singularly lacking in political talent and perspicacity. The only known case of second-phase Bolshevization is the XII Corps, where a Bolshevik leadership was activated by the front congress.[27] Otherwise the firm Bolshevik cohort consisted of the II Guards Corps, the Second Finnish Rifle Division (particularly the Sixth Regiment), and the 74th Infantry Division (XLI Corps).

That the guards corps should be more politicized than other surrounding units is not surprising, since they drew their replacements exclusively from Petrograd and otherwise were in close touch with their reserve units. On October 27 and 28 respectively the Petrograd MRC deputized two commissars to the Seventh Army, I. P. Vasianin and V. A. Upyr, along with a team of agitators, among them L. I. Gorbatenko, who were targeted on the guards units. A former Petrograd worker and Bolshevik activist, E. A. Krasnov, had also just returned from the capital, and Evgeniia Bosh, the flaming evangel of the Southwestern Regional Bureau, also materialized.[28] Thus from October 28 on a high concentration of politically experienced party workers made the rounds of units, addressed impromptu meetings, introduced resolutions, forced by-elections, and played on the mood of the masses with great vigor. A command report of November 1 on the Third Guards Division bears witness:

> The Bolshevik Lt. Gorbatenko, having arrived with a delegation from the reserve battalion, in the course of 24 hours conducted agitation among the soldiers of the [Volynskii] regiment promoting Bolshevik ideas. They assembled a series of illegal meetings, and today worked over a crowd of 100-200 men and appeared before the regimental committee, allowing no one else to speak, but shouted threats and slogans, forcing the committee to request the regimental commander to call a regimental assembly for tomorrow. In denying the request, I cited the order forbidding meetings.[29]

By November 2 the Bolsheviks had succeeded in forcing new elections and calling a corps assembly, which adopted a resolution on Soviet power and the creation of an MRC.[30] However, even energetic Bolsheviks could not create a situation out of whole cloth. The guards units were already in a state of turmoil because Commissar Surguchev was trying to extract

[27] See Popov, *Rasskaz o nezabyvaemom*, pp. 70ff.

[28] See *PVRK* 1:188, 191, 207, and 243, and *ORA*, p. 43 (report of commander of Guards Rifle Division of November 1, complaining of Bolshevik agitators).

[29] *ORA*, p. 42.

[30] Both Vasianin and Bosh addressed this assembly. See *VRKDA*, pp. 361-62. See also Krasnov's memoirs in *ONFV*, pp. 183-84.

loyalty resolutions from every unit of the Seventh Army.[31] In the I Guards Corps, with no visible Bolshevik presence, an assembly of regimental and divisional committees on October 29 declared its solidarity with the Petrograd garrison and the Second Congress of Soviets, voted down the resolution of the Southwestern Front Committee, and condemned sending troops to rescue the Provisional Government.[32] In the Third Guards Infantry Division (II Corps), staff units were very agitated over a plan to retire some of their units which had been approved by the divisional committee and demanded the complete reelection of all the committees in the corps and a corps congress. On October 28, they elected a Bolshevik deputy to the corps committee and registered a protest over the arrest of several telegraph operators who disseminated copies of the proclamations of the Petrograd MRC. In addition they accused the division committee of shelving a resolution on a general armistice instead of submitting it to regimental assemblies for discussion. Clumsy efforts by the regular committees to control communications or to sidetrack sensitive issues to prevent contagion with Bolshevism produced the opposite result.[33]

The Bolsheviks quickly exploited their control of the II Guards Corps to undertake further revolutionary action. The local Soviet and garrison in Vinnitsa had assumed power before the Petrograd uprising and engaged in a pitched battle with government troops who regained control on October 30. In nearby Zhmerinka was the rear depot of the Guards Sappers, and on November 1 Vasianin in his capacity as "people's commissar" ordered the corps MRC to reinforce Zhmerinka and retake Vinnitsa. The assignment was given to the Keksgolmskii and Third Guards Rifle regiments and units of the Artillery Brigade, who carried it out with dispatch. General Tsykovich, commander of the Seventh Army, on November 6 ruefully informed the front commander, General Volodchenko, that "they have turned the area around Zhmerinka into a little Kronshtadt."[34] The II Guards Corps

[31] Resolutions of protest in *VOSRU* 2:493 (Egerskii Regiment) and *VRKDA*, p. 360 ("meeting" of Third Guards Infantry Division of November 1).

[32] *ORA*, pp. 29-30. The first two points were obviously taken from the radiogram proclamation of the Petrograd MRC, and others are likewise derivable from the communications in circulation. On committees that were Left, but not Bolshevik, see below.

[33] Recounted in division staff report of October 28, *VKDA*, pp. 38-89. A resolution of one of the meetings on November 1 stated: "We categorically protest the actions of the corps, divisional, and regimental committees, hiding radio telegrams and information on events from units and handing out false information from the Provisional Government. . . . We demand the reelection of all committees" (*VRKDA*, pp. 359-60).

[34] *TrSh* 2:78. For other details, see staff survey of November 5 of Second Guards Division in *ORA*, p. 62, and newspaper account of Vinnitsa battle in *VOSRU* 2:494. See also above, p. 300.

remained securely in the hands of its Bolshevik MRC and sent a solid block of deputies to the front congress.[35]

Their control, however, did not extend to the I Guards Corps, which for most of November remained in the hands of its former leadership. The latter had already moved sharply left and had sent a deputy, Apraksin, to the Second Congress of Soviets. Apraksin returned from the Soviet Congress on November 7 with a full report, which was very harsh on the former government and the Petrograd KSRR, but claimed that the Bolsheviks, far from establishing a dictatorship, favored the Vikzhel formula for an all-socialist government. A corps assembly passed a resolution in favor of this formula, but reacted ambiguously to the idea of forming an MRC (16 votes in favor, 8 against, 8 abstentions). When a *nakaz* was worked out in preparation for the front congress under Apraksin's guidance, it still favored an all-socialist government, land, peace, and "an end to fratricidal war" (the standard positions of the conciliationists). That Apraksin was not a Right Bolshevik is proven by the fact that in all sincerity, though inaccurately, he claimed that Chernov had successfully negotiated an end to the Gatchina affair.[36]

The XXII Corps makes an interesting case study because both the government and the Bolsheviks tried and failed to turn it into a reliable source of military support. The Third Finnish Rifle Division was shipped out toward Petrograd on October 30, and the First Division was slated to follow; staff units had been sent on in advance and were temporarily located in Orsha, where they remained ensconced until they became embroiled in the battle for control of Stavka. Archival materials reflect a very energetic bid by the Bolshevik-dominated Sixth Regiment to win over their Second Division for revolutionary action while the rest of the corps was being rapidly fed into the railway system. Accompanying this development, taking advantage of the temporary absence of the staff, was a massive wave of destructive attacks, joined by the local peasantry, on every large estate in the region. A corps assembly had met on October 27 and passed a resolution of support for the government of the conventional type. However, on the same date 600 soldiers of the Sixth Regiment also met and approved the Petrograd uprising. On October 28, agitators fanned out to all units of the corps, calling for "demonstrations" and distributing leaflets with the text of the radiograms of the Petrograd MRC; on October 29 a series of meetings in other regiments were held which took positions of one kind of another in response. In vain the division committee tried to

[35] See documents in *VKDA*, pp. 411-16.

[36] See division committee *protokoly*, TsGVIA, f. 2322, op. 7, ed. khr. 2, ll. 26, 37, and 39.

curb this activity and secure approval for a loyalist resolution. By October 30 the Eighth Regiment had come out in support of the Sixth, posted controls over its officers, and scheduled a mass meeting to decide on the formation of an MRC; in the Fifth Regiment, six companies supported the Bolshevik uprising and six supported the Provisional Government. By November 2 the Fifth and Seventh regiments were on record in support of the Sixth Regiment, but with that the wave of agitation crested and rapidly receded. The Seventh Regiment merely "welcomed" the initiative, but decided against an open demonstration, while the Eighth Regiment revoked its previous decision and forced the resignation of its MRC. This regiment had been distressed over the removal of corps headquarters to the rear and had drawn up a petition to the army commissar to join it. Apparently they did not yet have confidence in the durability of the new power in Petrograd and did not wish to let slip the opportunity to escape front-line service. The sappers battalion rejected the idea of a demonstration against the Provisional Government, while the artillery units were split and decided to send a deputation to Petrograd for information.[37]

The First Finnish Rifle Division revealed an almost total indifference to events—the commander averred that not more than fifteen to twenty soldiers could be gathered by agitators in favor of the Petrograd coup and that the masses were hostile to them. A division assembly met to consider a loyalist resolution, but it was sidetracked by the demand of the 17th Regiment for consideration of its own resolution: it protested the disbanding of their former Fifth Division, which had been amalgamated with the First. The assembly was deeply divided over the issue, and the division committee was unable to get the discussion back on track. In other words, particular grievances took precedence over seemingly much more important political issues, reflecting a general disenchantment with politics, unless concrete visceral results were discernible. Against this wall of particularism, the campaign of the Sixth Regiment foundered.[38]

The Third Division departed without incident and was successfully insulated from events on its long journey northward, even taking part in action against the local Bolshevik revolt in Vinnitsa, but on arriving in Luga, after Kerensky's defeat, it turned Bolshevik.[39] A Bolshevik emissary from the Petrograd MRC had tried his hand at persuasion on November 4 or 5, but the division refused to halt its journey northward. They promised

[37] All in TsGVIA, f. 2222, op. 1, ed. khr. 1066, ll. 484-547 (staff reports), and ed. khr. 1185, ll. 197 and 198 (committee documents of loyalist content).

[38] *Ibid.*, l. 200.

[39] *Ibid.*, l. 209 (return of a deputation to the capital on November 11 led to by-elections on November 16; a visit to factories and barracks had convinced them that "the majority of the soldiers support the Bolsheviks").

only to clarify the situation before engaging in any military action. The prospect of getting as far away from the front as possible was too tempting to complicate it with politics.[40] The materials on the XXII Corps illustrate how difficult it is to make overarching generalizations on soldier reactions to Petrograd events and how much depended on the particular conjunctions of factors. In all situations, however, individual units displayed remarkable solidarity and refused to allow themselves to be used as extensions of the politics of outsiders. They very much wanted to participate in events, to be fully informed, and to influence the outcome, but on their own terms. In the existing confusion there was no reason to rush to judgment.

As far as can be ascertained, the 74th Division of the XLI Corps was the only other unit of the Seventh Army to be in favor of the Petrograd uprising.[41] Popov, a Bolshevik activist of the XII Corps, which he portrays as under Bolshevik influence, is quite vague about concrete developments during the October crisis and most of November, but he claims, probably accurately, that a Bolshevik delegation attended the front congress, which would indicate some committee turnovers; however, a corps congress that formed a Bolshevik-dominated MRC took place only in early December. The meeting place was guarded with units of the 11th and 19th divisions with posted machine guns, as Ukrainian units had just taken over front headquarters at Berdichev; the MRC suspected collusion of the command and the old committees to deny power to the Bolsheviks.[42]

On most other units the record is silent. One hears nothing of by-elections or congresses in non-Bolshevik units, and when the Seventh Army Committee finally called for a new army congress on November 17, it did not call for new elections. Bolshevik memoirs take on a very embattled character toward the end of November and early December, not only with respect to Ukrainian advances but also with respect to hostile committees in rival units such as the VII Siberian Corps. It is possible that the army committee had consciously sought to deny the Bolsheviks the arena in which they thrived, namely, electoral contests, but if such is the case the Bolsheviks did not push for them energetically. Why this was so is not at all clear, but it illustrates that the Bolsheviks required the legitimacy of democratic organs to wield power effectively and in the case of the Seventh

[40] Delegates' report of November 9 in *PVRK* 2:322-23.

[41] An assembly of October 31 of the entire division voted "All power to the Soviet" and elected an MRC. See *ORA*, pp. 36-37, and *VRKDA*, p. 411 (*protokol* No. 29 of December 1 of MRC).

[42] See Popov, *Rasskaz o nezabyvaemom*, pp. 75-76. By the end of November there were functioning MRCs also in the Third Caucasus and XLI Corps, but under what circumstances is not clear, nor is it clear that they were Bolshevik-dominated (see *VRKDA*, pp. 413-14 and 435-36, where routine sessions are numbered 5 and 8 respectively as of December 1 and 9).

Army, failing to achieve this, were obliged to rely on force alone. Consequently, in spite of a wealth of experienced party personnel and the same favorable factors as the Eleventh Army and elsewhere, the Bolsheviks failed to extend their influence much beyond the units they already controlled in late October.

Finally, by the third week in November the Bolshevik "Commissar" Vasianin became impatient and "ordered" the MRC of the Sixth Finnish Rifle Regiment to occupy Proskurov, the army headquarters and seat of the army committee, much as the Latvian brigades had occupied Valka. The attempt to bring in other units of the Second Division failed utterly, and the staff was protected by cossack and shock units. But like the Latvians the Seventh Army Bolsheviks managed to talk their way in rather than fight. The cossacks were swayed to neutrality by the promise that they would receive orders permitting them to go home. The shock units were disarmed by a clever ploy: while part of the Bolsheviks' negotiating team engaged the officers in abusive argument, others mixed with the soldiers of the shock unit and inquired whether they had received payouts for not receiving their full rations, as was the practice in infantry units. Immediately the soldiers were aroused against their officers and no longer posed a danger to the Bolshevik occupation of Proskurov. A provisional MRC for the Seventh Army was set up and took charge of staff operations, but so far as can be determined the Bolsheviks won over no new following. The congress scheduled by the old committee was successfully called off, and a congress under MRC sponsorship on the basis of new elections was held in Kamenets-Podolsk on December 2. Of 750 deputies, 500 were Bolshevik and most of the rest were Ukrainian and nonparty (nothing is mentioned of Left S.R.'s). Unreconstructed units probably boycotted the assembly, but also a new Bolshevik wave must have followed the proclamation of a general armistice on November 22. A solid cohort of Bolshevik functionaries presided over the proceedings—N. N. Kuzmin, the commissar for the Southwestern Front, Vasianin and Upyr, commissars for the Seventh Army, V. A. Malakovskii, the MRC chairman of the Sixth Finnish Rifle Regiment, and E. I. Krasnov, representative from the Second Guards Division. The major concern of the congress was the shaping contest with the Don Republic and the Ukrainian Rada; the Rada now claimed all power on the Southwestern Front and interdicted supplies and free access to core Russia. The much-depleted Seventh Army was now concerned above all with survival and battling the Ukrainian Republic to get home.[43]

[43] Details are entirely in memoirs of Malakovskii, Krasnov, and Tuzhikov in *ONFV*, pp. 163-212, and in Popov, pp. 80-95. The last available issue of *Iz7A* is November 19, with

☆

A sector as remote and vast as the Rumanian Front, comprising four armies (Eighth, Ninth, Sixth, Fourth), eighteen corps, and nearly fifty divisions, was even less likely to be affected by the politics of the center if not immune to the more spontaneous expressions of determination to achieve peace. For a good half of the units on this front this seemed to be true, but based more on inference from the sketchy staff surveys than on concrete knowledge. So far as can be determined the radioed messages from Smolnyi did not often get through to primary units, travelers were few, and committees and commissars filtered information reaching the ranks. Thus the radical impulses and peace hopes had to find other outlets, such as plundering local estates, threats to officers, and fraternization. An extensive survey of the Rumanian Front for this period notes for a few units a "worsening of the situation in connection with events in Petrograd and Moscow," sometimes linked to hopes for peace, sometimes expressed in sympathy for the Bolsheviks or Soviet power, but by no means yielding a uniform picture; on well over half the units, only various forms of disorders are recorded. Of the XVI Corps (Eighth Army) it comments that "the masses secretly sympathize with the Bolshevik uprising, connecting it with hopes for peace," but the survey also observes that "the mood is generally expectant, impatiently awaiting the meeting of the Constituent Assembly on which they lay all their hopes." The final summary states: "The Bolshevik current has spread significantly, though in general the mood is anxious, not yet fully defined and inconsistent. But a conscious recognition of Bolshevism has been created and as a consequence its application—fraternization."[44] There are fewer references to Soviet power than one might expect, but most units were probably still unaware that a congress had taken place or that the new government was based on the Soviets. The sanitized version reaching them still portrayed the Bolsheviks and the Petrograd garrison as having "seized power" in order to preempt the Constituent Assembly. That the masses should nevertheless perceive Bolshevism in a positive light is a measure of their disenchantment with the Provisional Government and the democratic leadership. But in several instances Bolshevism was attacked because Lenin was quoted as conceding that peace could not be obtained immediately. The 160th Division was said to be disenchanted with the Bolsheviks, who "promised immediate peace, but so far haven't got it."[45]

---

the old committee still in charge. *IzVK7*, the organ of the MRC, appeared from November 23.

[44] *ORA*, p. 79.

[45] *Ibid.*, pp. 73, 76 (front survey of November 8) and 144 (report on XVI Corps of November 18).

That a positive image of the Bolsheviks did not necessarily translate into votes is evident from the Constituent Assembly election results on the Rumanian Front. The Bolsheviks received only 24 percent of the total for the front as a whole, 15 percent in the Sixth Army, and only 11 percent in the Ninth (where the Ukrainians polled 20 percent), whereas the S.R.'s received 46.4 percent for the front and 62.7 and 63 percent for the latter two armies respectively.[46] Though some committee organs crowed that this refuted the notion of a "wave of Bolshevism," the Bolsheviks invariably did much better in elections to army and front congresses in the month of November and early December. As one soldier put it: "On peace we are all Bolsheviks, on everything else we are S.R.'s."[47]

That the Bolsheviks had a far less secure hold on the Rumanian Front than on any other did not mean, however, that otherwise the dynamic factors were not more or less the same, or that committee revolutions, even if belated, did not express the same popular goals. New leftist coalitions often pledged to carry out or follow in practice the decrees of Sovnarkom or the orders of the new Commander in Chief, Krylenko, but withheld formal recognition in favor of the idea of an all-socialist coalition. Moreover, Ukrainianization, which involved between 15 and 20 percent of the troops and transformed entire regiments and divisions into purely Ukrainian units, was a more potent factor in the Eighth and Ninth armies than anywhere else on the front. Yet on most points the platform of the Ukrainians was not unlike that of the Bolsheviks and other leftist factions. In the politics of congresses and committees, they allied themselves sometimes with the former, sometimes with the latter, but seldom with the defensists. Finally, there were as many distinctive patterns between armies, corps, and divisions as elsewhere, though the specific weight of Bolshevism was usually far less. The Ninth and Fourth armies were relatively unpoliticized for most of November, while loyalist committees struggled against various forms of spontaneous disintegration (somewhat resembling the Tenth and Seventh armies). The Eighth Army, however, had several divisions and one corps that had declared themselves for Soviet power before the Petrograd uprising (32nd and 165th divisions, XXXIII Corps) and several more afterward.[48]

[46] *IzFR*, November 25 and 28. The Mensheviks characteristically received 2-4%; the Kadets, 1.5-2%; Muslims 2-3%; and all others less than 1%. The participation rate was higher here than on any other front, reaching 78% in the Sixth Army (177 districts reporting). See *VGr*, November 27.

[47] *Ibid.*, November 22 and December 13. On the congress election results, see below, p. 370.

[48] See Frenkin, *Revoliutsionnoe dvizhenie*, pp. 253 and 258, for the first three; *ORA*, pp. 55 and 143, and *BMRF*, pp. 173-74, for latter.

The Bolshevik forces in the Eighth Army were well poised to respond to the uprising, as on October 28-30 they held a conference chaired by a loyal Leninist, B. I. Solers; 297 delegates were said to represent 7,000 party members and 77 different organizations, a higher total than even the Fifth Army. I. F. Kuchmin of the 13th Transamur Regiment had just returned from Petrograd where he had been fully informed about the Bolshevik plans for an uprising; it is also clear that the conference knew about the radiograms of the Petrograd MRC, so that the selective version of events being circulated by the loyalist committees could be effectively countered. The conference appointed a five-man MRC headed by Kuchmin and instructed all those present to organize their units in support of the Petrograd MRC.[49] Kuchmin promptly carried out his mission in his home regiment: on October 28 in the 13th Transamur Regiment an MRC claimed to be in control, and no orders were to be obeyed without its authority. As in the Sixth Finnish Rifle Regiment, it planned to organize a series of flying meetings in various units, collect resolutions on Soviet power, and then force by-elections in the committees, taking the entire XXXIII Corps by storm.

Since Bolsheviks already enjoyed significant influence in many units, the prospects for success seemed bright. Nevertheless, the campaign yielded very modest results and did not lead to a complete turnover in the committees for two more weeks. Kuchmin tried to generate momentum by staging "negotiations" of his regiment with the Germans and inviting other regiments to join them; it was suggested that fraternization should be conducted by specially elected MRCs. The 16th and 14th regiments followed suit, but the meeting in the 14th was said to be poorly attended, and a later one reversed the decision. Although the affair attracted great attention and even promoted sympathy for Soviet power and peace, other units remained very cautious toward the Bolsheviks of the 13th Regiment. For example, there were stormy meetings in the First Transamur Division that passed resolutions in favor of Soviet power, but the division was reserved toward the Bolshevik agitators and did not fall in with the fraternization or the election of MRCs; its attention was riveted to the Constituent Assembly elections, which they expected to resolve everything. The Second Transamur Division held by-elections, but S.R.'s were elected, not Bolsheviks. Even the very turbulent 117th Infantry Division calmed down, declined the invitation to take a position on Soviet power, and seemed more interested in the outcome of the Constituent Assembly elections. These soldiers were obviously averse to "stirring up party strife"

[49] See Frenkin, *Revoliutsionnoe dvizhenie*, pp. 248-49; text of resolution supporting Petrograd MRC in *ORA*, pp. 25-26.

or running the risk of civil war so near to the event that would certainly bring peace.[50]

Since a multi-party MRC already existed on the corps level in response to an initiative of Rumcherod, the Bolsheviks refocused their campaign on recalling MRC members who did not support Soviet power. A renewed effort was undertaken by the Bolsheviks of the Second Transamur Division, who sent emissaries to other units; on November 12 they convoked an ad hoc assembly of all units of the division who supported the recall movement. It resolved that "in view of the inability of the present MRC of the XXXIII Corps to measure up to this task, we demand its total replacement by nominees of directly elected committees."[51] On November 17 the corps commander reported to Eighth Army headquarters that an assembly of MRCs from regimental to corps level was discussing armistice strategy, guided by the Bolsheviks. To keep watch on the proceedings, he himself agreed to initiate contact with the German side.[52] Again the armistice issue worked powerfully to give the Bolsheviks a tighter hold on the organs of power. The chairman of the corps MRC, as of November 20, was the experienced Bolshevik Ia. M. Muravnik, though just when the turnover occurred is not clear.[53]

Given the initial advantages of the Bolsheviks and their unquestioned visibility on this sector of the front, it is perhaps puzzling why it took them so long to gain control of the committee apparatus of the XXXIII Corps and why there were so many evidences of ambivalence toward them on the part of the soldiers. The soldier masses enthusiastically supported the Bolshevik program and hailed their efforts to promote peace, but did not necessarily trust their leadership. This peculiar attitude was also expressed at an assembly of peasant organizations in a division of the Fourth Army. They passed a resolution threatening that if the other socialist parties did not adopt the Bolshevik program they would drop their own support of the idea of an "all-socialist coalition" and recognize Sovnarkom; at the same time they strongly condemned party strife and urged the socialist parties to find a common language.[54] A deputy to the congress of the Eighth Army from an artillery unit expressed it even better:

> The comrades demand a practical solution to the question of the war. Theoretical considerations have long since ceased to interest us. We

[50] From staff reports of XXXIII Corps of November 3 and 10 in *BMRF*, pp. 126-67 and 143-45.

[51] *VRKDA*, pp. 476-77.

[52] See *ORA*, p. 140.

[53] See *VRKDA*, p. 481.

[54] *BMRF*, p. 166.

> simply can fight no longer, so give us any kind of peace. That also expresses our view on power. We have no faith in individual persons, neither Kerensky nor Lenin. We are conditional Bolsheviks—whoever gives us peace we'll support.[55]

The Constituent Assembly elections revealed that the Bolsheviks had more support in the Eighth Army than in any other army on the front, but still polled only 24.3 percent, whereas the S.R.'s received 46 percent and the Ukrainians 21 percent. It was another story, however, at the congress of the Eighth Army which assembled on November 25: hard-core Bolsheviks like Solers and Kuchmin were in charge, and on the key issues the Bolsheviks outvoted their rivals two to one. Even a resolution approving the closing down of the S.R. press was passed 175 to 76.[56]

Of all the armies on the front, the Sixth Army proved to have the most resolute, non-Bolshevik leadership and in timely fashion discarded conventional committee politics for the only reasonable alternative to incipient Bolshevism, namely, an all-socialist coalition based on peace, land, and the democratization of the command structure. As noted above, the IV Siberian Corps of this army had anticipated the Vikzhel-OAK program in its resolution of October 14 at a corps assembly. The corps was also one of the first on this front to renovate its leadership through by-elections, so that the accumulated radicalism of the masses was given political form and content well before the October coup. In connection with the formation of an MRC on October 28 (a response to the Rumanian Front initiative, not to the Petrograd MRC), the architects of the leftist program, the Social Democratic (Menshevik) Internationalists, directly took over the leadership in the corps and conveyed the same radical impulse to the army level.[57]

A similar committee revolution took place in the IV Army Corps on November 2. Originally the corps committee had taken a loyalist position; however, they convoked a corps assembly of 188 representatives to deal with the refusal of the Guriiskii Regiment to take up a position on the line, and an unexpected outpouring of militant left sentiment resulted. The agenda was revised to consider the "current moment" and the election of new representatives to the army committee. The political resolution accepted Soviet power as a *fait accompli* and harshly condemned the "criminal shedding of the people's blood" without identifying the guilty party. It did, however, insist that the Soviet Congress, presumed to be still in session, include representatives of "all the democracy" and the "entire

[55] *Iz2S8*, November 27.

[56] See *ibid.*, November 29 and December 1. On Constituent Assembly elections, see *IzFR*, November 29. For the likely reason for the results, see below, pp. 386-87.

[57] See above, p. 317.

people,'' apparently alluding to the absence of the Peasant Soviet and a full representation of the front. The accommodationist spirit was also reflected in the balance of the newly elected committee members between Bolsheviks and Left S.R.'s; at the same time, the assembly took a firm line on the rebellion of the Guriiskii Regiment, not allowing themselves to be misled by their claim to be ''Bolsheviks.'' The Guriiskiis responded sarcastically: ''We congratulate the comrade Bolsheviks on their revolution and ask that they have us replaced at the front so that we too can defend Freedom and the Revolution in the rear.''[58] The new leadership in both the IV Siberian and IV Army corps was based on an alliance of Left S.R.'s, Social Democratic (Menshevik) Internationalists, and Bolsheviks, all of whom seemed gratified by the new arrangements and drew their inspiration more from specific front attitudes than from the national leadership; many of the leaders of all the fractions were subsequently active on the army and front level.[59] Both formed vigorous MRCs that took charge of their units, designated ''commissars'' to lower levels, initiated a whole series of command changes, and immersed themselves in questions of supply, munitions, restraining the wave of pogroms, and ordinary committee work.[60]

Since the front committee (the ''front section'' of Rumcherod) had called for the formation of MRCs on October 26 and otherwise struck a course emphasizing independence of the national leadership, one might be misled into crediting them for setting the new independent course. However, a closer study of the available materials reveals that the front section of Rumcherod did not enjoy a great deal of influence on the lower levels and that the latter were developing their own strategies independently. The organ of the Sixth Army Committee, *Voin-Grazhdanin* (*VGr*), publicized only the positions of the army committee and for a number of days either ignored or treated lightly the front initiatives. The army committee under the vigorous leadership of its new chairman, the Menshevik Internationalist Greiber, staked out its own position and flat-out rejected Rumcherod's appeal to put a battalion from each corps at the disposal of the front MRC. Clearly the army committee regarded its own authority, not that of the front organs, as binding in the Sixth Army. An expanded session of lower committees of the Sixth Army met on October 29 and endorsed the army

[58] From *protokol* in *VRKDA*, pp. 473-75, except for the final quotation, which is from reference to same incident in committee *protokol* of the IV Siberian Corps for November 1 (TsGVIA, f. 2282, op. 4, ed. khr. 11, l. 30).

[59] See list of members of the Sixth Army MRC in *VRKDA*, p. 476, compared with above cited sources, which produces several names from each party fraction.

[60] See further *protokoly* of the IV Siberian Corps in TsGVIA, f. 2282, op. 4, ed. khr. 11, ll. 31ff., and *VRKDA*, p. 477 (*protokol* of MRC of IV Army Corps of November 15).

committee resolution of the 27 ("united democratic government without census elements"), but also resolved that civil war was to be avoided at all costs and that accredited representatives should finally be sent to the Second Congress, presumed still to be in session. The architects of the new line were Greiber and Liperovskii, who had earlier formulated the Vikzhel-like political program of the Sixth Army Social Democratic (Menshevik) Internationalists. Greiber's address to the body in support of the resolution made a deep impression. He stressed above all that the idea of coalition had outlived itself, that an all-socialist government must include Bolsheviks (distancing himself from his own party's Central Committee), and that the vigorous pursuit of peace negotiations took precedence over everything else. The army committee, he informed the assembly, had already urged VTsIK to utilize the Skobelev mission to Paris to persuade the Allies to enter into peace negotiations and to withdraw formally from the alliance if they refused.[61]

Two days later the same session hotly discussed the proposal of the IV Siberian Corps to form an army MRC, which the former S.R. majority on the army committee took as an expression of "lack of confidence" in their leadership and an infringement on the "unity of all the democracy." *Voin-Grazhdanin*, now in the hands of the new leadership, noted sarcastically that the assembly was not carried away by the "revolutionary mysticism" of the old majority and frankly acknowledged that the credibility problem of the leadership could be repaired only through a freshly created organ drawing on new representatives from the lower units. Thus, two new representatives from each corps and one from each division and rear garrison were drawn into the army committee, and this expanded body selected the MRC. Because this process took time, it was November 7 before the selecting body could be convoked. By then it had been determined that the MRC should reflect parity between the three major political parties (S.R.'s, Mensheviks, and Bolsheviks), each allotted four seats, and one each for Muslims, Poles, and Ukrainians. Most of those chosen were identifiable Left Internationalists: Degtiarev and Kobozev were Left S.R.'s from the IV Siberian and IV Army corps respectively; Greiber, Rozin, and Zhuravskii were Menshevik Internationalists; and Vorob'ev, Khomkin, and

[61] *VGr*, October 31. The prominence in the leadership of the Rumanian Front of the United Social Democrats (primarily Menshevik Internationalists) is evident from their list for the Constituent Assembly elections in *VGr*, October 29, which besides Greiber and Liperovskii includes Iamolev (editor of *VGr*, "Uncle Pavel"), Ladyzhinskii (editor of *IzFR*), Veselkov of Rumcherod, Perekrestov and Nakhamkin of the OAK, and several others who were active in army committees. On the Internationalists forming a considerable caucus within this group and already enjoying considerable influence early in October, see the account of their separate conference in *VGr*, October 1, which represented a membership of 1,263 in the Sixth Army.

Orlovskii were Bolsheviks. It is interesting to note that Liperovskii was given an advisory vote and, still in his capacity as government commissar, informed lower units that "all orders and telegrams [of the Sixth Army's MRC] carrying the signature of Chairman Greiber or his two co-chairmen, Zhuravskii and Vorob'ev, are subject to immediate and exact execution."[62]

Greiber and Liperovskii, the architects of these new arrangements, were obviously trying to fill the void in power in the sharply changing situation. Once the MRC was in place, it backed the OAK-Vikzhel strategy and in effect implemented it in the Sixth Army by drawing in the participation of Left S.R.'s and Bolsheviks. At its first session the MRC adopted an eight-point program that included all the essentials of the Vikzhel platform, adding only complete controls over production and democratization of the Army. The MRC made very clear that it expected all persons and institutions to be subject to its authority and that all orders of the command were to be counter-signed by the MRC chairman or his designee, not excluding operative orders and those on troop movements.[63]

Soon the new coalition was put to the test over the question of the armistice and the assumption of the Supreme Command by Krylenko. All fractions of the MRC favored armistice negotiations in principle, but Krylenko had also directed the disbanding of the OAK as a tool of the former Stavka. At a joint session of the MRC and the army committee of November 15, the majority split with the Bolsheviks, agreeing to follow Krylenko's directives on armistice negotiations in practice, but not to recognize him as Commander in Chief, since, they argued, only an authoritative government which included all socialist parties and enjoyed the full participation of the front through its designated organ, the OAK, could treat with the Germans as equals and avert a dictated peace. Although the arguments were cogently and moderately presented, the Bolsheviks on the MRC took exception: only by recognizing Sovnarkom and Soviet power could such unity and authority be achieved. In fact, the Sixth Army MRC initiated armistice negotiations on the same date, designating Liperovskii and the Bolshevik Vorob'ev as their plenipotentiaries. On November 21 an olive branch was again held out to the Bolsheviks by agreeing to recognize Krylenko as Commander in Chief *when* all socialist parties were included in the government; in the meantime they would follow his directives without recognizing Sovnarkom. Bolsheviks Orlovskii and Vorob'ev urged their opponents to swallow their pride and accept the verdict of the revolutionary workers and soldiers of Petrograd. The Menshevik Iakovlev replied, "We will help the Bolsheviks make peace, but that doesn't mean we won't

[62] *VGr*, November 9, and *VRKDA*, November 12.

[63] *Protokol* of November 8 in *VGr*, November 12.

criticize them when they are wrong.'' Liperovskii argued that the Constituent Assembly, whose elections had just been concluded, should be the final arbiter on all questions.[64]

The arbiter in the Sixth Army, however, was not to be the Constituent Assembly, but a congress which met on November 26. The Bolsheviks elected 240 of the 695 deputies, or around 34 percent, while the S.R.'s won 49 percent and the United Social Democrats (Mensheviks) won 15 percent; however, 130 of the S.R.'s were Left S.R.'s and another 93 were Ukrainian socialists, who on key issues voted with the Bolsheviks. Despite their favorable position, several incidents revealed that the Bolsheviks were indecisive and lacking in leadership. The resolution of the Left S.R.'s, which favored a separate peace if the Allies proved recalcitrant, was handily passed 324 votes to 252, whereas a Menshevik Internationalist resolution was decisively defeated (''only the Constituent Assembly can make peace''). A different alignment occurred on the question of the Constituent Assembly and power, since the Left S.R.'s felt compelled to support the Menshevik Internationalist formula of unlimited sovereignty, and only the Bolsheviks opposed it. It was nevertheless defeated by a few votes, whereupon the Bolsheviks and Ukrainians presented a new resolution that recognized the authority of the Constituent Assembly only if it carried out the longings of the masses on land and peace as embodied in the land and peace decrees. An unfriendly amendment, sponsored by the Menshevik Internationalists, was defeated by 12 votes, while the resolution itself passed by 275 to 235. Thus, the Bolsheviks were able to prove that on any given issue they could command a majority. Greiber was still very prominent in the proceedings, vigorously defending his policies as chairman of both the army committee and the MRC against hostile interlocutions. The Bolsheviks grudgingly acknowledged that on practically every issue the Bolsheviks had backed Greiber's policies. On his part, he pledged his complete support to the new army committee on which the Bolsheviks and Left S.R.'s would enjoy a comfortable majority (53 out of 80 places). His magnanimity won him a standing ovation at the conclusion of his report.[65] The new leadership was constructed not unlike the old, with the center of gravity shifting slightly in favor of the Bolsheviks. No one could dispute that the Menshevik Internationalists had a near monopoly of talent, and Greiber and Liperovskii continued to exercise key functions in the new dispensation, which was preoccupied with problems of supply, demobilization, and the organized return of the army to Russian soil.

[64] *Ibid.*, November 24 and 25.

[65] All in *ibid.*, December 7. On the new MRC were three Bolsheviks, 12 Left S.R.'s, 17 regular S.R.'s, 10 United Social Democrats, and 10 ''Internationalists.''

The materials on the Sixth Army include rich information on the social, educational, and occupational profile of the participants, broken down by party affiliation. Thus there were 463 Great Russians, 116 Ukrainians, 25 White Russians, 23 Jews, 13 Latvians, 12 Poles, and a sprinkling of Tatars and other nationalities. Of the assembly 68 (9.6 percent) had attended institutions of higher education, 83 (11.7 percent) had attended secondary schools, and the rest, primary school or less (562, or 79.6 percent). As might be expected, the Mensheviks had the highest ratio of those with higher and secondary education (23 and 10 out of 78 deputies supplying information) most of whom followed white-collar professions. The remaining number were workers with party experience. Only 4 of the Bolsheviks had acquired a higher education and only 8 had a secondary education; 110 out of 183 by this count were workers and 46 were peasants, but only 26 characterized themselves as "old workers." The S.R.'s had a comparable raw number of educated types as the Mensheviks (24 and 19), but 105 workers and 85 peasants. The Ukrainians' profile resembled that of the Bolsheviks. One striking feature is that workers by far represented the largest social contingent in a predominantly peasant army, reflecting their higher general degree of culture and political experience; moreover, two-thirds of their number characterized themselves as skilled workers (carpenters, lathe operators, metal workers, etc.). It demonstrates once again that in all democratic organizations there was always a considerable social distinction between those elected and those electing them, but in this case, reflecting the popular upsurge, the intelligentsia element had yielded pride of place to those who lived by their labor.[66]

The vigorous response of the front leadership to the October coup appeared to be motivated by the same independent radicalism and disenchantment with coalition politics as the Sixth Army, but a closer analysis reveals that the substance was little more than a salvage operation. Though the front committee disassociated itself from the Provisional Government, its basic concern in creating an MRC appears to have been to steal the Bolsheviks' thunder and to create a strong substitute authority on the Rumanian Front. It sought more to dampen the mass reaction than to capture its radical spirit. Absent in its initial appeal was any reference to the urgency of peace or any other social issue (though the Constituent Assembly was to meet at all costs). The membership of the MRC included the two front commissars Tizengausen and Andrianov and otherwise comprised the existing leadership of the Front Section of Rumcherod, headed by the defensist S. R. Lodkipanidze (a representative of General Shcherbachev, a certain Colonel Dubiaga, was given an advisory vote). Though factional

[66] All in *ibid.*

politics seems not to have played a major role, a moderate Bolshevik named Baranov was included, who joined in the condemnation of the Bolshevik uprising.[67] The MRC platform still avoided sensitive issues and announced its chief purpose to be maintaining order and crushing anarchy. It claimed unequivocally, however, that the command was subject to its authority in all matters except operative, though only troop movements *to* the front could be construed as such. The MRC insisted on the right to remove commanders who resisted their authority. The appeal to all units to form their own MRCs and assume similar functions would seem to be a revolutionary measure, but obviously it envisaged a hierarchy of MRCs directly subject to the front MRC that was to command its own military force. The "congress" which convened on October 31 to finalize the new arrangements did not in fact constitute a "committee revolution," since it consisted of two representatives from existing committees down to the divisional level. Thus, it short-circuited the process by which mass ferment could alter the structure of power. It is not surprising that 80 of the 140 delegates were S.R.'s (no Lefts recorded), 40 were United S.D.'s (mainly Menshevik Internationalists), and only 25 were Bolsheviks. The congress featured little in the way of meaningful debate or political maneuvering. The speeches and topics were carefully pre-selected: Andrianov gave the major address, which was indeed bold for a government commissar but showed little practical imagination. Though he pictured the Bolsheviks as fanatics and irresponsible anarchists, Andrianov was just as harsh on the old VTsIK for making concessions to the bourgeois partners (sacrificing Chernov, approving the death penalty, acquiescing to the personality cult of Kerensky, relinquishing control over foreign policy), but on the crucial issue of war and peace he had nothing to say. He conceded that Bolshevism was an inevitable release for the mass mood in the absence of leadership by the political parties, but strangely held them responsible for putting a stop to pogroms and the pilfering of state supplies.

The proceedings began to get out of hand when a number of units gave reports that were sharply critical of the Provisional Government and deplored the use of armed force against the Bolsheviks. The Mensheviks intervened with a resolution blaming the coalition for creating the conditions that led to the coup; they proposed as a political solution an "all-democratic coalition" committed to land and peace. The Petrograd KSRR was acknowledged as the authoritative organ to rebuild a government, but should include Bolsheviks. The resolution was both behind and ahead of events, doubtless due to the garbled state of communications, but the sponsors had apparently secured the support of the Bolsheviks for this

[67] All in *IzFR*, October 27. Other points which follow, *passim*.

resolution as part of a total package to maintain a united front of Social Democrats against the S.R.'s. Suddenly the composition of the MRC became a subject of debate before the main resolution could be brought to a vote. The Menshevik-Bolshevik caucus insisted on three places for each of the major parties, which would put the S.R.'s in the minority. The S.R.'s protested that there was only one Social Democratic Party, and they could distribute their allotted three places between themselves as they saw fit. The Mensheviks and Bolsheviks threatened a walkout, and the S.R.'s yielded, provided the Ukrainians were also given three places; the Menshevik-Bolshevik bloc agreed, provided they went to a Ukrainian S.R., a Menshevik, and a Bolshevik respectively. The S.R.'s finally buckled, but immediately took their revenge: they moved an amendment to the main motion sharply condemning the Bolshevik uprising, which carried by a small margin. Naturally the Bolsheviks walked out, leaving the Mensheviks high and dry.

Although the S.R.'s had worked a power play worthy of the Bolsheviks, it was a formula for political disaster. The front committee was now aligned with the last-ditch KSRR-OAK strategy which had advanced Chernov as premier, but they had forfeited the much-needed talent of the Menshevik Internationalists. None of the respective armies responded to the front leadership's favorite idea of "revolutionary divisions" under the control of the front MRC or to any other of its policy positions. The Rumanian Front MRC was merely a cipher in the OAK strategy, constantly overestimating its authority but in practice impotent. Even its once-important connection with the Odessa-based Rumcherod lost all significance; power in the region was now split three ways—between the Ukrainian Rada (recognized by the Military District), a Bolshevik MRC, and a few local soviets that still recognized Rumcherod. The front MRC scarcely seemed politically active in November except to protest the disbanding of the OAK on November 16.

On November 24 a scratch Bolshevik unit of the 48th Division took over the headquarters of the Fourth Army in Roman, liquidating the former army committee (on which there is otherwise no information). On December 1 an army congress was held which was controlled by a Bolshevik-Left S.R. majority. In the Ninth Army an army conference of November 18-20 revealed substantial increases in the representation of Bolsheviks and Left S.R.'s, persuading the old committee to call for a series of corps congresses and an official army congress; the latter met on December 2 with a Bolshevik-Left S.R. majority. With Bolshevik-led leftist coalitions acquiring control in the Sixth and Eighth armies by the end of the month, the front MRC was totally isolated. Even General Shcherbachev no longer paid any attention to it, making his own arrangements with the Ukrainian

Rada for transforming his remaining units into their nationality components. On November 24 an MRC of staff units of front headquarters demanded that the front MRC resign "or we won't be responsible for the consequences." On November 29 a similar threat was made by the garrisons of Iassy and Sokol; they were particularly offended by the fact that "Kerensky's commissars" still lorded it over the front MRC with a palace guard of "revolutionary divisions." Bolshevik units formed their own MRC, and on December 2, accompanied by a guard of only twenty soldiers, "arrested" the old MRC. Two days later General Shcherbachev, with a force of nationality units, struck back and rounded up the Bolsheviks in the name of the Ukrainian Rada. In the course of it, the Bolshevik commissar of Sovnarkom, the veteran Kronshtadt Bolshevik S. Roshal, was brutally murdered.[68]

[68] See *ibid.*, November 26 and 29, and Frenkin, *Russkaia Armiia v revoliutsii*, pp. 634-35.

CHAPTER XI

PEACE AND DENOUEMENT (NOVEMBER-DECEMBER 1917)

ALTHOUGH the first two weeks of "Soviet power" revealed the enormous appeal of the Bolshevik program and the irreparable demise of the old democratic leadership, the Bolsheviks were far from having consolidated support either in Petrograd or at the front. "Soviet power" had generated high expectations, but the fear of civil war and impatience with party strife had thwarted Lenin's design of an all-Bolshevik government behind the facade of Soviet legitimacy, and the effort had even fragmented his own party following. Bolsheviks at the front received conflicting cues and were divided in their own counsels. Only in the Second Army had they gained uncontested control of the committee structure, the only possible fulcrum of effective power; elsewhere they were obliged either to share power with other leftist fractions or to fall short of it altogether. Even in the Fifth Army, where the Bolsheviks held a tenuous majority, they were restrained by inner doubts, the uncertain mood of the masses, and the residual strength of their opponents.

As long as they were mired in the Vikzhel negotiations, the Bolsheviks in Petrograd could not translate their ascendancy at the Second Congress into effective rule. The very notion of Soviet power during this interregnum was compromised, and for a time it looked as if the Bolsheviks would have to be satisfied with the only viable alternative, an "all-socialist government," until the Constituent Assembly. A sign of the Bolsheviks' discomfiture was their failure to follow up the decrees and proclamations of the first twenty-four hours with any significant sequels either to inspire the masses or to guide their own cohorts. Bolsheviks at the front were largely left to their own devices.[1]

[1] All Soviet collections reflect this hiatus. In *VRKDA*, in the section entitled "Rukovodstvo bol'shevistskoi partii i tsentral'nykh organov sovetsoi vlasti" (pp. 21ff.), the first seven documents are the directives of the Petrograd MRC, and the decrees and proclamations of the Second Congress of October 25-26. For the following days until November 8 there is

Lenin's hands were untied when the Mensheviks and S.R.'s obligingly laid down unacceptable conditions for entering a socialist coalition, thus covering the traces of his own intransigence. When the Vikzhel negotiations broke off, he regained control of his Central Committee, the defecting commissars returned to their posts, and the way was open for the Left S.R.'s to enter the government or Sovnarkom. No one was more aware of the political perils of the moment than Lenin. Clearly some dramatic new step was necessary to recover the lost momentum and to restore confidence at the front that Soviet power meant peace.

On November 8 Lenin struck upon the device that was to accomplish his purposes. At 5:00 A.M., acting on behalf of Sovnarkom, he formally instructed Acting Commander in Chief Dukhonin via direct wire to "contact the enemy military authorities with an offer of the immediate cessation of hostilities for the purpose of opening up peace negotiations" and to keep Sovnarkom informed of his progress. The terms of an armistice were to be worked out by field commanders but referred to Sovnarkom before signing.[2] Dukhonin temporized for most of the day while consulting the OAK, his front commanders, and the Allied military representatives at Stavka to work out a counter-strategy. Dukhonin and the OAK leaders tried to persuade themselves that neither the Allies nor the Germans would take the Bolsheviks' stratagem seriously, as it was so obviously a desperate move to repair their waning fortunes; in fact, it was a mortal blow to Stavka from which it was never to recover.[3] Before the entire army and the country Stavka had been maneuvered into rejecting an "order" intended to bring about peace, thus exposing its "counter-revolutionary" designs and advertising the pacifistic credentials of the Soviet government. The OAK was also obliged to reveal its colors by supporting Dukhonin against the Soviet government and peace.

At 12:30 that night Lenin, Stalin, and Krylenko, speaking for Sovnarkom, demanded a response to the previous directive, refusing to be put off by the claim that the communication was suspect because it was not sent in cipher and lacked the proper number and date. Dukhonin insisted

---

only the appeal of the Petrograd MRC for forces to combat the Krasnov expedition, but otherwise nothing addressed to the military Bolsheviks, the front MRCs, or organs of Soviet power in the region of the front; see also *BPB*, pp. 403-49 (for the entire month of November, only one routine letter of the Secretariat to a front unit; to the 48th Division on November 2), and *TrSh* 1:3-30 (only information bulletins and the Declaration of the Rights of the Peoples of the World of November 2).

[2] *Dekrety sovetskoi vlasti*, 2 vols. (Moscow, 1957), 1:53. Though this communication is cited elsewhere (e.g., Polikarpov, *Prolog grazhdanskoi voiny*, p. 164), this is the only available full text.

[3] For Stavka documents of this period, see "Nakanune peremiriia," *KA* 23 (1927): 195-249.

that he could not act upon the directive without knowing the Allied response to the Peace Decree of October 26, whether the Rumanian Army had consented, whether the Germans alone or all the Central Powers were concerned, and whether a separate peace was contemplated should the Allies refuse to cooperate. The Sovnarkom spokesmen dismissed these as peripheral questions and once more ordered Dukhonin "immediately and without further obstruction to undertake formal negotiations for an armistice between all the belligerent powers." Finally cornered, Dukhonin replied that although he personally now considered a speedy peace essential to the interests of Russia, only an authoritative central government of all Russia was entitled to undertake such a far-reaching step. (This was his first admission that he did not recognize Sovnarkom as a legitimate government, another coup for Lenin.) The People's Commissars responded that Dukhonin was removed as Commander in Chief for insubordination.[4]

Within an hour, over the signature of Lenin and Krylenko, an unciphered radiogram to "all regimental, divisional, corps, and army committees, and all soldiers of the revolutionary army and sailors of the fleet" recounted in full the exchanges with Dukhonin and announced the appointment of Krylenko as the People's Commander in Chief. Moreover, it included an astounding invitation that was well calculated to arrest the attention of every last soldier at the front: "Let each regiment on the front lines immediately elect plenipotentiaries for the formal initiation of negotiations for an armistice with the adversary. The Soviet of People's Commissars [Sovnarkom] hereby gives you this authority."[5] Once again the potent content of the appeal was proof against attempts to conceal it from the troops, as violent reprisals would ensue if the soldiers felt deceived.

In fact, there is more than adequate documentation that the appeal was promptly circulated through staff channels and the committee network on many sectors of the front. Moreover, the full text was carried in *IzFR* on November 10, in *IzOA* and *IzGr* on November 11, and in VG on November 12, and German intelligence also relayed it to every sector of the front.[6] In the XV Corps (Third Army, Western Front) the MRC called a session

[4] *ORA*, pp. 84-85, and elsewhere. Lenin's strategy comes out in his report to the VTsIK of November 10, where he argues that "until Dukhonin is unmasked and replaced, the Army cannot be sure that we mean business about an internationalist peace policy" (*ibid.*, pp. 87-88).

[5] *Ibid.*, p. 86, and other Soviet publications.

[6] On Ludendorff's so informing the government on November 10 (O.S.; November 24, N.S.), see AA, WK 2f, No. 1, WSVR ("Waffenstillstandverhandlungen mit Russland," 10 vols.), 2:73. This invaluable collection, in the archives of the Foreign Ministry of the German Empire, contains a wealth of documentation on the armistice negotiations, since its section attached to the Grosseshauptquartier received copies of all military intelligence reports and communications concerning intelligence.

on receipt of the radiogram (20:00 hours, November 9), and within two and a half hours it worked out and distributed to all lower units a five-point instruction on how to initiate and conduct negotiations.[7] The committee of the 32nd Division (Eighth Army, Rumanian Front) reacted just as expeditiously, choosing negotiators and proposing a cease-fire to the enemy, which led to a signed agreement on November 11; in both cases the Russian side pledged to obtain cease-fires in adjacent sectors if the Austro-Germans would do the same on their side.[8]

The Grenadier Corps MRC, an exceptionally well documented instance, also responded promptly to the Sovnarkom invitation. The negotiations took place on November 14, and within a few hours a simple cease-fire agreement was signed, of which they informed Commander in Chief Krylenko and the Second Army MRC the same day.[9] The preliminaries were settled at a brief meeting in the neutral zone between German staff officers of the division opposite and designees of the corps MRC. The Germans stipulated that no fraternization should occur during the talks, but were otherwise forthcoming. That evening the Germans sent over a formal invitation naming a time and place where the Russian delegation was to cross over to the German side. The MRC, on its part, issued a proclamation to the soldiers, exhorting them to "restrain yourselves from individual undertakings" during the proceedings. At the suggested time, after exchanging cordialities, the German escorts blindfolded the Russian plenipotentiaries and conducted them to a railroad-car salon several kilometers by truck to the rear.

The incongruity of bemedalled and bemonacled senior German officers parleying as equals with common Russian soldier-delegates did not hinder the business-like conduct of the matter at hand. The Germans presented their model text (prescribed by the intelligence branch, or *Nachrichtendienst*), but the Russians countered with their own, which was used as a basis. The agreement consisted of three simple parts: first, a determination that a cease-fire was to remain in effect until one of the two parties ter-

[7] *VRKDA*, pp. 268-69; the same document was intercepted by German military intelligence, which had broken the cipher of the Russian military radio and teletype communications (see AA, WK 2f, No. 1, WSVR 2:107).

[8] *ORA*, pp. 106 and 113. That the instructions, even prior to contact with the Germans were known to the latter's intelligence, see *BKA*, 2. BLD, Ab. 1a 5:7, "Nachrichten über feindliche Heere. Nachrichtendienst und Feindearbeiter für Russland," Fach 3 (Report of the Intelligence Section of the Eighth German Army of November 26, N.S.). Besides some intelligence information redundant with those in AA, WSVR, the archives of lower military units contain the detailed instructions to the unit *Nachrichtenoffiziere* and other valuable pieces of intelligence information, such as radio intercepts.

[9] For Petrov's detailed account, see *BOB*, pp. 358-61; for text of telegram to Krylenko, see *VRKDA*, p. 274; for a contemporary account and documents, see *IzGr*, November 15.

minated it on two days' notice; second, terms defining the sector affected and forbidding overflights, balloon observations, major reinforcements, or changes in weaponry (especially artillery); and third, a compromise between the German and Russian points of view, a stipulation that contacts between troops of the respective sides would be allowed only at prescribed places between the wires. It appears the Germans deviated from their own guidelines to humor the Russians. At the conclusion of the solemnities the Germans offered a modest repast and plied the Russians with flattering questions about "their revolution." The officers accompanied the Russians back to the neutral zone, cordial to the very end, while on the other side of the wire soldiers had congregated, eagerly awaiting the signal to celebrate.[10]

Documents in Soviet publications are informative though spare, whereas German archival sources yield abundant, comprehensive material. They confirm the nearly universal impact of the Sovnarkom broadcast and demonstrate that it was indeed the turning point, not only transforming the inchoate peace longings into an effective practical strategy, but also cementing the soldiers' loyalty to Sovnarkom and the MRCs as duly constituted organs of Soviet power. The German high command, and Ludendorff in particular, had long held high hopes that the Bolshevik advent to power would result in a separate peace releasing their armies for the Western Front. Up to this point, however, they had relied on their civilian contacts in Stockholm (the efforts of Parvus, Scheidemann, and Erzberger through the Bolshevik intermediaries Vorovskii and Ganetskii) to ensnare the Bolsheviks through their utopian schemes for world revolution.[11] When German military intelligence intercepted the Sovnarkom radiogram (as Lenin confidently expected), the German high command within hours issued informational bulletins and brief instructions to the network of intelligence officers on how to handle the situation. Ludendorff boasted that they no longer had to worry about the resistance of the Russian generalship, who would "now be compelled to undertake negotiations against their will" under massive pressure from the Russian soldiers, "whose longing for peace surpasses the imagination."[12]

On November 12 more detailed guidelines (*Richtlinien*) were issued, stipulating that the "present situation is to be exploited with the utmost vigor through all means of propaganda," the goal of which was defined as a comprehensive armistice agreement. Supplementary instructions in-

[10] For terms, see *IzGr*, November 19, and AA, WK, 2f, No. 1, WSVR, 1:2.

[11] There are abundant documents on these negotiations, some of them previously utilized by investigators, in *ibid.*, entire Band 1; for the most complete account, see Wolfgang Steglich, *Die Freidenspolitik der Mittelmächte 1917/18*, 2 vols. (Wiesbaden, 1964), chap. 4.

[12] AA, WK 2f, No. 1, WSVR, 2:78. For other points, see *ibid.*, 1:52 and 73.

cluded an absolute proscription on fraternization (dangerous for Austrian troops), and the discussion of troop movements, airplane observation, and replacements.[13] The results, reported hourly, were periodically compiled by the Intelligence Section at Supreme Headquarters (Section III-b of the Grosses Hauptquartier), which makes it possible to follow them in considerable detail.[14] Thus one can establish that by the time of the Grenadier cease-fire (November 14) at least seven other agreements had been formally negotiated and signed (122nd and 182nd divisions of the Special Army; the Sixth, Eighth, 133rd, and 137th divisions of the XV Corps of the Third Army; and the 69th Division of the Tenth Army), while twenty or so verbal pledges, as well as countless unofficial expressions of interest, were registered. In the days that followed, local armistices were concluded with the First and Second Turkestan divisions (Special Army), the 15th Siberian and 129th Infantry divisions (Second Army), and a number of others in the Fourth and Fifth armies (Rumanian and Northern fronts respectively).[15]

Improvised contacts between the wire were systematically cultivated from the German side by intelligence officers who requested to talk with authorized representatives of the Russians (*Bevollmächtigte*); individual Russian soldiers and officers often promised to secure the latter and generated pressure for more formal negotiations (instances in the 194th Division of the Special Army, the Sixth Siberian and 50th Infantry divisions of the Eleventh Army, 76th Division of the Fifth Army, and the Caucasus Grenadier Division of the Tenth Army). The Germans often inquired whether the Russian soldiers were aware of the telegrams of their leaders, Lenin and Krylenko, which further intimidated the Russian command. Probing written inquiries or small parties advancing to the wire under a white flag often initiated discussions from the Russian side. Only the Ninth Army on the Rumanian Front seemed immune to such overtures, which the German intelligence attributed to particularly effective counter-meas-

[13] BKA, 2. BLD, Ab. 1a, 39:7, Fach 3, instructions of the Intelligence Section of the Eighth German Army of November 23 and 25, supplemented on November 26, 27, and 29, which concerned such things as forbidding Russian soldiers to cross the wire, or contact between German and Russian soldiers without officers present.

[14] There are five comprehensive surveys of the front, army by army and division by division, from November 27 to December 2 (November 14-19, O.S.), separate surveys by General Mackensen for the Rumanian Front, and many reports on individual situations. The former consist of terse, one-sentence characterizations of contacts with Russian units; the latter are more detailed reports on the more important negotiations. (For the comprehensive surveys, see AA, WK 2f, No. 1, WSVR, 2:90 and 161; 3:33 and 148; 4:109-10; for details culled from these reports, further references will not be given. Since there are two complete surveys dated November 27 and none for November 28 and 29, reports for the latter dates may be missing from the file; daily reports resume on November 30.)

[15] *Ibid.*, 2:20, 35, 105; 3:33, 90, and 148.

ures by the Russian command and the committees. Here and there probes were broken up by artillery or machine-gun fire (Fourth Amur Border Division, Eighth Army, 46th Division, Eleventh Army), though in one case the guilty party was a visiting French officer who was lynched for his pains; in another case an officer who shot down an Austrian negotiator was raised over the trenches to invite retaliation (XI Corps, Special Army; and 30th Division, Sixth Army, respectively). Numerous instances of resulting confrontations are recorded, such as unexplained machine-gun fire (also 30th Division) and arrests of officers (100th Division, Special Army; 19th Division, Eighth Army).[16]

The Germans, of course, adjudged their *Friedensaktion* a brilliant success and the Bolsheviks their most valuable ally, but by the same token Lenin was calculatedly exploiting their services to promote his own revolution. For both of them the objective was to utilize the momentum of the masses to break down the remaining resistance of the command and the prowar committeemen. As in the case of the Kornilov affair, the soldiers needed little instruction on how to proceed—they needed only to prod their officers and committees to undertake the formal arrangements after they had prepared the ground; the pressure was continued until the agreements were solemnized. At the same time they could see to it that the negotiations were extended outward and upward until agreements blanketed entire armies and the front, ending in a general armistice and the initiation of peace negotiations between the respective governments. All this was perfectly clear to ordinary soldiers, and the enthusiasm and disciplined restraint they manifested while engaging in appropriate actions is remarkable indeed. The highly efficient informal networks kept them informed of everything that was going on around them, and the slightest attempt by diehard officers or committeemen to engage in subterfuge or counter-propaganda was condemned to futility or violent resolution.

Only on the role of fraternization was there a significant divergence between soldier sentiment and the strategy of German Intelligence. They could not understand why, if an internationalist peace based on the brotherhood of peoples was about to be consummated, they could not exchange regalements and mingle as happily with their trenchmates of the other side as they had in April. Their vexing determination to fraternize was noted frequently in the above reports and became a major sore spot in many of the negotiations. The Germans found it difficult to maintain the strictures of the *Richtlinien* in this regard without causing undue friction, and thus the usual compromise was to concede carefully supervised contact between the wires at designated points. Once soldiers understood that unauthorized

[16] All examples culled from comprehensive reports.

fraternization threatened to disrupt the fragile cease-fires, they observed the rules impeccably.[17] The Bolsheviks had a vested interest in adhering to the agreements, and therefore MRCs or individual Bolsheviks went to great lengths to terminate fraternization, while, paradoxically, loyalist committees, such as the IV Corps of the Sixth Army, readily promoted it (since it obviously disorganized the enemy and was the sole weapon they had left).[18]

The tangible effect of the armistice campaign on the power balance at the front can be seen most clearly in the case of the 32nd Division on the Rumanian Front, where the Bolsheviks had as yet made few inroads. The 32nd Division had an average profile in 1917, phases of turbulence and recovery, and a modest Bolshevik presence, but turbulence revived again after the Kornilov affair.[19] The Bolsheviks, however, were not visibly active when a rather unique ''committee revolution'' took place: instead of forming a nonpartisan MRC, as did most units on the Rumanian Front, on November 7 the committee restructured itself as a ''soviet'' on a more-or-less ''federative'' principle—twelve deputies representing companies, five representing a soldier-peasant Soviet, three representing a Ukrainian Rada, and one each representing a Muslim group, support and staff units, and each of the major political parties.[20]

The genesis of the revolution is unclear, but that it was conceived as a ''peace action'' is evident in the formation of a ''commission'' on fraternization and the decision to initiate formal negotiations with the enemy prior to the receipt of the Sovnarkom radiogram. Another peculiarity of the affair was that it enjoyed the benediction and participation of the divisional commander, who was himself a member of the Soviet and approved the action for which he was later generously praised in this ''Soviet's'' report to Commander in Chief Krylenko.[21] The Sovnarkom radiogram was an ex post facto, marvelous legitimization of what had already been initiated. Nothing in the entire affair bespeaks a specific Bolshevik influence, but it bears a striking resemblance to some of the spontaneous peace actions of late September and early October.

[17] The same was true for the other pitfall, the allurements of alcohol. On the first day one report noted that ''the negotiators came back thoroughly drunk''; thereafter the Germans ceased supplying alcohol, and the MRCs imposed strict rules against it, which the soldiers for the most part gracefully accepted (see *ORA*, p. 126, Stavka survey for November 13).

[18] See *VRKDA*, pp. 483, 478, and 479 (resolutions of committees of the 40th Infantry and Tenth Siberian Rifle divisions of November 16 and 17 respectively).

[19] See *RDRA*, pp. 155, 292, and 348, and above, pp. 247-48. Its neighboring division in the XI Corps, the 165th, had a history of incorrigible Bolshevism but was quiescent in October. See *RDRA*, p. 155, and Frenkin, *Revoliutsionnoe dvizhenie*, pp. 100 and 168.

[20] *ORA*, p. 67 (*protokol* of session of combined committees of November 7).

[21] See *ibid.*, pp. 67, 80, and 132.

The Austro-German intelligence knew the intentions of the 32nd Division Soviet to extend the scope of its activities to include other units, since they had intercepted its resolution when it was conveyed by telegraph to XI Corps headquarters, and thus immediately proposed that the cease-fire cover the entire Russian XI Corps, naming a suitable meeting place behind the Austrian lines. Not only was a Russian negotiating team from all three divisions of the XI Corps (12th, 32nd, 165th) assembled by the following day (November 10), but a German intelligence report of the same evening states "The events in the Russian XI Corps are attracting attention and spreading to the South, . . . the 79th Division [XIII Corps] is already preparing for negotiations." The message was probably spreading rapidly enough on the Russian side, but German intelligence broadcast it all along the front, and on the sector of the Sixth Army, far to the south, it persuaded the 40th Division to enter into negotiations the very next day.[22]

General Mackensen, who supervised intelligence operations for the Austro-Hungarian armies in Rumania, reported to his superiors on the brilliant prospects for peace negotiations in the entire Russian Eighth Army, since the two remaining corps, the XXIII and the XXXIII, were known to be Bolshevik-penetrated and "the universal desire for peace can no longer be withstood." He predicted definitive peace arrangements before the meeting of the Russian Constituent Assembly, after which the Bolsheviks were expendable. Likewise exultant was the *Nachrichtenoffizier*, who conducted the negotiations with the XI Corps and reported:

> The delegates were brought by car and my report in the spirit of the *Richtlinien* was well received. I was able to inform them that their chief, Krylenko, who would very soon begin energetic negotiations for a general armistice, was today to arrive at headquarters. The delegates wholeheartedly approved the procedure recommended by Lenin for negotiations at the front and stressed that Russia in its own interests must have peace to protect its freedom. . . . Should the Entente refuse the offer of an immediate armistice, [the delegates claimed] then Russia is prepared to concede a separate peace with the Central Powers without reservations. Present-day Russia will never again fight for the interests of the English and the French. The government that has given them peace and land will never more be overthrown. . . . The delegates of the MRC of the XI Corps formally requested me to contact by telegraph our Supreme Command and in their name to request a renunciation of annexationist goals in the East, which would immensely promote the cause of peace between Russia

[22] AA, WK 2f, No. 1, WSVR, 2:118 and 199 (two reports of General Mackensen of November 27 (November 14, O.S.).

> and the Central Powers. . . . The delegates stated that they would this very evening inform their higher command of the results of the present negotiations and tomorrow morning will dispatch a special envoy to report to Krylenko.[23]

While it is true that the German negotiator was a skilled professional and the Russian delegates were but neophytes, their bold self-assurance and pretensions to high diplomacy cannot but evoke admiration. Since the same alacrity to assume grave responsibility for the fate of the nation was evident in many other negotiations along the front, this must be accounted another of those remarkable moments of collective awareness comparable to the abdication crisis and the Kornilov affair. (The motivations of individual negotiators is immaterial, as they were by force of circumstances playing out a role on behalf of the masses; nevertheless, most of the negotiators, even staff officer consultants, seem to have become caught up in the grandeur of their mission.) The armistice ferment achieved what the Soviet Congress, the land and peace decrees, the Vikzhel negotiations, and even the Constituent Assembly elections failed to achieve, namely, the legitimization of the Soviet government and an eagerness to collaborate in its efforts for peace.

Again the 32nd Division serves as an excellent example. Within two days the activists of the division secured the ouster of the old corps committee and its reconstruction along the lines of their own soviet. Though not Bolshevik at the outset, they now cherished a cult of Lenin and Krylenko, unequivocally recognized the authority of Sovnarkom, and repudiated that of the OAK and the Rumanian Front MRC.[24] German intelligence also intercepted a telegraphed declaration of the XXIII Corps of support for Sovnarkom until the Constituent Assembly, though it still evinced a fear of civil war; a staff report for the Eighth Army of November 19 dolefully notes that it was a good corps spoiled by the armistice negotiations.[25] The XXXIII Corps, long plagued by Bolshevik agitation, withstood it for a time but succumbed as a result of the armistice. It held a congress on November 17, concerning which the corps commander reported: "Today at 3:30 hours deputies of the congress appeared before me and declared that the congress had decided to organize an armistice on our front; for this purpose an Austrian commander is to appear at 14:00

[23] *Ibid.*, 2:127 (November 14/27). For Mackensen's report, see *ibid.*, 2:122.

[24] *ORA*, pp. 132-33. A command report of early November refers to sympathy for the Bolsheviks in the XI Corps, but this was meant to describe the soldiers' mood, not as a party-political identification (*VOSRU* 2:476).

[25] *BMRF*, p. 163, and *VOSRU* 2:402. German intelligence has no record of dealings with this corps, but for the radio intercept, see AA, WK 2f, No. 1, WSVR, 2:95.

hours on the sector of the 406th Regiment.''[26] He also noted that the congress had taken on a ''Bolshevik hue,'' and indeed the veteran Bolshevik Muravnik was elected the new chairman of the corps MRC.

The XVI Corps, also of the Eighth Army, was in reserve in early November and thus not actively in contact with the Austro-Germans; instead they were tearing up the Moldavian countryside together with local peasants and more preoccupied with *samogon* (distilling) and plundering estates than with the armistice.[27] In connection with elections to the forthcoming army congress (November 20), the Bolshevized 161st Regiment staged ''demonstrations,'' marching with music from regiment to regiment, holding meetings, broadcasting the slogans ''Long live the People's Commissars!'' and ''Down with the War!'' There is no question but that the campaign was bearing fruit, but it seemed unrelated to the flurry of armistice activity taking place some distance away. Nevertheless, the corps commander reported:

> The steps undertaken by Krylenko on behalf of peace have won more and more adherents for the Bolsheviks among the masses. In the opinion of many soldiers the command and all the political parties except the Bolsheviks are working hand in hand with the Allies to prevent an early peace. The less-conscious element, seeing from the Bolsheviks concrete steps toward peace, now place in them all their hopes. They see in fraternization simply a step in that direction. . . . The soldiers are now saying they will never again return to the front lines because the war is as good as over.[28]

Thus, it is fairly certain that the striking victory of the Bolsheviks at the Eighth Army Congress (see above), after having fared so poorly in the Constituent Assembly elections, was in no small measure due to the bold stroke of Lenin and Krylenko in appealing directly to the masses to become involved in promoting peace. In fact, the first action of the congress on November 21 was to form a ''Parleying Commission'' composed of representatives from each corps and ''technical advisers'' from the staff, appealing to Krylenko's directive. The attached resolution stated: ''The armistice must have as its aim a democratic peace and must be accompanied

[26] *ORA*, p. 140. Once again a commander was dragged into negotiations against his will; he gracefully exited when the Austrians produced a staff officer instead of a commander to conduct the negotiations.

[27] *Ibid.*, p. 79 (front survey of November 8). On plundering continuing to be a serious problem in the entire XVI Corps throughout November, see *VRKDA*, p. 510 (MRC *protokol* of December 6).

[28] *VOSRU* 2:400 (n.d., but early November).

by organized fraternization to unite our proletariat with that of all the belligerent countries.''[29]

The result was not everywhere so visible and dramatic as in the Eighth Army, but the widespread catalytic effect of the armistice appeal in consolidating the authority of Sovnarkom and entrenching Bolshevik leadership in the MRCs has been observed in a number of examples in the last two chapters (in the Fifth and Special armies, for example). That this was due less to the direct intervention of organized Bolsheviks at the front than to the radicalizing effect of the radiogram is most clear in the Third Army. The XV Corps, which reacted instantaneously to the Sovnarkom radiogram, was nevertheless cool to Bolshevik emissaries from the XXXV Corps who showed up at a corps congress in November; the same emissaries raised the armistice question at the congress of the XX Corps on November 16, and as a result a twelve-man parleying commission was formed and instructions were worked out. Yet the congress on all other issues took a temporizing, non-Bolshevik position and still favored an all-socialist coalition. It appears that over the next two weeks, however, the Bolsheviks succeeded in exploiting the armistice issue to discredit the conciliatory majority of the army committee, as elections to the army congress at the end of the month produced an overwhelming and militant Bolshevik majority.[30]

In the case of the Tenth Army the impact of the armistice appeal was demonstrated at the congress, which was in session when the radiogram arrived. It expressed its gratitude to Sovnarkom for ''undertaking direct negotiations through its commissars and the Commander in Chief and insisting on an armistice on all fronts.''[31] The newly elected MRC contacted the German army group chief, General Eichhorn, by radio on November 18 to propose negotiations.[32] The Special Army Committee, it will be recalled, condemned Dukhonin for his rejection of Sovnarkom directives, which doubtless encouraged other initiatives from below. The 122nd Division was one of the first to conclude an agreement, and the two Turkestan divisions followed on November 17; there is no further record of armistice agreements on that level, but German intelligence records intensive negotiations in nine out of thirteen divisions in this sector by the time they were superseded by the army-level negotiations on November 18.[33]

[29] *BMRF*, p. 171.

[30] See *VKDA*, pp. 421 and 424 (*protokoly* of respective sessions), and *VRKDA*, p. 301 (announcement on November 28 to troops of XXV Corps of forthcoming congress).

[31] *ORA*, p. 99.

[32] *TrSh* 2:27; for German intelligence as acquainted with proceedings through radio intercepts, see AA, WK 2f, No. 1, WSVR, 3:114 and 117.

[33] *Ibid.*, 3:30 (survey for November 30, N.S.).

The armistice agreement signed by representatives of the Special Army MRC and General Linsingen, commander of the Austro-Hungarian Third Army, was by far the most comprehensive to that date and covered 100 kilometers of front; furthermore, Linsingen used his good offices to extend the agreement 50 kilometers northward to the Pripet River, which was defended by a German army group commanded by General Woyrsch. Consisting of nine articles, besides the now-standard items (geographical limits, two-day termination notice, no crossing the neutral zone, supervised fraternization at specified points), it regulated in somewhat more detail the permissibility of working on fortifications (repairs only, and none on wire barriers) and overflights (only at high altitudes during specified hours), and proscribed troop movements for three days except routine rotation on the line. It also established a mechanism and rules for dealing with violations. The Germans had by now, contrary to their original *Richtlinien*, reconciled themselves to regulated fraternization and limits on their rights to move troops and other military actions behind their own lines.[34] Since there were no similar guidelines laid down from above for the Russian negotiators, the terms were purely the result of the pragmatic reasoning of the negotiators, and one must credit them with considerable bargaining skill in taking advantage of the fact that the Germans were just as anxious as they for an armistice.

Though the German calculation was undoubtedly correct that the armistice ferment was moving the Russian Army ineluctably toward self-liquidation and a dictated peace, Lenin and Krylenko were more concerned with their proximate political objectives. It was imperative to keep Sovnarkom's leadership at the center of attention and maintain the image of decisive action. The strategy was to circumvent Stavka and the command structure by carrying the flag of Sovnarkom directly to the front. In his first order as People's Commissar of War and Commander in Chief, Krylenko announced that he was departing for the front to make peace.[35] On the evening of November 11, in the company of ten officers and fifty armed sailors and Red Guardsmen, he arrived in Pskov and summoned General Cheremisov to his salon wagon. When the latter refused, his entourage continued to Dvinsk and repeated the charade with General Boldyrev. Again rebuffed, Krylenko assembled the army committee, which had just taken an equivocal position on the armistice question, causing a rupture within the all-Bolshevik MRC, and made a fiery speech branding three enemies to be overcome: the Germans, hunger, and the counter-revolu-

[34] Text of agreement in *ibid.*, 3:62 and *TrSh* 2:86-87; for report of the MRC to Krylenko of November 19, see *VRKDA*, pp. 382-83.

[35] *AFRK*, November 21 (first issue replacing *AFSR*).

tionary nest at Stavka. The Germans, he boasted, would be neutralized by the offer of an armistice, hunger would be resolved by the heroic measures of Sovnarkom, but he personally would conduct the struggle against the counter-revolutionary Kornilovite Dukhonin and boasted that "the masses are ready to make peace over the corpses of the commanding staff."[36]

Krylenko's presence apparently overawed the dissidents in the army committee, as he selected a team of negotiators from their midst and headed for the sector of the XIX Corps, where he informed the 23rd Landwehr Division that he was prepared to treat with the army group commander, Eichhorn, or even the German Supreme Commander, on the question of a general armistice. Though the reply required the approval of Ludendorff and Kaiser Wilhelm, it was ready by 3:30 A.M. the following morning, empowering Eastern Front Commander General Hoffmann to meet with the Russians at Brest Litovsk on November 19.[37] Without awaiting the German reply, Krylenko telegraphed of his activities to all units of the army and charged army committees with removing any generals who did not fully cooperate. Furthermore, he now declared the OAK dispersed and laid on the Mogilev Soviet the obligation of finding a way to remove Dukhonin from Stavka without bloodshed. A follow-up message declared: "Comrades! The realization of peace is at hand! It is within our grasp. . . . Brand with contempt the appeals of the miserable gang of General Dukhonin and his bourgeois and pseudo-socialist camp-followers!"[38]

Krylenko's highly unorthodox behavior was well calculated to achieve his chief purpose: to discredit the command and the OAK and to establish Sovnarkom and himself personally as the sole arbiters of peace. Once he had secured a positive reply from the Germans, all opposition to his efforts on the Northern Front withered, particularly in the Fifth Army Committee, and with impunity he was now able to remove both Cheremisov and Boldyrev from command. Their replacements were not yet stalwart Bolsheviks, but this action served to intimidate lower commanders. (Novitskii was moved up to front chief from the Twelfth Army command, and a General Antipov, a corps commander in the Sixth Army, was appointed to command the Fifth Army.)

Events were taking their own course on the Western Front, completely apart from Krylenko's efforts. On November 13 the front MRC put the question point-blank to General Baluev: "Do you recognize the authority

[36] *KA* 23:222-23 (full report of Boldyrev to Levitskii, Dukhonin's deputy, n.d.). For a parallel, less complete account of Baranovskii (Quartermaster of the Northern Front) of November 13, see *ORA*, pp. 110-11.

[37] AA, WK 2f, No. 1, WSVR, 2:10 and 24.

[38] *Ibid.*, 2:52 for radio intercept version; published in *AFRK*, November 21. The first message is cited in report of Baranovskii of November 15 in *ORA*, p. 126.

of the MRC? If so, it is suggested to you to enter into negotiations on the question of an armistice immediately and so order all your subordinate commanders.''[39] Baluev flat-out refused, declaring he did not recognize the MRC's authority in such a vital question of state and that if it insisted he requested that he be relieved of his command. The MRC removed him without hesitation and nominated the Bolshevik commander of the 12th Turkestan Rifle Division, General V. V. Kamenshchikov, as his replacement. Baluev formally relinquished his post despite an urgent plea from Dukhonin to resist by any means possible. Thus the renovation of the commanding staff with pliant or pro-Bolshevik types was a major dividend of the strategy of Lenin and Krylenko.

Kamenshchikov immediately issued a fourteen-point instruction to all units on how to form armistice commissions, choose negotiating teams, define terms of armistice agreements, organize fraternization, and so on. The instruction coincides in so many points with those often adopted on all fronts both before and after the question of reciprocal influence arises. The only instance where the influence of Kamenshckikov's instruction can be documented is that of the Rumanian Front negotiations (see below); it is probable that in most instances the uniform exigencies and requirements of the situation led to similar pragmatic solutions.[40]

The armistice agreement on the Western Front, arrived at on November 19, was by far the most comprehensive in scale until the conclusion of the general armistice on December 4. It superseded all negotiations then under way in all three armies (Second, Third, Tenth) and was treated with great solemnity by both sides, almost as if their efforts were more definitive than the Brest negotiations. The Russian delegation, consisting of two representatives of each army, three from the front, and several more from lower units that insisted on being included, was headed by a soldier by the name of Shchukin, who by all the surviving accounts conducted himself with great authority and skill. Two general staff officers accompanied the delegation as technical consultants, to whom Petrov pays generous tribute for their efficiency and expertise in framing the terms.

The accounts of Petrov of the Second Army and Lukianov of the Third Army, as well as an official staff report, are all anxious to portray the Russian negotiators as tough, disciplined defenders of Russian interests, forcing adoption of their own much more elaborate draft on the astounded and condescending German negotiators, who were headed by Eichhorn's

[39] *KA* 23:216 (Val'ter, Chief of Staff of Western Front—Stavka, November 12). German intercept, AA, WK 2f, No. 1, WSVR, 2:20 and 48.

[40] Text in *ibid.*, 2:46 (German intercept), and *VRKDA*, pp. 272-73.

deputy, General-Major Sauberzweig.[41] The Russians were adamant on two points, the permissibility of fraternization and the forbidding of major troop movements or changes in strength while the armistice was in effect. They probably exaggerated their tactical victory on fraternization, because the formula was no different from that of a number of local agreements and had already figured in Kamenshchikov's instructions.

The Germans, however, were very anxious to preserve their maximum freedom of action on strategic military decisions, as they were already undertaking major troop transfers to the Western Front, and this was regarded as the chief purpose of a general armistice.[42] The Russian negotiators, on the other hand, were determined not to allow the Central Powers to take advantage of a regional armistice to shift troops to still-active sectors to the detriment of their comrades; in addition, they were quite conscious that internationalist principles dictated a general peace, which should not be endangered by untying the German hands in the East to undertake an offensive in the West. In the Grenadier's armistice, contrary to Petrov's explicit advice, Konobeev, the Grenadier negotiator, had yielded on the question of troop transfers to keep the talks from breaking down. Thus the Germans were in a cocky mood, and a deadlock after hours of passionate discussion seemed in prospect. During a long pause while the Germans were supposedly conducting higher-level consultations, the Russian delegation, with the help of their staff officers, worked out a new position that they felt would preserve the substance of their goals while skirting the most controversial areas. To their surprise the Germans were forthcoming and an agreement was quickly concluded. The compromise formula simply omitted any reference to a strategic argumentation (which the original Russian version had spelled out in detail), but it proscribed "major transfers" to or from the front covered by the armistice, defined not in the document itself but in a separate unpublished undertaking as not more than four divisions (twenty-five German divisions were on the sector covered by the agreement). The Russians were very proud of having outwitted the German imperialists, though in reality there was very little hope of enforcing this provision.[43]

[41] For various accounts, see *BOB*, pp. 361-70 (Petrov); *IzVK3*, November 25 and 29 (Lukianov); and *TrSh* 2:34-36 (staff version of Western Front Headquarters); for German record see AA, WK 2f, No. 1, WSVR, 3:116, 117, 129, and 143 (arrangements for meeting only).

[42] See Petrov's version in *BOB*, p. 359; for Ludendorff's explicit order not to discuss troop transfers, see AA, WK 2f, No. 1, WSVR, 2:141.

[43] Text in AA, WK 2f, No. 1, WSVR, 4:39; *IzVK3*, November 24; and *VOSRB* 2:254-56. The German transmission emphasized that the separate codicile on troop movements would be kept strictly secret, though it was openly boasted of in *IzVK3*, November 29.

The spreading blanket of local and regional cease-fires monopolized the attention of those affected, which made the proceedings at Brest Litovsk seem anticlimactic and almost irrelevant. Even the Bolshevik-dominated Western Front MRC totally ignored them, and references in the committee press and other front sources are few. Recounting the Brest negotiations here would serve no purpose, because the technical and psychological aspects are no different from those already covered and the strategy of the Soviet side to parlay them into a world revolution has been more than adequately covered in available works.[44] Let it be noted only that General Hoffmann was attempting to confine the discussions to purely technical aspects of the cessation of hostilities, dragging them out as long as possible to allow the parallel negotiations to gather momentum, and thus to maneuver the Russians into a disadvantageous posture without binding commitments on future peace negotiations.[45] Thus the formal talks initiated on November 19 in Brest were broken off on November 23 so that the Russians could return to Petrograd for further instructions. A ten-day general cease-fire was agreed to, which Krylenko solemnly announced upon arriving at Stavka, but this was hardly impressive compared with other more binding arrangements. Most divisions in the Fifth Army had bilateral agreements by this time, and though the record is strangely incomplete for the Twelfth Army (nothing on the German side), the all-Bolshevik MRC had issued a five-point instruction on the conduct of negotiations on November 12; once fully accredited by the army congress, the MRC circulated them through staff facilities on November 17.[46]

In the meantime, with the sinking fortunes of Stavka and the proclamation of the Don and Ukrainian republics (October 30 and November 7 respectively), the commanders of the Southwestern and Rumanian fronts, Generals Volodchenko and Shcherbachev, were persuaded that it was prudent to make their own arrangements with the Germans. Of the Southwestern Front there is scant record, though negotiations were begun on November 22. On November 20 Shcherbachev announced the initiation of armistice negotiations with the Germans in close cooperation with the Rumanian Front MRC (non-Bolshevik, it will be recalled) and the Ru-

[44] See Steglich, Freidenspolitik, chap. 4; John W. Wheeler-Bennet, *Brest-Litovsk: The Forgotten Peace, March 1918* (London, 1938), chap. 3; and Richard K. Debo, *Revolution and Survival: The Foreign Policy of Soviet Russia 1917-18* (Toronto, 1979), chap 1. German documents are in AA, WK 2f, No. 1, WSVR, 4:136ff., and entire Band 5.

[45] AA, WK 2f, No. 1, WSVR, 3:5 (internal Foreign Ministry communication of November 30 that refers to instructions of General Hoffmann).

[46] *VRKDA*, pp. 47 and 158-59 for orders of Krylenko and of Twelfth Army MRC respectively. On local armistices in the Fifth and Twelfth armies, see AA, WK 2f, No. 1, WSVR, 2:157.

manian government, and invited representatives of the Ukrainian and Don republics as observers. What prompted Shcherbachev to this sudden step is not entirely clear, but he already knew that Stavka was living on borrowed time. More important, he followed the progress of the negotiations on the Western Front closely and was briefed on the draft proposals of the delegation by a staff officer of the front headquarters. Perhaps he saw the advantages of taking charge of the situation before he suffered the fate of Baluev.[47] In any event, he was totally unable to halt the spread of local armistice agreements.

The front and army MRCs were apparently yielding to the same considerations, though only the case of the Sixth Army can be documented. The MRC had tried to hold the line against local armistice negotiations by claiming that only the OAK could speak for the entire Army and was competent to deal with the question. Their position was undercut, however, when the OAK on November 12 announced that because of disagreements among the leading democratic politicians it was renouncing any further effort to construct a national government.[48]

Though details are lacking, the full cooperation of all the leading democratic organizations on the Rumanian Front is evident in the makeup of the Russian delegation: Liperovskii, former government commissar to the Sixth Army, was named by Shcherbachev as the chief negotiator to be aided by two representatives of the front MRC, one of them the conciliator Bolshevik Vorobev. The full delegation included General Kel'chevskii, commander of the Ninth Army; the former commissar, Tizengausen; and others from each of the army MRCs, as well as official representatives of the Ukrainian Republic and the Rumanian Army (the latter were low-level staff officers).

The Germans were forthcoming, as Ludendorff was determined to settle Rumania's fate separately and had expressly forbidden the Brest negotiators to discuss it. General Mackensen was instructed to find out whether the Russians spoke for the Rumanian Army as well, and General Kel'chevskii answered affirmatively. When the Russians were asked point-blank whether they regarded the Brest negotiations as binding, they replied that they did not recognize the authority of Sovnarkom; thus both sides agreed they were merely negotiating a de facto armistice between the respective armies of the Rumanian Front, whereas comprehensive peace negotiations were

[47] On Shcherbachev's staff communications reflecting the extent of his information, see *KA* 23:228-31, 236-38, and 242-46; announcement of armistice negotiations in *VGr*, November 22.

[48] *VGr*, November 19 (record of MRC session of November 15).

deferred to the Constituent Assembly.[49] Again the question of troop transfers became the chief sticking point, threatening an impasse, but the Germans suggested a formula that the Russians found acceptable: no troop transfers were to be permitted after December 5 unless orders for them had been filed before that date, but not to exceed 10 percent of the total forces. The face-saving formula facilitated a quick agreement, which was signed on November 25.[50] This was the last of the regional armistices that preceded the final armistice by at least a week and were regarded by all parties as conclusive. The soldiers were persuaded that their intervention, as legitimate agents of the Soviet government, had brought them about.

☆

Although the Sovnarkom radiogram of November 8 was a mortal blow, neither Dukhonin nor the democratic leadership assembled at Stavka at once perceived its implications. The OAK issued its own radiogram "To all! To all! To all!" branding the tactics of Lenin and Trotsky as an admission they could not deliver on their promise of peace, since none of the powers recognized them as an accredited government. Genuine peace, the OAK claimed, could only be worked out by "all the democracy," which it insisted was embodied in its own proposal of an interim government headed by Chernov.[51] The OAK reckoned on the backing of most of the armies of the Southwestern and Rumanian fronts, as well as of the Third and Tenth armies of the Western Front. Chernov and other political figures (Gotz, Skobelev, Zenzinov) were at that moment at Stavka conferring with the OAK on the construction of a national government in lieu of the Vikzhel failure, while the Don and Ukrainian republics made clear their rejection of any compromise with Sovnarkom. Thus, Dukhonin was under the dangerous illusion that he was in a strong position. With his encouragement, the Allied missions to Stavka submitted a collective statement reminding Stavka in the name of their respective governments of the solemn obligations of the alliance laid down in September of 1914, under which each party agreed not to enter into separate peace negotiations with the enemy. Otherwise the "most serious consequences" might result.[52] Dukhonin mistakenly thought he could utilize the Allied note as leverage against Lenin's government, as he conveyed the note's text to the latter through a lower-level official in the War Ministry, General Marushevskii,

[49] *Ibid.*, December 1, which carries extensive material on the negotiations including the draft proposal of the Russians. For the German documents, including instructions to General Mackensen from the Intelligence Section of the Grosseshauptquartier, see AA, WK 2f, No. 1, WSVR, 4:13-15 and 22 (does not include a record of the negotiations).

[50] Text in *VGr*, December 1.

[51] *KA* 23:196.

[52] French and Russian text in *ibid.*, pp. 201-2.

with whom he had maintained contact on supply and other practical matters. Blaming the Allied "threat" directly on the radiogram of November 9, Dukhonin argued that peace was possible only through agreement of all the belligerent powers through their duly constituted state organs, which Stavka and the democratic organs still represented but Sovnarkom did not; piecemeal negotiations of military units at the front would have no standing in international law. To Marushevskii he expressed his confidence that the radiogram would have no effect whatsoever because of "the common sense of the mass of Russian soldiers," and Stavka was "not an island of isolated personal opinions and impressions."[53] He repeated the same arguments to his wavering front chiefs, as well as in two futile proclamations on November 12 to the political parties and the soldiers respectively: the parties were enjoined to reconstruct a valid state authority, and the soldiers were told "not to surrender your dearly bought freedom to Wilhelm's autocracy."[54]

The OAK had played the card of Chernov's premiership on November 8, but by the following day it was clear that less than half the armies endorsed the step. The Ukrainian Rada magnanimously supported the OAK's efforts if they were based on the principle of a "federation" of nationalities, but an irretrievable blow came from the quarter least expected—the central committees of the S.R. and Menshevik parties, who on November 10 pronounced their veto on Chernov's candidacy. On November 11 the OAK acknowledged the failure of its political initiative and announced that it was reverting to "routine business" and a "purely *ideinyi* struggle" against Bolshevism.[55] All Dukhonin's calculations for the reconstruction of a non-Bolshevik Russian state had now suffered shipwreck.

Strengthened by the positive response of the Germans, Krylenko on November 12 pronounced his ominous threat to liquidate Stavka and the OAK. Up to this point Stavka and the OAK had considered themselves militarily invulnerable. The Mogilev Soviet, with its sizeable garrison, had been staunchly loyal (a Bundist-S.R. majority and a quiescent Bolshevik minority). The First Finnish Rifle Division was now stationed at Orsha, the only railroad access to Stavka, and its committees had all recently passed loyalist resolutions. The Fourth Siberian Cossack Regiment, two companies of Orenburg Cossacks, and two shock battalions had also been moved into the vicinity to offset the doubtful loyalty of the St. George's battalions. Thus on November 12 Dukhonin confidently ordered the Finnish

[53] *Ibid.*, p. 204.

[54] Texts in *ibid.*, pp. 218-19.

[55] For details on the politics of Stavka's demise, see Stankevich, *Vospominaniia*, pp. 284-301; Lelevich, *Oktiabr' v stavke*, entire work, but esp. chaps. 4 and 5, and *BOAK*, included as "Prilozhenie" (Appendix) to the latter.

Rifle units to interdict any Bolshevik forces that might try to move on Stavka.[56] The OAK, despite its discomfiture, still pledged not to allow Stavka to be taken by force, because it was still the vital technical center of the Russian Army, which alone preserved the framework of the Russian state.

Thereafter Dukhonin's support began to wane rapidly. First came the shock of the removal in rapid succession of generals Cheremisov, Boldyrev, and Baluev, effectively amputating Dukhonin's command of the Northern and Western fronts. Despite his desperate efforts to halt them, armistice negotiations were cropping up everywhere, those of the Western Front and the Special Army representing the most serious challenges. The Southwestern Front had thus far been considered a rock of support, but on November 11 the front committee reluctantly informed the OAK:

> The wave of Bolshevism in the most recent days has reached the front, and their demagogic slogans are carrying the masses with them by an irresistible force. . . . The directive to Dukhonin to undertake armistice negotiations, and the subsequent appeal to the soldiers to undertake them on their own, has for the most part brought on terrible unrest.[57]

It stated flatly that if an all-socialist government pledged to immediate armistice negotiations were not formed within the next twenty-four hours, the result would be utter chaos.

All these adverse developments must have been weighing heavily on Dukhonin's spirits in the ensuing days. Therefore, when the Italian military representative informed him on November 18 that the Allies now conceded to the Russians the right to conclude a separate armistice and were at that moment in touch with Sovnarkom over the Brest negotiations, Dukhonin eagerly grasped at the straw. He immediately notified his front chiefs, prematurely publicizing the offer, and at a special assembly of his staff and the remaining democratic representatives he declared himself in favor of a bargain with the Bolsheviks to achieve unified negotiations with the Germans.[58] He wanted nothing for himself, Dukhonin pleaded with evident sincerity, and would peacefully surrender his office to the agreed-upon successor. The democratic cohort—a rump OAK, the Mogilev Soviet, and the soldiers' committees of all the hitherto loyal units—bit hard on this announcement, passing resolutions of "no civil war" and preparing to negotiate with Krylenko, whose force was rapidly approaching.

[56] See his telegraphed order in *KA* 23:223.

[57] Lelevich, "Prilozhenie," *BOAK*, November 11.

[58] See *KA* 23:236-40 (direct wire communications with front chiefs of November 18).

At this point Dukhonin would undoubtedly have been relieved at the prospect of a peaceful transfer of power to Bolsheviks, so it was a cruel shock when the Allied military representatives informed him a few hours later that their Italian colleague was in error, that they had granted no such dispensation, and that therefore they expected Dukhonin to carry out his obligations to the Allies as formerly.[59] The panic that presaged the end now set in. Krylenko's force of some 3,000 sailors and garrison troops (Litovskiis and Finlandskiis) was poised just beyond Orsha for a decisive thrust. The XVII Corps, still strung out along the rail line, offered no resistance, Vikzhel reneged on a pledge to block the tracks, and the First Finnish Rifle Division now assumed a stance of "neutrality" in the political struggle. Dukhonin, with the encouragement of the departing democratic leaders, Stankevich in particular, began to load up cars and trucks with Stavka's technical equipment to head southward, unsuccessfully pleading with the Ukrainian Rada for safe haven. To his chagrin the staff and auto units, the Mogilev Soviet, and the St. George's Cavaliers refused to allow his caravan to move out. A crisis had taken place in an all-night session of the Mogilev Soviet, which resulted in the recognition of Sovnarkom and of Krylenko as Commander in Chief, and in the formation of a Bolshevik-dominated MRC. The OAK, rebuffed in its attempt at good offices, declared itself disbanded until the convocation of a new all-army congress, and its membership dispersed.[60]

Dukhonin, persuaded by his Quartermaster General Dietrichs (to "save the dignity of a non-political Stavka"), now reconciled himself to a peaceful surrender and the humiliation of arrest. The ever-resourceful Stankevich contrived to obtain a car for his escape, but Dukhonin refused; when the shock units offered to fight to the finish if he would "clear out the *komitetshchina*," he again declined, and provided them with orders to the Caucasus Front. The remaining politicians, staff, and committeemen all melted away without any effort by Dukhonin to restrain them. Thus, when on the morning of November 20 the trainloads of Krylenko's force pulled in to the Mogilev station, there was no resistance. During the night the Mogilev MRC took Dukhonin and his remaining staff into protective custody, but alerted in the morning to the lynching mood of the Baltic sailors and garrison soldiers, the MRC spirited him secretly to Krylenko's salon car. A mob soon assembled, crying for blood. Krylenko did his best to defend his prisoner with his eloquence at the threshold of the railroad car,

[59] *Ibid.*, pp. 240-41 (retractions of Dukhonin and the key refutation of General Berthelot, military attaché of France to the Rumanian government).

[60] See Lelevich, pp. 75ff., who utilizes an officer's detailed eyewitness account, and Stankevich, pp. 298-300. Lelevich, as a member of the Mogilev Soviet, also knew many of the details firsthand or through acquaintances.

but this brought only a brief reprieve. The mob, further enraged by the news that Kornilov and the Bykhov prisoners had escaped with Dukhonin's complicity, swarmed over the railroad car, beat on it with rifles, broke through the windows, and roughly thrust Krylenko and other defenders aside; in a matter of seconds they dragged the unfortunate Dukhonin out to the platform, mercilessly beat him, and ran him through with bayonets. His body was stripped and exposed to repeated profanations, the Bolshevik commander apparently unable to prevent it.[61]

Krylenko wasted no time on regrets and set about organizing his own "Revolutionary Stavka," broadcasting victory proclamations and keeping warm the expectation of imminent peace. Proforma, an All-Army MRC was compounded from the most deserving Bolsheviks at hand, and the wily, Bolshevik-leaning General Bonch-Bruevich, currently the commandant of the Mogilev garrison, was appointed his Chief of Staff. Nevertheless, Stavka as the brain and technical center of the Russian Army had ceased to exist. Most of the communications equipment and specialists were gone, direct wire connections (except those with Petrograd) ceased functioning, and little military or political leadership other than hortatory was in evidence. No sooner was the book closed on the old war with the signing of a general armistice on December 4 than Krylenko was obliged to turn his attention to the internal war—toward an ever more aggressive Ukrainian Republic, toward the new counter-revolutionary centers on the Don and in the Urals, and toward the as yet un-Bolshevized Rumanian and Southwestern fronts.[62] All this need not concern us, because our story is the end of the Old Army, and in the course of December its lifeblood drained away. So long as the armistice negotiations were still in progress and the Constituent Assembly elections were not yet concluded, the soldiers and their committees had maintained a sense of order and restraint, and to speak of a mass departure for the rear would be premature. But with the final armistice all but signed, counter-revolutionary Stavka now liquidated, and a final round of congresses bringing in a new levy of leadership which recognized the legitimacy of the Soviet government, the mass of

[61] There are no eyewitness accounts by parties sympathetic to Dukhonin, but the grisly details were recounted by the Bolsheviks themselves in several versions in *AFRK*, November 23, and 26 and December 1, and in *RS*, November 26. Polikarpov cites the depositions of Krylenko himself and General Odinsov, a general staff officer who accompanied Krylenko and hoped to persuade Dukhonin to surrender peacefully (pp. 261-65); Odinstov testified that Krylenko did everything humanly possible to prevent the murder but was physically thrust aside. Another account, "Gen. Dukhonin v stavke," *Minuvshie gody*, No. 1-3 (1918), is not based on eyewitnesses and only provides details on the desecration of the corpse (p. 308).

[62] All this can be followed in the official organ of the MRC at Stavka, *RS*, from November 26 on. The absence of meaningful orders and directives is palpable.

soldiers saw no point in remaining in the trenches. The titanic flow of these masses homeward through the capillaries of a much-depleted transportation system, piled on top and clinging precariously to the sides of the railroad cars, the wood-fueled engines scarcely able to move under the burden, countless local clashes with Ukrainians, cossacks and proto-Whites, blocking, or competing for, the right-of-way—all this must be left to the reader's imagination or to some future chronicler. Other worthy themes, such as the ineffectual efforts of the new Bolshevik MRCs to cope with unaccustomed tasks of administration and command over a much-diminished raw material or the greatly improvised "democratization" measures (elections of officers and so forth), the rebaptizing of the Army in "Red" guise, or the emergence in these developments of a new cut of future Red commanders and commissars must be left unexplored. The essential story of this work has been told and should not be unduly lengthened. The Old Army in democratic garb had lived fitfully on for nine weary months after the March trauma, had once more in June made a final, futile effort, convulsed, and given up the ghost. The peasants in gray coats, the cells that made up the living tissue, had acquired a "conscious" life and strength of their own and had risen up against the organs that had hitherto been their brains and heart. The vision of Soviet power and peace had provided them with the justification of their collective revolt, but once these goals had in their eyes been consummated, the millions of cells became simply peasants, anxious to be repatriated to their families and accustomed way of life; with the grand redistribution of land in prospect they could now tangibly anticipate the fulfillment of their peasant utopian dream.

☆

Formal historiographical conclusions seem almost superfluous, inasmuch as the method here has been to allow the materials themselves to convey the most pertinent images and truths. It would be disingenuous, however, for the author to claim that his own perceptions and judgments have not entered into the selection and treatment of the evidence, and he willingly assumes responsibility for the final result. He can only claim to have been as faithful to the facts and their unprejudiced reconstruction as his own capacities have allowed. The major import of this work presumes to be the part played by the soldier masses, and secondarily by the "intellectuals in uniform" or committee activists, in the refashioning of society and political authority in the new "democratic Russia." The end results of "Bolshevism" and "Soviet power" were far more a reflection of the spontaneous forces of revolution, as opposed to the rational constructs of ideologues and political leaders, than either Soviet or Western historiography have characteristically acknowledged. The March events gave the peasants in uniform a vision of land and peace, of their definitive social liberation, but above all of their own collective power to attain such results, and they were not inclined to surrender this vision until the task was accomplished. The intellectuals and activists who staffed the committees were inspired by a like vision and regarded themselves as its legitimate spokesmen, but they failed to perceive how their applications of it in practice, particularly on the war but also on the pace and character of the social revolution, were at odds with those of their constituency. "Revolutionary democracy" could function effectively only if this gap could somehow be bridged, but events were to demonstrate that this would require radical readjustment of outlook. The formation of the Coalition Government and the sponsorship of the ill-starred offensive brought about the parting of the ways, and the unorganized soldier masses, bitterly disillusioned with their leadership, found in Bolshevik slogans the sought-for surrogate. Party Bolshevism at the front was suppressed in July and August more thoroughly than in the rear, but the threat of the revived Right and the rigidity of the socialist leadership served to resuscitate it in the course of the Kornilov affair. The Kornilov affair immeasurably confirmed the peasant soldier in his own picture of things and whetted his determination to force the revolutionary institutions to respond to his overwhelming desire for peace and social settlement. Both Soviet power and the Constituent Assembly were potent symbols of these aspirations, just as Kerensky and Coalition became discarded alternatives, but ultimately the soldier's vote was for any authority (including "Nicholas himself") that would promise and deliver a speedy peace. Though the trench soldiers were anxious to get home as expeditiously as possible, it would be erroneous to conclude that they simply ignored the political consequences. They ardently wished for their aspirations to be sanctioned by legitimate authority, and their actions often bespoke such a concern. Paradoxically, the evidence shows that neither the proclamation of Soviet power nor the land and peace decrees nor the elections to the Constituent Assembly generated that assurance: conflicting information and the imminent prospect of civil war "within the democracy" had obscured the significance of these developments, and the formula of an "all-socialist government" was viewed as no more than a holding action. But the invitation to open negotiations directly across the trenches in the name of Soviet-based power fired the soldiers' imagination as nothing else, and in the end legitimized the authority of Sovnarkom and the Bolshevik-dominated MRCs. Lenin and his closest cohorts may be credited with cleverly devising the formula that worked, but in the final analysis it evoked a very conditional endorsement of Bolshevik ascendancy—only "insofar as" and "to the extent that" it paved the way to land and peace. The Bolsheviks' momentary success can be attributed to their boldness in adopting the program of the masses without qualification. They were to pay a dear price for this tactic in the near future, but that is the subject for another study. The portrait of "Bolshevism" here is necessarily incomplete and viewed strictly as it pertains to the dynamics of the Revolution of 1917 at the front; it should not be projected into the future. The evidence here confirms the version of other recent studies of a multifaceted political force still in a state of gestation with revolving, not fixed, content.[63] Front Bolshevism and front Bolsheviks certainly entered into the matrix of the future party-state in a substantial way, but the precise contribution can be determined only by future studies. While many soldiers (more from the rear than from the front) did carry their "Bolshevism" back to the villages and towns, and often helped tip the balance against the S.R.'s and Whites, countless others (indeed the vast majority) soon shed the identification under the influence of other domestic concerns. Existing studies confirm that only a small fraction of the mass levy of 1917 were permanently to make their careers in the Communist Party and state.[64] On the other hand, the Bolsheviks of the military organizations—front and rear—were to make a substantial contribution, particularly to the Red Army and the security organs, but except for the better-known names, such as Krylenko and Antonov-Ovseenko, a special study would be required to establish the exact character and extent of that contribution. The hectic months of October through December were a period of political testing which only the strong of will and mentally alert could endure. The qualities that were sorted out were of a piece with the Civil War experience and became permanent features of the future system.

The dominant theme of this study, however, has been the Revolution of 1917 itself and the social matrix on which it thrived. The overriding theme has been the soldiers' longing for peace, which conditioned all other aspects of their behavior. But it is hoped that it has been sufficiently stressed that the peace aspirations were but a part of the way the soldiers looked at the world in general, as scions of a peasant culture with its indigenous parochial concerns. The war was simply one more intrusion into this private world of the demands of the holders of political and social power, robbing them of their lives and substance. The social concerns may have been at times obscured by the striving for peace, but they were ever present in the soldiers' thinking, as evidenced in their favorite retort: "What good is land and freedom to me if I'm dead?" The attachment of the soldier peasants

[63] Above all Rabinowitch, but also the works of Koenker, Wade, and Raleigh (see Bibliography).

[64] See T. H. Rigby, *Communist Party Membership in the U.S.S.R. 1917-67* (Princeton, 1968), pp. 351ff., and Leonard Schapiro, *The Communist Party of the Soviet Union* (New York, 1960), p. 237.

to the land and the village way of life was expressed in many more ways than could be treated here, such as the reluctance of the over-forties to return from their spring leave and their significant participation in the affairs of the village skhod, such as taking in the landlord's hay and carting off his cattle and possessions. Moreover, in the region of the front the soldiers were often partners in the agrarian revolution, if they did not directly instigate its most violent actions, a theme regrettably passed over. In fact, the soldiers' assumption that the Revolution signified the definitive end of landowning society and its unjust laws was clearly expressed from the very first weeks of March, and the fading prospect of its speedy realization simply fired their determination to end the war promptly so that the more fundamental matter could be attended to. This underlying assumption of a radical inversion of all former social and political relationships can be regarded as the leitmotif of this study and perhaps its essential historiographical contribution.

SOURCE ABBREVIATIONS AND BIBLIOGRAPHY

FOR A DISCUSSION of sources, see "Review of Souces" in the previous volume *The End of the Imperial Army: The Old Army and the Soldiers' Revolt (March-April 1917)* (Princeton, 1980), pp. 381-86.

SOURCE ABBREVIATIONS

Journals

AR *Arkhiv Russkoi Revoliutsii*
BA *Belyi Arkhiv*
By *Byloe*
FO *Forschungen zur Osteuropäischen Geschichte*
IA *Istoricheskii Arkhiv*
IS *Istoriia SSSR*
IZ *Istoricheskie Zapiski*
KA *Krasnyi Arkhiv*
KL *Krasnaia Letopis'*
LR *Letopis' Revoliutsii* (Kharkov)
PR *Proletarskaia Revoliutsiia*

Newspapers of 1917

AFRK *Armiia i Flot Rabochei i Kresti'anskoi Rossii*. November 21-December 31. Organ of Commissariat of Military and Naval Affairs.

AFSR *Armiia i Flot Svobodnoi Rossii*. Organ of War Ministry (replacing *Russkii Invalid* in 1917).

BOA *Biulleten' Biuro Ispolnitel'nogo Komiteta Osoboi Armii*. November 24-December 3. Replaces *IzOA*.

BOAK *Biulleten' Obshchearmeiskogo Komiteta*. Nos. 1-21, October 31-November 17. Organ of All-Army Committee at Stavka. Nos. 4-10, 15-18, and 21, reprinted in Lelevich, *Oktiabr' v Stavka*, Prilozhenie.

BVO *Biulleten' Vserossiiskoi Konferentsii Frontovykh i Tylovykh Voennykh Organizatsii RSDRP*. Nos. 1-5, June 16-24. Bulletins of the All-Russian Conference of Bolshevik Military Organizations.

BZF *Biulleten' Voenno-revoliutsionnogo Komiteta Zapadnogo Fronta*. Nos. 1-19(?), November. Information sheet of the Western Front Military Revolutionary Committee.

Fr *Front*. May 6-November 19. Organ of the Executive Committee of the Front Congress of the Western Front.

GO *Golos Okopa*. April 27-December. Organ of Committee of the XXXII Corps, Eleventh Army, Southwestern Front.

Go3A *Golos 3-i Armii*. Organ of Third Army Committee, Western Front.

GoFr *Golos Fronta*. September 1-November 26. Organ of Committee of the Southwestern Front.

GoXA *Golos X. Armii*. June 25-November 11. Organ of Tenth Army Committee, Western Front.

Iz1A *Izvestiia Armeiskogo Ispolnitel'nogo Komiteta 1-i Armii*. November 21-December 6. Organ of First Army Committee, Northern Front.

Iz2S8 *Izvestiia 2-go S"ezda 8-oi Armii*. Nos. 1-9, November 23-December 3. Information sheet of Eighth Army Congress.

Iz5A *Izvestiia Armeiskogo Ispolnitel'nogo Komiteta 5-i Armii*. April 18-December 31. Organ of Fifth Army Committee, Northern Front.

Iz7A *Izvestiia Armeiskogo Komiteta 7-i Armii*. May 20-November 18. Organ of Seventh Army Committee, Southwestern Front.

Iz8A *Izvestiia Armeiskogo Komiteta 8-oi Armii*. April 20-November 21. Organ of Eighth Army Committee, Southwestern Front, subsequently, Rumanian Front.

Iz9A *Izvestiia Armeiskogo Komiteta 9-i Armii*. May 1-December 12. Organ of Ninth Army Committee, Southwestern Front.

IzFR *Izvestiia Frontovogo Otdela Rumcheroda*. September 20-December 2. Organ of Front Section of Regional Soviet of Rumanian Front (Rumcherod).

IzGr *Izvestiia Ispolnitel'nogo Komiteta Grenaderskogo Korpusa*. June 23-December 20. Organ of Committee of the Grenadier Corps, Second Army, Western Front.

IzOA *Izvestiia Vybornykh Soveta Osoboi Armii*. April 4-November 22. Organ of Special Army Committee, Southwestern Front.

IzPS *Izvestiia Petrogradskogo Soveta Rabochikh i Soldatskikh Deputatov*. Organ of the Petrograd Soviet.

IzSK *Izvestiia Komiteta Sibirskogo Armeiskogo Korpusa*. October 8(?)-25. Organ of Committee of IV Siberian Corps, Sixth Army, Rumanian Front.

IzVIu *Izvestiia Voenno-revoliutsionnogo Komiteta Iugozapadnogo Fronta*. Nos. 1-6, November 28-December 3. Information sheet of Military Revolutionary Committee of the Southwestern Front.

IzVK3 *Izvestiia Voenno-revoliutsionnogo Komiteta 3-i Armii*. November

22-December 30. Organ of Military Revolutionary Committee of the Third Army, Western Front.

IzVK7 *Izvestiia Voenno-Revoliutsionnogo Komiteta 7-i Armii*. November 23, 1917-January 19, 1918. Organ of the Military Revolutionary Committee of the Seventh Army, Southwestern Front.

NZh *Novaia Zhizn'*. Independent socialist newspaper, Petrograd.

ON *Okopnyi Nabat*. July 23-August 20. Continuation of *OP*.

OP *Okopnaia Pravda*. April 30-July 21, October 12-December(?). Organ of the Bolshevik Military Organization of the Twelfth Army, published by Bolsheviks of the 436th Novoladozhskii Regiment.

Pr *Pravda*. Central organ of the Bolshevik Party, Petrograd.

RF *Rizhskii Front*. July 6-November 19. Organ of Iskosol, the Twelfth Army Committee, Northern Front.

RS *Revoliutsionnaia Stavka*. November 26, 1917-January 27, 1918. Organ of the Military Revolutionary Committee at Stavka.

SP *Soldatskaia Pravda*. April 17-July 5, October 27-December 30. Organ of the Military Organization of the Bolshevik Party. Replaced on July 23 by *Rabochii i Soldat* and on August 9 by *Soldat*.

SS *Soldatskoe Slovo*. Nonparty defensist newspaper, Petrograd.

VGr *Voin-Grazhdanin*. May 2-December 30. Organ of the Sixth Army Committee, Rumanian Front.

VOA *Vestnik Osoboi Armii*. March 1-September 8. Staff organ of the Special Army, Southwestern Front.

VSO *Vestnik Glavnogo Komiteta Soiuza Ofitserov Armii i Flota*. Nos. 1-5, June 14-August 24. Organ of the Officers' Union at Stavka.

VVK *Vestnik V Armeiskogo Korpusa*. June 1-16, September 17-December 6. Organ of the Committee of the V Corps, Eleventh Army, Southwestern Front.

VVP *Vestnik Vremennogo Pravitel'stva*. Organ of the Provisional Government.

Basic Published Sources, Documentary and Memoir Collections, Serial Monographs

BMRF *Bol'sheviki Moldavii i rumynskogo fronta v bor'be za vlast' sovetov (mart 1917-janvar' 1918). Dokumenty i materialy*. Kishinev, 1967.

BOB *V bor'be za Oktiabriu v Belorussii i na zapadnom fronte. Vospominaniia aktivnykh uchastnikov*. Minsk, 1957.

BPB *Bor'ba partii bol'shevikov za armiiu v sotsialisticheskoi revoliutsii. Sbornik dokumentov*. Moscow, 1977.

KPLOR *Kommunisticheskaia partiia Latvii v oktiabr'skoi revoliutsii 1917. Dokumenty i materialy*. Riga, 1963.

OHLK *Österreich-Ungarns Letzter Krieg 1914-1918*. 7 vols. Published by the Österreichs Ministerium für Heereswesen. Vienna, 1930-38. Cited in this work is Vol. 6: *Das Kriegsjahr 1917* (1936).

ONFV *Oktiabr' na fronte. Vospominaniia*. Moscow, 1967.

ORA *Oktiabr'skaia revoliutsiia i armiia. 25 oktiabria 1917 g.-mart 1918 g. Sbornik dokumentov*. Edited by L. S. Gaponenko. Moscow, 1973.

PSPZ *Petrogradskii Soviet Rabochikh i Soldatskikh Deputatov. Protokoly zasedanii ispolnitel'nogo komiteta i biuro i. k.* Edited by B. Ia. Nalivaiskii. Moscow-Leningrad, 1925.

PSTsK *Perepiska sekretariata TsK RSDRP(B) s mestnymi organizatsiiami (mart-oktiabr' 1917 g.). Sbornik dokumentov*. Moscow, 1957. (Cited as *PSTsK* 1, since it is an open series.)

———. *(noiabr' 1917g.-fevral' 1918 g.)*. (Cited as *PSTsK* 2.)

PVRK *Petrogradskii voenno-revoliutsionnyi komitet. Dokumenty i materialy*. 3 vols. Edited by D. A. Chugaev et al. Moscow, 1966-67.

RazA *Razlozhenie armii v 1917 godu*. Edited by N. E. Kakurin and Ia. A. Iakovlev. Moscow, 1925.

RDRA *Revoliutsionnoe dvizhenie v russkoi armii v 1917 g. 27 fevralia-24 oktiabria. Sbornik dokumentov*. Edited by L. S. Gaponenko. Moscow, 1925.

RMVTs *Rossiia v mirovoi voine 1914-1918 goda (v tsifrakh)*. Published by the Tsentral'noe Statisticheskoe Upravlenie, Otdel Voennoi Statistiki (Central Statistical Administration, Section on Military Statistics). Moscow, 1925.

RPG *The Russian Provisional Government 1917: Documents*. Edited by Robert Browder and Alexander Kerensky. 3 vols. Stanford, Calif., 1961.

RWK *Der Weltkrieg 1914 bis 1918. Die militärische Operationen zu Lande*. 12 vols. Vols. 1-9 published by the Reichsarchiv; vols. 10-11 by the Kriegsminsterium; and vols. 12-13, by the Oberkommando des Heeres. Cited in this work are:

Vol. 11: *Die Kriegsführung im Herbst 1916 und im Winter 1917* (1938).

Vol. 12: *Die Kriegsführung im Frühjahr 1917* (1939).

Vol. 13: *Die Kriegsführung im Sommer und Herbst 1917* (1942).

TrSh *Triumfal'noe shestvie sovetskoi vlasti*. Edited by D. A. Chugaev et al. 2 vols. Moscow, 1963.

VKDA *Voiskovye komitety deistvuiushchei armii. Mart 1917 g.-mart 1918 g.*. Edited by L. M. Gavrilov et al. Moscow, 1982.

VOSR *Velikaia oktiabr'skaia sotsialisticheskaia revoliutsiia. Dokumenty i materialy*. Edited by A. L. Sidorov et al. Moscow, 1957-62. Documentary series in unnumbered volumes. Cited in this work are:

Revoliutsionnoe dvizhenie v aprele 1917 g. Aprel'skii krizis (1958). (Cited as *VOSR. Aprel'skii krizis.*)

Revoliutsionnoe dvizhenie v Rossii v mai-Iiun'e 1917 g. Iiun'skaia demonstratsiia (1959). (Cited as *VOSR. Mai-iiun'.*)

Revoliutsionnoe dvizhenie v Rossii v iiule 1917 g. Iiul'skii krizis (1959). (Cited as *VOSR. Iiul'.*)

Revoliutsionnoe dvizhenie v Rossii v avguste 1917 g. Razgrom kornilovskogo miatezha (1959). (Cited as *VOSR. Avgust.*)

Revoliutsionnoe dvizhenie v Rossii v sentiabre. Obshchenatsional'nyi krizis (1959). Cited as *VOSR Sentiabr'.*

Revoliutsionnoe dvizhenie v Rossii nakanune Oktiabr'skogo vooruzhennogo vosstaniia (1-24 oktiabria 1917 g.) (1962). (Cited as *VOSR. Nakanune* oktiabria.)

Oktiabr'skoe vooruzhennoe vosstanie v Petrograde (1957). (Cited as *VOSR. Oktiabr'skoe vosstanie.*)

VOSRB *Velikaia oktiabr'skaia sotsialisticheskaia revoliutsiia v Belorussii. Dokumenty i materialy.* 2 vols. Edited by T. S. Gorbunov et al. Minsk, 1957. Separate titles are:

Vol. 1: *Belorussiia v period podgotovki sotsialisticheskoi revoliutsii (fevral'-oktiabr' 1917 g.).*

Vol. 2: *Pobeda sotsialisticheskoi revoliutsii i uprochenie sovetskoi vlasti v Belorussii.*

VOSRU *Velikaia oktiabr'skaia sotsialisticheskaia revoliutsiia na Ukraine. Fevral' 1917-aprel' 1918. Sbornik dokumentov i materialov.* 3 vols. Edited by S. M. Korolivskii. Kiev, 1955-57. Cited in this work are:

Vol. 1: *Podgotovka velikoi oktiabr'skoi sotsialisticheskoi revoliutsii na Ukraine. Sbornik dokumentov i materialov* (1955).

Vol. 2: *Pobeda velikoi oktiabr'skoi sotsialisticheskoi revoliutsii i ustanovlenie sovetskoi vlasti na Ukraine. Oktiabr'-dekabr' 1917 g.* (1957).

VRKDA *Voenno-revoliutsionnye komitety deistvuiushchei armii. 25 oktiabria 1917 g.-mart 1918 g.* Edited by L. M. Gavrilov et al. Moscow, 1977.

Archival Sources

AA Politisches Archiv des Auswärtigen Amtes. German Foreign Ministry Archives, Bonn, Germany. Utilized were:

Weltkrieg. Aktenzeichen 2f, No. 1. "Waffenstillstand verhandlungen mit Russland." Band 1-10. (Cited as WK 2f, No. 1, WSVR.)

Weltkrieg. Az No. 2. Geheim. "Friedenstimmungen und Aktionen zur Vermittlung des Friedens." Band 40-44 (June, 1917). (Cited as WK, No. 2. Geheim FAVF.)

Weltkrieg. Geheim (without further designation). "Geheime Berichte des Vertreters des Auswärtiges Amtes im Grossen Hauptquartier an den Stattsekretär über die militärische Lage." Band 37-39 and Adhang 1. (Cited as WK Geheim [undesignated]. GBAA.)

BKA Bayersiches Kriegsarchiv. Bavarian Military Archives, Munich, Germany. Utilized were:

A.O.K. der Südarmee. No. 19. Abteilung Ia. Band 4 Akt 7, Fach 1. "Gefechtbericht für die Schlacht bei Brzezany-Koniuchy am 29. 6. 1917."

2. Bayerischen Landwehr Division. Abt. Ia. Band 5 and 39. "Nachrichten über den Feind." Riga Front. (Cited as 2. BLD, Ab. 1a.)

14. Bayerische Infantrie Division. Abt. Ia. Band 24. "Spionage, Stimmung der Truppen des Feindes." Riga Front.

Bayerische Ersatz Division. Band 38. "Feindlage und Stimmung." Band 39. "Waffenstillstand, Nachrichtenwesen." Sereth Front, Galicia.

HI Hoover Institution on War, Revolution, and Peace. Stanford, California. Memoirs, personal papers, and miscellaneous unpublished manuscripts and documents.

Akintievskii, Gen. Konstantin Kon. Memoirs of, 1884-1962 (in English).

Alekseev, Gen. Mikhail Vasilevich. Miscellaneous papers, 1905-18. Little of use on 1917.

Bastunov, Vladimir. Headquarters of IX Corps, Kiev Military District and Second Army, Western Front. Orders, personnel rosters, casualty reports, 1897-1917.

Budberg, Baron A. P. "Vospominaniia o voine 1914-17 gg."

Bylevskii Papers, Nos. 1-10. Invaluable military morale reports, September-October 1917, mainly Northern Front.

Iunakov, N. L. "Moi poslednye mesiatsy v deistvuiushchei armii. Oktiabr'-dekabr' 1917 goda."

Lukomskii, Gen. Aleksei Sergeevich. Papers, 1914-39. 1917 materials superseded by published works.

Miller, Gen. E. K. "Pokazaniia gen. leitenanta E. K. Millera." Invaluable deposition on the occasion of his arrest by soldiers of the XXVI Corps, Ninth Army, Southwestern Front, on April 6, 1917.

Nicolaevsky, Boris Ivanovich. "Kornilovskie dni." Transcript of reports to Moscow Committee of the Kadet Party of F. F. Kokoshkin and N. M. Kishkin on the cabinet discussions of the "Kornilov rebellion."

———. "Zagovor Kornilova. Stati (vyrezki)." Collection of articles printed in the émigré press by participants in the Kornilov Affair, assembled by B. I. Nicolaevsky.

Shinkarenko-Brusilov, Col. N. V. Memoirs of 1917.

Solski (Solskii), Waclaw. "1917 god v zapadnoi oblasti i na zapadnom fronte." A Polish socialist close to Bolsheviks and activist in Minsk Soviet and on Western Front.

Uperov, V. V. Materials relating to a deputation of the Ninth Army, Rumanian Front, to Petrograd to inspect arms factories and to the formation of soldiers' committees in the 25th Division of that army in March, 1917. (Not utilized because discovered subsequently, but relevant to themes treated in the previous volume.)

Vakar, N. P. "Zagovor Kornilova." Correspondence, interviews, and article clippings assembled by Vakar for his articles on the subject. (In Nicolaevsky Archive.)

Voitinskii (Woytinsky), Vladimir. "Gody pobedy i porazhenii." 3 vols. Invaluable memoirs. Earlier and more extensive account of 1917 than published memoirs (see Woytinsky, *Stormy Passage*, below, under "Autobiographies etc.").

RA Archive of Russian and Eastern European History and Culture. Columbia University, New York.

Aprelev, B. P. "Zametki o sobytiiakh v Rossii 1917-1918-1919 g.g." Diary.

Danilchenko, Col. P. V. "Materialy dlia istorii po chasti zapasnogo bataliona L. Gv. Izmailovskago Polka do marta, 1917 g." In Archive of the Izmailovskii Regiment.

Finlandskii Guards Regiment. Archive. Regimental orders and miscellaneous documents on 1917, including B. V. Sergeev's field book-diary for April-August.

Khagondokov, K. N. "Vospominaniia."

Kirkhgof, Col. F. F. "Vospominaniia adiutanta komendanta glavnoi kvartiry shtaba verkhovnogo glavnokommanduiushchago."

Makhrov, Col. P. "Razval russkago fronta v 1917 g. i nemetskaia okkupatsiia Ukraina v 1918 g." Memoirs.

———. Miscellaneous documents, chiefly regimental orders, pertaining to the 13th Siberian Rifle Regiment, Twelfth Army, Northern Front.

Maslovskii, Gen. Evgenii Vasilevich. "Nekotorye stranitsy moei zhizni."

Messner, Col. Evgenii Eduardovich. ''Vospominaniia gen. shtaba polkovnika E. E. Messnera.''

Mitrofanov, Poruchik Oleg Pavlovich. ''Den' za den'. Karmannaia zapisnaia knizhka na 1917 goda.'' Diary, January-July.

Petrushevskii, Col. B. A. ''Dnevnik velikoi voiny, 1914-17 g.g.'' Diary.

Pronin, Col. V. ''Gen Lavr Geor. Kornilov.''

———. ''Miting Gen. Brusilova.''

Raupakh, R. R. Materials of the Extraordinary Investigative Commission of the Provisional Government on the Kornilov affair. Depositions, telegrams, orders, mainly relating to the armies of the Southwestern Front. Twenty-five titled and untitled folders. Those utilized in this work are:

''Materialy o sobytiiakh v gorodakh Berdicheve i Zhitomire.''

''Materialy otnosiashchie k delu o gen. Erdele.''

''Pokazanie Gen. ot Infantrii Lavra Geor. Kornilova.''

''Razsledovanie o sobytiiakh 27 i 28 avgusta 1917 g. v Berdicheve.''

''Razsledovanie o sobytiiakh 27-28 avgusta v Zhitomire.''

Untitled folder relating to events in Seventh Army, including deposition of General Selivachev.

Savchenko, I. G. ''Okopnye Dumy. Iz vospominaii.''

Shapkin, V. V. ''Poslednye dni stavki verkhovnago.''

Shatilov, Gen. P. N. Autobiography and memoirs of 1917.

Tikhobrazov, Dmitri Nikitich. ''V stavke posle revoliustsii (1917 g.). Iz vospominanii gen. shtaba. polkovnika Tikhobrazova.''

Timichenko-Ruban, Vladimir Nikitich. ''Stranitsy proshlago (vospominaniia).''

TsGVIA Tsentral'nyi Gosudarstvennyi Voenno-Istoricheskii Arkhiv (Central State Military-Historical Archive). The standard Soviet practice is followed in designating *fond* (f.), *opis'* (op.), and *delo* (d.); leaf or sheet numbers are designated with letter ''l.'' or ''ll.'' for inclusive pages. (More recently, Soviet archives are employing the designation ''ed. khr.'' instead of *delo*.) Utilized in this volume are:

f. 2179, op. 4, ed. khr. 2 and 6. Committee documents, Grenadier Corps, Second Army, Western Front.

f. 2222, op. 1, d. 2. Corps Committee journal, XXII Corps, Seventh Army, Southwestern Front.

———, ed. khr. 1066. Staff communications of the First, Third, Fifth Finnish Rifle and 159th Infantry divisions, XXII Corps.

———, ed. khr. 1185. Divisional and regimental committee documents, XXII Corps.

———, ed. khr. 1189. Staff documents of XXII Corps.

f. 2240, op. 5, d. 1. Miscellaneous committee documents of the XXXI Corps, Third Army, Western Front, after May, Special Army, Southwestern Front.

f. 2241, op. 1, d. 6. Depositions to the military prosecutor occasioned by the arrest of commander of the 520th Fokstanskii Regiment, XXXI Corps, Third Army, Western Front, by his own soldiers on March 15, 1917.

f. 2282, op. 4, ed. khr. 11. Corps Committee journal of the IV Siberian Corps, Sixth Army, Southwestern Front, August-November.

———, op. 6, d. 3. Miscellaneous staff and committee documents of the IV Siberian Corps.

f. 2283, op. 1, ed. khr. 12. Proceedings of military court of IV Siberian Corps of September 19, 1917, against nine soldiers of the 40th Siberian Rifle Regiment for agitation against the Provisional Government.

f. 2322, op. 7, ed. khr. 2. Staff documents of the Second Guards Infantry Division, I Guards Corps, Special Army, after May, Seventh Army, Southwestern Front.

———, ed. khr. 4. *Protokoly* (proceedings) of the Committee of the Second Guards Infantry Division.

f. 2326, op. 4, d. 4. Committee documents and *protokoly* of Third Grenadier Division, XXIII Corps, Eleventh Army, Southwestern Front.

———, d. 6. Proceedings of the *Osvedomitel'naia Kommissiia* (an information and conciliation committee organ), Third Grenadier Division.

f. 2327, op. 4, d. 1. Staff documents of Fifth Grenadier Division, Grenadier Corps, Second Army, Western Front.

f. 2333, op. 1, ed. khr. 1. Committee documents of the Third Infantry Division, XVII Corps, Eleventh Army, Southwestern Front.

f. 2335, op. 1, d. 282. Investigative materials, chiefly depositions of Military-Revolutionary Court of August 2-5 against soldier Arsenii Nikitin of the Fifth Infantry Division, IX Corps, Second Army, Western Front.

f. 2376, op. 1, d. 2. *Protokoly* of the Committee of the 46th Infantry Division, XXV Corps, Eleventh Army, Southwestern Front.

f. 2434, op. 2, d. 282. Staff documents of the 121st Division, XIII Corps, Fifth Army, Northern Front.

f. 2443, op. 1, d. 1. Miscellaneous staff and committee documents of the 130th Division, XXXI Corps, Special Army, Southwestern Front.

f. 2486, op. 1, ed. khr. 2. Miscellaneous staff and committee documents of the 186th Division, XLIII Corps, Twelfth Army, Northern Front.

f. 2938, op. 1, d. 23, part 1. Daily orders of the 329th Buzuliiskii Regiment, 83rd Division, XXXI Corps, Third Army, Western Front, from May on, Special Army, Southwestern Front. March-June, 1917.

f. 2573, op. 1, ed. khr. 2. Statutes and *protokoly* of Committee of the Volynskii Guards Regiment, Third Guards Infantry Division, II Guards Corps, Special, Eleventh, and Seventh armies in succession, Southwestern Front.

f. 3054, op. 2, d. 23, parts 1 and 2. Committee *protokoly* and daily orders of the 517th Batumskii Regiment, XXXI Corps, Third Army, Western Front, from May on, Special Army, Southwestern Front.

Bibliography

Documentary Collections and Published Sources

IN BOOKS

Akhun, M. I., and Petrov, V. A., eds. *Bol'sheviki i armiia 1905-1917. Voennaia organizatsiia pri peterburgskom komitete*. Leningrad, 1929.

Anikeev, V. V., ed. *Dokumenty velikogo oktiabria. Istoricheskii ocherk*. Moscow, 1977.

Chaadaeva, O. N., ed. *Soldatskie pis'ma 1917 goda*. Moscow, 1927.

Drezen, A. K., ed. *Bol'shevizatsiia petrogradskogo garnizona 1917 goda. Sbornik materialov i dokumentov*. Leningrad, 1932.

Gemmp, F. G. *Nachrichtendienst und Spionage des Heeres*. Microfilm of typescript at HI. Agents' reports and other valuable intelligence materials with extensive commentary.

Gosudarstvennoe soveshchanie. Stenograficheskii otchet. Edited by Ia. A. Iakovlev. Moscow, 1930. Stenographic record of State Conference of August 12-15, 1917, in Moscow.

Ilin-Zhenevskii, A. F., ed. *Pochemu soldaty i matrosy stali pod znamena oktiabria*. Leningrad, 1933. Soldiers' letters.

Kerensky, A. F. *Delo kornilova*. Moscow, 1919. Transcript of Kerensky's testimony to the Extraordinary Investigative Commission on the Kornilov affair, with Kerensky's commentary.

———. *Prelude to Bolshevism: The Kornilov Rebellion*. New York, 1919. Translation of above.

———. *Prikazy po armii ministra Kerenskago i ego rechi*. Petrograd, 1917.

Kolerov, V. A., and Sinani, B. S., eds. *Kornilovskie dni. Biulleteny vremennogo voennogo komiteta pri Ts. Isp. Kom. S.R. i S.D.s 28 avgusta po 4 sentiabria 1917 g*. Petrograd, 1917. Invaluable documentation of Kornilov affair.

Krastyn, Ia. P., and Spreslis, A. A. *Latyshskie strelki v bor'be za sovetskuiu vlast' v 1917-1920 gg. Vospominaniia i dokumenty*. Riga, 1962.

Lenin, V. I. *Sochineniia*. 3rd edition. 30 vols. and supplements. Edited by L. B. Kamenev and N. I. Bukharin. Moscow-Leningrad, 1927-33. Edition with the best notes, additional documents, and scholarly apparatus.

Matveev, F. I. *Iz zapisnoi knigi deputata 176 pekh. polka. Petrogradskii Sovet, mart-mai 1917 g*. Moscow-Leningrad, 1932. Only available record of sessions of Soldiers' Section of the Soviet.

Pervyi vserossiiskii s"ezd Sovetov R. i S. D. Stenograficheskii otchet. Edited by V. N. Rakhmetov and N. P. Miamlin. 2 vols. Moscow-Leningrad, 1930-31.

Protokoly tsentral'nogo komiteta RSDRP(B), avgust 1917-fevral' 1918. Moscow, 1958.

Put' k oktiabriu. Sbornik statei, vospominanii i dokumentov. 5 vols. Moscow, 1923-26.

Revoliutsiia 1917 g. v istoricheskikh dokumentakh. Tiflis, 1930. Telegraph communications of staff headquarters on Caucasus Front.

Russia. Army. Glavnyi shtab. Telegrams, June-November, 1917. Originals in bound volume, main library of Columbia University.

Sbornik ukazov i postanovlenii Vremennogo Pravitel'stva. 2 vols. Petrograd, 1917-18.

Sef, S. N., ed. *Revoliutsiia 1917 goda v Zakavkaz'e. Sbornik dokumentov i materialov*. Tiflis, 1927. Mainly proceedings of army and regional Soviet congresses.

S"ezd predstavitelei armeiskikh i tylovykh organizatsii Severnogo Fronta. Protokoly zasedanii. Petrograd, 1917.

Shestoi s"ezd RSDRP(bol'shevikov), avgust 1917 goda. Protokoly. Moscow, 1950.

Shliapnikov, A. G. *Semnadtsatyi god*. 4 vols. Moscow, 1923-31. To richly documented text are appended seminal documents as supplements. Indispensable.

Sidorov, A. L., ed. *Revoliutsionnoe dvizhenie v armii i na flote v gody mirovoi voiny 1914-fevral' 1917. Sbornik dokumentov*. Moscow, 1967.

Soveshchanie delegatov fronta v Petrograde 1917. Stenograficheskii otchet zasedanii, 24 apr-4 mai 1917. Petrograd, 1917.

Stenograficheskii otchet zasedanii Vserossiiskogo s"ezda ofitserskikh deputatov armii i flota v g. Petrograde s 8 po 27 maia 1917 g. Petrograd, 1917.

Volfovich, M., and Maksimov, A., eds. *Tsarskaia armiia v period mirovoi voiny i fevral'skoi revoliutsii (materialy).* Kazan, 1932.

Vserossiiskoe soveshchanie sovetov rabochikh i soldatskikh deputatov, 1917. Stenograficheskii otchet. Edited by M. N. Tsapenko and Ia. A. Iakovlev. Moscow, 1927.

Vtoroi vserossiiskii s"ezd sovetov rabochikh i soldatskikh deputatov. Sbornik dokumentov. Edited by D. A. Chugaev, A. F. Butenko et al. Moscow, 1957.

Vtoroi vserossiiskii s"ezd sovetov R. i S.D. Protokoly. Edited by K. G. Kotel'nikov. Moscow-Leningrad, 1928.

Zhurnaly zasedanii Vremennogo Pravitel'stva. Petrograd, 1917.

IN PERIODICALS

"Aprel'skie dni v Petrograde." *KA* 33 (1929): 34-81.

"Armiia i oktiabrskaia revoliutsiia." *Sovetskii Arkhiv*, No. 6 (1968): 58-65.

"Armiia v period podgotovki i provedeniia velikoi oktiabr'skoi sotsialisticheskoi revoliutsii." *KA* 84 (1937): 135-87.

"Biulleteny biuro voennykh komissarov (1917-1918 gg.)." *KR* 33 (1929): 249-54.

"Bolshevistskaia rabota vo flote i armii nakanune fevral'skoi revoliutsii." *PR* 29 (1924): 75-94.

"Bolshevizatsiia fronta v prediiul'skie dni 1917 g." *KA* 58 (1933): 86-100.

"Delegaty petrogradskogo garnizona na fronte (dekabr' 1917 g.)." *KA* 85 (1937): 29-58.

"Fevral'skaia revoliutsiia i okhrannoe otdelenie." *By* 29 (1918): 158-76.

"Fevral'skaia revoliutsiia 1917 goda." *KA* 21 and 22 (1927): 3-78 and 3-70.

"Fevral'skaia revoliutsiia v Petrograde (28 fevralia-1 marta 1917 g." *KA* 41-42 (1930): 62-102.

"Golosa iz okopov (soldatskie pis'ma 1915-16 gg.)." *KL* 25 (1928): 112-18.

"Iz dnevnika gen. B. G. Boldyreva." *KA* 23 (1927): 250-73.

"Iz dnevnika gen. M. V. Alekseeva" in collection *Russkii istoricheskii arkhiv*. Edited by Ian Slavik. Prague, 1929.

"Iz dnevnika gen. V. I. Selivacheva." *KA* 9 and 10 (1925): 108-31 and 138-74.

"Iz ofitserskikh pisem s fronta v 1917 g." *KA* 50-51 (1932): 194-210.

"Iz zhizni revoliutsii na fronte." *BA* 4 (1928): 72-81.

"K istorii kornilovshchiny (v prilozhenii dokladu L. Kornilova ot 23 apr. voennomu ministru Guchkovu i ego doklad Vremennomu Pravitel'stvu)." *KL* 10 (1924): 201-17.

"Na fronte v predoktiabr'skie dni. Po sekretnym materialam stavki." *KL* 6 (1923): 9-64. Mainly full *protokol* of Stavka Conference of July 1917 (available elsewhere).

"Nakanune peremiriia." *KA* 23 (1927): 195-249.

"Nastroenie armii nakanune oktiabr'skogo perevorota (pis'ma soldatov s fronta)." *KL* 13 (1925): 227-38.

"Oktiabr' na fronte." *KA* 23 and 24 (1927): 149-94 and 71-101.

"Oktiabr'skii perevorot i stavka." *KA* 7 and 9 (1925): 153-75 and 156-70.

"Otchet komissarov IX Armii I. Kirienko I. A. Chekotilo." *BA* 1 (1926): 13-34.

"Politicheskoe polozhenie Rossii nakanune fevral'skoi revoliutsii v zhandarmskom osveshchenii." *KA* 17 (1926): 3-35.

"Pravda grenaderskaia." *KL* 44-45 (1931): 67-71.

"Prikaz No. 2." *KA* 27 (1929): 214-19.

"Revoliutsiia na fronte." *LR* 10 (1925): 69-96. Staff communications on key political events of 35th Artillery Brigade.

"Revoliutsionnaia propaganda v armii 1916-17 gg." *KA* 17 (1926): 36-50.

"Revoliutsionnoe dvizhenie v voiskakh vo vremia mirovoi voiny." *KA* 4 (1923): 417-24.

"Ruskaia armiia nakanune revoliutsii." *By* 29 (1918): 151-57.

"Stavka i minsterstvo inostrannikh del." *KA* 30 (1928): 5-45.

"Telegrammy i razgovory po telegrafe mezhdu Pskovom, Stavkoi i Petrogradom otnosiashchimi k obstoiatel'stvam v koikh proizoshlo otreshenie." *Russkaia Letopis'*, 3 (1922). Nearly all available elsewhere, though pivotal.

"V.I. Dukhonin v Stavke (po neopublikovannym dannym)." *Golos Minuvshego*, 1-3 (1918): 289-308.

"Verkhovnoe komanovanie v pervye dni revoliutsii." *KA* 5 (1924): 213-40.

"Vokrug 'Gatchiny'." *KA* 9 (1925): 171-94.

"V tsarskoi armii nakanune fevral'skoi burzhuazno-demokraticheskoi revoliutsii." *KA* 81 (1937): 105-20.

Autobiographies, Memoirs, Personal Accounts, Diaries

BOOKS

Anet, Claude. *Through the Russian Revolution: Notes of an Eye-Witness from 12th March to 30th May*. London, 1917.

Antonov-Ovseenko, V. A. *V semnadtsatom godv*. Moscow, 1933.

Bochkareva, Maria. Yasha: My Life as Peasant, Officer, and Exile. New York, 1919.

Bonch-Bruevich, Gen. M. D. *From Tsarist General to Red Army Commander*. Moscow, 1966.

Brusilov, Gen. A. A. *Moi vospominaniia*. Moscow-Leningrad, 1929.

———. *A Soldier's Notebook, 1914-18*. London, 1930.

Chemodanov, G. *Poslednye dni staroi armii*. Moscow, 1926.

Denikin, Gen. Anton I. *Put' russkogo ofitsera*. New York, 1953.

Draudin, T. A. *Boevyi put' latyshskoi strelkovoi divisii v dni oktiabria i v gody grazhdanskoi voiny*. Riga, 1960.

Eremin, K. G. *Soldatskie versty. Voennye memuary*. Moscow, 1960.

Geroi oktiabria. Moscow, 1967. Memoirs of Moscow Military Organization of Bolsheviks.

Gerua, Gen. B. V. *Vospominaniia o moei zhizni*. 2 vols. Paris, 1969.

Grazkin, Dmitri Iu. *Okopnaia Pravda*. Moscow, 1933.

Gurko, Gen. V. I. (Gen. Basil Gourko). *Memories and Impressions of War and Revolution in Russia 1914-17*. London, 1918.

Hindenburg, Paul von. *Out of My Life*. London, 1933.

Hoffmann, Gen. Max. *Die Aufzeichnungen des Generalmaiors Max Hoffmann*. 2 vols. Berlin, 1930.

Ignatiev, Gen. A. A. *Piat'desiat let v stroiu*. 2 vols. Moscow, 1955.

Ilin-Zhenevskii, A. F. *Ot fevralia k zakvatu vlasti (vospominaniia o 1917 g.)*. Leningrad, 1927.

———. *From the February Revolution to the October Revolution, 1917*. New York, 1931.

Kal'nitskii, Ia. *Ot fevralia k oktiabriu. Vospominaniia frontovika*. Moscow, 1926.

Kamenskii, V., ed. *Leib-egeriia v voinu 1914-1917 gg. Sbornik materialov*. 2 vols. Paris, 1935. Chiefly memoirs.

Kerensky, A. F. *The Catastrophe: Kerensky's Own Story of the Russian Revolution*. New York, 1927.

———. *Russia and History's Turning Point*. New York, 1965.

Knorin, V. *1917 god v Belorussii i na zapadnom fronte*. Minsk, 1925.

Knox, Gen. Alfred. *With the Russian Army, 1914-1917*. 2 vols. London, 1921.

Kondzerovskii, P. K. *V stavke verkhovnogo 1914-1917 gg*. Paris, 1967.

Krasnov, Gen. P. N. *From the Double Eagle to the Red Flag*. 2 vols. New York, 1928. Autobiographical novel.

Krylenko, N. *Pochemu pobezhdala russkaia revoliutsionaia armiia*. Petrograd, 1917.

Kuropatkin, Gen. A. N. *Zapiski generala Kuropatkina o russko-iapanskoi voine. Itogi voiny*. Berlin, 1909.

Littauer, Vladimir S. *Russian Hussar*. London, 1965.

Lobanov-Rostovsky, Prince A. *The Grinding Mill*. New York, 1935.

Lomonosov, V. Iu. *Vospominaniia o fevral'skoi revoliutsii 1917 goda*. Stockholm-Berlin, n.d. (1921?)

Ludendorff, Gen. Eric von. *Ludendorff's Own Story: August, 1914—November, 1918*. 2 vols. New York and London, 1919.

Lugin, N. (Fedor Stepun). *Iz pisem praporshchika-artillerista*. Moscow, 1918.

Lukomskii, Gen. A. S. *Vospominaniia*. 2 vols. Berlin, 1922.

Miliukov, P. N. *Vospominaniia (1859-1917)*. 2 vols. New York, 1955.

Mstislavskii, S. (Maslovskii). *Piat' dnei. Nachalo i konets fevral'skoi revoliutsii*. Berlin, 1922.

Muravnik, Ia. *Vos'maia armiia Rumfronta. Oktiabr'skaia revoliutsiia*. Kharkov, 1922.

Os'kin, D. *Zapiski soldata*. Moscow, 1929.

Pares, Sir Bernard. *My Russian Memoirs*. London, 1931.

Petrov, N. G. *Bolsheviki na zapadnom fronte v 1917 g. Vospominaniia*. Moscow, 1959.

Pireiko, A. *Na fronte imperialisticheskoi voiny*. Moscow, 1925.

Podvoiskii, N. I. *God 1917*. Moscow, 1958.

Polivanov, Gen. A. A. *Iz dnevnikov i vospominanii po dolzhnosti voennogo ministra i ego pomoshchnika 1907-1916*. Moscow, 1924.

Polovtsev, Gen. Petr Aleksandrovich. *Dni zatmeniia*. Paris, n.d.

———. *Glory and Downfall: Reminiscences of a Russian General*. London, 1935. Extended full autobiography.

Popov, F. V. *Rasskaz o nezabyvaemom (zapiski bol'shevika)*. Kiev, 1961.

Popov, Konstantin S. *Vospominaniia kavkazskago grenadera 1914-20*. Belgrad, 1925.

Posevin, Stepan. *Gibel' imperii. Severnyi front (iz dnevnika shtabofitsera dlia poruchenii)*. Riga, 1922.

Rodzianko, Paul. *Tattered Banners*. London, 1939.

Savinkov, B. V. *K delu Kornilova*. Paris, 1919.

Semenov, G. (Vasil'ev). *Voennaia i boevaia rabota partii sotsialistov-revoliutsionerov za 1917-1918 g.g*. Berlin, 1921-22.

Shil'nikov, Gen. I. F. *1-aia zabailkal'skaia kazachaia diviziia v velikoi evropeiskoi voine 1914-18 gg*. Harbin, 1933.

Shklovskii, Viktor. *Revoliutsiia i front*. Petrograd, 1921.

Sorokin, F. D. *Gvardeiskii ekipazh v fevral'skie dni 1917 goda*. Moscow, 1932.

Stankevich, V. B. *Vospominaniia 1914-1919 gg*. Berlin, 1920.

Stepun, Fedor. *Byvshee i nesbyvsheesia*. 2 vols. New York, 1956.

———. *Iz pisem praporshchika-artilerista*. Odessa, 1919.

Sukhanov, N. N. *Zapiski o revoliutsii*. 7 vols. Berlin, 1922-23.

Sukhomlinov, Gen. V. *Vospominaniia*. Berlin, 1924.

Tarasov-Rodionov, Aleksei. *February 1917*. New York, 1931.

Tornau, Baron S. A. *S rodnym polkom (1914-1917 gg.)*. Berin, 1923.

Tsereteli, I. G. *Vospominaniia o fevral'skoi revoliutsii*. 2 vols. Paris, 1963.

Val', E. G. *K istorii belogo dvizheniia (deialtel'nost' general-ad'iutanta Shcherbacheva)*. Tallin, Estonia, 1935.

V boiakh za vlast' sovetov. Iz istorii komanda "Dvintsev," uchastnikov oktiabr'skikh boev 1917 g. v Moskve. Sbornik vospominanii i dokumentov. Moscow, 1937. Memoirs of activists in Fifth Army, Northern Front.

Verkhovskii, Gen. A. I. *Na trudnom perevale*. Moscow, 1959. Memoirs, completely different, written many years later.

———. *Rossiia na Golgofe (iz pokhodnogo dnevnika 1914-1918)*. Petrograd, 1918. Diary.

Vertsinskii, Gen. E. A. *God revoliutsii. Vospominaniia ofitsera general'nogo shtaba za 1917-18 g*. Tallin, Estonia, 1929.

Vrangel', Gen. P. N. *Vospominaniia generala P. N. Vrangelia*. Frankfurt, Germany, 1969.

Wild, Max. *Secret Service on the Russian Front*. New York, 1932.

Woytinsky, W. S. *Stormy Passage. A Personal History Through Two Russian Revolutions*. Differs considerably in tone and content from Ms. memoirs (see Voitinskii, HI). New York, 1961.

IN PERIODICALS AND COLLECTIONS

Alekseev (pseud.). "Iz vospominanii o fevral'skoi revoliutsii na Rumynskom Fronte." *LR* 22 (1927): 66-74.

Budovskii, I. "Oktiabr' na Rumynskom Fronte." *LR* 8 (1924): 44-49.

Degtiarev, L. S. "Oktiabr' Rumynskogo Fronta (po lichnym vospominaniiam)." *KL* 6 (1923): 207-78.

Dubenskii, D. N. "Kak priozoshel perevorot v Rossii. Zapiski-dnevniki." *Ruskaia Letopis'* 4 (1922): 11-112.

Fomin, B. V. "Pervye mesiatsy posle fevral'skoi revoliutsii zap. bataliona

Lb. Gv. Izmailovskogo polka.'' *Izmailovskaia Starina*, Nos. 27-28 (1937-38): 117-36 and 144-78.

———. ''Vospominaniia o fevral'skoi revoliutsii 1917 g.'' *Izmailovskaia Starina*, Nos. 16-18 (1933): 7-41, 31-60, and 58-87.

Glezer, D. ''Na fronte v 1917 g.'' *KL* 6 (1923): 202-7.

Golobev, Capt. M. ''Kornilovskoe vystuplenie. Ocherk ochevidtsa i uchastnika.'' *Izmailovskaia Starina*, No. 4 (1931): 42-46.

Grazkin, D. I. ''Okopnaia Pravda.'' *IA* No. 4 (1957): 168-83.

———. ''Revoliutsionnaia rabota v XII armii.'' *Voprosy Istorii*, No. 9 (1957): 3-16.

Guchkov, A. I. ''Iz vospominanii A. I. Guchkova.'' *Poslednye Novosti*, September 16, 1936ff. Serialized under various titles.

Kalinenok, M. A. ''Bol'sheviki VIII armii Rumynskogo Fronta v bor'be za vlast' Sovetov (sentiabr'-dekabr' 1917 g.'' In *Iz istorii revoliutsionnogo dvizheniia i sotialisticheskogo stroitel'stva Moldavii.* Kishinev, 1963.

Khaustov, F. I. ''Okopnaia Pravda (ocherk).'' *KL* 24 (1927): 108-14.

Kirpichnikov, T. ''Vosstanie l.g. Volynskogo polka.'' *By* 5-6 (1917): 5-15.

Klimovich, G. ''L. Gv. Moskovskii polk v voinu 1914-1917 gg.'' *Biulleten' L. Gv. Moskovskogo Polka*, Nos. 130-33 (September, 1951-April, 1952).

Klodt, Baron P. ''Lichnye vospominaniia.'' *Finlandets*, Nos. 21ff. (July, 1933ff.), serialized.

Kondriushkin, Ivan. ''Velikii oktiabr' na Rumynskom Fronte.'' *PR* 10 (1922): 425-42.

Krasnov, P. N. ''Na vnutrennom fronte.'' *AR* 1 (1922): 97-190.

Krylenko, Iu. ''Fevral'skaia revoliutsiia i staraia armiia.'' *PR* 61-62 (1927): 240-51.

Manakin, V. ''Shock Battalions of 1917: Reminiscences.'' *Russian Review* 14 (July and October, 1955): 214-32 and 332-44.

Remter [pseud.]. ''Epizody fevral'skoi revoliutsii na iugozapadnom fronte.'' *LR* 22 (1927): 54-65.

Savinkov, B. ''Gen. Kornilov (iz vospominanii).'' *By* 31 (1925): 182-97.

Sergeev, B. V. ''1917 god na fronte.'' *Finlandets*, Nos. 32ff. (1956), serialized.

Sokolov, N. N. ''Kak rodilsia prikaz No. 1.'' *Ogonek*, March 13, 1927.

Varentsova, O. ''Voennoe biuro pri MK bol'shevikov. Staraia armiia i kontrrevoliutsiia.'' In *Staryi bol'shevik* (Moscow, 1934).

Vatsetis, I. ''Latyshskie strelki v oktiabr'skoi revoliutsii. *Voina i Revoliustiia*, No. 10-11 (1927): 113-42.

Voronovich, N. "Zapiski predsedatelia soveta soldatskikh deputatov." *Arkhiv Grazhdanskoi Voiny* 2 (1922): 11-102.

Zaitsev, I. "Na fronte posle oktiabria (otryvki vospominanii)." *KR* 24 (1927): 52-57.

Studies and General Works

BOOKS

Andreev, A. M. *Soldatskie massy garnizonov russkoi armii v oktiabr'skoi revoliutsii*. Moscow, 1975.

Bazanov, S. N. *V bor'be za oktiabr' na severnom fronte: 5-ia armiia*. Moscow, 1985.

Burdzhalov, E. N. *Vtoraia russkaia revoliutsiia. Moskva, front periferiia*. Moscow, 1971.

———. *Vtoraia russkaia revoliutsiia. Vosstanie v Petrograde*. Moscow, 1967.

Chamberlin, W. H. *The Russian Revolution*. 2 vols. New York, 1935.

Danilov, Gen. Iu. N. *Rossiia v mirovoi voine, 1914-15 gg*. Berlin, 1924.

Denikin, Gen. Anton I. *Ocherki russkoi smuty*. 5 vols. Paris-Berlin, 1921-26.

———. *Russian Turmoil: Memoirs, Military Social, and Political*. London, 1922.

———. *Staraia armiia*. 2 vols. Paris, 1929-31.

Ezergailis, Andrew. *The Latvian Impact on the Bolshevik Revolution: The First Phase, September, 1917, to April, 1918*. Boulder, Colo., 1983.

Frenkin, M. S. *Revoliutsionnoe dvizhenie na rumynskom fronte 1917 g.-mart 1918*. Moscow, 1965.

———. *Russkaia armiia i revoliutsiia 1917-1918*. Munich, 1978.

———. *Zakvat vlasti bol'shevikami v Rossi i rol' tylovikh garnizonov*. Jerusalem, 1982.

Gaponenko, L. S. *Soldatskie massy zapadnogo fronta v bor'be za vlast' sovetov*. Moscow, 1953.

Gavrilov, L. M. *Soldatskie komitety v oktiabr'skoi revoliutsii (deistvuiushchaia armiia)*. Moscow, 1985.

———. Soldatskie massy deistvuiushchei armii v period podgotovleniia oktiabr'skoi sotsialisticheskoi revoliutsii. Dissertation. Moscow, 1969.

Getzler, Israel. *Kronstadt 1917-1921: The Fate of a Soviet Democracy*. London, 1983.

Gitsiu, M. M. *Deiatel'nost' soldatskikh sovetov i komitetov na rumynskom fronte i v Moldavii v 1917 g*. Kishinev, 1985.

Golovin, Gen. N. N. *Rossiiskaia kontr-revoliutsiia v 1917-1918 gg*. 5 vols., 12 parts. Tallin, Estonia, 1937.

———. *Voennye usiliia v mirovoi voine*. 2 vols. Paris, 1939.

Golub, P. A. *Partiia, armiia i revoliutsiia*. Moscow, 1967.

———. *Soldatskie massy iugozapadnogo fronta v bor'be za vlast' sovetov*. Kiev, 1958.

Hasegawa, Tsuyoshi. *The February Revolution: Petrograd, 1917*. Seattle, 1981.

Iakupov, I. M. *Bol'sheviki vo glave revoliutsionnykh soldatskikh mass 1917- ianvar' 1918*. Kiev, 1967.

———. *Bor'ba za armiiu v 1917 godu (deiatel'nost' bol'shevikov v prif-rontovykh okrugakh)*. Moscow, 1975.

———. *Partiia bol'shevikov v bor'be za armiiu v period dvoevlastiia*. Kiev, 1972.

Ivanov, N. Ia., *Kornilovshchina i ee razgrom*. Leningrad, 1965.

Kaimin', Ia. *Latyshskie strelki v bor'be za pobedu oktiabr'skoi revoliutsii*. Riga, 1967.

Kapushkov, S. G. *Bor'ba bol'shevistskoi partii za armiiu v period pervoi mirovoi voiny*. Moscow, 1957.

Kapustin, M. I. *Soldaty severnogo fronta v bor'be za vlast' sovetov*. Moscow, 1957.

———. *Zagovor generalov (iz istorii kornilovshchiny i ee razgroma)*. Moscow, 1968.

Katkov, George. *The Kornilov Affair: Kerensky and the Breakup of the Russian Army*. London and New York, 1980.

———. *Russia 1917: The February Revolution*. New York, 1967.

Keep, John L. M. *The Russian Revolution: A Study in Mass Mobilization*. New York, 1976.

Kersnovskii, A. A. *Istoriia russkoi armii*. 4 vols. Belgrade, 1933-38.

Koenker, Diane. *Moscow Workers and the 1917 Revolution*. Princeton, 1981.

Kritskii, M. A. *Kornilovskii udarnyi polk*. Paris, 1936.

Kuzmina, T. F. *Revoliutsionnoe dvizhenie soldatskikh mass tsentra Rossii nakanune oktiabria*. Moscow, 1978.

Lelevich G. (L. G. Kal'manson). *Oktiabr' v stavke*. Gomel, 1922.

Manikovskii, Gen. A. A. *Boevoe snabzhenie russkoi armii v mirovoi voiny*. 2 vols. Moscow, 1930.

Manukian, R. A. *Revoliutsionnaia rabota bol'shevikov v Kavkazskoi armii (fevral' 1917-fevral' 1918)*. Erivan, 1969.

Martynov, Gen. E. I. *Kornilov (popytka voennogo perevorota)*. Leningrad, 1927.

———. *Tsarskaia armiia v fevral'skom perevorote*. Leningrad, 1927.

Melgunov, S. P. *The Bolshevik Seizure of Power*. Santa Barbara, Calif., 1971.

———. *Kak bol'sheviki zakvatili vlast'*. Paris, 1953.

———. *Martovskie dni 1917 goda*. Paris, 1961.

Miller, V. I. *Soldatskie komitety russkoi armii v 1917 g*. Moscow, 1974.

Mints, I. I. *Istoriia velikogo oktiabria*. 3 vols. Moscow, 1967-73.

Muratov, Kh. I. *Revoliutsionnoe dvizhenie v russkoi armii v 1905-7 gg*. Moscow, 1955.

———. *Revoliutsionnoe dvizhenie v russkoi armii v 1917 godu*. Moscow, 1958.

Polikarpov, V. D. *Prolog grazhdanskoi voiny v Rossii, oktiabr' 1917-fevral' 1918*. Moscow, 1976.

Rabinovich, S. E. *Bor'ba za armiiu v 1917 g*. Moscow, 1930.

———. *Vserossiiskaia voennaia konferentsiia bol'shevikov 1917 goda*. Moscow, 1931.

Rabinowitch, Alexander. *The Bolsheviks Come to Power: The Revolutions of 1917 in Petrograd*. New York, 1976.

———. *Prelude to Revolution: The Petrograd Bolsheviks and the July 1917 Uprising*. Bloomington, Ind., 1968.

Raleigh, Donald. *Revolution on the Volga: 1917 in Saratov*. Bloomington, Ind., 1986.

Revoliutsionnoe dvizhenie v russkoi armii v gody pervoi russkoi revoliutsii. Sbornik statei. Edited by V. I. Konovalov. Moscow, 1955.

Ronge, Maximilian. *Kriegs- und Industriespionage*. Wien, 1930.

Rosenberg, William. *Liberals in the Russian Revolution: The Constitutional Democratic Party, 1917-1921*. Princeton, 1974.

Saul, Norman. *Sailors in Revolt: The Russian Baltic Fleet in 1917*. Lawrence, Kans., 1978.

Shurygin, F. A. *Revoliutsionnoe dvizhenie soldatskikh mass Severnogo fronta v 1917 g*. Moscow, 1958.

Spanocchi, L. *Das Ende des kaiserlichen russische Heeres*. Wien, 1932.

Steklov, A. P. *Revoliutsionnaia deiatel'nost' bol'shevistskikh organizatsii na Kavkazskom fronte 1914-1917 gg*. Tbilisi, 1969.

Stone, Norman. *The Eastern Front 1914-17*. London, 1975.

Vasil'ev, F. I., and Kazakov, A. S. *Strategicheskii ocherk voiny 1914-1918 gg. na Rumynskom fronte*. Moscow, 1922.

Vladimirova, Vera. *Kontrrevoliutsiia v 1917 g*. Moscow, 1924.

Wade, Rex. *Red Guards and the Workers' Militias in the Russian Revolution*. Stanford, Calif., 1984.

Wildman, Allan K. *The End of the Russian Imperial Army: The Old Army and the Soldiers' Revolt (March-April 1917)*. Princeton, 1980.

Zaionchkovskii, Gen. A. M. *Mirovaia voina 1914-1918 gg.* 2 vols. Moscow, 1938.

———. *Podgotovka Rossii k mirovoi voine.* Moscow, 1926.

———. *Strategicheskii ocherk voiny 1914-1918 gg.* 7 vols. Moscow, 1923. Vol. 6: *Period ot proryva iugozapadnogo fronta v mae 1916 g. do kontsa goda.* Vol. 7: *Kampaniia 1917-ogo goda.*

Zaionchkovskii, P. A. *Samoderzhavie i russkaia armiia na rubezhe XIX-XX stoletii.* Moscow, 1973.

ARTICLES AND CONTRIBUTIONS

Alekseeva, M. I. "Gazety 'Okopnaia Pravda' i 'Otkliki Pravdy' v bor'be za soldatskie massy posle iiulskikh dnei 1917 g." *Voprosy Istorii KPSS*, No. 5 (1964).

Anikeev, V. V. "Voennye organizatsii RSDRP(B) v 1917 g." *Voprosy Istorii KPSS*, No. 10 (1964): 109-17.

Anushkan, V. "A. A. Polivanov i ego 'Memuary.' " *By* 27-28 (1924): 286-300.

Arefin, S. "Razval armii." *BA* 4 (1928): 55-71.

Boyd, John. "The Origins of Order No. 1." *Soviet Studies* 19 (1967): 359-73.

Bushnell, John. "Peasants in Uniform: The Tsarist Army as a Peasant Society." *Journal of Social History* 13, No. 4 (October, 1979): 565-76.

———. "The Tsarist Officer Corps, 1881-1914: Customs, Duties, Inefficiency." *American Historical Review* 86, No. 4 (October, 1981): 753-80.

Drezen, A. K. "Petrogadskii garnizon v iiule i avguste 1917 g." *LR* 24 (1927): 191-223.

———. "Petrogradskii garnizon v oktiabre." *KL* 23 (1927): 101-33.

Feldman, R. S. "The Russian General Staff and the June 1917 Offensive." *Soviet Studies* 19 (1968): 526-43.

Ferro, Marc. "The Russian Soldier in 1917." *The Slavic Review*, 30 (1971): 483-512.

Fomin, V. "S''ezd deputatov armii i tyly Zapadnogo fronta v aprele 1917 g." *PR* 63 (1927): 164-80.

Gavrilov, L. M. "K voprosu o bol'shevizatsii soldatskikh komitetov deistvuiushchei armii v period podgotovki i pobedy oktiabria." *Voprosy Istorii KPSS*, No. 2 (1969): 89-99.

———. "Perepis' russkoi armii 25 oktiabria, 1917 g." *IS*, No. 2 (1964): 87-91.

Gavrilov, L. M. "Sostav reservov fronta nakanune oktiabria." *IS* No. 4 (1967): 18-29.

Geyer, Dietrich. "Die russische Räte und die Friedensfrage im Frühjahr und Sommer 1917." *Vierteljahrhefte für Zeitgeschichte* 5 (1957): 220-40.

Golub, P. "Bol'shevizatsiia soldatskikh mass v kanun oktiabria." *Voenno-Istoricheskii Zhurnal*, No. 5 (1967): 3-18.

Gorodetskii, E. N. "Demobilizatsiia armii v 1917-18 gg." *IS*, No. 1 (1958): 3-31.

Kedrov, M. "Vserossiiskaia konferentsiia voennykh organizatsii RSDRP (bol'shevikov)." *PR* 6 (1927): 226-27.

Keirim-Markus, M. "O polozhenii armii nakanune oktiabria (doneseniia komissarov Vremennago pravitel'stva i komandirov voinskikh chastei)." *IA*, No. 6 (1957): 35-60.

Kenez, Peter. "A Profile of the Pre-revolutionary Officer Corps." *California Slavic Studies* 7 (1973): 121-58.

Kitaev, P. "B. V. Savinkov i gen. Kornilov." *By* 31 (1925): 177-81.

Kochakov, B. M. "Sostav petrogradskogo garnizona v 1917 g." *Uchenye Zapiski Leningradskogo Gosudarstvennogo Universiteta* 24, No. 205, 1956, pp. 60-86.

Kutuzov, V. V. "Doneseniia komissarov vr. prav. i komandirov kak istochnik dlia izucheniia istorii revoliutsionnogo dvizheniia v russkoi armii (fevral'-oktriabr' 1917 g.)." In *Istochnikovedenie istorii sovetskogo obshchestva*. Moscow, 1964.

———. "Sostav voennoi organizatsii RSDRP(B) 6-go armeiskogo korpusa v oktiabr' 19017 g." *IA*, No. 5 (1961): 207-9.

Lazarev, M. S. "Likvidatsiia Stavki staroi armii kak ochaga kontr-revoliutsii." *Voprosy Istorii*, No. 3 (1968): 43-57.

Lisovoi, Ia. M. "A. Kerenskii v armii gen. Denikina." *BA* (1926) 1: 35-50.

———. "Itogi odnogo iz ugovorov (po vospominaniiam i dokumentam shtaba 28 pekhotnoi divizii)." *BA* 2-3 (1928): pp. 11-41.

———. "Revoliutsionnye generaly." *BA* 1 (1926): 51-70.

Miller, V. I. "Fevral'skaia revoliutsiia i vozniknovenie soldatskikh komitetov na fronte." In *Sverzhenie samoderzhaviia. Sbornik statei*. Moscow, 1970.

———. "Frontovoi s"ezd iugozapadnogo fronta (mai 1917 g.)" in *Istoricheskii opyt velikogo·oktiabria*. Moscow, 1975.

———. "Nachalo demokratizatsii staroi armii v dni fevral'skoi revoliutsii." *IS*, No. 6 (1966): 26-43.

———. "Stavka i soldatskie komitety v marte 1917 g." In *Oktiabr' i grazhdanskaia voina v SSSR. Sbornik statei*. Moscow, 1966.

Mukhov, F. V. "Vazhnaia veka v bor'be za revoliutsionnye soldatskie massy (k 50-letiiu Vserossiiskoi konferentsii frontovikh i tylovykh voennykh organizatsii RSDRP[B])." *Voprosy Istorii KPSS*, No. 5 (1967): 84-91.

Polikarpov, V. D. "Raboty N. V. Krylenko po istorii revoliutsii armii." *IZ* 94 (1974): pp. 304-64.

———. "Revoliutsionnye organy pri Stavke verkhovnogo glavkomanduiushchego (noiabr' 1917-mart 1918 g.)." *IZ* 86 (1970): 7-56.

Rabinovich, S. E. "Armeiskaia pechat' i bor'ba za armiiu." *Voina i Revoliutsiia*, No. 10-11 (1927): 109-32.

———. "Bol'shevistskaia voennaia organizatsiia v 1917 g." *PR* 77 (1928): 179-98.

———. "Deklaratsiia prav soldatov." *PR* 77 (1928): 35-57.

———. "Rabota bol'shevikov v armii v 1917 g." *Voina i Revoliutsiia*, No. 6 (1927): 96-108.

———. "Vserossiiskaia konferentsiia bol'shevistskikh voennykh organizatsii." *KL* 44 (1930): 46-75.

Ray, Oliver. "The Imperial Russian Army Officer." *Political Science Quarterly* 76 (December, 1961): 576-92.

Shankovskyi, L. "Disintegration of the Imperial Russian Army in 1917." *Ukrainian Quarterly* 13 (1957): 305-28.

Shliapnikov, A. N. "Iiul' na fronte." *PR* 53 (1926): 16-59.

———. "Iiun'skaia nastuplenie." *PR* 50 (1926): 5-50.

Sobolev, G. L. "Petrogradskii garnizon V 1917 g." *IZ* 88 (1971): 60-84.

Soliubskii, A. P. "Severnyi front v dni fevral'skoi revoliutsii." *IS*, No. 11 (1967): 18-26.

Stein, Hans-Peter. "Der Offizier des russischen Heeres." *FO* 13 (1967): 346-507.

Wettig, Gerhard. "Die Rolle der russischen Armee im revolutionären Machtkampf 1917." *FO* 12 (1967): 46-389.

Zhuravlev, G. I. "Bor'ba soldatskikh mass protiv letnogo nastupleniia na fronte (iiun'-iiul' 1917 g.)." *IZ* 61 (1957): 5-30.

INDEX

LIBRARY OF CONGRESS CATALOGING-IN-PUBLICATION DATA

Wildman, Allan K.
The end of the Russian Imperial Army.

Includes bibliographies and indexes.
Contents: v. 1. The old army and the soldiers' revolt (March-April)—v.
2. The road to Soviet power and peace.
1. Soviet Union—History—February Revolution, 1917.
2. Russia. Armii͡a—History. I. Title.
DK265.9.A6W54 947.084′1 79-84021
ISBN 0-691-05287-5 (v. 1)
ISBN 0-691-05504-1 (v. 2)